DICTIONARY

ITALIAN•ENGLISH
ENGLISH•ITALIAN

DICTIONARY
ITALIAN • ENGLISH
ENGLISH • ITALIAN

TIGER BOOKS INTERNATIONAL
LONDON

© Geddes & Grosset Ltd 1994

This edition published in 1994 by
Tiger Books International PLC, London

ISBN 1-85501-374 6

Printed and bound in Slovenia

Abbreviations | ## Abbreviazioni

abbr, abbrev	abbreviation	abbreviazione
adj	adjective	aggettivo
adv	adverb	avverbio
art	article	articolo
auto	automobile	automobile
aux	auxiliary	ausiliario
bot	botany	botanica
chem	chemistry	chimica
com	commerce	commercio
conj	conjunction	congiunzione
cul, culin	cooking term	espressione di cucina
dem	demonstrative	dimostrativo
excl	exclamation	esclamazione
f	feminine noun	sostantivo feminile
fam	colloquial term	espressione familiare
fig	figurative use	uso figurato
gr	grammar	grammatica
interj	interjection	interiezione
inv, invar	invariable	invariabile
law	law term	giurisprudenza
m	masculine noun	sostantivo maschile
mar	marine term	termine marittimo
med	medicine	medicina
mus	music	musica
n	noun	sostantivo
pl	plural	plurale
poss	possessive	possessivo
pron	pronoun	pronome
prep	preposition	preposizione
rel	relative	relativo
relig	religious	religioso
sl	slang	gergo
vi	intransitive verb	verbo intransitivo
vr	reflexive verb	verbo riflessivo
vt	transitive verb	verbo transitivo
vulg	vulgar	volgare

A

a *prep* to; in; at; on; by; with; for.

abate *m* abbot.

abbagliante *adj* dazzling.

abbagliare *vt* to dazzle.

abbaiare *m* bark; * *vi* to bark.

abbaino *m* dormer window.

abbandonare *vt* to abandon; to leave; to forsake; to desert; to drop; * *vr* ~**rsi** to give oneself up to.

abbandonato *adj* disused; marooned.

abbandono *m* desertion; neglect; retirement; withdrawal; abandon, abandonment; walkout.

abbassare *vt* to dim; to turn down; * *vi* to sink; * *vr* ~**rsi** to abase oneself; to stoop; to abate.

abbastanza *adj*, enough; fairly; * *adv* enough; reasonably; relatively; **avere** ~ **di** to have a bellyful of.

abbattere *vt* to cull; to fell; to dash (hopes).

abbattimento *m* despondency, dejection.

abbattuto *adj* crestfallen, dejected, despondent.

abbellire *vt* to adorn; to beautify; to embellish.

abbiente *adj* well-to-do

abbigliamento *m* clothing; dress.

abbindolare *vt* to take in.

abbonamento *m* subscription; season ticket; * *vr* ~**rsi** to subscribe.

abbonato *m* subscriber.

abbondante *adj* abundant; plentiful; copious; bountiful.

abbondanza *f* abundance; affluence; plenty; fullness.

abbondare *vi* to abound.

abbordare *vt* to accost.

abbreviare *vt* to abbreviate, to abridge.

abbreviazione *f* abbreviation.

abdicare (a) *vt* to abdicate.

abdicazione *f* abdication.

aberrazione *f* aberration.

abietto *adj* abject.

abile *adj* able, adept, adroit.

abilità *f* ability, aptitude.

abissale *adj* abysmal.

abisso *m* abyss.

abituare *vt* to accustom.

abituato *adj* accustomed.

abolire *vt* to abolish.

abolizione *f* abolition.

abominevole *adj* abominable.

a bordo *adv* aboard.

aborigeno *adj* aboriginal.

abortire *vi* to abort.

aborto *m* abortion.

aborrevole *adj* abhorrent.

aborrire *vt* to abhor.

abrasione *f* abrasion.

abrasivo *adj* abrasive.

abrogare *vt* to abrogate.

abside *f* apse.

abbozzare *vt* to draft.

abbozzo *m* draft.

abbozzo *m* sketch.

abbracciare *vt* to embrace; to hug; to span; to espouse.

abbraccio *m* cuddle; embrace; hug.

abbronzarsi *vr* to tan.

abbronzato *adj* tanned.

abbronzatura *f* suntan, tan.

abete *m* fir (tree), spruce; **legno di** ~ *m* deal.

abile *adj* artful; deft; skilled, skilful.

abilità *f* ability; knack; skill; ~ **artistica** artistry.

abisso *m* gulf.

abitabile *adj* habitable, inhabitable.

abitante *m/f* inhabitant.

abitare *vt* to inhabit; (ghost) to haunt; * *vi* to live.

abitazione *f* habitation.

abito *m* dress; gown; ~ **da sera** *m* evening dress.

abituale *adj* habitual; ordinary; routine.

abituato *adj* accustomed.

abitudine *f* habit; custom; practice; way.

abiurare *vi* to recant.

abnegazione *f* self-sacrifice.

abortire *vi* to abort, miscarry.

aborto *m* abortion, miscarriage.

abrogare *vt* to revoke, to repeal.

abrogazione *f* repeal.

abusare *vt* to misuse; ~ **di** to abuse.

abusivo *adj* unauthorized, unlawful.

abuso *m* abuse, misuse.

acacia *f* acacia.

acaro *m* mite.

accademia *f* academy.

accademico *adj* academic; * *m* academic, academician.

accadere *vt* to befall; * *vi* to befall; to happen; to occur; to pass.

accampamento *m* camp; encampment.

accampare *vt* to encamp.

accanitamente *adv* hotly.

accanito *adj* fierce.

accanto *prep* beside; ~ **a** next to.

accantonare *vt* to shelve.

accaparrarsi *vr* to hog; to scoop.

accappatoio *m* bathrobe.

accarezzare *vt* to fondle; to pet; to stroke.

accartocciare *vt* to crumple.

accatastare *vt* to stack.

accecare *vt* to blind.

accedere a *vi* to assent to; to attain (office); to adhere (to); to access.

accelerare *vt* to accelerate; to hasten; to precipitate; * *vi* to accelerate.

acceleratore *m* accelerator.

accelerazione *f* acceleration.

accendere *vt* to switch on; to turn on; to put on; to light; to strike (a match); to ignite; to kindle.

accendino *m* cigarette lighter.

accennare *vt* to mention.

accenno *m* allusion.

accensione *f* ignition; **chiave dell'~** *f* ignition key.

accentato *adj* stressed.

accento *m* accent; ~ **irlandese** *m* brogue; emphasis.

accentuare *vt* to accentuate.

accerchiare *vt* to circle; to ring.

accertare *vt* ascertain.

acceso *adj* on.

accessibile *adj* accessible.

accessione *f* accession.

accesso *m* access; **divieto d'~** no entry; fit.

accessori *mpl* fittings; trimmings

accessorio *n* accessory; attachment; fitment.

accetta *f* hatchet.

accettabile *adj* acceptable.

accettare *vt* to accept; to take.

accettazione *f* acceptance; reception.

acciaieria *f* steelworks.

acciaio *m* steel.

accidentato *adj* bumpy; rugged; uneven.

accidia *f* sloth.

accidioso *adj* slothful.

accigliarsi *vr* to scowl.

acciottolare *vt* to rattle.

acciottolio *m* rattle.

acciuffare *vt* to nab.

acciuga *f* anchovy.

acclamare *vt* to acclaim.

acclamazioni *fpl* acclaim.

acclimatare *vt* to acclimatize; * *vr* ~**rsi** to acclimatize oneself.

accoglienza *f* acceptance.

accompagnamento *m* accompaniment.

accompagnare *vt* to accompany.

accompagnatore *m* accompanist (*mus*).

acconsentire a *vi* to acquiesce in.

accorciare *vt* to abridge.

accordo *m* agreement; **essere d'~ con** to agree.

acclamare *vt* to hail.

accoccolarsi *vr* to nestle.

accogliente *adj* cosy, snug.

accoglienza *f* welcome.

accogliere *vt* to welcome.

accolito *m* henchman.

accollarsi *vr* to shoulder.

accomodante *adj* easy-going.

accomodare *vt* to mend.

accompagnare *vt* to accompany.

accompagnato *adj* accompanied.

accompagnatore *m* chaperone.

acconciatura *f* hairstyle.

accondiscendere *vi* to condescend.

acconsentire *vi* to consent.

accontentare *vt* to indulge; to humour; to please.

accoppiamento *m* copulation; mating.

accoppiare *vt* to mate; * *vr* ~**rsi** to copulate; to mate.

accorciare *vt* to shorten; to curtail.

accordare *vt* to grant; to tune; * *vi* to tune.

accordatore *m* tuner.

accordo *m* agreement; deal; settlement.

accorgersi *vr* to notice.

accortezza *f* shrewdness.

accorto *adj* astute; shrewd; politic.

accovacciarsi *vr* to crouch.

accozzaglia *f* jumble.

accreditare *vt* to credit.

accrescere *vt* to increase; * *vr* ~**rsi** to increase.

accucciarsi *vr* to duck.

accumulare *vt* to accumulate, to amass; to store; to hoard; * *vt* ~**rsi** to accumulate.

accumulo *m* accumulation.

accuratezza *f* accuracy.

accurato *adj* accurate; careful.

accusa *f* accusation, charge, prosecution (*law*); allegation; **mettere sotto ~** to impeach.

accusare *vt* to accuse; to charge.

accusativo *m* (*gr*) accusative.

accusato *m* accused.

accusatore *m* accuser.

acerbo *adj* unripe.

acero *m* maple.

acetato *m* acetate.

aceto *m* vinegar.

acetosa *f* sorrel.

acidità *f* acidity; sourness.

acido *adj* acid; caustic; sour; * *m* acid.

acme *m* acme.

acne *f* acne.

acqua *f* water; ~ **dolce** fresh water; **tirare l'~** to flush.

acquaio *m* sink.

acquario *m* aquarium; **A~** Aquarius.

acquartieramento *m* billet.

acquatico *adj* aquatic.

acquattarsi *vr* to cower; to squat.

acquazzone *m* cloudburst; downpour; shower.

acquedotto *m* aquaduct.

acquerello *m* watercolour.

acquiescente *adj* acquiescent.

acquiescenza *f* acquiescence.

acquirente *m/f* purchaser.

acquisire *vt* to acquire.

acquistare *vt* to purchase.

acquisto *m* acquisition; purchase.

acquolina *f* drizzle; **che fa venire l'~ in bocca** *adj* mouthwatering

acquoso *adj* watery.

acre *adj* acrid; sour.

acrimonia *f* acrimony.

acro *m* acre.

acrobazia *f* stunt.

acustica *f* acoustics.

acute *adj* acute.

acutezza *f* smartness.

acuto *adj* sharp; keen; reedy.

adattamento *m* adaptation, adjustment.

adattare *vt* to adapt; * *vr* **~rsi** to acclimatize.

adatto *adj* appropriate; right; fit; suitable; becoming.

adattare *vt* to suit.

addebitare *vt* to debit.

addebito *m* debit.

addestramento *m* training.

addestrare *vt* to train; to school.

addetto *m* attaché.

addio *m* farewell; goodbye; * *adj* **d'~** parting.

addirittura *adv* actually; even.

addirsi *vt* to befit.

additivo *m* additive.

addizionare *vt* to add.

addizione *f* addition.

addolcire *vt* to sweeten

addolcirsi *vr* to mellow

addolcito *adj* mellow

addolorare *vt* to distress; to grieve; to pain;

addolorato *adj* sorrowful; pained.

addome *m* abdomen.

addomesticare *vt* to domesticate; to tame.

addomesticato *adj* tame.

addomesticazione *f* domestication.

addominale *adj* abdominal.

addormentarsi *vr* to fall asleep

addormentato *adj* asleep; sleeping.

addossarsi *vr* to take on.

adeguatamente *adv* suitably.

adeguato *adj* adequate.

adenoidi *fpl* adenoids.

aderente *m/f* adherent.

aderire *vi* to adhere.

adesione *f* adhesion.

adesivo *m* adhesive; sticker.

adesso *adv*, *conj* now.

adiacente *adj* adjacent.

adiposo *adj* adipose.

adolescenza *f* adolescence.

adolescente *m/f* adolescent, teenager.

adolescenziale *adj* teenage.

adoperare *vt* to use.

adorabile *adj* adorable, lovable.

adorare *vt* to adore; to worship.

adorato *adj* beloved.

adorazione *f* adoration; worship.

adottare *vt* to adopt.

adottato *adj* adopted.

adozione *f* adoption.

adulare *vi* to crawl; * *vt* to fawn upon.

adulazione *f* adulation.

adulterare *vt* to adulterate; to doctor.

adultero *adj* adulterous; * *m* adulterer.

adultera *f* adulteress.

adulterio *m* adultery.

adulto *adj* adult; * *m* adult, grown-up.

adunare *vt* to mass; * *vr* **~rsi** to mass.

aereo *adj* aerial.

aerobica *f* aerobics.

aeromobile *m* aircraft.

aeronatica *f* militare air force.

aeroporto *m* airport.

aerosol *m* aerosol.

affabile *adj* affable, amiable, good-natured.

affaccendarsi *vr* to bustle.

affamato *adj* hungry; starving, famished.

affare *m* affair; deal; bargain; snip.

affari *mpl* business; **uomo d'~** *m* businessman; **donna d'~** *f* businesswoman.

affascinante *adj* fascinating; glamorous; intriguing.

affascinare *vt* to fascinate; to captivate, to charm; to enthral.

affaticare *vt* to fatigue; to strain.

affatto *adv* at all; **niente ~** not in the least.

affermare *vt* to affirm; to assert; to state.

affermativo *adj* affirmative.

affermato *adj* successful.

affermazione *f* assertion, claim, affirmation.

afferrare *vt* to catch, to clasp; to grasp; to grab, to snatch; to seize.

affettare *vt* to slice; to affect.

affettato *adj* affected.

affettatrice *f* slicer.

affetto *m* affection; fondness.

affettuoso *adj* loving, warm-hearted.

affezionato *adj* affectionate, fond.

affidabile *adj* dependable, reliable.

affidare *vt* to entrust; (actor) to cast.

affidatario *adj*: **genitore ~** *m* foster parent.

affidavit *m inv* affidavit.

affievolirsi *vr* to dwindle.

affiggere *vt* to post.

affilare *vt* to sharpen.

affilato *adj* sharp.

affiliare *vt* to affiliate.

affiliazione *f* affiliation.

affinché *conj* so that.

affine *adj* (*ling*) cognate; related.

affinità *f* affinity.

affittare *vt* to lease; to let; to rent.

affitto *m* rent; **proprietà in ~** *f* leasehold; **contratto d'~** *m* tenancy.

affliggere *vt* to afflict.

afflitto *adj* doleful.

affluente *m* tributary.

afflusso *m* influx; onrush.

affogare *vt, vi* to drown.

affollare *vt* to crowd; to throng; * *vr* **~rsi** to cram.

affondare *vi* to founder; to sink.

affrancare *vt* to stamp, to frank.

affrancato *adj* prepaid.

affrancatura *f* postage.

affresco *m* fresco.

affrettare *vt* to quicken; * *vr* **~rsi** to hurry, to make haste.

affrettato *adj* hasty.

affrontare *vt* to broach; to confront; to deal with, to tackle; to face.

affronto *m* affront, slur, snub, slight.

affumicare *vt* to smoke.

affumicato *adj* smoked.

affusto *m* gun carriage.

aforisma *m* aphorism.

afoso *adj* close, sultry, muggy.

afrodisiaco *m* aphrodisiac.

agenda *f* diary.

agente *m/f* agent; **~ immobiliare** *m* estate agent.

agenzia *f* agency; **~ viaggi** *f* travel agency.

agevolazione *f* concession; ~ **fiscale** *f* tax relief.

agganciare *vt* to hook.

aggeggio *m* contraption; gadget.

aggettivo *m* adjective.

aggiungere *vt* to add.

agghiacciante *adj* gruesome, spine-chilling.

agghindarsi *vr* to preen.

aggiornare *vt* to update; to write up.

aggiornato *adj* up-to-date.

aggirare *vt* to circumvent; to skirt.

aggirarsi *vr* to prowl; ~ **furtivamente** *vi* to skulk; **chi si aggira furtivamente** *m* prowler.

aggiunta *f* addition, accession (to collection), adjunct.

aggiustare *vt* to adjust; to mend, to repair.

agglomerazione *f* agglomeration.

agglomerato *m* chipboard.

aggrapparsi *vr* to cling.

aggravamento *m* aggravation.

aggravare *vt* to aggravate.

aggraziato *adj* graceful.

aggredire *vt* to mug.

aggregare *vt* to affiliate.

aggressione *f* aggression.

aggressivo *adj* aggressive.

aggressore *m* aggressor; attacker.

aggrottare *vt* to contract; ~ **le sopracciglia** *vi* to knit one's brow, to frown.

aggrovigliare *vt* to tangle.

aggrumarsi *vr* to cake.

agguato *m* ambush; **stare in** ~ to lie in ambush.

agile *adj* agile; lithe; nimble.

agilità *f* agility.

agio *m* ease; **sentirsi a proprio** ~ to feel at one's ease.

agire *vi* to act.

agitare *vt* to agitate; to stir; to churn; to flail; * *vr* ~**rsi** to fidget; to dither; to wriggle.

agitato *adj* flustered.

agitatore *m* agitator.

agitazione *f* agitation.

agitazione *f* fuss, flurry; state; unrest; **stato di** ~ *m* fluster.

aglio *m* garlic; **spicchio d'**~ *m* clove of garlic.

agnello *m* lamb.

ago *m* needle.

agonia *f* death throes.

agonistico *adj* competitive.

agosto *m* August.

agricolo *adj* agricultural.

agricoltore *m* farmer.

agricoltura *f* agriculture, farming.

agrifoglio *m* holly.

agrume *m* citrus.

aguzzino *m* slave-driver.

aguzzo *adj* sharp.

ahi! *excl* ouch!.

ahimè! *excl* alas!.

aia *f* farmyard.

AIDS *m* AIDS.

airone *m* heron.

aitante *adj* upstanding.

aiuola *f* (garden) border; flower bed.

aiutante *m/f* assistant; help; ~ **di campo** aide-de-camp.

aiutare *vt* to assist, to aid, to help.

aiuto *m* aid, assistenza, help.

al di là *prep* beyond.

ala *f* wing; (*sport*) winger.

alabastro *m* alabaster.

alacremente *adj* busily.

alambicco *m* still.

alato *adj* winged.

alba *f* dawn, daybreak, sunrise.

albatro *m* albatross.

alberello *m* sapling.

albergatore *m* hotelier.

albergo *m* hotel.

albero *m* tree; ~ **da frutto** *m*

fruit tree; mast; (*mar*) spar; shaft; ~ **a gomiti** *m* crankshaft; ~ **a camme** *m* camshaft.

albicocca *f* apricot.

albicocco *m* apricot tree.

album *m* album.

alcali *m inv* alkali.

alcalino *adj* alkaline.

alce *m* elk, moose.

alchimia *f* alchemy.

alchimista *m* alchemist.

alcolico *adj* alcoholic.

alcolico *m* alcoholic; **bevande alcoliche** *fpl* liquor.

alcolismo *m* alcoholism.

alcolizzato *m* alcoholic.

alcool *m* alcohol, (*fam*) booze; ~ **denaturato** *m* methylated spirits.

alcova *f* alcove.

alcuno *adj* some; * *pron* **alcuni** some.

alfabetico *adj* alphabetical; **in ordine** ~ in alphabetical order.

alfabeto *m* alphabet; ~ **Morse** *m* Morse code.

alfiere *m* (chess) bishop.

algebra *f* algebra.

alghe *fpl* algae; seaweed.

aliante *m* glider; **volo con l'**~ *m* gliding.

alias *adv* alias.

alibi *m* alibi.

alienare *vt* to alienate.

alienazione *f* alienation.

alimentare *vt* to feed.

alimentari *m* grocery; **negoziante di** ~ *m* grocer.

alimentazione *f* diet; input.

alimenti *mpl* alimony.

aliscafo *m* hydrofoil.

alito *m* breath.

alitosi *f* halitosis.

allacciare *vt* to tie; to lace; to buckle; * *vr* ~**rsi** to buckle, to fasten.

allampanato *adj* weedy.

allargare *vt* to broaden.

allarmare *vt* to alarm.

allarme *m* alarm, alert; **falso** ~ *m* false alarm.

allarmista *m/f* alarmist; scaremonger; * *adj* panicky.

allattare *vt* to suckle; to feed; ~ **al seno** to breastfeed.

alleanza *f* alliance.

allearsi con *vr* to ally.

alleato *adj* allied; * *m* ally.

allegare *vt* to enclose; to append.

allegato *m* enclosure.

alleggerire *vt* to lighten; * *vr* ~**rsi di** to jettison.

allegoria *f* allegory.

allegorico *adj* allegorical.

allegramente *adv* gaily.

allegria *f* gaiety; merriment.

allegro *m* cheerful, jolly, merry; perky.

allenamento *m* training.

allenare *vt* to train, to coach.

allenato *adj* trained.

allenatore *m* trainer, coach.

allentare *vt* to loosen; to slacken; to weaken; * *vt* ~**rsi** to slacken.

allentato *adj* loose.

allergia *f* allergy.

allettante *adj* alluring; tantalizing; tempting.

allettare *vt* to allure; to entice.

allevamento *m* breeding; ~ **di pesci** *m* fish farm.

allevare *vt* to breed; to bring up; to raise; to foster.

allevatore *m* breeder.

alleviare *vt* to alleviate; to ease; to relieve.

allibratore *m* bookmaker.

allievo *m* pupil.

alligatore *m* alligator.

allineare *vt* to align.

allineato *adj* aligned; **non** ~ non-aligned.

allitterazione *f* alliteration.
allodola *f* lark, skylark.
alloggiamento *m* housing.
alloggiare *vt* to accommodate; to house; * *vi* to lodge; to stay.
alloggio *m* accommodation.
alludere a *vt* to allude.
allontanamento *m* estrangement.
allontanare *vt* to stave off.
allora *adv* then; **da ~** since.
alloro *m* bay, laurel.
allucinazione *f* hallucination.
alludere *vt* to hint.
alluminio *m* aluminium.
allungare *vt* to elongate; to lengthen.
allusione *f* allusion; hint.
alluvionale *adj* alluvial.
almanacco *m* almanac.
almeno *adv* at least.
alpinismo *m* climbing; mountaineering.
alpinista *m/f* climber; mountaineer.
alpino *adj* alpine.
alquanto *adv* somewhat.
altalena *f* swing; seesaw.
altare *m* altar.
alterco *m* wrangle.
alternante *adj* alternating.
alternare *vt* to alternate.
alternativa *f* alternative; **come ~** alternatively.
alternativo *adj* alternative.
alternato *adj* alternate.
alternatore *m* alternator.
altezza *f* height; headroom; highness; **essere all'~** to live up to.
altezzoso *adj* supercilious; snooty; lofty.
altitudine *f* altitude.
alto *adj* high; tall; treble; **in ~** aloft; **il più ~** topmost; **verso l'~** upwards; * *adv* **in ~** overhead; * *m* high.
altolocato *adj* grand.

altoparlante *m inv* loudspeaker; speaker.
altopiano *m* plateau.
altrettanto *adv* just as; likewise.
altrimenti *adv* else; otherwise.
altro *pron*: **un ~** another; other; **l'un l'~** one another; * *adj* other; more; * *adv* else.
altrove *adv* elsewhere.
altruista *adj* selfless; unselfish.
alveare *m* beehive, hive.
alzare *vt* to heighten; to raise; to turn up; * *vr* **~rsi** to rise; to stand up.
amaca *f* hammock.
amalgamare *vt* to amalgamate.
amante *m/f* lover; *f* mistress.
amare *vt* to love.
amaretto *m* macaroon.
amarezza *f* bitterness.
amarillide *f* amaryllis.
amaro *adj* bitter.
amazzone *f* horsewoman.
ambasciata *f* embassy.
ambasciatore *m* ambassador.
ambasciatrice *f* ambassadress.
ambedue *adj* both.
ambidestro *adj* ambidextrous.
ambientale *adj* environmental.
ambientalista *m/f* conservationist.
ambientarsi *vr* to find one's feet.
ambiente *m* environment; setting; **~ sociale** *m* milieu.
ambiguità *f inv* ambiguity.
ambiguo *adj* ambiguous; dubious.
ambito *m* scope.
ambizione *f* ambition.
ambizioso *adj* ambitious.
ambra *f*, *adj* amber.
ambulante *adj* itinerant.
ambulanza *f* ambulance.
ambulatorio *m* surgery.
ametista *f* amethyst.

amianto *m* asbestos.

amica *f* girlfriend.

amichevole *adj* amicable; friendly.

amicizia *f* friendship.

amico *m* friend; pal; **~ del cuore** bosom friend.

amicone *m* chum, crony.

amido *m* starch.

ammaccare *vt* to dent.

ammaccatura *f* dent.

ammalarsi *vr* to sicken.

ammanettare *vt* to shackle.

ammassarsi *vr* to flock.

ammazzare *vt* to kill.

ammettere *vt* to accept, to admit; **bisogna ~ che** admittedly.

ammiccare *vi* to wink.

amministrare *vt* to administrate; **~ male** to mismanage; to administer.

amministrativo *adj* administrative.

amministratore *m* administrator; trustee; **~ delegato** managing director.

amministrazione *f* administration; **~ della casa** *f* housekeeping; **cattiva ~** *f* mismanagement.

ammiragliato *m* admiralty.

ammiraglio *m* admiral.

ammirare *vt* to admire.

ammiratore *m* admirer; well-wisher.

ammirazione *f* admiration.

ammissibile *adj* admissible, allowable.

ammissione *f* acknowledgement, admission: entrance.

ammoniaca *f* ammonia.

ammettere *vt* to concede, to countenance, to brook; to grant; to own up.

ammissibile *adj* permissible.

ammobiliato *adj* furnished.

ammonimento *m* caveat.

ammonire *vt* to admonish; to caution.

ammontare *vi* to amount; **~ a** to amount to; * *vt* to total.

ammonitorio *adj* cautionary.

ammorbidente *m* softener.

ammorbidire *vt* to soften.

ammortizzabile *adj* redeemable.

ammortizzare *vt* to absorb.

ammortizzatore *m* shock absorber

ammucchiare *vt* to heap, to pile.

ammuffito *adj* mouldy.

ammutinamento *m* mutiny.

ammutinarsi *vr* to mutiny.

ammutolito *adj* tongue-tied.

amnesia *f* amnesia.

amnistia *f* amnesty.

amorale *adj* amoral.

amore *m* love; **vero ~** true love; **storia d' ~** *f* romance; **per ~** for the sake of; **malato d'~** *adj* lovesick.

amorfo *adj* amorphous.

amoroso *adj* amorous.

ampere *m inv* amp(ere).

ampiamente *adv* amply.

ampiamento *m* enlargement.

ampiezza *f* fullness.

ampio *adj* ample.

ampliare *vt* amplify; to enlarge; to widen.

amplificare *vt* amplify.

amplificatore *m* amplifier; **~ di segnale** booster.

amplificazione *f* amplification; **impianto di ~** *m* public address system.

ampolla *f* cruet.

ampolloso *adj* turgid.

amputare *vt* amputate.

amputazione *f* amputation.

amuleto *m* amulet.

anacardio *m* cashew.

anacronismo *m* anachronism.

anagrafe *f* registry office.

anagramma *m* anagram.

analcolico *m* soft drink; * *adj* non-alcoholic.

analfabeta *m/f, adj* illiterate.

analisi *f inv* analysis; ~ **del sangue** blood test; ~ **infinitesimale** *f* calculus.

analista *m/f* analyst; ~ **sistemi** systems analyst.

analitico *adj* analytic(al).

analizzare *vt* to analyse.

analogia *f* analogy.

analogico *adj* analogue.

analogo *adj* analogous.

ananas *m inv* pineapple.

anarchia *f* anarchy.

anarchico *adj* anarchic; * *m* anarchist.

anatema *m* anathema.

anatomia *f* anatomy.

anatomico *adj* anatomical.

anatra *f* duck; **maschio dell'~** *m* drake.

anatroccolo *m* duckling.

anca *f* hip.

ancestrale *adj* ancestral.

anche *adv* also; too; as well.

ancheggiare *vt* to wiggle one's hips.

ancora *adv* again; another; even; still; already; * *adj* more.

àncora *f* anchor.

ancoraggio *m* anchorage.

andamento *m* trend.

andare *vi* to go; ~ **a gattoni** to crawl; ~ **furtivamente** to creep; ~ **a destra** to bear right; ~ **avanti** to lead; * *vt* ~ **bene a** to fit; ~ **sù e giù** to pace.

andarsene *vi* to go (away).

andata *f* **biglietto di** ~ *m* single ticket.

andatura *f* going, gait, walk.

aneddoto *m* anecdote.

anelito *m* gasp.

anello *m* ring; ~ **di fidanzamento** *m* engagement ring; link.

anemia *f* anaemia.

anemico *adj* anaemic.

anemone *m* (*bot*) anemone.

anestetico *m* anaesthetic.

anestetista *m/f* anaesthetist.

aneto *m* dill.

anfibio *m̄* amphibian; amphibious.

anfiteatro *m* amphitheatre.

angelico *adj* angelic.

angelo *m* angel.

anglicismo *m* anglicism.

anglicizzare *vt* anglicize.

angolino *m* nook.

angolo *m* angle; corner; ~ **sperduto** *m* backwater.

angoscia *f* anguish; distress; * *vr* ~**rsi** to agonize over.

anguilla *f* eel.

anguria *f* watermelon.

angusto *adj* cramped; poky.

anice *m* aniseed.

anima *f* soul.

animale *adj* animal; * *m* animal; ~ **domestico** *m* pet; **animali nocivi** *mpl* vermin.

animare *vt* to animate; to pep up.

animato *m* boisterous; * *adj* animate(d).

animazione *f* animation.

animelle *fpl* sweetbreads.

animosità *f inv* animosity.

annaffiatoio *m* watering can.

annali *mpl* annals; records.

annata *f* vintage; year.

annegare *vt, vi* to drown.

annerire *vt* to blacken; * *vr* ~**rsi** to blacken.

annesso *m* annex.

annettare *vt* to annex.

annientamento *m* annihilation.

annientare *vt* to annihilate.

anniversario *m* anniversary.

anno *m* year; session; ~ **nuovo** *m* New Year; ~ **luce** *m* light year; **all'**~ per annum.

annodare *vt* to knot.

annoiare *vt* to bore.

annotare *vt* to annotate; to record.

annotazione *f* annotation.

annuale *adj* yearly.

annualità *f* annuity.

annuario *m* yearbook.

annullamento *m* annulment.

annullare *vt* to countermand; to abrogate, to annul; to invalidate; to nullify.

annunciare *vt* to announce.

annunciatore *m* newscaster.

annuncio *m* advertisement; accouncement; **annunci economici** *mpl* classified advertisements.

annuo *m* annual.

annusare *vt* to sniff.

anomalia *f* abnormality, anomaly.

anomalo *adj* anomalous.

anonimato *m* anonymity; obscurity.

anonimo *adj* anonymous; unnamed.

anoressia *f* anorexia.

anormale *adj* abnormal; freak.

anormalità *f* abnormality.

ansare *vi* to gasp.

ansia *f* anxiety.

ansimare *vi* to pant; to puff; to wheeze.

ansioso *adj* nervous; solicitous.

antagonismo *m* antagonism.

antagonista *m* antagonist.

antartico *adj* antarctic.

antecedente *adj* antecedent.

anteguerra *f* pre-war.

antenato *m* ancestor.

antenna *f* aerial, antenna; feeler.

anteprima *f* preview.

anteriore *adj* anterior; fore.

antiaderente *adj* non-stick.

antiaereo *adj* anti-aircraft.

antiappannante *m* demister.

antibiotico *m* antibiotic.

anticamera *f* antechamber.

antichità *f* antiquity.

anticiclone *m* anticyclone.

anticipare *vt* to advance; to forestall.

anticipo *m* andvance; down payment; **in ~** in advance or ahead; **dare un ~** to give an advance (loan); **pagato in ~** prepaid.

antico *adj* ancient, antique.

anticoncezionale *adj*, *m* contraceptive.

anticonformista *adj*, *m/f* nonconformist.

anticorpo *m* antibody.

antidolorifico *m* painkiller.

antidoto *m* antidote.

antieconomico *adj* uneconomic.

antifurto *m inv* burglar alarm.

antigelo *m* antifreeze.

antilope *f* antelope.

antincendio *adj*: **allarme ~** *f* fire alarm.

antiorario *adj*: **in senso ~** anticlockwise.

antipasto *m* hors d'oeuvres, starter.

antipatia *f* antipathy; dislike.

antipatico *adj* objectionable; unlovable.

antipodi *mpl* antipodes.

antiquariato *m* antiques; **pezzo d'~** *m* antique.

antiquario *m* antiquarian.

antiquato *adj* antiquated; dated; old-fashioned; stuffy.

antirrino *m* snapdragon.

antisemitico *adj* antisemitic.

antisettico *m*, *adj* antiseptic.

antisociale *adj* antisocial.

antistiminico *m* antihistamine.

antitesi *f inv* antithesis.

antologia *f* anthology; reader.

antracite *f* anthracite.

antropologia f anthropology.
anzianità f seniority.
anziano adj aged; elderly; old; * m elder.
aorta f aorta.
apartheid f apartheid.
apatia f apathy.
apatico adj apathetic; listless.
ape f bee.
aperitivo m aperitif.
aperto adj open; broad-minded; open-minded; gaping; **all'~** outdoor.
apertura f aperture; opening; spread.
apiario m apiary.
apice m prime.
apocalisse f Apocalypse.
apocrifo adj apocryphal.
apolide adj stateless.
apolitico adj apolitical.
apoplessia f apoplexy.
apoplettico adj apoplectic.
apostolico adj apostolic.
apostolo m apostle.
apostrofo m apostrophe.
apoteosi f apotheosis.
appagare vt to quench.
appaltatore m contractor.
appannarsi vr to mist up.
apparecchio m set; appliance; **~ acustico** m hearing aid; **~ ortodontico** m brace.
apparecchiare vt to lay (the table).
apparente adj outward; seeming.
apparentemente adv ostensibly.
apparenza f semblance.
apparire vi to appear; **~ indistintamente** to loom.
appariscente adj showy; **poco ~** inconspicuous.
appartamento m apartment; flat; suite.
appartato adj secluded.
appartenere vi to belong.

appassionante adj gripping.
appassionato adj devotee; enthusiastic; passionate; * m enthusiast.
appassire vi to droop; to fade; to wilt, to wither.
appellante m/f appellant; * vt **~rsi** (law) to appeal.
appello m appeal; muster.
appena adv barely; just; hardly; fresh, freshly; scarcely; **~ possibile** as soon as possible; * conj as soon as possible.
appendere vt to hang.
appendice f adjunct, appendage, appendix.
appetito m appetite.
appetitoso adj appetizing; luscious.
appezzamento m plot.
appianare vt to even; to settle; to patch up.
appiccicare vt to paste; * vr **~rsi** to stick.
appiccicoso adj clammy; sticky, glutinous.
applaudire vt to applaud; to clap.
applauso m applause, acclaim; clapping.
applicabile adj applicable.
applicare vt to enforce; * vr **~rsi** to apply.
applicato adj applied.
applicazione f application.
appoggiare vt to back; to lean; to support; to prop; to second; * vr **~rsi** to lean.
appoggio m backing; rest.
appollaiarsi vr to roost; to perch.
apporre vt affix, append.
apposito adj apposite.
apposizione f apposition.
apposta adv deliberately; on purpose.
apprendista m/f apprentice; trainee.

18

apprendistato *m* apprenticeship.

apprensione *f* apprehension; misgiving.

apprensivo *adj* apprehensive.

apprezzamento *m* appreciation.

apprezzare *vt* to appreciate.

approccio *m* approach.

approfittare *vi* to profit; ~ **di** to take advantage of.

approfondire *vt* to deepen.

approfondito *adj* thorough; close.

appropriarsi *vr*; ~ **di** to appropriate; ~ **indebitamente** to embezzle.

appropriatamente *adv* aptly.

appropriato *adj* apt; proper; suitable.

appropriazione *f* appropriation; ~ **indebita** embezzlement.

approssimativo *adj* approximate; rough.

approssimazione *f* approximation.

approvare *vt* to approve; to assent; to carry; to endorse; to subscribe; to pass.

approvazione *f* approbation, approval; endorsement.

approvvigionamento *m* procurement.

appuntamento *m* appointment; date; rendezvous.

appuntito *adj* pointed.

apribottiglie *m inv* bottle-opener.

aprile *m* April.

aprire *vt* to open; to unlock; ~ **facendo leva** *vt* to prise.

apriscatole *m inv* tin-opener.

aquila *f* eagle.

aquilino *adj* aquiline; hooked (nose).

aquilone *m* kite.

aquilotto *m* eaglet.

arabesco *n* arabesque.

arabile *adj* arable.

arabo *adj*, *m* arab.

arachide *f* peanut.

aragosta *f* lobster.

araldica *f* heraldry.

araldo *m* herald.

arancia *f* orange.

aranciata *f* orangeade.

arancio *m* orange tree; *adj* orange.

arare *vi*, *vt* to plough.

aratro *m* plough.

arazzo *m* tapestry.

arbitrario *adj* arbitrary.

arbitrato *m* arbitration.

arbitro *m* arbitrator; referee; umpire; **fare da** ~ to arbitrate.

arca *f* ark.

arcaico *adj* archaic.

arcangelo *m* archangel.

arcata *f* arcade.

archeologia *f* archeology.

archeologico *adj* archaeological.

archeologo *m* archaelogist.

architettare *vt* to engineer.

architetto *m* architect.

architettonico *adj* architectural.

architettura *f* architecture.

architrave *f* lintel.

archivi *mpl* records.

archiviare *vt* to file.

archivio *m* archives; file.

arciere *m* archer.

arcivescovado *m* archbishopric.

arcivescovo *m* archbishop.

arco *m* arch; bow; **tiro con l'**~ archery; * *adj* **ad** ~ arched.

arcobaleno *m* rainbow.

ardente *adj* ardent; aflame.

ardere *vi* to blaze; to glow.

ardesia *f* slate.

ardore *m* ardour.

arduo *adj* arduous.

area *f* area.
arena *f* arena, bullring.
arenaria *f* sandstone.
arenarsi *vr* run aground.
argano *m* winch.
argentato *adj* silvery.
argenteria *f* silver.
argentiere *m* silversmith.
argento *m* silver.
argilla *f* clay.
argine *m* embankment.
argomento *m* subject; topic.
arguto *adj* pithy; witty.
arguzia *f* wit, witticism.
aria *f* air; look; (*mus*) aria, (*auto*) choke; ~ **condizionata** *f* air-conditioning; **con ~ condizionata** *adj* air-conditioned; **senz' ~** *adj* airless.
aridità *f* dryness.
arido *adj* arid.
arieggiare *vt* air.
arieggiato *adj* airy.
ariete *m* ram; battering ram.
Ariete *m* Aries;
aringa *f* herring.
aristocratico *m* aristocrat; *adj* aristocratic.
aristocrazia *f* aristocracy.
aritmetica *f* arithmetic.
aritmetico *adj* arithmetical.
arlecchino *m* harlequin.
arma *f* weapon; ~ **da fuoco** firearm.
armadietto *m* cabinet; locker.
armadio *m* cupboard.
armaiolo *m* gunsmith.
armamentario *m* (*fig*) paraphernalia.
armamenti *mpl* armaments.
armare *vt* to arm.
armato *adj* armed; **uomo ~** gunman.
armatore *m* shipowner.
armatura *f* armour.
armeria *f* armoury.
armistizio *m* armistice.
armonia *f* concord; harmony.

armonica *f* harmonica; mouth-organ.
armonico *adj* harmonic.
armonioso *adj* harmonious.
armonizzare *vt*, *vi* to harmonize.
arnese *m* tool.
aroma *m* aroma.
aromatico *adj* aromatic.
arpa *f* harp.
arpione *m* harpoon.
arpista *f* harpist.
arrabbiare *vt* **far ~** to make someone angry; to enrage.
arrabbiatissimo *adj*: **essere ~** to fume.
arrabbiato *adj* angry.
arrampicarsi *vr* to climb, to clamber.
arrancare *vi* to plod.
arredamento *m* decor.
arredare *vt* to furnish.
arredatore *m* interior designer.
arrendersi *vr* to surrender.
arrestare *vt* to arrest; to apprehend; to stem; to stop, to stunt.
arresto *m* arrest; stop; ~ **cardiaco** *m* heart failure.
arretrati *mpl* arrears.
arretrato *adj* back; backward; **cumulo di lavoro ~** *m* backlog; **numero ~** *m* back number.
arricchimento *m* enrichment.
arricchire *vt* to enrich.
arricciare *vt* to curl.
arringa *f* harangue.
arringare *vt* to harangue.
arrivare *vi* to arrive; to go; to get; to turn up.
arrivederci *excl* goodbye.
arrivo *m* arrival; **in ~** *adj* incoming.
arrogante *adj* arrogant.
arroganza *f* arrogance.
arrossare *vt* to redden.

arrossire *vi* to blush, to flush, to redden.

arrostire *vt* to roast.

arrosto *adj inv*, *m* roast.

arrotondare *vt* to round.

arruffare *vt* to ruffle.

arruffato *adj* dishevelled.

arrugginire *vi*, *vt* to rust.

arruolamento *m* conscription; enlistment.

arruolare *vt* to conscript; to enlist.

arsenale *m* arsenal.

arsenico *m* arsenic.

arte *f* art; craft; **le belle arti** *fpl* the fine arts; ~ **bellica** warfare.

arteria *f* artery.

arterioso *adj (anat)* arterial.

artico *adj* arctic.

articolare *vt* to articulate; ~ **male** *vi* to slur one's speech.

articolazione *f* articulation; joint; enunciation.

articolo *m* article; item; story.

artificiale *adj* artificial; man-made.

artigianato *m* handicraft.

artigiano *m* craftsman; artisan.

artigliere *m* gunner.

artiglieria *f* artillery; ordnance.

artiglio *m* claw; talon.

artista *m/f* artist; entertainer; performer.

artistico *adj* artistic.

arto *m* limb.

artrite *f* arthritis.

arzillo *adj* spry.

ascella *f* armpit.

ascendente *m* ascendancy.

ascensione *f* ascent, ascension.

ascensore *m* lift.

ascesa *f* rise.

ascesso *m* abscess.

aspetto *m* appearance.

ascetico *adj* ascetic.

ascia *f* axe.

asciugacapelli *m inv* hair-dryer.

asciugamano *m* towel.

asciugare *vt* to dry; to blot (ink).

asciutissimo *adj* bone-dry.

asciutto *adj* dry; sere.

ascoltare *vi* to listen.

asfaltare *vt* to surface.

asfalto *m* asphalt.

asfissia *f* asphyxia.

asfissiare *vt* asphyxiate; ~ **col gas** to gas.

asilo *m* asylum; ~ **nido** *m* crèche; kindergarten; ~ **infantile** *m* nursery school; playgroup.

asino *m* ass; donkey.

asma *f* asthma.

asmatico *adj* asthmatic.

asola *f* buttonhole.

asparago *m* asparagus.

aspettare *vt* to await; to expect; * *vi* to wait.

aspettativa *f* expectation.

aspetto *m* aspect; look; facet; **sotto certi** ~ in some respects.

aspirante *adj* would-be.

aspirare *vt* to aspirate; to aspire.

aspirazione *f* aspiration; suction.

aspirina *f* aspirin.

asportabile *adj* removable.

asportare *vt* to remove.

asprezza *f* acrimony.

aspro *adj* acerbic, bitter; tart; sharp, sour; pungent; rugged; harsh; acrimonious.

assegnare *vt* allocate, allot.

assaggiare *vt* to taste; to sample.

assalire *vt* to assail.

assalitore *m* assailant.

assaltare *vt* to assault; to hold up (a bank).

assalto *m* assault; **prendere d'~** *vt* to storm.

assaporare *vt* to savour; to taste.

assassina *f* murderess.

assassinare *vt* to assassinate; to murder.

assassinio *m* assassination; murder; foul play.

assassino *m* assassin; murderer; killer.

asse *f* board; axis; **~ da stiro** ironing board; **~ di pavimento** floorboard.

assediare *vt* to besiege.

assedio *m* siege; **stato d'~** *m* martial law.

assegnare *vt* to assign; to award; to set.

assegno *m* cheque; **libretto degli assegni** *m* cheque book; **~ in bianco** *m* blank cheque.

assemblea *f* assembly.

assennato *adj* sensible.

assente *adj* absent; faraway; * *m/f* absentee.

assenteismo *m* absenteeism .

assenza *f* absence.

asserire *vt* to affirm; to allege.

assetato *adj* thirsty.

assicurare *vt* to assure; to insure; to secure.

assicuratore *m* insurer; underwriter.

assicurazione *f* assurance; insurance; undertaking.

assiduo *adj* assiduous; sedulous.

assillare *vt* to beset; to harass; to harry; to nag.

assimilare *vt* to assimilate; to absorb.

assimilazione *f* assimilation.

assioma *m* axiom.

assiomatico *adj* axiomatic.

assistente *m/f* helper; *m* auxiliary; **~ sociale** *m/f* social worker.

assistenza *f* help; aid; **~ postoperatoria** aftercare; **servizio ~ clienti** after-sales service; **~ sociale** social work.

assistenziale *adj* welfare; **stato ~** *m* welfare state.

assistere *vt* to help; to minister to.

asso *m* ace; **avere un ~ nella manica** to have an ace up one's sleeve.

associare *vt* to associate; to couple.

associazione *f* association; fellowship; partnership.

assodato *adj* cut-and-dried.

assoggettato *adj* subject.

assolato *adj* sunny.

assolo *m* solo.

assolutamente *adv* absolutely.

assoluto *adj* absolute; uncompromising; unmitigated.

assoluzione *f* acquittal; absolution.

assolvere *vt* to discharge; to absolve from; to acquit.

assomigliare *vi* to look like; to take after.

assonnato *adj* drowsy; sleepy; **con aria ~** *adv* sleepily.

assorbente *m* sanitary towel; * *adj* absorbent.

assorbimento *m* absorption; takeover.

assorbire *vt* to absorb.

assordante *adj* deafening.

assordare *vt* to deafen.

assortimento *m* assortment.

assortito *adj* assorted; mixed.

assorto *adj* intent.

assuefare *vt* to inure.

assuefazione *f* addiction.

assumere *vt* to employ, to engage; to take on; * *vr* **~rsi** to take upon oneself.

assurdità *f* absurdity.

assurdo *adj* absurd; preposterous; * *m* (an) absurdity.

asta f pole; shaft; **salto con l'~** pole vault; **~ dell'olio** f dipstick; auction.

astante m/f bystander.

astemio adj abstemious; teetotal; * m teetotaller.

astenersi vr to refrain; * vi to abstain.

astenzione f abstention.

asterisco m asterisk; star.

asticella f stick.

astinenza f abstinence; selfdenial; **~ dall'alcool** f temperance.

astio m resentment; **guardare con ~** to glower.

astioso adj acrimonious.

astore m goshawk.

astratto adj abstract.

astrazione f abstraction.

astringente adj, m astringent.

astrologia f astrology.

astrologo m astrologer.

astronauta m/f astronaut; spaceman/woman.

astronomia f astronomy.

astronomico adj astronomical.

astronomo m astronomer.

astruso adj abstruse; recondite.

astuccio m case; **~ per matite** m pencil case.

astuto adj sly; wily.

astuzia f guile; trickery; ruse; slyness.

atavico adj ancestral.

ateismo m atheism.

ateo m atheist.

atipico adj unrepresentative.

atlante m atlas.

atleta m/f athlete.

atletico adj athletic.

atmosfera f atmosphere.

atmosferico adj atmospheric.

atomico adj atomic.

atomo m atom.

atout m inv trump.

atrio m lobby; concourse; vestibule.

atroce adj atrocious; excruciating; heinous.

atrocità f inv atrocity; enormity; outrage.

atrofia f atrophy.

attaccabrighe m/f inv troublemaker.

attaccamento m attachment.

attaccante m forward.

attaccare vt to affix; to charge (mil); to attach, to attack; to hitch up.

attacco m attack; strike; onslaught; fit; bout (illness); seizure; **~ improvviso** blitz; **~ massiccio** broadside.

attecchire vi to take; to root.

atteggiamento m attitude.

attendibile adj trustworthy; reputable.

attenersi vr to comply; to stick to.

attento adj careful; observant; watchful; **stare ~** to beware.

attenuante adj extenuating.

attenuare vt to attenuate; to assuage; extenuate; to tone down; * vr **~rsi** to moderate.

attenzione f attention; care; heed; caution.

atterraggio m landing; touchdown; **~ forzato** crash landing.

atterrare vi to land.

atterrire vt to appal.

attesa f wait; waiting; **lista d'~** waiting list; **sala d'~** waiting room; anticipation; expectancy, expectation; **in ~** adj expectant.

atteso adj due.

attestare vt to certify; to attest.

attestazione f certification.

attico m penthouse.

attiguo adj adjoining; **essere ~ a** to adjoin.

attinia f (zool) sea anemone.

attirare vt to attract; to draw;

~ con l'inganno to lure.

attivare *vt* activate.

attività *f* activity; business; pursuit.

attivo *adj* active; brisk.

attizzare *vt* to stoke.

attizzatoio *m* poker.

atto *m* act; **~ di proprietà** title deed.

attorcigliare *vt* to twist; * *vt* **~rsi** to coil; * *vr* to twist; to twine.

attorcigliato *adj* convoluted.

attore *m* actor; plaintiff.

attraente *adj* attractive; appealing; fetching; engaging.

attrattiva *f* attraction.

attraversare *vt* to cross; to span

attraverso *prep* across; through.

attrazione *f* attraction; pull.

attrezzare *vt* to equip.

attrezzatura *f* apparatus; equipment; gear; tackle; **~ da pesca** fishing tackle; (*pl*) amenities.

attrezzo *m* tool; **cassetta degli attrezzi** *f* toolbox.

attribuire *vt* attribute; ascribe; apportion; to give.

attributo *m* attribute.

attrice *f* actress.

attuabile *adj* viable.

attuale *adj* current; present; prevailing; up-to-date.

attualità *f*: **problemi d'~** *mpl* current affairs.

attualmente *adv* just now; currently.

attuare *vt* to implement.

attutire *vt* to deaden; to cushion.

attutito *adj* muted.

audace *adj* audacious; daring; bold.

audacia *f* audacity; boldness; daring; temerity.

auditorio *m* auditorium.

augurare *vt* to wish.

augurio *m* wish.

augusto *adj* august.

aula *f* classroom.

aumentare *vt* to augment; to increase; to grow; to gain; to heighten; * *vi* increase; to heighten; to rise; to accrue.

aumento *m* raise; gain; increase; rise; **~ di valore** *m* appreciation.

aura *f* aura.

aureola *f* halo.

ausiliare *adj* auxiliary.

ausiliario *adj, m* ancillary.

auspicio *m* omen; **sotto gli auspici** under the auspices.

austerità *f* austerity.

austero *adj* austere; stark.

autenticare *vt* to witness.

autenticità *f* authenticity.

autentico *adj* authentic.

autista *m* chauffeur; *m/f* driver.

autoaffondare *vt* to scuttle.

autoarticolato *m* articulated lorry.

autobiografia *f* autobiography.

autoblinda *f* armoured car.

autobus *m* bus.

autocarro *m* lorry: **~ della nettezza urbana** *m* dustcart.

autocercante *adj* homing.

autocisterna *f* tanker.

autocommiserazione *f* self-pity.

autocontrollo *m* self-control.

autocrata *m* autocrat.

autocratico *adj* autocratic.

autodidatta *adj* self-taught.

autodifesa *f* self-defence.

autodisciplina *f* self-discipline.

autografo *m* autograph.

automatico *adj* automatic.

automazione *f* automation.

automobile *f* car; **~ sportiva** sports car.

automobilista *m/f* motorist.

autonoleggio *m* car hire.

autonomia *f* autonomy; range.

autonomo *adj* self-governing.

autopompa *f* fire engine.

autopsia *f* autopsy; post-mortem.

autore *m* author; writer.

autorespiratore *m* autolung.

autorevole *adj* authoritative.

autorimessa *f* garage.

autorità *f* authority.

autoritario *adj* authoritarian.

autoritario *adj* bossy.

autoritratto *m* self-portrait.

autorizzare *vt* to authorize.

autorizzazione *f* authorization; clearance; permit; licence; leave.

autostop *m* hitchhiking; **fare l'~** to hitch (a lift), to hitchhike.

autostrada *f* motorway.

autosufficiente *adj* self-sufficient.

autotrasportatore *m* haulier.

autotrasporto *m* haulage.

autrice *f* authoress.

autunnale *adj* autumnal.

autunno *m* autumn.

avambraccio *m* forearm.

avamposto *m* outpost.

avances *fpl*: **fare delle ~ a** to make a pass at.

avanguardia *f* avant-garde; forefront; **d'~** *adj* avant-garde.

avanti *adv* ahead; forwards; **in ~** onwards; **in ~** *adj* forward; **più ~** further, farther.

avanzare *vi* advance; **~ a poco a poco** to edge forward.

avanzato *adj* advanced.

avanzi *mpl* leavings, leftovers, remains; dross

avanzo *m* remainder.

avarizia *f* avarice; meanness.

avaro *adj* avaricious; mean; * *m* miser.

avena *f* oats; **farina d'~** *f* oatmeal.

avere *vt* to have.

aviatore *m* flier.

aviazione *f* flying; aviation.

avidamente *adv* hungrily.

avidità *f* greed.

avido *adj* greedy, grasping; covetous.

aviofono *m* intercom.

aviorimessa *f* hangar.

avo *m* ancestor.

avocado *m* avocado.

avorio *m*, *adj* ivory.

avvalersi *vr*: **~ di** to avail oneself of.

avvallamento *m* subsidence.

avvallarsi *vr* to subside.

avvelenamento *m* poisoning; **~ del sangue** blood poisoning.

avvelenare *vt* to poison.

avvenimento *m* event; happening; incident.

avventarsi *vr* to go for.

avventato *adj* rash; unwise.

avvento *n* advent; coming.

avventura *f* adventure; affair.

avventuroso *adj* adventurous.

avverbio *m* adverb.

avversario *m* adversary; opponent; * *adj* opposing.

avversione *f* aversion; abomination, disgust.

avvertimento *m* warning.

avvertire *vt* to sense; to warn; alarm.

avviamento *m*; goodwill; **motorino d'~** *m* starter.

avviare *vt* to start.

avviato *adj*: **ben ~** going.

avvicinabile *adj* approachable.

avvicinare *vt* to approach; * *vr* **~rsi** to near.

avvilimento *m* abasement; humiliation; disheartenment.

avvilire *vt* to abase; to dishonour; to disgrace; to dishearten.

avvilito *adj* downcast; **essere ~** to mope.

avvincente *adj* absorbing; enthralling.

avvisare *vt* advise.

avviso *m* notice; advice.

avvitare *vt* to screw.

avvocato *m* advocate; lawyer; solicitor; attorney, barrister, counsel.

avvolgere *vt* to wind; to envelop; to coil; to swathe; to shroud.

avvoltoio *m* vulture.

azalea *f* azalea.

azienda *f* establishment.

azionare *vt* to drive; to power; to operate; to work.

azione *f* action; deed; share; **azioni** *fpl* holdings.

azionista *m/f* shareholder, stockholder.

azoto *m* nitrogen.

azzardo *m* gamble.

azzimato *adj* dapper; spruce.

azzuffarsi *vr* to brawl; to scuffle.

azzurro *adj* azure; blue.

B

babao *m* bogey man

babbo *m* pa(pa), dad(dy).

babbuino *m* baboon.

babordo *m* port.

bacca *f* berry.

baccano *m* hubbub; row.

baccello *m* pod.

bacchetta *f* baton; drumstick; wand; rod.

bacetto *m* peck.

baciare *vt* to kiss.

bacino *m* dock; pelvis; **~ carbonifero** coalfield; **~ idrico** reservoir.

bacio *m* kiss.

backgammon *m* backgammon.

baco *m* maggot.

badare *vt* to heed; to mind; **non ~ a** to discount.

badessa *f* abbess.

badia *f* abbey.

badminton *m* badminton

baffo *m*: **baffi** *mpl* moustache; whiskers.

bagaglio *m* baggage; **bagagli** *mpl* luggage.

bagliore *m* glare.

bagnante *m/f* bather.

bagnare *vt* to wet.

bagnato *adj* wet, soggy.

bagnino *m* lifeguard.

bagno *m* bath; **fare il ~** *vt* to bath; **fare il ~** *vt* to bathe; **stanza da ~** bathroom.

baia *f* bay; cove.

baionetta *f* bayonet.

baita *f* hut.

balaustrata *f* balustrade.

balbettare *vt, vi* to stutter, to stammer.

balbuzie *f* stammer, stutter.

balcone *m* balcony.

baldacchino *m* canopy; **letto a ~** four-poster (bed).

baldoria *f* spree; revelry; *vi* **far ~** to carouse; to revel.

balena *f* whale.

balestruccio *m* martin.

balia *f* wet nurse.

balistico *adj* ballistic.

balla *f* bale.

ballare *vt, vi* to dance.

ballata *f* ballad.

ballerina *f* ballerina.

ballerino *m* dancer.

ballo *m* dance; ball; **sala da ~** dance hall.

balsamico *adj* balmy.

balsamo *m* (hair) conditioner; balm.

baluardo *m* bulwark.

baluginare *vi* to glimmer.

balzare *vi* to pounce; to bound; to leap.

balzo *m* pounce; leap; bound.

bambinaia *f* nanny; baby-minder.

bambino *m* infant; baby; child (*pl* children); **~ che fa i primi passi** *m* toddler.

bambola *f* doll.

bambù *m* bamboo.

banale *adj* banal; mundane; commonplace; corny; run-of-the-mill.

banalità *f* platitude; *fpl* trivia.

banana *f* banana.

banano *m* banana tree.

banca *f* bank; **servirsi di una ~** *vi* to bank.

bancarella *f* stall.

bancarellista *m/f* stallholder.

bancaria *adj*; **attività ~** banking.

bancarotta *f* bankruptcy.

banchettare *vi* to feast.

banchetto *m* banquet; feast; spread.

banchiere *m* banker.

banchina *f* wharf.

banco *m* counter; pew; form; shoal; school (of fish); **~ degli imputati** *m* dock.

banconota *f* banknote.

banda *f* gang; band; bevy.

bandiera *f* flag; colours.

bandire *vt* to banish; to outlaw.

bandito *m* bandit.

banditore *m* auctioneer; town crier.

banjo *m inv* banjo.

bar *m* bar; café.

bara *f* coffin.

baracca *f* hut; shanty, shack.

baraonda *f* bedlam.

baratro *m* abyss.

barattare *vi, vt* to barter; to trade.

barattolo *m* jar; canister; **~ del tè** tea caddy.

barba *f* beard; **senza ~** *adj* clean-shaven; **~ corta** *f* stubble.

barbabietola *f* beet; beetroot; **~ da zucchero** *f* sugar beet.

barbaro *m* barbarian; * *adj* barbaric.

barbecue *m* barbecue.

barbiere *m* barber.

barbiturico *m* barbiturate.

barboncino *m* poodle.

barbuto *adj* bearded.

barca *f* boat.

barchino *m* punt.

barcollare *vi* to stagger; to reel.

bardare *vt* to harness.

bardatura *f* harness; trappings.

bardo *m* bard.

barella *f* stretcher.

barile *m* keg; barrel; cask.

barista *m/f* barman, barmaid, bartender.

baritono *m* baritone.

barlume *m* glimmer.

barmy *adj* suonato.

barocco *adj* baroque.

barometro *m* barometer.

barone *m* baron.

baronessa *f* baroness.

barra *f* tiller; **~ di comando** *f* joystick.

barricare *vt* to barricade.

barricata *f* barricade.

barriera *f* barrier.

baruffa *f* tussle; scrap.

basare *vt* to base.

base *f* base; basis; staple; grass roots; **buone basi** *fpl* good grounding.

baseball *m* baseball.
basilico *m* basil.
basilisco *m* basilisk.
bassifondi *mpl* slum area.
basso *adj* low; short; bass; * *m* (*mus*) bass.
bassopiano *m* lowland.
bassotto *m* dachshund.
bastardaggine *f* bastardy.
bastardo *m* bastard; (*sl*) sod; mongrel.
bastare *vi* to be enough; to suffice; **far ~** *vt* to eke out, to stretch.
bastione *m* rampart; **bastioni** *mpl* battlements.
bastoncino *m* stick; chopstick.
bastone *m* rod; club; cane; crook; staff; stick; **~ da passeggio** walking stick; **~ della tenda** *f* curtain rod.
battaglia *f* battle; **campo** *m* **di ~** battlefield.
battaglione *m* battalion.
battello *m* boat; **~ a ruote** *m* paddle steamer.
battente *m* knocker.
battere *vt* to hit; to beat; to flutter; **~ a macchina** to type; * *vi* to beat.
batteri *mpl* bacteria.
batteria *f* battery; drums; set.
batterista *m/f* drummer.
battesimo *m* baptism; christening.
battezzare *vt* to christen; to baptise.
battibecco *m* tiff; squabble.
battimano *m* clap.
battiscopa *m inv* skirting board.
battistero *m* baptistry.
battistrada *m inv* tread.
battito *m* beat; flutter; throb; **~ di ciglia** *m* blink.
battuta *f* quip; joke; sally.
batuffolo *m* wad.
baule *m* chest, trunk.

bauxite *f* bauxite.
bava *f* dribble; slime.
bavaglino *m* bib.
bavaglio *m* gag.
bazar *m* bazaar.
beatificare *vt* to beatify.
beatitudine *f* beatitude.
beccaccino *m* snipe.
beccare *vt* to peck.
beccata *f* peck.
becchino *m* gravedigger.
becco *m* bill, beak; spout.
becher *m* beaker.
befana *f* hag.
beffa *f* practical joke.
beffardo *adj* mocking; derisive; wry.
beffarsi *vr* to mock.
begonia *f* begonia.
beige *m inv* beige.
belare *vi* to baa, to bleat.
belato *m* bleat.
belladonna *f* deadly nightshade.
belletto *m* rouge.
bellezza *f* beauty.
bellicoso *adj* bellicose; truculent.
belligerante *adj* belligerent.
bello *adj* beautiful; handsome; good; good-looking, nice; nice-looking; lovely.
bemolle *adj* (*mus*) flat.
benché *conj* notwithstanding; though; although.
benda *f* blindfold.
bendare *vt* to blindfold.
bendato *adj* blindfold.
bendisposto *adj* well-disposed.
bene *m* good; welfare; * *excl* fine; * *adv* right; all right; well; * *adj* well; **voler ~ a** *vt* to love.
benedetto *adj* blessed.
benedicite *m* grace; **dire il ~** *vt* to say grace.
benedire *vt* to bless.
benedizione *f* benediction; blessing.

beneducato *adj* wellbred.

benefattore *m* benefactor.

beneficiario *m* beneficiary; payee.

beneficienza *f* charity.

benefico *adj* beneficient.

benessere *m* welfare, wellbeing.

benestante *adj* well-off.

benestare *m* assent; consent; **dare il ~ a qn** *vt* to give someone the go-ahead.

benevolenza *f* benevolence.

benevolo *adj* benevolent, benign.

beni *mpl* assets.

beniamino *m* pet, favourite.

benigno *adj* benign.

benino *adj*: **per ~** prim.

benvenuto *adj*, *m* welcome.

benvoluto *adj* popular.

benzina *f* petrol.

bere *m* drinking; * *vt* to drink; to imbibe; * *vi* to drink.

bernoccolo *m* bump.

berretto *m* cap; beret.

bersagliere *m* rifleman.

bersaglio *m* target; **~ per frecette** *m* dartboard.

bestemmia *f* curse; blasphemy.

bestemmiare *vi* o swear; to curse; to blaspheme.

bestemmiatore *m* blasphemer.

bestia *f* beast; **~ da soma** beast of burden.

bestiale *adj* bestial.

bestiame *m* livestock, cattle, stock.

bestiolina *f* creepy-crawly.

bestione *m* hulk.

betoniera *f* cement mixer.

bettola *f* dive.

betulla *f* birch.

bevanda *f* drink; **~ gasata** *f* pop.

bevitore *m* drinker.

biancastro *adj* whitish.

biancheria *f* laundry; **~ intima**

f lingerie, underwear.

bianco *adj* blank; white; * *m* white.

biancospino *m* hawthorn.

bibbia *f* bible.

bibita *f* drink.

biblico *adj* biblical.

bibliografia *f* bibliography.

biblioteca *f* library.

bibliotecario *m* librarian.

bicarbonato *m*: **~ di sodio** bicarbonate of soda.

bicchiere *m* glass; beaker; tumbler.

bicchierino *m* dram, nip.

bici *f inv* bike.

bicicletta *f* bicycle, cycle; **andare in ~** *vi* to cycle.

bicipite *m* biceps.

bidè *m inv* bidet.

bidello *m* janitor.

bidonata *f* raw deal.

bidone *m* drum; bin, dustbin.

bidonville *f inv* shanty town.

biennale *adj* biennial.

bifocali *adj* bifocal; **occhiali ~** *npl* bifocals.

biforcarsi *vr* to fork.

biforcazione *f* fork; bifurcation.

biforcuto *adj* forked.

bigamia *f* bigamy.

bigamo *m* bigamist.

bighellonare *vi* to loiter; to dawdle.

bighellone *m* loafer.

biglia *f* marble.

bigliardo *m* snooker.

bigliettaio *m* ticket collector.

biglietteria *f* ticket office.

biglietto *m* card; note; ticket.

bignè *m inv* éclair.

bigodino *m* curler, roller.

bikini *m inv* bikini.

bilancia *f* scales.

Bilancia *f* Libra;

bilanciare *vt* to offset.

bilancio *m* balance; budget; **~**

di esercizio balance sheet.
bilaterale *adj* bilateral.
bile *f* gall; bile.
biliardo *m* billiards; pool.
biliare *adj* bilious.
bilico *m*: **tenere in ~** to balance.
bilingue *adj* bilingual.
bilione *m* billion.
bimbo *m* baby.
binario *m* platform; track.
binocolo *m* binoculars.
biochimica *f* biochemistry.
biografia *f* biography.
biografico *adj* biographical.
biografo *m* biographer.
biologia *f* biology.
biologico *adj* biological.
biondo *m*, *adj* blond.
biossido *m* dioxide.
bipede *m* biped.
biposto *adj* two-seater.
birichinata *f* mischief.
birichino *adj* mischievous.
birillo *m* skittle.
birra *f* beer; ale; **~ bionda** *f* lager.
bis excl, *m inv* encore.
bisbetica *f* shrew.
bisbigliare *vt, vi* to whisper.
bisbiglio *m* whisper, whispering.
biscia *f* grass snake.
biscotto *m* biscuit.
bisecare *vt* to bisect.
bisestile *adj*: **anno ~** *m* leap year.
bisogno *m* need; want: **aver ~ di** *vt* to need.
bisognoso *adj* needy; deprived; impecunious.
bisonte *m* bison.
bistecca *f* steak; **~ di manzo** *f* steak; **~ di maiale** *f* porkchop.
bisticciare *vi* bicker; to spar; * *vt* **~rsi** to squabble.
bistrattare *vt* to mishandle.
bisturi *m inv* lancet; scalpel.

bitume *m* bitumen.
bivacco *m* bivouac.
bizzarria *f* quirk; oddity.
bizzarro *adj* droll; kinky; bizarre; weird.
blandire *vt* to wheedle.
blando *adj* bland.
blasé *adj* blasé.
blasfemo *adj* blasphemous.
blaterare *vi* to rattle on; * *vt* to prattle.
blatta *f* cockroach.
blazer *m* blazer.
bleso *adj*: **essere ~** *vi* to lisp; **pronuncia blesa** *f* lisp.
bloc-notes *m inv* notepad.
bloccare *vt* to block (up); to jam; to stop; * *vr* **~rsi** to stick; to stall.
bloccato *adj*: **~ dal ghiaccio** icebound.
blocchetto *m* pad.
blocco *m* bloc; block; blockade; freeze; **posto di ~** *m* checkpoint.
bluffare *vi* to bluff.
blusa *f* smock.
boa *f* buoy; boa.
bob *m inv* bobsleigh.
bobina *f* coil; spool; reel.
bocca *m* mouth; **guardare a ~ aperta** *vt* to gape.
boccaccia *f* trap.
boccale *m* mug.
boccaporto *m* hatch.
boccata *f* gulp.
bocchetta *f* nozzle.
bocchino *m* cigarette holder mouthpiece.
boccia *f*: **le bocce** bowls; **campo da bocce** bowling green.
bocciare *vt* to fail.
bocciolo *m* bud.
boccolo *m* ringlet.
boccone *m* morsel; mouthful.
body *m inv* leotard.
boia *m* hangman, executioner
boicottaggio *m* boycott.

boicottare *vt* to boycott, to black.

bolla *f* bubble.

bollettino *m* comuniqué; newsletter; bulletin.

bollire *vi* to boil; to seethe.

bollitore *m* kettle.

boma *m* boom.

bomba *f* bomb, bombshell; **~ incendiaria** *f* incendiary (bomb); **~ a orologieria** *f* time bomb.

bombardamento *m* bombardment.

bombardare *vt* to bomb; to bombard; to shell.

bombo *m* bumblebee.

bombola *f* gas cylinder.

bonificare *vt* to reclaim.

bontà *f* goodness.

boomerang *m inv* boomerang.

borbottare *vt, vi* to mutter; to mumble; to gabble.

borbottio *m* mutter.

bordare *vt* to edge.

bordeaux *adj* maroon.

bordeggiare *vi* to tack.

bordello *m* brothel.

bordo *m* edge, edging; surround; verge; (*mar*) tack; **fuori ~** *adj* overboard.

borghese *m* (*mil*) civilian; * *adj* bourgeois; **in ~** in plain clothes.

borghesia *f* bourgeosie; **dell'alta ~** *adj* upper-class.

borioso *m* prig.

borsa *f* handbag; pouch; bag; **~ di studio** bursary, grant, scholarship; **Borsa valori** *f* Stock Exchange.

borsaiolo *m* pickpocket.

borsellino *m* purse.

borsone *m* grip.

boscaglia *f* scrub; thicket.

boschetto *m* grove; coppice.

bosco *m* wood.

boscoso *adj* wooded; **zona boscosa** *f* woodland.

botanica *f* botany.

botanico *m* botanist; * *adj* botanic(al).

botola *f* trapdoor.

botta *f* bump; bash; **botte** *fpl* beating; hiding; butt.

botteghino *m* box office.

bottiglia *f* bottle.

bottino *m* loot; plunder; booty; spoil.

bottone *m* button; **~ automatico** *m* popper.

bouquet *m inv* bouquet.

boutique *f inv* boutique.

bovindo *m* bay window.

bovino *adj* bovine.

bowling *m* bowling; bowling alley.

box *m inv* playpen.

bozza *f* proof.

bozzolo *m* cocoon.

braccialetto *m* bracelet, bangle.

bracciante *m/f* farmhand.

bracciata *f* armful.

braccio *m* arm; jib; fathom.

bracciolo *m* armrest.

bracconaggio *m* poaching.

bracconiere *m* poacher.

brace *f* embers.

braciere *m* brazier.

bramare *vi* to yearn.

bramoso *adj* yearning.

branchia *f* gill.

branco *m* drove; gaggle (of geese); pride; pack.

brancolare *vi* to fumble.

brandello *m* shred.

brandire *vt* to flourish; to brandish; to swing.

brandy *m inv* brandy.

bravo *adj* good.

breccia *f* opening; breach.

breve *adj* brief; short.

brevettare *vt* to patent.

brevettato *adj* patented.

brevetto *m* patent.

brevità *f* brevity.

brezza *f* breeze; **~ marina** *f* sea breeze.

bric-a-brac *m* bric-a-brac.

briciola *f* breadcrumb; crumb.

briciolo *m* shred; scrap.

bricolage *m* do-it-yourself.

bridge *m* bridge.

brigata *f* brigade.

briglia *f* briglie; bridle; *fpl* harness.

brillante *adj* brilliant.

brillare *vi* to shine.

brillo *adj* merry; tipsy; tiddly.

brina *f* ftost; hoarfrost.

brindare *vt* to toast.

brindisi *m inv* toast; **qui ci vuole un ~!** this calls for a drink!

brio *m* liveliness.

brioso *adj* breezy.

brivido *m* shiver; thrill; shudder.

brocca *f* jug; pitcher.

broccato *m* brocade.

broccoli *mpl* broccoli.

brochure *f* brochure.

brodaglia *f* swill.

brodo *m* broth; stock; **~ ristretto** *m* consommé.

brodoso *adj* sloppy.

bronchiale *adj* bronchial.

bronchite *f* bronchitis.

broncio *m* pout; **tenere il ~** *vi* to sulk; **fare il ~** *vi* to pout.

brontolare *vi* to grumble; to grouse; to rumble.

brontolii *mpl* nagging.

brontolio *m* grumble.

brontolone *adj* nagging; * *m* nag.

bronzo *m* bronze.

brucare *vt* to crop.

bruciacchiare *vt* to singe; to scorch.

bruciacchiatura *f* scorch.

bruciapelo *adj*: **a ~** point-blank.

bruciare *vt* to burn; * *vi* to smart; to sting; to rankle.

bruciato *m* burning.

bruciatore *m* burner.

bruciatura *f* burn.

bruco *m* caterpillar.

brughiera *f* moor, heath.

brulicare *vi* to teem.

brumoso *adj* misty.

bruna *f* brunette.

bruscamente *adv* sharply; abruptly.

brusco *adj* abrupt, brusque, bluff, blunt, off-hand, curt; sharp; unceremonious; rude.

brutale *adj* brutal.

brutalità *f* brutality.

brutalmente *adv* roughly.

bruto *m*, brute; * *adj* brute; bad; ugly.

bruttezza *f* ugliness.

brutto *adj* bad; ugly.

bubble-gum *m inv* bubble gum.

buca *f* hole; pothole; pit; **~ di sabbia** *f* sandpit.

bucaneve *m inv* snowdrop.

bucare *vt* to hole; to prick.

bucato *m* washing.

buccia *f* peel; skin; rind; zest.

buco *m* hole.

bucolico *adj* bucolic.

buddismo *m* Buddhism.

budello *m* gut; **budella** *fpl* guts.

budino *m* pudding.

bue *m* ox.

bufalo *m* buffalo.

bufera *f* gale; **~ di neve** blizzard.

buffet *m inv* buffet.

buffo *adj* funny, comic.

buffone *m* buffoon; fool; jester.

buffoneria *f* antics.

bugia *f* lie; **~ pietosa** *f* white lie.

bugiardo *adj* lying; * *m m* liar; fibber.

buio *adj* dark; gloom; *m* dark; darkness; **~ pesto** pitch black.

bulbo *m* bulb; ~ **oculare** *m* eyeball; **a forma di** ~ *adj* bulbous.

bulldog *m inv* bulldog.

bulldozer *m inv* bulldozer.

bulletta *f* tack.

bullo *m* bully.

bullone *m* bolt.

bungalow *m inv* bungalow.

bunker *m inv* bunker.

buoi *mpl* oxen.

buongustaio *m* epicure; gourmet.

buono *m* coupon; token; ~ **premio** *m* gift voucher; *adj* kind-hearted; good.

burattino *m* puppet.

burbero *adj* gruff; surly.

burla *f* prank.

burlone *m* joker; tease.

burocrate *m/f* bureaucrat.

burocrazia *f* bureaucracy; (*fig*) red tape.

burrasca *f* squall.

burrascoso *adj* rough; stormy; tempestuous.

burro *m* butter.

burrone *m* gully; ravine.

bussare *vi* to knock; to tap; * *vt* to rap.

bussata *f* rap.

bussola *f* compass.

busta *f* envelope.

bustarella *f* backhander; bribe.

bustina *f* sachet.

busto *m* bust; girdle, corset.

buttafuori *m inv* bouncer;

buttar *vt:* ~ **fuori** to turf out; ~ **via** to throw away.

byte *m* byte.

C

cabina *f* booth; (lorry) cab; (plane) cabin; cubicle; ~ **di pilotaggio** cockpit, flight deck; ~ **telefonica** *f* (tele)phone booth, callbox.

cacao *m* cocoa; **burro di** ~ *m* lipsalve.

cacatoa *m inv* cockatoo.

caccia *f* hunt, hunting; chase; **una partita di** ~ *f* shoot.

cacciare *vi* to hunt.

cacciatore *m* hunter, huntsman.

cacciatorpediniere *m* destroyer.

cacciavite *m inv* screwdriver.

cachemire *m inv* cashmere.

cachi *m* khaki, persimmon.

cactus *m inv* cactus.

cadavere *m* (dead) body, cadaver, corpse.

cadaverico *adj* cadaverous; deathly.

cadente *adj* tumble-down.

cadenza *f* cadence; ~ **strascicata** *f* drawl.

cadere *vi* to fall; to topple over; to slump; * *vt* **lasciar** ~ to drop.

cadetto *m* cadet.

caduta *f* fall; slump.

caffè *m* café; coffee; **pausa per il** ~ *f* coffee break.

caffeina *f* caffeine.

caffettiera *f* coffee pot; ~ **a filtro** *f* percolator.

cagionevole *adj* unsound.

cagliare *vi* to curdle.

caglio *m* rennet.

cagna *f* bitch.

cagnolino *m* puppy; ~ **di lusso** *m* lapdog.

calabrone *m* hornet.

calamaro *m* squid.

calamità *f* calamity.

calamita *f* magnet.

calamitoso *adj* calamitous.

calare *vi* to drop; to wane; * *vt* to lower; to drop.

calca *f* squash.

calcagno *m* heel.

calcare *m* limestone.

calcatoio *m* ramrod.

calce *f* lime; **bianco di ~** *m* whitewash.

calcestruzzo *m* concrete; **rivestire di ~** *vt* to concrete.

calciatore *m* footballer.

calcificare *vt* to calcify.

calcio *m* kick; calcium; football; soccer; **dare un ~** *vt* to boot; to kick.

calcolabile *adj* calculable; computable.

calcolare *vt* to calculate; to compute; to reckon; **~ male** to misjudge; to miscalculate.

calcolatore *m* calculator.

calcoli *mpl* reckoning.

calcolo *m* calculation; computation; **~ biliare** *m* gallstone.

caldaia *f* boiler.

calderone *m* cauldron.

caldo *adj* hot, warm.

caleidoscopio *m* kaleidoscope.

calendario *m* calendar.

calendola *f* marigold.

calesse *m* trap.

calibrare *vt* to calibrate.

calibratura *f* calibration.

calibro *m* bore; calibre; gauge.

calice *m* chalice; goblet; glass.

calligra fia *f* calligraphy.

callista *m/f* chiropodist.

callo *m* corn.

calma *f* calm; cool; composure.

calmante *adj* soothing; sedative; * *m* sedative.

calmare *vt* to calm; to lull; to pacify; to steady; to soothe;

* *vr* **~rsi** *vr* to abate (storm); to simmer down, to calm down (person).

caloroso *adj* appreciative.

calmo *adj* calm; cool; untroubled.

calo *m* fall; drop.

calore *m* heat; warmth.

caloria *f* calorie.

calpestare *vt* to tread; to trample.

calunnia *f* aspersion; calumny; slander.

calunniare *vt* to slander; to malign.

calunnioso *adj* slanderous.

calvario *m* Calvary.

calvinista *m/f* calvinist.

calvizie *f* baldness.

calvo *adj* bald.

calza *f* stocking; calze; *fpl* hosiery.

calzante *m* shoehorn.

calzatura *f* footwear.

calzettone *m* sock.

calzino *m* sock, ankle sock.

calzolaio *m* cobbler; shoemaker.

calzoleria *f* shoeshop.

calzoncini *mpl* shorts.

camaleonte *m* chamaleon.

cambiamento *m* change; shift; **~ continuo** *m* flux.

cambiare *vt* to change; to switch; * *vi* to change.

cambio *m* change; exchange; **tasso di ~** *m* rate of exchange; **agente di ~** stockbroker; gear; **scatola del ~** *f* gearbox; **leva del ~** *f* gear lever.

camelia *f* camellia.

camera *f* room; chamber; (*pol* house; **~ da letto** *f* bedroom **~ degli ospiti** *f* guestroom; **~ dei bambini** *f* nursery; **~ os cura** *f* darkroom; **~ d'aria** inner tube.

cameraman *m inv* cameramar

cameratismo *m* companion-ship.

cameriera *f* waitress; maid, chambermaid.

cameriere *m* waiter; ~ **person-ale** *m* valet.

camerino *m* dressing room.

camicetta *f* blouse.

camicia *f* shirt; ~ **di forza** *f* straitjacket.

caminetto *m* fireplace.

camino *m* chimney.

camion *m inv* lorry, truck.

camioncino *m* pick-up truck.

camionista *m* truckdriver.

cammello *m* camel.

cammeo *m* cameo.

camminare *vi* walk; ~ **senza fretta** amble; ~ **su e giù** to pace; ~ **in punta dei piedi** to tiptoe; ~ **pesantemente** to tramp; ~ **come una papera** to waddle; ~ **a fatica** to wade; * *m* walking.

camminatore *m* walker.

camomilla *f* camomile.

camoscio *m* chamois; **pelle di** ~ *f* chamois leather.

campagna *f* country, country-side; campaign; ~ **di vendita** *f* sales drive; **fare una** ~ *vi* to campaign.

campagnolo *m* countryman.

campana *f* bell; **sordo come una** ~ *adj* stone-deaf.

campanello *m* bell; doorbell.

campanile *m* belfry; steeple.

campeggiare *vi* to camp.

campeggiatore *m* camper.

campeggio *m* camping; camp-site.

campestre *adj* cross-country.

campionato *m* championship; league.

campione *m* champion; sam-ple; specimen.

campo *m* ground, field; pitch; **lavoro sul** ~ *m* fieldwork; ~

da tennis tennis court.

campus *m inv* campus.

camuso *adj* snub-nosed.

canaglia *f* rabble.

canale *m* canal; channel.

canapa *f* hemp; ~ **indiana** can-nabis.

canarino *m* canary.

cancellare *vt* to cancel, to an-nul; to delete; to efface; to erase; to scratch; to obliterate; to scrub.

cancellata *f* railings.

cancellazione *f* cancellation.

cancelleria *f* stationery.

cancelletto girevole *m* turn-stile.

cancelliere *m* chancellor.

cancello *m* gate.

Cancer *m* Cancer.

cancerogeno *adj* carcinogenic.

canceroso *adj* cancerous.

cancrena *f* gangrene.

cancro *m* cancer.

candeggiare *vt* to bleach.

candeggina *f* bleach.

candela *f* candle; sparking plug.

candelabro *m* candelabra.

candeliere *m* candlestick.

candida *f* thrush.

candidato *m* candidate; appli-cant; entrant; nominee.

candidatura *f* candidacy.

candito *adj* candied.

candore *m* candour; whiteness.

cane *m* dog; ~ **per ciechi** *m* guide dog; ~ **pastore** *m* sheep-dog.

canfora *f* camphor.

canguro *m* kangaroo.

canile *m* kennel; ~ **municipale** *m* dog pound.

canino *adj* canine; ~ **superiore** *m* eyetooth.

canna *f* cane; crossbar; barrel (of gun); reed; ~ **d'India** *f* rat-tan; ~ **da pesca** *f* fishing rod;

~ **fumaria** f flue; ~ **da zuc-chero** f sugar cane.
cannella f cinnamon.
cannibale m/f cannibal.
cannibalismo m cannibalism.
cannone m canon.
cannoniera f gunboat.
cannuccia f straw.
canoa f canoe.
canone m canon; fee.
canonica f vicarage.
canonizzare vt to canonize.
canottiera f vest.
cantante m/f singer.
cantare vi to sing; to crow; * vt to sing; to chant.
canticchiare vt to hum.
cantiere m yard; ~ **navale** m dockyard, shipyard.
cantina f cellar; wine cellar.
canto m song; singing; crow; chant; ~ **funebre** m dirge.
cantone m canton.
canyon m inv canyon.
canzonatorio adj quizzical.
canzoncina f ditty.
canzone f song; ~ **folk** f folk-song.
caos m chaos.
caotico adj chaotic.
capace adj capable.
capacità f ability .
capo m head; **da ~ a** fresh.
capacità f capability; capacity; skill; fpl scope; power.
capanna f hut.
capanno m shed.
caparra f surety.
capelli mpl hair.
capezzale m bolster.
capezzolo m nipple.
capillare m capillary.
capire vt to understand; to comprehend; to take in; to figure out, to fathom; **far ~** to intimate; * vi to understand.
capital f capital (city).
capitale m (fin) capital.

capitalismo m capitalism.
capitalista m/f capitalist.
capitalizzare vt to capitalize.
capitano m captain, skipper.
capitare vi to happen.
capite m: **pro ~ per** capita.
capitolare vi to capitulate.
capitolazione f sellout.
capitolo m chapter.
capitombolo m tumble.
capo m boss, chie f; commander; leader; cape; head; headland; **a ~ scoperto** adj bareheaded; **da ~** adv over again; **a tre capi** adj three-ply.
capobanda m ringleader.
capocameriere m head waiter.
Capodanno m New Year's Day.
capodoglio m sperm whale.
capofamiglia m/f householder.
capofitto: a ~ adv headlong.
capogiro m dizziness.
capolavoro m masterpiece.
capolinea m terminal, terminus.
caporale m corporal.
caposquadra m foreman.
capovolgere vt to invert; to overturn; * vr ~**rsi** to turn over.
capovolto adj, adv upside down.
cappa f cape; cloak.
cappella f chapel.
cappellaio m hatter.
cappellano m chaplain.
cappello m hat.
cappero m caper.
cappio m loop; noose.
cappotto m coat.
cappuccio m cowl; hood.
capra f goat.
capraio m goatherd.
capretto m kid.
capriccio m caprice; capriccic fancy; whim.
capriccioso adj capricious temperamental.

Capricorno *m* Capricorn.
capri foglio *m* honeysuckle.
capriola *f* somersault.
capriolo *m* roebuck.
capro *m*: ~ **espiatorio** *m* scapegoat.
caprone *m* billy goat.
capsula *f* capsule.
carabina *f* rifle.
caracollare *vi* to prance.
caraffa *f* carafe, decanter.
caramella *f* sweet; candy; ~ **fondente** *f* fudge; ~ **mou** *f inv* toffee.
caramello *m* caramel.
carato *m* carat.
carattere *m* character; type; ~ **tipografico** *m* typeface.
caratteristica *f* feature; trait; * *adj* characteristic.
caratterizzare *vt* to characterize.
caratterizzazione *f* characterization.
carboidrato *m* carbohydrate.
carbonaio *m* coalman.
carboncino *m* charcoal.
carbone *m* coal; charcoal; ~ **coke** *m* coke.
carbonio *m* carbon.
carbonizzare *vt* carbonize; to char.
carburante *m* fuel; **rifornirsi di** ~ *vr* to refuel.
carburatore *m* carburettor.
carcassa *f* carcass.
carcerato *m* convict, jailbird.
carcere *m* jail, prison; **rimandere in** ~ *vt* to remand.
carceriere *m* jailer.
carcio fo *m* artichoke.
cardiaco *adj* cardiac.
cardinale *adj*, *m* cardinal.
cardine *m* hinge.
cardio *m* cockle.
cardo *m* thistle.
carenza *f* shortage.
carestia *f* famine.

carezza *f* caress; stroke.
carezzare *vt* to caress.
carica *f* (*mil*) charge; **affrancatura a** ~ **del destinatario** *f* freepost.
caricabatterie *m inv* charger.
caricare *vt* to load; to wind.
caricatore *m* magazine.
caricatura *f* caricature; **fare una** ~ **di** *vt* to caricature.
carico *m* load; cargo; shipment; burden; **persona a** ~ *f* dependant; * *adj* loaded.
carie *f* caries.
carino *adj* sweet, bonny, cute.
carisma *m* charisma.
carità *f* charity.
caritatevole *adj* beneficent; charitable.
carlino *m* pug.
carnagione *f* complexion.
carnale *adj* carnal.
carne *f* meat; flesh; **ben in** ~ buxom; **pezzo di** ~ *m* joint; ~ **macinata** *f* mince; **di** ~ *adj* meaty.
carne ficina *f* carnage.
carnevale *m* carnival.
carnivoro *adj* carnivorous.
carnoso *adj* fleshy.
caro *adj* dear; darling; expensive; **avere** ~ *vt* to cherish; **rendere** ~ *vt* to endear.
carogna *f* carrion.
carota *f* carrot.
carpa *f* carp.
carreggiata *f* carriageway.
carrello *m* trolley; ~ **elevatore** *m* fork-lift truck; ~ **d'atterraggio** *m* undercarriage.
carretto *m* cart.
carriera *f* career.
carriola *f* barrow, wheelbarrow.
carro *m* wagon; ~ **armato** *m* tank.
carrozza *f* coach; carriage.
carrozzeria *f* bodywork.

carta f paper; charter; map; ~ **bianca** f carte blanche; ~ **carbone** f carbon paper; ~ **di credito** f credit card; ~ **d'imbarco** f boarding card; ~ **da gioco** f playing card; ~ **assorbente** f blotting paper; ~ **stagnola** f foil; ~ **protocollo** f foolscap; ~ **oleata** f greaseproof paper, wax paper; ~ **igienica** f toilet paper; ~ **da lettere** f notepaper, writing paper; ~ **da pareti** f wallpaper; ~ **straccia** f waste paper; ~ **vetrata** f sandpaper; **carte** fpl cards; vt **dare le carte** to deal.

cartella f briefcase; folder; file; satchel; portfolio.

cartellino m docket.

cartello m placard; cartel; ~ **stradale** m roadsign.

cartilagine f cartilage; gristle.

cartilaginoso adj gristly.

cartogra fia f cartography.

cartolaio m stationer.

cartolina f postcard; ~ **d'auguri** f greetings card.

cartone m cardboard; carton; ~ **animato** m cartoon.

cartuccia f cartridge.

casa f house; home; household; (sl) pad; **amore per la ~** m domesticity; ~ **colonica** f farmhouse; ~ **viaggiante** f mobile home; **fatto in ~** adj homemade; **verso ~** adv homeward(s).

casaccio adj: **a ~** at random.

casalinga f housewife.

casamento m tenement.

cascarci vi to fall for (a trick, etc).

cascata f cascade; water fall; **cascate** fpl (water)falls.

casco m helmet, crash helmet.

casella f pigeonhole.

casellario m filing cabinet.

caserma f barracks; ~ **dei pompieri** f fire station.

casinò m inv casino.

casino m carry-on.

caso m (med, gr) case; chance; **per caso** adv by accident, by chance; **a ~** adj at random.

caso mai conj in case.

cassa f case, crate; checkout; till; ~ **comune** f pool.

cassa forte f safe; strongbox.

casseruola f casserole.

cassetta f cassette; ~ **delle lettere** f postbox; ~ **per i fiori** f window box.

cassetto m drawer.

cassettone m chest of drawers.

cassiere m cashier; teller.

cast m inv cast.

casta f caste.

castagna f chestnut; ~ **d'ippocastano** f conker.

castagno m chestnut tree.

castano adj chestnut.

castello m castle.

castigare vt to castigate; to chasten; to discipline.

castità f chastity.

casto adj chaste.

castoro m beaver.

castrare vt to castrate; to neuter.

castrazione f castration.

casuale adj casual; haphazard.

cataclisma m cataclysm.

catacombe fpl catacombs.

catalizzatore m catalyst.

catalogo m catalogue.

catamarano m catamaran.

catapecchia f slum.

catarifrangente m cat's eye; reflector.

catarro m catarrh.

catastro fe f catastrophe.

catechismo m catechism.

categoria f category; class; grade.

categorico adj categoric(al)

absolute; downright;.

catena *f* chain; range; ~ **di montaggio** *f* production line.

cateratta *f* cataract.

catodo *m* cathode.

catrame *m* tar.

cattedrale *f* cathedral.

cattiveria *f* mischie *f*; wickedness.

cattività *f* captivity.

cattivo *adj* bad; ill; evil; nasty; malicious; wicked.

cattolicesimo *m* Catholicism.

cattolico *adj, m* Catholic, Roman Catholic.

cattura *f* capture.

cauccciù *m* rubber.

causa *f* cause; law suit; ~ **giudiziaria** *f* litigation; **essere ~ di** *vt* to engender; **intentare ~** *vi* to sue; **a ~ di** *adj* due to. * *prep* owing to; on account of.

causare *vt* to cause; to bring about; to occasion.

caustico *adj* caustic; vitriolic.

cautamente *adv* warily.

cautela *f* wariness.

cauterizzare *vt* to cauterize; to sear.

cauto *adj* cautious; canny.

cauzione *f* bail.

cava *f* quarry; pit.

cavalcare *vt* to ride.

cavalcata *f* ride.

cavalcavia *m inv* overpass.

cavalcioni *prep*; **a ~ di** astride.

cavaliere *m* cavalier; horseman; knight.

cavalleresco *adj* chivalrous.

cavalleria *f* chivalry; cavalry.

cavallerizzo *m* rider.

cavalletta *f* grasshopper.

cavalletto *m* easel; trestle.

cavallina *f* leap frog.

cavallo *m* horse; horsepower; crotch; (chess) knight; **a ~** *adv* on horseback; **corse di cavalli** *fpl* horse-racing.

cavalloni *mpl* surf.

cavalluccio marino *m* seahorse.

cavarsela *vi* to cope; to pull through.

cavatappi *m inv* corkscrew.

caverna *f* cave, cavern.

cavia *f* guinea pig.

caviale *m* caviar.

caviglia *f* ankle.

cavillare *vi* to quibble.

cavillo *m* quibble.

cavità *f* hollow; pothole.

cavo *m* cable; **televisione via ~** cable television; * *adj* hollow.

cavolfiore *m* cauliflower.

cavolino *m*; **cavolini** *mpl* **di Bruxelles** Brussels sprouts.

cavolo *m* cabbage.

cazzo *m* prick.

cazzuola *f* trowel.

cece *m* chickpea.

cecità *f* blindness.

cedere *vt* to cede; to yield; * *vi* to give, to give in; to relent; to sink; to submit; to yield.

cediglia *f* cedilla.

cedro *m* cedar.

ce *f* **fone** *m* clout; slap.

celebrazione *f* celebration.

celebrità *f inv* celebrity; fame; stardom.

celeste *adj* blue, sky-blue; heavenly.

celestiale *adj* celestial.

celibato *m* celibacy.

celibe *adj* celibate (man); single.

cella *f* cell.

cello fan *m* cellophane.

cellulare *adj* cellular.

celluloide *f* celluloid.

cellulosa *f* cellulose.

cembalo *m* cymbal.

cementare *vt* to cement.

cemento *m* cement.

cena *f* dinner, supper.

cencio *m* rag.

cenere *f* ash.

cengia *f* ledge.

cenno *m* motion; wave; ~ **del capo** *m* nod; **chiamare con un** ~ *vt* to beckon; **salutare con un** ~ **della mano** *vt* to wave; **fare un** ~ **col capo** *vi* to nod.

cenotafio *m* cenotaph.

censimento *m* census.

censore *m* censor.

censorio *adj* censorious.

censura *f* censorship, censure.

censurare *vt* to censor, to censure.

centenario *m* centenary.

centenario *m*, *adj* centenarian.

centennale *adj* centennial.

centesimo *m* cent; hundredth; * *adj* hundredth.

centigrado *adj* centigrade.

centilitro *m* centilitre.

centimetro *m* centimetre.

cento *adj*, *m* hundred.

centrale *adj* central; middle; * *f* ~ **elettrica** *f* power station.

centralinista *m/f* operator.

centralino *m* switchboard.

centralizzare *vt* to centralize.

centrifuga *f* centrifuge; spin-dryer.

centrifugo *adj* centrifugal.

centro *m* centre; middle; ~ **civico rionale** *m* community centre; ~ **del bersaglio** *m* bull's-eye; ~ **commerciale** *m* shopping centre.

centurione *m* centurion.

cera *f* wax; polish; ~ **d'api** *f* beeswax; **statua di** ~ *f* waxwork; **museo delle cere** *m* waxworks; **dare la** ~ **a** *vt* to polish with wax.

ceralacca *f* sealing wax.

ceramica *f* ceramic; pottery.

cerata *m*; **cappello di** ~ sou'wester.

cerbiatto *m* fawn.

cerbottana *f* blowpipe.

cercare *vt* to try; to look for; ~ **a tastoni** to grope; to hunt for; * *vi* to search, to seek; to forage.

cerchio *m* circle; hoop; ring.

cereale *m* cereal.

cereali *mpl* grain.

cerebrale *adj* cerebral.

cerimonia *f* ceremony.

cerino *m* taper.

cerniera *f* hinge; zip.

cerotto *m* plaster.

certamente *adv* definitely.

certezza *f* certainty; sureness.

certificare *vt* to certify.

certificato *m* certificate; ~ **di nascita** birth certificate; ~ **di morte** death certificate.

certo *adj* certain; some; sure; * *pron* **certi** some.

certosino *m* Carthusian.

cerva *f* hind.

cervellata *f* saveloy.

cervello *m* brain; mastermind; **fare il lavaggio del** ~ **a** * *vt* to brainwash.

cervo *m* deer, stag; **carne di** ~ *f* venison.

cesareo *adj* Caesarian.

cesoie *fpl* shears.

cespuglio *m* bush, shrub.

cessare *vt* to cease; * *vi* to cease, to stop.

cessazione *f* cessation.

cesso *m* (*Brit fam*) bog.

cestino *m* basket.

cesto *m* hamper.

cetra *f* zither.

cetriolino *m* gherkin.

cetriolo *m* cucumber.

champagne *m inv* champagne.

che *rel pron* that; which; who, whom; * *conj* that; then; * *adj* what

che *f m inv* che *f*.

cherosene *m* kerosene; paraffin

cherubino *m* cherub.

chewing-gum *m inv* chewing gum.

chi *pron* who, whom; * *poss pron* **di ~** whose.

chiacchierare *vi* to chat, to chatter; to gossip; to jabber.

chiacchierata *f* chat.

chiacchiere *fpl* chatter.

chiacchierio *m* jabber.

chiacchierone *m* chatterbox.

chiamare *vt* to call; to name; to term.

chiamata *f* call; **~ alle armi** *f* (*mil*) call-up.

chiaramente *adv* clearly.

chiaretto *m* claret.

chiarezza *f* clarity; fairness.

chiarificazione *f* clarification.

chiarimento *m* explanation; **fornire un ~ a** *vt* to enlighten.

chiarire *vt* to clarify.

chiaro *adj* clear; articulate; fair; light; straightforward.

chiarore *m* flare.

chiaroveggente *m/f* clairvoyant.

chiasso *m* din.

chiassoso *adj* riotous.

chiatta *f* barge.

chiave *f* (*mus*) clef; wrench; **nota di ~** *f* keynote; **~ di sol** *f* treble clef; key; **~ di volta** *f* keystone; **~ fissa** *f* spanner; **chiudere a ~** *vt* to lock.

chiavistello *m* bolt; latch.

chiazza *f* blotch.

chic *adj* chic, classy; smart.

chicche *fpl* goodies.

chicchirichì *m* cock-a-doodle-do.

chicco *m* grain; bean; **~ di caffè** coffee bean.

chiedere *vt* to ask; **~ notizie di** to ask after; * *vr* **~rsi** to wonder; * *vi* **~ a gran voce** to clamour; **~ di** to inquire after.

chiesa *f* church.

chiffon *m* chiffon.

chiglia *f* keel.

chignon *m* bun.

chilo *m* kilo.

chilogrammo *m* kilogram(me).

chilometraggio *m* mileage.

chilometro *m* kilometre.

chimica *f* chemistry.

chimico *adj* chemical; * *m* chemist; **prodotto ~** chemical.

chinare *vt* to bow; to incline; * *vr* **chinarsi** to droop; to stoop.

chinino *m* quinine.

chioccia *f* broody hen.

chiocciola *f* snail.

chiodo *m* nail; spike; **~ fisso** *m* hobby-horse; **munire di chiodi** *vt* to spike.

chiodo *m* stud; nail.

chioma *f* hair.

chiosare *vt* to gloss.

chiosco *m* kiosk.

chiostro *m* cloister.

chip *m inv* silicon chip; microchip.

chiromante *m/f* fortune-teller.

chiromante *m/f* palmist.

chirurgia *f* surgery.

chirurgico *adj* surgical.

chirurgo *m* surgeon.

chitarra *f* guitar.

chitarrista *m/f* guitarist.

chiudere *vt* to close; to shut; * *vr* **~rsi** to shut.

chiunque *pron* anybody; who.

chiurlo *m* curlew.

chiusa *f* lock; sluice.

chiuso *adj* closed.

chiusura *f* close-down; close; closing; fastener, fastening.

ci **pers** *pron* us.

cialda *f* waffle.

ciambella *f* doughnut.

ciance *fpl* drivel.

cianfrusaglie *fpl* junk.

cianografia *f* blueprint.

cianuro *m* cyanide.

ciao *excl* hullo, hi!

ciarlare *vi* to waffle.

ciarlatano *m* quack.

ciarliero *adj* chatty.

ciascuno *adv* apiece; * *adj, pron, adv* each.

cibernetica *f* cybernetics.

cibo *m* fare, food; *(fam)* grub.

cicala *f* cicada.

cicalino *m* bleeper, buzzer.

cicatrice *f* scar.

cicatrizzarsi *vr* to scar.

ciclamino *m* cyclamen.

ciclismo *m* cycling.

ciclista *m/f* cyclist.

ciclo *m* cycle.

ciclomotore *m* moped.

ciclone *m* cyclone.

cicogna *f* stork.

cicoria *f* chicory.

cicuta *f* hemlock.

ciecamente *adv* blindly.

cieco *adj, m* blind; **vicolo ~** *m* blind alley.

cielo *m* heaven; sky.

cifra *f* figure; digit.

cifrare *vt* to code.

ciglio *m* eyelash, lash; side.

cigno *m* swan; **giovane ~** *m* cygnet.

cigolare *vi* to grate; to squeak.

cigolio *m* squeak.

ciliegia *f* cherry.

ciliegio *m* cherry tree.

cilindrico *adj* cylindrical.

cilindro *m* cylinder; top hat.

cima *f* crown (of hill); peak; summit; top.

cimitero *m* cemetery; churchyard; graveyard.

cimurro *m* distemper.

cincia *f* tit.

cinegiornale *m* newsreel.

cinema *m inv* cinema.

cinepresa *f* cine camera, movie camera.

cinetico *adj* kinetic.

cinghia *f* belt, strap; **~ della ventola** *f* fanbelt.

cinghiale *m* boar.

cinguettare *vi* to chirp; to twitter.

cinguettio *m* chirp; twitter.

cinico *adj* cynic(al); * *n* cynic.

cinismo *m* cynicism.

cinquanta *m, adj* fifty.

cinquantesimo *m, adj* fiftieth.

cinque *m, adj* five.

cinto *m*; **~ erniario** truss.

cintura *f* belt; **~ di sicurezza** *f* seatbelt, safety belt.

cinturino *m* strap.

ciò **dem** *pron* that; * *adv* **con ~** thereby.

ciocca *f* lock; strand.

cioccolato *m* chocolate.

cioè *adv* i.e.; namely.

ciondolare *vi* to loll.

ciottoli *mpl* shingle.

ciottolo *m* cobblestone; pebble.

cipiglio *m* frown.

cipolla *f* onion; *(med)* bunion; rose (of watering can).

cipresso *m* cypress.

cipria *f* face powder.

circa *adv* around; some; somewhere.

circo *m* circus.

circolare *adj, f* circular; * *vi* to circulate.

circolazione *f* circulation; **~ del sangue** *f* bloodstream.

circolo *m* club; clubhouse.

circoncidere *vt* to circumcise.

circoncisione *f* circumcision.

circondare *vt* to encircle; to surround.

circonferenza *f* girth; circumference.

circonflesso *adj* circumflex.

circonlocuzione *f* circumlocution.

circonvallazione *f* by-pass.

circoscrivere *vt* to circumscribe.

circoscrizione *f* precinct.

circospetto *adj* circumspect; guarded.

circostanza *f* circumstance.

circostanziato *adj* circumstantial.

circuito *m* circuit; **televisione a ~ chiuso** *f* closed-circuit television; **~ di gara** *m* speedway.

cirripede *m* barnacle.

cirrosi *f* cirrhosis.

cisposo *adj*; **dagli occhi cisposi** bleary-eyed.

cisterna *f* tank.

cisti *f inv* cyst.

cistifellea *f* gall bladder.

citante *m/f* (*law*) claimant.

citare *vt* to cite; **~ in giudizio** to subpoena; to sue; to quote; * *vi* to quote.

citazione *f* quotation; subpoena.

cito fono *m* entry phone.

citrico *adj* citric.

citrullo *m* sucker.

città *f inv* city, town.

cittadella *f* citadel.

cittadino *m* citizen; national; **semplice ~** *m* commoner.

ciuffo *m* clump; tuft.

civetta *f* flirt; owl.

civettuolo *adj* coy.

civico *adj* civic.

civile *adj* civil; urbane; **protezione ~** *f* civil defence.

civilizzare *vt* to civilize.

civiltà *f inv* civilization.

clacson *m inv* hooter, horn; **suonare il ~** *vt* to toot.

clamore *m* clamour.

clamoroso *adj* resounding.

clan *m inv* clan.

clandestino *adj* clandestine; undercover.

clarinetto *m* clarinet.

classe *f* class, form; style; **prima ~** *f* first class.

classico *adj* classic(al); standard.

classificare *vt* to classify; to categorize; to grade; to sort.

classificatore *m* binder.

classificazione *f* classification.

classista *m* class consciousness.

clausola *f* clause; proviso; **~ addizionale** *f* rider.

claustrofobia *f* claustrophobia.

claustrofobico *adj* claustrophobic.

clavicembalo *m* harpsichord.

clavicola *f* collarbone.

clemente *adj* clement.

clemenza *f* clemency.

cleptomania *f* kleptomania.

clericale *adj* (*rel*) clerical.

clero *m* clergy.

clessidra *f* hourglass.

cliente *m/f* client, customer.

clientela *f* custom; clientele.

clima *m* climate.

climatico *adj* climatic.

climatizzato *adj* air-conditioned.

clinica *f* clinic; nursing home.

clipper *m inv* clipper.

clorare *vt* to chlorinate.

cloro *m* chlorine.

cloro filla *f* chlorophyll.

cloroformio *m* chloroform.

clou *m inv* highlight.

club *m* club.

coabitare *vi* to cohabit.

coagulare *vt* to coagulate; * *vr* **~rsi** to clot, to coagulate.

coalizione *f* coalition.

cobalto *m* cobalt.

cobra *m inv* cobra.

cocaina *f* cocaine.

coccarda *f* rosette.

coccinella *f* ladybird.

cocciuto *adj* pig-headed; stubborn.

coccò *m*; **noce di ~** *f* coconut.

coccodè *m* cackle (of hen);

fare ~ *vi* to cackle.
coccodrillo *m* crocodile.
coccolare *vt* to cosset; to cuddle; to mollycoddle.
cocktail *m inv* cocktail.
cocomero *m* watermelon.
coda *f* queue; tail; tailback; **~ di cavallo** *f* ponytail.
codazzo *m* train.
codeina *f* codeine.
codice *m* code; cipher; **~ a barre** bar code; **~ di avviamento postale** *m* postcode.
codicillo *m* codicil.
coefficiente *m* coefficient.
coercizione *f* duress.
coerente *adj* consistent; coherent.
coerenza *f* coherence.
coesione *f* cohesion.
coesistenza *f* coexistence.
coesistere *vi* to coexist.
cofano *m* (*Brit*) bonnet.
cogliere *vt* to pluck; to pick; to seize.
cognac *m inv* cognac.
cognata *f* sister-in-law.
cognato *m* brother-in-law.
cognizione *f* cognition.
cognome *m* surname.
coincidenza *f* coincidence.
coincidere *vi* to coincide; to concur.
coinvolgere *vt* to involve.
colapasta *m inv* colander.
colare *vi* to run.
colazione *f*; **prima ~** breakfast; **seconda ~** lunch.
colera *f* cholera; **andare in ~** *vi* to throw a tantrum.
colesterolo *m* cholesterol.
colibrì *m inv* humming-bird.
colica *f* colic; gripe.
colla *f* gum; glue.
collaborare *vi* to collaborate.
collaboratore *m* (journal) contributor; collaborator.
collaborazione *f* collaboration.

collana *f* necklace; **~ a girocollo** *m* choker.
collant *m inv* tights, pantyhose.
collasso *m* collapse.
collaudare *vt* to test.
collaudo *m* test.
collazionare *vt* to collate.
colle *m* hill.
collega *m/f* colleague, associate.
collegamento *m* connection.
collegare *vt* to connect, to link; * *vt* to join; to relate; **~ a terra** (*elec*) to earth.
college *m* college; boarding school; **~ elettorale** *m* constituency.
collegiale *m/f* boarder.
collera *f* rage; temper.
colletta *f* whip-round.
collettivo *m* collective; * *adj* collective; corporate.
collezionista *m* collector.
collie *m inv* collie (dog).
collina *f* hill; foothill.
collinoso *adj* hilly.
collirio *m* eyedrops.
collo *m* collar; neck; instep.
collocare *vt* to locate; to site.
colloquio *m* interview.
colloso *adj* gluey.
collusione *f* collusion.
collutorio *m* gargle; mouthwash.
colmare *vt*: **~ qn di qc** *vt* to lavish something on somebody.
colombaia *f* dovecote.
colombo *m* dove.
colon *m inv* (*med*) colon.
colonnello *m* colonel.
colonia *f* colony; **acqua di ~** *f* eau de cologne.
coloniale *adj* colonial.
colonizzare *vt* to colonize; to settle.
colonizzatore *m* colonist.
colonna *f* column; pillar; **~ sonora** *f* soundtrack; **met-**

tere in ~ *vt* to tabulate.

colonnina *f* bollard.

colono *m* settler.

colorante *m* dye; stain.

colorare *vt* to colour.

colorazione *f* colouring.

colore *m* colour; (cards) suit; **dai colori vivaci** *adj* colourful.

colossale *adj* colossal, mammoth, monstrous.

colpa *f* blame, fault; guilt; **senza ~** *adj* guiltless.

colpetto *m* dab; pat; tap; flick, flip; prod; poke; **dare un ~** *vt* to flick; **dare dei colpetti leggeri** *vt* to pat; **dare un ~ a** *vt* to poke.

colpevole *m* culprit; * *adj* guilty; culpable; * *vt* riconoscere ~ to convict.

colpevolezza *f* guilt, culpability.

colpire *vt* to hit; to knock; to smite; to strike; to clout; to impress; **~ violentemente** to batter.

colpo *m* bang; blow; knock; hit; slam; stroke; thump; whack; coup; **~ secco** chop; **~ di punta** jab; **fare un bel ~** to make a killing; **colpi d'arma da fuoco** *mpl* gun fire; **~ di grazia** *m* deathblow; **~ giornalistico** *m* scoop; **~ mancato** *m* miss; **che fa ~** *adj* striking.

coltellata *f* stab.

coltello *m* knife; **~ a serramanico** jack-knife.

coltivare *vt* to cultivate; to grow, to farm, to till.

coltivatore *m* grower.

coltivazione *f* crop; cultivation.

colto *adj* cultured, learned, educated.

coltura *f* (*agr*, *biol*) culture; growing.

coma *m inv* coma.

comandamento *m* commandment.

comandare *vt* to command.

comando *m* control; command; order.

comatoso *adj* comatose.

combattente *m/f* combatant; fighter.

combattere *vi* to battle; * *vt* to combat; to fight.

combattimento *m* combat, fight, fighting.

combinare *vt* to combine.

combinazione *f* combination.

combustibile *adj* combustible; * *m* fuel.

combustione *f* combustion.

come *conj* as; * *adv* how; * *prep* like; * *adj* such as.

cometa *f* comet.

comico *adj* comic; * *m* comedian.

comignolo *m* chimney stack.

cominciare *vt* to begin, to commence; to start; to take up; * *vi* to begin; to get; to start.

comitato *m* committee; **~ elettorale** *m* caucus.

comizio *m* rally; **comizi elettorali** *mpl* hustings.

commando *m* commando.

commedia *f* comedy; play.

commemorare *vt* to commemorate.

commemorativo *adj* memorial.

commemorazione *f* commemoration.

commentare *vt* to commentate.

commento *m* comment; commentary.

commerciale *adj* commercial; trading.

commercialista *m* chartered accountant.

commerciante *m/f* dealer, merchant, trader.

commerciare *vi* to trade.

commercio *m* commerce, trade, trading.

commessa *f* saleswoman.

commesso *m* salesman.

commestibile *adj* edible, eatable.

commettere *vt* to commit.

commiserazione *f* commiseration.

commissariato *m* commissariat.

commissario *m*; **~ di bordo** *m* purser.

commissionare *vt* to commission.

commissione *f* commision; board; errand.

commosso *adj* affected, touched.

commovente *adj* appealing, moving, touching, emotive.

commozione *f* emotion; **~ cerebrale** *f* concussion.

commuovere *vt* to move, to touch.

commutare *vt* to commute.

comodità *f* convenience.

comodo *adj* comfortable; convenient; handy.

compagnia *f* company, society.

compagno *m* companion; comrade; mate; **~ di classe** *m* classmate; **~ di studi** *m* fellow student; **~ di viaggio** *m* fellow traveller.

comparativo *adj* (*gr*) comparative.

comparire *vi* to appear.

comparsa *f* appearance.

compassione *f* compassion, pity.

compassionevole *adj* compassionate.

compasso *m* compass; **~ a punte fisse** *m* dividers.

compatibile *adj* compatible.

compatire *vt* to pity; * *vi* to sympathize.

compatriota *m/f* compatriot, fellow countryman.

compatto *adj* compact.

compendiare *vt* abridge.

compensare *vt* to compensate.

compensato *m* plywood.

compenso *m* compensation.

competente *adj* competent, proficient.

competenza *f* competence, proficiency.

competere *vi* to compete.

compiacente *adj* compliant.

compiacimento *m* complacency.

compiaciuto *adj* complacent; smug, self-righteous.

compiere *vt* to do; to accomplish; to fulfil.

compilare *vt* to compile.

compilazione *f* compilation.

compimento *m* fulfilment.

compito *m* homework; job; task.

compleanno *m* birthday.

complementare *adj* complementary; subsidiary.

complemento *m* complement.

complessità *f inv* complexity; intricacy; sophistication; involvement.

complessivo *adj* aggregate.

complesso *m* complex; ensemble, entirety; group; hang-up. **nel ~** by and large.

completamente *adv* fully; totally; wholly, utterly; absolutely; right.

completamento *m* completion; accomplishment.

completare *vt* to complete; to fill in (form, etc).

completo *adj* complete; absolute; whole; unidivided; suit;

complicare *vt* to complicate.

complicato *adj* elaborate; involved.

complicazione *f* complication

complice *m/f* accomplice, accessory; **essere ~ di** *vt* to aid and abet.

complicità *f* complicity.

complimentarsi *vr* to compliment.

complimento *m* compliment.

complottare *vi, vt* to plot.

complotto *m* plot.

componente *adj* component; * *m* component; constituent.

comporre *vt* to compose.

comportamento *m* behaviour.

comportare *vt* to entail; * *vr* **~rsi** to act; to behave; **~ male** to misbehave.

composito *adj* composite.

compositore *m* composer; compositor.

composizione *f* composition; make-up.

composto *m* compound; * *adj* self-possessed; composed; compound; (*gr*) **parola composta** *f* compound.

comprare *vt* to buy.

compratore *m* buyer.

comprendere *vt* to comprise; to comprehend; to encompass.

comprensibile *adj* comprehensible, understandable.

comprensione *f* comprehension, appreciation, understanding; sympathy.

comprensivo *adj* understanding, sympathetic.

compressa *f* compress; tablet.

comprimere *vt* to compress.

compromesso *m* compromise.

comprovare *vt* to substantiate.

computer *m* computer; **personal ~** *m* personal computer.

comune *adj* common; routine; ordinary; * *m* borough; municipality; **in ~** *adj* communal; **in ~** *adv* jointly.

comunemente *adj* commonly.

comunicare *vt* to communi-cate; to impart; to commune.

comunicazione *f* communication; (road, etc); **di grande ~** arterial.

comunione *f* communion.

comunismo *m* communism.

comunista *m/f* communist.

comunità *f inv* community.

comunque *adv* anyhow; * *conj* however.

con *prep* with.

conato *m*; **avere dei conati di vomito** to retch.

concavo *adj* concave.

concedere *vt* allow.

concentramento *m* concentration; **campo di ~** *m* concentration camp.

concentrare *vt* to concentrate.

concentrato *m* concentrate; strong; **~ di frutta** *m* fruit squash.

concentrazione *f* concentration.

concentrico *adj* concentric.

concepibile *adj* conceivable.

concepimento *m* conception.

concepire *vt* to conceive.

concerto *m* concert, concerto, recital.

concessione *f* concession, franchise; **~ atta a placare** *f* sop.

concetto *m* concept.

conchiglia *f* shell.

conciare *vt* to cure.

conciliabile *adj* reconcilable.

conciliare *vt* to accommodate (differences).

conciliante *adj* accommodating, amenable .

concordare *vt* to agree, to conciliate; * *vi* to agree.

conciliatorio *adj* conciliatory.

conciliazione *f* conciliation.

concimare *vt* to manure.

concime *m* compost, manure.

conciso *adj* concise; crisp; terse.

concittadino *m* fellow citizen.

concludere *vt* to conclude; to clinch; * *vi* to conclude; to tie up.

conclusione *f* conclusion; **conclusioni** *fpl* findings.

conclusivo *adj* conclusive; closing.

concomitante *adj* concomitant.

concordanza *f* concordance.

concordare *vi* to settle.

concorrente *m/f* competitor; contestant, entrant.

concorrenza *f* competition.

concorrenziale *adj* competitive.

concorso *m* competition, contest.

concreto *adj* concrete.

concubina *f* concubine.

concupire *vt* to covet.

condanna *f* conviction, condemnation.

condannare *vt* to condemn; to sentence; to decry.

condensare *vt* to condense.

condensato *adj* potted.

condensazione *f* condensation.

condiglianze *fpl* condolences.

condimento *m* condiment, seasoning; dressing, relish; **~ per l'insalata** *m* salad dressing.

condire *vt* to dress, to season.

condiscendente *adj* condescending; acquiescent.

condiscendenza *f* compliance; **trattare con ~** *vt* to patronize

condividere *vt* to share.

condizionale *adj* conditional.

condizionare *vt* to condition.

condizionato *adj* qualified.

condizione *f* condition; state; **~ indispensabile** *f* precondition; **condizioni** *fpl* terms.

condotta *f* conduct; **cattiva ~** *f* misbehaviour, misconduct.

conducente *m* driver.

condurre *vt* to conduct; to lead; (ship) to sail.

conduttività *f* conductivity.

conduttore *m* (*phys*) conductor.

conduttura *f* conduit; pipeline; **~ principale** *f* main; **~ dell'acqua** *f* water main.

conduzione *f* conduction.

confederarsi *vr* to confederate.

confederato *adj* confederate.

confederazione *f* confederacy.

conferenza *f* talk; lecture; **~ stampa** *f* press conference; **tenere una ~** *vt* to lecture.

conferire *vt* to bestow, to confer.

conferma *f* confirmation.

confermare *vt* to confirm.

confessare *vt* to confess.

confessionale *m* confessional.

confessione *f* confession; denomination.

confessore *m* confessor.

confezionare *vt* to package; to tailor.

conficcare *vt* to stick; to plunge; to jab.

confidare *vt* to confide.

confidente *m* confidant.

confidenziale *adj* private.

configurazione *f* configuration.

confinante *adj* neighbouring.

confine *m* border, boundary, frontier,

confisca *f* confiscation; seizure.

confiscare *vt* to confiscate.

conflagrazione *f* conflagration.

conflitto *m* conflict; clash; strife.

confluenza *f* confluence.

confluire *vi* to merge; * *vt* to join.

confondere *vt* to confuse; to baffle.

conformarsi *vr* to conform.

conformità *f* conformity; compliance.

confortare *vt* to comfort.

conforto *m* comfort.

confusione *f* confusion, muddle; turmoil.

confuso *adj* confused; be fuddled; mixed-up.

confutare *vt* to disprove; to refute; to rebut.

congedare *vt* to dismiss.

congedo *m* dismissal; furlough.

congegno *m* device; contrivance.

congelamento *m* freezing, frostbite; **punto di ~** *m* freezing point

congelare *vt* to freeze; * *vr* **~rsi** to freeze.

congelato *adj* frozen, frostbitten.

congelatore *m* freezer, deep-freeze.

congenito *adj* congenital, inbred.

congestionato *adj* congested.

congestione *f* congestion.

congettura *f* conjecture, surmise, guesswork.

congetturare *vt* to conjecture, to surmise.

congiuntive *adj*, *m* subjunctive.

congiuntura *f* conjuncture; juncture.

congiunzione *f* conjunction.

congiura *f* conspiracy.

congiurare *vi* to conspire.

conglomerato *m* conglomerate.

congratularsi *vr* to congratulate.

congratulazioni *fpl* congratulations.

congregazione *f* congregation.

congresso *m* congress.

congruità *f* congruity.

congruo *adj* congruous.

coniare *vt* to mint.

conico *adj* conic(al).

conifera *f* conifer.

conifero *adj* coniferous.

conigliera *f* rabbit hutch.

coniglio *m* rabbit.

coniugale *adj* conjugal, matrimonial, marital.

coniugare *vt* to conjugate.

coniugato *adj* married.

coniugazione *f* conjugation.

connivente *adj*; **essere ~ in** to connive.

connivenza *f* connivance.

cono *m* cone.

conoscente *m/f* acquaintance.

conoscenza *f* acquaintance; knowledge; consciousness; **privo di ~** *adj* insensible.

conoscere *vt* become acquainted with; to know.

conosciuto *adj* familiar.

conquista *f* conquest.

conquistare *vt* to conquer; to win.

conquistatore *m* conqueror.

consacrare *vt* to consecrate, to hallow.

consacrazione *f* consecration.

consapevole *adj* aware; mindful.

consapevolezza *f* awareness.

consapevolmente *adv* wittingly.

consciamente *adv* knowingly.

consecutivo *adj* consecutive; successive.

consegna *f* delivery.

consegnare *vt* to consign; to hand over; to deliver; to turn in.

conseguente *adj* consequent.

conseguenza *f* consequence; after-effect; **conseguenze** *fpl* aftermath; **di ~** *adv* consequently.

consenso *m* consensus; acquiescence; agreement.

conserva f preserve.

conservante m preservative.

conservare vt to conserve, to preserve; to retain.

conservatore m conservative; curator (of museum); * adj conservative.

conservatorio m conservatory.

conservazione f conservation, preservation.

considerare vt to consider; to regard; to deliberate; to treat.

considerazione f consideration.

considerevole adj considerable, handsome, sizeable.

consigliabile adj advisable.

consigliare vt advise; to recommend.

consigliere m adviser; councillor, counsellor.

consigli mpl guidance.

consiglio m advice; council, counsel; (pol) **C~ dei Ministri** The Cabinet.

consistenza f consistency; texture.

consistere vi to consist.

consociato adj associate.

consolare adj consular; * vt to console.

consolato m consulate.

consolazione f consolation, comfort, solace.

console m consul.

consolidare vt to consolidate; * vr **~rsi** to strengthen.

consolidazione f consolidation.

consonante f consonant.

consorte m/f consort.

consorzio m consortium.

consueto adj customary.

consuetudine f custom.

consulente m/f adviser, consultant.

consulenza f consultancy.

consultare vt to consult; * vi to

refer; * vr to confer.

consultazione f consultation.

consultivo adj advisory.

consumare vt to consummate; to consume; to wear: * vi to fray; * vr **~rsi** to wear away.

consumato adj threadbare, worn.

consumatore m consumer.

consumazione f consummation.

consumista adj; **società ~** consumer society.

consumo m consumption; **beni di ~** mpl consumer goods.

consunto adj worn-out.

consunzione f (med) tuberculosis, consumption.

contabile m/f accountant, bookkeeper.

contabilità f accountancy, bookkeeping.

contachilometri m inv mileometer.

contadino m peasant, rustic.

contagioso adj catching, contagious.

contagocce m inv dropper.

contaminare vt to contaminate.

contaminato adj tainted.

contaminazione f contamination.

contanti mpl; **in ~** in cash.

contare vt to count; **~ su** to depend on, to rely on; to number * vi to count.

contatore m meter; **~ del gas** m gas meter.

contatto m contact; **lenti a ~** fpl contact lenses.

contattare vt to contact.

contatto m touch.

conte m count, earl.

contea f county, shire.

conteggio m count.

contegno m demeanour.

contegnoso adj demure.

contemplare *vt* to contemplate.

contemplativo *adj* contemplative.

contemplazione *f* contemplation.

contemporaneo *adj* contemporary, contemporaneous.

contendente *m/f* contender.

contendere *vi* to contend; * *vr* ~**rsi** to vie.

contenere *vt* to contain.

contenitore *m* container, holder.

contentare *vt* to suit.

contentezza *f* content, contentment.

contentissimo *adj* delighted.

contento *adj* content; contented; glad; happy; pleased; **tutto** ~ chuffed.

contenuto *m* contents.

contenzioso *adj* contentious.

contessa *f* countess.

contestare *vt* to contest; to dispute; to query.

contestatore *m* protestor.

contesto *m* context.

contiguo *adj* contiguous; adjoining; **essere** ~ **a** *vt* to adjoin.

continentale *adj* continental.

continente *m* continent; mainland.

contingente *m* contingent.

contingenza *f* contingency.

continuare *vt* to carry on, to continue; * *vi* to continue; to go on.

continuazione *f* continuance, continuation.

continuità *f* continuity.

continuo *adj* continual; continuous; constant; non-stop.

conto *m* account; bill; **dover rendere** ~ **a qn** to be answerable to someone; **non tenere** ~ **di** to override; **per** ~ **di** on behalf of; ~ **in banca** *m* bank account; ~ **scoperto** overdraft; **estratto** ~ statement; ~ **spese** *m* expense account; **rendersi** ~ **di** *vr* to realize.

contorcere *vt* to contort; * *vr* ~**rsi** to squirm; to writhe.

contorno *m* contour, outline.

contorsione *f* contortion.

contrabbandare *vt* to smuggle.

contrabbandiere *m* smuggler.

contrabbando *m* contraband; smuggling.

contraccambiare *vt* to reciprocate; to requite.

contraccezione *f* contraception, birth control.

contraddire *vt* to contradict,

contraddittorio *adj* contradictory, conflicting; inconsistent.

contraddizione *f* contradiction.

contraereo *adj*; **fuoco** ~ *m* flak.

contrafatto *adj* counterfeit.

contraffare *vt* to counterfeit, to forge.

contraffattore *m* forger.

contraffazione *f* forgery.

contrafforte *m* buttress.

contrappeso *m* counterbalance.

contrariare *vt* to put out.

contrariato *adj* disgruntled.

contrario *m* contrary, opposite; * *adj* contrary; **al** ~ conversely.

contrarre *vt* to contract; to incur.

contrarsi *vr* to twitch.

contrastante *adj* contrasting.

contrastare *vi* to contrast.

contrasto *m* contrast.

contrattare *vi* to bargain, to haggle.

contrattempo *m* contretemps, upset.

contratto *m* contract; ~ **d' affitto** *m* lease.

contrattuale *adj* contractual.

contravvenire *vt* to contravene; to flout.

contravvenzione *f* contravention.

contrazione *f* contraction.

contribuente *m/f* taxpayer.

contribuire *vi, vt* to contribute; **che contribuisce** *adj* contributory.

contribuzione *f* contribution.

contro *prep* against, versus.

controbilianciare *vt* to counterbalance.

controcultura *f* underground.

controfigura *f* stand-in.

controfiletto *m* sirloin.

controfirmare *vt* countersign.

controllare *vt* to check; to inspect; to control; to test.

controllo *m* control; inspection; ~ **delle nascite** *m* birth control; **visita di** ~ *f (med)* checkup.

controllore *m* inspector.

controproducente *adj* counterproductive.

controversia *f* controversy, dispute.

controverso *adj* controversial.

contumacia *f* default.

contusione *f* contusion.

conurbazione *f* conurbation.

convalescente *adj, m/f* convalescent.

convalescenza *f* convalescence; recuperation; **fare la** ~ to convalesce.

convalescenziario *m* sanatorium.

convalidare *vt* to authenticate; to validate.

convegno *m* conference; ~ **galante** *m* assignation.

convenire *vi* to convene.

convento *m* convent.

convenuto *adj* agreed; * *m* respondent.

convenzionale *adj* conventional.

convenzione *f* convention.

convergente *adj* convergent.

convergenza *f* convergence.

convergere *vi* to converge.

conversare *vi* to converse.

conversazione *f* talk; conversation; ~ **mondana** *f* small talk; ~ **brillante** *f* repartee.

conversione *f (rel)* conversion.

convertibile *adj* convertible.

convertire *vt* to convert.

convertito *m* convert.

convertitore *m* converter.

convesso *adj* convex.

convettore *m* convector.

convezione *f* convection.

convincente *adj* convincing; cogent; forcible.

convincere *vt* to convince; to coax; ~ **con le buone** to cajole.

convinto *adj* staunch.

convinzione *f* conviction; belief.

convocare *vt* to summon; to convoke; to convene.

convoglio *m* convoy.

convulsione *f* convulsion.

convulso *adj* convulsive.

cooperare *vi* to cooperate.

cooperativa *f* cooperative.

cooperativo *adj* cooperative.

cooperazione *f* cooperation.

cooptare *vt* to coopt.

coordinamento *m* liaison; * *vt* to coordinate.

coordinata *f* coordinate.

coordinatore *m* coordinator.

coordinazione *f* coordination.

coperchio *m* cover, lid.

coperta *f* blanket; deck; **coperte** *fpl* bedclothes; ~ **termica** *f* electric blanket.

coperto *adj* cloudy, overcast; ~

di vegetazione overgrown.

copertura *f* cover, covering.

copia *f* copy.

copiare *vt* to copy; to crib.

copiatrice *f* copier.

copione *m* scenario, script.

copioso *adj* profuse.

coppia *f* couple, pair, twosome.

copricapo *m* headdress.

copri fuoco *m* curfew.

copriletto *m* bedspread, counterpane.

coprimozzo *m* hubcap.

coprire *vt* to cover; to defray.

coraggio *m* courage, bravery; pluck; spirit; valour; ~ **dato da alcolici** *m* Dutch courage.

coraggioso *adj* brave, courageous, plucky, valiant.

corale *adj* choral.

corallino *m* coral reef.

corallo *m* coral.

corda *f* cord; string; rope; chord; ~ **del bucato** *f* clothes line: ~ **da acrobata** *f* tightrope.

cordame *m* rigging.

cordiale *m* cordial; * *adj* cordial, genial.

cordialità *f* friendliness.

cordicella *f* twine.

cordone *m* cord; ~ **ombelicale** *m* umbilical cord.

coreografia *f* choreography.

coreografo *m* choreographer.

coriaceo *adj* thick-skinned.

coriandoli *mpl* confetti.

coriandolo *m* coriander.

corista *m/f* chorister.

cornacchia *f* crow.

cornamusa *f* bagpipes; **suonatore di** ~ *m* piper.

cornea *f* cornea.

cornetta *f* cornet.

cornetto *m* croissant; cornet.

cornice *f* frame.

cornicione *m* cornice.

corno *m* horn.

coro *m* choir; chorus.

corollario *m* corollary.

corona *f* crown.

coronario *adj* cornoary.

coroncina *f* coronet.

coroner *m inv* coroner.

corpino *m* bodice.

corpo *m* body; corps.

corporale *adj* corporal, corporeal.

corporatura *f* build; frame.

corporazione *f* guild.

corpulento *adj* corpulent, portly.

corpulenza *f* corpulence.

corredino *m* layette.

correggere *vt* to correct; to emend; to right; to mark.

correlare *vt* to correlate.

correlativo *adj* correlative.

correlato *adj* interrelated.

correlazione *f* correlation.

corrente *adj* current; fluent; running; * *f* current; flow.

correo *m* co-respondent.

correre *vi* to race; to run; * *vt* to run.

correttezza *f* fair play.

correttivo *adj* corrective; remedial.

corretto *adj* correct; right.

correzione *f* correction; emendation.

corrida *f* bull fight.

corridoio *m* corridor.

corridore *m* runner; racer.

corriera *f* coach.

corriere *m* carrier; courier.

corrimano *m* handrail, rail.

corrispondente *m/f* correspondent; pen friend; * *adj* corresponding.

corrispondenza *f* correspondence; **vendita per** ~ *f* mail order.

corrispondere *vi* to correspond; to match; to tally; * *vt* to correspond.

corroborare *vt* to corroborate.

corroborazione *f* corroboration.

corrodere *vt* to corrode; * *vr* ~**rsi** to corrode.

corrompere *vt* to corrupt; to bribe; to debauch.

corrosione *f* corrosion.

corrosivo *adj* corrosive.

corrotto *adj* corrupt.

corruttibile *adj* corruptible.

corruzione *f* corruption; bribery.

corsa *f* dash; race; run; racing.

corsia *f* ward.

corsivo *adj* italic.

corso *m* course; ~ **serale** *m* evening class; **moneta a ~ legale** *f* legal tender; **in ~** *adj* ongoing.

corte *f* court; ~ **marziale** *f* court-martial.

corteccia *f* bark.

corteggiamento *m* courtship.

corteggiare *vt* to court, to woo.

corteggiatore *m* suitor.

corteo *m* cortège; ~ **in maschera** *m* pageant.

cortese *adj* courteous, gracious.

cortesia *f* courtesy.

cortigiano *m* courtier.

cortile *m* courtyard; quadrangle; yard; backyard; ~ **per la ricreazione** *m* playground.

cortisone *m* cortisone.

corto *adj* short.

cortocircuito *m* short circuit.

corvo *m* crow; raven; rook.

cosa *pron* what; * *f* thing.

coscia *f* thigh; haunch; leg; ~ **di pollo** *f* drumstick.

cosciente *adj* conscious.

coscienza *f* conscience.

coscienzioso *adj* conscientious; painstaking.

coscritto *m* conscript.

così *adv* so; ~ ~ so-so; such; thus; that.

cosiddetto *adj* so-called.

cosmetico *adj*, *m* cosmetic.

cosmico *adj* cosmic.

cosmo *m* cosmos.

cosmonauta *m/f* cosmonaut, spaceman.

cosmopolita *adj*, *m/f* cosmopolitan.

cospargere *vt* to sprinkle; to spread; ~ **di sabbia** to sand.

cospicuo *adj* conspicuous.

cospiratore *m* conspirator.

costa *f* coast.

costante *adj* constant; steady; equable.

costantemente *adv* consistently.

costanza *f* constancy.

costare *vt* to cost.

costellazione *f* constellation.

costernazione *f* consternation.

costiero *adj* coastal; inshore.

costituire *vt* to constitute.

costituzionale *adj* constitutional.

costituzione *f* constitution.

costo *m* cost.

costola *f* rib.

costoletta *f* chop.

costoso *adj* costly, expensive.

costringere *vt* to constrain; to compel; to impel; to coerce; to constrict.

costrizione *f* compulsion; constraint; constriction.

costruire *vt* to construct, to build.

costruttore *m* builder.

costruzione *f* building, construction, edifice; ~ **annessa** *f* outhouse.

costume *m* costume; fancy dress; outfit; custom; wont; ~ **da bagno** bathing costume swimsuit.

cotenna *f* rind; ~ **arrostita** crackling.

cotogna *f* quince.

cotogno *m* quince tree.

cotoletta *f* cutlet.

cotonare *vt* to backcomb.

cotone *m* cotton; ~ **idrofilo** *m* cotton wool.

cotonificio *m* cotton mill.

cotta *f* crush; surplice.

cottage *m* cottage.

cottimo *m*: **lavoro a** ~ *m* piecework.

cotto *adj* cooked; **poco** ~ underdone.

cottura *f* baking.

coupé *m inv* (*auto*) coupé.

covare *vt* to brood; to incubate; to harbour; * *vi* ~ (**sotto la cenere**) to smoulder.

covata *f* brood.

covo *m* den; haunt.

covone *m* sheaf.

cowboy *m inv* cowboy.

cozza *f* mussel.

cracker *m* cracker.

crampo *m* cramp.

cranio *m* skull.

crasso *adj* crass.

cratere *m* crater.

cravatta *f* tie.

creare *vt* to create.

creatività *f* creativity.

creativo *adj* creative.

creatore *m* creator.

creatura *f* creature.

creazione *f* creation; brainchild.

credente *m/f* believer.

credenza *f* dresser; sideboard; credence.

credenziali *vfpl* credentials.

credere *vt* to believe; to feel; to reckon; to understand; **non** ~ to disbelieve; * *vi* to believe; to think.

credibile *adj* credible; believable.

credibilità *f* credibility.

credito *m* credit; **lettera di** ~ *f* letter of credit.

creditore *m* creditor.

credo *m* creed.

credulità *f* credulity; gullibility.

credulo *adj* credulous.

credulone *adj* gullible.

crema *f* cream; ~ **pasticcera** *f* custard; **color** ~ *adj, f inv* cream; ~ **per il viso** *f* face cream.

cremare *vt* cremate.

crematorio *m* crematorium.

cremazione *f* cremation.

cremisi *adj* crimson.

cremoso *adj* creamy.

creosoto *m* creosote.

crepa *f* crack; cleft.

crepaccio *m* crevasse; chasm.

crepuscolo *m* dusk, night fall, twilight.

crescente *adj* growing; increasing; rising.

crescere *vi* to grow.

crescione *m* cress.

crescita *f* growth.

cresima *f* confirmation.

cresimare *vt* to confirm.

crespo *m* crêpe; * *adj* fuzzy, frizzy.

cresta *f* crest; ridge.

cretino *m* cretin.

cric *m inv* jack.

cricca *f* clique.

criceto *m* hamster.

cricket *m* cricket.

criminale *m/f, adj* criminal, felon.

criminalità *f* crime.

crimine *m* felony.

crinale *m* ridge.

criniera *f* mane.

cripta *f* crypt.

crisi *f* crisis; turn.

cristalleria *f* glassware.

cristallino *adj* crystal-clear, cristalline.

cristallizzare *vt* to crystalize; * *vr* ~**rsi** to crystallize.

cristallo *m* crystal.

cristianesimo *m* Christianity.

cristianità *f* Christianity, Christendom.

cristiano *m*, *adj* Christian.

Cristo *m* Christ.

criterio *m* criterion; yardstick.

critica *f* criticism.

criticare *vt* to criticize; to fault; to slate.

critico *m* critic, critique; * *adj* critical.

criticone *m* faultfinder.

crivellare *vt* to riddle.

croccante *adj* crisp, crunchy.

crocchetta *f* croquette.

croce *f* cross.

crociata *f* crusade.

crociato *m* crusader.

crociera *f* cruise.

crocifiggere *vt* to crucify.

crocifissione *f* crucifixion.

crocifisso *m* crucifix.

croco *m* crocus.

crogiolarsi *vr* to bask.

crogiolo *m* crucible.

crollare *vi* to collapse; to keel over; to slump.

crollo *m* collapse; slump.

cromatico *adj* chromatic.

cromato *adj*: **metallo** ~ *m* chrome.

cronaca *f* chronicle.

cronico *adj* chronic.

cronista *m* reporter.

cronologia *f* chronology.

cronologico *adj* chronological.

cronometrare *vt* to time.

cronometro *m* chronometer; stopwatch.

croquet *m* croquet.

crosta *f* crust; scab.

crostaceo *m* crustacean, shellfish.

crostata *f* tart.

crotalo *m* rattlesnake.

cruciale *adj* crucial.

cruciverba *m inv* crossword.

crudele *adj* cruel; unkind

crudeltà *f* cruelty.

crudo *adj* raw; uncooked.

crumiro *m* blackleg; scab.

crup *m* croup.

crusca *f* bran.

cruscotto *m* dashboard.

cubico *adj* cubic.

cubo *m* cube.

cuccetta *f* couchette; bunk, berth; sleeper.

cucchiaiata *f* spoonful.

cucchiaino *m* teaspoon.

cucchiaio *m* spoon; ~ **da portata** serving spoon.

cucciolata *f* litter.

cucciolo *m* pup, cub.

cucina *f* cooker, cookery; kitchen; ~ **componibile** *f* fitted kitchen.

cucire *vt* to stitch, to sew; * *vi* to sew; **macchina da** ~ *f* sewing machine.

cucito *m* needlework.

cucitrice *f* stapler.

cucitura *f* seam.

cuculo *m* cuckoo.

cuffia *f* earphones, headphones; bathing cap; bonnet.

cugino *m* cousin.

cui *rel pron* **il** ~ whose.

culinario *adj* culinary.

culla *f* crib, cradle, cot; ~ **trasportabile** carrycot.

cullare *vt* to rock.

culminare *vi* to culminate.

culmine *m* culmination; acme; climax.

culo *m* (*sl*) bum, arse.

culto *m* cult.

cultura *f* culture, learning, edification.

culturale *adj* cultural.

cumino *m* caraway, cumin.

cumulativo *adj* cumulative.

cumulo *m* drift.

cuneo *m* wedge.

cunetta *f* dip; gutter.

cuocere *vt* to cook; ~ **al forno**

to bake; ~ **in bianco** to poach.

cuoco *m* cook.

cuoio *m* hide, leather; ~ **capelluto** *m* scalp.

cuore *m* heart; **prendersi a ~** to befriend; **di ~** *adv* heartily; **dal ~ tenero** *adj* soft-hearted.

cupo *adj* gloomy, glum.

cupola *f* dome.

cura *f* cure; **aver ~ di** *vt* to groom.

curare *vt* to care for; to tend; to treat.

curato *m* curate.

curcuma *f* turmeric.

curiosare *vi* to browse; to snoop, to pry.

curiosità *f inv* curio; curiosity.

curioso *adj* curious; inquisitive, nos(e)y.

curriculum vitae *m inv* curriculum vitae.

curry *m* curry.

cursore *m* cursor.

curva *f* curve, bend, turn, turning.

curvare *vt* to curve.

curvatura *f* curvature; camber; warp.

cuscinetto *m* pad.

cuscino *m* cushion.

custode *m/f* custodian, attendant.

custodia *f* case; custody.

D

da *prep* to; out; off; since; from, by, for.

dado *m* die, dice; nut.

daino *m* deer; **femmina di ~** *f* doe; fallow deer.

dalia *f* dahlia.

daltonico *adj* colour-blind.

damigella *f* damsel; ~ **d'onore** bridesmaid.

dandy *m* dandy.

dannazione *f* damnation.

danneggiare *vt* to harm, to hurt; to impair.

danno *m* harm; **danni** *mpl* breakage, havoc.

dannoso *adj* detrimental.

danza *f* dancing; ~ **classica** ballet.

danzare *vi* to dance.

danze *f* dance.

dappertutto *adv* everywhere; throughout.

dapprima *adv* at first.

dardo *m* dart.

dare *vt* to give; ~ **su** to overlook; * *vi* to give.

darsena *f* dock.

darsi *adv*:**può darsi** it may be.

data *f* date.

database *m* database.

datare *vt* to date.

dati *mpl* data.

dativo *m* dative.

datore *m*: ~ **di lavoro** employer.

dattero *m* date.

dattilografia *f* typing.

dattilografo *m* typist.

dattiloscritto *m* typescript; * *adj* typewritten.

davanti *adv* ahead; * *prep* by; * *m* front, fore; * *adj* front.

davanzale *m* windowsill, sill, window ledge.

davvero *adv* really.

dazio *m* duty.

dea *f* goddess.

debilitare *vt* to debilitate.

debitamente *adv* duly.
debito *m* debt.
debitore *m* debtor.
debole *adj* weak, frail, feeble; * *m* penchant; foible
debolezza *f* weakness, frailty, feebleness.
debutto *m* debut.
decadente *adj* decadent.
decadenza *f* decadence.
decaffeinato *adj* decaffeinated.
decapitare *vt* to decapitate, to behead.
decapitazione *f* decapitation.
decappottabile *adj*, *f* (*auto*) convertible.
deceduto *adj* deceased.
decelerare *vt* to decelerate.
decennio *m* decade.
decente *adj* decent, proper.
decentramento *m* decentralization, devolution.
decenza *f* decency.
decesso *m* decease, demise.
decibel *m inv* decibel.
decidere *vt* to decide; to elect; to resolve; ~ **su** adjudicate.
deciduo *adj* deciduous.
decifrare *vt* to decipher.
decimale *adj*, *m* decimal.
decimare *vt* to decimate.
decimo *adj*, *m* tenth.
decisione *f* decision.
decisivo *adj* decisive.
deciso *adj* decided; set.
declamare *vt*, *vi* declaim.
declamazione *f* declamation.
declinare *vt*, *vi* to decline.
declinazione *f* declension.
declino *m* decline.
decodificare *vt* to decode.
decollare *vi* to take off.
decollato *adj* airborne.
decollo *m* takeoff
decomporre *vt* to decompose.
decomposizione *f* decomposition, decay.

decompressione *f* decompression.
decongestionante *m* decongestant.
decorare *vt* to decorate, to deck.
decorativo *adj* decorative.
decoratore *m* decorator.
decorazione *f* decoration; garnish.
decoro *m* decorum, propriety.
decoroso *adj* decorous, seemly.
decrepito *adj* decrepit.
decrescrere *vi* to decrease.
decretare *vt* to decree, to rule.
decreto *m* decree.
decurtare *vt* to dock.
dedica *f* dedication; inscription.
dedicare *vt* to dedicate, to devote; to give.
dedizione *f* dedication.
dedurre *vt* to deduce, to gather; to infer; to deduct.
deduzione *f* inference; deduction.
defecare *vi* to defecate.
deferente *adj* deferential, dutiful.
deferenza *f* deference.
defezionare *vi* to defect.
defezione *f* defection.
deficiente *adj* brainless.
deficit *m inv* deficit.
definibile *adj* definable.
definire *vt* to define; to class; to settle; to finalize.
definitivo *adj* definitive, definite; firm.
definito *adj* defined; **ben ~** clear-cut.
definizione *f* definition.
deflazione *f* deflation.
deflorare *vt* to deflower.
deformare *vt* to deform; to warp.
deforme *adj* misshapen.
deformità *f* deformity.
defraudare *vt* to defraud.

defunto *adj* late.

degenerare *vi* to degenerate.

degenerato *adj, m* degenerate.

degenza *f* stay.

deglutizione *f* swallow.

degnarsi *vr* to deign, to condescend.

degradante *adj* degrading.

degradare *vt* to degrade, to demote.

degradazione *f* degradation.

degustazione *f* tasting; ~ **dei vini** *f* wine-tasting.

delegare *vt* to delegate, to depute.

delegato *m* delegate; commissioner.

delegazione *f* delegation.

delfino *m* dolphin.

deliberare *vi* to deliberate.

deliberazione *f* deliberation.

delicatezza *f* delicacy.

delicato *adj* delicate.

delimitare *vt* to delimit.

delineare *vt* to delineate.

delineazione *f* delineation.

delinquente *m* delinquent.

delinquenza *f* delinquency.

delinquenziale *adj* delinquent.

delirante *adj* delirious.

delirio *m* delirium.

delitto *m* crime.

delizia *f* delight.

delizioso *adj* charming, delightful, delicious, delectable, scrumptious.

delta *m inv* delta.

deltaplano *m* hang-gliding.

delucidare *vt* to elucidate.

deludente *adj* disappointing.

deludere *vt* to disappoint.

delusione *f* disappointment; comedown.

deluso *adj* disappointed.

demagogo *m* demagogue.

demarcazione *f* demarcation.

demistificare *vt* to debunk.

democratico *m, adj* democrat(ic).

democrazia *f* democracy.

demolire *vt* to demolish, to pull down, to knock down; to scrap.

demolizione *f* demolition.

demonio *m* demon, fiend.

demoralizzare *vt* to demoralize.

demoralizzato *adj* dispirited.

denaro *m* money; (stockings) denier.

denigrare *vt* to disparage.

denigratorio *adj* disparaging.

denominatore *m* denominator.

denotare *vt* to denote.

densità *f inv* density.

denso *adj* dense.

dente *m* tooth; cog; ~ **d'arresto** *m* ratchet; ~ **del giudizio** *m* wisdom tooth; **mal di denti** *m* toothache; ~ **di leone** *m* dandelion; **mettere i denti** *vi* to teethe.

dentiera *f* dentures.

dentifricio *m* toothpaste.

dentista *m/f* dentist.

dentistico *adj* dental.

dentro *prep* into; within; inside; * *adv* inside.

denudare *vt* to denude.

denuncia *f* denunciation.

denunciare *vt* to denounce; to report.

denutrito *adj* underfed, undernourished.

denutrizione *f* malnutrition.

deodorante *m* deodorant.

deodorare *vt* to deodorize.

deperibile *adj* perishable.

depilatore *m* hair remover.

depliant *m inv* brochure.

deplorare *vt* to deplore.

deplorevole *adj* deplorable; regrettable; sad.

deportare *vt* to deport.

deportazione *f* deportation.

depositante *m/f* depositor.

depositare *vt* to deposit; * *vr* ~**rsi** to settle.

deposito *m* deposit; depot; store; repository; warehouse; ~ **segreto** *m* cache, ~ **auto** *m* car pound.

deposizione *f* deposition; statement.

depravare *vt* to deprave.

depravato *adj* depraved.

depravazione *f* depravation.

deprecare *vt* to deprecate.

depredazione *f* depredation.

depressione *f* depression; low.

depresso *adj* depressed, downhearted.

deprezzamento *m* depreciation.

deprezzarsi *vr* to depreciate.

deprimente *adj* gloomy.

deprimere *vt* to depress.

depurare *vt* to purify.

depurazione *f* purification.

deputazione *f* deputation.

deragliare *vt*: **far** ~ to derail.

deretano *m* posterior.

deridere *vt* to deride.

derisione *f* derision.

deriva *f* drift; leeway; **alla** ~ *adj* adrift; **andare alla** ~ *vi* to drift.

derivare *vt* to derive; * *vi* ~ **da** to arise from.

derivato *adj, m* derivative.

derivazione *f* derivation.

dermatite *f* dermatitis.

dermatologia *f* dermatology.

derrick *m inv* derrick.

derubare *vt* to rob.

descrittivo *adj* descriptive.

descrivere *vt* to describe.

descrizione *f* description.

desertico *adj* desert.

deserto *m* desert; wilderness.

desiderabile *adj* desirable.

desiderare *vt* to desire; to wish; to want; to long for; to lust after; ~ **disperatamente** to crave; ~ **moltissimo** to hunger after; * *vi* to wish.

desiderio *m* desire; wish; longing; ~ **intenso** yearning; ~ **incontrollabile** *m* compulsion; **avere molto** ~ **di** *vt* to hanker after.

desideroso *adj* desirous, wishful.

designare *vt* to designate.

desinenza *f* ending.

desistere *vi* to desist.

desolato *adj* bleak, desolate, dreary.

desolazione *f* desolation.

despota *m* despot.

dessert *m inv* dessert, pudding.

destinare *vt* to intend; to earmark.

destinatario *m* recipient.

destinato *adj* destined.

destinazione *f* destination.

destino *m* destiny, fate, lot; doom.

destra *f* right.

destrezza *f* dexterity; ~ **di mano** *f* sleight of hand; **fare giochi di** ~ *vi* to juggle.

destro *adj* right; dext(e)rous.

detective *m*: ~ **privato** *m* private detective.

detenuto *m* inmate.

detenzione *f* detention; custody; ~ **preventiva** *f* remand.

deterioramento *m* deterioration.

deteriorarsi *vr* to deteriorate, to decay.

determinare *vt* to determine.

determinazione *f* determination, resolution.

deterrente *m* deterrent.

detersivo *m* detergent; soap powder.

detestabile *adj* detestable.

detestabile *adj* obnoxious, vile.

detestare *vt* to detest, to loathe.

detonare *vi* to detonate.

detonatore *m* detonator.
detonazione *f* detonation.
detrimento *m* detriment.
detriti *mpl* debris.
dettagliante *m* retailer.
dettagliare *vt* to detail.
dettaglio *m* detail; **al ~** *adj*
(com) retail; **vendere al ~** *vt*
to retail.
dettare *vt* to dictate.
dettatura *f* dictation.
detto *m* saying.
deturpare *vt* to blemish; to defile, to deface.
devastare *vt* to devastate; to
ravage.
devastatore *adj* devastating.
devastazione *f* devastation;
ravage.
deviare *vi* to deviate, to divert,
to deflect.
deviatore *m* signalman.
deviazione *f* deviation, diversion, detour.
devolvere *vt* to devolve.
devoto *adj* devoted, devout.
devozione *f* devotion.
di *prep* of; any.
diabete *m* diabetes.
diabetico *adj*, *m* diabetic.
diabolico *adj* devilish, diaboli-
cal, fiendish.
diacono *m* deacon.
diadema *m* diadem, tiara.
diaframma *m* diaphragm; midriff.
diagnosi *f inv* diagnosis.
diagnosticare *vt* to diagnose.
diagnostico *adj* diagnostic.
diagonale *adj* diagonal.
diagramma *m* diagram.
dialetto *m* dialect.
dialisi *f* dialysis.
dialogo *m* dialogue.
diamantaio *m* diamond cutter.
diamante *m* diamond.
diametrale *adj* diametrical.
diametro *m* diameter.

diapason *m inv* tuning fork.
diapositiva *f* slide, transparency.
diario *m* diary.
diarrea *f* diarrhoea.
diavoletto *m* imp.
diavolo *m* devil.
dibattere *vt* to debate; * *vr* **~rsi**
to flounder.
dibattito *m* debate.
dicembre *m* December.
diceria *f* hearsay.
dichiarare *vi* (cards) to bid; * *vt*
to declare.
dichiarazione *f* declaration;
pronouncement; statement; **~
dei redditi** *f* tax return.
diciannovesimo *adj*, *m* nineteenth
diciassette *adj*, *m* seventeen.
diciassettesimo *adj*, *m* seventeenth.
diciottesimo *adj*, *m* eighteenth.
diciotto *adj*, *m* eighteen.
didattico *adj* educational, didactic.
dieci *adj*, *m inv* ten.
diesis *m* (mus) sharp; **in ~** *adv*
(mus) sharp.
dieta *f* diet; **seguire una ~** *vi*
to diet.
dietetico *adj* dietary.
dietro *prep* behind; * *m* back.
difendere *vt* to defend; to
champion; to plead.
difensivo *adj* defensive.
difesa *f* defence.
difetto *m* defect; shortcoming;
flaw, failing, fault.
difettoso *adj* defective, faulty,
imperfect.
diffamare *vt* to libel, to vilify,
to smear.
diffamatorio *adj* libellous.
diffamazione *f* defamation, libel.
differenza *f* difference.

differenziale *adj, m* differential.

differire *vi* to differ.

difficile *adj* difficult, hard, tricky, stiff.

difficoltà *f inv* difficulty.

diffidare *vt* to distrust, to mistrust.

diffidente *adj* distrustful, mistrustful, wary.

diffidenza *f* distrust, mistrust.

diffondere *vt* to diffuse; to popularize; * *vi* **~rsi** to waft.

diffrazione *f* diffraction.

diffusione *f* diffusion.

diffuso *adj* widespread; prevalent; rife.

difterite *f* diphtheria.

diga *f* dyke.

digeribile *adj* digestible.

digerire *vt* to digest.

digestione *f* digestion.

digestivo *adj* digestive.

digitale *adj* digital; * *f* foxglove.

digiunare *vi* to fast.

digiuno *m* fast.

dignità *f* dignity.

dignitario *m* dignitary.

dignitoso *adj* dignified.

digressione *f* digression.

digrignare *vt*: **~ i denti** to gnash one's teeth.

dilaniare *vt* to claw to pieces.

dilatare *vt* to dilate.

dilemma *m* dilemma.

dilettante *m/f* amateur.

dilettarsi *vr* to dabble.

diligente *adj* diligent, industrious.

diligenza *f* diligence.

diluire *vt* to dilute.

diluvio *m* deluge.

dimagrante *adj* slimming.

dimenare *vt* to wag; to waggle.

dimensione *f* dimension; **dimensioni** *fpl* size.

dimenticare *vi* to forget.

dimentico *adj* unmindful.

dimettersi *vr* to resign, to quit.

dimezzare *vt* to halve.

diminuire *vt* to diminish; to decrease; to lessen; to abate; * *vi* to decrease; to dwindle; to reduce; to lessen.

diminuzione *f* decrease.

dimissioni *fpl* resignation.

dimora *f* dwelling, abode.

dimorare *vi* to dwell.

dimostrabile *adj* demonstrable.

dimostrare *vt* to demonstrate; to prove.

dinamica *f* dynamics.

dinamico *adj* dynamic.

dinamismo *m* go, pep.

dinamitardo *m* bomber.

dinamite *f* dynamite.

dinamo *f inv* dynamo.

dinastia *f* dynasty.

dingo *m* dingo.

diniego *m* denial.

dinoccolato *adj* lanky; **camminare ~** *vi* to slouch.

dinosauro *m* dinosaur.

dintorni *mpl* environs.

dio *m* god; **per amor di D~!** *excl* for God's sake!

diocesi *f inv* diocese.

dipanare *vt* to unravel.

dipendente *m/f* employee.

dipendenza *f* dependence, reliance.

dipendere *vi* to depend; **~ da** to be contingent on.

dipingere *vt* to paint.

diploma *m* diploma.

diplomatico *m, adj* diplomat.

diplomato *adj* trained.

diplomazia *f* diplomacy.

dipsomania *f* dipsomania.

diradarsi *vr* to thin.

diramarsi *vr* to branch.

dire *vt* to speak; to tell; to say **va detto che** *adv* admittedly; * *vi* to say.

direttamente *adv* directly squarely; straight.

direttiva *f* directive.

direttive *fpl* guidelines.

diretto *adj* direct; first hand; non-stop; ~ **a** *adv* bound for; **essere** ~ **a** *vi* to make for.

direttore *m* editor; (*mus*) conductor.

direttrice *f* manageress.

direzione *f* direction, way; leadership; administration.

dirigente *m/f* executive, director; * *adj* managerial.

dirigere *vt* to direct; to administer; (*mus*) to conduct; to run.

diritto *m* right; law; ~ **civile** civil law; ~ **comune** common law; **dare** ~ **a** *vt* to entitle; * *adj* right; straight; * *adv* straight.

diritti *mpl* dues; ~ **d'autore** *mpl* copyright.

dirottamento *m* hijack.

dirottare *vt* to hijack.

dirottatore *m* hijacker.

dirotto *adj*: **piovere a** ~ *vi* to pelt with rain; **sta piovendo a** ~ it's pouring with rain.

disabitato *adj* uninhabited.

disaccordo *m* discord; **essere in** ~ *vi* to disagree.

disadattato *m* misfit; maladjusted.

disadorno *adj* unadorned.

disagio *m* discomfort.

disamorato *adj* disaffected.

disapprovare *vi* to disapprove.

disapprovazione *f* disapproval, disfavour.

disarcionare *vt* to toss.

disarmante *adj* disarming.

disarmare *vt* to disarm.

disarmato *adj* unarmed.

disarmo *m* disarmament.

disastro *m* disaster; washout.

disastroso *adj* disastrous, dire, ruinous.

disattento *adj* inattentive, unheeding.

disattenzione *f* carelessness.

disavventura *f* misadventure.

discanto *m* descant.

discarica *f* dump, tip.

discendente *m/f* descendant.

discepolo *m* disciple.

discernere *vt* to discern.

discernimento *m* discrimination, discernment.

discesa *f* descent; **in** ~ *adv* downhill.

dischetto *m* floppy disk.

disciplina *f* discipline.

disciplinare *adj* disciplinary.

disco *m* disc, discus; record; ~ **volante** *m* flying saucer.

discolpa *f* exoneration.

discolpare *vt* to exonerate; to clear.

disconoscimento *m* disclaimer.

discordante *adj* discordant.

discordanza *f* disagreement; variance.

discordare *vi* to differ.

discordia *f*: **pomo della** ~ *m* bone of contention.

discorsivo *m* discursive.

discorso *m* discourse, speech, address.

discoteca *f* disco.

discredito *m* discredit.

discrepanza *f* discrepancy.

discreto *adj* discreet; unobtrusive; fair.

discrezionale *adj* discretionary.

discrezione *f* discretion.

discriminazione *f* discrimination; **fare** ~ **tra** *vt* to discriminate.

discussione *f* discussion; argument.

discutere *vt* to discuss.

discutibile *adj* arguable, debatable, questionable.

disdegno *m* disdain.

disegnare *vt* to draw.

disegnatore *m* designer; ~ **tecnico** *m* draughtsman.

disegno *m* drawing, design, picture, pattern.

diserbante *m* weedkiller.

diseredare *vt* to disinherit.

disertore *m* deserter.

diserzione *f* desertion.

disfare *vt* to undo, to unpack; * *vr* ~**rsi di** to part with.

disfatta *f* rout.

disgelo *m* thaw.

disgrazia *f* misfortune.

disgraziato *adj* unlucky; wretched.

disgustare *vt* to disgust.

disgusto *m* disgust.

disgustoso *adj* disgusting; foul.

disidratare *vt* to dehydrate.

disidratato *adj* dehydrated.

disillusione *f* disenchantment.

disincantare *vt* to disenchant.

disincantato *adj* disenchanted.

disincarnato *adj* disembodied.

disinfettante *m* disinfectant.

disinfettare *vt* to disinfect.

disingannare *vt* to disillusion, to disabuse.

disinganno *m* disillusion.

disinnescare *vt* to defuse.

disinnestare *vt* to disengage.

disintegrarsi *vr* to disintegrate.

disinteressato *adj* disinterested.

disinvolto *adj* effortless; unconstrained; glib; nonchalant; **gioviale e** ~ debonair.

disinvoltura *f* ease; aplomb.

dislessico *adj* word-blind.

disoccupato *adj* unemployed, jobless.

disoccupazione *f* unemployment.

disonestà *f* dishonesty.

disonesto *adj* dishonest; crooked.

disonorare *vt* to dishonour, to disgrace, to shame.

disonore *m* dishonour, disgrace.

disonorevole *adj* dishonourable, discreditable.

disordinato *adj* disorderly, untidy.

disordine *m* disorder, clutter, untidiness, mess; **in** ~ in disarray.

disordini *mpl* (*pol*) disturbance, riot.

disorganizzato *adj* disorganized, unorganized.

disorganizzazione *f* disorganization.

disorientare *vt* to bewilder.

disorientato *adj* disorientated.

disossare *vt* to fillet.

dispari *adj inv* odd.

disparità *f inv* disparity.

dispendio *m* expenditure.

dispendioso *adj* extravagant, wasteful.

dispensa *f* dispensation; pantry, larder.

dispensare *vt* to dispense.

dispensario *m* dispensary.

dispepsia *f* dispepsia.

dispeptico *adj* dyspeptic.

disperare *vi* to despair.

disperato *adj* desperate, despairing, hopeless; **un caso** ~ *m* a dead loss.

disperazione *f* despair, desperation.

disperdere *vt* to disperse; * *vr* ~**rsi** to scatter.

dispersione *f* dispersal.

dispetto *m* spite; **far** ~ **a** *vt* to spite.

dispettoso *adj* spiteful.

dispiacente *adj* sorry.

dispiacere *vt* to displease; * *vr* ~**rsi** to be sorry, to regret; * *m* chagrin, displeasure.

disponibile *adj* available; disposable.

disponibilità *f* willingness.
disporre *vt* to dispose; * *vi* ~ **di** to command.
dispositivo *m* device.
disposizione *f* arrangement; layout; ~ **naturale** *f* flair.
disposto *adj* disposed, willing; ~ **a fare** prepared to do.
dispotico *adj* domineering, despotic.
dispotismo *m* despotism.
disprezzare *vt* to despise; to scorn.
disprezzo *m* contempt, scorn.
disputa *f* dispute, contention.
disputarsi *vr* to dispute.
disquisizione *f* disquisition.
disseminare *vt* to disseminate.
dissenso *m* dissension, dissent.
dissenteria *f* dysentery.
dissentire *vi* to dissent.
dissertazione *f* dissertation.
dissidente *m* dissenter, dissident.
dissimile *adj* dissimilar, unlike.
dissimulazione *f* dissimulation.
dissipare *vt* to disssipate, to dispel; to allay.
dissipazione *f* dissipation.
dissociare *vt* to dissociate.
dissolutezza *f* debauchery.
dissoluto *adj* debauched, dissolute, loose, rakish.
dissolvere *vt* to dissolve.
dissomiglianza *f* dissimilarity.
dissonanza *f* dissonance.
dissotterrare *vt* to unearth.
dissuadere *vt* to deter, to dissuade.
distaccamento *m* detachment; secondment.
distaccare *vt* to second.
distaccato *adj* withdrawn, cool.
distacco *m* detachment.
distante *adj* distant; * *adv* off; * *adj* far.

distanza *f* distance; **a** ~ *adv* apart.
distanziare *vt* to distance, to space.
distendersi *vr* to unwind.
distensione *f* detente.
distesa *f* expanse, stretch; tract.
disteso *adj* recumbent; outstretched.
distico *m* couplet.
distillare *vt* to distil.
distillazione *f* distillation.
distilleria *f* distillery.
distinguere *vt* to distinguish, to differentiate, to discriminate.
distintivo *m* badge.
distinto *adj* distinct.
distinzione *f* distinction; **senza distinzioni** *adv* regardless.
distogliere *vt* to remove; ~ **da** to avert from.
distorcere *vt* to distort.
distorsione *f* distortion.
distrarre *vt* to distract, to divert.
distratto *adj* distracted; forgetful; absent-minded.
distrazione *f* distraction; absent-mindedness, oversight; amusement.
distretto *m* district.
distribuire *vt* to distribute; to give out.
distributore *m* distributor; ~ **automatico** *m* vending machine.
distribuzione *f* distribution.
districare *vt* to extricate.
distruggere *vt* to destroy; to wreck.
distruttivo *adj* destructive.
distrutto *adj* destroyed; shattered, zonked.
distruzione *f* destruction.
disturbare *vt* to disturb; to trouble.

disturbo *m* disturbance; static; **fare azione di ~** *vt* to heckle.

disubbidiente *adj* disobedient, naughty.

disubbidienza *f* disobedience.

disubbidire *vt* to disobey.

disuguale *adj* unequal.

disuso *m* disuse; **essere in ~** *vi* to be in abeyance; **cadere in ~** *vi* to fall into disuse.

ditale *m* thimble.

dito *m* finger; **~ del piede** *m* toe.

ditta *f* firm.

dittatore *m* dictator.

dittatoriale *adj* dictatorial.

dittatura *f* dictatorship.

dittongo *m* diphthong.

diuretico *adj* diuretic.

divagare *vi* to digress, to ramble.

divampare *vi* to blaze, to flame.

divano *m* couch, settee.

divenire *vi* to become.

diventare *vi* to become; **~ grande** to grow up.

divergente *adj* divergent.

divergenza *f* divergence.

divergere *vi* to diverge.

diversamente *adv* otherwise, other than.

diversificare *vi* to diversify.

diversità *f* diversity.

diverso *adj* different; **diversi** *adj* sundry.

divertente *adj* amusing, entertaining.

divertimento *m* amusement, enjoyment, fun.

divertire *vt* amuse; * *vr* **~rsi** to enjoy oneself, to have a good time.

dividendo *m* dividend.

dividere *vt* to divide, to split, to share.

divieto *m* ban.

divinità *f* divinity, godhead, deity.

divino *adj* divine, heavenly, godlike.

divisa *f* uniform, strip.

divisibile *adj* divisible.

divisione *f* division.

diviso *adj* divided.

divisore *m* divisor.

divo *m* star; **~ del cinema** *m* film star.

divorare *vt* to devour, to wolf.

divorziare *vt*, *vi* to divorce.

divorziato *adj* divorced; * *m* divorcee.

divorzio *m* divorce.

divulgare *vt* to divulge; to leak.

dizionario *m* dictionary; **~ dei sinonimi** *m* thesaurus.

dizione *f* diction, elocution.

doccia *f* shower; **fare la ~** *vi* to shower.

docente *adj* teaching; * *m* **~ universitario** lecturer, don.

docile *adj* docile.

documentare *vt* to document.

documentario *adj*, *m* documentary.

documento *m* document; **documenti** *mpl* papers.

dodicesimo *adj*, *m* twelfth.

dodici *adj*, *m inv* twelve.

dogana *f* customs; **esente da ~** *adj* duty free.

doganiere *m* customs officer.

doglie *fpl* labour; **avere le ~** *vi* to be in labour.

dogma *m* dogma.

dogmatico *adj* dogmatic, opinionated.

dolce *adj* sweet; gentle; soft; **dalla voce ~** *adv* soft-spoken; * *m* sweet, pudding;

dolcemente *adv* gently.

dolcezza *f* sweetness.

dolcificante *m* sweetener.

dolciumi *mpl* confectionery.

dollaro *m* dollar.

dolore *m* ache, pain; grief, sorrow, woe; **~ acuto** *m* pang immenso ~ *m* heartbreak; ~ **atroce** *m* agony.

doloroso *adj* painful, sore.

domanda *f* question; inquiry; query; application; **fare una** ~ *vi* to ask a question.

domandarsi *vt* to wonder.

domani *adv*, *m inv* tomorrow.

domare *vt* to tame.

domenica *f* Sunday, Sabbath.

domestico *adj* domestic; * *m* servant.

domicilio *m* abode, domicile.

dominante *adj* dominant, uppermost.

dominare *vt* to dominate; to control; to subdue; to master.

dominazione *f* domination.

dominio *m* dominion, domain, domino.

donare *vt* to donate.

donatore *m* contributor; donor; ~ **di sangue** blood donor.

donazione *f* endowment, donation.

donchisciottesco *adj* quixotic.

dondolare *vt* to swing; to dangle; * *vi* to swing; to rock.

dondolo *adj*: **sedia a** ~ *f* rocking chair.

dongiovanni *m inv* ladykiller.

donna *f* woman; ~ **d'affari** *f* businesswoman.

donnaiolo *m* philanderer.

donnola *f* weasel.

dono *m* gift; ~ **del cielo** *m* godsend.

dopo *prep* after; * *adv* after; next; ~**tutto** after all; afterwards.

dopobarba *m inv* aftershave.

doppiamente *adv* doubly.

doppiare *vt* to dub.

doppio *adj* dual, double; towold; **camera doppia** *f* double room; understudy.

dorare *vt* to gild.

doratura *f* gilding, gilt.

dormire *vi* to sleep, to slumber.

dormitorio *m* dormitory.

dorso *m* backstroke.

dosare *vt* to dose.

dose *f* dose.

dossier *m inv* dossier; (*law*) brief.

dotare *vt* to endow.

dotato *adj* gifted.

dote *f* dowry; accomplishment; **doti** *fpl* abilities.

dotto *adj* scholarly.

dottore *m* doctor; (*univ*) bachelor.

dottoressa *f* (*univ*) bachelor.

dottrina *f* doctrine.

dottrinale *m* doctrinal.

double-face *adj* reversible.

dove *adv* where, whereabouts; * *conj* where.

dovere *mod.vb* to have to; to owe; **io devo** I must; * *m* stint.

dovunque *conj* wherever.

dovuto *adj* due.

dozzina *f* dozen.

draga *f* dredge.

dragamine *m inv* minesweeper.

dragare *vt* to drag, to dredge.

drago *m* dragon.

dragoncello *m* tarragon.

dramatico *adj* dramatic.

dramma *m* drama.

drammatizzare *vt* to dramatize.

drammaturgo *m* playwright, dramatist.

drappeggiare *vt* to drape.

drappo *m* cloth; ~ **funebre** *m* pall.

drastico *adj* drastic.

drenaggio *m* drain, drainage.

drenare *vt* to drain.

dribbling *m* dribble.

dritto *adj* erect; * *adv* upright.

droga *f* drug, dope; spice.

drogare *vt* to drug; to spice.

drogato *m* addict, junkie.

dubbio *adj* dubious; * *m* doubt.
dubitare *vt* to doubt.
duca *m* duke.
duchessa *f* duchess.
due *m* two; * *adj* two; **tutti e ~**
  both; **a ~ porte** two-door;
  * *adv* **~ volte** twice.
duello *m* duel.
duetto *m* duet.
dumping *m* dumping.
duna *f* dune.
duodenale *adj* duodenal.
duodeno *m* duodenum.
duplicare *vt* to duplicate.

duplicato *m* duplicate.
duplice *adj* dual.
duplicità *f* duplicity.
durante *prep* during.
durare *vi* to last, to wear.
durata *f* length, duration.
duraturo *adj* enduring, lasting.
durevole *adj* durable.
durevolezza *f* durability.
durezza *f* hardness.
duro *adj* hard, stiff; trying; **~
  d'orecchio** hard of hearing; **~
  di cuore** hard-hearted.

E

e *conj* and.
ebanista *m/f* cabinet-maker.
ebano *m* ebony.
ebbrezza *f* intoxication.
ebollizione *f* boiling; **punto di
  ~** *m* boiling point.
ebraico *adj, m* Hebrew.
ebrea *f* Jewess.
ebreo *m* Jew, Hebrew; * *adj*
  Jewish, Hebrew.
eccedenza *f* excess; **~ di popolazione** *f* overspill.
eccedere *vt* to exceed.
eccellente *adj* excellent.
eccellenza *f* excellence; **la Sua
  E~** His Excellency.
eccentricità *f* eccentricity.
eccentrico *m* eccentric; crank;
  freak; * *adj* eccentric.
eccessivamente *adv* unduly.
eccessivo *adj* excessive, inordinate.
eccesso *m* excess.
eccetto *prep* except.
eccezionale *adj* grand; outstanding; exceptional; bumper; preeminent; swell.

eccezionalmente *adv* unique-
  ly; extra.
eccezione *f* exception.
eccitabile *adj* excitable.
eccitare *vt* to excite.
eccitato *adj* excited.
eccitazione *f* excitement.
ecclesiastico *adj* ecclesiastica
echeggiare *vi* to echo.
eclettico *adj* eclectic.
eclissare *vt* to eclipse; to ou
  shine, to overshadow; t
  dwarf.
eclissi *f inv* eclipse.
eco *m/f* echo.
ecografia *f* ultrasound, scan.
ecologia *f* ecology.
economia *f* economy, econom
  ics; **fare ~** *vi* to economize.
economico *adj* economica
  inexpensive.
economista *m/f* economist.
economo *m* bursar.
eczema *m* eczema.
edera *f* ivy.
edificare *vt* to edify.
edificio *m* building, edifice.

editore *m* publisher.
editoria *f* publishing.
editoriale *m* editorial.
editto *m* edict.
edizione *f* edition.
edonismo *m* hedonism.
educare *vt* to educate.
educato *adj* polite.
educazione *f* education; politeness; upbringing; **(buona)** ~ *f*
  breeding, good manners; ~ **fi-**
  sica *f* physical education.
effeminatezza *f* effeminacy.
effeminato *adj* effeminate.
effervescente *adj* effervescent,
  fizzy.
effervescenza *f* fizz.
effettivo *adj* actual; virtual.
effetto *m* effect; spin (of ball);
  ~ **sonoro** *m* sound effect; **ef-**
  fetti personali *mpl* belongings; **non fare più** ~ *vi* to
  wear off;
effettuare *vt* to effect.
efficace *adj* effective, effectual.
efficacia *f* effectiveness, efficacy.
efficiente *adj* efficient; busi-
  ness-like.
efficienza *f* efficiency.
effigie *f* effigy.
effimero *adj* ephemeral.
eglefino *m* haddock.
egli *pron.*
ego *m* ego.
egocentrico *adj* self-centred.
egoismo *m* egoism, selfishness.
egoista *m/f* egoist; * *adj* selfish.
egotismo *m* egotism.
egotista *m/f* egotist.
egualitario *adj* egalitarian.
eiaculare *vt* to ejaculate.
eiaculazione *f* ejaculation.
elaborare *vt* to elaborate; to
  evolve; to hatch (a plot).
elaborato *adj* fancy.
elaboratore *m* computer.
elaborazione *f* elaboration; ~

dei dati *f* data processing; ~
  della parola *f* word processing.
elasticità *f* elasticity, stretch.
elastico *adj* elastic; resilient;
  * *m* elastic; rubber band.
elefante *m* elephant.
elegante *adj* elegant; dressy;
  smart; snappy; stylish; posh;
  abiti eleganti *mpl* finery.
elegantemente *adv* smartly.
eleganza *f* elegance, smartness.
eleggere *vt* to elect.
eleggibile *adj* elegible.
eleggibilità *f* elegibility.
elegia *f* elegy.
elementare *adj* elementary.
elemento *m* element.
elemosina *f* alms.
elencare *vt* to list.
elenco *m* list; directory; ~ **tele-**
  fonico *m* telephone directory/
  book.
elettorale *adj* electoral; **fare**
  un giro ~ *vt* to canvass.
elettorato *m* electorate.
elettore *m* constituent, voter.
elettricista *m* electrician.
elettricità *f* electricity.
elettrico *adj* electric(al); * *m*
  impianto ~ wiring.
elettrificare *vt* to electrify.
elettrodo *m* electrode.
elettrolisi *f* electrolysis.
elettrone *m* electron.
elettronica *f* electronics.
elettronico *adj* electronic.
elevare *vt* to elevate.
elevazione *f* elevation.
elezione *f* election.
elezioni *fpl* elections; ~ **legis-**
  lative *fpl* general election; ~
  suppletive *fpl* bye-election.
elica *f* screw, propeller.
elicottero *m* helicopter, chopper.
eliminare *vt* to eliminate; to
  remove.

eliminazione *f* elimination; disposal; removal.

elio *m* helium.

elisir *m inv* elixir.

élite *f inv* élite.

ella *pron* she.

ellittico *adj* elliptic(al).

elogio *m* eulogy; praise.

eloquente *adj* eloquent.

eloquenza *f* eloquence.

eludere *vt* to elude; to evade; to sidestep.

emaciato *adj* emaciated; gaunt.

emanare *vt* to exude; to shed.

emancipare *vt* to emancipate.

emancipazione *f* emancipation.

emarginato *m* drop-out; outcast.

ematologia *f* haematology.

embargo *m* embargo.

emblema *m* emblem.

emblematico *adj* emblematic.

embolia *f* bends.

embrione *m* embryo.

emendamento *m* amendment.

emendare *vt* amend.

emergenza *f* emergency.

emergere *vi* to emerge.

emetico *m* emetic.

emettere *vt* to emit; to issue; to release.

emicrania *f* migraine.

emigrante *m/f* emigrant.

emigrare *vi* to emigrate.

emigrazione *f* emigration.

eminente *adj* eminent; great; distinguished.

eminenza *f* eminence.

emirato *m* emirate.

emisfero *m* hemisphere.

emissario *m* emissary.

emissione *f* emission; issue; release.

emittente *f* transmitter.

emofilia *f* haemophilia.

emoglobia *f* haemaglobin.

emolumento *m* emolument.

emorragia *f* bleeding; haemorrhage; ~ **nasale** *f* nosebleed.

emorroidi *fpl* haemorrhoids, piles.

emotivo *adj* emotional (person), emotive (film, etc).

emozionante *adj* exciting.

emozionato *adj* excited; agog with excitement.

emozione *f* emotion.

empietà *f* impiety.

empio *adj* impious; godless.

empirico *adj* empirical.

emù *m inv* emu.

emulare *vt* to emulate.

emulsionare *vt* to emulsify.

emulsione *f* emulsion.

enciclica *f* encyclical.

enciclopedia *f* encyclopaedia.

encomio *m* commendation.

endemico *adj* endemic.

endovenoso *adj* intravenous.

energia *f* energy.

energico *adj* energetic, spirited; strenuous.

enfasi *f* emphasis, stress.

enfatico *adj* emphatic.

enigma *m* enigma.

enigmatico *adj* enigmatic, cryptic.

ennesimo *adj* umpteenth.

enorme *adj* enormous, huge, tremendous, terrific.

enormità *f* immensity.

ente *m* corporation.

enterite *f* entiritis.

entità *f inv* entity.

entourage *m inv* entourage.

entrambi *adj* both; either.

entrare *vi* to enter, to go in, to come in; **lasciare** ~ to admit; * *vt* to enter, to go in; **questo non c'entra** this doesn't enter into it.

entrata *f* entrance, entry, hall

entroterra *m* (Australia) outback; **nell'**~ *adv* inland.

entusiasmare *vt* to thrill; * *vr* ~**rsi** to enthuse.

entusiasmo *m* enthusiasm, keenness, zest.

entusiasta *adj* keen.

enumerare *vt* to enumerate.

enunciare *vt* to enunciate.

enzima *m* enzyme.

epatite *f* hepatitis.

epico *adj* epic.

epidemia *f* epidemic.

epidemico *adj* epidemic.

Epifania *f* Epiphany.

epilessia *f* epilepsy.

epilettico *adj, m* epileptic

epilogo *m* epilogue.

episcopale *adj* episcopal.

episcopaliano *adj, m* Episco-palian.

episodio *m* episode, incident.

epistola *f* epistle.

epiteto *m* epithet.

epoca *f* epoch, day, age.

epopea *f* epic.

equatore *m* equator.

equatoriale *adj* equatorial.

equazione *f* equation.

equestre *adj* equestrian.

equidistante *adj* equidistant.

equilatero *adj* equilateral.

equilibrato *adj* level-headed.

equilibrio *m* equilibrium; bal-ance; **tenere in** ~ *vt* to bal-ance.

equinozio *m* equinox.

equipaggiamento *m* kit.

equipaggiare *vt* to fit out.

equipaggio *m* crew.

équipe *f inv* team; **lavoro d'**~ *m* teamwork.

equità *f* equity.

equitazione *f* riding; horse-manship; **scuola di** ~ *f* riding school.

equivalente *m/f* counterpart; * *adj* equivalent.

equivalere *vi* to be tanta-mount.

equivoco *m* misapprehension; * *adj* equivocal; underhand; **giocare sull'**~ *vi* to equivocate.

equo *adj* equitable.

era *f* era, age, time.

eradicare *vt* to root out.

erba *f* grass; (marijuana) pot; ~ **cipollina** chives; ~ **aromati-ca** *f* herb; **in** ~ budding.

erbaccia *f* weed.

erbaceo *adj* herbaceous.

erbivoro *adj, m* herbivorous.

erborista *m/f* herbalist.

erboso *adj* grassy.

erede *m* heir, heiress.

eredità *f* heredity, heritage; in-heritance, legacy; **lasciare in** ~ *vt* to bequeath.

ereditare *vt* to inherit.

ereditario *adj* hereditary.

eremita *m* hermit.

eremitaggio *m* hermitage.

eresia *f* heresy.

eretico *adj, m* heretic.

erezione *f* erection.

ergastolo *m* life imprisonment.

erica *f* heather.

erigere *vt* to erect, to raise.

ermellino *m* ermine, stoat.

ermetico *adj* hermetic; air-tight.

ernia *f* hernia.

erodere *vt* to erode.

eroe *m* hero.

eroico *adj* heroic.

eroina *f* heroin; heroine.

eroismo *m* heroism.

erotico *adj* erotic.

erpice *m* harrow.

erroneamente *adv* wrongly.

erroneo *adj* erroneous.

errore *m* error; mistake; falla-cy; ~ **di stampa** *m* erratum, misprint; ~ **giudiziario** *m* miscarriage of justice;

erudito *adj* erudite.

erudizione *f* erudition, scholar-ship.

eruzione *f* eruption; **essere in ~** *vi* to erupt.

esacerbare *vt* to exacerbate.

esagerare *vt* to exaggerate; to overstate; to overdo; to stretch.

esagerato *adj* undue.

esagerazione *f* exaggeration.

esagonale *adj* hexagonal.

esagono *m* hexagon.

esalazione *f* fume.

esaltare *vt* to exalt.

esaltato *adj* exalted.

esame *m* examination; test; **~ di guida** *m* driving test; **~ di ammissione** *m* entrance examination.

esaminare *vt* to examine; to vet; to survey; **~ a fondo** to follow up.

esaminatore *m* examiner.

esangue *adj* bloodless.

esasperante *adj* aggravating.

esasperare *vt* to exasperate.

esasperazione *f* exasperation.

esattamente *adv* exactly.

esattezza *f* accuracy, exactness, exactitude.

esatto *adj* exact, accurate, spot-on.

esattore *m* (tax) collector; **~ delle imposte** *m* tax collector.

esauriente *adj* exhaustive, comprehensive.

esaurientemente *adv* at length.

esaurimento *m* exhaustion; **~ nervoso** *m* nervous breakdown.

esaurire *vt* to deplete; to exhaust.

esaurito *adj* exhausted; spent; out of print.

esca *f* bait.

eschimese *adj* Eskimo; **cane ~** *m* husky (dog).

esclamare *vt* to exclaim, to ejaculate.

esclamazione *f* exclamation, ejaculation.

escludere *vt* to exclude, to debar, to except.

esclusione *f* exclusion.

esclusivo *adj* exclusive, select; sole.

escogitare *vt* to devise; to contrive; to think up.

escrementi *mpl* excrement; (animals) droppings.

escursione *f* excursion; outing; ramble; **~ a piedi** *f* hike; **fare escursioni** *vi* to ramble.

escursionista *m/f* rambler.

esecrabile *adj* execrable.

esecutivo *adj* executive.

esecutore *m* executor.

esecuzione *f* execution.

eseguire *vt* to do, to execute; to perform.

esempio *m* example, instance.

esemplare *adj* exemplary.

esemplificare *vt* to exemplify.

esentare *vt* to exempt.

esente *adj* exempt.

esenzione *f* exemption.

esercitare *vt* to exercise; to drill; to exert; to ply; * *vr* **~rsi** to practise.

esercitazione *f* drill.

esercito *m* military, army.

esercizio *m* exercise, practice.

esibirsi *vr* to appear; to perform.

esibizionista *m/f* show-off.

esigente *adj* exacting, demanding.

esigenza *f* requirement.

esigere *vt* to expect; to demand; to exact.

esile *adj* slim.

esiliare *vt* to exile.

esilio *m* exile.

esistante *adj* halting.

esistente *adj* existent; extant.

esistenza *f* existence.

esistenziale *adj* existential.

esistenzialismo *m* existentialism.

esistere *vi* to exist.

esitante *adj* hesitant; tentative.

esitare *vi* to hestitate; to dither.

esitazione *f* hesitation.

esito *m* outcome.

esodo *m* exodus.

esofago *m* oesophagus.

esonerare *vt* to excuse.

esorbitante *adj* exorbitant; extortionate.

esorcismo *m* exorcism.

esorcizzare *vt* to exorcise.

esortare *vt* to exhort.

esoterico *adj* esoteric.

esotico *adj* exotic.

espandere *vt* to expand.

espansione *f* expansion.

espansivo *adj* expansive, effusive, gushing, demonstrative.

espatriato *adj, m* expatriate.

espediente *m* expedient.

espellere *vt* to expel; to eject.

esperienza *f* experience.

esperimentare *vt* to experience.

esperimento *m* experiment.

esperto *adj* accomplished; experienced; expert; * *m* expert; adept; troubleshooter; pundit.

espiare *vi* to atone for.

espiazione *f* atonement.

espirare *vt* to exhale.

esplicativo *adj* explanatory.

esplicitamente *adv* specifically.

esplicito *adj* explicit.

esplodere *vi* to explode; * *vt* to blow up.

esplorare *vt* to explore; to prospect.

esploratore *m* explorer.

esplorazione *f* exploration.

esplosione *f* explosion; blast.

esplosivo *adj, m* explosive.

esponente *m/f* exponent.

esporre *vt* to expose; to exhibit; to display; to show; to expound.

esportare *vt* to export.

esportatore *m* exporter.

esportazione *f* export.

esposimetro *m* exposure meter.

espositore *m* exhibitor.

esposizione *f* display, exposition; show; exposure.

esposto *adj* exposed.

espressione *f* expression.

espressivo *adj* expressive.

espresso *adj* express.

esprimere *vt* to express; to air; to phrase; to voice; * *vr* ~**rsi** to express oneself; **chi non sa** ~ *adj* inarticulate.

espropriare *vt* to expropriate.

esproprio *m* expropriation.

espulsione *f* expulsion, ejection.

espurgare *vt* to expurgate; to bowdlerize.

essenza *f* essence.

essenziale *adj* essential.

essenzialmente *adv* primarily.

essere *vi* to be; * *m* being.

essi *pers pron* they.

essiccare *vt* to dry.

essiccato *adj* dried; desiccated.

essistenza *f* being.

esso *m* it.

est *m* east; * *adv* verso ~ eastwards.

estasi *f inv* ecstasy; rapture; **mandare in** ~ *vt* to entrance.

estasiare *vt* to enrapture; to ravish.

estasiato *adj* rapturous.

estate *f* summer; **piena** ~ *f* midsummer.

estatico *adj* ecstatic.

estendersi *vr* to reach; to range; ~ **disordinatamente** to straggle.

estensione *f* extent.

estenuante *adj* gruelling; wearisome.

esterno *adj* external, exterior; outside; outward; outer; * *m* external, exterior; outside; **collaboratore ~** *m* freelance.

estero *adj* foreign; overseas; **all'~** *adv* overseas; **andare all'~** *vi* to go abroad.

esteso *adj* extensive.

estetico *adj* aesthetic.

estinguere *vt* to quench; to write off.

estinto *adj* extinct.

estintore *m* extinguisher; fire extinguisher.

estinzione *f* extinction.

estirpare *vt* to extirpate.

estorcere *vt* to extort.

estorsione *f* extortion.

estradare *vt* to extradite.

estradizione *f* extradition.

estramurale *adj* extramural.

estraneo *adj* foreign; alien; extraneous; * *m* outsider.

estrarre *vi* to abstract; * *vt* to mine; to draw; to extract.

estratto *m* excerpt.

estrazione *f* extraction; draw; **~ mineraria** *f* mining.

estremamente *adv* highly; exceedingly.

estremista *m/f* extremist.

estremità *f* end, extremity.

estremo *adj* far; extreme; utmost; * *m* extreme.

estrinseco *adj* extrinsic.

estrogeno *m* oestrogen.

estroverso *adj*, *m* extrovert.

estuario *m* estuary.

esuberante *adj* exuberant.

esuberanza *f* exuberance.

esule *m/f* exile.

esultante *adj* elated, jubilant.

esultanza *f* elation, jubilation.

esultare *vi* to exult.

esumare *vt* to exhume.

età *f inv* age.

etere *m* ether.

eternamente *adv* forever.

eternità *f* eternity.

eterno *adj* eternal; everlasting; timeless.

eterodosso *adj* unorthodox.

eterogeneo *adj* heterogeneous.

eterosessuale *adj*, straight; *n f* heterosexual; (*fam*) straight.

etica *f* ethics.

etichetta *f* label; tag; etiquette.

etico *adj* ethical.

etimologia *f* etymology.

etimologico *adj* etymological.

etnico *adj* ethnic.

eucalipto *m* gum tree; eucalyptus.

Eucaristia *f* Eucharist.

eufemismo *m* euphemism.

euforia *f* euphoria.

eunuco *m* eunuch.

eutanasia *f* euthanasia.

evacuare *vt* to evacuate.

evacuazione *f* evacuation.

evadere *vi* to escape; to break out; to abscond; * *vt* to evade.

evidente *adj* apparent.

evangelico *adj* evangelic(al).

evangelista *m* evangelist.

evaporare *vi* to evaporate.

evaporazione *f* evaporation.

evasione *f* evasion; escape; breakout; escapism.

evasivo *adj* evasive; non-committal.

evento *m* occurrence.

eventuale *adj* eventual.

eventualità *f* eventuality.

evidente *adj* evident; plain; overt.

evitabile *adj* avoidable.

evitare *vt* to avoid; to shun; to miss; to eschew.

evocare *vt* to evoke.

evocativo *adj* evocative.

evoluzione *f* evolution.

evolversi *vr* to evolve.

extra *adj* extra.
extra-coniugale *adj* extramarital.

extrasensoriale *adj* extrasensory.
extraterrestre *m* alien.

F

---

fa *adv* ago; **quanto tempo ~?** how long ago?
fabbrica *f* factory; mill; works; **~ di birra** brewery.
fabbricante *m* manufacturer; **~ di birra** brewer.
fabbricare *vt* to manufacture; to make; to fabricate.
fabbricazione *f* manufacture; fabrication.
fabbro *m* smith; blacksmith; locksmith.
faccenda *f* chore; matter; affair; **faccende** *fpl* housework.
facchino *m* porter.
faccia *f* face; side; **~ tosta** *f* cheek (impudence); **a ~ in giù** *adj* prone.
facciale *adj* facial.
facciata *f* facade.
faceto *adj* facetious.
facile *adj* easy; effortless.
facilità *f* facility; easiness.
facilitare *vt* to facilitate; to ease.
facilmente *adv* easily.
facoltà *f inv* faculty; school.
facoltativo *adj* optional.
facsimile *m* facsimile; fax.
factotum *m* dogsbody.
faesite *f* hardboard.
faggio *m* beech.
fagiano *m* pheasant.
fagiolino *m* French bean.
fagiolo *m* bean; **~ bianco** *m* haricot.
faglia *f* (*geol*) fault.
fagotto *m* bassoon; bundle;

fare un ~ di *vt* to bundle.
fai da te *m* do-it-yourself.
faida *f* feud.
falce *f* scythe, sickle.
falciare *vt* to mow, to scythe.
falciatrice *f* mower.
falco *m* hawk, falcon; **~ pescatore** *m* osprey.
falconiera *f* falconry.
falegname *m* carpenter, joiner.
falegnameria *f* carpentry, joinery, woodwork.
falla *f* hole.
fallace *adj* fallacious.
fallibile *adj* fallible.
fallibilità *f* fallibility.
fallico *adj* phallic.
fallimento *m* failure.
fallire *vi* to fail, to abort, to backfire.
fallito *adj* abortive; bankrupt; * *m* bankrupt.
fallo *m* foul.
falò *m* bonfire.
falsificare *vt* to falsify, to fake, to fiddle; to cook (the books).
falsità *f* falsity, untruth.
falso *adj* false, fake, hollow, deceitful, dud, two-faced, untrue, spurious.
fama *f* fame.
fame *f* hunger; **sciopero della ~** *m* hunger strike; **aver ~** *vi* to be hungry; **morire di ~** *vi* to starve.
famelico *adj* ravenous.
famigerato *adj* notorious.
famiglia *f* family, household.

familiare *adj* familiar; homely; colloquial; **espressione ~** *f* colloquialism.

familiarità *f* familiarity.

familiarizzarsi *vr* to familiarize.

famoso *adj* famous, famed, noted.

fan *m* fan.

fanale *m* headlight.

fanatico *m* fanatic; buff; bigot; * *adj* fanatic; bigoted; hooked.

fanatismo *m* fanaticism.

fanciulla *f* maiden.

fanciullesco *adj* boyish.

fanciullo *m* boy.

fanello *m* linnet.

fanfara *f* fanfare.

fanfaronata *f* bluster.

fango *m* mud.

fangoso *adj* muddy.

fannullone *m* bum; layabout.

fantascienza *f* science fiction.

fantasia *f* fantasy.

fantasioso *adj* fanciful; whimsical.

fantasma *m* ghost, apparition, phantom; spook; * *adj* phantom; **abitato dai fantasmi** haunted.

fantasticare *vi* to fantasize.

fantasticheria *f* reverie.

fantastico *adj* fantastic, super.

fante *m* jack, knave.

fanteria *f* infantry.

fantino *m* jockey.

farabutto *m* scoundrel.

faraone *m* Pharoah.

farcire *vt* to stuff.

fare *vt* to do; to make; **~ lo stupido** to act the fool; * *vt, vi* **~ male** to hurt.

faretra *f* quiver.

farfalla *f* bow tie; butterfly.

farina *f* flour; meal.

farinoso *adj* powdery.

farmaceutico *adj* pharmaceutical.

farmacia *f* dispensary, pharmacy.

farmacista *m/f* chemist, pharmacist.

farneticare *vi* to rave.

faro *m* lighthouse; beacon; **~ antinebbia** *m* foglamp.

farsa *f* farce.

farsi *vr* to get.

fascia *f* bandage.

fascia *f* sling.

fasciare *vt* to strap.

fascino *m* glamour, fascination, allure, charm, mystique.

fascio *m* sheaf.

fascismo *m* fascism.

fascista *m/f* fascist.

fase *f* phase.

fastidio *m* annoyance.

fastidioso *adj* troublesome.

fasto *m* pomp.

fasullo *adj* bogus, fake, phoney.

fata *f* fairy.

fatale *adj* fatal; vital.

fatalismo *m* fatalism.

fatica *f* fatigue; toil.

faticare *vi* to labour, to toil, to slog.

faticata *f* slog.

faticoso *adj* strenuous, uphill, tough, tiring, laborious.

fatidico *adj* fateful.

fatiscente *adj* derelict.

fattibile *adj* workable.

fattibilità *f* feasibility.

fatto *pp* done; * *m* fact; * *adj* **ben ~** shapely.

fattore *m* bailiff; factor.

fattoria *f* farm; **piccola ~** (*Scot*) croft.

fattorino *m* errand boy.

fattura *f* bill, invoice; workmanship.

fatturare *vt* to invoice.

fatuo *adj* fatuous.

fauna *f* fauna.

fautore *m* campaigner.

fava *f* broad bean.

favo *m* honeycomb.

favola *f* fable.

favoloso *adj* fabulous.

favore *m* favour; **a ~ di** *prep* for.

favorevole *adj* favourable; auspicious.

favorire *vt* to favour, to further, to farther; to advance; to be conducive to.

favoritismo *m* favouritism.

favorito *adj* favoured, favourite.

fax *m* fax.

fazione *f* faction.

fazzolettino *m*: ~ **di carta** tissue.

fazzoletto *m* handkerchief.

fazzolettone *m* bandanna.

febbraio *m* February.

febbre *f* fever.

febbrile *adj* feverish.

feccia *f* dregs, scum.

feci *fpl* faeces.

fecondare *vt* to fertilize.

fecondo *adj* fertile; **in età feconda** of childbearing age.

fede *f* faith, belief; wedding ring.

fedele *adj* faithful; true; regular; accurate; * *m/f* churchgoer, worshipper.

fedeltà *f* faithfulness, fidelity; accuracy.

federa *f* pillowcase, pillowslip.

federale *adj* federal.

federare *vt* to federate.

federazione *f* federation.

feed-back *m* feed-back.

fegato *m* liver; mettle.

felce *f* fern; bracken.

felice *adj* happy.

felicissimo *adj* overjoyed.

felicità *f* bliss, happiness.

felino *adj* feline.

felpa *f* plush; sweatshirt.

feltro *m* felt.

femmina *adj*, *f* female.

femminile *adj* feminine, womanly.

femminista *m/f* feminist; movimento ~ *m* women's liberation.

femminuccia *f* cissy.

fendente *m* hack.

fenice *f* phoenix.

fenico *adj*; **acido ~** carbolic acid.

fenicottero *m* flamingo.

fenomenale *adj* phenomenal.

fenomeno *m* phenomenon.

feriale *adj*; **giorno ~** *m* weekday.

ferire *vt* to hurt, to injure, to wound.

ferita *f* wound; hurt; injury; ~ **superficiale** *f* flesh wound.

ferito *adj* wounded.

fermabloc *m inv* clipboard.

fermacarte *m inv* paperweight.

fermaglio *m* clip, paperclip.

fermare *vt* to halt; to stop; to stay; to waylay; * *vi* to halt; * *vr* ~**si** to stop; (car) to pull in, to pull up.

fermata *f* stop; halt; ~ **d'autobus** bus stop.

fermentare *vi* to ferment; **mettere a ~** to brew.

fermentazione *f* brew.

fermento *m* ferment.

fermezza *f* firmness.

fermo *adj* firm; still; steady; stationary; **tenere ~** *vt* to steady.

feroce *adj* ferocious, fierce.

ferocia *f* ferocity, fierceness; savagery.

ferraglia *f* scrap.

ferramenta *fpl* hardware.

ferrare *vt* to shoe (a horse).

ferreo *adj* unswerving.

ferriera *f* ironworks.

ferro *m* iron; ~ **di cavallo** *m* horseshoe; ~ **da calza** *m* knitting needle; **minerale di ~** *m* iron ore.

ferrovia *f* railway.

ferroviere *m* railwayman.
fertile *adj* fertile.
fertilità *f* fertility.
fertilizzare *vt* to fertilize.
fervente *adj* fervent, fervid.
fervore *m* fervour.
fessura *f* fissure; chink; crepice; slot; slit; split.
festa *f* party, feast, festival, festivity, fête, gala; **di ~** *adj* festive.
festeggiamenti *mpl* rejoicings.
festeggiare *vt* to celebrate.
festival *m inv* festival.
fetale *adj* foetal.
fetente *m/f* stinker.
feticcio *m* fetish.
feticista *m/f* fetishist.
fetido *adj* fetid.
feto *m* foetus.
fetta *f* slice; **~ biscottata** *f* rusk.
fettuccia *f* tape.
feudale *adj* feudal.
feudalismo *m* feudalism.
fiaba *f* fairy tale.
fiaccare *vt* to wear down; to sap.
fiacco *adj* sluggish.
fiala *f* vial, phial.
fiamma *f* flame; pennant: **in fiamme** *adj* burning; ablaze, aflame, alight.
fiammeggiante *adj* lurid.
fiammella *f*: **di sicurezza** *f* pilot light.
fiammifero *m* match; **scatola per fiammiferi** *f* matchbox.
fiancheggiare *vt* to flank; to border.
fianco *m* side; flank; **fianchi** *mpl* loins; **di ~** *adv* edgeways, abreast.
fiaschetta *f* flask.
fiasco *m* flask, fiasco; flop.
fiato *m* wind; breath; **senza ~** *adj* breathless.
fibbia *f* buckle.

fibra *f* fibre; **~ di vetro** *f* fibreglass.
fibroso *adj* stringy.
ficcanaso *m/f inv* busy-body; snooper
ficcare *vt* to jam, to ram.
fico *m* fig.
fidanzamento *m* engagement; betrothal.
fidanzare *vt* to betroth.
fidanzata *f* fiancée.
fidanzato *m* boyfriend; fiancé; * *adj* engaged.
fidarsi *vr* to trust.
fidato *adj* trusted, trusty.
fiducia *f* trust, confidence.
fiducioso *adj* hopeful, trustful.
fienile *m* hayloft.
fieno *m* hay; **raffreddore da ~** *m* hay fever.
fiera *f* fair; show; **~ campionaria** *f* trade fair.
fievole *adj* faint.
figlia *f* daughter.
figliare *vi* to calve.
figliastra *f* step-daughter.
figliastro *m* step-son.
figlio *m* son; **senza figli** *adj* childless.
figlioccia *f* goddaughter.
figlioccio *m* godchild, godson.
figura *f* figure; **~ rappresentativa** *f* figurehead.
figurare *vi* to figure.
figurativo *adj* figurative; **linguaggio ~** *m* imagery.
fila *f* line, row, tier, file.
filamento *m* filament.
filantropia *f* philanthropy.
filantropico *adj* philanthropic; charitable.
filantropo *m* philanthropist.
filare *vi* to belt; * *vt* to spin.
filarmonico *adj* philharmonic.
filastrocca *f* nursery rhyme.
filatelia *f* philately.
filato *m* yarn.
filatoio *m* spinning wheel.

filetto *m* fillet.

filiale *adj* filial.

filigrana *f* filigree; watermark.

film *m inv* film, motion picture, movie.

filmare *vt* to film.

filmina *f* filmstrip.

filo *m* thread; string; wire; flex; wisp; ~ **spinato** *m* barbed wire; ~ **elettrico** *m* lead; **fili argentati** *mpl* tinsel.

filocomunista *m* (*pol*) fellow traveller.

filologia *f* philology.

filologo *m* philologist.

filosofare *vi* to philosophize.

filosofia *f* philosophy.

filosofico *adj* philosophic(al).

filosofo *m* philosopher.

filtrare *vt* to percolate; to filter; * *vi* to percolate; to permeate; to seep.

filtro *m* filter; **con ~** *adj* filter-tipped.

finale *adj* final; eventual; finale; closing; ultimate; * *f* (*sport*) final.

finalista *m/f* finalist.

finalmente *adv* at last.

finanza *f* finance.

finanziare *vt* to finance; to fund.

finanziario *adj* financial.

finanziatore *m* financier.

finché *conj* until.

fine *adj* fine; acute; **senza ~** endless; * *f* end; close; ending; finish; ~ **delle trasmissioni** *f* close-down; **porre ~ a** *vt* to end; **alla ~** *adv* finally.

finemente *adv* finely.

finestra *f* window; ~ **a saliscendi** *f* sash window.

finestrino *m* window.

finezza *f* finesse.

fingere *vi* to fake, to pretend; to sham; * *vt* to pretend; to sham; ~ **di non vedere** to ignore.

finire *vt* to finish; * *vi* to finish, to end.

finito *adj* over; through; finite.

fino *adj* fine; * *prep* ~ **a** until.

finocchio *m* fennel; (*fam*) queer, poof.

finora *adv* hitherto; so far.

finto *adj* dummy, mock.

finzione *f* fiction, make-believe.

fioco *adj* dim.

fionda *f* catapult, sling.

fioraio *m* florist.

fiordo *m* fjord.

fiore *m* flower; bloom; **fiori** *mpl* (cards) clubs; blossom; **in fiore** *adj* flowery.

fiorente *adj* flourishing, thriving.

fioretto *m* foil.

fiorire *vi* to flower; to bloom.

firma *f* signature.

firmamento *m* firmament.

firmare *vt* to sign, to autograph; * *vi* to sign.

firmatario *m* signatory.

fisarmonica *f* accordion.

fiscale *adj* fiscal.

fischi *mpl* jeer.

fischiare *vt* to jeer, to boo; * *vi* to whistle.

fischiettare *vt* to whistle.

fischio *m* whistle; catcall.

fisica *f* physics.

fisicamente *adv* bodily.

fisico *adj* physical; * *m* physicist; physique.

fisiologia *f* physiology.

fisiologico *adj* physiological.

fisiologo *m* physiologist.

fisioterapia *f* physiotherapy.

fissare *vt* to fix; to peg; ~ **con chiodi** to tack.

fissazione *f* fixation.

fisso *adj* fixed; set; steady.

fitta *f* twinge, stab; ~ **al fianco** *f* stitch.

fittizio *adj* fictitious.

fitto *adj* close.

fiume *m* river, stream.
fiutare *vt* to scent.
fiuto *m* smell; ~ **negli affari** business acumen.
flaccido *adj* flabby, flaccid.
flagello *m* curse, scourge.
flagrante *adj* flagrant; **in** ~ red-handed.
flanella *f* flannel.
flash *m inv* flash, flash cube; newsflash.
flatulenza *f* flatulence, wind.
flautista *m/f* flautist.
flauto *m* flute, recorder.
fleboclisi *f* drip.
flemma *f* phlegm.
flemmatico *adj* phlegmatic.
flessibile *adj* flexible; supple, limber.
flessibilità *f* flexibility.
flipper *m* pinball machine.
flirt *m inv* flirtation.
flora *f* flora.
floreale *adj* floral.
florido *adj* florid.
floscio *adj* floppy.
floscio *adj* limp.
flotta *f* fleet.
flottiglia *f* flotilla.
fluidità *f* fluidity.
fluido *adj*, *m* fluid.
fluire *vi* to flow.
fluorescente *adj* fluorescent.
fluoruro *m* fluoride.
flusso *m* flow; ~ **di cassa** (*com*) cash flow.
fluttuare *vi* to fluctuate.
fluttuazione *f* fluctuation.
fobia *f* phobia.
foca *f* seal.
focale *adj* focal.
focena *f* porpoise.
focolaio *m* (*fig*) hotbed.
focolare *m* hearth; fireplace; **angolo del** ~ *m* fireside.
focoso *adj* hot.
fodera *f* lining.
foderare *vt* to line.

foderato *adj* lined.
fodero *m* scabbard.
foglia *f* leaf.
fogliame *m* foliage.
foglietto *m* slip.
foglio *m* folio, leaf (of paper), sheet.
fogna *f* sewer; **acque di** ~ *fpl* sewage.
fohn *m* hairdrier; **asciugare con il** ~ *vt* to blow-dry.
folata *f* gust.
folclore *m* folklore.
folla *f* crowd; mob.
folle *adj* crazy, insane; *vi* **andare in** ~ to coast; * *f* (*auto*) neutral; *m* madman.
follemente *adv* madly.
folletto *m* goblin, elf, pixie.
follia *f* insanity, madness.
folto *adj* bushy.
fomentare *vt* to foment.
fondale *m* backcloth.
fondamentale *adj* fundamental, basic; seminal.
fondamento *m* grounding.
fondare *vt* to establish, to found.
fondatore *m* founder.
fondazione *f* foundation, endowment.
fondente *m* fondant.
fondere *vi* to fuse; to melt, to smelt; * *vr* ~**rsi** to blend, to merge.
fonderia *f* foundry.
fondina *f* holster.
fondo *m* fund; bottom; sediment; ~ **per le piccole spese** *m* petty cash; **senza** ~ *adj* bottomless.
fondi *mpl* grounds.
fonema *m* phoneme.
fonetica *f* phonetics.
fonetico *adj* phonetic.
fontana *f* fountain.
fonte *m* spring, source; ~ **battesimale** *m* font.

footing *m* jogging; **fare ~** *vi* to jog.

foraggio *m* feed, fodder, forage, chaff.

forare *vt* to pierce; to punch.

forbici *fpl* scissors; **~ per potare** *fpl* secateurs.

forbicina *f* earwig.

forcella *f* crotch; wishbone.

forchetta *f* fork.

forcina *f* hairpin.

forcipe *m* forceps.

forcone *m* pitchfork.

foresta *f* forest.

forestale *adj* forest; **guardia ~** *f* forester.

forestiero *m* stranger.

forfora *f* dandruff.

forgiare *vt* to forge.

foriero *m* harbinger.

forma *f* shape; fitness; form; **in ~** *adj* fit.

formaggio *m* cheese; **piatto per il ~** *m* cheeseboard.

formale *adj* formal, ceremonial, ceremonious.

formalità *f inv* formality; **mancanza di ~** *f* informality.

formare *vt* to form, to shape.

formativo *adj* formative.

formato *m* format.

formattare *vt* to format.

formazione *f* formation; education; background.

formica *f* ant.

formicaio *m* anthill.

formichiere *m* anteater.

formicolare *vi* to tingle.

formicolio *m* tingle, tingling, pins and needles.

formidabile *adj* formidable.

formoso *adj* curvaceous.

formula *f* formula.

formulare *vt* to formulate; to word.

formulazione *f* wording.

fornace *f* forge; furnace; kiln.

fornaio *m* baker.

fornello *m* gas ring.

fornire *vt* to furnish, to provide, to supply.

fornitore *m* supplier, stockist, tradesman, purveyor

fornitura *f* supply, provision.

forno *m* oven.

foro *m* forum.

foro *m* hole, bore.

forse *adj* perhaps; * *adv* maybe.

forsennato *adj* frenzied; berserk.

forte *adj* forceful.

forte *m* (*mus*) forte; hard; loud; strong.

fortezza *f* fortress, stronghold.

fortificare *vt* to fortify.

fortificato *adj* walled.

fortificazione *f* fortification.

fortuito *adj* fortuitous.

fortuito *adj* accidental, incidental.

fortuna *f* luck; fortune; **colpo di ~** lucky break, fluke.

fortunatamente *adv* luckily.

fortunato *adj* fortunate, lucky.

foruncolo *m* spot, pimple, boil; **pieno di foruncoli** *adj* spotty.

forza *f* force; might; power; strength; coercion; leverage; **le forze armate** *fpl* the forces; **~ d'animo** *f* fortitude; **a ~ di** by dint of; **~ di volontà** *f* willpower.

forzare *vt* to force; to break into.

forzato *adj* forced.

foschia *f* haze, mist.

fosfato *m* phosphate.

fosforescente *adj* phosphorescent.

fosforo *m* phosphorus.

fossa *f* ditch.

fossato *m* moat.

fossetta *f* dimple.

fossile *adj, m* fossil

fosso *m* ditch, trench.

foto *f inv* shot.

fotocopia *f* photocopy.

fotocopiare *vt* to photocopy.

fotocopiatrice *f* photocopier.

fotogenico *adj* photogenic.

fotografare *vt* to photograph, to snap.

fotografia *f* picture; photograph, photography.

fotografico *adj* photographic.

fotografo *m* photographer.

fotomontaggio *m* photomontage.

fotosintesi *f* photosynthesis.

fottere *vt* to fuck.

foulard *m inv* scarf, cravat.

foyer *m inv* foyer.

fra *prep* between.

fracasso *m* crash, smash, noise, racket.

fradicio *adj* sodden.

fragile *adj* fragile, breakable, brittle.

fragilità *f* fragility.

fragola *f* strawberry.

fragoroso *adj* uproarious.

fragrante *adj* fragrant.

fragranza *f* fragrance.

fraintendere *vt* to be at cross-purposes.

fraintendere *vt* to misunderstand, to misconstrue.

frammentario *adj* fragmentary, piecemeal.

frammento *m* fragment; chip; snippet.

frammischiare *vt* to intermingle.

frana *f* landslide.

franchezza *f* frankness; openness; **brutale ~** bluntness.

franchigia *f* franchise.

franco *m* franc, frank; * *adj* candid; straightforward; outspoken; (*com*) free; **essere ~ con qn** to be open with somebody.

francobollo *m* stamp, postage stamp.

frangente *m* breaker (wave).

frangia *f* fringe.

frangiflutti *m inv* breakwater.

frangivento *m* windbreak.

frantumare *vt* to crush; to shatter, to smash.

frappé *m inv* milkshake.

frasario *m* phrase book.

frase *f* sentence; phrase; **~ di moda** catch phrase; **~ fatta** *f* cliché.

frassino *m* (*bot*) ash.

frastagliato *adj* rugged.

frate *m* friar.

fratellastro *m* step-brother.

fratello *m* brother.

fratello *m* brother, sibling.

fraternità *f* brotherhood, fraternity.

fraternizzare *vi* to fraternize.

fraterno *adj* fraternal, brotherly.

fratricida *adj*, *m/f* fratricide.

frattaglie *fpl* giblets; offal.

frattempo *adv*: **nel ~** in the meantime, in the meanwhile.

frattura *f* fracture.

fraudolento *adj* fraudulent.

frazione *f* fraction.

freccia *f* arrow; indicator; **mettere la freccia** *vi* to indicate

frecciata *f* gibe; **lanciare frecciate a** *vi* to gibe.

freddo *adj* cold, chill; stand-offish; * *m* cold, chill.

fregare *vt* to pinch, to nick.

fregata *f* frigate.

fregio *m* frieze.

fremere *vi* to thrill.

fremito *m* thrill.

frenare *vt* to curb; to control; * *vi* to brake.

frenesia *f* frenzy.

frenetico *adj* frenzied, frantic.

freno *m* brake; curb; **~ a mano** *m* handbrake; **agire da freno**

su *vi* to act as a disincentive; **porre ~ a** *vt* to crack down on; **tenere a ~** *vt* to restrain.

frequentare *vt* to attend; to frequent; to haunt; to consort (with); to patronize.

frequente *adj* frequent.

frequenza *f* frequency; attendance.

freschezza *f* freshness.

fresco *adj* fresh; crisp; cool; chilly; **mettere in ~** *vt* to chill.

frescura *f* cool.

fresia *f* freesia.

fretta *f* hurry, haste, rush; **in ~ e furia** *adv* hastily; **fare in ~** *vi* to hurry; **far ~** *vt* to rush; **fare ~ a** *vt* to hustle.

frettoloso *adj* hurried; cursory.

friggere *vt* to fry.

frigido *adj* frigid.

frignare *vi* to blubber.

frigo *m* fridge.

frigorifero *m* refrigerator.

fringuello *m* finch, chaffinch.

frittata *f* omelet(te).

frittella *f* fritter; pancake.

fritto *adj* fried.

frivolezza *f* frivolity; triviality; levity.

frivolo *adj* frivolous, flighty.

frizione *f* friction; clutch; **premere la ~** *vi* to declutch.

frizzante *adj* sparkling.

frizzare *vi* to fizz.

frocio *m* (*Amer fam*) fag.

frodo *m*: **cacciare di ~** *vt, vi* to poach.

fronda *f* frond.

frondoso *adj* leafy.

frontale *adj* frontal.

fronte *m* front; *f* forehead; *f* brow; **essere di ~ a** *vt* to face; **fare ~ a** *vt* to face up to; **di ~** *prep* facing; **di ~** *adv* opposite.

frontespizio *m* title page.

frontiera *f* frontier.

frontone *m* gable.

frottola *f* fib; cock-and-bull story.

frugale *adj* frugal; abstemious.

frugalmente *adv* sparingly.

frugare *vt* to delve; * *vi* to rummage; to rifle through.

frullare *vt* to whisk.

frullatore *m* mixer; blender; liquidizer; **passare al ~** *vt* to liquidize.

frullino *m* whisk.

frumento *m* corn; wheat.

frusciare *vi* to rustle.

fruscio *m* rustle.

frusta *f* whip.

frustare *vt* to flog, to lash, to whip.

frustata *f* lash.

frustino *m* riding crop.

frustrare *vt* to frustrate; to foil.

frustrato *adj* frustrated.

frustrazione *f* frustration.

frutta *f* fruit.

fruttare *vt* to yield.

frutteto *m* orchard.

fruttifero *adj* fruitful.

fruttivendolo *m* fruiterer, greengrocer.

frutto *m* fruit; **frutti di mare** *mpl* seafood.

fruttuoso *adj* fruitful.

fucilare *vt* to shoot.

fucilazione *f* shooting.

fucile *m* gun, rifle; **~ ad aria compressa** air gun; **~ da caccia** *m* shotgun.

fucina *f* smithy.

fuco *m* drone.

fucsia *f* fuchsia.

fuga *f* flight; escape; fugue; **~ romantica** *f* elopement; **~ precipitosa** *f* stampede.

fuggifuggi *m* debacle.

fuggire *vi* to abscond; to elope; to flee; * *vt* to flee.

fuggitivo *adj, m* fugitive, runaway.

fulcro *m* hub, fulcrum.

fuliggine *f* soot; **granellino di ~** *m* smut.

fulminare *vt* to electrocute; *vt* **~ con lo sguardo** to glare at.

fulmine *m* lightning, bolt of lightning, thunderbolt.

fulvo *m*, *adj* fawn.

fumante *adj* smoking.

fumare *vt* to smoke; * *vi* to smoke; to steam; **vietato ~** no smoking.

fumatore *m* smoker.

fumo *m* smoke, smoking; **senza ~** *adj* smokeless; **emettere ~** *vt* to fume.

fumoso *adj* smoky.

fune *f* rope.

funebre *adj*: **carro ~** *m* hearse.

funerale *m* funeral.

funereo *adj* funereal.

fungo *m* mushroom; **~ velenoso** *m* toadstool; **~ del legno** *m* dry rot.

funivia *f* cable-car.

funzionale *adj* functional.

funzionamento *m* function; **cattivo ~** *m* malfunction.

funzionare *vi* to operate; to work; to run; *vt* **far ~** to operate.

funzionario *m* official; **~ del fisco** assessor.

funzione *f* function; service.

fuoco *m* fire; focus; **~ incrociato** crossfire; **cessate il ~** ceasefire; **resistente al ~** *adj* fireproof; **fuochi d'artificio** *mpl* fireworks.

fuori *adv* outside; out; * *prep* out; **~ di** outside.

fuoribordo *adj* outboard.

fuorigioco *adj*; **in ~** offside.

fuorilegge *m* outlaw.

furberia *f* craftiness.

furbizia *f* cunning.

furbo *adj* crafty, cunning, artful, **essere più ~ di** *vt* to outwit

furetto *m* ferret.

furfante *m* knave.

furgone *m* van.

furia *f* fury, rage.

furibondo *adj* wild, livid; **rendere ~** *vt* to incense.

furiere *m* quartermaster.

furioso *adj* furious; raging; **rendere ~** *vt* to infuriate.

furtivamente *adv* by stealth; **procedere ~** *vi* to sidle.

furtivo *adj* furtive, stealthy, surreptitious.

furto *m* theft; snatch; larceny; **~ con scasso** burglary.

fusa *fpl* purr; **far le ~** *vi* to purr.

fusciacca *f* sash.

fusibile *m* fuse; **scatola dei fusibili** *f* fusebox.

fusione *f* fusion; merger; **punto di ~** *m* melting point.

fuso *m* spindle; * *adj* molten.

fusoliera *f* fuselage.

fustigazione *f* flogging.

fusto *m* he-man.

futile *adj* futile, self-defeating.

futilità *f* futility.

futuro *adj* future; prospective; coming; succeeding; elect; * *m* future.

G

gabardine *m inv* gabardine.

gabbia *f* cage; hutch; **mettere in ~** *vt* to cage.

gabbiano *m* (sea)gull.

gabinetto *m* lavatory, water closet, toilet, washroom.

gaffe *f inv* faux pas, blunder, clanger, boob.

gag *f inv* gag.

gaiamente *adv* merrily.

gala *m* gala.

galante *adj* gallant.

galassia *f* galaxy.

galea *f* galley.

galla *adv*: **a ~** afloat.

galleggiamento *m* floating; **linea di ~** *f* waterline.

galleggiante *m* float, ballcock; * *adj* buoyant.

galleggiare *vi* to float.

galleria *f* gallery, arcade; tunnel; **~ d'arte** art gallery.

galletto *m* cockerel.

gallina *f* hen.

gallo *m* cock, rooster.

gallone *m* gallon.

galoppare *vi* to gallop.

galoppo *m* gallop; **piccolo ~** *m* canter.

galvanizzare *vt* to galvanize.

gamba *f* leg.

gamberetto *m* shrimp.

gambero *m* prawn; crayfish.

gamberone *m*: **gamberoni** *mpl* scampi.

gambetto *m* gambit.

gambo *m* shank, stalk.

gamma *f* range, gamut.

gancio *m* hook; catch; clasp.

gangster *m inv* gangster.

gara *f* contest, competition.

garage *m inv* garage.

garantire *vt* to guarantee; to ensure; to secure; * *vi* to vouch.

garanzia *f* guarantee; warranty; (*fin*) collateral.

garbato *adj* graceful, suave,

garbo *m* grace.

gareggiare *vt* to race.

gargarismo *m* gargle; **fare i gargarismi** *vi* to gargle.

gargolla *f* gargoyle.

garitta *f* sentrybox.

garofano *m* carnation; **chiodo di ~** *m* clove.

garza *f* gauze, lint.

gas *m inv* gas; throttle; **impianto di produzione del ~** *m* gasworks.

gasolio *m* diesel.

gassato *adj* carbonated; **non ~** *adj* still.

gassoso *adj* gassy, gaseous.

gastrico *adj* gastric.

gastronomico *adj* gastronomic.

gattino *m* kitten.

gatto *m* cat, tomcat.

gazza *f* magpie.

gazzella *f* gazelle.

gazzetta *f* gazette.

gel *m inv* gel.

gelare *vt, vi* to freeze.

gelata *f* freeze.

gelatina *f* jelly; gelatine; **~ esplosiva** *f* gelignite.

gelato *m* ice, ice cream.

gelido *adj* frosty; freezing, raw.

gelo *m* frost.

gelone *m* chilblain.

gelosia *f* jealousy.

geloso *adj* jealous.

gelso *m* mulberry (tree); **mora di ~** mulberry fruit.

gelsomino *m* jasmine.

Gemelli *mpl* Gemini.

gemello *adj, m* twin.

gemere *vi* to moan, to groan, to wail.

gemito *m* moan, groan, wail.

gemma *f* gem.

gemogliare *vi* to sprout.

gene *m* gene.

genealogia *f* genealogy.

genealogico *adj* genealogical.

general *m* general; **~ di brigata** brigadier; * *adj* general, overall.

generalità *f inv* generality.

generalizzare *vi* to generalize.

generalizzazione *f* generalization.

generalmente *adv* in general, generally.

generare *vt* to generate; to sire.

generatore *m* generator.

generazione *f* generation.

genere *m* gender; kind, sort, genus.

generi *mpl*: ~ **alimentari** *mpl* foodstuffs.

generico *adj* generic; sweeping.

genero *m* son-in-law.

generosità *f* generosity.

generoso *adj* generous.

genetica *f* genetics.

gengiva *f* gum.

geniale *adj* brainy.

genio *m* genius.

genitali *mpl* genitals.

genitivo *m* genitive.

genitore *m* parent; ~ **affidatario** *m* foster parent; **dei genitori** *adj* parental.

gennaio *m* January.

gentaglia *f* (*fam*) hoi polloi, riff-raff.

gente *f* people, folk.

gentile *adj* kind, nice, good, obliging, thoughtful; * *m* gentile.

gentilezza *f* kindness, civility.

gentiluomo *m* gentleman.

genuflettersi *vr* to genuflect.

genuino *adj* genuine, sterling.

geografia *f* geography.

geografico *adj* geographic(al).

geografo *m* geographer.

geologia *f* geology.

geologico *adj* geological.

geologo *m* geologist.

geometria *f* geometry.

geometrico *adj* geometric(al).

geranio *m* geranium.

gerarchia *f* hierarchy.

gergo *m* jargon, parlance, slang.

geriatrico *adj* geriatric.

germinare *vi* to germinate.

germoglio *m* shoot, sprout, off-shoot; **germogli di soia** *mpl* beansprouts.

geroglifico *adj*, *m* hieroglyphic.

gessato *adj* pinstripe.

gesso *m* chalk; plaster; (*med*) cast.

gestazione *f* gestation.

gesticolare *vi* to gesticulate; to wave.

gestione *f* management, running, administration .

gestire *vt* to manage, to run, to administer.

gesto *m* gesture, sign; **ampio ~** *m* sweep.

gestore *m* manager; ~ **di un pub** *m* publican.

Gesù *m* Jesus.

gesuita *m* Jesuit.

gettare *vt* to throw; to chuck; to sprout; to cast.

getto *m* jet, spray.

geyser *m inv* geyser.

ghepardo *m* cheetah.

gheriglio *m* kernel.

gherone *m* gusset.

ghiacciaia *f* cooler.

ghiacciaio *m* glacier.

ghiacciato *adj* icy.

ghiaccio *m* ice; ~ **invisibile** *m* black ice.

ghiacciolo *m* icicle.

ghiaia *f* gravel.

ghianda *f* acorn.

ghiandaia *f* jay.

ghiandola *f* gland.

ghigliottina *f* guillotine.

ghigliottinare *vt* to guillotine.

ghiottone *m* glutton.

ghiottoneria *f* delicacy; gluttony.

ghirlanda *f* garland, wreath.

ghiro *m* dormouse.

ghisa *f* cast iron.

già *adv* already; yet.

giacca *f* jacket; ~ **a vento** *f* anorak, windcheater.

giacimento *m* deposit; ~ **petrolifero** *m* oilfield.

giacinto *m* hyacinth; ~ **dei boschi** bluebell.

giada *f* jade.

giaguaro *m* jaguar.

giaietto *m* jet.

giallastro *adj* yellowish; sallow.

giallo *adj*, * *m* yellow; (traffic lights) amber.

giardinaggio *m* gardening.

giardiniere *m* gardener.

giardino *m* garden.

giarrettiera *f* garter.

giavellotto *m* javelin.

gibbone *m* gibbon.

giga *f* jig.

gigante *m* giant.

gigantesco *adj* gigantic, monster.

giglio *m* lily.

gin *m inv* gin.

ginecologo *m* gynaecologist.

ginepro *m* juniper.

ginestra *f* broom; ~ **spinosa** *f* gorse.

gingillarsi *vi* to dilly-dally.

ginnasta *m/f* gymnast.

ginnastica *f* gym, gymnastics.

ginnastico *adj* gymnastic.

ginocchio *m* knee.

giocare *vt*, *vi* to play; ~ **chiassosamente** *vi* to romp; ~ **(d'azzardo)** *vt*, *vi* to gamble.

giocatore *m* player; ~ **d'azzardo** gambler.

giocattolo *m* toy.

giocherellare *vt* to toy with, to fiddle.

giocherellone *adj* playful.

gioco *m* game; play; ~ **chiassoso** *m* romp; ~ **di carte** *m* card game; **doppio** ~ *m* double-dealing; ~ **d'azzardo** *m* gambling.

giocoliere *m* juggler.

giocoso *adj* frolicsome.

giogo *m* yoke.

gioia *f* joy, glee; *vt* **riempire di** ~ to delight.

gioielliere *m* jeweller.

gioiello *m* jewel; **gioielli** *mpl* jewellery.

giornalaio *m* newsagent.

giornale *m* (news)paper; ~ **radio** *m* news.

giornaliero *adj* daily.

giornalismo *m* journalism.

giornalista *m/f* journalist, columnist.

giornata *f* day.

giorno *m* day, daytime; ~ **per** ~ day by day; **di** ~ by day; **buon** ~ *excl* good morning; **un** ~ *adv* sometime.

giostra *f* merry-go-round, roundabout, carousel.

giovane *adj* young; **più** ~ junior; * *m* youth.

giovanile *adj* juvenile, youthful.

giovanotto *m* youngster.

giovare *vt* to benefit.

giovedì *m inv* Thursday.

giovenca *f* heifer.

gioventù *f* youth.

gioviale *adj* jovial, hearty, jocular, convivial.

giovialità *f* heartiness.

giovinezza *f* youthfulness.

giraffa *f* giraffe.

giramondo *m/f* rover.

girare *vt* to revolve; to spin; to turn; (cheque) to endorse; * *vi* to revolve; to turn; ~ **furtivamente** to lurk: ~ **in cerca di clienti** (eg taxi) to cruise; * *vr* ~**rsi** to turn round; to swivel.

girasole *m* sunflower.

girata *f* endorsement.

giretto *m* spin.

girevole *adj* revolving.

girino *m* tadpole.

giro *m* tour; round; circuit; turn; walk; ride; run; spin; tour; lap; ~ **in macchina** *m* drive; ~ **d'affari** *m* turnover; **presa in** ~ *f* taunt; **in** ~ *adv* about, around; **prendere in** ~ *vt* to taunt.

gironzolare *vi* to roam; to stroll around; to wander.

girovagare *vt* per to wander.

gita *f* jaunt; excursion; trip.

giù *adv* down; **in** ~ downwards.

giubileo *m* jubilee.

giubilo *m* exultation.

giudicare *vt* to judge; to deem; to adjudicate.

giudice *m* judge.

giudiziario *adj* judicial; **azione giudiziaria** *f* prosecution.

giudizio *m* judgement; estimation.

giudizioso *adj* judicious.

giugno *m* June.

giumenta *f* mare.

giunca *f* junk.

giunco *m* rush.

giungla *f* jungle, wilderness.

giunta *f* junta.

giuntare *vt* to splice.

giuntura *f* join.

giuramento *m* oath.

giurare *vt* to swear, to vow; * *vi* to swear.

giurato *m* juror.

giuria *f* jury; panel.

giurisdizione *f* jurisdiction.

giurisprudenza *f* jurisprudence.

giustamente *adv* right.

giustapposizione *f* juxtaposition.

giustificabile *adj* justifiable.

giustificare *vt* to justify.

giustificazione *f* justification; warrant.

giustizia *f* justice.

giustiziare *vt* to execute.

giusto *adj* right; just; fair; proper.

glaciale *adj* glacial; frosty.

gladiatore *m* gladiator.

glassa *f* icing.

glassare *vt* to ice.

glicerina *f* glycerine.

globale *adj* global; comprehensive; blanket.

globo *m* globe.

globulo *m* corpuscle.

gloria *f* glory, kudos.

glorificare *vt* to glorify.

glorificazione *f* glorification.

glorioso *adj* glorious.

glossa *f* gloss.

glossario *m* glossary.

glucosio *m* glucose.

gnocco *m* dumpling.

gnomo *m* gnome.

gnu *m inv* gnu.

goal *m inv* goal.

gobba *f* hump.

gobbo *adj* hunch-backed; * *m* hunch-back.

goccia *f* drop, drip.

goccino *m* dash.

gocciolare *vi* to trickle.

gocciolina *f* droplet.

godere *vt* to enjoy.

godimento *m* enjoyment.

goffo *adj* clumsy, gauche, awkward, ungainly.

goffrare *vt* to emboss.

gola *f* throat, gullet; gorge.

golf *m* golf; **mazza da** ~ *f* golf club; **circolo di** ~ *m* golf club; **campo di** ~ *m* golf course; **giocatore di** ~ *m* golfer.

golfo *m* gulf.

goloso *adj* greedy.

gomitata *f* nudge, dig.

gomito *m* elbow; *(tech)* crank; **alzare il** ~ *vi* to booze.

gomma *f* rubber; tyre; ~ **a terra** *f* flat (tyre).

gommapiuma *f* foam rubber.

gommone *m* dinghy.

gondola *f* gondola.

gondoliere *m* gondolier.

gonfiabile *adj* inflatable.

gonfiare *vt* to inflate; to distend; * *vr* ~**rsi** to billow (sails); to swell.

gonfio *adj* swollen; puffy, bloated; **essere ~ di** *vi* to bulge.

gonfiore *m* swelling.

gong *m inv* gong.

gongolare *vi* to gloat.

gonna *f* skirt; ~ **pantalone** *f inv* culottes.

gonorrea *f* gonorrhoea.

gonzo *m* dupe.

gorgogliare *vi* to gurgle.

gorgoglio *m* gurgle.

gorilla *m inv* gorilla.

gormless *adj* tonto.

gotico *adj* gothic.

gotta *f* gout.

governante *f* governess; housekeeper.

governare *vt* to rule, to govern; (animals) to tend, to groom.

governatore *m* governor.

governo *m* government; administration.

gozzo *m* (*ornith*) crop.

gracchiare *vt* to rasp.

gracidare *vi* to croak.

gradazione *f* gradation; ~ **alcolica** *f* strength.

gradevole *adj* pleasant; ~ **al palato** palatable.

gradiente *m* gradient.

gradino *m* step.

gradito *adj* welcome; acceptable; **non ~** unwelcome.

grado *m* degree; grade; rank.

graduale *adj* gradual.

gradualmente *adv* little by little.

graduare *vt* to grade.

graffetta *f* staple.

graffiare *vt* to scratch; to claw.

graffio *m* scratch.

graffiti *mpl* graffiti.

grafica *f* graphics.

grafico *adj* graphic(al); * *m* graph.

grammatica *f* grammar.

grammaticale *adj* grammatical.

grammo *m* gram.

grammofono *m* gramophone.

grana *f* grain.

granaio *m* granary.

granata *f* grenade.

granatiere *m* grenadier.

granchio *m* crab.

grandangolare *adj* wide-angle.

grande *adj* big, large, great.

grandezza *f* greatness.

grandinare *vi* to hail.

grandine *f* hail; **chicco di ~** *m* hailstone.

grandiosità *f* grandeur.

grandioso *adj* grandiose.

granello *m* granule, grain.

granito *m* granite.

grano *m* corn, wheat; **campo di ~** *m* cornfield.

granturco *m* maize; **fiocchi di ~** *mpl* cornflakes; **farina finissima di ~** *f* cornflour.

granulare *vt* to granulate.

grappolo *m* bunch, cluster.

grassetto *adj* bold (type).

grasso *m* grease.

grasso *m* fat; ~ **dell'arrosto** *m* dripping; ~ **di balena** blubber; * *adj* fat, fatty; **piante grasse** *fpl* succulent plants.

grassoccio *adj* rotund.

grassotello *adj* podgy.

grata *f* grid, grate, grating.

graticcio *m* trellis.

graticola *f* gridiron.

gratifica *f* bonus.

gratis *adv* gratis.

gratitudine *f* gratitude, thankfulness.

grato *adj* grateful; appreciative; thankful.

grattacapo *m* (*fig*) headache.

grattacielo *m* skyscraper.

grattare *vt* to grate; * *vi* to scrape, to scratch.

gratuito *adj* free; gratuitous.
gravame *m* onus.
gravare *vt* to tax.
grave *adj* grave; serious; acute.
gravidanza *f* pregnancy.
gravido *adj* pregnant.
gravità *f* gravity.
gravitare *vi* to gravitate.
gravitazione *f* gravitation.
gravoso *adj* onerous.
grazia *f* grace; **grazie** *fpl* thanks;
grazioso *adj* pretty.
greco *adj* Greek.
gregge *m* flock, herd.
greggio *adj* unrefined, raw.
grembiule *m* apron, pinafore.
grembo *m* lap, womb.
grezzo *adj* crude.
grida *fpl* shouting.
gridare *vi, vt* to cry, to shout.
grido *m* cry; shout; **~ di incoraggiamento** *m* cheer.
griffone *m* griffin.
grigio *m* grey; * *adj* grey, drab.
griglia *f* grill; **cuocere alla ~**
vt to grill.
grilletto *m* trigger.
grillo *m* cricket.
grinta *f* drive.
gronda *f* eaves.
grondaia *f* gutter.
grondare *vt* to stream.
groppa *f* rump.
grossa *f* gross.
grossista *m/f* wholesaler.
grosso *adj* big; thick.
grossolanamente *adv* roughly.
grossolano *adj* gross; crude;
earthy.
grotta *f* grotto; cave.
grottesco *adj* grotesque.
groviglio *m* entanglement, tangle.
gru *f inv* crane.
gruccia *f* (coat)hanger.
grugnire *vi* to grunt.
grugnito *m* grunt.
grumo *m* clot, lump.

gruppo *m* group; cluster; batch;
~ sanguigno blood group.
gruzzolo *m* hoard; nest egg.
guadagnare *vt* to earn; to gain.
guadagno *m* gain; return;
guadagni *mpl* earnings.
guadare *vt* to ford.
guado *m* ford.
guai *mpl* trouble.
guaina *f* sheath.
guaio *m* scrape, fix.
guaire *vi* to whine.
guaito *m* whine.
guancia *f* cheek.
guanciale *m* pillow.
guanto *m* glove; gauntlet.
guantoni *mpl* boxing gloves.
guardacaccia *m inv* gamekeeper.
guardacoste *m inv* coastguard.
guardalinee *m inv* linesman.
guardare *vi* to look; to watch;
~ i bambini to baby sit; * *vt*
to look; to survey; to watch; to
view; **~ con occhi vogliosi** to
leer.
guardaroba *m inv* wardrobe;
cloakroom.
guardia *f* guard; watch; **~ del
corpo** bodyguard; **corpo di ~**
m guardroom; **~ forestale** *f*
ranger; **cane da ~** *m* watchdog; **fare la ~ a** *vt* to guard.
guardiano *m* watchman; keeper.
guaribile *adj* curable.
guarigione *f* cure.
guarire *vt* to cure; to heal.
guarnigione *f* garrison.
guarnire *vt* to garnish.
guarnizione *f* gasket.
guastafeste *m/f inv* spoilsport,
kill-joy.
guastare *vt* to vitiate; * *vr* **~rsi**
vr to go off, to spoil.
guasto *m* breakdown.
guerra *f* war; **~ civile** *f* civil
war.

guerriero *m* warrior.
guerriglia *f* guerrilla warfare.
guerrigliero *m* guerrilla.
gufo *m* owl.
guglia *f* spire.
guida *f* leader; guide; guidebook; driving; guidance; runner.
guidare *vt* to drive; to guide; to steer; to lead.
guidatore *m* driver.
guinzaglio *m* leash, lead.

gulasch *m inv* goulash.
guru *m inv* guru.
guscio *m* shell; husk; ~ **d'uovo** *m* eggshell; ~ **di noce** *m* nutshell.
gustare *vt* to relish.
gusto *m* flavour; taste; relish; **di** ~ *adv* heartily; **di** ~ *adj* tasteful; **di cattivo** ~ *adj* tasteless.
gutturale *adj* guttural.

H

habitat *m inv* habitat; home.
hamburger *m inv* hamburger.
handicap *m* handicap.
handicappato *adj* handicapped.
harem *m inv* harem.
hascisc *m* hash(ish).
herpes *m inv* cold sore; ~ **zoster** *m* (*med*) shingles.

hi-fi *m inv* hi-fi.
hobby *m inv* hobby.
hockey *m* hockey.
hostess *f inv* stewardess.
hostess *f inv* hostess.
hot dog *m inv* hot dog.
hotel *m inv* hotel.
house boat *f inv* houseboat.

I

ibrido *adj*, *m* hybrid.
iceberg *m inv* iceberg.
icona *f* icon.
iconoclasta *adj*, *m* iconoclast(ic).
idea *f* idea; notion; **mezza** ~ *f* inkling; ~ **brillante** *f* brainwave; ~ **sbagliata** *f* misconception.
ideale *adj*, *m* ideal.
idealista *m/f* idealist.
idem *adv* ditto.
identico *adj* identical.
identificare *vt* to identify; to equate.
identità *f inv* identity.

ideologia *f* ideology.
idillico *adj* idyllic.
idillio *m* idyll.
idiomatico *adj* idiomatic(al); **frase idiomatica** *f* idiom.
idiota *m/f* idiot; moron.
idolatrare *vt* to idolize.
idolatria *f* idolatry.
idolo *m* idol.
idoneità *f* fitness.
idrante *m* hydrant.
idraulica *f* hydraulics.
idraulico *adj* hydraulic; * *m* plumber.
idrico *adj* water; **impianto** ~ *m* waterworks.

idroelettrico *adj* hydroelectric.
idrofobia *f* hydrophobia.
idrofobo *adj* rabid.
idrogeno *m* hydrogen.
idrovolante *m* seaplane.
iena *f* hyena.
ieri *adv* yesterday.
iettatore *m* jinx.
igiene *f* hygiene.
igienico *adj* hygienic.
igloo *m inv* igloo.
ignaro *adj* oblivious, unaware.
ignizione *f* ignition.
ignobile *adj* ignoble, base.
ignominia *f* ignominy.
ignominioso *adj* ignominious.
ignorante *adj* ignorant; * *m/f* ignoramus.
ignoranza *f* ignorance.
gnorare *vt* to ignore; to disregard; to be unacquainted with.
ignoto *adj* nameless; unknown.
il *def art* the.
ilarità *f* hilarity, mirth.
illecito *adj* illicit, unlawful.
illegale *adj* illegal.
illegalità *f* illegality.
illeggibile *adj* illegible; unreadable; **grafia ~** *f* scrawl.
illegittimità *f* illegitimacy.
illegittimo *adj* illegitimate.
illeso *adj* unharmed.
illimitato *adj* limitless, boundless, unlimited.
illogico *adj* illogical.
illudere *vt* to delude.
illuminare *vt* to illuminate, to light.
illuminato *adj* enlightened.
illuminazione *f* lighting, illumination.
Illuminismo *m* Enlightenment.
illusione *f* illusion; delusion.
illusorio *adj* illusory; unrealistic.
illustrare *vt* to illustrate.
illustrativo *adj* illustrative.

illustrato *adj* pictorial; **libro ~** *m* picture book.
illustrazione *f* illustration.
illustre *adj* illustrious.
imbacuccare *vt* to muffle.
imballaggio *m* packing; **materiale da ~** *m* packing material.
imballare *vt* to pack.
imbalsamare *vt* to embalm.
imbarazzante *adj* embarrassing, awkward.
imbarazzato *adj* embarrassed; sheepish.
imbarazzo *m* embarrassment; **mettere in ~** *vt* to embarrass.
imbarcare *vt* to embark; to ship; * *vr* **~rsi** to board.
imbarco *m* embarkation.
imbastire *vt* (sewing) to baste, to tack.
imbastitura *f* tacking; **punto di ~** *m* tack.
imbattuto *adj* undefeated.
imbavagliare *vt* to gag.
imbecille *m* imbecile.
imbevere *vt* to imbue.
imbiancare *vt* to whitewash.
imbianchino *m* painter.
imboscata *f* ambush; **fare un'~ a** *vt* to ambush.
imbottigliare *vt* to bottle.
imbottire *vt* to stuff, to pad.
imbottitura *f* stuffing, padding.
imbrattare *vt* to smudge, to daub.
imbrogliare *vt* to cheat, to embroil, to hoodwink.
imbroglio *m* cheat, fiddle.
imbroglione *m* cheat, swindler, fiddler.
imbronciato *adj* morose; sulky; in a huff.
imbuto *m* funnel.
imitare *vt* to imitate, to impersonate, to copy, to mimic.
imitativo *adj* imitative.

imitatore *m* mimic.

imitazione *f* imitation; fake; takeoff; **imitazioni** *fpl* mimicry.

immacolato *adj* pristine.

immagazzinamento *m* storage.

immagazzinare *vt* to store.

immaginabile *adj* imaginable.

immaginare *vt* to imagine; to picture; to visualize; **s'immagini!** *excl* think nothing of it!

immaginario *adj* imaginary, fictional.

immaginazione *f* imagination; **ricco di ~** *adj* imaginative.

immagine *f* image.

immancabile *adj* unfailing.

immangiabile *adj* inedible, unpalatable.

immatricolare *vt* to enrol, to register; * *vr* ~**rsi** to matriculate.

immatricolazione *f* enrolment, matriculation.

immaturo *adj* immature; callow.

immediato *adj* immediate, instant.

immenso *adj* immense.

immergere *vt* to immerse, to duck, to dip, to steep, to plunge.

immeritato *adj* undeserved, unmerited,

immersione *f* immersion; ~ **con autorespiratore** *f* skindiving.

immerso *adj* engrossed.

immigrato *m* immigrant.

immigrazione *f* immigration.

imminente *adj* imminent, forthcoming.

immischiarsi *vr* to meddle.

immissione *f* intake.

immobile *adj* immobile, motionless, still.

immobilità *f* immobility, stillness.

immondizie *fpl* rubbish.

immorale *adj* immoral.

immoralità *f* immorality.

immortalare *vt* to immortalize.

immortale *adj* immortal.

immortalità *f* immortality.

immotivato *adj* unmotivated.

immune *adj* immune.

immunità *f* immunity.

immunizzare *vt* to immunize.

immutabile *adj* unchanging, immutable.

impacchettare *vt* to parcel.

impacciato *adj* self-conscious, wooden.

impadronirsi *vr* to master (e.g. a language)

impalcatura *f* scaffolding.

impalpabile *adj* impalpable.

impappinarsi *vr* to flounder.

imparare *vt* to learn.

impareggiabile *adj* matchless, peerless.

imparentato *adj* related, kindred.

imparziale *adj* impartial, fair, unbiased, detached.

imparzialità *f* impartiality, fairness.

impasse *f* impasse.

impassibile *adj* impassive, unemotional; deadpan; stolid; **dalla faccia ~** poker-faced.

impastare *vt* to knead.

impasto *m* dough, paste.

impatto *m* impact.

impaurire *vt* to scare.

impaurito *adj* frightened.

impaziente *adj* impatient.

impazienza *f* impatience.

impazzire *vi* to go mad; **far ~** to *vt* madden.

impeccabile *adj* impeccable; immaculate; faultless.

impedimento *m* impediment.

impedire *vt* to stop, to hinder.

impegnare *vt* to pledge, to pawn; * *vr* ~**rsi** to covenant.

impegno *m* commitment; bond; engagement.

impellente *adj* compelling.

impenetrabile *adj* impenetrable.

impenitente *adj* unrepentant.

impennarsi *vr* to rear.

impensabile *adj* unthinkable.

imperativo *adj* imperative.

imperatore *m* emperor.

imperatrice *f* empress.

impercettibile *adj* imperceptible.

imperdonabile *adj* unforgivable, inexcusable.

imperfetto *adj* imperfect.

imperfezione *f* imperfection, blemish.

imperiale *adj* imperial.

imperialismo *m* imperialism.

imperioso *adj* imperious.

imperituro *adj* undying.

impermeabile *adj* impermeable; mackintosh, raincoat.

impero *m* empire.

imperscrutabile *adj* inscrutable.

impersonale *adj* impersonal.

imperterrito *adj* undaunted, undismayed.

impertinente *adj* impertinent, pert, cocky.

impertinenza *f* impertinence, backchat.

imperturbabile *adj* imperturbable.

imperturbato *adj* undisturbed.

imperversare *vi* to be rife.

impervio *adj* impervious.

impestare *vt* to foul.

impetuosità *f* impetuosity.

impetuoso *adj* impetuous, hotheaded.

impiallacciatura *f* veneer.

impianto *m* plant; **impianti ~ elettrico** *m* wiring; *mpl* fixtures.

impiastro *m* poultice.

impiccare *vt* to hang.

impiccione *m* meddler.

impiegare *vt* to employ.

impiegato *m* clerk, office worker.

impiego *m* job, position; use.

impietrito *adj* petrified.

impigliare *vt* to entangle; to pile.

implacabile *adj* implacable, relentless, unrelenting.

implicare *vt* to implicate, to imply.

implicazione *f* implication.

implicito *adj* implicit.

implorare *vt* to implore, to entreat, to beseech; * *vi* to plead.

imponente *adj* imposing, impressive, awe-inspiring; towering.

imponibile *adj* taxable.

impopolare *adj* unpopular.

imporre *vt* to impose; to levy; * *vr* **imporsi che sa ~** to be assertive; to put one's foot down.

importante *adj* important; momentous; weighty; **il più ~** foremost.

importanza *f* importance; **avere più ~ di** *vt* to outweigh.

importare *vt* to import; * *vi* to matter; **non mi importa** I don't care.

importatore *m* importer.

importazione *f* import, importation.

importo *m* amount.

importunare *vt* to importune, to worry.

importuno *adj* importunate.

imposizione *f* imposition.

impossibile *adj* impossible; hopeless.

impossibilità *f* impossibility.

imposta *f* tax; levy; **~ sul reddito** *f* income tax; **~ indiret**

ta *f* excise; **esente da ~** *adj* tax-free.

impostazione *f* layout.

imposto *adj* enforced.

impostore *m* impostor, sham.

impotente *adj* impotent, powerless.

impotenza *f* impotence.

impoverire *vt* to impoverish.

impoverito *adj* impoverished.

impraticabile *adj* impracticable.

imprecazione *f* expletive, imprecation.

impreciso *adj* imprecise.

impregnare *vt* to impregnate, to steep.

impregnato *adj* impregnated; **~ d'acqua** waterlogged.

impregnazione *f* impregnation.

imprenditore *m* entrepreneur.

impreparato *adj* unprepared.

impresa *f* concern; undertaking, venture; enterprise; exploit; feat; **imprese** *fpl* doings.

impressionabile *adj* impressionable.

impressione *f* impression, feeling, hunch; **fare ~ a** *vt* to impress.

imprevedibile *adj* unforeseeable, unpredictable.

imprevidente *adj* improvident.

imprevisto *adj* unforeseen.

imprigionare *vt* to imprison, to incarcerate.

imprimere *vt* to imprint.

improbabile *adj* improbable, unlikely.

improbabilità *f* improbability, unlikelihood.

improduttivo *adj* unproductive.

impronta *f* print; **~ digitale** *f* fingerprint.

impronunciabile *adj* unpronounceable.

improperi *mpl* abuse.

improvvisamente *adv* all at once.

improvvisare *vi* to improvise; ** vt* to improvise, to ad-lib, to extemporize.

improvvisato *adj* impromptu, ad-lib, makeshift, extempore

improvviso *adj* sudden, snap.

imprudente *adj* imprudent, ill-advised, injudicious.

imprudenza *f* imprudence.

impudico *adj* immodest.

impugnare *vt* to impugn.

impugnatura *f* hilt.

impulsivo *adj* impulsive.

impulso *m* impulse, urge.

impunemente *adv* with impunity.

impunito *adj* unpunished.

impurità *f inv* impurity.

impuro *adj* impure.

imputare *vt* to indict.

imputato *m* defendant, accused.

imputazione *f* charge, indictment.

incidente *m* accident.

incidere su *vt* affect.

in *prep* in; into; **~ vettura** *adv* aboard.

inabilità *f* inability.

inabitabile *adj* uninhabitable.

inaccessibile *adj* inaccessible.

inadatto *adj* inappropriate, unfit, unsuitable

inadeguato *adj* inadequate.

inadempiente *adj* defaulting; **risultare ~** *vi* to default.

inafferrabile *adj* elusive.

inalare *vt* to inhale.

inalterabile *adj* unalterable.

inalterato *adj* unaltered.

inamidare *vt* to starch.

inammissibile *adj* inadmissible.

inanimato *adj* inanimate.

inapplicabile *adj* inapplicable.

inaridire *vt* to parch.

inasprire *vt* to embitter.

inattaccabile *adj* impregnable, watertight.

inatteso *adj* unexpected.

inattività *f* inactivity.

inattivo *adj* inactive, idle.

inattuabile *adj* unworkable.

inaudito *adj* unheard-of.

inaugurale *adj* inaugural, maiden.

inaugurare *vt* to inaugurate.

inaugurazione *f* inauguration, opening.

inavvicinabile *adj* unapproachable.

inazione *f* inaction.

incagliarsi *vr* (*naut*) to ground.

incalcolabile *adj* incalculable.

incallito *adj* horny.

incalzare *vt* to ply.

incancrenito *adj* ingrained.

incandescente *adj* incandescent, white-hot.

incandescenza *f* glow.

incantare *vt* to enchant.

incantesimo *m* enchantment, spell, incantation.

incantevole *adj* enchanting, ravishing.

incanto *m* charm.

incapace *adj* incapable, unable, helpless; **rendere ~** *vt* to incapacitate.

incapacità *f* incapacity.

incaricare *vt* to commission.

incarico *m* assignment.

incarnare *vt* to embody, to epitomize.

incarnato *adj* incarnate.

incarnazione *f* incarnation, embodiment.

incartare *vt* to wrap.

incassare *vt* to cash.

incastellatura *f* housing.

incastrare *vt* to embed.

incatenare *vt* to chain, to fetter.

incauto *adj* incautious.

incavato *adj* cavernous.

incavolato *adj* ratty.

incendiario *adj* incendiary, inflamatory.

incendio *m* fire, blaze; **~ doloso** *m* arson.

inceneritore *m* incinerator.

incenso *m* incense.

incentivo *m* incentive, inducement.

incepparsi *vr* to jam, to stick.

incerato; telone ~ *m* tarpaulin.

incertezza *f* uncertainty, suspense.

incerto *adj* unsure, uncertain, touch-and-go.

incessante *adj* incessant, ceaseless, unremitting, unceasing.

incesto *m* incest.

incestuoso *adj* incestuous.

inchiesta *f* inquest, inquiry.

inchinarsi *vr* to bow.

inchino *m* curtsey; bow; **fare un ~** *vi* to curtsey.

inchiodare *vt* to nail.

inchiodato *adj* rooted.

inchiostro *m* ink.

inciampare *vi* to trip, to stumble.

incidente *m* accident; mishap; crash; **avere un ~** *vi* to crash.

incidenza *f* incidence.

incidere *vt* to incise; to engrave; to cut (a record); to carve; to inscribe; to lance; to score; **~ all'acquaforte** to etch.

incinta *adj* pregnant, expecting.

incipiente *adj* incipient.

incipriarsi *vr* to powder.

incisione *f* incision; cut; engraving; **~ all'acquaforte** etching; **~ su legno** *f* woodcut.

incisivo *adj* incisive.

incitare *vt* to incite.

incivile *adj* uncivil.

inciviso *m* incisor.

inclemente *adj* inclement.

inclinare *vt* to tilt, to slant.

inclinato *adj* slanting, sloping; **essere ~** *vi* to slope.

inclinazione *f* inclination, bent.

includere *vt* to include.

inclusione *f* inclusion.

incluso *adj* including, inclusive.

incoerente *adj* incoherent.

incoerenza *f* incoherence, inconsistency.

incognito *m*: **in ~** *adj* incognito.

incollare *vt* to glue, to gum, to stick.

incolore *adj* colourless.

incolpare *vt* to blame.

incolto *adj* uncultivated, fallow; uneducated.

incolume *adj* uninjured, untouched.

incombente *adj* impending.

incominciare *vt, vi* to begin.

incommensurabile *adj* immeasurable.

incomodare *vt* to inconvenience.

incomparabile *adj* incomparable.

incompatibile *adj* incompatible.

incompatibilità *f* incompatibility.

incompetente *adj* incompetent.

incompetenza *f* incompetence.

incompiuto *adj* unfinished.

incompleto *adj* incomplete.

incomprensibile *adj* incomprehensible; **parole incomprensibili** *fpl* gibberish.

inconcludente *adj* inconclusive.

incondizionato *adj* unconditional, wholehearted, unqualified, unreserved.

inconfondibile *adj* unmistakable.

incongruo *adj* incongruous.

inconorazione *f* coronation.

inconsapevolmente *adv* unknowingly.

inconscio *adj, n* unconscious.

inconsolabile *adj* inconsolable.

incontestato *adj* unchallenged.

incontinente *adj* incontinent.

incontinenza *f* incontinence.

incontrare *vt* to meet, to encounter.

incontrastato *adj* undisputed.

incontro *m* encounter; meeting; match; (boxing) bout.

incontrollabile *adj* uncontrollable, compulsive.

incontrollato *adj* unchecked.

incontrovertibile *adj* incontrovertible, indisputable.

inconveniente *m* drawback.

incoraggiamento *m* encouragement.

incoraggiare *vt* to encourage.

incordare *vt* to string.

incornare *vt* to gore.

incorniciare *vt* to frame.

incoronare *vt* to crown.

incorporare *vt* to incorporate.

incorporazione *f* incorporation.

incorreggibile *adj* incorrigible, hopeless.

incorruttibile *adj* incorruptible.

incostante *adj* erratic.

incredibile *adj* incredible, unbelievable.

incredibilmente *adv* amazingly.

incredulità *f* incredulity, disbelief.

incredulo *adj* incredulous.

incremento m increment, increase; **forte ~** boom.

increscioso adj untoward.

increspare vt to pucker, to ripple.

increspatura f ripple.

incriminare vt to incriminate.

incrinare vt to crack.

incrociare vt to cross.

incrociatore m cruiser.

incrocio m crossing, crossroads, junction; crossbreed.

incrollabile adj unwavering.

incrostare vt to encrust, to cake.

incubatrice f incubator.

incubo m nightmare.

incudine f anvil.

inculcare vt to inculcate.

incurabile adj incurable, terminal.

incuriosire vt to intrigue.

incursione f incursion, inroad, foray, swoop; **fare un'~** vi to swoop.

incurvarsi vi to sag.

incustodito adj unattended.

indaco m, adj indigo.

indagare vt to investigate, to inquire (into).

indagine f investigation; survey.

indebolire vt to weaken, to enfeeble; * vr **~rsi** to weaken.

indecente adj indecent, rude.

indecenza f indecency.

indecisione f indecision.

indeciso adj undecided; indecisive; doubtful.

indecoroso adj unseemly.

indefinibile adj indefinible.

indefinito adj indefinite; undefined; nondescript.

indegno adj undeserving, unworthy.

indelebile adj indelible.

indelicato adj indelicate, tactless.

indenne adj unscathed.

indennità f allowance; compensation.

indennizzare vt to indemnify.

indennizzo m indemnity.

indentificazione f identification.

indescrivibile adj indescribable.

indeterminato adj indeterminate, undetermined.

indicare vt to indicate; to point; to state; to tell; to say; to quote; * vi to say.

indicativo adj indicative.

indicazione f indication; clue; **~ stradale** f signpost.

indice m index; forefinger, index finger.

indicibile adj unspeakable.

indietreggiare vi to recoil.

indietro adv behind; back, backwards; **fare marcia ~** vi to back, to reverse; **restare ~** vi to lag; **marcia indietra** f reverse (gear).

indifeso adj defenceless, unprotected.

indifferente adj indifferent cold, uninterested, unmoved.

indifferenza f indifference, disregard.

indigeno adj indigenous, native, aboriginal, indigenous * m native.

indigente adj destitute; * m pauper.

indigenza f destitution.

indigenza f penury.

indigestione f indigestion.

indignato adj indignant.

indignazione f indignation.

indimenticabile adj unforgetable.

indipendente adj independent; self-contained.

indipendenza f independence

indire vt to call.

indiretto *adj* indirect, roundabout.

indirizzare *vt* to address; ~ **male** to misdirect.

indirizzario *m* mailing list.

indirizzo *m* address.

indisciplinato *adj* unruly, undisciplined.

indiscreto *adj* indiscreet.

indiscrezione *f* indiscretion.

indiscriminato *adj* indiscriminate.

indiscusso *adj* unquestioned.

indiscutibile *adj* unquestionable.

indispensabile *adj* indispensable.

indisposizione *f* indisposition, ailment.

indisposto *adj* indisposed, ill, unwell, poorly.

indistinguibile *adj* indistinguishable.

indistinto *adj* indistinct; **una massa indistinta** *f* blur.

indistruttibile *adj* indestructible.

indivia *f* endive.

individuale *adj* individual, one-man.

individualità *f* individuality.

individuare *vt* to detect, to pick out.

individuo *m* individual.

indivisibile *adj* indivisible.

indizio *m* clue, lead, pointer, sign.

indole *f* disposition, temper.

indolente *adj* indolent, workshy.

indolenza *f* indolence, lethargy.

indolenzito *adj* sore, stiff.

indolore *adj* painless.

indomabile *adj* indomitable.

indomato *adj* untamed.

indossare *vt* to wear; to model.

indossatore *m* model.

indottrinamento *m* indoctrination.

indottrinare *vt* to indoctrinate.

indovinare *vt, vi* to guess.

indovinello *m* riddle, conundrum.

indovino *m* soothsayer.

indubbiamente *adv* doubtless.

indubbio *adj* undoubted.

indubitabile *adj* indubitable.

indugiare *vi* to linger.

indulgente *adj* indulgent, lenient, soft.

indulgenza *f* indulgence.

indumento *m* garment.

indurire *vt* to harden; * *vr* ~**rsi** to set.

industria *f* industry, trade.

industriale *adj* industrial; **zona** ~ *f* industrial estate; * *m* industrialist.

industrializzare *vt* to industrialize.

induzione *f* induction.

inebetito *adj* dopey.

inebriante *adj* heady.

inebriare *vt* to intoxicate.

inedia *f* starvation.

inedito *adj* unpublished.

ineffabile *adj* ineffable.

inefficace *adj* ineffective, ineffectual.

inefficiente *adj* inefficient.

inefficienza *f* inefficiency.

ineguaglianza *f* inequality.

ineguale *adj* uneven.

ineleggibile *adj* ineligible.

inequivocabile *adj* unequivocal.

inerpicarsi *vr* to scramble.

inerte *adj* inert.

inerzia *f* inertia.

inesatezza *f* inaccuracy.

inesatto *adj* inaccurate.

inesauribile *adj* inexhaustible.

inesercitato *adj* unpractised.

inesistente *adj* non-existent.

inesorabile *adj* inexorable.

inesperienza *f* inexperience.

inesperto *adj* inexperienced; unskilful.

inesplicabile *adj* unaccountable.

inesplorato *adj* unexplored.

inesploso *adj* unexploded; live.

inespressivo *adj* expressionless.

inesprimibile *adj* inexpressable.

inestimabile *adj* inestimable, invaluable; **di valore ~** priceless.

inestricabile *adj* inextricable.

inettitudine *f* ineptitude.

inetto *adj* inept.

inevitabile *adj* inevitable, unavoidable, inescapable.

inevitabilmente *adv* inevitably.

infallibile *adj* infallible, foolproof, surefire, unerring.

infallibilità *f* infallibility.

infame *adj* infamous.

infamia *f* infamy.

infangare *vt* to soil; to taint.

infanticidio *m* infanticide.

infantile *adj* infantile, babyish, childish.

infanzia *f* infancy, childhood; **prima ~** *f* babyhood.

infarinatura *f* smattering.

infarto *m* heart attack.

infastidire *vt* to annoy, to bother.

infaticabile *adj* indefatigable, untiring.

infatti *adv* indeed.

infatuato *adj* infatuated.

infatuazione *f* infatuation.

infausto *adj* ill-fated, inauspicious, ominous.

infedele *adj* unfaithful, infidel; * *m* infidel.

infedeltà *f inv* unfaithfulness, infidelity.

infelice *adj* unhappy, miserable.

infelicità *f* unhappiness.

infeltrito *adj* matted.

inferiore *adj* inferior, lower.

inferiorità *f* inferiority.

infermeria *f* infirmary, sickbay.

infermiere *m* nurse.

infermità *f inv* affliction; **~ mentale** *f* insanity.

infermo *adj* infirm.

infernale *adj* infernal, hellish.

inferno *m* hell.

inferriata *f* grille.

infestare *vt* to infest.

infettare *vt* to infect.

infettivo *adj* infectious.

infezione *f* infection.

infiammabile *adj* flammable.

infiammare *vt* to inflame.

infiammazione *f* inflamation.

infilare *vt* to thread; to string; to tuck; to cram.

infiltrarsi *vr* to infiltrate.

infilzare *vt* to spike.

infine *adv* lastly.

infinità *f* infinity.

infinitivo *adj* infinitive.

infinito *adj* infinite; * *m* infinitive.

infittirsi *vi* to thicken.

inflazione *f* inflation.

inflessibile *adj* inflexible; adamant.

inflessibilità *f* inflexibility.

inflessione *f* inflection.

infliggere *vt* to inflict.

influente *adj* influential.

influenza *f* influence, influenza, sway, clout.

influenzare *vt* to influence, to sway, to swing.

influire su *vt* to affect.

infocato *adj* fiery.

infondato *adj* groundless, baseless, unfounded

infondere *vt* to infuse.

inforcatura *f* crotch.

informale *adj* informal, casual.

informare *vt* to acquaint, to apprise.

ingiurie *fpl* abuse

ingiurioso *adj* abusive.

ingresso *m* entrance; admission, admittance.

inimicarsi *vr* to antagonize.

informare *vt* to inform; **~ male** to misinform; * *vr* **~rsi** to inquire.

informatica *f* computer science.

informato *adj* knowledgeable.

informatore *m* informant.

informazioni *fpl* information.

informe *adj* shapeless.

infossato *adj* sunken.

infradiciare *vt* to douse.

inframmezzare *vt* to intersperse.

infrangere *vt* to infringe.

infrangibile *adj* unbreakable, shatter-proof.

infrarosso *adj* infra-red.

infrastruttura *f* infrastructure.

infrazione *f* offence, infraction.

infrequente *adj* infrequent.

infruttuoso *adj* unfruitful, barren.

infuriare *vi* to storm; * *vr* **~rsi** to rage.

infusione *f* infusion; **lasciare in ~** *vt* to infuse.

infuso *m* brew; **fare un ~ di** *vt* to brew.

ingaggiare *vt* to engage.

ingannare *vt* to deceive, to fool, to hoax, to trick, to dupe.

ingannevole *adj* deceptive.

inganno *m* trick, deceit, deception; **trarre in ~** *vt* to mislead.

ingarbugliare *vt* to scramble.

ingarbugliato *adj* garbled.

ingegnere *m* engineer; **~ civile** *m* civil engineer.

ingegneria *f* engineering.

ingegnosità *f* ingenuity.

ingegnoso *adj* ingenious.

ingenuo *adj* naïve, ingenuous, artless, simple, childlike.

inghiottire *vt* to swallow; to gulp (down); to engulf; * *vi* to swallow.

inginocchiarsi *vr* to kneel.

inginocchiatoio *m* hassock.

ingiunzione *f* injunction.

ingiurioso *adj* invidious; hurtful.

ingiustificato *adj* unjustified,

ingiustizia *f* injustice.

ingiusto *adj* wrong, wrongful, unfair, unjust.

inglorioso *adj* inglorious.

ingollare *vt* to bolt (food).

ingombrante *adj* cumbersome; * *vt* to clutter; to encumber.

ingorgo *f* blockage; bottleneck; traffic jam.

ingovernabile *adj* ungovernable.

ingozzare *vt* to guzzle.

ingrandimento *m* enlargement.

ingrandire *vt* to enlarge, to magnify.

ingrassare *vt* to fatten.

ingratitudine *f* ingratitude.

ingrato *adj* ungrateful, thankless.

ingraziarsi *vr* to ingratiate.

ingrediente *m* ingredient.

ingresso *m* entrance, entry.

ingrosso *adj*: **all'~** *adv* wholesale.

ingualcibile *adj* crease-resistant.

inguine *m* groin.

inibire *vt* to inhibit.

inibito *adj* inhibited.

inibizione *f* inhibition.

iniettare *vt* to inject.

iniettato *adj* injected; **~ di sangue** bloodshot.

iniezione *f* injection, shot.

inimicizia *f* enmity.

inimitabile *adj* inimitable.

inimmaginabile *adj* unimaginable, inconceivable.

inintelligibile *adj* unintelligible.

ininterrotto *adj* unbroken, uninterrupted.

iniquità *f* iniquity.

iniquo *adj* iniquitous, inequitable.

iniziale *f, adj* initial.

iniziare *vt* to begin, to start; to initiate; * *vi* to begin.

iniziativa *f* initiative, enterprise.

iniziazione *f* initiation.

inizio *m* beginning, commencement; onset; outset; start; **sapevo fin dall'~** I knew all along; **all'~** *adv* initially.

innaffiare *vt* to water.

innamorare *vt* to enamour; * *vr* ~**rsi** to fall in love.

innanzi *adv* ahead; **d'ora ~** henceforth; **~ tutto** firstly.

innato *adj* innate, in-born.

innaturale *adj* unearthly, unnatural.

innegabile *adj* undeniable.

innervosire *vt* to fluster, to rattle.

innestare *vt* to graft, to implant; to engage.

innesto *m* graft.

inno *m* hymn, anthem.

innocente *adj* innocent.

innocenza *f* innocence.

innocuo *adj* innocuous, harmless.

innominabile *adj* unmentionable.

innovazione *f* innovation; **fare delle innovazioni** *vi* to innovate.

innumerevole *adj* innumerable, countless.

inoculare *vt* to inoculate.

inoculazione *f* inoculation.

inodore *adj* odourless, scentless.

inoffensivo *adj* unoffending, inoffensive.

inoltrare *vt* to forward.

inoltre *adv* furthermore, besides, moreover.

inondare *vt* to inundate, to flood, to swamp.

inondazione *f* inundation, flood.

inopportuno *adj* inopportune, unsuitable; ill-timed.

inorganico *adj* inorganic.

inorridire *vt* to horrify.

inorridito *adj* aghast.

inospitale *adj* inhospitable.

inosservato *adj* unnoticed, unobserved, unseen.

inossidabile *adj* stainless.

input *m* input.

inquietante *adj* disquieting.

inquieto *adj* uneasy.

inquietudine *f* disquiet.

inquilino *m* tenant, occupant, occupier.

inquinamento *m* pollution.

inquinare *vt* to pollute.

inquisizione *f* inquisition.

insalata *f* salad; **~ di cavolo bianco** coleslaw.

insalatiera *f* salad bowl.

insalubre *adj* unhygienic.

insaponare *vt* to soap.

insaponato *adj* soapy.

insaziabile *adj* insatiable, avid.

inscatolare *vt* to tin.

insediamento *m* settlement.

insediarsi *vr* to settle.

insegna *f* ensign.

insegna *f* standard.

insegne *fpl* insignia; **~ reali** *fpl* regalia.

insegnamento *m* teaching.

insegnante *m/f* teacher; *m* master, schoolmaster; *f* schoolmistress; **~ privato** *m* tutor.

insegnare *vt*, *vi* to teach.

inseguimento *m* chase, pursuit.

inseguire *vt* to chase, to pursue; to stalk.

inseminazione *f* insemination.

insenatura *f* inlet, creek.

insensato *adj* senseless, foolish, hare-brained; mindless.

insensibile *adj* insensitive, unfeeling, callous.

inseparabile *adj* inseparable.

inserire *vt* to insert.

inserto *m* insert.

inservibile *adj* dud; **arnese ~** *m* dud.

inserviente *m* orderly.

inserzione *f* insertion; advertisement.

insetticida *m* insecticide.

insetto *m* insect, bug; **~ nocivo** *m* pest.

insicurezza *f* insecurity.

insidioso *adj* insidious.

insieme *adv*, *adj* together; **mettere ~** *vt* to pool; * *m* aggregate.

insignificante *adj* insignificant; inconsequential; fiddling; niggling; trifling; petty.

insincerità *f* insincerity.

insincero *adj* insincere.

insinuare *vt* to insinuate; * *vr* **~rsi** to worm.

insinuazione *f* insinuation, innuendo.

insipido *adj* insipid, flavourless, tasteless.

insistente *adj* insistent; nagging (pain, etc).

insistenza *f* insistence.

insistere *vi* to insist; * *vt* to insist; to urge.

insoddisfacente *adj* unsatisfying.

insoddisfatto *adj* dissatisfied.

insoddisfazione *f* dissatisfaction.

insolazione *f* sunstroke.

insolente *adj* insolent.

insolenza *f* insolence.

insolito *adj* uncommon, unusual.

insolubile *adj* insoluble.

insoluto *adj* outstanding.

insolvente *adj* insolvent.

insolvenza *f* insolvency.

insondabile *adj* unfathomable.

insonne *adj* sleepless.

insonnia *f* insomnia.

insopportabile *adj* insufferable, unendurable, unbearable; beastly.

insormontabile *adj* insurmountable.

insorto *m* insurgent.

insostenibile *adj* untenable.

insostituibile *adj* irreplaceable.

insperato *adj* unhoped-for.

inspiegabile *adj* inexplicable.

inspiegato *adj* unexplained.

instabile *adj* unstable, unsettled.

instabilità *f* instability.

installare *vt* to install.

installatore *m* fitter.

installazione *f* installation.

instancabile *adj* tireless, unflagging.

instillare *vt* to instil.

insubordinato *adj* insubordinate.

insubordinazione *f* insubordination.

insuccesso *m* failure.

insufficiente *adj* insufficient, unsatisfactory.

insufficienza *f* insufficiency, deficiency.

insulare *adj* insular.

insulina *f* insulin.

insulso *adj* dull, inane.

insultante *adj* insulting.

insultare *vt* to insult, to abuse; to revile.

insulti *mpl* abuse.

insulto *m* insult.

insuperabile *adj* insuperable.

insuperato *adj* unbroken, un-equalled.

insurrezione *f* insurrection, uprising.

intaccare *vt* to notch.

intaglio *m* carving.

intarsiare *vt* to inlay.

intarsiato *adj* inlaid.

intasamento *m* snarl-up.

intasare *vt* to clog.

intascare *vt* to pocket.

intatto *adj* intact, unbroken, undamaged, unimpaired.

integrale *adj* wholemeal.

integrante *adj* integral.

integrare *vt* to integrate, to supplement, to eke out; * *vr* ~rsi to fit in.

integrazione *f* integration.

integrità *f* integrity.

intelletto *m* intellect.

intellettuale *m/f*, *adj* intellectual.

intelligente *adj* intelligent, clever.

intelligenza *f* intelligence, cleverness, wit.

intellighenzia *f* intelligentsia.

intelligibile *adj* intelligible.

intendere *vt* to intend, to mean.

intenditore *m* connoisseur.

intensificare *vt* to intensify, to escalate.

intensificazione *f* escalation.

intensità *f inv.* intensity; brilliance.

intensivo *adj* intensive.

intenso *adj* intense, acute, heavy.

intento *adj*, *m* intent.

intenzionale *adj* intentional.

intenzionato *adj*: **ben** ~ well-intentioned.

intenzione *f* intent, intention;

avere ~ **di** *vi* to intend.

interazione *f* interaction, interplay.

intercedere *vi* to intercede.

intercessione *f* intercession.

intercettare *vt* to intercept; to tap.

interessante *adj* interesting.

interessare *vt* to interest; * *vr* ~rsi di to care about.

interesse *m* interest; expediency; **tasso di** ~ *m* interest rate; ~ **personale** *m* self-interest.

interferenza *f* interference.

interferire *vt* to interfere.

interiezione *f* interjection.

interiora *fpl* entrails.

interiore *adj* inner, inward.

interlocutore *m* speaker.

intermediario *m* intermediary, go-between.

intermedio *adj* intermediate, in-between.

interminabile *adj* interminable, endless, unending, never-ending.

intermittente *adj* intermittent.

internazionale *adj* international.

interno *m* inside; interior; internal; *(tel)* extension; * *adj* interior; inland; *adv* **all'**~ indoors, within.

intero *adj* entire, whole.

interporre *vt* to interpose.

interpretare *vt* to interpret; to render; to play; to act; to construe; ~ **male** to misinterpret.

interpretazione *f* interpretation, performance.

interprete *m/f* interpreter.

interregno *m* interregnum.

interrogante *m/f* questioner.

interrogare *vt* to interrogate, to cross-examine; to quiz, to question.

interrogativo *adj* interrogative, quizzical; **punto ~** *m* question mark.

interrogatorio *m* interrogation.

interrompere *vt* to interrupt; to butt in; to discontinue; to abort; * *vi* to interrupt.

interruttore *m* switch.

interruzione *f* interruption, intermission.

intersecare *vt* to intersect.

intersezione *f* intersection.

interurbano *adj* long-distance.

intervallo *m* interval, interlude, break, recess, lapse, gap, half-time; **~ di tempo** *m* time-lag.

intervenire *vt* to intervene.

intervento *m* intervention; operation.

intervista *f* interview.

intervistatore *m* interviewer.

intesa *f* understanding.

intestato *adj* intestate.

intestinale *adj* intestinal.

intestino *m* intestine; bowels; gut.

intimidire *vt* to intimidate, to browbeat, to overawe, to cow.

intimità *f* intimacy.

intimo *adj* intimate, close; **più ~** inmost, innermost.

intitolare *vt* to entitle.

intollerabile *adj* intolerable.

intollerante *adj* intolerant.

intolleranza *f* intolerance.

intonacare *vt* to plaster.

intonacatore *m* plasterer.

intonaco *m* plaster.

intonarsi *vr* to match, to tone.

intonazione *f* intonation, pitch.

intontimento *m* stupor.

intontire *vt* to stupefy.

intontito *adj* groggy.

ntoppo *m* hitch, snag, hold-up.

ntorbidire *vt* to cloud.

ntorno a prep about, around; round; * *adv* around.

intorpidimento *m* numbness.

intorpidire *vt* to numb, to dull.

intorpidito *adj* torpid, numb, dead.

intossicazione *f* poisoning; **~ alimentare** *f* food poisoning.

intraducibile *adj* untranslatable.

intralcio *m* hindrance.

intransigenza *f* intransigence.

intransitabile *adj* impassable.

intransitivo *adj* intransitive.

intrappolare *vt* to trap, to corner.

intraprendente *adj* enterprising, go-ahead.

intraprendere *vt* to wage.

intrattabile *adj* unmanageable, intractable.

intrattenere *vt* to entertain, to regale.

intravedere *vt* to glimpse.

intrecciare *vt* to braid, to plait; to entwine; to intertwine; to weave; **intrecciati** *adj* crisscross; * *vr* **~rsi** to interlock.

intrepido *adj* intrepid, fearless.

intricato *adj* intricate.

intrigante *m* schemer; * *adj* scheming.

intrigo *m* intrigue.

intrinseco *adj* intrinsic, inherent.

introdurre *vt* to introduce.

introduttivo *adj* introductory.

introduzione *f* introduction.

introiti *mpl* takings.

intromettersi *vr* to intrude, to interfere.

intromissione *f* interference.

introspezione *f* introspection.

introvabile *adj* unobtainable.

introverso *m* introvert.

intrusione *f* intrusion.

intruso *m* intruder, interloper, gatecrasher.

intuire *vt* to sense, to divine.

intuitivo *adj* intuitive.

intuito *m* intuition.

inumanità *f* inhumanity.

inumano *adj* inhuman.

inumidire *vt* to damp, to dampen, to moisten.

inutile *adj* useless, unnecessary, worthless, pointless, needless.

inutilità *f* uselessness.

inutilizzato *adj* unused.

invadente *adj* obtrusive, officious.

invadere *vt* to invade; to overrun; * *vi* to encroach.

invalido *adj* disabled; invalid; * *m* invalid.

invano *adv* to no avail.

invariabile *adj* invariable.

invariato *adj* unchanged.

invasare *vt* to pot.

invasione *f* invasion.

invasore *m* invader.

invece *adv* instead; ~ di in lieu of.

invecchiare *vi* to age.

inveire *vi* to rail (against).

invendibile *adj* unsaleable.

invenduto *adj* unsold.

inventare *vt* to invent; to make up; to concoct (a story).

inventario *m* inventory, stocktaking.

inventivo *adj* inventive.

inventore *m* inventor.

invenzione *f* invention.

invernale *adj* winter, wintry.

inverno *m* winter; **pieno** ~ *m* midwinter.

inverosimile *adj* unlikely.

inversione *f* inversion, reversal.

inverso *m* converse; * *adj* inverse, reverse.

invertebrato *m* invertebrate.

invertire *vt* to reverse; to switch.

investigatore *m* investigator, detective.

investimento *m* investment.

investire *vt* to invest.

inveterato *adj* inveterate, confirmed.

invettiva *f* invective.

inviare *vt* to send, to dispatch.

inviato *m* envoy.

invidia *f* envy.

invidiabile *adj* enviable; **poco** ~ unenviable.

invidiare *vt* to grudge, to begrudge.

invidioso *adj* envious.

invincibile *adj* invincible, unconquerable.

invio *m* dispatch.

inviolabile *adj* inviolable.

invisibile *adj* invisible.

invitante *adj* inviting.

invitare *vt* to invite; to ask out; to take out.

invitato *m* guest.

invito *m* invitation.

invocare *vt* to invoke.

involontario *adj* involuntary.

involontario *adj* inadvertent, accidental, unwitting, unintentional.

involtino di fegato *m* faggot.

invulnerabile *adj* invulnerable.

inzuppare *vt* to drench, to soak, to dunk.

inzuppato *adj* waterlogged.

io *pron* I.

iodio *m* iodine.

iperbole *f* hyperbole.

ipermercato *m* hypermarket.

ipersensibile *adj* highly strung.

ipertensione *f* hypertension.

ipnosi *f* hypnosis.

ipnotico *adj* hypnotic.

ipnotismo *m* hypnotism.

ipnotizzare *vt* to hynotize, to mesmerize.

ipocondria *f* hypochondria.

ipocondriaco *m* hypochondriac

ipocrisia *f* hypocrisy.

ipocrita *m/f* hypocrite;

ipocrito *adj* hypocritical; **discorsi ipocriti** *mpl* cant.

ipodermico *adj* hypodermic.

ipoteca *f* mortgage.

ipotecare *vt* to mortgage.

ipotesi *f inv* hypothesis.

ipotetico *adj* hypothetical.

ippocastano *m* horse chestnut.

ippoglosso *m* halibut.

ippopotamo *m* hippopotamus.

ira *f* wrath.

irascibile *adj* irascible, cantankerous, bad-tempered, sharp-tempered.

irato *adj* irate.

iride *f* iris.

iris *f inv* iris.

ironia *f* irony.

ironico *adj* ironic.

irradiare *vt* to irradiate.

irraggiare *vt* to radiate.

irraggiungibile *adj* unattainable.

irragionevole *adj* irrational.

irragionevole *adj* unreasonable.

irrazionale *adj* unreasonable.

irreale *adj* unreal.

irreconciliabile *adj* irreconcilable.

irrecuperabile *adj* irretrievable.

irrefrenabile *adj* irrepressible.

irrefutabile *adj* unanswerable.

irregolare *adj* irregular.

irregolarità *f inv* irregularity.

irreligioso *adj* irreligious.

irremovibile *adj* unshakable.

irreparabile *adj* irrepairable.

irreprensibile *adj* blameless

irreprensibile *adj* irreproachable, unimpeachable.

irrequieto *adj* restive, restless, fidgety; **persona irrequieta** *f* fidget.

irresistibile *adj* irresistible.

irresoluto *adj* irresolute.

irresponsabile *adj* irresponsible, feckless.

irrestringibile *adj* unshrinkable.

irriconoscibile *adj* unrecognizable.

irrigare *vt* to irrigate.

irrigazione *f* irrigation.

irrigidire *vt* to stiffen; * *vr* ~**rsi** to stiffen.

irriguardoso *adj* inconsiderate, unthinking.

irrilevante *adj* immaterial.

irripetibile *adj* unrepeatable.

irrisorio *adj* paltry.

irritabile *adj* irritable, petulant, testy.

irritante *adj* irritating, annoying, aggravating; **sostanza ~** *f* irritant.

irritare *vt* to irritate, to aggravate, to vex.

irritato *adj* irritated, vexed.

irritazione *f* irritation.

irriverente *adj* irreverent, disrespectful, flippant.

irriverenza *f* irreverence.

irrompere *vi* (*fig*) to erupt.

irruvidire *vt* to roughen.

irruzione *f* raid; **fare ~ in** to raid *vt*.

iscrivere *vt* to enrol; * *vr* ~**rsi** to register; to enter for.

iscrizione *f* inscription; enrolment; membership; lettering.

Islam *m inv* Islam.

isola *f* island, isle.

isolamento *m* insulation; isolation, seclusion.

isolano *m* islander.

isolare *vt* to insulate; to isolate.

isolato *adj* insulated; marooned; ~ **acusticamente** soundproof.

ispessire *vt* to thicken.

ispettore *m* inspector.

ispezione *f* inspection.

ispido *adj* shaggy.

ispirare *vt* to inspire.

ispirazione *f* inspiration.

issare *vt* to hoist.

istantaneo *adj* instantaneous.

istante *m* instant.

isterectomia *f* hysterectomy.

isterico *adj* hysterical; **crisi isterica** *f inv* hysterics.

isterismo *m* hysteria.

istigare *vt* to instigate.

istigazione *f* instigation.

istintivo *adj* instinctive.

istinto *m* instinct.

istituire *vt* to institute, to establish.

istituto *m* institute, home; **~ superiore** *m* college.

istituzione *f* institution, establishment.

istmo *m* isthmus.

istrionico *adj* histrionic.

istruire *vt* to instruct, to educate.

istruttivo *adj* instructive.

istruttore *m* instructor.

istruzione *f* instruction, education, schooling; **~ superiore** *f* further education; **dare istruzioni a** *vt* to brief.

itinerante *adj* travelling.

itinerario *m* itinerary, route.

itterizia *f* jaundice.

iuta *f* jute.

IVA *f* VAT.

J

jazz *m* jazz.

jeans *mpl* jeans; **tessuto ~ m** denim.

jeep *f inv* jeep.

jet *m inv* jet.

jolly *m* joker.

judo *m* judo.

juke-box *m inv* juke-box.

K

K.O. *m inv* knock-out.

karate *m* karate.

ketchup *m* ketchup.

kilt *m inv* kilt.

kolossal *m* spectacular.

L

la *pron* her.

là *adv* there.

labbro *m* lip.

labirinto *m* labyrinth, maze.

laboratorio *m* laboratory.

laburista *adj* labour.

lacca *f* lacquer, hairspray.

laccetto *m* tab.

lacchè *m inv* lackey, footman.

laccio *m* (shoe)lace; tether.

lacerante *adj* piercing.

lacerare *vt* to lacerate.

laconico *adj* laconic.

lacrima *f* tear; **in lacrime** *adj* tearful.

lacrimogeno *adj*; **gas ~** *m* teargas.

lacuna *f* hiatus.

ladro *m* thief, burglar, crook.

ladruncolo *m* filcher.

laggiù *adv* yonder.

laghetto *m* pond.

lagnanza *f* grievance.

lago *m* lake, (*Scot*) loch.

laguna *f* lagoon.

laico *m* layman; **laici** *mpl* laity; * *adj* lay, secular.

laim *m* lime.

lama *f* blade.

lamb's wool *m* lambswool.

lambire *vi* to lap; * *vt* to wash

lamé *m inv* lamé.

lamentare *vt* to lament, to bewail, to bemoan; * *vr* **~rsi** to complain.

lamentela *f* complaint.

lamento *m* lament.

lamiera *f* sheet; **~ ondulata** *f* corrugated iron.

laminato *adj* laminated.

lampada *f* lamp; **~ a spirito** *f* blowlamp.

lampadario *m* chandelier.

lampadina *f* (light) bulb.

lampante *adj* self-evident.

lampeggiare *vi* to flash.

lampeggio *m*: **~ diffuso** sheet lightning.

lampo *m* flash; lightning.

lampone *m* raspberry, raspberry bush.

lana *f* wool; **di ~** *adj* woollen; **indumenti di ~** *mpl* woollens.

lancetta *f* pointer.

lancia *f* lance, spear.

lanciare *vt* to throw, to toss, to cast, to fling, to shoot, to bowl,

to pitch; * *vr* **~rsi** to dart, to dive.

lancinante *adj* stabbing, shooting.

lancio *m* throw; launch, blast-off; **rampa di ~** *f* launching pad.

languido *adj* languid; lackadaisical; **con gli occhi languidi** dewy-eyed.

languire *vi* to languish, to pine.

lanoso *adj* woolly.

lanterna *f* lantern.

lapidare *vt* to stone; to pelt with stones.

lapide *f* gravestone; tablet.

lapis *m* pencil.

lardo *m* lard.

larghezza *f* width, breadth, broadness; **nel senso della ~** *adv* breadthwise.

largo *adj* broad, wide; **al ~** offshore.

larice *m* larch.

laringe *f* larynx.

laringite *f* laryngitis.

larva *f* larva, grub.

lasciapassare *m inv* pass.

lasciare *vt* to leave, to let; to vacate, to quit; * *vr* **~rsi** to part.

lascito *m* bequest.

lascivo *adj* lascivious; lecherous; wanton.

laser *m inv* laser.

lassativo *m* laxative.

lasso *m*: **~ di tempo** *m* lag.

lastra *f* slab.

lastricare *vt* to pave.

latente *adj* latent, dormant.

laterale *adj* lateral, side, sideways.

latitudine *f* latitude.

lato *m* side.

latrare *vi* to bay.

latta *f* can, tinplate.

latte *m* milk; **~ in polvere** *m* dried milk; **~ cagliato** *m* curd(s); ~ **concentrato** *m* evaporated milk; ~ **detergente** *m* cleanser.

latteo *adj* milky; **Via Lattea** *f* Milky Way.

lattina *f* can, tin.

lattuga *f* lettuce.

laurea *f* degree; **consegna delle lauree** *f* graduation; * *vr* ~**rsi** to graduate.

laureato *m* graduate.

lava *f* lava.

lavabile *adj* washable.

lavabo *m* washbasin.

lavacristallo *m* windscreen washer.

lavaggio *m* washing; ~ **auto** car wash.

lavagna *f* blackboard.

lavanda *f* lavender.

lavanderia *f* laundry; ~ **automatica** *f* launderette.

lavandino *m* basin.

lavare *vt* to wash; to bathe (a wound); to sluice; to launder; ~ **a secco** to dry-clean; * *vi* ~ **i piatti** to do the washing up; * *vr* ~**rsi** to wash.

lavastoviglie *f inv* dishwasher.

lavata *f* wash.

lavativo *m* slacker.

lavatrice *f* washing machine.

lavello *m* sink; **piano del** ~ *m* draining board.

lavorare *vi* to work; to labour; ~ **troppo** to overwork.

lavoratore *m* worker; ~ **accanito** *m* workaholic.

lavoretto *m* odd job.

lavoro *m* work; job; labour; **duro** ~ *m* graft; **lavori stradali** *mpl* roadworks.

forza ~ *f* workforce; ~ **eccessivo** *m* overwork; ~ **preparatorio** *m* groundwork; **ora di** ~ *f* manhour.

leader *m* leader.

leale *adj* loyal.

lealtà *f* loyalty, allegiance.

lebbra *f* leprosy.

lebbroso *m* leper.

lecca lecca *m inv* lollipop.

leccapiedi *m/f* sycophant.

leccare *vt* to lick, to lap.

leccata *f* lick.

leccornia *f* titbit.

ledere *vt* to impinge on.

lega *f* league; ~ **per saldatura** *f* solder.

legale *adj* legal, lawful; * *f* **medicina** ~ *f* forensic medicine.

legalità *f* legality.

legalizzare *vt* to legalize.

legalmente *adv* legally.

legame *m* link, bond.

legamento *m* ligament.

legare *vt* to tie, to fasten, to bind, to rope, to strap, to tether, to lash; ~ **stretto** to truss.

legato *adj* bound.

legatura *f* slur.

legazione *f* legation.

legge *f* law; **senza leggi** *adj* lawless.

leggenda *f* legend.

leggendario *adj* legendary.

leggere *vt, vi* to read, to peruse.

leggermente *adv* lightly, slightly.

leggero *adj* light, flimsy, lightweight; faint; *vi* **prendere alla leggera** to trifle with.

leggibile *adj* legible; readable.

leggio *m* music stand.

legiferare *vt* to legislate.

legione *f* legion.

legislativo *adj* legislative; **corpo** ~ *m* legislature.

legislatore *m* legislator.

legislazione *f* legislation.

legittimare *vt* to legitimize.

legittimità *f* legitimacy.

legittimo *adj* legitimate; rightful.

legna *f* wood; ~ **da ardere** firewood.

legname *m* timber.

legno *m* wood; **di ~** *adj* wooden; **legni** *mpl* (*mus*) woodwind.

lei *pron* her, she; **di ~** hers; * *pers pron* you.

lendine *f* nit.

lente *f* lens; **~ d'ingrandimento** *f* magnifying glass.

lentezza *f* slowness.

lenticchia *f* lentil.

lentiggine *f* freckle.

lentigginoso *adj* freckled.

lento *adj* slow, sluggish; slack; backward (child).

lenza *f* fishing line.

lenzuolo *m* sheet.

leone *m* lion.

leonessa *f* lioness.

leopardo *m* leopard.

leporino *adj*: **labbro ~** *m* harelip.

lepre *f* hare.

lesbica *f* lesbian; (*sl*) dyke.

lesbico *adj* lesbian.

lesione *f* lesion; hurt.

lessare *vt* to boil.

lessico *m* lexicon.

letale *adj* lethal.

letame *m* muck.

letargico *adj* lethargic.

letargo *m* hibernation; **cadere in ~** *vi* to hibernate.

lettera *f* letter; **~ d'accompagnamento** *f* covering letter; **~ d'amore** *f* love letter; **lettere** *fpl* the arts; **dire** *or* **scrivere ~ per ~** *vi* to spell.

letterale *adj* literal.

letterario *adj* literary.

letteratura *f* literature.

lettino *m* cot.

letto *m* bed; **~ di piume** *m* feather bed; **~ di morte** *m* deathbed; **costretto a ~** *adj* bedridden.

lettore *m* reader.

lettura *f* reading; perusal; **sala di ~** *f* reading room.

leucemia *f* leukaemia.

leucisco *m*: **~ rosso** *m* roach.

leva *f* lever.

levatura *f* stature.

levigatezza *f* smoothness.

levriero *m* greyhound.

lezione *f* lesson.

lezioni *fpl* tuition.

li *pers pron* them.

lì *adv* there.

libbra *f* pound.

libellula *f* dragonfly.

liberale *adj* liberal.

liberalità *f* liberality; largesse.

liberamente *adv* freely.

liberare *vt* to liberate, to free, to unleash; to clear.

liberazione *f* liberation; deliverance; * *excl* **che ~!** good riddance!

libero *adj* free, unattached, unoccupied, vacant; **stanza libera** *f* vacancy; **segnale di ~** *m* dialling tone; **stile ~** (swim) crawl.

liberoscambismo *m* free trade.

libertà *f* liberty, freedom; **~ condizionale** *f* probation; **~ provvisoria** *f* parole; **in ~** *adv* at large.

libertino *m* libertine, rake.

libidine *f* lust.

libidinoso *adj* lustful, prurient; **espressione libidinosa** *f* leer.

libido *f inv* libido.

libraio *m* bookseller.

librarsi *vi* to soar; * *vr* to hover.

libreria *f* bookshop; bookcase.

libretto *m* libretto; booklet; **~ di circolazione** *m* logbook; **~ di risparmio** *m* passbook;

libro *m* book; **~ di testo** *m* textbook.

licenza *f* licence; leave.

licenziamento *m* dismissal; discharge; redundancy.

licenziare *vt* to dismiss, to sack, to fire, to discharge.
licenziato *adj* redundant.
licenzioso *adj* licentious.
lichene *m* lichen.
lieto *adj* pleased, glad, joyful, joyous.
lievitare *vi* to rise; **far ~** *vt* to leaven.
lievito *m* yeast; **~ in polvere** *m* baking powder.
ligneo *adj* ligneous.
ligustro *m* privet.
lilla *m inv* lilac.
lima *f* file.
limare *vt* to file.
limetta *f*: **~ di carta** *f* emery board; **~ per le unghie** *f* nail-file.
limetta *f* lime.
limitare *vt* to limit, to restrict, to confine.
limitazione *f* limitation, check.
limite *m* limit; **~ di velocità** *m* speed limit.
limiti *mpl* bounds.
limo *m* silt.
limonata *f* lemonade.
limone *m* lemon; **albero di ~** *m* lemon tree.
limousine *f inv* limousine.
limpido *adj* limpid.
lince *f* lynx; **dagli occhi di ~** *adj* eagle-eyed.
linciare *vt* to lynch.
linea *f* line; figure; **~ di demarcazione** *f* borderline; **~ secondaria** *f* (*rail*) branch line; **~ principale** *f* mainline.
lineare *adj* linear.
linfa *f* sap, lymph.
lingotto *m* ingot; **oro in lingotti** *m* bullion.
lingua *f* language; tongue; **~ madre** *f* mother tongue; **avere la ~ sciolta** *vt* to have the gift of the gab.
linguaggio *m* language, speech.

linguetta *f* flap, tab.
linguista *m/f* linguist.
linguistica *f* linguistics.
linguistico *adj* linguistic.
linimento *m* liniment.
lino *m* flax; linen; **seme di ~** *m* linseed.
linoleum *m* linoleum.
liofilizzato *adj* freeze-dried.
liquidare *vt* to liquidate; to clear; to sell off.
liquidazione *f* liquidation.
liquido *adj*, *m* liquid.
liquirizia *f* liquorice.
liquore *m* liqueur.
liquori *mpl* spirits.
lirico *adj* lyrical; operatic.
lisca *f* fishbone.
lisciare *vt* to smooth.
liscio *adj* smooth, smoothly, even, straight.
lista *f* list; roll; **~ nera** *f* blacklist; **~ dei vini** *f* wine list.
listino *m*: **~ prezzi** *m* price list.
litania *f* litany.
lite *f* row.
litigare *vi* to argue, to quarrel, to row, to wrangle, to fall out.
litigio *m* quarrel.
litigioso *adj* litigious, quarrelsome.
litografia *f* lithograph, lithography.
litorale *m* coast, coastline.
litre *m* litro.
liturgia *f* liturgy.
liuto *m* lute.
livellare *vt* to level; to equalize.
livello *m* level; **a ~ di** *adv* flush with; **ad alto ~** *adj* top level.
livido *m* bruise; * *adj* livid; **farsi un ~ a** *vt* to bruise.
livrea *f* livery.
lo *pron* him.
lobo *m* lobe.
locale *adj* local; **anestesia ~** *f* local anaesthetic; **amministrazione ~** *f* local government.

locali *mpl* premises.

località *f inv* locality.

localizzare *vt* to localize; **~ con esatezza** to pinpoint.

locanda *f* inn.

locandiere *m* innkeeper.

locomotiva *f* locomotive, engine.

locusta *f* locust.

lodare *vt* to praise, to commend.

lodevole *adj* laudable, praiseworthy, commendable, creditable, worthy.

loggia *f* lodge.

logica *f* logic.

logico *adk* logical.

logo *m inv* logo.

logoramento *m* wear.

logorarsi *vr* to wear out.

logoro *adj* effete.

lombaggine *f* lumbago.

lombata *f* loin.

lombrico *m* earthworm.

longevità *f* longevity.

longitudine *f* longitude.

lontananza *f* distance.

lontano *adj* distant, far, faraway; **più ~** farthest, furthest; *adv* farthest, furthest.

lontra *f* otter.

loquace *adj* loquacious, talkative, voluble, garrulous, comunicative.

loquacità *f* loquacity.

lordo *adj* gross.

loro pers *pron* you; them; * *poss adj* your(s), their; * *pron* your(s).

losanga *f* lozenge.

losco *adj* shifty.

lotta *f* fight; combat; battle; struggle; **~ libera** *f* wrestling.

lottare *vt* to fight, to struggle; * *vi* to struggle, to battle, to wrestle.

lottatore *m* wrestler.

lotteria *f* lottery, draw, sweepstake.

lotto *m* lot; **~ di terreno** *m* plot.

lozione *f* lotion.

lubrificante *m* lubricant.

lubrificare *vt* to lubricate, to grease.

lucchetto *m* padlock.

luccicare *vi* to glisten, to glitter, to gleam, to shimmer.

luccichio *m* gleam.

luccio *m* pike.

lucciola *f* firefly.

luce *f* light; **~ di giorno** *f* daylight; **~ di posizione** *f* sidelight.

lucente *adj* shining; gleaming; **~ e liscio** sleek.

lucentezza *f* gloss, shine, sheen.

lucernario *m* skylight.

lucertola *f* lizard.

lucidare *vt* to polish, to buff.

lucidato *adj* polished.

lucidata *f* polish.

lucido *adj* shiny, glossy; lucid; * *m* polish; **~ da scarpe** bootpolish.

lucrativo *adj* lucrative.

luglio *m* July.

lugubre *adj* lugubrious, mournful.

lui *pron* him, he.

lumaca *f* slug.

lume *m* **di candela** candlelight.

luminosità *f* brightness.

luminoso *adj* luminous, bright.

luna *f* moon; **~ piena** *f* full moon; **~ park** *m inv* funfair; **~ di miele** *f* honeymoon; **chiaro di ~** *f* moonlight.

lunare *adj* lunar.

lunatico *adj* moody.

lunedì *m inv* Monday.

lunga *f*: **di gran ~** far and away.

lunghezza *f* length; **per la ~** *adv* lengthways.

lungo *adj* long, lengthy, full-length.

lungomare *m* esplanade, prom(enade), front, seafront.

lungometraggio *m*: **a ~** *adj* full-length.

luogo *m* place; scene; **~ d'incontro** *m* venue; **fuori ~** *adj* inappropriate.

lupo *m* wolf.

luppolo *m* hop.

lusinga *f* flattery; **persuadere con le lusinghe** *vt* to inveigle.

lusingare *vt* to flatter.

lusinghe *fpl* flattery.

lusinghiero *adj* flattering, complimentary.

lusso *m* luxury.

lussuoso *adj* luxurious.

lussureggiante *adj* lush, luxuriant.

lustrare *vt* to shine, to polish.

lustrino *m* sequin, spangle.

lustro *m* lustre.

lutto *m* mourning; bereavement; **in ~** *adj* bereaved.

M

ma *conj* but; yet.

macabro *adj* grim; sick.

macadam *m*: **~ al catrame** *m* tarmac.

maccheroni *mpl* macaroni.

macchia *f* spot, smudge, stain; blot; taint; slur; **~ d'olio** *f* oil slick; **senza ~** *adj* unblemished.

macchiare *vt* to mark, to stain, to spot, to blot.

macchiato *adj* spotted.

macchina *f* machine; car; **~ fotografica** *f* camera; **~ a tre porte** *f* hatchback; **~ da scrivere** *f* typewriter.

macchinari *mpl* machinery.

macchinazione *f* machination.

macchinista *m* engine driver.

macchiolina *f* fleck, speck.

macedonia *f* fruit salad.

macellaio *m* butcher.

macellare *vt* to butcher, to slaughter.

macellazione *f* slaughter.

macelleria *f* butcher's shop.

macello *m* shambles.

macerare *vt* to macerate.

macerie *fpl* rubble.

macigno *m* boulder.

macina *f* millstone.

macinare *vt* to grind, to mill.

macinino *m* grinder.

macis *m*, *f* mace.

madre *f* mother.

madrelingua *f* native language.

madreperla *f* mother-of-pearl.

madrina *f* godmother.

maestà *f* majesty.

maestoso *adj* majestic, stately.

maestra *f* teacher, schoolmistress.

maestria *f* craftsmanship.

maestro *m* maestro; teacher, schoolmaster.

maga *f* sorceress.

magazzino *m* warehouse; stockroom; **grande ~** *m* department store; **~ doganale** *m* bonded warehouse.

maggio *m* May.

maggiorana *f* marjoram.

maggioranza *f* majority.

maggiordomo *m* butler.

maggiore *adj* elder, eldest; senior; extra; major; **mia sorella ~** my big sister; ***** *m* major.

magia *f* magic.

magico *adj* magic.

magistrale *adj* masterly.

magistrato *m* magistrate.

magistratura *f* judiciary.

maglia *f* jersey; stitch; mesh; **lavorare a** ~ *vi* to knit.

maglieria *f* knitwear.

maglietta *f* T-shirt.

maglione *m* jumper, sweater.

magnaccia *m inv* pimp.

magnanimità *f* magnanimity.

magnanimo *adj* magnanimous.

magnate *m* magnate, tycoon.

magnesia *f* magnesia.

magnesio *m* magnesium.

magnetico *adj* magnetic.

magnetismo *m* magnetism.

magnificare *vt* to extol.

magnificenza *f* magnificence.

magnifico *adj* magnificent, grand.

magniloquente *adj* bombastic.

mago *m* magician, wizard.

magro *adj* thin, lean, meagre; ~ **e forte** wiry.

mai *adv* never, ever.

maiale *m* pig, pork.

maionese *f* mayonnaise.

maiuscolo *adj* capital.

mal *m*: ~ **di mare** *m* seasickness; ~ **d'auto** *m* carsickness; **avere il** ~ **di mare** *vi* to be seasick.

malaccorto *adj* misguided.

malandato *adj* shabby.

malaria *f* malaria.

malaticcio *adj* sickly, unhealthy.

malato *adj* ill, sick, diseased.

malattia *f* illness, sickness, disease, malady

malavita *f* underworld.

malcontento *adj, m* malcontent.

male *m* harm, wrong, evil; **i mali** *mpl* the ills; **andato a** ~ *adj* off; **far** ~ *vi* to hurt.

maledetto *adj* damned, accursed, bloody.

maledire *vt* to curse.

maledizione *f* curse.

maleducato *adj* bad-mannered, ill-bred.

maleducazione *f* rudeness.

malefico *adj* malign.

malessere *m* malaise.

malevolenza *f* ill-will.

malevolo *adj* malevolent, acrimonious.

malfamato *adj* low, seamy.

malgrado *prep* despite; * *conj* in spite of.

maligno *adj* malignant, nasty, snide, spiteful, vicious.

malinconia *f* melancholy.

malinconico *adj* melancholy.

malincuore *adj*: **a** ~ *adv* unwillingly.

malinteso *m* misunderstanding, mix-up.

malizia *f* malice.

malizioso *adj* mischievous, roguish.

malleabile *adj* malleable, pliable.

malmenare *vt* to manhandle.

malridotto *adj* tatty.

malsano *adj* unhealthy.

malsicuro *adj* insecure.

malto *m* malt.

maltrattare *vt* to maltreat, to mistreat, to ill-treat.

malva *f* mallow; * *adj* mauve.

malvagio *adj* evil, evil-minded, wicked.

malvolentieri *adv* unwillingly, grudgingly.

malvone *m* hollyhock.

mamma *f* (*inf*) mummy; ~ **mia!** **futura** ~ *f* mother-to-be; *excl* oh dear!

mammella *f* breast; udder.

mammifero *m* mammal.

mammut *m inv* mammoth.

manager *m inv* manager.

manata *f* slap; **dare una** ~ **a** *vt* to whack.

mancante *adj* missing, deficient.

mancanza *f* lack; deficiency; want; default; **in ~ di** *prep* failing.

mancare *vt* to miss; * *vi* to lack; to want; to fail; to pass away, to pass on.

mancia *f* tip; gratuity; **dare la ~ a** *vt* to tip.

manciata *f* handful.

mancino *adj* left-handed.

mandare *vt* to send; **~ tutto all'aria** to upset the apple cart.

mandarino *m* mandarin; mandarine, tangerine.

mandato *m* writ; warrant; mandate; **~ di morte** *m* death warrant; **~ di comparizione** *m* summons.

mandolino *m* mandolin.

mandorla *f* almond.

mandria *f* herd.

mandrillo *m* wolf.

maneggevole *adj* manageable, manoeuvrable; **poco ~** unwieldy.

maneggiare *vt* to handle; to wield; to ply.

maneggio *m* stables.

manetta *f* manacle.

manette *fpl* handcuffs.

manganello *m* cudgel, truncheon, cosh.

manganese *m* manganese.

mangiabile *adj* edible.

mangiare *vt* to eat; **dare da ~ a** *vt* to feed.

mangiata *f* feed.

mangiatoia *f* manger, crib, trough.

mangime *m* feed.

mango *m* mango.

mania *f* mania, craze.

maniaco *adj* manic; * *m* maniac.

manica *f* sleeve; **la M~** the English Channel; **giro della ~** armhole; **senza maniche** *adj* sleeveless.

manichino *m* dummy.

manico *m* handle.

manicomio *m* madhouse, asylum.

manicotto *m* muff.

manicure *f inv* manicure.

maniera *f* manner.

maniero *m* manor.

manifestante *m* demonstrator.

manifestare *vt* to demonstrate, to manifest, to evince.

manifestazione *f* demonstration, manifestation, show.

manifesto *m* manifesto, poster.

manigoldo *m* ruffian.

manipolare *vt* to manipulate.

manipolazione *f* manipulation.

manna *f* godsend.

mannaggia *escl* blast.

mannaia *f* chopper, cleaver.

mano *f* hand; coat (of paint); **lavorazione a ~** *f* handiwork; **stretta di ~** *f* handshake; **a portata di ~** *adj* at hand; **a mani vuote** empty-handed; **di seconda ~** second-hand.

manodopera *f* labour, manpower.

manomettere *vi* to tamper.

manopola *f* knob.

manoscritto *m* manuscript.

manovale *m* labourer.

manovra *f* manoeuvre.

manovrare *vi*, *vt* to manoeuvre.

mansarda *f* attic.

mantella *f* cloak.

mantello *m* cape.

mantenere *vt* to maintain; to support; to keep; to hold; **~ i contatti con** to liaise.

mantenimento *m* maintenance.

mantice *m* bellows.

manuale *m* handbook, guide, manual; * *adj* manual.

manubrio *m* handlebars; dumbbell.

manufatto *m* artefact.

manutenzione *f* maintenance; upkeep.

manzo *m* beef; steer.

mappa *f* map; **tracciare una ~** *vt* to map.

mappamondo *m* globe.

maratona *f* marathon.

marca *f* make, brand.

marcato *adj* pronounced; rugged.

marcatore *m* marker.

marchiare *vt* to brand.

marchio *m* hallmark, trademark.

marcia *f* gear; march.

marciapiede *m* pavement.

marciare *vi* to march.

marcio *adj* rotten.

marcire *vi* to rot.

marciume *m* rot.

marco *m* mark.

mare *m* sea; **~ lungo** *m* swell; **d'alto ~** *adj* ocean-going.

marea *f* tide; **alta ~** *f* high tide; **di ~** *adj* tidal.

maresciallo *m* marshall.

margarina *f* margarine.

marginale *adj* marginal.

margine *m* border, margin.

marijuana *f* marijuana.

marina *f* navy; marina, marine; **~ mercantile** *f* merchant navy.

marinaio *m* sailor, mariner, seaman.

marinare *vt* to marinate; **~ la scuola** to play truant.

marinaresco *adj*: **canzone marinaresca** *f* shanty.

marinata *f* marinade.

marino *adj* marine.

marito *m* husband.

marittimo *adj* maritime.

marketing *m* marketing.

marmellata *f* jam; **~ di arance** *f* marmalade.

marmo *m* marble.

marrone *adj* brown; **~ rossiccio** *inv* russet.

marsupiale *m*, *adj* marsupial.

marsupio *m* pouch.

martedì *m inv* Tuesday; **~ grasso** *m* Shrove Tuesday.

martellare *vt* to hammer.

martello *m* hammer; **~ da fabbro** *m* sledgehammer; **~ pneumatico** *m* pneumatic drill.

martin *m inv*: **~ pescatore** *m* kingfisher.

martire *m* martyr.

martirio *m* martyrdom.

martora *f* marten.

marzapane *m* marzipan.

marziale *adj* martial.

marzo *m* March.

mascalzone *m* rogue, rascal; villain.

mascara *m inv* mascara.

mascella *f* jaw.

maschera *f* mask; usherette; **festa in ~** *f* fancy dress party; **~ antigas** *f* gasmask.

mascherare *vt* to mask; to disguise; to gloss over.

mascherata *f* masquerade.

maschiaccio *m* tomboy.

maschile *adj* male, masculine; * *m* masculine.

maschilismo *m* chauvinism.

maschilista *m* chauvinist.

maschio *adj*, *m* male; (*zool*) buck.

masochista *m/f* masochist.

mass media *m* pl mass media.

massa *f* mass, body, bulk.

massacrare *vt* to massacre, to slaughter.

massacro *m* massacre, slaughter.

massaggiare *vt* to massage.

massaggiatore *m* masseur.

massaggiatrice *f* masseuse.
massaggio *m* massage.
massiccio *adj* massive.
massima *f* maxim.
massimizzare *vt* to maximize.
massimo *adj* utmost, maximum; * *m* utmost.
massone *m* mason; freemason.
massoneria *f* masonry; freemasonry.
mastello *m* tub.
masticare *vt* to masticate, to chew.
mastino *m* inglese *m* mastiff.
mastro *m* master; libro ~ *m* ledger.
masturbarsi *vr* to masturbate.
masturbatore *m* wanker.
masturbazione *f* masturbation.
matassa *f* skein.
matematica *f* mathematics, maths.
matematico *adj* mathematical; * *m* mathematician.
materasso *m* mattress.
materia *f* matter; subject.
materiale *adj* material; bodily; * *m* material.
materialismo *m* materialism.
maternità *f* motherhood, maternity.
materno *adj* motherly, maternal.
matinée *f inv* matinée.
matita *f* pencil.
matrice *f* stencil, counterfoil, stub.
matricola *f* fresher.
matrigna *f* step-mother.
matrimoniale *adj* matrimonial; **letto ~** *m* double bed; **camera ~** *f* double room.
matrimonio *m* marriage; wedding; **certificato di ~** *m* marriage certificate.
mattatoio *m* slaughterhouse.
matterello *m* rolling pin.

mattina *f* morning, forenoon.
matto *adj* crazy, lunatic; * *m* lunatic, (*sl*) nut, nutcase.
mattone *m* brick.
mattonella *f* tile.
mattutino *m* matins.
maturare *vi* to ripen, to mellow; * *vr* **~rsi** to mature.
maturità *f* maturity.
maturo *adj* mature, ripe, mellow.
matusa *m inv* old fogey, square.
mausoleo *m* mausoleum.
mazza *f* club (golf), bat; mace.
mazzo *m* bunch.
mazzolino *m* posy, spray.
mazzuolo *m* mallet.
me *pron* me.
meccanica *f* mechanics.
meccanico *m* mechanic, engineer; * *adj* mechanical.
meccanismo *m* mechanism, works.
meccanizzare *vt* to mechanize.
mecenate *m/f* patron.
medaglia *f* medal.
medaglione *m* medallion; locket.
media *mpl* media; * *f* average; **sopra la ~** *adj* above par.
mediare *vt* to mediate.
mediatore *m* mediator; broker.
mediazione *f* mediation; brokerage.
medicare *vt* to medicate.
medicato *adj* medicated.
medicina *f* medicine; drug.
medicinale *adj* medicinal; * *m* drug.
medico *m* doctor; physician; **~ di famiglia** *m* family doctor; * *adj* medical.
medievale *adj* medieval.
medio *adj* average, medium, mean, middling.
mediocre *adj* mediocre, middling, pedestrian.
mediocrità *f* mediocrity.

meditare *vi* to meditate, to cogitate.

meditativo *adj* meditative.

meditazione *f* meditation.

mediterraneo *adj* Mediterranean.

medusa *f* jellyfish.

megafono *m* megaphone.

megalomane *m/f* megalomaniac.

meglio *adv* better, best; ~ **così** so much the better.

mela *f* apple; ~ **selvatica** *f* crab apple.

melagrana *f* pomegranate.

melanzana *f* aubergine.

melassa *f* treacle, molasses.

melma *f* slime, ooze, mire.

melmoso *adj* slimy.

melo *m* apple tree.

melodia *f* melody, tune.

melodioso *adj* melodious, tuneful.

melodramma *m* melodrama.

melone *m* melon.

membrana *f* membrane.

membro *m* member, fellow.

memorabile *adj* memorable; **giorno** ~ *m* red-letter day.

memorandum *m* *inv* memorandum.

memoria *f* memory; **imparare a** ~ *vt* to memorize; **a** ~ *adv* by rote.

mendicante *m/f* beggar.

mendicare *vt* to beg.

menestrello *m* minstrel.

meningite *f* meningitis.

meno *prep* less; minus; * *adj* fewer; less; * *adv* least; less; * *pron* less; * **a** ~ **che** *conj* unless.

menomazione *f* handicap, disability.

menopausa *f* menopause.

mensa *f* canteen.

mensile *adj* monthly.

mensola *f* bracket; cantilever;

~ **del caminetto** *f* mantelpiece.

menta *f* mint; ~ **peperita** *f* peppermint.

mentale *adj* mental.

mentalità *f* *inv* mentality.

mentalmente *adv* mentally.

mente *f* mind; **di** ~ **aperta** *adj* open-minded.

mentire *vi* to lie.

mento *m* chin; **doppio** ~ *m* double chin.

mentore *m* mentor.

mentre *conj* as, whereas, while.

menù *m* *inv* menu.

menzione *f* mention.

menzogna *f* lie, falsehood.

meraviglia *f* marvel.

meraviglioso *adj* marvellous, great, smashing.

mercantile *adj* mercantile.

mercato *m* market, marketplace; ~ **nero** black market; ~ **azionario** *m* stock market.

merce *f* merchandise.

mercenario *adj*, *m* mercenary.

merceria *f* haberdashery.

merciaio *m* haberdasher.

merci *fpl* goods.

mercoledì *m* *inv* Wednesday.

mercurio *m* mercury, quicksilver.

merda *f* shit.

meridiana *f* sundial; * *adj*, *m* meridian.

meridionale *adj* south.

meridione *m* south.

meringa *f* meringue.

meritare *vt* to merit, to deserve.

meritatamente *adv* deservedly.

meritato *adj* well-deserved.

meritevole *adj* deserving.

merito *m* merit.

meritocrazia *f* meritocracy.

meritorio *adj* meritorious.

merlango *m* whiting.

merlo *m* blackbird.

merluzzo *m* cod; **olio di fegato di ~** *m* cod-liver-oil.

meschinità *f* pettiness, narrow-mindedness;

meschino *adj* mean, narrow-minded, sordid.

mescolanza *f* mix.

mescolare *vt* to mix, to shuffle, to jumble, to mingle, to stir; * *vr* **~rsi** to hobnob.

mescolata *f* shuffle.

mese *m* month.

messa *f* mass.

messaggero *m* messenger.

messaggio *m* message.

messale *m* missal.

messinscena *f* act, sham.

mestiere *m* craft.

mestiere *m* occupation, trade.

mesto *adj* rueful.

mestolo *m* ladle, scoop.

mestruazione *f* menstruation.

mestruazioni *fpl* period.

meta *f* destination; (rugby) try.

metà *f inv* half; * *adj* half; mid; **a ~ prezzo** *adj*, *adv* half-price; **a ~ strada** *adj* halfway.

metabolismo *m* metabolism.

metafisica *f* metaphysics.

metafisico *adj* metaphysical.

metafora *f* metaphor.

metaforico *adj* metaphoric(al).

metallico *adj* metallic.

metallo *m* metal.

metallurgia *f* metallurgy.

metamorfosi *f inv* metamorphosis.

metano *m* methane.

metanolo *m* wood alcohol.

meteora *f* meteor.

meteorite *m* meteorite.

meteorologia *f* meteorology.

meteorologico *adj* meteorological.

meteorologo *m* weatherman.

meticcio *m* half-caste.

metodico *adj* methodical.

metodo *m* method.

metraggio *m* footage.

metrico *adj* metric.

metro *m* metre; **~ a nastro** *m* tape measure.

metrò *m inv* underground railway.

metropoli *f inv* metropolis.

metropolitana *f* underground railway.

metropolitano *adj* metropolitan.

mettere *vt* to put; **~ insieme** to lump together; to concoct; **~ via** to put away; to stand; to place; * *vr* **~rsi** to don.

mezz'ora *f* half-hour.

mezzaluna *f* half-moon, crescent.

mezzanino *m* mezzanine.

mezzanotte *f* midnight.

mezzo *m* middle, medium, mean ; *adj* half; **in ~ a** *prep* midst.

mezzi *mpl* wherewithal.

mezzogiorno *m* noon, midday.

mi *pron* me.

mia poss *adj* my.

miagolare *vi* to mew.

miagolio *m* mew.

micidiale *adj* deadly; murderous.

micio *m* pussy.

microbo *m* germ, microbe.

microfono *m* microphone.

microonda *f* microwave.

microscopico *adj* microscopic.

microscopio *m* microscope.

midollo *m* marrow.

miele *m* honey.

mietere *vt* to reap.

mietitore *m* reaper.

mietitrice *f* (combine) harvester.

miglio *m* mile; millet.

miglioramento *m* improvement.

migliorare *vt* to improve; t

better; * *vi* to improve.

migliore *adj* better, best, topmost; * *m* best.

migrare *vi* to migrate.

migratore *adj* migratory.

migrazione *f* migration.

milionario *m* millionaire.

milione *m* million.

milionesimo *m* millionth.

militante *m/f* militant.

militare *adj* military; * *vi* to militate.

milizia *f* militia.

mille *adj, m* thousand.

millennio *m* millennium.

millepiedi *m inv* centipede, millipede.

millesimo *adj, m* thousandth.

milligrammo *m* milligramme.

millilitro *m* millilitre.

millimetro *m* millimetre.

milza *f* spleen.

mimare *vt, vi* to mime.

mimetizzazione *f* camouflage.

mimo *m* mime.

mina *f* mine.

minaccia *f* threat, menace.

minacciare *vt* to threaten, to menace.

minaccioso *adj* menacing, forbidding.

minare *vt* to mine; to undermine.

minato *m*: **campo ~** minefield.

minatore *m* miner, coalminer.

minerale *m* mineral; **acqua ~** *f* mineral water; **~ grezzo** *m* ore; * *adj* mineral.

mineralogia *f* mineralogy.

minestra *f* soup.

mingherlino *m* weakling; * *adj* skinny.

miniatura *f* miniature.

miniera *f* mine; **~ di carbone** coalmine, colliery.

minima *f* minimum.

minimizzare *m* understatement; * *vt* to minimize; to play

down, to underplay, to soft-pedal.

minimo *adj* least; minimal; * *m* least; **andare al ~** *vi* to tick over.

ministeriale *adj* ministerial.

ministero *m* ministry.

ministro *m* minister; clergyman; **Primo ~** *m* Prime Minister.

minoranza *f* minority.

minore *adj* minor, lesser, younger.

minorenne *m/f* minor, juvenile; * under-age.

minorile *adj* juvenile.

minuetto *m* minuet.

minugia *f*: **corda di ~** catgut.

minuscolo *adj* tiny, minute, dainty, diminutive, slight.

minuto *adj* minute, tiny; fine; **minuta e graziosa** petite; * *m* minute.

minuzioso *adj* thorough.

mio *poss adj* my; *poss pron* mine.

miope *adj* short-sighted, nearsighted, myopic.

miopia *f* short-sightedness.

miracolo *m* miracle, wonder.

miracoloso *adj* miraculous.

miraggio *m* mirage.

miriade *f* myriad.

mirino *m* viewfinder, sight.

mirra *f* myrrh.

mirtillo *m* bilberry.

mirto *m* myrtle.

misantropo *m* misanthropist.

miscela *f* mixture, blend.

miscellanea *f* miscellany.

mischia *f* scrum.

mischiare *vt* to blend.

miscuglio *m* concoction.

miseria *f* poverty, want, misery; pittance.

misericordia *f* mercy.

misericordioso *adj* merciful.

misero *adj* poor.

misfatto *m* misdeed.
misogino *m* misogynist.
missile *m* missile.
missionario *m* missionary.
missione *f* mission.
misterioso *adj* mysterious.
mistero *m* mystery.
mistico *adj* mystic(al); * *m* mystic.
misto *adj* mixed.
mistura *f* mixture.
misura *f* size; measure, measurement; step; **fatto su ~** *adj* tailor-made.
misurare *vt* to measure; to gauge.
misurazione *f* measurement.
mite *adj* mild; meek.
mitigare *vt* to mitigate.
mitigazione *f* mitigation.
mito *m* myth.
mitologia *f* mythology.
mitra *f* mitre.
mitragliatore *m* submachine gun.
mitragliatrice *f* machine gun.
mittente *m/f* sender.
mobile *adj* mobile, moving.
mobili *mpl* furniture, furnishings.
mobilità *f* mobility.
mobilitare *vt* to mobilize.
mocassino *m* moccasin.
moccio *m* snot.
moccioso *m* brat; * *adj* snotty.
moda *f* fashion, vogue; **alla ~** *adj* fashionable; **fuori ~** *adj* unfashionable, out-of-date.
modanatura *f* moulding.
modellare *vt* to model, to fashion.
modello *m* pattern; model; mock-up.
moderare *vt* to temper.
moderato *adj* moderate; sparing; * *m* moderate.
moderazione *f* moderation.
modernizzare *vt* to modernize.

modernizzazione *f* modernization.
moderno *adj* modern.
modestia *f* modesty.
modesto *adj* modest, unassuming.
modifica *f* modification.
modificare *vt* to modify.
modista *f* milliner.
modo *m* way; mode; fashion; (*gr*) mood; **grosso ~** *adv* broadly; **in questo ~** so; **in qualche ~** somehow.
modulare *vt* to modulate.
modulazione *f* modulation.
modulo *m* form; module.
moffetta *f* skunk.
mogano *m* mahogany.
moglie *f* wife.
mohair *m* mohair.
molare *m* molar.
molecola *f* molecule.
molestare *vt* to molest.
molla *f* spring; **a ~** *adj* clockwork.
mollare *vt* to release; to ditch.
molle *adj* limp.
molleggiato *adj* springy.
molletta *f* clothes peg, peg; hairclip.
mollo *m*: **mettere a ~** *vt* to soak.
mollusco *m* mollusc.
molo *m* jetty, quay.
moltiplicare *vt* to multiply.
moltitudine *f* host, throng, multitude.
molto *adj* much; * *pron* much; **sto ~ meglio** I am a great deal better; * *adv* a lot; very; much.
molti *pron* many.
momentaneo *adj* momentary.
momento *m* moment; momentum; time; **dell'ultimo ~** *adj* last minute.
monaco *m* monk.
monarca *m* monarch.
monarchia *f* monarchy.

monastero *m* monastery.

monastico *adj* monastic.

mondano *adj* worldly.

mondiale *adj* world, world-wide.

mondo *m* world.

monello *m* urchin.

moneta *f* coin; currency.

monetario *adj* monetary.

mongolfiera *f* hot air balloon.

mongoloide *m/f* mongol.

monitor *m inv* monitor.

monocolo *m* monocle.

monocromatico *adj* mono-chrome.

monografico *adj*: **saggio ~** *m* memoir.

monografio *m* monograph.

monolocale *adj*: **appartamento ~** *m* studio apartment.

monologo *m* monologue.

monopattino *m* scooter.

monopolio *m* monopoly.

monopolizzare *vt* to monopolize.

monosillabo *m* monosyllable.

monossido *m* monoxide.

monotonia *f* monotony; sameness; flatness.

monotono *adj* monotonous, drab, humdrum, unvaried.

monouso *adj* disposable; throwaway.

monsone *m* monsoon.

montacarichi *m* lift, elevator, hoist.

montaggio *m* assembly; **catena di ~** assembly line.

montagna *f* mountain; **montagne russe** big dipper.

montagnoso *adj* mountainous.

montante *adj* rising; incoming (tide); * *m* upright.

montare *vt* to assemble; to mount.

montato *adj* assembled; big-headed.

montatura *f* frame.

monte *m* mount; **~ di pietà** *m* pawnshop.

monticello *m* knoll.

montone *m* ram; sheepskin; *m* mutton.

montuoso *adj* mountainous; **zona ~** *f* highlands.

monumentale *adj* monumental.

monumento *m* monument, memorial.

moquette *f* (fitted) carpet.

mora *f* bramble; blackberry.

morale *adj* moral; **principi morali** *mpl* morals; * *m* morale.

moraleggiante *adj* sanctimonious.

moraleggiare *vi* to moralize.

moralista *m* moralist.

moralità *f* morality.

morbidezza *f* softness.

morbido *adj* soft.

morbillo *m* measles.

morboso *adj* morbid.

mordere *vt* to bite.

morente *adj* dying.

morfina *f* morphine.

morire *vi* to die.

mormorare *vt*, *vi* to murmur.

mormorio *m* murmur; babbling.

moroso *m* defaulter.

morsa *f* vice.

morsetto *m* clamp; **stringere con un ~** *vt* to clamp.

morso *m* bite; bit (horse).

mortaio *m* mortar.

mortale *adj* mortal; deadly; killing; *m/f* mortal.

mortalità *f* mortality.

morte *f* death; dying.

mortificare *vt* to mortify.

mortificato *adj* contrite.

mortificazione *f* mortification, contrition.

morto *adj* dead.

mosaico *m* mosaic.

mosca *f* fly.
moscerino *m* midge.
moschea *f* mosque.
moscone *m* bluebottle.
mossa *f* move.
mostra *f* display; exhibition.
mostrare *vt* to show
mostro *m* monster.
mostruosità *f* monstruosity.
mostruoso *adj* monstrous.
motel *m inv* motel.
motivare *vt* to motivate.
motivazione *f* motivation.
motivo *m* reason, motive, grounds, cause, motif, score.
moto *m* motion.
moto *f inv.* (*fam*) motorbike.
motocicletta *f* motor-cycle.
motocross *m* motocross; **gara di ~** *f* scramble.
motolancia *f* launch.
motore *m* motor, engine.
motoscafo *m* motorboat; **~ da corsa** *m* speedboat.
motteggiare *vi* to quip.
motto *m* motto.
mousse *f inv* mousse.
movibile *adj* movable.
movimentato *adj* eventful, hectic; **una carriera movimentata** *f* a chequered career.
movimento *m* movement, motion.
mozzafiato *adj* breathtaking.
mozzare *vt* to dock.
mozzicone *m* cigarette end, cigarette butt, stub.
mozzo *m* hub.
mucca *f* cow.
mucchio *m* heap, pile, mound, stack.
muco *m* mucus.
mucoso *adj* mucous.
muffa *f* fungus, mildew, mould.
muffola *f* mitten.
muggire *vi* to bellow, to low, to moo.
muggito *m* bellow, moo.

mughetto *m* lily of the valley.
mugnaio *m* miller.
mugugnare *vi* to bellyache.
mugugno *m* grouse.
mulinello *m* eddy; reel.
mulino *m* mill; **~ a vento** *m* windmill.
mulo *m* mule.
multa *f* fine; **~ per sosta vietata** *f* parking ticket.
multare *vt* to fine.
multiplo *adj, m* multiple.
moltiplicazione *f* multiplication.
mummia *f* mummy.
municipale *adj* municipal.
municipio *m* town hall.
munificenza *f* munificence.
munifico *adj* bountiful.
munizioni *fpl* munitions.
muovere *vt* to move; to wriggle; * *vi* to move; * *vr* **~rsi** to stir.
murale *adj* mural; **pittura ~** *f* mural.
muratore *m* bricklayer, builder, mason.
muratura *f* masonry.
muro *m* wall.
musa *f* muse.
muschio *m* moss; musk; **bacca del ~** *f* cranberry.
muscolare *adj* muscular.
muscolo *m* muscle.
muscoli brawn.
muscoloso *adj* sinewy.
muscoso *adj* mossy.
museo *m* museum, gallery.
museruola *f* muzzle.
musica *f* music; **~ pop** *f* pop music.
musicale *adj* musical.
musicista *m/f* musician.
muso *m* muzzle, smout; face.
mussola *f* muslin.
mussolina *f* gossamer.
muta *f* moulting; **fare la ~** *vi* to moult.
mutabile *adj* fickle.

mutamento *m* switch.
mutande *fpl* pants, knickers.
mutandine *fpl* panties, briefs.
mutante *adj*, *m* mutant.
mutare *vi* to change.
mutazione *f* mutation; **subire una ~** *vi* to mutate.

mutevole *adj* changing.
mutilare *vt* to mutilate.
mutilato *m* cripple; **lasciare ~** *vt* to cripple.
mutilazione *f* mutilation.
mutismo *m* dumbness.
muto *adj* mute, dumb.

N

nacchere *fpl* castanets.
naftalina *f* naphthalene; **pallina di ~** *f* mothball.
nailon *m* nylon.
nano *m* midget, dwarf.
napalm *m* napalm.
nappa *f* tassel.
narciso *m* narcissus.
narcotico *adj*, *m* narcotic.
narice *f* nostril.
narrare *vt* to narrate.
narrativa *f* fiction.
narrativo *adj* narrative.
narrazione *f* narration, narrative.
nasale *adj* nasal.
nascita *f* birth; **luogo di ~** *m* birthplace; **diritto di ~** birthright.
nascondere *vt* to hide, to conceal, to cover, to screen, to secrete.
nascondiglio *m* hiding place, hideaway.
nascosto *adj* hidden, covert.
nasello *m* hake.
naso *m* nose.
nastro *m* ribbon; tape; **~ adesivo** *m* adhesive tape; **~ isolante** *m* insulating tape; **~ trasportatore** *m* conveyor belt.
nasturzio *m* nasturtium.
nata *adj* née; **~ Brown** née Brown.

Natale *m* Christmas, Xmas; * **biglietto di ~** *m* Christmas card; **canto di ~** *m* carol.
natale *adj* native.
natali *mpl* parentage.
natica *f* buttock.
Natività *f* Nativity
nativo *m* native
nato *adj* born; **~ morto** *adj* stillborn.
natura *f* nature; wildlife; **~ morta** *f* still life.
naturale *adj* natural; unaffected; **in grandezza ~** *adj* lifesized.
naturalista *m/f* naturalist.
naturalizzare *vt* to naturalize.
naturalmente *adv* of course.
naufragio *m* (ship)wreck; sinking.
naufrago *m* castaway.
nausea *f* nausea; **fino alla ~** ad nauseam.
nauseabondo *adj* nauseous.
nauseare *vt* to nauseate, to sicken.
nauseato *adj* squeamish, queasy.
nautico *adj* nautical.
navale *adj* naval.
navata *f* nave, aisle.
nave *f* ship, boat; **~ traghetto** *f* car ferry; **~ ammiraglia** *f* flagship; **~ da guerra** battleship, warship; **~ cisterna** *f*

tanker; ~ **in disarmo** f hulk.

navetta f shuttle.

navigare vt to navigate; * vi to navigate, to sail.

navigazione f navigation, shipping; **tecnica di ~** f seamanship.

nazionale adj national; **a livello ~** nationwide.

nazionalismo m nationalism.

nazionalista adj, m/ f nationalist.

nazionalità f inv nationality.

nazionalizzare vt to nationalize.

nazione f nation.

nazista adj, m/ f Nazi.

né conj neither, nor; * adv nor, neither, either; * adj neither.

neanche adv either; * conj neither.

nebbia f fog.

nebbioso adj foggy.

nebuloso adj nebulous.

nécessaire m case, kit; ~ **da toilette** m inv toilet bag.

necessariamente adv necessarily.

necessario adj necessary; * **rendere ~** vt to necessitate.

necessità f necessity, must.

necrofago adj necrophagous; **animale ~** m scavenger.

necrologio m obituary.

nefasto adj fatal.

negare vt to deny.

negativa f (gr; foto) negative.

negativo adj negative.

negazione f negation, negative.

négligé m inv negligee.

negligente adj negligent, careless, remiss, slack.

negligenza f negligence, malpractice, slackness.

negoziante m/ f storekeeper.

negozio m shop.

negra f Negress.

negro adj, m Negro.

nemico m enemy, foe.

nemmeno conj neither.

neo m mole, beauty spot.

neon m neon; **insegna al ~** f neon light.

neonato adj newborn, baby.

nepotismo m nepotism.

neppure conj neither.

nero adj, m black.

nervo m nerve.

nervoso adj nervous, jumpy.

nesso m relationship; **senza ~** adj unrelated.

nessuno pron none, nobody.

nettamente adv outright.

nettare m nectar.

netto adj net, outright, pronounced.

netturbino m dustman.

neutrale adj neutral.

neutralità f neutrality.

neutralizzare vt to neutralize, to counteract.

neutro adj neuter, neutral.

neutrone m neutron; **bomba a ~** f neutron bomb.

neve f snow; **palla di ~** f snowball; **pupazzo di ~** m snowman.

nevicare vi to snow.

nevischio m sleet.

nevoso adj snowy.

nevrosi f inv neurosis.

nevrotico adj, m neurotic.

nicchia f niche.

nichel m nickel.

nichilista m/ f nihilist.

nicotina f nicotine.

nidificare vi to nest.

nido m nest; ~ **d'aquila** m eyrie; ~ **d'ape** m honeycomb.

niente pron none; * excl non f ~ never mind.

night m inv nightclub.

ninfea f waterlily.

ninfomane adj, f nymphomaniac.

ninnananna f lullaby.

ninnolo *m* trinket, bauble.

nipote *m* nephew; *f* niece; *m/ f* grandchild.

nipotina *f* granddaughter.

nipotino *m* grandson.

nitido *adj* clear, sharp.

nitrire *vi* to neigh, to whinny.

nitrito *m* neigh.

no *adv* no; * *adj* nessuno.

nobile *adj*, *m* noble.

nobiltà *f* nobility; **piccola ~** *f* gentry.

nobiluomo *m* nobleman.

nocca *f* knuckle.

nocciola *f* hazelnut; * *adj* hazel.

nocciolina *f* peanut.

nocciolo *m* hazel tree.

noce *f* walnut; *m* walnut tree; **~ moscata** *f* nutmeg.

nocivo *adj* noxious, harmful.

nodo *m* knot, crux.

nodoso *adj* knotty, gnarled.

nodulo *m* lump.

noi *pers pron* us, .we

noia *f* bore; boredom.

noioso *m* bore; * *adj* dull, boring, tedious; **diventare ~** *vi* to pall.

noleggiare *vt* to hire, to rent, to charter.

noleggio *m* hire, charter.

nolo *m* rental, freight.

nomade *m/ f* nomad.

nome *m* name, first name, forename; **secondo ~** *m* middle name; **~ da ragazza** *m* maiden name; **~ depositato** *m* trade name.

nomina *f* nomination.

nominale *adj* nominal.

nominare *vt* to name, to nominate.

nominativo *adj*, *m* nominative.

non *adv* not.

noncurante *adj* heedless.

nondimeno *adv* nonetheless.

nonna *f* grandmother, granny.

nonno *m* grandfather, granddad.

nonni *mpl* grandparents.

nono *adj*, *m* ninth.

nonostante *conj* in spite of; * *prep* notwithstanding; **ciò ~** *adv* nevertheless, notwithstanding.

nontiscordardimé *m inv* forget-me-not.

nord *adj* north; **del ~** northern, northerly; **verso ~** northerly; * *adv* northwards; * *m* north.

nordest *m* northeast.

nordovest *m* northwest.

norma *f* norm; **~ di vita** *f* ethos; **~ del regolamento comunale** *f* by-law.

normale *adj* normal.

normalmente *adv* ordinarily.

nostalgia *f* nostalgia; **avere la ~ di casa** *vt* to be homesick.

nostalgico *adj* wistful.

nostro *adj* our; * *pron* ours.

nostromo *m* boatswain.

nota *f* note.

notaio *m* notary; conveyancer.

notare *vt* to note, to spot.

notazione *f* notation.

notevole *adj* notable, substantial, remarkable.

notevolmente *adv* notably.

notifica *f* notification.

notificare *vt* to notify; to serve (warrant, etc).

notizia *f* news, word.

notiziario *m* news.

notizie *fpl* news.

noto *adj* well-known; distinguished.

notorietà *f* notoriety.

notte *f* night, night-time; **di ~** by night, overnight; * *excl* **buona ~** good night; * *adv* ogni ~ nightly; * *adj* di ogni ~ nightly.

notturno *adj* nocturnal.

novantesimo *adj*, *m* ninetieth.

nove *adj, m inv* nine.
diciannove *adj, m inv* nineteen.
novembre *m* November.
novità *f* novelty.
novizio *m* novice.
nozione *f* notion.
nozze *fpl* wedding.
nube *f* cloud.
nubile *adj* single or unmarried woman; celibate (woman).
nuca *f* nape.
nucleare *adj* nuclear.
nucleo *m* nucleus, core.
nudista *adj, m/ f* nudist.
nudità *f* nudity.
nudo *adj* nude, naked, bare.
nulla *m* nil, naught.
nullità *f* nonentity, nobody.
nullo *adj* null, void, invalid.
numerale *m* numeral.
numerare *vt* to number.
numerico *adj* numerical.
numero *m* number; size; issue; turn; ~ **di telefono** *m* telephone number.
numeroso *adj* numerous.
nunzio *m* nuncio; ~ **apostolico** *m* legate.
nuocere *vt* to harm.
nuora *f* daughter-in-law.
nuotare *vt, vi* to swim.
nuotata *f* swim.
nuotatina *f* dip.
nuoto *m* swimming.
nuovo *adj* new; ~ **arrivato** *m* newcomer; * **di** ~ *adv* anew.
nutriente *adj* nourishing, nutritious.
nutrimento *m* nourishment, sustenance.
nutrire *vt* to nourish, to feed, to nurture, to foster, to cherish (a hope, etc).
nuvola *f* cloud.
nuvoloso *adj* cloudy.
nuziale *adj* nuptial, bridal.

O

o *conj* or, either.
oasi *f inv* oasis.
obbligare *vt* to oblige.
obbligato *adj* indebted.
obbligatorio *adj* mandatory, set, obligatory, compulsory.
obbligazione *f* debenture.
obbligo *m* obligation.
oberato *adj* overwhelmed; ~ **di debiti** burdened with debts.
obesità *f* obesity.
obeso *adj* obese, gross.
obiettare *vt* to object.
obiettivo *adj* objective, unprejudiced; * *m* target; lens.
obiezione *f* objection; * **sollevare** ~ **i** *vi* to demur.
obitorio *m* morgue, mortuary.
oblio *m* oblivion.
obliquo *adj* oblique.
oblò *m inv* porthole.
oblungo *adj* oblong.
oboe *m* oboe.
obsoleto *adj* obsolete.
oca *f* goose; **maschio dell'~** *m* gander; **pelle d'~** *f* goose pimples.
occasionale *adj* occasional.
occasione *f* occasion, chance, opportunity.
occhiali *mpl* glasses, spectacles, goggles; ~ **da sole** *mp* dark glasses, sunglasses.
occhiata *f* look, glance; **dar un'~ a** *vt* to glance.
occhieggiare *vt* to ogle.

occhiello *m* buttonhole.

occhio *m* eye; **chiudere un ~ su** *vt* to overlook.

occidentale *adj* west, western.

occorrente *adj, m* requisite.

occultamento *m* cover-up.

occupare *vt* to take up, to occupy.

occuparsi *vr* to deal with, to look after, to attend to.

occupato *adj* busy.

occupatore *m* occupier; **~ abusivo** *m* squatter.

occupazione *f* occupation, employment.

oceanico *adj* oceanic.

oceano *m* ocean.

ocra *f* ochre.

oculista *m/f* oculist.

ode *f* ode.

odiare *vt* to hate.

odio *m* hatred, hate.

odioso *adj* hateful, horrid, odious.

odissea *f* odyssey.

odontoiatria *f* dentistry.

odore *m* odour, smell; **~ forte** *m* tang.

offendere *vt* to offend.

offensivo *adj* offensive.

offerta *f* bid, offer, contribution, tender; **~e** *fpl* bidding (auction).

offesa *f* offence.

offeso *adj* upset.

officina *f* garage, workshop.

offrire *vt* to offer, to treat, to bid, to tender, to stand; **~si** *vr* to volunteer.

offset *m inv* offset.

offuscare *vt* to blur.

oftalmico *adj* ophthalmic.

oggetto *m* object, (*comm*) re; **~ esposto** *m* exhibit.

oggi *adv, m inv* today.

oggigiorno *adv* nowadays.

ogni *adj* every, each.

ognuno *pron* each, everybody.

oleandro *m* oleander.

oleoso *adj* oily.

olfatto *m* smell.

oliare *vt* to oil.

oliatore *m* oilcan.

olio *m* oil; **quadro a ~** *m* oil painting; **~ d'oliva** *m* olive oil; **~ solare** *m* suntan oil; **~ di ricino** castor oil.

oliva *f* olive.

olmo *m* elm.

olocausto *m* holocaust.

oltraggiare *vt* to revile.

oltraggiare *vt* to outrage.

oltre *prep* besides, aside from, beyond, past;* *adv* farther; **andare ~** *vt* to overshoot.

oltremarino *adj, m* ultramarine.

oltrepassare *vt* to overstep.

omaggio *m* homage; **in ~** complimentary.

ombelico *m* navel.

ombra *f* shade, shadow.

ombrello *m* umbrella, brolly (*fam Brit*).

ombretto *m* eyeshadow.

ombroso *adj* shady, skittish.

omelia *f* homily.

omeopatia *f* homoeopathy.

omeopatico *m* homoeopath.

omeopatico *adj* homoeopathic.

omettere *vt* to omit.

omicida *adj* homicidal.

omicidio *m* murder, homicide; **~ colposo** *m* manslaughter.

omissione *f* omission.

omogeneità *f* homogeneity.

omogeneo *adj* smooth, homogeneous.

omonimo *m* homonym, namesake.

omosessuale *adj, m/f* homosexual, (*fam*) gay.

oncia *f* ounce.

onda *f* wave; **~ anomala** *f* tidal wave; **lunghezza d'~** *f* wavelength; * **a ~ lunga** *adj* long-wave; **a onde corte** *adj* short-wave; **a onde medie** *adj* medium-wave.

ondata *f* tide, wave, gush, surge; **~ di caldo** *f* heatwave.

ondeggiamento *m* sway.

ondeggiare *vi* to sway.

ondulato *adj* corrugated, undulating, wavy.

onere *m* burden, onus.

onestà *f* honesty.

onesto *adj* honest, straight, square.

onisco *m* woodlouse.

onnipotente *adj* omnipotent.

onnipresente *adj* ubiquitous.

onnivoro *adj* omnivorous.

onorare *vt* to grace, to honour.

onorario *adj* honorary.

onorario *m* fee, retainer.

onore *m* honour, credit; **Vostro ~** *m* Your Worship.

onorevole *adj* honourable.

opaco *adj* opaque, matt.

opale *m/f* opal.

opera *f* work, opera.

operaio *adj* blue-collar; **classe ~ a** *f* working class; ** m* worker, workman.

operare *vi* to operate.

operativo *adj* operational, operative.

operazione *f* operation, transaction.

operoso *adj* industrious.

opinione *f* opinion, belief.

oppio *m* opium.

opporsi *vr* to oppose.

opportunista *m/f* opportunist.

opportuno *adj* fitting, timely, opportune, expedient.

opposizione *f* opposition.

opposto *m, adj* opposite.

oppressione *f* oppression.

oppressivo *adj* oppressive.

oppressore *m* oppressor.

opprimente *adj* oppressive, heavy.

opprimere *vt* to oppress, to burden.

optare *vi* to opt (for).

opulento *adj* opulent.

opuscolo *m* booklet, pamphlet.

opzione *f* option.

ora *adv, conj* now; ** f* hour, time, period; **ogni ~** hourly.

oracolo *m* oracle.

orale *adj, m* oral.

oralmente *adv* orally.

orario *m* timetable, schedule; **in senso ~** *adv* clockwise; **fuso ~** *m* time zone.

oratore *m* speaker, orator.

orazione *f* oration.

orbettino *m* slowworm.

orbita *f* orbit; socket.

orbitare *vi* to orbit.

orchestra *f* orchestra.

orchestrale *adj* orchestral.

orchestrare *vt* to score music.

orchidea *f* orchid.

orco *m* bogey man, ogre.

orda *f* horde.

ordinanza *f* odinance.

ordinare *vt* to order; to ordain.

ordinario *adj* ordinary.

ordinato *adj* neat, orderly, tidy.

ordinazione *f* order, order form; ordination.

ordine *m* order, command; tidiness; **~ gerarchico** *m* pecking order; **~ pubblico** *m* law and order; **di prim'~** *adj* first rate; **mettere in ~** *vt* to tidy.

orecchiabile *adj* catchword.

orecchino *m* earring.

orecchio *m* ear; **che non ha** *adj* tone-deaf; **suonare a ~** to play by ear; **mal d'~i** *m* earache.

orecchioni *mpl* mumps.

orefice *m* goldsmith.

orfano *adj, m* orphan.

orfanotrofio *m* orphanage.

organetto *m* barrel organ.

organico *adj* organic.

organigramma *m* flow chart.

organismo *m* organism.

organista *m/f* organist

organizzare *vt* to organize, to arrange, to plan, to put on, to run.

organizzazione *f* organization, outfit.

organo *m* organ.

orgasmo *m* orgasm, climax.

orgia *f* orgy.

orgoglio *m* pride.

orgoglioso *adj* proud.

orientale *adj* oriental, easterly, eastern.

orientare *vt* to orientate.

oriente *m* east.

orifizio *m* orifice.

origano *m* oregano.

originale *adj, m* original.

originalità *f* originality.

origine *f* origin; **avere ~ in** *vi* to originate from.

origliare *vt* to eavesdrop.

orina *f* urine.

orinare *vi* to urinate.

orizzontale *adj* horizontal.

orizzonte *m* horizon.

orlo *m* rim, brim, brink, verge, edge; hem.

orma *f* trail, track, footprint.

ormeggiare *vi* to berth, to moor, to tie up.

ormeggio *m* berth.

ormone *m* hormone.

ornamentale *adj* ornamental.

ornamento *m* ornament.

ornare *vt* to ornament.

ornato *adj* ornate.

ornitologo *m* bird watcher.

oro *m* gold; **tempi d'~** *mpl* heyday; **d'~** *adj* golden.

orologiaio *m* watchmaker.

orologio *m* clock; **~ da polso** *m* wristwatch.

oroscopo *m* horoscope.

orrendo *adj* ghastly, horrendous, lurid.

orribile *adj* horrible, hideous.

orrore *m* horror; **film dell'~** *m inv* horror film.

orsacchiotto *m* teddy bear.

orso *m* bear.

ortaggio *m* vegetable.

ortensia *f* hydrangea.

ortica *f* nettle.

orticaria *f* rash.

orticoltore *m* horticulturist.

orticoltura *f* horticulture.

orto *m* vegetable garden, kitchen garden.

ortodossia *f* orthodoxy.

ortodosso *adj* orthodox.

ortografia *f* orthography.

ortografia *f* spelling.

ortopedia *f* orthopaedics.

ortopedico *adj* orthopaedic.

orzaiolo *m* sty(e).

orzo *m* barley.

osare *vt* to dare.

oscenità *f* obscenity.

osceno *adj* obscene, lewd.

oscillare *vi* to vacillate.

oscillare *vi* to sway, to oscillate, to waver, to seesaw.

oscillazione *f* swing.

oscurare *vt* to obscure, to darken.

oscurità *f* dark, darkness, blackness.

oscuro *adj* obscure.

ospedale *m* hospital.

ospitale *adj* hospitable.

ospitalità *f* hospitality.

ospitare *vt* to put up.

ospite *m/f* host, guest, visitor.

ospizio *m* hospice.

osseo *adj* bony.

osservanza *f* observance.

osservare *vt* to remark, to observe.

osservatore *m* observer.

osservatorio *m* observatory.

osservazione *f* remark, observation, comment; **punto d'~** *m* vantage point.

ossessionare *vt* to obsess.
ossessivo *adj* obsessive.
ossidare *vt* to tarnish, to oxidize.
ossificarsi *vr* to ossify.
ossigeno *m* oxygen.
osso *m* bone.
ostacolare *vt* to thwart, to hamper, to impede.
ostacolo *m* hurdle, stumbling block, obstacle.
ostaggio *m* hostage.
ostello *m* hostel.
ostentazione *f* flourish.
osteopatia *f* osteopathy.
osteria *f* (*fam*) boozer.
ostetrica *f* midwife.
ostetricia *f* midwifery.
ostia *f* host; wafer.
ostile *adj* hostile, unfriendly, inimical.
ostilità *f* hostility.
ostinato *adj* obstinate, wilful.
ostinazione *f* wilfulness.
ostracizzare *vt* to ostracize.
ostrica *f* oyster.
ostruire *vt* to obstruct.
ostruzione *f* obstruction.
ottagono *m* octagon.
ottano *m* octane.
ottanta *adj, m* eighty.
ottantesimo *adj* eightieth.

ottava *f* octave.
ottavino *m* piccolo.
ottavo *adj* eighth.
ottenere *vt* to gain, to get, to obtain.
ottenibile *adj* obtainable.
ottica *f* optics.
ottico *m* optician; * *adj* optic(al).
ottimale *adj* optimum.
ottimista *adj* optimistic, sanguine; * *m/f* optimist.
ottimistico *adj* optimistic.
ottimo *adj* fine.
otto *adj, m* eight; **oggi a ~** a week today.
ottobre *m* October.
ottone *m* brass.
ottundere *vt* to dull.
otturare *vt* to fill.
otturatore *m* shutter.
otturazione *f* filling.
ottuso *adj* obtuse, thick, dull.
ouverture *f inv* overture.
ovaia *f* ovary.
ovale *adj, m* oval.
overdose *f inv* overdose.
ovest *adj, m* west, westward.
ovile *m* sheepfold.
ovvio *adj* obvious.
oziare *vi* to laze.
ozono *m* ozone.

P

pacato *adj* subdued, sedate.
pacchiano *adj* tawdry.
pace *f* peace, calm.
pacificare *vt* to mollify.
padella *f* frying pan; bedpan.
padiglione *m* pavilion, summerhouse.
padre *m* father.
padrino *m* godfather.
padrona *f* mistress.

padronanza *f* mastery, grasp
padrone *m* boss, master.
paesaggio *m* scenery, lan
scape.
paese *m* land, country, villag
abitante di ~ *m* villager.
paesino *m* hamlet.
paffuto *adj* chubby.
paga *f* wages.
pagabile *adj* due.

pagamento *m* payment; ~ **unico** *m* lump sum.

pagano *m* heathen.

pagare *vi*, *vt* to pay; **far** ~ to charge; **pagherò** I.O.U.; **far** ~ **troppo** *vi* to overcharge; **da** ~ *adj* owing.

pagella *f* report.

pagina *f* page; **prima** ~ *f* front page.

paglia *f* straw; **copertura di** ~ *f* thatch.

pagliaccio *m* clown.

pagliaio *m* haystack.

paglierino *adj* straw-coloured, buff.

paglietta *f* boater.

paio *m* pair.

pala *f* shovel.

palafreniere *m* groom.

palazzo *m* mansion; ~ **per uffici** *m* office block.

palco *m* stage, dais, (theatre) box; (*zool*) antler; ~ **dell'orchestra** *m* bandstand; ~ **improvvisato** *m* soapbox.

palese *adj* glaring, manifest, undisguised.

palestra *f* gym.

paletta *f* spade, slice, scoop.

palio *m* contest; **mettere in** ~ *vt* to raffle.

palissandro *m* rosewood.

palizzata *f* stockade.

palla *f* ball; ~ **di canone** *f* cannonball; ~ **di neve** *f* snowball.

pallacanestro *f* basketball.

pallavolo *f* volleyball.

pallido *adj* pale, wan.

palloncino *m* balloon; (**alcotest**) breathalyzer.

pallone *m* ball.

palo *m* stake, goalpost.

palpebra *f* eyelid.

palpitare *vi* to beat, to throb.

palude *f* swamp, bog, marsh.

paludoso *adj* marshy, swampy; **zona paludosa** *f* fen.

pancetta *f* bacon; **una fettina di** ~ *f* rasher of bacon.

panchina *f* bench.

pancia *f* belly, tummy.

panciotto *m* waistcoat.

pane *m* bread, loaf; ~ **tostato** *m* toast; ~ **integrale** brown bread; ~ **di Spagna** *m* sponge (cake).

pangrattato *m* breadcrumbs.

panico *m* flap.

panificio *m* bakery.

panino *m* roll, sandwich; ~ **dolce** *m* bun.

panna *f* cream; ~ **montata** *f* whipped cream.

panno *m* baize.

pannocchia *f* corn on the cob.

pantaloni *mpl* trousers.

pantano *m* morass.

pantofola *f* slipper.

papà *m* (*inf*) dad(dy).

papalina *f* skullcap.

pappa *f* mush, feed.

pappagallino *m* budgerigar.

papparsi *vr* to scoff.

parabrezza *m* *inv* windscreen.

paracenere *m* fender.

paradiso *m* heaven, paradise.

parafango *m* mudguard.

parafulmine *m* lightning conductor.

paragonare *vt* to liken, to compare.

paragone *m* comparison.

paralume *m* shade.

paralume *m* lampshade.

paramento *m* vestment.

paramontura *f* facing.

paranco *m* tackle.

paraocchi *mpl* blinkers.

parapiglia *f* scramble; ~ **generale** *f* free-for-all.

parare *vt* to save.

parascolastico *adj* extracurricular.

parasole *m* sunshade.

parassita *m/f* hanger-on.

parata f parade; (sport) save; ~ **militare** f tattoo; ~ **aerea** f flypast.

paraurti m inv bumper.

paravento m screen.

parco m park; ~ **comunale** m common.

parecchio adj several; **parecchi** adj umpteen.

pareggiare vi to equalize, to draw, to tie.

pareggio m draw, tie, equalizer.

parente m/f relation, relative; ~ **più stretto** m next of kin; ~ **acquisito** m in-law; **parenti** mpl kin.

parentela f relationship.

parentesi f inv bracket.

parere vi to seem; **a quanto pare** adv seemingly, apparently; * ~ m opinion.

parete f wall.

pari adj, equal, even; **essere alla ~ con** vi to be level with; **ragazza alla ~** f au pair.

paria m inv untouchable.

parlamentare m/f member of parliament; ~ **di secondo piano** m backbencher.

parlare vi to talk, to tell, to speak; ~ **a vanvera** to babble.

parlata f speech.

parodia f travesty, burlesque.

parola f word; **parole** fpl lyrics; **senza ~** adj speechless; ~ **d'ordine** f watchword; ~ **per ~** adj, adv verbatim.

parolaccia f swearword, four-letter word; **parolacce** fpl bad language.

parrucca f wig.

parrucchiere m hairdresser.

parrucchino m toupee.

parsimonia f thrift.

parsimonioso adj thrifty.

parte f part, share, side; **da qualche ~** adv somewhere;

da ~ adv aside; **da queste parti** adv hereabouts; **in gran ~** adv largely; **dall'altra ~** adv, prep across; **d'altra ~** then again; **a ~** adj, adv apart.

partecipare vi to participate; ~ **al dolore** vi to commiserate.

partecipazione f participation, involvement.

parteggiare vi to side.

partenza f departure.

particolare adj special, especial, distinctive; * m detail.

partire vi to leave, to depart, to start.

partita f lot, consignment; match, game; ~ **a quattro** f foursome; ~ **doppia** adj double-entry.

partitura f score.

parto m birth, confinement.

partorire vt to give birth, to bear.

parvenu m inv upstart.

pascolare vi to graze.

Pasqua f Easter.

passaggio m lift; ~ **pedonale** m walkway; **di ~** adj through.

passamontagna m inv balaclava.

passare vi, vt to pass, to go by; to relay; to strain.

passata f wipe.

passatempo m hobby.

passe-partout m inv skeleton key.

passeggero adj fleeting.

passeggiare vi to walk.

passeggiata f walk.

passeggiatina f stroll.

passera f flounder.

passerella f gangway, foot bridge.

passero m sparrow.

passino m strainer.

passionale adj passionate, sultry.

passione f eagerness.

passo *m* step, pace, stride, tread, footstep; **fare un ~** *vi* to step; **~ lento** *m* crawl; **~ stretto** *m* defile; **camminare a grandi passi** *vi* to stride;

pastella *f* batter.

pastello *m* crayon.

pasticceria *f* cake shop.

pasticciere *m* confectioner.

pasticcino *m* cake.

pasticcio *m* pie; hash, mess, botch, (*fam*) cock-up; **fare un ~ di** *vt* to botch; to bungle.

pastiglia *f* lozenge.

pasto *m* meal; **~ a prezzo fisso** *m* table d'hôte.

pastoie *fpl* shackles.

pastone *m* mash.

pastorale *m* crook (bishop's).

pastore *m* shepherd; clergyman, vicar.

patata *f* potato, (*fam*) spud; **patate lesse** *fpl* boiled potatoes; **~ fritta** *f* chip.

patatina *f* crisp.

patella *f* limpet.

patente *f* licence; **~ di guida** *f* driving licence.

paternità *f* fatherhood.

paterno *adj* fatherly.

patibolo *m* scaffold, gallows.

patria *f* home, homeland, fatherland.

patrigno *m* step-father.

patrimonio *m* heritage, estate, wealth.

pattinaggio *m* skating; **~ sul ghiaccio** *m* ice-skating; **pista di ~** *f* rink.

pattinare *vi* to skate.

pattino *m* skate; **~ a rotelle** *m* roller skate.

pattumiera *f* dustpan.

paura *f* fear; **avere ~ di** *vt* to fear.

pauroso *adj* fearful.

pausa *f* stop, rest.

pavimentare *vt* to floor.

pavimento *m* floor.

pavoneggiarsi *vr* to swagger, to strut.

paziente *m*, *adj* patient; **~ esterno** *m* outpatient.

pazienza *f* forbearance.

pazzia *f* madness, folly, fad, lunacy.

pazzo *adj* demented, mad, insane, lunatic.

peccaminoso *adj* sinful.

peccare *vi* to sin.

peccato *m* shame, sin.

peccatore *m* sinner.

pecora *f* ewe, sheep; **~ nera** *f* black sheep.

peculiarità *f inv* idiosyncracy.

pedaggio *m* toll.

pedagogia *f* education.

pedinare *vt* to shadow, to tail, to trail.

peggio *adj*, *adv*, *m/f* worse, worst.

peggiorare *vt* to worsen, to compound.

peggiore *adj*, *m/f* worse, worst.

pelare *vt* to fleece, to rip off.

pelle *f* skin, leather; **~ di mucca** cowhide; **lasciarci la ~** *vi* to bite the dust.

pellerossa *m/f* redskin; **giovane guerriero ~** *m* brave.

pelliccia *f* fur, fur coat.

pellicciaio *m* furrier.

pellicina *f* cuticle.

pellicola *f* skin, film.

pelo *m* hair, fur, bristle, nap; **senza peli** *adj* hairless.

peloso *adj* hairy, furry.

peluche *f* plush; **di ~** *adj* fluffy.

peluria *f* fluff, fuzz.

pena *f* punishment; **~ capitale** *f* capital punishment; **~ di morte** death penalty.

pendenza *f* slant, incline; **essere in ~** *vi* to dip.

pendere *vi* to slant, to hang, to lean.

pendio m slope, tilt, hillside.

pendolare m commuter; **fare il ~** vi to commute.

penetrare vt to penetrate.

penitenza f forfeit.

penna f pen; feather; **~ a sfera** ballpoint pen.

pennarello m felt-tip pen.

pennellata f dab.

pennello m brush; **~ da barba** m shaving brush.

pennino m nib.

pennone m flagpole.

penoso adj distressing, lamentable, grievous.

pensare vi to think, to expect.

pensatore m thinker.

pensiero m thought, thinking.

pensieroso adj thoughtful.

pensionante m/f boarder, lodger.

pensionato adj retired; * m pensioner.

pensione f pension, retirement; superannuation; boarding house; **mandare in ~** vt to retire; **andare in ~** vi to retire; **~ familiare** f guesthouse; **essere a ~ da** to board.

pentagramma m staff.

Pentecoste f Whit.

pentimento m repentance.

pentirsi vr to repent, to rue.

pentito adj repentant.

pentola f saucepan.

penzolare vi to swing.

pepe m pepper; **~ della Giamaica** allspice.

per prep for, from, to, through.

percepibile adj discernible, noticeable.

perchè conj why, because, what for.

perciò adv thus.

percorrere vt to walk.

percorso m route.

percuotere vt to thrash.

perdente m underdog.

perdente m/f loser.

perdere vt to lose; to miss; to leak; to forfeit; to shed; to waste.

perdersi vt to go astray.

perdita f waste; leak; write-off; loss.

perdonabile adj excusable.

perdonare vt to forgive, to condone.

perdono m forgiveness.

perfetto adj perfect, flawless.

perfido adj wicked.

perfino adv even.

pergamena f scroll.

pericolo m danger, distress; **mettere in ~** vt to jeopardize, to endanger.

pericoloso adj dangerous, unsafe.

periferia f suburbia, outskirts.

periferico adj outlying.

periodico m journal.

periodo m period, spell, time.

perizia f expertise, survey.

perlina f bead.

perlustrare vt to search.

permaloso adj touchy.

permanente adj permanent.

permesso m leave.

permettere vt to allow, to enable; * vr **~rsi** afford.

permissività f laxity.

permissivo adj lax.

perno m swivel.

perplessità f bewilderment.

perplesso adj puzzled, bemused; **lasciare ~** vt to mystify, to fox.

perquisire vt to frisk, to search.

perquisizione f search.

perseguitare vt to dog, to hound; **~ ingiustamente** vt to victimize.

perseverare vi to soldier on.

persiana f shutter.

persistente adj lingering, niggling.

personaggio *m* character.
personale *m* staff.
personificazione *f* epitome.
perspicace *adj* discerning, acute.
perspicacia *f* acumen, insight.
pessimo *adj* abominable.
persuadere *vt* to persuade, to induce.
pertinente *adj* relevant; **non ~** *adj* irrelevant.
pertinenza *f* relevance.
pertosse *f* whooping cough.
pesante *adj* heavy, hefty.
pesantemente *adv* heavily.
pesare *vt*, *vi* to weigh.
pesca *f* fishing.
pescare *vi*, *vt* to fish.
pescatore *m* fisherman.
pesce *m* fish; **~ rosso** *m* gold fish.
pescecane *m* shark.
peschereccio *m* trawler.
pescivendolo *m* fishmonger.
pesciolino *m* small fish; **~ d'acqua dolce** *m* minnow.
pesista *m* weightlifter.
peso *m* weight, encumbrance; **~ leggero** *m* lightweight; **eccedenza di ~** *f* overweight; **~ medio** *m* middle weight; **sostenere il ~ di** *vt* to bear the brunt of.
pessimo *adj* wretched, lousy.
pestare *vi* to tread, to stamp.
peste *f* terror, scamp.
petardo *m* cracker, banger, squib.
petroliera *f* oil tanker.
petrolio *m* oil.
pettegolezze *fpl* gossip.
pettegolo *m* gossip.
pettinare *vt* to comb.
pettinato *m* worsted.
pettinatura *f* hairdo.
pettine *m* comb; (*zool*) scallop.
pettirosso *m* robin.
petto *m* breast, chest, bust, bos-

om; **~ a doppio ~** *adj* double-breasted.
pezzetto *m* scrap.
pezzo *m* piece, bit, snatch; **bel ~** *m* chunk; **venire in pezzi** *vi* to come apart; **~ grosso** *m* bigwig.
piacente *adj* good-looking.
piacere *vt* to please; **non ~** *vt* to dislike; * *m* pleasure; **~!** how do you do!; **mi fa molto ~ vedere**… I am glad to see….
piacevole *adj* nice, agreeable.
piaga *f* blight, sore.
piagnucolare *vi* to snivel, to whimper, to grizzle.
piagnucolio *m* whimper.
piagnucoloso *adj* snivelling.
pianerottolo *m* landing.
piangere *vt*, *vi* to cry, to weep, to howl, to mourn.
piano *m* floor, storey; scheme; **primo ~** *m* close-up, foreground; **al ~ inferiore** *adj* downstairs; * *adv* slowly; * *adj* slow; level.
pianta *f* map; plant; **~ del piede** *f* sole (of foot).
piantare *vt* to drop, to jilt.
piantato *adj* planted; **ben ~** *adj* strapping, burly.
pianterreno *m* ground floor.
piantime *m* seedling.
pianto *m* cry.
piastra *f* hotplate.
piastrella *f* tile; **a piastrelle** *adj* tiled.
piastrellare *vt* to tile.
piattino *m* saucer.
piatto *m* plate, dish; turntable; * *adj* flat, level.
piazza *f* square.
piazzale *m* forecourt.
piazzare *vt* to station.
piccante *adj* spicy, hot.
picche *fpl* spades.
picchiare *vt* to thump, to hit, to sock, to bash.

picchiata *f* nosedive, swoop; scendere in ~ *vi* to swoop.

picchio *m* woodpecker.

piccione *m* pigeon; ~ **viaggiatore** *m* carrier pigeon.

picco *m* peak; **a** ~ *adj* sheer.

piccolezza *f* smallness.

piccolino *adj* smallish.

piccolo *adj* small, little; **farsi** ~ **per la paura** *vi* to cringe.

piccozza *f* ice axe.

pidocchio *m* louse.

piede *m* foot; ~ **di porco** *m* crowbar; **a piedi** *adj* walking; **in piedi** *adj* standing.

piedestallo *m* mount.

piega *f* crease, fold, twist.

piegare *vt* to bend, to fold; * *vr* ~**rsi** to bend, to fold.

pieghevole *adj* collapsible, folding.

pieno *adj* full.

pietanza *f* dish.

pietoso *adj* sorry.

pietra *f* stone; ~ **miliare** *f* milestone; ~ **angolare** *f* cornerstone; ~ **tombale** *f* tombstone; **mettiamoci una ~ sopra** let bygones be bygones.

pietrisco *m* grit.

pigione *f* rent.

pigna *f* cone.

pignolo *adj* fastidious, fussy, finicky, niggling.

pigrizia *f* laziness, idleness.

pigro *adj* lazy, idle.

pila *f* battery, torch.

pilota *m* pilot; **secondo ~** *m* copilot; ~ **collaudatore** *m* test pilot.

pince *f inv* tuck, dart.

ping-pong *m* table tennis.

pinguedine *f* stoutness.

pinna *f* fin, flipper.

pinza *f* tongs.

pinzette *fpl* tweezers.

pio *adj* godly.

pioggerella *f* drizzle.

pioggia *f* rain.

piolo *m* rung.

piombo *m* lead.

piovano *adj* of rain; **acqua piovana** *f* rainwater.

piovere *vi* to rain.

piovigginare *vi* to drizzle.

piovoso *adj* wet, rainy.

piovra *f* octopus.

pipa *f* pipe; ~ **di radica** *f* briar pipe.

pipistrello *m* bat.

piroetta *f* twirl.

pirofilo *adj* ovenproof.

piroscafo *m* steamer; ~ **da carico** *m* freighter.

piscina *f* swimming pool, baths.

pisolino *m* doze, nap; **schiacciare un ~** *vi* to nap.

pista *f* scent; track; runway; ~ **d'atterraggio** *f* landing strip; ~ **di patinaggio** *f* ice rink, skating rink.

pistola *f* pistol, gun.

pitagorico *adj* Pythagoric; **tavola pitagorica** *f* multiplication table.

pittoresco *adj* scenic.

più *adv*, *adj* more, most; **in ~** *adj* extra, spare; **sempre di ~** more and more.

piuma *f* feather; **piume** *fpl* down.

piumone *m* duvet.

piuttosto *adv* sooner, somewhat, rather.

pizzicare *vt* to nip, to sting.

pizzico *m* nip, touch.

pizzo *m* lace.

placare *vt* to salve, to appease; * *vr* ~**rsi** to abate.

placenta *f* afterbirth.

plaid *m inv* rug.

planare *vi* to glide.

planata *f* glide.

plasmare *vt* to mould.

plastica *f* plastic; ~ **facciale** *f* face-lift.

platea *f* (*teat*) stalls.

plotone *m* squad; ~ **d'esecu-zione** *m* firing squad.

poco *m* a little; **pochi** *mpl* few; **a ~ a ~** inch by inch.

podere *m* holding.

podio *m* rostrum.

poesia *f* verse.

poggiare *vi* to rest.

poggio *m* hillock.

poi *adv* then.

poiana *f* buzzard.

poichè *conj* inasmuch as, for.

pois *m inv* spot; **a ~** *adj* spotted.

polemico *adj* argumentative.

polena *f* (*naut*) figurehead.

polizia *f* police, (*fam*) fuzz; **agente di ~** (*Brit*) constable; **corpo di ~** *m* constabulary.

poliziotto *m* policemen, (*fam*) cop, bobby.

polizza *f* policy; ~ **d'assicura-zione** *f* insurance policy.

pollaio *m* hen-house.

pollame *m* fowl.

pollice *m* inch; thumb.

pollo *m* chicken.

polmone *m* lung.

polo *m* pole; ~ **nord** *m* North Pole.

polpetta *f* rissole; ~ **di carne** *f* meatball.

polpettone *m* meatloaf.

polsino *m* cuff, wristband.

polso *m* wrist.

poltiglia *f* slush.

poltrona *f* armchair.

polvere *f* dust, powder; ~ **da sparo** *f* gunpowder.

polveroso *adj* dusty.

pomellato *adj* dappled.

pomeriggio *m* afternoon.

pomo *m* knob.

pomodoro *m* tomato.

pompa *f* pump; pomp; **impre-sario di pompe funebri** *m* undertaker.

pompelmo *m* grapefruit.

pompiere *m* fireman; **corpo dei pompieri** *m* fire brigade.

ponce *m* punch; **specie di ~** *m* toddy.

ponente *m* west; **di ~** *adj* westerly.

ponte *m* bridge; ~ **sospeso** *m* suspension bridge; ~ **aereo** *m* airlift.

popolo *m* people.

poppa *f* stern; **a ~** *adj* aft, astern.

porcellana *f* china.

porcellino *m* piglet; ~ **d'India** *m* guinea pig.

porcile *m* sty.

porco *m* pig, hog.

porre *vt* to lay, to set.

porro *m* wart; leek.

porta *f* door, gateway; ~ **d'in-gresso** *f* front door; ~ **poste-riore** backdoor; ~ **a vento** *f* swinging door.

portacenere *m inv* ashtray.

portachiavi *m inv* key-ring.

portacipria *m inv* compact.

portaerei *f inv* aircraft carrier.

portafinestra *f* French window.

portafoglio *m* wallet.

portafortuna *m inv* mascot.

portamento *m* carriage, bear-ing, deportment.

portaoggetti *m inv* **vano ~** *m* glove compartment.

portapane *m inv* **cassetta ~** *f* breadbin.

portare *vt* to carry, to get, to waft; ~ **a termine** to accomplish.

posta *f* post; ~ aerea airmail.

portare *vt* to wear, to carry, to take, to bring, to bear; ~ **avan-ti** *vt* to carry on.

portasciugamano *m* towel rail.

portasigarette *m inv* cigarette case.

portata *f* extent, range, reach, course; **di vasta ~** *adj* far-reaching.

portatore *m* bearer, carrier.

portauovo *m* eggcup.

portavoce *m inv* spokeman, mouthpiece.

portellone *m* door; **~ posteriore** *m* tailgate.

portiere *m* porter, doorman; goalkeeper; **~ in livrea** *m* commissionaire.

portinaio *m* caretaker,janitor.

portineria *f* lodge.

porto *m* port, harbour; **~ di mare** *m* seaport; **franco di ~** *adj* carriage-free.

portuale *m* docker.

porzione *f* helping.

posare *vt* to lay, to model.

posata *f* cutlery.

posato *adj* staid.

posatoio *m* roost.

posizione *f* position, viewpoint, stand, situation, setting.

posologia *f* dosage.

possedere *vt* to own, to have.

possente *adj* mighty.

possesso *m* tenure.

possessore *m* holder.

possibile *adj* possible

possibilità *f inv* possibility; **~** *fpl* scope.

posta *f* post, mail.

postagiro *m* giro.

posteggio *m* parking; **~ di taxi** *m* taxi rank.

posteriore *adj* hind, hindquarters, back, rear; **la parte ~** *f* the rear.

postilla *f* footnote.

posto *m* seat, room, spot; **in nessun ~** *adv* nowhere.

pot-pourri *m inv* (*mus*) medley.

potabile *adj* drinkable.

potere *vt* to be able to; * *m* power.

precedente *m* precedent; sen-za precedenti *adj* all-time.

povero *adj* poor.

povertà *f* poverty.

pozzo *m* well; **~ nero** *m* cesspit; **~ petrolifero** *m* oil well.

pranzare *vi* to dine.

pranzo *m* lunch, feast.

prateria *f* grassland.

praticamente *adv* virtually.

pratico *adj* practical, sensible down-to earth, versed; **privo di senso ~** impractical:

prato *m* meadow, lawn.

preannunciare *vt* to herald.

preavvertire *vt* to forewarn.

preavviso *m* notice.

precario *adj* precarious, uneasy.

precedente *adj* former, foregoing, old; **precedenti penali** *mpl* (criminal) record.

precedenza *f* precedence; **dare la ~** *vt* to give way.

precedere *vt* to antedate.

precipitare *vi* to crash (plane)

precipitarsi *vr* to rush.

precipitazioni *fpl* rainfall.

precisione *f* accuracy.

preciso *adj* accurate.

prego *excl* not at all.

precoce *adj* forward, early.

precursore *m* forerunner.

predilezione *f* fondness.

predire *vt* to pretell.

predisposto *adj* susceptible.

prefazione *f* foreword.

preferire *vt* to prefer.

preferito *adj* favourite.

prefisso *m* dialling code.

perforatrice *f* drill.

pregustamento *m* foretaste.

prelievo *m* withdrawal.

preliminare *adj* exploratory.

prematuro *adj* untimely, early.

premeditato *adj* deliberate.

premere *vt* to squeeze.

premiare *vt* to reward.

preminente *adj* leading.

premio *m* prize, award, bonus: **primo ~** *m* jackpot; **~ per il peggior contendente** *m* booby prize.

premunirsi *vr* to hedge one's bets.

premura *f* rush.

premuroso *adj* attentive, considerate.

prenatale *adj* antenatal.

prendere *vt* to take, to get, to acquire, to catch; **andare a ~** *vt* to fetch; **~ gusto a** *vt* to acquire a taste for; **~ freddo** *vi* to catch cold; **~ fuoco** *vi* to catch fire.

prenotare *vt* to reserve, to book.

prenotazione *f* reservation.

preoccupante *adj* worrying, disturbing.

preoccupare *vt* to worry, to trouble; * *vr* **~rsi** to mind, to worry, to fret.

preoccupato *adj* worried.

preoccupazione *f* worry, concern, care.

preponderante *adj* overriding.

prepotente *adj* overbearing, high-handed; **fare il ~** *vi* to bully.

prepuzio *m* foreskin.

presa *f* hold, grasp, grip; socket; **~ d'aria** vent; **~ multipla** *f* adaptor.

presagire *vi* to bode.

presentatore *m* announcer, TV host, compère.

presentare *vt* to introduce, to submit, to show, to table; * *vr* **~rsi** to arise, to stand.

presentazione *f* introduction.

presente *adj*, *m* present; **con la ~** *adv* herewith.

presentimento *m* foreboding.

preservativo *m* condom, sheath.

preside *m* headmaster, dean.

presidente *m* president, chairman.

presiedere *vt* to chair.

pressante *adj* urgent.

presso *adj* near, c/o; **nei pressi** *adv* thereabouts.

pressione *f* pressure, strain; **~ del sangue** blood pressure; **gruppo di ~** *m* lobby.

prestare *vt* to lend, to loan, to spare.

prestigiatore *m* conjurer.

prestigio *m* prestige; **fare giochi di ~** *vi* to conjure.

prestito *m* loan; **prendere in ~** *vt* to borrow.

presto *adv* early, soon.

presunto *adj* supposed.

presuntuoso *adj* overconfident.

pretendente *m/f* claimant.

pretendere *vt* to expect, to claim.

pretenzioso *adj* ostentatious.

pretesa *f* claim; **pretese** *fpl* affectation.

prevalere *vi* to prevail; **~ su** *vt* to get the better of, to overrule.

prevedere *vt* to foresee, to forecast, to envisage, to anticipate; **era da ~** it was bound to happen.

prevedibile *adj* foreseeable.

preventivare *vt* to estimate.

preventivo *m* estimate.

previdenza *f* foresight, forethought.

previsione *f* forecast; **previsioni del tempo** *fpl* weather forecast.

prezioso *adj* valuable.

prezzo *m* price; **a ~ ridotto** *adj* cut-rate; **a buon ~** *adj* cheap.

prigione *f* prison, jail, lock-up.

prigionia *f* captivity.

prigioniero *m*, *adj* captive.

prima *adv* before, beforehand, sooner; **sulle prime** *adv* at first; * *m* first.

primavera *f* spring, springtime.

primo *adj* first, early, former.

primula *f* cowslip.

principale *adj* main, chief, arch; **ruolo ~** *m* lead; **prodotto ~** *m* staple.

principalmente *adv* mainly.

principe *m* prince; **~ ereditario** *m* crown prince.

principiante *m/f* beginner, learner.

principio *m* beginning, inception; principle, tenet.

privare *vt* to deprive.

privazione *f* deprivation; **privazioni** *fpl* hardship.

privo *adj* wanting, devoid.

probabile *adj* probable, likely; **è ~ che si arrabbi** he's liable to get angry.

probabilità *f inv* probability, chance, likelihood; **~ fpl** odds.

problema *m* problem; **problemi** *mpl* trouble.

proboscide *f* trunk.

procedere *vi* to proceed; **~ velocemente** *vi* to speed along; **~ lentamente** *vi* to crawl.

processare *vt* to try.

processo *m* trial, process.

procione *m* raccoon.

procuratore *m* attorney.

prode *adj* stalwart.

prodezza *f* feat.

prodotto *m* product, comodity.

produzione *f* production, output, generation.

profanare *vt* to desecrate.

profanazione *f* desecration.

professionale *adj* professional, vocational.

professore *m* professor, teacher.

profondità *f* depth.

profondo *adj* deep, sound; **poco ~** *adj* shallow.

profugo *m* refugee.

profumare *vt* to scent.

profumato *adj* scented, redolent.

profumo *m* scent, smell.

profusione *f* profusion; **a ~** *adv* galore.

progenitori *mpl* forefathers.

progettare *vt* to design.

progetto *m* design.

programma *m* programme, syllabus, schedule.

programmare *vt* to time.

programmazione *f* programming.

progredire *vi* advance.

progresso *m* progress, advance; **fare ~** *vi* to make headway.

prontezza *f* alacrity.

proibire *vt* to forbid, to ban.

proiettare *vt* to screen.

proiettile *m* bullet; **a prova di ~** *adj* bulletproof.

prole *f* brood, young, issue, offspring.

prolisso *adj* long-winded.

prolunga *f* extension.

prolungare *vt* to lengthen, to extend.

promemoria *m inv* memo.

promotore *m* sponsor.

promozione *f* sponsorship.

promuovere *vt* to sponsor.

pronosticare *vt* to tip.

prontamente *adv* readily.

prontezza *f* readiness.

pronto *adj* ready; **~!** *excl* (*tel*) hullo.

pronunciare *vt* to pronounce, to utter.

propaganda *f* propaganda; **~ elettorale** *f* electioneering.

propagandista *m/f* canvasser.

propagare *vt* to spread.

propagazione *f* spread.

propenso *adj* inclined; **poco ~** *adj* disinclined

proporzionato *adj* commensurate.

proposito *m* intention; subject; **a ~ di** *prep* about, concerning; **a ~ ...** by the way....

pseudonimo *m* alias.

proposizione *f* clause (*gr*), proposition.

proprietà *f* ownership; **~ assoluta** *f* freehold.

proprietaria *f* landlady.

proprietario *m* owner, landlord; **~ terriero** *m* landowner.

proprio *adj* own; * *adv* just; **che lavora in ~** *adj* self-employed; **amor ~** *m* self-esteem.

prosperare *vi* to thrive, to flourish.

proroga *f* reprieve, grace; **concedere una ~** *vt* to reprieve.

prosciugamento *m* drainage.

prosciugare *vt* to drain.

prosciutto *m* ham; **~ affumicato** *m* gammon.

prossimamente *m inv* trailer.

prossimo *adj* next, forthcoming, coming.

proteggere *vt* to shield.

protesta *f* outcry.

protestare *vi* to protest, to remonstrate.

protezione *f* guard.

protrarsi *vi* to overrun.

prova *f* test, rehearsal, trial, fitting; **~ ardua** *f* ordeal.

provare *vt* to rehearse; to feel; to try.

provenire *vi* to emanate.

provetta *f* test-tube.

provino *m* audition.

provocante *adj* saucy.

provocare *vt* to provoke, to bring about, to spark.

provocatorio *adj* challenging.

provvedere *vt* to cater for.

provvedimento *m* measure.

provvisorio *adj* temporary, interim.

provvista *f* store, stock.

prua *f* fore, bow.

prudente *adj* careful, cautious.

prudenza *f* caution.

prudere *vi* to itch.

prugnola *f* sloe.

prugnolo *m* blackthorn.

prurito *m* itch.

pseudonimo *m* nom de plume.

puah *excl* ugh.

pubblicare *vt* to publish, to issue.

pubblicazione *f* publication; **pubblicazioni matrimoniali** *fpl* banns.

pubblicità *f* commercial, advertisement, advertising; **fare ~** *vi* to advertise.

pubblico *m* audience.

pugilato *m* boxing.

pugile *m* boxer; **fare il ~** *vi* to box.

pugnalare *vt* to stab.

pugnale *m* dagger.

pugno *m* fist.

pula *f* husk, chaff.

pulce *f* flea.

pulcino *m* chick.

puledra *f* filly.

puledro *m* foal, colt.

pulire *vt* to clean, to cleanse, to wipe.

pulitissimo *adj* spotless.

pulito *adj* clean.

pulizia *f* cleaning, cleanliness, cleanness.

pullman *m* coach.

pulsare *vi* to throb.

pungente *adj* cutting, nippy, acid, acrid.

pungere *vt* to bite (insect), to sting.

pungiglione *f* sting.

punire *vt* to chastise, to discipline.

punta *f* tip, tinge, bit (tool), barb, spike; **~ del dito** *f* fingertip.

puntare *vt* to aim; to back (a horse).

puntata *f* stake; instalment, episode; **opera a puntate** *f* serial.

punteggiare *vt* to dot.

punteggio *m* score.

punteruolo *m* awl.

puntina *f* stylus.

puntino *m* spot.

punto *m* dot, point, stop, stitch; **~ esclamativo** *m* exclamation mark; **~ morto** *m* deadlock; **~ e virgola** semi-colon; **due punti** (*typ*) colon; **~ morto** *m* standstill; **~ nero** blackhead; **~ cieco** or **~ debole** blind spot; **~ d'appoggio** *m* foothold; **a tal ~ che** *adv* insomuch.

puntone *m* rafter.

puntura *f* sting, bite (insect).

punzecchiare *vt* to needle.

pupazzo *m* puppet; **~ di neve** *m* snowman.

puré *m* mash.

pure *adv* also.

puro *adj* pure, sheer, mere, unadulterated.

purosangue *adj inv, m/f inv* thoroughbred.

purtroppo *adv* unluckily.

pusillanime *adj* fainthearted.

putiferio *m* rumpus, row, stink.

putrefarsi *vr* to decay.

puttana *f* prostitute, whore.

puzzare *vi* to smell, to stink, to reek.

puzzle *m* (jigsaw) puzzle.

puzzo *m* stench, reek, stink, smell.

puzzolente *adj* smelly, rank

Q

qua *adv* here.

qua qua *m* quack; **fare ~** *vi* to quack.

quacchero *adj, m* Quaker.

quaderno *m* exercise book.

quadrangolo *m* quadrangle.

quadrante *m* dial, face (of watch, etc), quadrant.

quadrato *adj, m* square.

quadrigemino *adj*: **gemello ~** *m* quadruplet.

quadrilatero *adj* quadrilateral.

quadro *m* square; painting, picture; **~ di comando** *m* console; **quadri** *mpl* (cards) diamonds.

quadrupede *m* quadruped.

quadruplo *adj* quadruple, fourfold.

quaglia *f* quail.

qualche *adj* some.

qualcosa *pron* something.

qualcuno *pron* anybody, somebody.

quei *dem adj* those.

quale *adj* what, which.

qualifica *f* qualification.

qualificare *vt* to qualify.

qualificato *adj* qualified.

qualità *f* quality.

qualsiasi *adj* any; **~ cosa** *pron* whatever; **in ~ momento** *conj* whenever.

quando *adv, conj* when.

quantità *f inv* quantity; **piccola ~** *f* modicum; **comprare in grande ~** *vt* to buy in bulk.

quantitativo *adj* quantitative

quanto *adj* how much; **quanti**

adj how many; tanti **quanti** as many as; **~ a** *adv* as to, as for; **~ a me** as for me.

quaranta *m inv* forty.

quarantena *f* quarantine.

quarantesimo *adj, m* fortieth.

quartetto *m* quartet.

quartier *m* quarter; **~ generale** *m* headquarters; **~ residenziale** *m* housing estate.

quarto *m* quarter, fourth; * *adj* fourth; **un ~ d'ora** *m* a quarter of an hour.

quarzo *m* quartz.

quasi *adv* almost, nearly; **~ tutto** *pron* most.

quattordicesimo *adj, m* fourteenth.

quattordici *adj, m* fourteen.

quattro *adj, m* four; **dividere in ~** *vt* to quarter.

quel *adj* that; **quelli** *pron* those.

quercia *f* oak.

questo *dem adj, dem pron* this;

questi *dem adj, dem pron* these; **con ~** *adv* hereby.

questionario *m* questionnaire.

questione *f* question.

questore *m* commissioner of police.

qui *adv* here; **da ~ in avanti** *adv* hereafter.

quietare *vt* to hush.

quindi *adv* therefore, consequently.

quindicesimo *adj* fifteenth.

quindici *m, adj* fifteen; **~ giorni** *m* fortnight.

quinte *fpl* wings; **dietro le ~** *adj, adv* offstage.

quintetto *m* quintet.

quinto *adj, m* fifth.

quiz *m inv* quiz.

quorum *m inv* quorum.

quota *f* quota, dues; **~ di ammissione** *f* entrance fee.

quotidiano *adj, m* daily.

quoziente *m* quotient.

quadrare *vi* to square.

R

rabarbaro *m* rhubarb.

rabbia *f* anger; rabies; **con ~** *adv* angrily.

rabbino *m* rabbi.

rabbrividire *vi* to shiver, to wince, to shudder; **che fa ~** creepy.

raccapricciante *adj* grisly, bloodcurdling.

racchetta *f* racket; **~ da tennis** *f* tennis racket.

racchiudere *vt* to encase.

raccogliere *vt* to collect, to pick up, to gather.

raccolta *f* collection, set:

raccolto *m* crop, harvest; **fare il ~ di** *vt* to harvest.

raccomandabile *adj* advisable; **poco ~** *adj* disreputable.

raccomandare *vt* to recommend; **mi raccomando!** be sure!.

raccomandata *f* registered letter.

raccomandazione *f* recommendation.

raccontare *vt* to relate, to tell, to recount.

racconto *m* story, yarn.

raccordo *m* connection; **binario di ~** *m* siding.

rachitismo *m* rickets.

racimolare *vt* to glean.

racket *m inv* racket.

radar *m* radar.
raddobbare *vt* to refit.
raddobbo *m* refit.
raddoppiare *vt* to double, to redouble.
raddrizzare *vt* to straighten, to right, to unbend.
radere *vt* to shave; to raze.
radersi *vr* to shave.
radiale *adj* radial.
radiante *adj* radiant.
radiatore *m* radiator.
radiazione *f* radiation.
radicale *adj* radical, sweeping * *m/f* radical.
radicare *vi* to root.
radicato *adj* entrenched.
radice *f* root.
radio *f* radio; * *m* radium.
radioamatore *m* radio ham.
radioattività *f* radioactivity.
radioattivo *adj* radioactive; **pioggia radioattiva** *f* fallout.
radiografia *f* X-ray, radiography.
radiologo *m* radiographer.
radioso *adj* sunny.
rado *adj* sparse.
radunare *vt* to assemble, to rally, to gather, to muster.
radunarsi *vr* to congregate, to collect.
raduno *m* gathering, rally, meeting.
radura *f* clearing.
rafano *m* horseradish.
raffermo *adj* stale.
raffica *f* gust, volley, flurry; ~ **di vento** *f* blast of wind; ~ **di domande** *f* barrage of questions.
raffinare *vt* to refine.
raffinatezza *f* refinement, polish.
raffinato *adj* polished, cultured, sophisticated.
raffineria *f* refinery.
rafforzare *vt* to fortify.

raffreddare *vt* to cool.
raffreddore *m* cold.
rafia *f* raffia.
raganella *f* rattle.
ragazza *f* girl; **di** ~ *adj* girlish.
ragazzino *m* kid.
ragazzo *m* boy, lad; boyfriend.
raggelante *adj* withering.
raggio *m* spoke; radius; ray, beam; ~ **di luna** *m* moonbeam; **a lungo** ~ *adj* long-range.
raggirare *vt* to bamboozle.
raggiro *m* swindle; **indurre con raggiri** *vt* to con.
raggiungere *vt* to hit, to attain, to reach.
raggiungibile *adj* attainable.
raggruppare *vt* to group.
ragionamento *m* reasoning.
ragionare *vi* to reason.
ragione *f* reason, sense; **aver** ~ *vi* to be right.
ragionevole *adj* reasonable, thinking, rational.
ragioniere *m/f* accountant
ragioneria *f* accountancy
ragliare *vi* to bray.
raglio *m* bray.
ragnatela *f* web, spider-web, cobweb.
ragno *m* spider.
rallegrare *vt* to gladden.
rallegrarsi *vr* to rejoice, to brighten.
rallentare *vt*, *vi* to slow (down).
rally *m inv* rally.
ramato *adj* auburn.
rame *m* copper.
ramificare *vi* to ramify.
ramificazione *f* ramification.
rammarico *m* regret.
rammendare *vt* to darn.
rammendo *m* mending. darn.
rammentare *vt* to recollect.
ramo *m* branch, bough.
ramoscello *m* sprig, twig.
rampa *f* ramp, flight (of stairs); ~ **di lancio** *f* launch pad.

rampante *adj* rampant.
rampicante *f* creeper.
rana *f* frog; **nuoto a ~ m** breast-stroke.
ranch *m inv* ranch.
rancido *adj* rancid, rank.
rancore *m* grudge, ill feeling, rancour.
randagio *adj* stray.
randello *m* club, bludgeon.
rango *m* standing.
rantolo *m* rattle.
ranuncolo *m* buttercup.
rapa *f* turnip.
rapace *adj* predatory.
rapare *vt* to crop.
rapida *f* rapids.
rapire *vt* to abduct, to kidnap.
rapitore *m* abductor, kidnapper.
rapporti *mpl* dealings.
rapporto *m* report, relation, rapport, ratio; **rapporti** *mpl* intercourse; **rapporti sessuali** *mpl* sex.
rapprendersi *vr* to congeal.
rappresaglie *fpl* reprisals, retaliation.
rappresentante *m* representative.
rappresentare *vt* to represent, to enact, to depict, to perform.
rappresentativo *adj* representative.
rappresentazione *f* performance, representation.
rapsodia *f* rhapsody.
raramente *adv* seldom.
rarità *f* rarity.
raro *adj* rare; **sono rari** they are few and far between.
raschiare *vt* to scrape.
raschiatura *f* scrape.
raschietto *m* scraper.
raso *m* satin.
rasoio *m* razor; **~ elettrico** *m* shaver.
raspa *f* rasp.

raspare *vt* to rasp.
rassegnato *adj* resigned.
rassicurante *adj* reassuring, soothing.
rassicurare *vt* to reassure.
rastrellare *vt* to rake.
rastrelliera *f* rack.
rastrello *m* rake.
rata *f* instalment.
ratifica *f* ratification.
ratificare *vt* to ratify.
ratto *m* rat.
rattoppare *vt* to patch (up).
rattristare *vt* to sadden.
rauco *adj* hoarse, husky, rough, raucous.
ravanello *m* radish.
ravvivare *vt* to liven up, to enliven, to brighten.
razionale *adj* rational.
razionalità *f* rationality.
razionalizzare *vt* to rationalize.
razionare *vt* to ration.
razione *f* ration.
razza *f* race, strain, breed; skate; (fish) razza, ray.
razziale *adj* racial.
razzismo *m* racism.
razzista *m/f* racialist.
razzo *m* rocket.
re *m inv* king.
reagire *vi* to react.
reale *adj* real, actual, royal.
reali *mpl* royalty.
realismo *m* realism.
realista *m/f* realist; royalist.
realistico *adj* realistic, lifelike.
realizzabile *adj* feasible.
realizzare *vt* to realize, accomplish, to achieve; * **~rsi** to come to fruition.
realizzazione *f* accomplishment, achievement, realization.
realtà *f* reality; **in ~** in fact.
reattore *m* reactor; **~ autofertilizzante** *m* breeder.

reazionario *m* reactionary, die-hard; * *adj* reactionary.

reazione *f* reaction, after-effect; **~ a catena** *f* chain reaction; **motore a ~** *m* jet engine; **~ violenta** *f* backlash.

rebbio *m* prong.

rebus *m* puzzle.

recalcitrante *adj* recalcitrant.

recalcitrare *vt* to balk.

recensione *f* notice.

recensire *vt* to review.

recensore *m* reviewer.

recente *adj* recent.

reception *f inv* reception.

recessione *f* recession.

recintare *vt* to enclose, to fence.

recinto *m* fence, compound, enclosure, paddock, pen.

recipiente *m* vessel, receptacle.

reciproco *adj* mutual, reciprocal.

reciso *adj* cut.

recita *f* recital.

recitare *vt, vi* to recite.

reclamizzare *vt* to publicize.

reclusione *f* imprisonment, confinement.

recluso *adj* recluse.

recluta *f* recruit.

reclutamento *m* recruitment.

reclutare *vt* to recruit.

record *m inv* record.

recriminare *vt* to recriminate.

recriminazione *f* recrimination.

redazionale *adj* editorial.

redditività *f* profitability.

redditizio *adj* profitable.

reddito *m* income, revenue.

Redentore *m* Redeemer.

redenzione *f* redemption.

redigere *vt* to edit.

redimere *vt* to redeem.

redine *f* rein.

referendum *m inv* referendum.

referenza *f* reference; **referenze** *fpl* credentials, testimonial.

refettorio *m* refectory.

refrigerante *m* coolant.

refrigerare *vt* to refrigerate.

regalare *vt* to give.

regale *adj* regal.

regalo *m* gift.

regata *f* regatta.

reggente *m/f* regent.

reggenza *f* regency.

reggere a *vt* to stand.

reggimento *m* regiment.

reggiseno *m* bra; brassiere.

regime *m* régime.

regina *f* queen.

regionale *adj* regional.

regione *f* region.

regista *m* producer.

registrare *vt* to register, to record, to tape, to enter.

registratore *m* tape recorder, recorder; **~ a cassette** *m* cassette recorder.

registrazione *f* registration.

registro *m* record, register.

regnare *vi* to rule, to reign.

regno *m* kingdom, reign, realm.

regola *f* rule; **~ principale** *f* golden rule.

regolamento *m* rule; settlement, regulation.

regolare *vt* to regulate, to set to readjust; * *adj* regular even.

regolarità *f* regularity.

regolatore *m* regulator; **~ luminoso** *m* dimmer switch.

regredire *vi* to regress.

regressivo *adj* regressive.

regresso *m* regression.

reincarnazione *f* reincarnation.

reintegrare *vt* to reinstate.

reinvestire *vt* to plough back.

reiterare *vt* to reiterate.

reiterazione *f* reiteration.

relativo *adj* relative, pertaining, comparative.

relax *m* relaxation.

relazione *f* paper; relation, relationship.

relè *m* relay.

relegare *vt* to relegate.

relegazione *f* relegation.

religione *f* religion.

religioso *adj* religious, holy.

reliquia *f* relic.

relitto *m* wreck; **relitti** *mpl* wreckage.

remare *vi* to row, to scull.

rematore *m* rower.

reminiscenza *f* reminiscence.

remissione *f* remission.

remissivo *adj* subservient.

remo *m* oar.

remoto *adj* remote.

remunerativo *adj* gainful.

renale *adj* renal.

rendere *vt* to render.

rendimento *m* performance, output.

rene *m* kidney.

renna *f* reindeer.

reparto *m* unit, department.

reperto *m* exhibit.

repertorio *m* repertory, repertoire.

replica *f* repeat, replica.

reportage *m inv* report.

repressione *f* suppression, repression.

repressivo *adj* repressive.

represso *adj* pent-up.

reprimere *vt* to suppress, to repress, to quell, to clamp down.

repubblica *f* republic.

repubblicano *m* republican.

reputazione *f* reputation, repute

requisire *vt* to comandeer, to requisition.

requisizione *f* requisition.

resa *f* surrender; yield, return.

rescindere *vt* to rescind.

rescissione *f* termination

residente *adj*, *m* resident.

residenza *f* residence.

residuo *m* residue; * *adj* residual.

resina *f* resin.

resinoso *adj* resinous.

resistente *adj* tough, hardwearing, strong.

resistenza *f* resistance, endurance, strength, stamina.

resistere *vt* to resist, to withstand.

respingente *m* buffer.

respingere *vt* to repulse, to repel, to spurn, to quash.

respirare *vt* to breathe.

respiratore *m* respirator; **~ a tubo** *m* snorkel.

respiratorio *adj* respiratory.

respirazione *f* breathing, respiration.

respiro *m* breath, breathing; **dare ~ a** *vt* to give respite to; **attimo di ~** breathing space.

responsabile *adj* responsible, liable.

responsabilità *f* responsibility, liability.

ressa *f* crush, rush.

restare *vt* to stay, to remain.

restaurare *vt* to restore.

Restaurazione *f* Restoration.

restauro *m* renovation, restoration.

resti *mpl* remains.

restio *adj* reluctant.

restituire *vt* to give back, to repay, to return, to restore.

restituzione *f* restitution.

resto *m* rest, change, remainder, remnant.

restringere *vt* to narrow; * *vr* **~rsi** to shrink.

restrittivo *adj* restrictive.

restrizione *f* restriction, restraint.

retata *f* roundup, catch, haul.

rete *f* net, network, grid; **~ metallica** *f* netting.

reticella *f* hairnet.
reticenze *f* reticence.
reticolato *m* lattice.
retina *f* retina.
retorica *f* rhetoric.
retorico *adj* rhetorical.
retribuzione *f* retribution.
retro *m* back.
retrocucina *m inv* scullery.
retrodatare *vt* to backdate.
retrogrado *adj* retrograde.
retromarcia *f* reverse.
retroscena *f* backstage.
retrospettiva *f* retrospective.
retrospettivo *adj* retrospec-
    tive; **giudizio ~** *m* hindsight.
retrovisore *m* rear-view mir-
    ror.
rettangolare *adj* rectangular.
rettangolo *m* rectangle, oblong.
rettifica *f* rectification.
rettificare *vt* to rectify.
rettile *m* reptile.
rettilineo *adj* rectilinear.
rettitudine *f* righteousness,
    rectitude.
retto *m* upright; rectum; * *adj*
    right.
rettore *m* vice-chancellor, rec-
    tor.
reumatico *adj* rheumatic.
reumatismo *m* rheumatism.
reverendo *m* Reverend.
reverente *adj* reverent, rever-
    ential.
revisionare *vt* to service, to
    overhaul.
revisione *f* review, service, re-
    vision, overhaul; **fare una ~
    di** *vt* to review; **~ dei conti** *f*
    audit; **fare una ~ di** *vt* to au-
    dit.
revisore *m* reviser; **~ dei con-
    ti** auditor.
revocare *vt* to revoke, to lift.
riabilitare *vt* to rehabilitate.
riabilitazione *f* rehabilitation.
riadattarsi *vr* to readjust.

rianimare *vt* to revive.
rianimazione *f* reanimation;
    centro di ~ *m* intensive care
    unit.
riaprire *vt* to reopen.
riarmo *m* rearmament.
riarso *adj* parched.
riassicurare *vt* to reinsure.
riassumere *vt* to sum up, to
    outline.
riassunto *m* summary, résumé.
ribalta *f* flap; **luci della ~** *fpl*
    footlights.
ribaltabile *adj* reclining.
ribaltare *vt* to capsize.
ribattere *vt* to retort.
ribattino *m* rivet.
ribellarsi *vr* to revolt, to rebel.
ribelle *adj* rebel, rebellious,
    wayward, defiant, insurgent;
    * *m/f* rebel.
ribellione *f* rebellion.
ribes *m inv* currant.
ribrezzo *m* loathing.
ricadere *vi* to relapse.
ricaduta *f* relapse.
ricamare *vt* to embroider.
ricambiare *vt* to repay.
ricambio *m* relay, refill; **pezzo
    di ~** *m* spare part.
ricamo *m* embroidery; **saggio
    di ~** *m* sampler.
ricapitolare *vt*, *vi* to recapitu-
    late.
ricaricare *vt* to recharge.
ricattare *vt* to blackmail.
ricatto *m* blackmail.
ricavato *m* proceeds.
ricchezza *f* wealth, richness
    ricchezze *fpl* riches.
riccio *m* hedgehog; * *adj* curly
ricciolo *m* curl.
ricco *adj* wealthy, rich.
ricerca *f* research, search
    quest, hunt; **fare ~** *vi* to re
    search; **andare alla ~ di** *vi* t
    scout around for; **~ di merca**
    to *f* market research.

ricercato *adj* elaborate.
ricetta *f* prescription, recipe.
ricettario *m* cookery book.
ricevere *vt* to receive, to get.
ricevimento *m* reception.
ricevitore *m* receiver.
ricevuta *f* receipt.
richiamare *vt* to phone back, to retrieve, to recall.
richiamo *m* recall, catchword, (*med*) booster, lure; **uccello di ~** *m* decoy.
richiedere *vt* to request, to require.
richiesta *f* request, demand.
richiesto *adj* sought-after.
ricognitore *m* scout.
ricognizione *f* reconnaissance; **fare una ~** *vi, vt* to reconnoitre.
ricomparire *vi* to reappear.
ricompensa *f* recompense, reward.
ricompensare *vt* to recompense.
riconciliare *vt* to reconcile.
riconciliazione *f* reconciliation.
riconoscente *adj* thankful.
riconoscenza *f* gratefulness.
riconoscere *vt* to recognize, to know.
riconoscimento *m* recognition.
riconsiderare *vt* to reconsider.
ricoprire *vt* to recover, to coat.
ricordare *vt* to recall, to remember, to remind.
ricordo *m* souvenir, recollection, keepsake, memory; **~ di famiglia** *m* heirloom.
ricorrente *adj* recurrent.
ricorrenza *f* recurrence.
ricorrere to return; ~ in giudizio *vi* to prosecute.
ricorso *m* recourse, resort; **far ~ a** *vt* to resort to.
ricostituente *m* tonic.
ricostruire *vt* to rebuild, to reconstruct.

ricoverato *m* inpatient.
ricreazione *f* recreation.
ricuperare *vt* to salvage, to recover, to retrieve, to repossess.
ricupero *m* retrieval, recovery.
ridacchiare *vi* to chuckle, to titter, to snigger, to cackle, to giggle.
ridere *vi* to laugh, to scoff.
ridicolo *m* ridicule; **mettere in ~** *vt* to ridicule; * *adj* laughable, ridiculous.
ridondante *adj* redundant.
ridondanza *f* redundancy.
ridotto *adj* diminished.
ridurre *vt* to reduce, to cut, to lower, to whittle away; **~ drasticamente** *vt* to axe.
riduzione *f* cut, cutback, reduction.
rielezione *f* reelection.
riempire *vt* to fill, to refill to stuff.
rientranza *f* recess.
rientro *m* reentry.
rievocare *vt* to conjure up.
riferimento *m* reference; **punto di ~** *m* landmark; **con ~ a** with reference to.
riferirsi *vr* to refer; **~ a** to pertain to.
riffa *f* raffle; **di ~** *or* **di raffa** by hook or by crook.
rifinitura *f* finish.
rifiutare *vt* to refuse, to turn down, to rebuff.
rifiuto *m* refusal, rebuff, denial; **rifiuti** *mpl* litter.
riflessione *f* reflection.
riflessivo *adj* reflexive.
riflesso *m* reflection, reflex.
riflettere *vt* to mirror, to think over, to reflect.
riflettore *m* searchlight, floodlight, spotlight.
rifluire *vi* to ebb.
riflusso *m* ebb.
riforma *f* reform.

Riforma f Reformation.
riformare vt to reform.
riformatore m reformer.
riformatorio m borstal.
riformista m/f reformist.
rifornire vt to stock, to replenish.
rifrangere vt to refract.
rifrazione f refraction.
rifugiato m refugee; **~ politico** m defector.
rifugio m shelter, haven, refuge, retreat; **~ antiatomico** m fallout shelter.
riga f stripe, line, (hair) parting.
rigare vt to streak, to rule.
rigato adj lined.
rigenerare vt to regenerate.
rigenerato adj regenerate.
rigenerazione f regeneration.
rigetto m rejection.
righello m ruler.
rigidezza f rigidity.
rigidità f stiffness.
rigido adj rigid, stiff, hard, strict, intemperate.
rigonfiamento m bulge.
rigore m rigour; **a ~ di termini** adv strictly speaking.
rigoroso adj stringent, rigorous.
riguadagnare vt to regain.
riguardante prep respecting.
riguardare vt to regard, to concern.
riguardo m regard; **~ a** prep regarding, concerning; **senza ~** adv regardless.
rilanciare vt to reflate.
rilasciare vt to release, to issue.
rilascio m release, issue.
rilassare vt to relax; * vr **~rsi** to relax.
rilassato adj relaxed, (fam) laid-back.
rilegare vt to bind.

rilegato adj bound.
rilegatore m bookbinder.
rilegatura f binding.
rilevamento m survey.
rilievo m relief; **mettere in ~** vt to stress.
riluttante adj unwilling.
riluttanza f reluctance, disinclination.
rima f rhyme; **far ~ con** vi to rhyme.
rimandare vt to postpone, to put off, to defer, to delay, to refer.
rimando m cross-reference.
rimanere vi to stay, to remain.
rimbalzare vi to bounce, to rebound, to ricochet.
rimbalzo m bounce, ricochet; **di ~** adv on the rebound.
rimbombare vi to reverberate.
rimbombo m reverberation.
rimborsare vt to refund, to reimburse, to pay back.
rimborso m reimbursement, repayment, refund, rebate.
rimediare vt to remedy, to make up for.
rimedio m remedy.
rimessa f remittance.
rimettere vt to remit.
rimodellare vt to remodel.
rimorchiare vt to tow, to pick up.
rimorchiatore m tug.
rimorchio m tow, trailer; **cavo per ~** m towrope.
rimorso m remorse.
rimostrare vi to expostulate.
rimozione f removal.
rimpatriare vt to repatriate.
rimpiangere vt to regret.
rimpianto m regret.
rimpiazzare vt to replace.
rimpinzarsi vr to gorge.
rimproverare vt to reprimand to reproach, to blame, to reprehend.

rimprovero *m* rebuke, reprimand, reproach; **di ~** *adj* reproachful.

rimuginare *vt* to mull over; * *vi* to brood.

rimunerare *vt* to rimunerate.

rimunerazione *f* remuneration.

rimuovere *vt* to remove, to dislodge.

Rinascimento *m* Renaissance.

rinchiudere *vt* to confine, to pen.

rinforzare *vt* to strengthen, to toughen, to boost, to brace, to reinforce.

rinforzo *m* brace.

rinfrescante *adj* cooling.

rinfrescare *vi, vt* to freshen, to refresh.

rinfusa *f*: **alla ~** *adj* higgledy-piggledy.

ring *m inv* boxing ring.

ringhiare *vi* to growl, to snarl.

ringhiera *f* banisters.

ringhio *m* snarl, growl.

ringiovanire *vt* to rejuvenate.

ringraziamento *m* thanksgiving.

ringraziare *vt* to thank.

rinnegare *vt* to disown.

rinnegato *m* renegade.

rinnovare *vt* to refurbish, to renovate, to renew.

rinnovo *m* renewal.

rinoceronte *m* rhinoceros.

rinomanza *f* renown.

rinomato *adj* renowned.

rinsecchirsi *vr* to shrivel.

rintoccare *vi* to strike.

rintocco *m* stroke, chime; **~ funebre** *m* knell.

rintracciare *vt* to trace.

rinuncia *f* renunciation.

rinunciare *vt* to renounce, to surrender, to relinquish, to waive, to give up, to forgo.

invigorire *vt* to exhilarate.

iorganizzare *vt* to reorganize.

riorganizzazione *f* reorganization.

riparabile *adj* reparable.

riparare *vt* to repair, to fix, to redress; to shelter, to shade.

riparazione *f* reparation, repair, redress.

riparo *m* cover, refuge, shelter.

ripartire *vt* to mete out.

ripassare *vt* to revise.

ripasso *m* revision.

ripensare *vi* to think over; **ripensandoci** in retrospect.

ripercorrere *vt* to retrace.

ripercussioni *fpl* repercussions.

ripetere *vt* to repeat; * *vr* **~rsi** to recur.

ripetizione *f* repetition.

ripetutamente *adv* repeatedly.

ripiano *m* shelf.

ripicca *f* pique.

ripido *adj* steep.

ripiegare *vt* to refold; **~ su** to fall back on.

ripieno *m* stuffing, filling.

riportare *vt* to report, (*math*) to carry.

riporto *m* carry-over; **cane da ~** *m* retriever.

riposante *adj* restful.

riposare *vi* to rest, to stand, to repose; * *vr* **~rsi** to rest.

riposo *m* rest, repose.

ripostiglio *m* boxroom.

riprendere *vt* to recapture, to retake, to resume.

riprendersi *vi* to recover.

ripresa *f* resumption, take, upturn, recovery.

ripristino *m* revival.

riprodurre *vt* to reproduce ; * *vr* **~rsi** to breed.

riproduzione *f* reproduction.

riprovevole *adj* reprehensible.

ripudiare *vt* to repudiate.

ripugnante *adj* repulsive, loathsome, repugnant.

ripugnanza f distaste, repugnance, repulsion.

ripulsione f repulsion.

riqualificare vi, vt to retrain.

riqualificazione f retraining.

risaia f paddy field.

risalire vi to reascend; ~ **a** vi to date from.

risalto m prominence; **dare ~ a** vt to feature.

risata f laugh, laughter; ~ **fragorosa** f guffaw.

risatina f snigger; ~ **stupida** f titter.

riscaldamento m heating.

riscattare vt to ransom.

riscatto m ransom.

rischiare vt to risk, to venture, to hazard, to chance.

rischio m risk, hazard, chance.

rischioso adj risky, hazardous.

risciacquare vt to rinse, to swill.

risciò m inv rickshaw.

risentimento m resentment; **pieno di ~** adj resentful.

risentirsi vr to resent.

riserbo m reserve.

riserva f reservation, reserve, qualification; **di ~** adj spare.

riservare vt to reserve, to book.

riservato adj confidential, secretive, cagey, classified.

risiedere vi to reside.

risma f ream.

riso m rice.

risolare vt to sole.

risolino m giggle, snigger; ~ **stridulo** cackle.

risolutezza f resolve.

risoluto adj resolute, unfaltering, determined, purposeful, steadfast.

risoluzione f resolution.

risolvere vt to resolve, to solve, to sort out.

risonante adj resonant.

risonanza f resonance.

risonare vi to resound.

risorsa f resource.

risparmiare vt to spare, to save.

risparmiatore m saver.

risparmio m saving; **libretto di ~** m savings account; **cassa di ~** f savings bank.

rispecchiare vt to reflect.

rispettabile adj respectable.

rispettabilità f respectability.

rispettare vt to respect; **far ~** vt to enforce.

rispettivo adj respective.

rispetto m respect; ~ **a** prep vis-à-vis; ~ **di sé** m self-respect; **mancanza di ~** f disrespect.

rispettoso adj respectful, dutiful; ~ **delle leggi** adj law-abiding.

risplendente adj resplendent.

rispondere vi to answer, to respond, to reply, to counter; ~ **male a qn** vi to snap somebody's head off.

risposarsi vr to remarry.

risposta f reply, response, retort.

rissa f brawl, fracas.

ristabilire vt to reestablish; * vr ~**rsi** to recuperate.

ristagno m stagnation.

ristampa f reprint, reissue.

ristorante m restaurant.

ristoro m refreshment.

ristrutturare vt to convert.

ristrutturazione f conversion.

risultare vi to result, to emerge, to ensue.

risultato m result, upshot; **avere come ~** vi to result.

risuonare vi to ring.

risurrezione f resurrection.

risuscitare vt to resuscitate.

risvegliare vt to stir.

risveglio m awakening, revival.

risvolto m lapel.

ritagliare *vt* to clip.

ritaglio *m* snip, cutting, clipping.

ritardare *vt* to hold up, to delay.

ritardatario *m* latecomer.

ritardato *adj* retarded.

ritardo *m* delay; **in ~** *adj* late.

ritenere *vt* to rank, to opine.

ritentivo *adj* retentive.

ritenuto *adj*: **essere ~ ricco** *vi* to be reputed to be rich.

ritenzione *f* retention.

ritirare *vt* to withdraw, to retract, to take back; * *vr* **~rsi** to retire, to retreat, to secede.

ritiro *m* withdrawal.

ritmico *adj* rhythmical.

ritmo *m* rhythm, beat, swing.

rito *m* rite, ceremonial.

ritoccare *vt* to retouch, touch up.

ritornare *vi* to revert, to go back.

ritornello *m* chorus, refrain.

ritorno *m* return; **biglietto andata e ~** *m* return ticket; **essere di ~** to be back.

ritrarre *vt* to portray; * *vr* **~rsi** to recede.

ritrasmettere *vt* to relay.

ritrattare *vt* to retract.

ritrattazione *f* recantation.

ritratto *m* portrait.

ritrovarsi *vr* to rendezvous.

ritto *adj* upright.

rituale *adj*, *m* ritual.

riunione *f* meeting, reunion.

riunire *vt* to rally, to reunite, to reunite; * *vr* **~rsi** to riunite, to sit.

riuscire *vi* to succeed.

riuscita *f* success.

riuscito *adj* successful; **non ~** *adj* unsuccessful.

riva *f* bank (river); **~ del mare** *f* seashore.

rivale *adj*, *m* rival.

rivaleggiare *vt* to rival.

rivalità *f* rivalry.

rivalutare *vt* to revalue.

rivedere *vt* to revise.

rivelare *vt* to give away, to disclose, to reveal; * *vr* **~rsi** to turn out, to prove.

rivelato *adj* revealed; **mai ~** *adj* untold.

rivelatore *m* detector, indicator; * *adj* revealing, telltale.

rivelazione *f* revelation, disclosure.

rivendicare *vt* to stake, to claim.

riversare *vt* to disgorge; * *vr* **~rsi** to surge.

rivestimento *m* facing, casing.

rivestire *vt* to cover; **~ con materiale isolante** *vt* to lag.

rivettare *vt* to rivet.

rivista *f* magazine, review.

rivolo *m* trickle.

rivolta *f* revolt.

rivoltante *adj* revolting.

rivoltare *vt* to revolt.

rivoltella *f* gun, revolver.

rivoltoso *m* rioter.

rivoluzionario *adj*, *m* revolutionary.

rivoluzione *f* revolution.

rizzarsi *vi* to bristle.

roano *m* roan.

roba *f* stuff, things.

robbia *f* madder.

robot *m inv* robot.

robustezza *f* sturdiness.

robusto *adj* stout, sturdy, robust, hardy.

roccia *f* rock.

roccioso *adj* rocky.

rock *m* rock.

roditore *m* rodent.

rododendro *m* rhododendrum.

rognone *m* kidney.

rognoso *adj* mangy.

romantico *adj* romantic.

romanziere *m* novelist.

romanzo *m* novel.
rombo *m* rhombus; boom, rumble; ~ **di tuono** *m* thunderclap.
romice *m* dock.
rompere *vt* to snap, to break, to rupture; * *vr* **~rsi** to break.
rompicapo *m* puzzle.
rondella *f* washer.
rondine *f* swallow.
rondone *m* swift.
ronzare *vi* to drone, to hum, to buzz.
ronzino *m* nag.
ronzio *m* drone, buzz, hum.
rosa *f* rose; * *adj, m inv* pink; ~ **selvatica** brier.
rosaio *m* rosebed.
rosario *m* rosary.
rosato *adj* rosy; **vino ~** *m* rosé wine.
rosbif *m* roast beef.
roseo *adj* rosy.
rosicchiare *vt* to gnaw, to nibble.
rosmarino *m* rosemary.
rosolare *vt* to brown.
rosone *m* rose.
rospo *m* toad.
rosseggiare *vi* to glow.
rossetto *m* lipstick.
rossiccio *adj* reddish, ginger.
rosso *adj, m* red.
rossore *m* redness, blush, flush.
rosticceria *f* takeaway.
rotaia *f* rail.
rotare *vi* to rotate.
rotatoria *f* roundabout.
rotazione *f* rotation.
roteare *vi* to gyrate, to wheel; **far ~** *vt* to twirl.
rotella *f* caster, roller.
rotolare *vi, vt* to roll; * *vr* **~rsi** to wallow.
rotolo *m* scroll, coil, roll.
rotondo *adj* round.
rotta *f* course, route.
rottame *m* write-off.

rotto *adj* broken.
rottura *f* severance, rupture, break.
rotula *f* knee-cap.
roulette *f* roulette.
roulotte *f inv* caravan.
round *m inv* round.
routine *f* routine.
rovente *adj* red-hot.
rovescia *f* lapel; **alla ~** *adj* inside out; **conto alla ~** *m* countdown.
rovesciamento *m* overthrow.
rovesciare *vt* to tip, to topple, to spill, to upset, to overthrow: * *vr* **~rsi** to tip.
rovescio *m* reverse, (*sport*) backhand, purl.
rovina *f* ruin, undoing, downfall.
rovinare *vt* to spoil, to ruin.
rovistare *vi* to rummage, to ransack.
rovo *m* bramble bush.
royalty *m inv* royalty.
rozzo *adj* boorish, uncouth, rough.
rubacchiare *vt* to pilfer, to filch.
rubamazzo *m* snap.
rubare *vt* to steal.
rubicondo *adj* ruddy.
rubinetto *m* tap, (water) cock.
rubino *adj, m* ruby.
rublo *m* rouble.
rubrica *f* rubric.
rudere *m* ruin.
rudimentale *adj* rough and ready.
rudimento *m* rudiment.
ruga *f* wrinkle, line.
rugby *m* rugby.
ruggine *f* rust.
rugginoso *adj* rusty.
ruggire *vi* to roar.
ruggito *m* roar.
rugiada *f* dew.
rullare *vi* to taxi.
rullino *m* film, roll.

rullo *m* roller; **~ compressore** *m* steamroller.

rum *m inv* rum.

ruminare *vi* to ruminate, to chew over.

rumore *m* noise, sound; **~ metallico** *m* clank, clang; **~ secco** *m* rattle; **produrre un ~ metallico** *vi* to jangle.

rumorosamente *adv* noisily.

rumoroso *adj* vociferous, noisy.

ruolo *m* role.

ruota *f* wheel; **~ di scorta** *f* spare wheel; **andare a ~ libera** *vi* to freewheel; **~ dentata** *f* gearwheel.

rupe *f* crag.

rurale *adj* rural.

ruscelletto *m* rivulet.

ruscello *m* stream, brook.

ruspante *adj* free-range.

russare *vi* to snore.

rustico *adj* rustic.

rusticone *m* bumpkin.

ruta *f* rue.

ruttare *vi* to belch, to burp.

rutto *m* burp, belch.

ruvidità *f* roughness.

ruvido *adj* rough, coarse.

ruzzolare *vi* to tumble.

S

sabato *m* Saturday, Sabbath.

sabbia *f* sand; **sacco di ~** *m* sandbag; **sabbie mobili** *fpl* quicksand.

sabbiare *vt* to sandblast.

sabbioso *adj* sandy.

sabotaggio *m* sabotage.

sabotare *vt* to sabotage.

saccarina *f* saccharin.

saccheggiare *vt* to sack, to raid, to pillage, to loot.

saccheggiatore *m* marauder.

saccheggio *m* sack, plunder.

sacchetto *m* carrier bag, bag.

sacco *m* sack; **~ a pelo** *m* sleeping bag.

sacerdotale *adj* priestly.

sacerdote *m* clergyman.

sacerdotessa *f* priestess.

sacerdozio *m* priesthood.

sacramento *m* sacrament.

sacrificale *adj* sacrificial.

sacrificare *vt* to sacrifice.

sacrificio *m* sacrifice.

sacrilegio *m* sacrilege.

sacrilego *adj* sacrilegious.

sacro *adj* sacred.

sacrosanto *adj* sacrosanct.

sadico *m* sadist.

sadico *adj* sadistic.

sadismo *m* sadism.

safari *m inv* safari.

saga *f* saga.

saggezza *f* wisdom.

saggio *adj* wise; * *m* essay; sage.

Sagittario *m* Sagittarius.

sagoma *f* silhouette, template.

sagrestano *m* sexton.

sagrestia *f* vestry.

sagù *m* sago.

sala *f* room, hall; **~ da ballo** *f* ballroom; **~ d'udienza** *f* courtroom; **~ di regia** (*TV, radio*) *f* control room; **~ di comando** (*naut, mil*) *f* control room; **~ d'attesa** *f* departure lounge; airport lounge.

salamandra *f* salamander.

salame *m* salami, sausage.

salamoia *f* brine; **mettere in ~** *vt* to souse.

salare *vt* to salt, to cure.

salariato *m* wage earner.

salato *adj* savoury, salty; **piatto ~** *m* savoury.

saldamente *adv* steadily, fast.

saldare *vt* to weld, to solder; to settle, to pay off; **lampada a benzina per ~** *f* blowlamp.

saldarsi *vr* to set.

saldatura *f* weld.

saldo *adj* steady, firm; * *m* balance.

sale *m* salt.

salgemma *m* rock salt.

salice *m* willow; **~ piangente** *m* weeping willow.

salicone *m* pussy willow.

saliente *adj* salient.

saliera *f* salt cellar.

salina *f* saltworks.

salino *adj* saline.

salire *vt, vi* to ascend, to mount, to climb, to go up ; **~ su** to board.

salita *f* rise, climb, slope, ascension; **in ~** *adj* uphill.

saliva *f* saliva.

salivare *vi* to salivate.

salma *f* corpse.

salmo *m* psalm.

salmone *m* salmon.

salnitro *m* saltpeter.

salone *m* salon, saloon, lounge, hall.

saloon *m inv* saloon.

salopette *f inv* dungarees.

salotto *m* parlour, drawing room, sitting room.

salpare *vi* to set sail.

salsa *f* sauce; **~ indiana** *f* chutney.

salsetta *f* dip.

salsiccia *f* sausage, banger.

saltare *vi, vt* to jump; * *vi* to spring, to skip; **~ con un balzo** *vi* to vault; **far ~** *vt* to blast.

saltatore *m* jumper.

saltellare *vi* to skip, to caper, to hop, to cavort.

saltello *m* skip, hop.

salto *m* jump, spring; **fare un ~** *vi* to pop in; **~ mortale** *m* somersault.

saltuario *adj* casual (labour).

salubre *adj* wholesome, salubrious.

salumeria *f* delicatessen.

salutare *adj* salutary; * *vt* to salute, to greet.

salute *f* health.

saluto *m* greeting, salute; **distinti saluti** *mpl* yours sincerely.

salva *f* salvo.

salvacondotto *m* safe-conduct.

salvadanaio *m* piggy bank.

salvaguardare *vt* to safeguard.

salvaguardia *f* safeguard.

salvare *vt* to save, to rescue.

salvataggio *m* salvage, rescue; **lancia di ~** *f* lifeboat; **giubbotto di ~** *m* life jacket; **sagola di ~** *f* lifeline.

salvatore *m* saviour.

salvezza *f* salvation, boon.

salvia *f* sage.

salvo prep save; * *adj* safe.

sambuco *m* elder; **bacca di ~** *f* elderberry.

San Silvestro *m*: **la notte di ~** *f* New Year's Eve.

sancire *vt* to sanction.

sandalo *m* sandal.

sandwich *m* sandwich.

sangue *m* blood; **~ freddo** *m* sangfroid; **al ~** *adj* rare.

sanguinaccio *m* black pudding.

sanguinante *adj* bleeding, bloody.

sanguinare *vi* to bleed.

sanguinario *adj* bloodthirsty.

sanguinoso *adj* gory.

sanguisuga *f* leech, bloodsucker.

sanità *f* soundness; **~ mentale** *f* sanity.

sano *adj* healthy, sound; **~ e salvo** *adj* safe and sound, unhurt; **~ di mente** *adj* sane.

santificare *vt* to sanctify.

santità *f* sanctity, godliness, holiness.

santo *m* saint; * *adj* saintly, holy; **lo Spirito S~** *m* the Holy Ghost.

santuario *m* sanctuary, shrine.

sanzione *f* sanction.

sapere *vi* to know, to smell (of), to hear; **io non so nuotare** I can't swim; * *m* knowledge.

sapientone *m* smart aleck, know-all.

saponata *f* soap suds.

sapone *m* soap.

sapore *m* taste, flavour, savour; **~ forte** *m* tang.

saporito *adj* tasty.

saracinesca *f* shutter.

sarcasmo *m* sarcasm.

sarcastico *adj* sarcastic.

sarcofago *m* sarcophagus.

sardina *f* sardine, pilchard.

sardonico *adj* sardonic.

sarta *f* seamstress.

sarto *m* tailor, dressmaker.

sassofono *m* saxophone.

sassoso *adj* stony.

Satana *m* Satan.

satanico *adj* satanic.

satellite *m* satellite.

satira *f* satire, lampoon.

satireggiare *vi* to satirize.

satirico *adj* satirical; **scrittore ~** *m* satirist.

satiro *m* satyr.

saturare *vt* to saturate.

savana *f* savannah.

saziare *vt* to satiate.

sazio *adj* replete.

sbaciucchiarsi *vr* to smooch.

sbadigliare *vi* to yawn.

sbadiglio *m* yawn.

sbagliare *vt* to make a mistake, to err; * *vr* **~rsi** to slip up, to mistake.

sbagliato *adj* wrong.

sbaglio *m* mistake, slip.

sballottare *vt* to toss, to jostle, to buffet.

sbalordire *vt* to stagger, to astound.

sbalorditivo *adj* staggering.

sbalordito *adj* flabbergasted.

sbaragliare *vt* to rout.

sbarazzare *vt* to rid.

sbarazzarsi *vr* to throw off.

sbarcare *vi* to disembark, to land.

sbarco *m* landing, disembarkation.

sbarra *f* rail, bar.

sbarramento *m* barrage.

sbarrare *vt* to bar, to cross; **~ gli occhi** *vi* to goggle; **~ contro** *vt* to strike.

sbattere *vt*, *vi* to bang, to slam, to flap, to bump; **~ le palpebre** *vt* to blink; **andare a ~ contro** *vt* to blunder into.

sbavare *vi* to slaver, to drool, to slobber.

sbiadirsi *vr* to fade.

sbiancare *vt* to whiten; **~ in viso** *vi* to blanch.

sbigottire *vt* to dumbfound.

sbigottito *adj* aghast.

sbilanciarsi *vr* to overbalance.

sbilenco *adj* lop-sided.

sbirciare *vi* to peek, to peep.

sbloccare *vt* to unblock.

sbornia *f* drunkenness; **postumi di una ~** *mpl* hangover.

sborsare *vt* to disburse, to fork out.

sbottonare *vt* to unbutton.

sbranare *vt* to savage, to maul.

sbriciolare *vt* to crumble; * *vr* **~rsi** to crumble.

sbrigare *vt* to deal with, to polish off.

sbrigativo *adj* brisk.
sbrinare *vt* to defrost.
sbrindellato *adj* bedraggled.
sbrodolare *vt* to dribble.
sbrogliare *vt* to untangle, to disentangle.
sbronzo *adj* drunk, tight.
sbucciapatate *m* potato peeler.
sbucciare *vt* to peel, to skin.
sbuffare *vi* to snort, to chug.
sbuffata *f* snort.
scacchi *mpl* chess; **pezzo degli ~** *m* chessman.
scacchiera *f* chessboard.
scacciare *vt* to oust.
scacco *m* check (chess); **~ matto** *m* checkmate.
scadente *adj* shoddy, third-rate, ropy.
scadenza *f* expiry, deadline.
scadere *vi* to fall due, to lapse, to expire.
scaduto *adj* out-of-date, overdue.
scaffalature *fpl* shelving.
scafo *m* hull.
scagionare *vt* to vindicate; * *m* vindication.
scaglia *f* scale, flake.
scagliare *vt* to sling, to hurl.
scaglionare *vt* to stagger.
scala *f* scale, ladder, staircase; **~ di sicurezza** *f* fire escape; **su vasta ~** *adj* full-scale; **~ cronologica** *f* timescale; **in grande ~** *adj* large scale; **~ mobile** *f* escalator.
scalare *vt* to scale, to climb.
scalata *f* climb.
scaldabagno *m* water-heater, geyser.
scaldare *vt* to warm, to heat; **~ con aromi** *vt* to mull; * *vr* **~rsi** to warm up.
scaldavivande *m inv* hotplate.
scaletta *f* stile.
scalfittura *f* score.
scalino *m* stair.

scalo *m* slipway.
scalogno *m* shallot.
scalpello *m* chisel.
scalpitare *vt* to paw the ground.
scalpore *m* sensation, stir, furore.
scaltrezza *f* wiliness.
scaltro *adj* knowing, wily.
scalzo *adj* barefoot(ed).
scambiare *vt* to swap, to exchange.
scambio *m* exchange, swap, interchange; **libero ~** *m* free trade.
scamosciata *adj* oil-tanned; **pelle ~** *f* suede.
scampanellata *f* ring.
scampanio *m* peal.
scampare *vt* to escape.
scampolo *m* remnant.
scanalatura *f* slot.
scandagliare *vt* to plumb.
scandaglio *m* sounding, sounding line.
scandalizzare *vt* to scandalize, to shock.
scandalo *m* scandal.
scandaloso *adj* shocking, outrageous, scandalous.
scandire *vi* to scan.
scansafatiche *m/f* shirker.
scansare *vt* to shirk.
scapolo *adj* unmarried; * *m* bachelor.
scappare *vi* to escape, to abscond; **lasciarsi ~** *vr* to blurt out.
scappatella *f* escapade.
scappatoia *f* loophole.
scarabeo *m* beetle.
scarabocchiare *vt* to scribble, to doodle.
scarabocchio *m* scribble, doodle.
scarafaggio *m* cockroach.
scaramuccia *f* skirmish.
scaraventare *vt* to dash.

scardinare *vt* to unhinge.

scarica *f* discharge.

scaricare *vt* to dump, to unload, to discharge.

scaricatore *m* unloader; **~ di porto** *m* stevedore.

scarico *m* drain, plughole, outlet; **tubazione di ~** *f* wastepipe: **tubo di ~** *m* drainpipe; **gas di ~** *m* exhaust; * *adj* flat battery.

scarlattina *f* scarlet fever.

scarlatto *adj, m* scarlet.

scarmigliato *adj* unkempt.

scarpa *f* shoe; **scarpe da ginnastica** *fpl* trainers.

scarpata *f* scarp, escarpment.

scarpetta *f* bootee.

scarpone *m* boot, brogue; **~ da sci** *m* ski boot.

scarsità *f* dearth, scarcity, scarceness.

scarso *adj* slender, scant, scarce, sparse.

scartare *vt* to push aside, to unwrap, to discard, to reject.

scartavetrare *vt* to sand.

scarto *m* reject; **di ~** *adj* waste, trashy.

scartoffie *fpl* bumf.

scassato *adj* dilapidated.

scassinatore *m* housebreaker.

scatenare *vt* to trigger (off); * *vr* **~rsi** to go on the rampage, to let rip.

scatola *f* tin, box.

scattare *vi* to click.

scatto *m* click; **muoversi a scatti** *vr* to jerk; **a scatti** *adj* jerky.

scavare *vt* to excavate, to dig, to sink, to channel, to gouge, to hollow; **~ gallerie** to burrow.

scavatore *m* digger.

scavezzacollo *m* daredevil.

scavo *m* excavation, dig, cutting (railway, etc).

scegliere *vt* to single out, to select, to cull (fruit), to choose, to pick.

sceicco *m* sheik.

scellerato *m* miscreant.

scellino *m* shilling.

scelta *f* selection, pick, option, choice; * *adj* select.

scemo *m* nit, twit.

scena *f* scene.

scendere *vt, vi* to come down, to descend.

sceneggiatura *f* screenplay.

sceriffo *m* sheriff.

scervellarsi *vr* to rack one's brains.

scervellato *m* scatterbrain.

scetticismo *m* scepticism.

scettico *m* sceptic; * *adj* sceptical.

scettro *m* sceptre.

scheda *f* index card.

scheggia *f* sliver, splinter.

scheggiare *vt* to chip; * *vr* **~rsi** to splinter.

scheggiatura *f* chip.

scheletrico *adj* scraggy.

scheletro *m* skeleton.

schematico *adj* schematic.

scherma *f* fencing.

schermo *m* screen.

scherno *m* mockery.

scherzare *vi* to joke, to kid, to jest.

scherzetto *m* caper.

scherzo *m* joke, lark, trick, jest, hoax.

schiaccianoci *m inv* nutcrackers.

schiacciante *adj* damning, overwhelming.

schiacciare *vt* to swat, to squash, to mash, to crush.

schiaffeggiare *vt* to smack.

schiaffo *m* slap, smack, buffet; **dare uno ~ a** *vt* to slap.

schiarirsi *vr* to brighten.

schiavitù *f* slavery.

schiavo *m* slave; **rendere ~** *vt* to enslave.

schiena *f* back.

schiera *f* array.

schieramento *m* array.

schierare *vt* to deploy, to marshall.

schietto *adj* frank, outright, forthright.

schiffo *m* cuff.

schifoso *adj* lousy, rotten.

schioccare *vt* to snap.

schiocco *m* snap, pop, smack.

schiudersi *vr* to unfold, to hatch (egg).

schiuma *f* froth, foam, lather.

schiumare *vt* to skim; * *vi* to froth.

schiumeggiare *vi* to foam.

schiumoso *adj* frothy.

schivare *vt* to dodge.

schivata *f* dodge; **fare una ~** *vi* to duck.

schizofrenia *f* schizophrenia.

schizzare *vt* to splash, to squirt; to sketch.

schizzinoso *adj* choosy, fussy.

schizzo *m* squirt; sketch.

schooner *m inv* schooner.

sci *m inv* ski, skiing.

scia *f* wake, trail.

sciacallo *m* jackal.

sciacquare *vt* to rinse.

sciacquatura *f* rinse.

sciacquone *m* flush.

sciagurato *m* wretch.

scialbo *m* dowdy.

scialle *m* wrap, shawl.

scialuppa *f* sloop.

sciamare *vi* to swarm.

sciame *m* swarm.

sciarada *f* charade.

sciare *vi* to ski.

sciarlatano *m* charlatan.

sciarpa *f* scarf.

sciatica *f* sciatica.

sciatore *m* skier.

sciatto *adj* slipshod, slovenly.

sciattone *m* slob.

scientifico *adj* scientific.

scienza *f* science.

scienziato *m* scientist.

scimitarra *f* scimitar.

scimmia *f* monkey, ape.

scimpanzé *m inv* chimpanzee.

scintilla *f* spark.

scintillante *adj* scintillating.

scintillare *vi* to twinkle, to sparkle, to glint.

scintillio *m* twinkle, glint, sparkle.

scioccare *vt* to shock.

sciocchezza *f* silliness, trifle.

sciocco *m* fool; * *adj* silly, soppy, daft, nonsensical.

sciogliere *vt* to melt, to dissolve, to disband, to untie; **~ da** *vt* to absolve from.

scioglilingua *m inv* tongue-twister.

scioglimento *m* dissolution.

scioltezza *f* fluency.

sciolto *adj* loose, runny.

scioperante *m/f* striker.

scioperare *vi* to strike.

sciopero *m* strike, stoppage.

sciovinismo *m* chauvinism.

sciovinista *m/f* chauvinist.

scipito *adj* vapid.

scippatore *m* bag-snatcher.

scisma *m* schism.

scissione *f* split.

scissionista *adj* breakaway.

sciupare *vt* to mar.

scivolare *vi* to slide, to slip.

scivolata *f* slip.

scivolo *m* slide, chute; **~ a spirale** *m* helter skelter.

scivolone *m* slide.

scivoloso *adj* slippery.

sclerosi *f* sclerosis.

scocciato *adj* narked.

scocciatura *f* drag.

scodella *f* bowl.

scodinzolare *vi* to wag.

scogliera *f* reef, cliff.

scoiato *adj* skinned.

scoiattolo *m* squirrel.

scolara *f* schoolgirl.

scolaro *m* schoolboy.

scolastico *adj* scholastic.

scollato *adj* low-cut.

scollatura *f* cleavage.

scolorimento *m* discoloration.

scolorire *vt* to discolour.

scolpare *vt* to exculpate.

scolpire *vi*, *vt* to sculpt, to carve.

scombussolamento *m* disruption.

scombussolare *vt* to disrupt, to upset, to unsettle.

scombussolato *adj* upset.

scommessa *f* wager, bet.

scommettere *vi*, *vt* to bet, to wager.

scomodità *f* inconvenience.

scomodo *adj* uncomfortable, inconvenient.

scompagnato *adj* odd.

scomparire *vi* to die out, to disappear.

scomparsa *f* disappearance.

scomparso *adj* defunct.

scompartimento *m* compartment.

scompigliare *vt* to mess up.

scomposto *adj* dishevelled; **sdraiarsi/sedersi in modo ~** *vr* to sprawl.

scomunica *f* excommunication.

scomunicare *vt* to excommunicate.

sconcertante *adj* uncanny, puzzling, confusing.

sconcertare *vt* to abash, to disconcert, to nonplus.

sconcertato *adj* abashed; embarrassed.

sconcezze *fpl* smut.

sconcio *adj* smutty.

sconfiggere *vt* to vanquish, to defeat.

sconfinato *adj* unbounded.

sconfitta *f* defeat, beating.

scongelare *vt* to thaw.

sconnesso *adj* unconnected, desultory.

sconosciuto *adj* strange, unknown, unfamiliar; * *m* stranger.

sconsiderato *adj* thoughtless.

sconsigliabile *adj* inadvisable.

sconsolato *adj* disconsolate, forlorn.

scontato *adj* discounted, foreseen; **un risultato ~** *m* a foregone conclusion; **dare per ~** *vi* to take for granted.

scontentezza *f* discontent.

scontento *adj* discontent, discontented.

sconto *m* discount.

scontrarsi *vr* to crash, to collide, to clash.

scontro *m* clash, smash, collision, confrontation.

scontroso *adj* sullen, bloody-minded.

sconveniente *adj* unbecoming.

sconvolgere *vt* to convulse.

sconvolgimento *m* upheaval.

sconvolto *adj* deranged, shattered.

scooter *m inv* scooter.

scopa *f* broom; **~ di filacce** *f* mop.

scopare *vt*, *vi* to sweep, to brush.

scopata *f* sweep.

scoperta *f* discovery, detection, find: **~ decisiva** *f* breakthrough.

scoperto *adj* exposed.

scopo *m* purpose, point, end, goal; **senza ~** *adj* aimless.

scoppiare *vi* to burst, to break out; **far ~** *vt* to pop, to burst; **~ a piangere** *vi* to burst into tears.

scoppiettare *vi* to sputter, to crackle.

scoppiettio *m* crackle.

scoppio *m* blowout, outbreak, outburst.

scoprire *vt* to uncover, to find out, to rumble, to discover.

scoraggiamento *m* discouragement.

scoraggiante *adj* discouraging, daunting.

scoraggiare *vt* to discourage, to dishearten.

scorbutico *adj* grumpy.

scorbuto *m* scurvy.

scoreggia *f* fart.

scoreggiare *vi* to fart.

scorgere *vt* to spy, to descry.

scorie *fpl* slag.

Scorpione *m* Scorpio.

scorpione *m* scorpion.

scorrere *vi* to run, to stream, to course.

scorrettezza *f* impropriety.

scorretto *adj* incorrect, improper; **gioco ~** *m* foul play.

scorrevole *adj* sliding, fluent.

scorso *adj* last.

scorta *f* stockpile, escort.

scortare *vt* to escort.

scortese *adj* discourteous, unkind, impolite.

scortesia *f* impoliteness, discourtesy.

scorticare *vt* to scrape, to graze.

scorticatura *f* graze.

scossa *f* jolt, tremor, shake, shock.

scotch *m inv* adhesive tape, sellotape.

scotennare *vt* to scalp.

scottare *vt* to scald, to blanch.

scottato *adj* sunburnt.

scottatura *f* scald, sunburn.

scovolino *m* pipe cleaner.

scozzese *adj* Scottish; **tessuto ~** *m* plaid.

screditare *vt* to discredit; * *vr* **~rsi** to cheapen oneself.

scremare *vt* to skim.

scremato *adj* skimmed.

screpolatura *f* chap.

screziato *adj* speckled.

scriba *m* scribe.

scribacchiare *vt* to scrawl.

scribacchino *m* hack.

scricchiolare *vi* to crunch, to creak.

scricchiolio *m* creak, crunch.

scricciolo *m* wren.

scrigno *m* casket.

scrittore *m* writer.

scrittura *f* writing, handwriting, script; **Sacre scritture** *fpl* Scripture.

scrivania *f* desk, writing desk.

scrivere *vt, vi* to write, to pen; * *m* writing.

scroccare *vi* to sponge, to scrounge, to cadge.

scroccone *m/f* scrounger, sponger, cadger.

scrofa *f* sow.

scrollata *f* shaking.

scrostarsi *vr* to flake.

scrostato *adj* flakey.

scroto *m* scrotum.

scrupolo *m* scruple, qualm compunction; **senza scrupoli** *adj* unscrupulous.

scrupoloso *adj* scrupulous.

scrutare *vt* to scan, to peer, to eye, to scrutinize.

scrutinio *m* scrutiny.

scuderia *f* stable.

scudo *m* shield.

sculacciare *vt* to spank, to smack.

scultore *m* sculptor.

scultura *f* sculpture; **~ in legno** *f* woodcarving.

scuola *f* school; **~ superiore privata** *f* public school; **~ serale** *f* night school; **~ di perfezionamento** *f* finishing school; **~ guida** *f* driving school; **~ d'arte** *f* art school

scuotere *vt* to shake, to rouse.

scuro *adj* dark; **di colorito ~** *adj* swarthy.

scurrile *adj* scurrilous.

scusa *f* excuse; **scuse** *fpl* apology; **di ~** *adj* apologetic; **~! scusi!** *excl* sorry!.

scusare *vt* to excuse; * *vr* **~rsi** to apologize.

sdegnare *vt* to disdain.

sdegno *m* outrage.

sdegnoso *adj* disdainful.

sdentato *adj* toothless.

sdoganamento *m* clearance.

sdolcinato *adj* sloppy.

sdraiarsi *vr* to lie down.

sdraiato *adj* lying; **essere ~** *vi* to recline.

sdrucciolevole *adj* slippery.

se *conj* if, whether.

se stessi *pers pron* themselves.

secca *f* shallow; **in ~** *adv* aground.

seccante *adj* tiresome, irksome.

seccare *vt* to dry.

seccato *adj* cross.

seccatura *f* bother, nuisance.

secchezza *f* dryness.

secchio *m* pail, (coal) scuttle, bucket.

secco *adj* dry.

secernare *vt* to secrete.

secessione *f* secession.

secolare *adj* secular.

secolo *m* century.

secondario *adj* secondary, incidental; prodotto ~ *m* spin-off; **scuola ~** *f* secondary school.

secondino *m* screw.

secondo *prep* according to, under; * *adj, m* second.

secretaire *m* bureau.

secrezione *f* secretion, discharge.

sedano *m* celery.

sedativo *m, adj* sedative.

sede *f* seat, head office; **~ vescovile** *f* see.

sedentario *adj* sedentary.

sedere *vi* to sit; **far ~** *vt* to seat; * *m* bottom, backside; * *vr* **~rsi** to sit.

sedia *f* chair, seat; **~ a rotelle** *f* wheelchair; **~ a sdraio** *f* deckchair.

sedicente *adj* self-styled.

sedicesimo *adj, m* sixteenth.

sedici *adj, m* sixteen.

sedile *m* seat.

sedimento *m* sediment, lees.

sedizione *f* sedition.

sedizioso *adj* seditious.

seducente *adj* glamorous, seductive.

sedurre *vt* to seduce.

seduta *f* sitting, session.

seduttore *m* seducer.

seduzione *f* seduction.

sega *f* saw.

segale *f* rye.

segare *vt* to saw.

segatura *f* sawdust.

seggio *m* seat.

seggiolino *m* seat; **~ eiettabile** *m* ejector seat.

seggiolone *m* high chair.

segheria *f* sawmill.

seghettato *adj* serrated, jagged.

seghetto *m* hacksaw.

segmento *m* segment.

segnalare *vt, vi* to signal.

segnale *m* signal, sign; **~ acustico** *m* bleep.

segnalibro *m* bookmark.

segnare *vt* to show, to write down, to score, to mark.

segnato *adj* marked; **~ dalle intemperie** *adj* weather-beaten.

segnatura *f* signature.

segnavento *m inv* weathervane.

segno *m* indicator, token, tick, sign, mark.

segregare *vt* to segregate, to sequester.

segregazione f segregation.
segreta f dungeon.
segretariato m secretariate.
segretario m secretary; ~ **comunale** m town clerk.
segreteria telefonica f answering machine.
segretezza f secrecy.
segretissimo adj top-secret.
segreto adj secret, sneaking; * m secret.
seguace m/f follower.
seguente adj following.
segugio m bloodhound, sleuth, hound.
seguire vt to follow; * vi to ensue.
seguito m retinue, sequel, following; **in** ~ adv thereafter, afterwards.
sei adj, m six.
selezionare vt to select.
selezione f selection.
self-service adj inv self-service.
sella f saddle; **senza** ~ adj bareback.
sellaio m sadler.
sellare vt to saddle.
sellino m seat; ~ **posteriore** m pillion.
seltz m inv soda.
selvaggina f game.
selvaggio adj uncivilized, wild, savage; * m savage.
selvatico adj wild.
semaforo m traffic lights.
semantica f semantics.
sembianza f guise.
sembrare vi to seem, to appear, to look; **voler** ~ vt to purport.
seme m seed, pip.
semestrale adj half-yearly.
semiasse m axle.
semicerchio m semicircle.
semicircolare adj semicircular.
semiconduttore m semiconductor.

semifinale f semifinal.
semina f sowing.
seminare vt to sow, to seed.
seminario m seminar, seminary.
seminterrato m basement.
semiprezioso adj semiprecious.
semolino m semolina.
semplice adj simple, plain, easy.
semplicemente adv simply, merely.
sempliciotto m simpleton.
semplicità f simplicity.
semplificare vt to simplify.
semplificazione f simplification.
sempre adv always, ever; **per** ~ adv forever; ~ **più veloce** adv faster and faster.
sempreverde m/f evergreen.
senape f mustard.
senato m senate.
senatore m senator.
senile adj senile.
senilità f senility.
senna f senna.
senno m sense.
seno m bosom, breast; sinus; ~ **scoperto** adj topless.
sensale m/f middleman; ~ **d matrimoni** m matchmaker.
sensazione f sensation, fee' feeling.
sensibile adj tender, sensitiv
sensibilità f sensitivity.
senso m sense, feeling; **priv di sensi** adj senseless; **senz** ~ adj meaningless; **buon** ~ common sense.
sensuale adj sensual.
sensualità f sensuality.
sentenza f sentence.
sentenzioso adj sententious
sentiero m track, trail, path
sentimentale adj sentiment
sentimento m sentiment, fee

ing; **~ falso** *m* bathos.

sentinella *f* sentry, look-out.

sentire *vt* to feel, to hear, to catch; **~ odore di** *vt* to smell; **~ per caso** *vt* to overhear.

sentito *adj* warm.

senza *prep* without, apart from.

separabile *adj* separable.

separare *vt* to separate, to part.

separatamente *adv* separately.

separato *adj* separate, estranged, discrete; **vivere separati** to live apart.

separazione *f* separation, parting.

sepolcro *m* sepulchre.

sepoltura *f* burial.

seppellimento *m* interment.

seppellire *vt* to bury, to inter.

seppia *f* cuttlefish.

sequenza *f* sequence, clip.

sequestrare *vt* to impound, to sequestrate.

sequestro *m* attachment; **~ di persona** *m* kidnapping.

sera *f* evening.

serata *f* evening.

serbatoio *m* tank, cistern; **~ del carburante** *m* fuel tank.

serenata *f* serenade; **fare la ~ a** *vt* to serenade.

serenità *f* serenity, equanimity.

sereno *adj* serene, halcyon, calm.

serge *f* serge.

sergente *m* sergeant.

serie *f inv* succession, series, run.

serigrafia *f* silk-screen printing.

serio *adj* serious, earnest.

sermone *m* sermon.

serpeggiante *adj* winding.

serpeggiare *vi* to meander.

serpente *m* snake, serpent.

serpentina *f* serpentine.

serra *f* hot-house, greenhouse, conservatory.

serraglio *m* seraglio; menagerie.

serrata *f* lockout.

serratura *f* lock; **buco della ~** *m* keyhole.

servile *adj* servile; menial.

servire *vi* to wait, to serve, to dish.

servizio *m* service, (press, radio, TV) coverage; **~ da tè** *m* tea service.

servo *m* servant; **~ favorito** *m* minion.

sessanta *adj, m* sixty.

sessantesimo *adj, m* sixtieth.

sessismo *m* sexism.

sessista *adj* sexist.

sesso *m* sex.

sessuale *adj* sexual.

sessualità *f* sexuality.

sestante *m* sextant.

sestetto *m* sextet.

sesto *adj, m* sixth.

set *m inv* set.

seta *f* silk; **baco da ~** *m* silkworm.

setacciare *vt* to scour, to sieve, to sift.

setaccio *m* sieve, riddle.

sete *f* thirst.

setola *f* bristle.

setoloso *adj* bristly.

setta *f* sect.

settanta *adj, m* seventy.

settantesimo *adj, m* seventieth.

settario *adj* sectarian.

sette *adj, m* seven.

settembre *m* September.

settentrionale *adj* northern.

settentrione *m* north.

setter *m inv* setter.

setticemia *f* septicaemia.

settico *adj* septic.

settimana *f* week; **fine ~** *m inv* weekend.

settimanale *adj, m* weekly.

settimo *adj, m* seventh.

settore *m* sector.

severità *f* strictness, harshness, severity.

severo *adj* severe, harsh, strict.

sexy *adj inv* sexy.

sezionamento *m* dissection.

sezionare *vt* to dissect.

sezione *f* section, department; ~ **trasversale** *f* cross-section.

sfaccettatura *f* facet.

sfacchinata *f* drudgery.

sfacciataggine *f* forwardness.

sfacciato *adj* blatant, brazen, barefaced.

sfacelo *m* dilapidation.

sfarzo *m* pageantry.

sfavorevole *adj* unfavourable, adverse.

sfortuna *f* adversity.

simile *adj* alike.

sfera *f* sphere.

sferico *adj* spherical.

sferragliare *vi* to clatter, to rattle.

sfibrato *adj* jaded.

sfida *f* dare, defiance, challenge.

sfidante *m/f* challenger.

sfidare *vt* to defy to brave, to dare, to challenge.

sfigurare *vt* to disfigure.

sfilare *vt* to unthread; * *vi* to parade; ~ **davanti** *vi* to file past.

sfilata *f* parade, marchpast; ~ **di moda** fashion show.

sfinge *f* sphinx.

sfiorare *vi* to touch on, to brush.

sfocato *adj* fuzzy, hazy.

sfoderato *adj* unlined.

sfogare *vt* to vent.

sfoggiare *vt* to flaunt.

sfogliare *vt* to flip through.

sfogo *m* rash.

sfolgorare *vi* to glare, to flare.

sfondo *m* background.

sformato *adj* baggy.

sfortunatamente *adv* unfortunately, unhappily.

sfortunato *adj* hapless, unlucky, unfortunate.

sforzarsi *vr* to strive, to exert oneself.

sforzo *m* stress, exertion, effort.

sfrattare *vt* to evict.

sfratto *m* eviction.

sfrecciare *vi* to zoom off.

sfregare *vt* to rub, to chafe, to scour.

sfregiare *vt* to deface, to slash, to scar.

sfrenato *adj* unrestrained.

sfrigolare *vi* to sizzle.

sfrontatezza *f* effrontery, impudence.

sfrontato *adj* unashamed, brash, impudent.

sfruttamento *m* exploitation.

sfruttare *vt* to tap, to exploit.

sfruttato *adj* exploited; **non ~** *adj* untapped.

sfuggire *vi* to slip, to escape.

sfumatura *f* tint, nuance, overtone.

sgabello *m* stool.

sgambettare *vi* to scamper, to frolic.

sganciare *vt* to unhook, to uncouple.

sgangherato *adj* ramshackle.

sgarbato *adj* churlish, bad mannered.

sgargiante *adj* garish.

sgarrare *vi* to lapse.

sgattaiolare *vi* to sneak; ~ **via** *vi* to scuttle off.

sgobbare *vi* to slave, to plod.

sgobbone *m* slogger.

sgocciolare *vi* to drip.

sgombero *m* clearance.

sgombrare *vt* to clear.

sgombro *adj* clear; * *m* mackerel.

sgomentare *vt* to dismay.

sgomento *m* dismay; * *adj* dismayed.

sgonfiare *vt* to deflate.

sgonfio *adj* flat.

sgorgante *adj* gushing.

sgorgare *vi* to well up, to gush.

sgradevole *adj* undesirable, distasteful, nasty; **oggetto ~ alla vista** *adj* eyesore.

sgradevolezza *f* unpleasantness.

sgranare *vt* to shell.

sgranocchiare *vt* to munch, to crunch.

sgridare *vt* to scold.

sguaiato *adj* ribald.

sgualcire *vt* to crease.

sgualdrina *f* tart, slut.

sguardo *m* look, gaze; **~ fisso** *m* stare; **~ passeggero** *m* glimpse.

sguazzare *vi* to paddle, to dabble.

shampoo *m inv* shampoo.

shearling *m* sheepskin.

sherry *m inv* sherry.

shock *m inv* shock.

show-room *m inv* showroom.

si *pers pron* itself, themselves.

sì *adv*, *m* yes, yeah.

sibilare *vi* to hiss.

sibilo *m* hiss.

siccità *f* drought.

siccome *conj* since.

sicomoro *m* sycamore.

sicurezza *f* safety, security; **di massima ~** *adj* gilt-edged (stocks, etc).

sicuro *adj* sure, safe, secure, confident; **~ di se** *adj* self-confident; **una cosa ~** *f* a cinch.

sidro *m* cider.

siepe *f* hedge.

siero *m* serum.

sifilide *f* syphilis.

sifone *m* siphon.

sigaretta *f* cigarette, (*fam*) fag.

sigaro *m* cigar; **~ spuntato** *m* cheroot.

sigillare *vt* to seal.

sigillo *m* seal.

sigla *f* abbreviation; **~ editoriale** *f* imprint.

significare *vt* to signify, to mean.

significativo *adj* meaningful, significant.

significato *m* meaning, significance, purport.

signora *f* lady, madam, Mrs.; **da ~** *adj* ladylike.

signore *m* sir, gentleman, lord, Mr.

signorina *f* Miss.

silenziatore *m* silencer.

silenzio *m* silence, quiet, hush.

silenziosamente *adv* softly.

silenzioso *adj* quiet, silent.

silfo *m* sylph.

silice *f* flint.

sillaba *f* syllable.

sillogismo *m* syllogism.

silo *m* silo.

siluro *m* torpedo.

silvicoltura *f* forestry.

simboleggiare *vt* to symbolize.

simbolico *adj* symbolic, token.

simbolo *m* symbol.

simile *adj* similar, comparable, like; **simili** *mpl* fellow men.

similitudine *f* simile.

simmetria *f* symmetry.

simmetrico *adj* symmetrical.

simpatia *f* liking, fellow feeling; **prendere in ~** *vt* to take to.

simpatico *adj* likeable, nice, congenial.

simposio *m* symposium.

simulare *vt* to simulate, to feign.

simulato *adj* sham.

simulazione *f* simulation.

simultaneo *adj* simultaneous, concurrent.

sinagoga *m* sinagogue.

sincerità *f* sincerity.

sincero *adj* sincere, true, heart-felt.

sincronizzare *vt* to synchronize.

sindaca *f* mayoress.

sindacalismo *m* trade unionism.

sindacalista *m/f* trade unionist, unionist.

sindacalizzare *vt* to unionize.

sindacato *m* syndicate, trade union, union.

sindaco *m* mayor.

sindrome *f* syndrome.

sinecura *f* sinecure.

sinfonia *f* symphony.

singhiozzare *vi* to sob.

singhiozzo *m* sob, hiccup; **avere il ~** *vi* to hiccup.

singolare *adj* singular, quaint.

singolarità *f* singularity.

singolo *adj* single; * *m* singles (tennis).

sinistra *f* left hand; **a ~** *adv* on the left.

sinistro *adj* left, eerie, sinister, spooky.

sinodo *m* synod.

sinonimo *m* synonym, byword; * *adj* synonymous.

sinossi *f inv* synopsis.

sintassi *f* syntax.

sintesi *f inv* synthesis.

sintomo *m* symptom.

sintonizzatore *m* tuner.

sinuoso *adj* sinuous.

sirena *f* siren, hooter, mermaid.

siringa *f* syringe.

siringare *vt* to syringe.

sistema *m* system.

sistemare *vt* to settle, to position, to fix, to arrange.

sistematico *adj* systematic.

sistemazione *f* accommodation, arrangement.

sit-in *m inv* sit-in.

situare *vt* to place.

situato *adj* situated.

situazione *f* situation; **~ critica** *f* plight.

skate-board *m inv* skateboard.

sketch *m inv* sketch; **~ satirico** *m* skit.

slacciare *vt* to undo, to unfasten.

slam *m inv* slam.

slang *m* slang.

sleale *adj* treacherous, disloyal.

slealtà *f* treachery, disloyalty.

slegato *adj* disjointed.

slip *m inv* pants, underpants, briefs.

slitta *f* sled, sledge, sleigh.

slittamento *m* skid.

slittare *vi* to skid.

slittino *m* toboggan.

slogan *m inv* slogan.

slogare *vt* to wrench, to strain, to dislocate; * *vr* **~rsi** to twist, to sprain.

slogatura *f* dislocation, sprain.

smagliare *vt* to ladder.

smagliatura *f* run.

smaltare *vt* to enamel.

smalto *m* enamel, glaze; **~ per unghie** *m* nail varnish.

smammare *vi* to push off.

smarrire *vt* to mislay, to misplace; * *vr* **~rsi** to stray.

smarrito *adj* lost; **ufficio oggetti smarriti** *m* lost property office.

smascherare *vt* to unmask, to expose.

smembrare *vt* to dismember.

smemoratezza *f* forgetfulness.

smentire *vt* to belie, to deny, to disclaim.

smentita *f* disclaimer.

smeraldo *m* emerald.

smeriglio *m* emery.

smerlare *vt* to scallop.

smerlo *m* scallop.

smettere *vt* to quit, to stop.

smidollato *adj* spineless.

sminuire *vt* to understate, to detract, to belittle.

smistare *vt* to sort, to shunt.

smisurato *adj* immense.

smoderato *adj* immoderate.

smog *m inv* smog.

smontare *vt* to take down, to dismantle, to dismount.

smorfia *f* grimace.

smorto *adj* pasty.

smottamento *m* landslip.

smussare *vt* to dull, to bevel.

smussatura *f* bevel.

snazionalizzare *vt* to denationalize.

snellezza *f* slenderness.

snello *adj* trim, slender.

snervante *adj* nerve-racking.

snervare *vt* to enervate.

snidare *vt* to ferret out.

sniffare *vt* to sniff.

snob *m/f inv* snob; * *adj* snobbish, snob, genteel.

snobbare *vt* to snub, to slight.

snobismo *m* snobbery.

sobbalzare *vi* to lurch, to jolt.

sobbalzo *m* lurch, start, jerk.

sobbollire *vi* to simmer.

sobborgo *m* suburb.

sobrietà *f* sobriety.

sobrio *adj* sober.

socchiuso *adj* ajar.

soccombere *vi* to succumb.

soccorrere *vt* to help, to aid.

soccorso *m* help; **pronto ~** *m* first aid.

socialismo *m* socialism.

socialista *m/f* socialist.

società *f inv* society, company, corporation; **~ per azioni** *f* joint stock company.

socievole *adj* sociable; **poco ~** *adj* unsociable.

socio *m* partner, member.

sociologia *f* sociology.

sociologico *adj* sociological.

sociologo *m* sociologist.

soda *f* soda.

soddisfacente *adj* satisfactory, gratifying.

soddisfare *vt* to satisfy, to content, to gratify, to meet.

soddisfatto *adj* satisfied; **~ di sé** *adj* self-satisfied.

soddisfazione *f* satisfaction, gratification, fulfilment.

sodio *m* sodium.

sodo *adj* hard-boiled.

sofà *m inv* sofa.

sofferente *adj* ailing.

sofferenza *f* affliction, suffering.

soffiare *vi* to puff, to blow.

soffiata *f* tip-off.

soffice *adj* soft.

soffietto *m* bellows.

soffio *m* puff.

soffitta *f* attic, garret, loft.

soffitto *m* ceiling.

soffocamento *m* asphyxiation.

soffocante *adj* sweltering, overpowering, stifling,

soffocare *vt* to suffocate, to stifle, to choke, to cramp.

soffocazione *f* suffocation.

soffrire *vt, vi* to suffer.

sofisticare *vt* to adulterate.

sofisticato *adj* sophisticated.

software *m* software.

soggettivo *adj* subjective.

soggetto *m* subject; **~ a** *adj* subject to, prone to, liable to.

sogghignare *vi* to sneer.

sogghigno *m* sneer.

soggiogare *vt* to subjugate.

soggiorno *m* living room; stay.

soglia *f* threshold, doorstep.

sogliola *f* sole.

sognare *vt, vi* to dream, to muse; **~ ad occhi aperti** *vi* to daydream.

sognatore *m* dreamer.

sogno *m* dream, fantasy; **mondo dei sogni** *m* cloud-cuckooland; **di ~** *adj* dreamy.

soia f soya.
solamente adv only.
solare adj solar.
solarium m inv solarium.
solcare vt to furrow.
solco m rut, groove, furrow.
soldato m soldier; ~ **semplice** m private.
soldo m penny, cent; **soldi** mpl money, cash; **senza un** ~ adj penniless.
sole m sun; **prendere il** ~ vi to sunbathe; **senza** ~ adj sunless; **luce del** ~ f sunlight, sunshine.
solecismo m solecism.
soleggiato adj sunny.
solenne adj solemn.
solennità f inv solemnity.
solennizzare vt to solemnize.
soletta f insole.
solfato m sulphate.
solforico adj sulphuric.
solfuro m sulphide.
solidarietà f solidarity.
solidificare vt to solidify.
solidità f solidity.
solido adj solid, sturdy; * m solid.
soliloquio m soliloquy.
solista m/f soloist.
solitario adj solitary, lonely; * m solitaire.
solito adj stock, usual, accustomed; **di** ~ adv usually.
solitudine f solitude, loneliness.
sollecitare vt to solicit, to invite.
sollecito m reminder; * adj expeditious.
sollecitudine f solicitude.
solletico m tickle; **far il** ~ **a** vt to tickle; **che soffre il** ~ adj ticklish.
sollevare vt to raise, to lift, to uplift, to bring up; ~ **con una leva** vt to pry.

sollievo m relief.
solo adj alone, single, very; * conj but, only.
solstizio m solstice.
soltanto adv only, just.
solubile adj soluble, (coffee) instant.
soluzione f solution.
solvente adj, m solvent.
solvenza f solvency.
somaro m dunce.
somiglianza f similarity, resemblance, likeness.
somigliare vt to resemble.
somma f sum, amount.
sommare vt to add.
sommario m abstract.
sommergere vt to submerge, to overwhelm; * vr ~**rsi** to sink.
sommergibile m submarine.
sommersione f submersion.
somministrare vt to dose, to administer.
somministrazione f administration.
sommo adj supreme, paramount.
sommossa f riot, rising.
sonaglio m rattle.
sonata f sonata.
sonda f probe.
sondaggio m poll; ~ **di opinioni** m opinion poll.
sondare vt to sound, to probe.
sonetto m sonnet.
sonico adj sonic.
sonnambulismo m sleepwalking, somnambulism.
sonnambulo m sleepwalker, somnambulist.
sonnecchiare vi to snooze, to doze, to drowse.
sonnellino m snooze.
sonnifero m sleeping pill.
sonno m slumber, sleep.
sonnolento adj sleepy, dozy.
sonnolenza f sleepiness, somnolence, drowsiness.

sonoro *adj* sonorous.

sontuoso *adj* palatial, sumptuous, plush.

soporifero *adj* soporific.

soppiantare *vt* to supplant, to supersede.

soppiatto; di ~ *adv* stealthily.

sopportabile *adj* bearable, endurable.

sopportare *vt* to bear, to stand, to endure.

sopportazione *f* tolerance.

sopprimere *vt* to suppress, to put down.

sopra *prep* over, above, on; **di ~** *adj* upstairs; **piano di ~** *m* upstairs.

soprabito *m* overcoat.

sopracciglio *m* eyebrow.

sopraelevato *adj* overhead.

sopraffare *vt* to overpower, to overwhelm.

sopraggiungere *vi* to intervene.

soprammenzionato *adj* abovementioned.

soprannaturale *adj, m* supernatural.

soprannome *m* nickname.

soprannominare *vt* to nickname.

soprano *m/f* soprano.

sopratetto *m* flysheet.

sopratutto *adv* above all.

sopravvalutare *vt* to overrate, to overestimate.

sopravvenire *vi* to supervene.

sopravvivenza *f* subsistence.

sopravvivere *vt, vi* to survive; **~ a** *vt* to outlive.

soprintendente *m/f* superintendent.

sorbetto *m* sorbet, sherbet.

sordido *adj* sordid.

sordità *f* deafness.

sordo *adj* deaf.

sordomuto *adj* deaf-and-dumb.

sorella *f* sister, sibling; **da ~** *adv* sisterly.

sorellastra *f* step-sister.

sorgente *f* spring, source, fount.

sorgere *vi* to rise, to spring; * *m* rise.

soriano *m* tabby cat.

sormontabile *adj* surmountable.

sormontare *vt* to surmount, to top.

sorpassare *vt, vi* to pass, to outstrip.

sorpassato *adj* outdated, outmoded.

sorprendente *adj* surprising, startling, astonishing

sorprendere *vt* to surprise, to catch.

sorpresa *f* surprise; **bella ~** *f* windfall.

sorpresina *f* treat.

sorridere *vi* to smile; **~ in modo sciocco** *vi* to simper; **~ radiosamente** *vi* to beam; **~ compiaciuto** *vi* to smirk.

sorrisetto *m* smile; **~ sciocco** *m* simper.

sorriso *m* smile; **~ compiaciuto** *m* smirk; **largo ~** *m* grin; **fare un largo ~** *vi* to grin.

sorsata *f* draught.

sorseggiare *vt* to sip.

sorso *m* sip.

sorte *f* fate, lot.

sorteggio *m* draw.

sorvegliante *m/f* supervisor, overseer.

sorveglianza *f* supervision, watch.

sorvegliare *vt* to supervise, to invigilate, to oversee.

S.O.S. *m* S.O.S.

sosia *m inv* double.

sospendere *vt* to suspend, to stay, to adjourn.

sospensione *f* suspension, stoppage, adjournment; **~ dell'esecuzione** *f* stay of execution.

sospeso *adj* suspended; **in ~** *adj*

pending; **essere in ~** *vi* to be in abeyance.

sospettare *vt* to suspect.

sospetto *m* suspicion; * *adj* suspect, fishy.

sospettoso *adj* suspicious.

sospirare *vi* to sigh.

sospiro *m* sigh.

sosta *f* stop, stopover, halt.

sostantivo *adj* substantive; * *m* noun, substantive.

sostanza *f* substance.

sostanziale *adj* substantial.

sostanzioso *adj* substantial, filling.

sostegno *m* support, prop, mainstay.

sostenere *vt* to support, to sustain, to contend, to uphold.

sostenibile *adj* tenable.

sostenitore *m* supporter, backer, campaigner, advocate.

sostentamento *m* livelihood.

sostituire *vt* to substitute, to deputize, to replace.

sostituto *m* replacement, substitute; * *adj* deputy.

sostituzione *f* substitution.

sottaceti *mpl* pickles; **mettere sottaceto** *vt* to pickle.

sotterfugio *m* subterfuge.

sotterraneo *adj* subterranean, underground.

sottigliezza *f* subtlety.

sottile *adj* subtle, thin, fine.

sottilmente *adv* subtly.

sotto *adv*, *prep* under, underneath, below, beneath.

sottobicchiere *m* coaster.

sottobosco *m* undergrowth.

sottoesposto *adj* underexposed.

sottolineare *vt* to underline, to emphasize.

sottomano *adj* handy.

sottomarino *adj* underwater.

sottomesso *adj* submissive.

sottomettere *vt* to subdue.

sottomissione *f* submission, subjection.

sottopassaggio *m* subway, underpass.

sottopeso *adj* underweight.

sottoporre *vt* to subject.

sottoprodotto *m* by-product.

sottoscritto *adj*, *m* undersigned.

sottoscrivere *vt* to sign, to underwrite.

sottosegretario *m* undersecretary.

sottosopra *adj*, *adv* topsy-turvy, upside down.

sottosviluppato *adj* underdeveloped.

sottotitolo *m* subtitle, caption.

sottovalutare *vt* to undervalue, to underestimate, to underrate.

sottovento *adj* lee, leeward.

sottoveste *f* slip, petticoat.

sottrarre *vt* to subtract.

sottrazione *f* subtraction.

sottufficiale *m* non-commissioned officer; **~ di marina** *m* petty officer.

soufflé *m inv* soufflé.

souvenir *m inv* souvenir.

soviet *m inv* soviet.

sovietico *adj* soviet.

sovrabbondanza *f* surfeit, glut.

sovraccaricare *vt* to overload.

sovraffollato *adj* overcrowded.

sovranità *f* sovereignty.

sovrano *m* ruler, sovereign; * *adj* sovereign.

sovrappiù: *m* **di ~** *adj* surplus.

sovrapporsi *vr* to overlap.

sovrapposizione *f* overlap.

sovrapprezzo *m* surcharge.

sovrastruttura *f* superstructure.

sovrumano *adj* superhuman.

sovvenzionare *vt* to subsidize.

sovvenzione *f* grant, subsidy.

sovversione *f* subversion.

sovversivo *adj, m* subversive.

sovvertire *vt* to subvert.

spaccare *vt* to split, to chop; * *vr* ~**rsi** to split.

spaccatura *f* rift.

spacciare *vt* to peddle.

spacciatore *m* (drug) pusher; pedlar.

spacco *m* slit, vent, split.

spaccone *m* braggart.

spada *f* sword; **pesce** ~ *m* swordfish.

spadaccino *m* swordsman.

spadino *m* rapier.

spadroneggiare *vt* to domineer.

spaghetti *mpl* spaghetti.

spago *m* string.

spalancarsi *vr* to gape.

spalancato *adj* yawning, wide open.

spalare *vt* to shovel.

spalla *f* shoulder; **alzata di spalle** *f* shrug.

spallina *f* strap.

spalmare *vt* to smear, to spread.

spandersi *vr* to spread.

spaniel *m inv* spaniel.

spanna *f* span.

sparare *vt* to fire, to shoot.

sparatoria *f* shooting.

spareggio *m* disparity; **partita di** ~ *f* play-off.

spargere *vt* to strew.

spargimento *m* scattering; ~ **di sangue** *m* bloodshed.

sparlare *vi* to backbite.

sparo *m* shot, gunshot.

sparpagliare *vt* to scatter.

spartano *adj* spartan.

spartiacque *m* watershed.

spartizione *f* share-out.

sparviero *m* sparrowhawk.

pasmo *m* spasm.

pasmodico *adj* spasmodic.

passionato *adj* dispassionate.

spassosissimo *adj* hilarious.

spastico *m, adj* spastic.

spatola *f* spatula.

spauracchio *m* bugbear.

spavalderia *f* bravado.

spaventapasseri *m inv* scarecrow.

spaventare *vt* to frighten, to startle, to scare.

spaventato *adj* frightened.

spavento *m* scare, fright.

spaventoso *adj* frightening, abysmal, horrific.

spaziale *adj* spatial; **veicolo** ~ *m* spacecraft.

spazio *m* room, space, gap; ~ **cosmico** *m* outer space.

spazioso *adj* spacious, roomy.

spazzacamino *m* chimney sweep.

spazzaneve *m inv* snowplough.

spazzare *vt, vi* to sweep.

spazzatura *f* trash, rubbish.

spazzola *f* brush; ~ **per capelli** *f* hairbrush.

spazzolare *vt* to brush.

spazzolino *m* small brush; ~ **da denti** *m* toothbrush; ~ **da unghie** *m* nailbrush.

specchio *m* mirror, looking glass.

speciale *adj* special.

specialista *m/f* (*med*) consultant, specialist.

specialità *f inv* speciality.

specializzato *adj* specialist, skilled.

specializzazione *f* specialization; **di** ~ **dopo la laurea** *adj* post-graduate.

specie *f inv* sort, species.

specificare *vt* to specify; ~ **uno per uno** *vt* to itemize.

specificazione *f* specification.

specifico *adj* specific.

specioso *adj* specious.

speculare *vi* to speculate, to profiteer.

speculativo *adj* speculative.

speculatore *m* profiteer.

spedire *vt* to ship, to send, to dispatch; ~ **per posta** *vt* to post, to mail.

spedizione *f* trek, expedition, dispatch.

spedizioniere *m* shipper.

spegnere *vt* to switch off, to extinguish, to blow out (candle); * *vr* ~**rsi** to die down.

spellare *vt* to skin; ~**rsi** to peel.

spendaccione *m* spendthrift.

spendere *vt* to spend, to expend.

spennare *vt* to pluck.

spensierato *adj* happy-go-lucky, light hearted, carefree.

spento *adj* dull, off.

speranza *f* hope.

sperare *vt* to hope.

sperduto *adj* godforsaken.

spergiurare *vt* to perjure.

spergiuro *m* perjury.

spericolato *adj* reckless.

sperimentale *adj* experimental.

sperimentare *vt* to test.

sperma *m* sperm, semen.

speronare *vt* to ram.

sperone *m* spur.

sperperare *vt* to squander.

spesa *f* expense, shopping, groceries, outlay; **fare la** ~ *vi* to shop.

spesso *adj* thick; * *adv* often.

spessore *m* thickness.

spettacolo *m* spectacle, show, entertainment; **il mondo dello** ~ *m* show business.

spettare *vi* to be due, to appertain.

spettatore *m* spectator, onlooker.

spettinato *adj* uncombed.

spettrale *adj* spectral.

spettro *m* spectre.

spezie *fpl* spice.

spezzato *adj* broken.

spezzone *m* extract.

spia *f* spy; **fare la** ~ **a** *vi* to sneak on; ~ **luminosa** *f* warning light.

spiacevole *adj* unpleasant, disagreeable.

spiaggia *f* seaside, beach.

spianare *vt* to smooth, to level, to flatten.

spiare *vi* to peep, to spy.

spicchio *m* gore (in skirt), segment.

spiccioli *m pl* small change.

spiedino *m* kebab.

spiedo *m* spit, skewer.

spiegabile *adj* explicable.

spiegare *vt* to unfold, to spread, to explain.

spiegazione *f* explanation, elucidation.

spiegazzare *vt* to screw up, to crinkle.

spietato *adj* pitiless, ruthless, remorseless.

spifferare *vt* to blab.

spiffero *m* draught.

spigliato *adj* racy, jaunty.

spigoloso *adj* angular.

spilla *f* brooch; ~ **di balia** *f* safety pin.

spillo *m* pin; **fissare con uno** ~ *vt* to pin.

spilorcio *adj* stingy.

spilungone *adj* lanky.

spina *f* plug, thorn, prickle; ~ **dorsale** *f* spine, backbone; **alla** ~ *adj* on draught.

spinaci *mpl* spinach.

spinale *adj* spinal.

spinello *m* joint.

spinetta *f* spinet.

spingere *vt* to push, to propel, to shove, to drive; ~ **con forza** *vt* to thrust.

spinoso *adj* thorny, prickly, spiky.

spinta *f* push, impetus, boost.

spinto *adj* suggestive, risqué, bawdy, naughty.

spintone *m* thrust, shove.

spionaggio *m* spying, espionage.

spioncino *m* peephole.

spione *m* telltale, sneak.

spirale *adj* spiral; * *f* spiral, (contraceptive) coil.

spirare *vi* to expire.

spiritista *m/f* spiritualist.

spirito *m* spirit.

spiritosaggine *f* wisecrack.

spiritoso *adj* humorous.

spirituale *adj* spiritual.

spiritualità *f* spirituality.

splendido *adj* splendid, stunning, gorgeous.

splendore *m* radiance, splendour.

spogliare *vt* to undress, to despoil, to divest, to strip; * *vr* ~rsi to strip.

spogliarellista *m/f* stripper.

spogliarello *m* striptease.

spoglio *adj* bare.

spola *f* shuttle; **fare la ~ tra** *vi* to ply between, to shuttle.

spolverare *vt*, *vi* to dust.

sponda *f* shore.

sponsor *m/f inv*.

sponsorizzare *vt* to sponsor.

sponsorizzazione *f* sponsorship.

spontaneamente *adv* voluntarily.

spontaneità *f* spontaneity.

spontaneo *adj* unstudied, spontaneous.

spopolamento *m* depopulation.

spopolare *vt* to depopulate.

sporadico *adj* sporadic.

sporcare *vt* to soil, to foul, to smear.

sporcizia *f* dirtiness.

sporco *adj* dirty, smutty; * *m* dirt.

sporgente *adj* overhanging.

sporgenza *f* ledge.

sporgere *vi* to protrude, to stick out, to jut (out), to overhang.

sport *m inv* sport; ~ **invernali** *mpl* winter sports.

sportello *m* door; ~ **automatico** *m* cash dispenser.

sportiva *f* sportswoman.

sportivo *m* sportsman.

sposa *f* bride.

sposare *vt* to wed, to marry; * *vr* ~rsi to marry.

sposato *adj* married.

sposo *m* spouse, bridegroom.

spossessare *vt* to dispossess.

spostare *vt* to budge, to shift, to move, to displace.

spot *m inv* spotlight.

spratto *m* sprat.

spray *m inv* spray.

sprecare *vt* to fritter (away), to waste.

sprecato *adj* misspent.

spreco *m* wastage, waste.

sprecone *adj* wasteful.

spregevole *adj* contemptible, despicable.

spregiativo *adj* derogatory.

spremere *vt* to squeeze.

sprezzante *adj* scornful, scathing, contemptuous.

sprigionare *vt* to give off.

sprint *m inv* sprint.

spronare *vt* to spur, to urge on, to goad.

sprone *m* yoke, boost, spur.

sproporzionato *adj* disproportionate.

sprovvisto *adj* lacking; **essere colto (preso) alla ~** to be taken aback, unawares.

spruzzare *vt* to spray, to squirt.

spruzzatina *f* sprinkling.

spruzzo *m* splash, spray.

spudorato *adj* shameless.

spugna *f* towelling, sponge; **lavare con una ~** *vt* to sponge.

spugnoso *adj* spongy.

spumoso *adj* foamy.

spuntare *vt* to tick, to trim; ~ denti *vt* to cut teeth; * *vi* to dawn (day).

spuntata *f* trim.

spuntino *m* snack.

spurgare *vt* to bleed (radiators, etc).

sputacchiare *vi* to splutter.

sputare *vt, vi* to spit.

sputo *m* spit, spittle.

squadra *f* team, side; ~ **di armati** *f* posse.

squadrare *vt* to square.

squadrone *m* troop, squadron.

squalificare *vt* to disqualify.

squallido *adj* seedy, sleazy, squalid, dingy.

squallore *m* squalor.

squalo *m* shark.

squama *f* scale.

squamare *vt* to scale.

squarciare *vt* to gash.

squarcio *m* gash.

squash *m* squash.

squaw *f inv* squaw.

squilibrato *adj* unbalanced.

squilibrio *m* imbalance.

squillo *m* ring.

squisito *adj* exquisite.

squittio *m* squeak.

squittire *vi* to peep, to squeak.

sradicare *vt* to eradicate, to uproot.

srotolare *vt* to unwind, to unroll.

stabile *adj* stable.

stabilimento *m* plant.

stabilire *vt* to establish, to set, to stipulate, to name.

stabilità *f* stability.

stabilito *adj* set.

stabilizzare *vt* to stabilize.

staccabile *adj* detachable.

staccare *vt* to unplug, to disconnect, to detach; * *vr* ~**rsi** to come off.

staccato *adj* unattached, detached, loose.

stadera *f* steelyard.

stadio *m* stage.

staffa *f* stirrup.

stagionare *vt* to season.

stagionato *adj* ripe.

stagione *f* season; **di** ~ *adj* seasonable; **bassa** ~ *f* off season.

stagnante *adj* slack, stagnant.

stagnare *vi* to stagnate.

stagno *adj* watertight; * *m* tin.

stalagmite *f* stalagmite.

stalattite *f* stalactite.

stalla *f* stable, stall, barn, cowshed.

stallo *m* stalemate; **andare in** ~ *vi* to stall.

stallone *m* stud, stallion.

stame *m* stamen.

stampa *f* press, print, printing; **stampe** *fpl* printed matter; **agenzia** ~ *f* news agency.

stampante *m* printer.

stampare *vt* to print.

stampatello *m* printing.

stampato *m* print.

stampella *f* crutch.

stampo *m* cast, mould.

stancare *vt* to tire; * *vr* ~**rsi** to flag.

stanchezza *f* tiredness, weariness, fatigue.

stanco *adj* weary, tired; ~ **morto** *adj* dead tired.

stand *m inv* stall, stand.

standard *adj, m inv* standard.

standing *m* financial standing.

stantio *adj* stale, musty.

stantuffo *m* piston.

stanza *f* room.

stanziamento *m* allocation.

stanziare *vt* to station.

stappare *vt* to uncork.

stare *vi* to stay, to stand; ~ **i piedi** *vi* to stand; ~ **per (far qc)** *vi* to be about to (do something).

starnutire *vi* to sneeze.

starnuto *m* sneeze.

starter *m inv* starter.

stasera *adv* tonight.

statico *adj* static.

statista *m* statesman.

statistica *f* statistics.

statistico *adj* statistical.

stato *m* status, state.

statua *f* statue.

statuario *adj* statuesque, statuary.

statura *f* stature.

status *m* status.

statuto *m* statute, charter.

stazionario *adj* stationary,

stazione *f* station; ~ **di servizio** *f* service station.

stecca *f* slat, splint, cue.

steeplechase *m inv* steeplechase.

stella *f* star; ~ **filante** *f* streamer; ~ **di mare** *f* starfish.

stellato *adj* starry.

stelo *m* stem.

stendardo *m* banner.

stendere *vt* to stretch, to lay.

stendibiancheria *m inv* clothes horse.

stenografia *f* stenography, shorthand.

stenografo *m* stenographer.

stentato *adj* laboured; **parlare un inglese** ~ *vt* to speak broken English.

sterco *m* dung.

stereo *m inv* stereo, hi-fi.

stereofonia *f* stereo.

stereotipo *m* stereotype.

sterile *adj* barren, sterile.

sterilità *f* sterility.

sterilizzare *vt* to sterilize.

sterlina *f* pound (sterling).

sterminare *vt* to exterminate.

sterminio *m* extermination.

sterno *m* sternum, breastbone.

sterzare *vi* to swerve, to steer.

sterzata *f* swerve.

sterzo *m* lock.

stesso *adj* self, same, self-same, very, own * *pron* same * *adv* anyhow.

stetoscopio *m* stethoscope.

steward *m inv* steward.

stia *f* coop.

stigma *m* stigma.

stigmatizzare *vt* to stigmatize.

stile *m* style, panache.

stiletto *m* stiletto.

stima *f* esteem, valuation, estimation.

stimabile *adj* reputable.

stimare *vt* to treasure, to esteem.

stimato *adj* valued.

stimolante *m* stimulant; *adj* stimulating, piquant, challenging.

stimolare *vt* to stimulate, to whet, to arouse.

stimolazione *f* stimulation.

stimolo *m* stimulus, fillip; **essere di** ~ **a** *vi* to prod.

stinco *m* shank, shin.

stipare *vt* to cram; ~ **di** *vt* to pack.

stipato *adj* crammed.

stipendio *m* wages, salary.

stipulazione *f* stipulation.

stiracchiarsi *vr* to stretch.

stirare *vt* to press, to iron; (muscles) to flex; * *m* ironing.

stirpe *f* stock, lineage, ancestry.

stitichezza *f* constipation.

stitico *adj* constipated.

stiva *f* hold.

stivale *m* boot.

stivare *vt* to stow.

stizzito *adj* peeved.

stizzoso *adj* peevish.

stock *m* stock.

stoffa *f* fabric, cloth, material; **negoziante di** ~ *m* draper.

stoicismo *m* stoicism.

**stoico n stoic; * *adj* stoical.

stola *f* stole.

stomaco *m* stomach; **bruciore di ~** *m* heartburn.

stonare *vt* to jar.

stonato *adj* flat, off-key.

stop *m* stop sign; **il fanalino dello ~** *m* brakelight.

stoppia *f* stubble.

stoppino *m* wick.

stordire *vt* to daze.

stordito *adj* light headed, in a daze, dazed.

storia *f* story, history; **storie** *fpl* fuss.

storico *adj* historic(al); * *m* historian.

storione *m* sturgeon.

storno *adj* starling.

storpiare *vt* to maim.

storta *f* retort.

storto *adj* crooked, awry; **guardare qn ~** *vt* to look askance at somebody; **con le gambe storte** *adj* bandy-legged.

strabico *adj* cross-eyed; **essere ~** *vi* to squint.

strabismo *m* squint, cast.

stracciare *vt* to shred.

stracciato *adj* ragged.

straccio *m* duster, rag; **passare lo ~** *vt* to mop.

strada *f* street, road, way; **~ transitabile** *f* thoroughfare; **portare qn su una brutta ~** to lead astray; **~ secondaria** *f* byway; **~ principale** *f* main road; **a metà ~** *adv* midway.

stradina *f* lane.

strafare *m* overkill.

strage *f* slaughter.

strambo *adj* rum.

stramoderno *adj* new-fangled.

strangolamento *m* strangulation.

strangolare *vt* to strangle.

straniero *m* alien, foreigner; * *adj* alien, foreign.

strano *adj* strange, peculiar, odd.

straordinario *adj* extraordinary; * *m* overtime.

strapazzare *vt* to overwork, (*culin*) to scramble.

strappare *vt* to tear, to rip, to wrench, to snatch;

strappo *m* strain, rip, tear.

straripare *vi* to flood.

strascicare *vt* to shuffle, to drawl.

strascicato *adj* trailing; **un passo ~** *m* shuffle.

stratagemma *m* stratagem, ploy.

strategia *f* strategy.

strategico *adj* strategic.

strato *m* stratum, ply, layer; **~ sottile** *m* film.

strattone *m* tug, wrench; **dare uno ~ a** *vt* to tug.

stravagante *adj* extravagant, outlandish, flamboyant.

stravaganze *f* extravagance.

stravedere *vi* to dote.

stravolto *adj* distraught.

straziante *adj* harrowing.

strega *f* witch; **caccia alle streghe** *f* witch-hunt.

stregare *vt* to bewitch.

stregone *m* sorcerer.

stregoneria *f* witchcraft, sorcery.

stremare *vt* to exhaust.

strepitoso *adj* roaring.

stress *m* stress.

stressante *adj* stressful.

stretta *f* squeeze.

strettamente *adv* closely.

stretto *adj* tight, strict, narrow; * *m* strait, sound.

striare *vt* to streak.

stricnina *f* strychnine.

stridere *vi* to screech.

stridio *m* rasp.

strido *m* screech.

stridulo *adj* shrill, grating.

strillare *vi* to yell, to bawl, to screech, to shriek.

strillo *m* scream, shriek, squeal.

striminzito *adj* stunted, puny.

strimpellare *vt* to strum.

stringa *f* shoelace.

stringente *adj* stringent.

stringere *vt* to tighten, to grip, to clench; * *vr* ~**rsi** to narrow.

striscia *f* streak, strip, band; **striscie pedonali** *fpl* pedestrian crossing.

strisciare *vi* to creep, to trail; ~ **di fronte a** *vi* to grovel.

striscio *m* smear; **di** ~ *adj* glancing.

striscione *m* banner.

stritolare *vt* to mangle.

strizzare *vt* to squeeze, to wring.

strizzata *f* squeeze.

strizzatina *f*: **una** ~ **d'occhio** *f* wink.

strizzatoio *m* mangle.

strofinaccio *m* dishcloth.

strofinamento *m* rub.

strofinare *vt* to scrub, to rub.

strofinata *f* scrub.

strombettare *vi* to blare.

stroncare *vt* to scotch, to quash.

stronza *f* bitch.

stronzio *m* strontium.

stronzo *m* turd, pig.

stropicciare *vt* to wrinkle.

strozzare *vt* to throttle, to strangle.

strozzatore *m* strangler.

struggente *adj* poignant.

strumentale *adj* instrumental.

strumento *m* instrument, tool.

struttura *f* structure, shell, framework.

strutturare *vt* to structure.

struzzo *m* ostrich.

stucchevole *adj* sickly.

stucco *m* stucco, putty.

studente *m* student; ~ **universitario** *m* undergraduate.

studiare *vt, vi* to study, to read.

studio *m* studio, study, practice.

studioso *adj* studious; * *m* scholar.

stufa *f* fire, heater, stove; ~ **a gas** *f* gasfire; ~ **elettrica** *f* electric fire.

stufare *vt* to stew.

stufato *m* stew.

stufo *adj* fed-up.

stunt-man *m inv* stuntman.

stupefacente *m* drug.

stupendo *adj* stupendous, wonderful, terrific.

stupidità *f* stupidity.

stupido *adj* stupid, witless, idiotic.

stupire *vt* to stupefy, to amaze, to astonish; * *vr* ~**rsi** to wonder, to marvel.

stupore *m* wonder, astonishment, amazement.

stuprare *vt* to rape.

stupratore *m* rapist.

stupro *m* rape.

sturalavandini *m inv* plunger.

stuzzicadenti *m inv* toothpick.

stuzzicare *vt* to tease, to bait.

su *adv* up, above; * *prep* over, on.

subacqueo *adj* underwater.

subaffittare *vt, vi* to sublet.

subalterno *adj, m* subordinate.

subappaltare *vt* to subcontract.

subconscio *m* subconscious.

subcosciente *adj* subconscious.

subdolo *adj* devious.

subentrante *adj* incoming.

subire *vt* to undergo, to sustain.

subito *adv* at once, straight away, forthwith.

sublimare *vt* to sublimate.

sublime *adj* sublime.

subliminale *adj* subliminal.

subnormale *adj* subnormal.

subordinare *vt* to subordinate.

subordinato *adj, m* subordinate.

subordinazione *f* subordination.

suburbano *adj* suburban.

succedere *vi* to happen, to transpire, to succeed.

successione *f* succession, sequence.

successivo *adj* subsequent, succeeding, next.

successo *m* success, hit.

successone *m* smash.

successore *m* successor.

succhiare *vt, vi* to suck.

succinto *adj* succinct, scanty.

succo *m* juice, gist; **~ di frutta** *m* fruit juice.

succoso *adj* juicy.

succulento *adj* succulent.

sud *adj, m* south; **del ~** *adj* southerly, southern; **verso ~** *adv* southward(s).

sudare *vt, vi* to sweat.

sudario *m* shroud.

suddetto *adj* aforementioned.

suddito *m* subject.

suddividere *vt* to subdivide.

sudicio *m* filth; * *adj* grimy, grubby.

sudiciume *m* grime, filth.

sudore *m* sweat.

sufficiente *adj* sufficient, enough, adequate.

sufficienza *f* enough; (*scol*) pass mark.

suffragetta *f* suffragette.

suffragio *m* suffrage.

suffumicare *vt* to fumigate.

suggerimento *m* tip, suggestion.

suggerire *vt* to suggest, to prompt.

suggeritore *m* prompter.

sughero *m* cork.

sugo *m* sauce; **~ dell'arrosto** *m* gravy.

suicida *adj* suicidal; * *m/f* suicide.

suicidio *m* suicide.

suini *mpl* swine.

suite *f inv* suite.

sultanina *f* sultana; **uva ~** *f* sultana.

sultano *m* sultan.

suo poss *adj, pron* your(s), her(s), his, its.

suocera *f* mother-in-law.

suocero *m* father-in-law.

suola *f* sole.

suonare *vt, vi* to sound, to play, to ring, to blow (trumpet, etc).

suono *m* sound; **~ acuto** *m* twang

suora *f* nun, sister.

superare *vt* to pass, to top, to excel, to surpass, to weather, to exceed, to clear, to overtake; **~ numericamente** *vt* to outnumber.

superbo *adj* superb, haughty.

superficiale *adj* superficial, perfunctory, facile.

superficie *f* top, surface; **risalire in ~** *vi* to surface.

superfluo *adj* superfluous.

superiore *adj* upper, senior, advanced; * *m/f* superior.

superiorità *f* superiority.

superlativo *adj, m* superlative.

supermercato *m* supermarket.

superpetroliera *f* supertanker.

superpotenza *f* superpower.

supersonico *adj* supersonic.

superstite *m/f* survivor.

superstizione *f* superstition.

superstizioso *adj* superstitious.

superuomo *m* superman.

supino *adj* supine.

supplementare *adj* supplementary, additional, backup, extra.

supplemento *m* supplement.

supplica *f* supplication, plea, entreaty.

supplicare *vt* to beg, to appeal

supporre *vt* to presume, to suppose, to guess, to assume.

supportabile *adj* tolerable, bearable.

supportare *vt* to bear.

supporto *m* strut.

supposizione *f* assumption, supposition, guess.

supposta *f* suppository.

suppurare *vi* to fester.

supremazia *f* supremacy.

supremo *adj* ultimate, crowning.

surf *m* surfboard.

surgelare *vt* to freeze.

surgelato *adj* frozen.

surplus *m inv* surplus.

surreale *adj* surrealistic.

surrealismo *m* surrealism.

surrogato *adj*, *m* surrogate.

suscettibilità *f* susceptibility, sensibility.

susina *f* plum, damson.

susino *m* plum tree.

suspense *m* suspense.

sussidiario *m* subsidiary.

sussidio *m* help; ~ **di disoccupazione** *m* dole.

sutura *f* suture.

svago *m* leisure.

svaligiare *vt* to rifle, to burgle.

svalutazione *f* devaluation.

svanire *vi* to vanish.

svantaggiato *adj* underprivileged.

svantaggio *m* disadvantage.

svantaggioso *adj* disadvantageous.

svariato *adj* diverse, multifarious.

svasato *adj* flared.

svastica *f* swastika.

sveglia *f* alarm.

svegliare *vt* to awake, to rouse; * *vr* ~**rsi** to wake; ~ **troppo tardi** to oversleep.

sveglio *adj* awake, smart, alert, quick-witted; **completamente** ~ *adj* wide-awake.

svelare *vt* to unveil.

svelto *adj* agile, smart.

svendita *f* sale.

svenimento *m* swoon, faint.

svenire *vi* to swoon, to faint.

sventolare *vt* to wave.

sventrare *vt* to gut.

sventurato *adj* luckless.

sverniciare *vt* to strip.

svestire *vt* to disrobe.

svezzare *vt* to wean.

sviare *vt* to sidetrack.

svignarsela *vi* to skive off, to slink away, to bolt.

svilire *vt* to debase.

sviluppare *vt* to develop; * *vr* ~**rsi** to develop; ~ **rapidamente** to mushroom.

sviluppo *m* development, twist.

svista *f* oversight, lapse.

svitare *vt* to unscrew.

svogliato *adj* half-hearted.

svolazzare *vi* to flit, to flutter.

svolazzo *m* flourish.

svolgere *vt* to perform.

svuotare *vt* to drain.

swing *m* swing.

T

tabaccaio *m* tobacconist.

tabacchiera *f* snuffbox.

tabacco *m* tobacco; ~ **da fiuto** *m* snuff.

tabella *f* chart, schedule, table.

tabellone *m* billboard, scoreboard.

tabernacolo *m* tabernacle.

tabù *m inv* taboo.
tabulatore *m* tabulator.
tacca *f* notch.
taccagno *adj* miserly.
taccheggiare *vi* to shoplift.
taccheggiatore *m* shoplifter.
tacchino *m* turkey.
tacco *m* heel.
taccola *f* jackdaw.
taccuino *m* notebook.
tacere *vi* to keep quiet; **far ~** *vt* to silence.
tachimetro *m* speedometer.
tacito *adj* tacit, unwritten.
taciturno *adj* taciturn.
tafano *m* horsefly.
tafferuglio *m* scuffle, scrimmage.
taffettà *m* taffeta.
taglia *f* size; **~ forte** *f* outsize.
tagliaboschi *m inv* woodcutter, woodsman.
tagliaerba *m inv* lawnmower.
taglialegna *m inv* lumberjack.
tagliare *vt* to cut, to slice, to sever, to hack, to chop, to carve.
tagliatelle *fpl* noodles.
tagliaunghie *m* clippers.
tagliente *adj* cutting, sharp, keen; **non ~** *adj* blunt.
tagliere *m* chopping board, breadboard.
taglietto *m* nick.
taglio *m* cut, cutback, slash; **a doppio ~** *adj* double-edged; **~ di capelli** *m* haircut.
tailleur *m inv* suit.
talco *m* talc, talcum powder.
tale *adj* such.
talea *f* cutting.
talento *m* talent; **di ~** *adj* talented.
talismano *m* talisman.
talmente *adv* such.
talpa *f* mole.
tamburellare *vt* to drum.
tamburino *m* tambourine.

tamburo *m* drum.
tamponamento *m* plugging; **~ a catena** *m* pile-up.
tamponare *vt* to dab.
tampone *m* tampon, wad, swab.
tana *f* warren, hole (fox, etc), burrow, den, lair.
tanga *m inv* G-string.
tangente *f* tangent.
tangibile *adj* tangible.
tanto *adj*, *pron* much, many; **ogni ~** *adv* now and then.
tappa *f* stage, leg.
tappare *vt* to bung, to cap, to cork, to plug.
tappetino *m* mat; **~ da bagno** bathmat.
tappeto *m* carpet, rug.
tappezzare *vt* to paper.
tappezzeria *f* upholstery.
tappo *m* top, bung, stopper, spigot, plug.
tarantola *f* tarantula.
tarchiato *adj* squat.
tardi *adj* late.
targa *f* plate.
tariffa *f* rate, tariff, fare, charge; **~ ridotta** *f* off-peak rate.
tarlo *m* woodworm.
tarma *f* moth.
tartan *m inv* tartan.
tartaro *m* tartar.
tartaruga *f* tortoise; **guscio di ~** *m* tortoiseshell; **~ acquatica** *f* turtle.
tartufo *m* truffle.
tasca *f* pocket.
tascabile *m* paperback.
tassa *f* duty, tax; **~ doganale** *f* customs duty.
tassare *vt* to tax.
tassativo *adj* imperative.
tassazione *f* taxation.
tassista *m/f* taxi-driver.
tasso *m* rate; badger; yew.
tastare *vt* to feel, to finger.

tastiera *f* keyboard.

tasto *m* key.

tattica *f* tactic, tactics.

tattico *adj* tactical.

tatto *m* touch, tact, feel.

tatuaggio *m* tattoo.

tatuare *vt* to tattoo.

tautologia *f* tautology.

tautologico *adj* tautological.

taverna *f* tavern.

tavola *f* table, plank; ~ **calda** *f* snack-bar.

tavolino *m* coffee table.

tavolo *m* table; ~ **da carte** card table.

tavolozza *f* palette.

taxi *m inv* taxi, cab.

tazza *f* cup; ~ **da tè** *f* teacup.

tazzone *m* mug.

tè *m inv* tea; ~ **al limone** *m inv* lemon tea.

teatrale *adj* theatrical.

teatro *m* theatre; **abitué del** ~ *m/f* theatregoer; ~ **lirico** *m* opera house.

tecnica *f* skill, technique.

tecnicità *f* technicality.

tecnico *m* technician; * *adj* technical.

tecnologia *f* technology.

tecnologico *adj* technological.

tedio *m* tedium.

tee *m inv* tee.

teenager *m/f inv* teenager.

tegola *f* tile.

teiera *f* teapot.

tek *m* teak.

tela *f* web, canvas; ~ **indiana** *f* cheesecloth; ~ **grezza** calico.

telaio *m* frame, loom, chassis.

telecomando *m* remote control.

telecomunicazioni *fpl* telecommunications.

telecronaca *f* commentary.

telecronista *m/f* commentator.

telefonare *vi* to phone, to ring, to call.

telefonata *f* telephone call.

telefonista *m/f* telephonist.

telefono *m* telephone, phone; ~ **pubblico** *m* payphone; ~ **rosso** *m* hotline.

telegiornale *m* TV news.

telegrafico *adj* telegraphic.

telegrafo *m* telegraph.

telegramma *m* telegram.

telenovella *f* soap opera.

telepatia *f* telepathy.

telescopio *m* telescope.

telespettatore *m* viewer.

televisione *f* television; **trasmettere per** ~ *vt* to televise.

televisore *m* television set.

telex *m inv* telex.

telone *m* tarpaulin; ~ **impermeabile** *m* groundsheet.

tema *m* theme.

temerario *adj* foolhardy.

temere *vt vi* to fear, to dread.

tempera *f* distemper.

temperamatite *m inv* sharpener.

temperamento *m* temperament, temper.

temperare *vt* to sharpen.

temperato *adj* temperate.

temperatura *f* temperature.

temperino *m* penknife.

tempesta *f* tempest, storm.

tempestare *vt* to pelt.

tempestivo *adj* prompt.

tempia *f* temple.

tempio *m* temple.

tempismo *m* timing.

tempo *m* time; weather; tense; ~ **libero** *m* spare time, leisure; **appena in** ~ in the nick of time; **a** ~ **pieno** *adj*, *adv* full-time.

temporale *m* storm, thunderstorm; **da** ~ *adj* thundery.

temporaneamente *adv* temporarily.

tenace *adj* tenacious, dogged.

tenacia *f* tenacity.

tenda *f* tent, curtain; **grande ~** *f* marquee; **~ avvolgibile** *f* blind.

tendenza *f* tendency, inclination, drift, bias.

tendenziosa *adj* tendentious; **una domanda ~** *f* a leading question.

tender *m inv* tender.

tendere *vt* to tend, to stretch, to strain, to tense, to extend; **tendere a** *vi* to be inclined to.

tendine *m* tendon, sinew; **~ del ginocchio** *m* hamstring.

tendone *m* awning; **~ del circo** *m* big top.

tenente *m* lieutenant.

tenere *vt* to keep, to stock, to retain, to carry, to hold, to have; **~ stretto** *vt* to clutch; **~ fede a** *vt* to abide by.

tenerezza *f* tenderness, gentleness, endearment.

tenero *adj* tender, endearing.

tenia *f* tapeworm.

tennis *m* tennis.

tennista *m/f* tennis player.

tenore *m* tenor.

tenorile *adj* tenor.

tensione *f* tension, stress, strain; **mancanza di ~** *f* slackness.

tentacolo *m* tentacle.

tentare *vt* to tempt, to attempt, to endeavour.

tentativo *m* endeavour, go, bid, try, attempt.

tentazione *f* temptation.

tentoni *adv* gropingly; **andare a ~** *vi* to fumble.

tenue *adj* tenuous, subdued.

tenuta *f* attire, estate.

teologia *f* theology.

teologico *adj* theological.

teologo *m* theologian.

teorema *m* theorem.

teoretico *adj* theoretical.

teoria *f* theory; **in ~** in theory, in the abstract.

teorico *m* theorist.

teorizzare *vi* to theorize.

teppista *m/f* hooligan, thug, hoodlum.

terapeutica *f* therapeutics.

terapeutico *adj* therapeutic.

terapia *f* therapy.

terapista *m/f* therapist.

tergicristallo *m* windscreen wiper.

tergiversare *vi* to prevaricate, to hedge.

tergo *m* back; **a ~** *adv* overleaf.

termale *adj* thermal; **stazione ~** *f* spa.

terminal *m* air terminal

terminale *adj*, *m* terminal.

terminare *vi*, *vt* to end, to terminate.

termine *m* term, limit, end; **portare a ~** *vt* to pull off; **a lungo ~** *adj* long-term; **~ improprio** *m* misnomer; **senza mezzi termini** *adv* bluntly.

termite *f* termite.

termometro *m* thermometer.

termoresistente *adj* heat-resistant.

termosifone *m* radiator.

termostato *m* thermostat.

terra *f* land, ground, earth; **per via di ~** *adv*, *adj* overland; **di ~ cotta** *adj* earthen; **a ~** *adj* ashore; **scendere a ~** *vi* to go ashore.

terraglie *fpl* earthenware.

terraiolo *m* landlubber.

terrazza *f* patio, terrace.

terremoto *m* earthquake.

terreno *m* ground, land, terrain, soil; **~ coltivabile** *m* farmland.

terrestre *adj* terrestrial; **forze terrestri** *fpl* land forces.

terribile *adj* terrible, frightful, awful, appalling.

terriccio *m* loam.

terrier *m inv* terrier.

terrificare *vt* to terrify.
territoriale *adj* territorial.
territorio *m* territory.
terrore *m* terror, dread.
terrorismo *m* terrorism.
terrorista *m/f* terrorist.
terrorizzare *vt* to terrorize.
terzo *adj*, *m* third.
teschio *m* skull.
tesi *f inv* thesis, contention.
teso *adj* tense, fraught, uptight, taut, edgy.
tesoriere *m* treasurer.
tesoro *m* treasure; exchequer; darling, sweetheart.
tessera *f* card.
tessere *vt*, *vi* to weave.
tessile *adj* textile.
tessitore *m* spinner.
tessitura *f* weaving.
tessuti *mpl* textiles.
tessuto *f* fabric, cloth, tissue, material.
test *m* test; **Pap ~** *m* cervical smear.
testa *f* head; **essere in ~** *vi* to be in the lead; **in ~** *adj* leading; **mal di ~** *m* headache.
testamento *m* testament, will.
testardaggine *f* stubbornness.
testardo *adj* headstrong.
testata *f* warhead; butt; **dare una ~** *vt* to butt.
testicolo *m* testicle.
testimone *m* witness; **banco dei testimoni** *m* witness box; **~ oculare** *m* eyewitness.
testimonianza *f* evidence, testimony.
testimoniare *vi* to testify, to witness.
testo *m* text.
testuale *adj* textual.
tetano *m* tetanus.
tetro *adj* bleak, dismal, sombre.
tetta *f* tit, boob.
tettarella *f* teat.
tetto *m* roof; **senza ~** *adj* home-

less; **~ apribile** *m* sunroof; **mettere il ~** *vi* to roof.
thermos *m inv* vacuum flask, thermos flask.
thriller *m inv* thriller.
tibia *f* shinbone.
tic *m inv* tic, twitch; **~ tac** *m inv* tick.
ticchettare *vi* to tick.
tiepido *adj* tepid, lukewarm.
tifo *m* typhus.
tifone *m* typhoon.
tifoso *m* fan, supporter.
tiglio *m* lime.
tigre *f* tiger, tigress.
timbrare *vt* to stamp.
timbro *m* stamp; **~ postale** *m* postmark.
timer *m inv* timer.
timidezza *f* timidity, shyness, diffidence.
timido *adj* shy, diffident, bashful, timid.
timo *m* thyme.
timone *m* rudder, helm.
timoniere *m* cox.
timore *m* fear; **~ reverenziale** *m* awe; **nel ~ che** *conj* lest.
timoroso *adj* apprehensive.
timpano *m* eardrum.
tingere *vt* to stain, to tint, to dye, to colour.
tino *m* vat.
tinta *f* paint, hue.
tintarella *f* suntan.
tintinnare *vi* to tinkle, to clink, to chink.
tintinnio *m* clink, ping, clatter.
tintore *m* dyer.
tintoria *f* dye-works.
tintura *f* dye.
tipico *adj* typical.
tipo *m* type, fellow, class, sort.
tipografo *m* printer, typographer.
tirannia *f* tyranny.
tirannico *adj* tyrannical.
tiranno *m* tyrant.

tirante m guy rope.

tirare vi to pull, to strain, to draw; ~ **avanti** vi to go ahead; ~ **su** vt to hitch up.

tirata f pull, tirade.

tirato adj haggard.

tiratore m shot; **franco ~** m sniper; ~ **scelto** m marksman.

tirchio adj tight-fisted.

tirocinante m/f trainee.

tirocinio m apprenticeship; **fare ~** vi to train.

tiroide f thyroid.

titillare vt to titillate.

titolare m bearer, occupant, occupier.

titolo m title, designation, stock; bond; **titoli di testa** mpl credits.

tizio m chap, bloke, guy.

tizzone m cinder.

toccare vt to touch.

tocco adj touched; * m touch.

toga f gown.

togliere vi to take away, to remove.

toilette f inv toilet, dressing table; ~ **per uomini** f gents; **articoli da ~** mpl toiletries.

tollerante adj tolerant.

tolleranza f tolerance.

tollerare vt to tolerate, to suffer.

tomaia f upper.

tomba f tomb, grave.

tombola f bingo.

tomo m tome.

tonaca f cassock, habit, frock.

tonalità f shade.

tonare vi to thunder.

tonfo m splash, thud, thump.

tonica f tonic; **acqua ~** f tonic water.

tonificante adj invigorating, bracing.

tonnellaggio m tonnage.

tonnellata f ton.

tonno m tuna.

tono m tone.

tonsilla f tonsil.

tonsillite f tonsillitis.

tonsura f tonsure.

tonto adj stupid; * m fool, jerk.

topazio m topaz.

topo m mouse; ~ **campagnolo** m field mouse; ~ **di biblioteca** m bookworm.

topografia f topography.

toporagno m shrew.

toppa f patch.

torace m thorax.

torba f peat.

torbido adj murky.

torchio m press.

torcia f torch.

torcicollo m crick in the neck, stiff neck.

tordo m thrush.

torello m bullock.

torero m bullfighter.

tormentare vt to torment, to badger, to pester, to plague.

tormento m torment.

tornado m inv tornado.

tornante m hairpin bend.

tornare vi to return; ~ **indietro** vi to turn back.

torneo m tournament.

tornio m lathe.

tornire vt to turn.

toro m bull.

Toro m Taurus.

torre f tower, (chess) rook; ~ **di guardia** f watchtower; ~ **di controllo** f control tower.

torrefare vt to roast (coffee).

torrente m torrent.

torrenziale adj torrential.

torretta f turret.

torrido adj torrid.

torrione m keep.

torrone m nougat.

torso m torso.

torsolo m stalk, core.

torta f pie, cake.

torto m wrong; **far ~ a** vt to wrong.

tortora *f* turtledove.

tortuoso *adj* circuitous, tortuous.

tortura *f* torture.

torturare *vt* to torture.

torvo *adj* grim; **sguardo ~** *m* scowl.

tosare *vt* to shear, to clip (dog, etc).

tosasiepi *m* hedge clippers.

tosse *f* cough.

tossico *adj* toxic.

tossicodipendente *m/f* drug addict.

tossicodipendenza *f* addiction.

tossicomane *m/f* addict.

tossina *f* toxin.

tossire *vi* to cough.

tostapane *m inv* toaster.

tostare *vt* to toast.

totale *adj* total, utter; * *m* total.

totalità *f* totality.

totalitario *adj* totalitarian.

tournée *f* tour.

tovaglia *f* tablecloth.

tovagliolo *m* napkin, serviette.

tozzo *adj* thickset.

tra *prep* between; **~ poco** *adv* shortly.

traballante *adj* rickety, shaky.

traballare *vi* to wobble.

traboccare *vi* to overflow, to slop, to brim over.

trabocchetto *m* booby trap.

tracagnotto *adj* dumpy.

tracannare *vt* to swill.

traccia *f* smear, trace; **essere sulle traccie di** *vt* to track.

tracciare *vt* to chart, to trace, to plot.

trachea *f* trachea, windpipe.

tracolla *f* strap.

tradimento *m* betrayal, treason.

tradire *vt* to betray, to shop.

traditore *m* traitor.

tradizionale *adj* traditional.

tradizione *f* tradition; **tradizioni** *fpl* lore.

tradurre *vt, vi* to translate.

traduttore *m* translator.

traduzione *f* translation.

trafficante *m/f* trafficker.

trafficare *vi* to traffic.

traffico *m* traffic.

trafficone *m* wheeler-dealer.

trafiggere *vt* to transfix, to spear, to impale.

trafila *f* rigmarole.

tragedia *f* tragedy.

traghetto *m* ferry.

tragicamente *adv* tragically.

tragico *adj* tragic.

tragicommedia *f* tragicomedy.

tragitto *m* haul, run.

traguardo *m* finishing line, finish, winning post.

tram *m inv* tram.

trama *f* story, plot, weave.

tramare *vi* to scheme.

trambusto *m* commotion, bustle, uproar, palaver.

tramezzino *m* sandwich.

tramontare *vi* to set.

tramonto *m* sundown, sunset.

tramortire *vt* to stun.

trampolino *m* springboard, diving board.

trampolo *m* stilt.

tran tran *m* routine.

trance *f inv* trance.

tranello *m* catch, decoy, pitfall.

trangugiare *vt* to gobble.

tranne *prep* except, but, bar.

tranquillamente *adv* happily.

tranquillante *m* tranquillizer.

tranquillità *f* ease.

tranquillo *adj* leisurely, quiet, tranquil.

transatlantico *m* liner.

transatlantico *adj* transatlantic.

transistor *m inv* transistor.

transitivo *adj* transitive.

transito *m* transit.

transitorio *adj* transient.

transizione *f* transition.

trantran *m* grind.

trapanare *vt* to drill.

trapano *m* drill.

trapezio *m* trapeze.

trapiantare *vt* to transplant.

trapianto *m* transplant.

trappola *f* trap, snare; ~ **mortale** *f* deathtrap.

trapunta *f* quilt; ~ **di piuma** *f* eiderdown.

trasalire *vi* to start, to flinch.

trasandatezza *f* shabbiness.

trasandato *adj* scruffy, sloppy.

trascendere *vt* to transcend.

trascinante *adj* rousing.

trascinare *vt* to haul, to drag, to lug; ~ **a fatica** to heave; * *vr* ~**rsi** to trudge.

trascorrere *vi* to elapse, to spend.

trascrizione *f* transcription.

trascurabile *adj* unimportant, negligible.

trascurare *vt* to neglect, to overlook, to disregard.

trascuratezza *f* neglect.

trasferibile *adj* transferable.

trasferimento *m* transfer.

trasferire *vt* to shift, to transfer.

trasferta *f* transfer; **giocare in** ~ *vi* (*sport*) to play away.

trasformare *vt* adapt, to turn, to transform, to change.

trasformatore *m* transformer.

trasformazione *f* transformation.

trasfusione *f* transfusion; ~ **di sangue** *f* blood transfusion.

trasgredire *vt* to transgress.

trasgressione *f* misdemeanour.

trasgressore *m* offender.

traslocare *vt, vi* to move.

trasloco *m* removal, move.

trasmettere *vt* to transmit, to convey, to broadcast; * *vr* ~**rsi** (sound) to carry.

trasmissione *f* transmission, drive, broadcast; ~ **anteriore** *f* front-wheel drive.

trasparente *adj* transparent, see-through, clear, sheer.

trasparenza *f* transparency.

traspirare *vi* to perspire, to transpire.

traspirazione *f* perspiration.

trasportare *vt* to convey, to transport.

trasporto *m* transport, transportation, conveyance.

trastullarsi *vr* to tinker.

trasudare *vt* to ooze.

tratta *f* (bank) draft.

trattamento *m* treatment; ~ **del viso** *m* facial.

trattare *vt* to treat, to process, to transact, to handle, to negotiate.

trattatello *m* tract.

trattativa *f* negotiation.

trattato *m* treaty, treatise.

trattenere *vt* to detain, to withhold, to restrain, to keep.

trattenimento *m* entertainment.

trattenuta *f* stoppage.

trattino *m* dash, hyphen.

tratto *m* stretch, reach, section, line; **tutto d'un** ~ all at once.

trattore *m* tractor.

trauma *m* trauma.

traumatizzante *adj* traumatic.

travagliato *adj* troubled.

travasare *vt* to siphon, to decant.

trave *f* beam, girder.

traveller's cheque *m inv* traveller's cheque.

traversa *f* rung.

traversata *f* crossing.

traversina *f* sleeper.

traverso *adj* cross; **di** ~ *adj*

adv askew, sidelong.

travestimento *m* disguise.

travestire *vt* to disguise.

travestito *m* transvestite; * *adj* (in) drag.

travisare *vt* to misrepresent.

trazione *f* traction.

tre *adj, m* three; **vincere per ~ volte** consecutive to get a hat-trick.

trebbiare *vt* to thresh.

treccia *f* plait, braid.

treccina *f* pigtail.

tredicesimo *adj, m* thirteenth.

tredici *adj, m inv* thirteen.

tredimensionale *adj* three-dimensional.

tregua *f* respite, lull, truce.

tremare *vi* to quiver, to tremble, to quake.

tremendo *adj* dreadful, tremendous.

trementina *f* turpentine.

tremito *m* tremble, trembling.

tremolare *vi* to flicker.

tremolio *m* flicker.

trench *m inv* trench coat.

treno *m* train; **~ postale** *m* mail train.

trenta *adj, m* thirty.

trentesimo *adj, m* thirtieth.

trepidazione *f* trepidation.

treppiede *m* tripod.

tresca *f* intrigue.

triangolare *adj* triangular.

triangolo *m* triangle.

tribale *adj* tribal.

tribolazione *f* tribulation.

tribordo *m* starboard.

tribù *f* tribe.

tribuna *f* gallery; **~ coperta** *f* grandstand.

tribunale *m* law court, tribunal.

tributo *m* tribute.

tricheco *m* walrus.

triciclo *m* tricycle.

tricofizia *f* ringworm.

trifoglio *m* shamrock, clover.

trigonometria *f* trigonometry.

trillare *vi* to trill.

trillo *m* trill.

trilogia *f* trilogy.

trimestrale *adj* quarterly.

trimestre *m* term.

trincea *f* trench.

trinciante *m* carving knife.

trinciare *vt* to shred.

Trinità *f* Trinity.

trio *m* trio.

trionfale *adj* triumphal.

trionfante *adj* triumphant.

trionfo *m* triumph.

trip *m inv* trip.

triplicare *vt* to treble.

triplice *adj* triple; **in ~ copia** *adj* triplicate.

triplo *adj* triple, treble.

trippa *f* tripe.

triste *adj* sad, woeful.

tristezza *f* misery, sadness.

tritacarne *m inv* mincer.

tritare *vt* to mince.

trito *adj* hackneyed, trite.

tritone *m* newt.

trivellare *vt* to bore.

trivellazione *f* drilling; **impianto di ~** *m* oil rig.

trofeo *m* trophy.

tromba *f* trumpet, bugle; **~ d'aria** *f* whirlwind.

trombone *m* trombone; daffodil.

trombosi *f* thrombosis; **~ coronarica** *f* coronary.

troncare *vt* to sever.

tronco *m* log, trunk.

troncone *m* stump.

trono *m* throne.

tropicale *adj* tropical.

troppo *adv* too.

troppopieno *m* overflow.

trota *f* trout; **~ salmonata** *f* salmon trout.

trottare *vi* to trot.

trotto *m* trot.

trottola *f* top.
troupe *f* troupe.
trovare *vt* to find; **venire a ~** * *vi* to come round; * *vr* **~rsi** to stand.
trovata *f* gimmick.
trovatello *m* foundling.
truccare *vt* to rig.
trucchetto *m* dodge.
trucco *m* trick, hocus-pocus, make-up.
trucidare *vt* to slaughter.
truciolo *m* (wood) shaving.
truffa *f* fraud, confidence trick, swindle.
truffare *vt* to swindle.
truffatore *m* con man.
truppe *fpl* troops.
trust *m inv* trust.
tu pers *pron* you.
tuba *f* tuba.
tubare *vi* to coo.
tubature *fpl* piping.
tubazione *f* tubing.
tubercolosi *f* tuberculosis.
tubo *m* tube, pipe; **~ di gomma** *m* hose(pipe); **~ a raggi catodici** *m* cathode-ray tube.
tuffarsi *vr* to plunge, to dive.
tuffatore *m* diver.
tuffo *m* plunge, dive; **tuffi** *mpl* diving.
tugurio *m* hovel.
tulipano *m* tulip.
tumore *m* tumour, growth.
tumultuare *vi* riot.
tumultuoso *adj* tumultuous.
tunica *f* robe, tunic.
tunnel *m inv* tunnel.

tuo poss *adj, pron* your(s).
tuonare *vi* to rant.
tuono *m* thunder.
tuorlo *m* yolk.
turbante *m* turban.
turbare *vt* to agitate, to upset, to perturb.
turbato *adj* upset, disturbed.
turbina *f* turbine.
turbinare *vi* to eddy.
turbinio *m* swirl.
turbolento *adj* turbulent, rowdy, obstreperous.
turbolenza *f* turbulence.
turchese *adj, m* turquoise.
turismo *m* sightseeing, tourism, touring; **ufficio del ~** *m* tourist office.
turista *m/f* tourist.
turistico *adj* tourist; **attrazioni turistiche** *fpl* sights.
turno *m* shift, turn; **~ di notte** *m* nightshift.
tuta *f* overalls; **~ da ginnastica** *f* tracksuit.
tutela *f* guardianship.
tutina *f* rompers.
tutore *m* guardian.
tuttavia *conj* however, yet, all the same, nevertheless; * *adv* though.
tutto *adj* all, every, any; * *pron* everything, everybody; * *m* whole; **ci sedemmo tutti quanti** we all sat down; **~ sommato** altogether; **in ~** *prep* throughout.
tuttofare *m* handyman.
twist *m* twist.

U

ubbidiente *adj* obedient.
ubbidienza *f* obedience.
ubbidire *vi, vt* to obey.

ubicazione *f* site.
ubriachezza *f* drunkenness.
ubriaco *adj* drunk, inebriated

(*fam*) plastered, (*fam*) pissed; ~ **fradicio** *adj* dead drunk; * *m* drunk.

ubriacone *m* drunkard.

uccelliera *f* aviary.

uccellino *m* fledgling.

uccello *m* bird.

uccidere *vt* to kill, to slay.

uccisione *f* killing.

udibile *adj* audible; **non** ~ *adj* inaudible.

udienza *f* hearing, audience.

udito *m* hearing.

ufficiale *adj* official; * *m* officer; ~ **giudiziario** *m* bailiff; ~ **di stato civile** *m* registrar.

ufficiare *vi* to officiate.

ufficio *m* office, bureau; ~ **postale** *m* post office; **orario d'~** *m* office hours; **d'~** *adj* clerical; **lavoro d'~** *m* paperwork.

ufficioso *adj* unofficial.

uguaglianza *f* equality.

uguagliare *vt* to touch, to match, to equal.

uguale *m/f* match; * *adj* equal.

ugualmente *adv* equally.

ulcera *f* ulcer.

ulivo *m* olive tree.

ulteriore *adj* ulterior, further, farther.

ultimamente *adv* lately.

ultimatum *m inv* ultimatum.

ultimo *adj* last, latter, final; **negli ultimi ultimi** *adv* latterly.

ululare *vi* to howl.

ululato *m* howl.

umanamente *adv* humanly.

umanista *m/f* humanist.

umanità *f* humanity, mankind.

umanitario *adj* humanitarian, humane.

umano *adj* human; **essere** ~ *m* human (being).

umidità *f* humidity, wet, moisture, dampness.

umido *adj* damp, humid, moist,

wet; ~ **e freddo** *adj* dank.

umile *adj* lowly, humble.

umiliare *vt* to demean, to humiliate, to humble.

umiliazione *f* indignity, humiliation.

umilmente *adv* humbly.

umiltà *f* humility.

umore *m* mood, frame of mind, humour.

umorismo *m* humour.

umorista *m/f* humorist.

unanime *adj* unamity.

unanimità *f* unanimity.

uncinetto *m* crochet.

undicesimo *adj*, *m* eleventh.

undici *adj*, *m* eleven.

ungere *vt* to anoint, to grease, (*culin*) to baste.

unghia *f* fingernail, nail, claw.

unguento *m* ointment, salve.

unico *adj* sole, unique, one, single; **a senso** ~ *adj* one-way.

unicorno *m* unicorn.

unificante *adj* cohesive.

unificare *vt* to unify, to unite.

unificazione *f* unification.

uniforme *adj* uniform.

uniformemente *adv* evenly.

uniformità *f* uniformity.

unilaterale *adj* one-sided, unilateral.

unione *f* union, unity.

unire *vt* to join, to unify, to unite; * *vr* ~**rsi** to join, to coalesce.

unisono *m* unison.

unità *f inv* unit, unity.

unito *adj* united; **in tinta unita** *adj* plain.

universale *adj* universal.

università *f* university.

universo *m* universe.

univoco *adj* one-to-one.

uno *adj*, *m* one; **l'~ o l'altro** *adj* either; **a** ~ **a** ~ *adv* singly.

unto *m* grease; * *adj* greasy.

untuoso *adj* greasy, smarmy.

unzione *f* unction.

uomo *m* (*pl* **uomini**) man, fellow; ~ **d'affari** *m* businessman; **da** ~ *adj* men's.

uovo *m* egg; ~ **in camicia** *m* poached egg; ~ **sodo** *m* boiled egg; **uova di pesce** *fpl* roe, spawn; **deporre le uova** *vi* to spawn; ~ **di Pasqua** *m* Easter egg.

uragano *m* hurricane.

uranio *m* uranium.

urbano *adj* urban.

urgente *adj* urgent.

urgenza *f* urgency.

urlare *vi, vt* to howl, to bellow, to yell, to scream.

urlo *m* scream, yell, wail, bellow.

urna *f* urn.

urogallo *m* grouse.

urtare *vt* to bang against, to jar, to impinge on.

usabile *adj* expendabile.

usanza *f* usage.

usare *vt* to use.

usato *adj* used, spent.

uscente *adj* outgoing.

usciere *m* usher.

uscire *vi* to go out.

uscita *f* exit, release; ~ **di sicurezza** *f* emergency exit.

usignolo *m* nightingale.

uso *m* usage, use, wear; **a doppio** ~ *adj* dual purpose.

ustione *f* burn.

usura *f* wear, usury; ~ **per attrito** *f* attrition.

usuraio *m* usurer.

usurpare *vt* to usurp, to encroach.

utensile *m* utensil, implement.

utero *m* uterus, womb; ~ **collo dell'utero** *m* cervix.

utile *adj* useful, helpful; **essere** ~ **a qn** *vi* to stand somebody in good stead.

utilità *f* usefulness, utility.

utilizzabile *adj* usable.

utilizzare *vt* to utilize.

uva *f* grapes; ~ **passa** *f* currant; **una chicca d'**~ *f* grape; ~ **un grappolo d'**~ *m* a bunch of grapes; ~ **spina** *f* gooseberry.

uvetta *f* raisin.

V

vacanza *f* vacation, holiday; ~ **organizzata** *f* package holiday.

vacca *f* cow.

vaccinare *vt* to vaccinate.

vaccinazione *f* vaccination.

vaccino *m* vaccine.

vacillante *adj* rocky, shaky, wavering, unsteady.

vacillare *vi* to totter, to falter.

vacuo *adj* blank, vacant, vacuous.

vagabondo *m* tramp, vagabond, vagrant;* *adj* roving.

vagamente *adj* dimly.

vagare *vi* to rove, to drift.

vagina *f* vagina.

vaglia *m* draft; ~ **postale** *f* money order.

vagliare *vt* to screen.

vago *adj* faint, woolly, vague, remote, shadowy.

vagone *m* carriage, wagon.

vaiolo *m* smallpox.

valanga *f* spate, avalanche.

valere *vi* to be worth.

validità *f* validity, soundness.

valido *adj* valid, sound, worthwhile; **non ~** *adj* invalid.

valutare *f* to appraise.

valigia *f* suitcase, case; **fare le valigie** *vt* to pack.

valle *f* valley, dale.

vallone *m* glen.

valore *m* value, worth; **~ nominale** *m* face value.

valorizzare *vt* to enhance.

valoroso *adj* manful.

valuta *f* currency; **~ estera** *f* foreign currency, exchange.

valutare *vt* to assess, to evaluate, to value, to estimate.

valutazione *f* valuation, appraisal, assessment, estimate.

valvola *f* valve.

valzer *m inv* waltz.

vampiro *m* vampire.

vandalismo *m* vandalism.

vandalizzare *vt* to vandalize.

vandalo *m* vandal.

vanga *f* spade.

vangare *vt* to dig.

vangelo *m* gospel.

vaniglia *f* vanilla.

vanità *f inv* vanity, conceit.

vanitoso *adj* vain, conceited.

vano *m* space; **~ della porta** *m* doorway; * *adj* vain, fruitless.

vantaggio *m* advantage, perk, benefit; **vantaggi** *mpl* fringe benefits; **trarre ~** *vi* to benefit, to capitalize on; **vantaggioso** *adj* advantageous.

vantare *vt* to boast; **che si vanta sempre** *adj* boastful; *vr* **~rsi** to brag.

vanteria *f* boast.

vapore *m* vapour, steam; **cuocere a ~** *vt* to steam.

vaporizzare *vt* to vapourize.

varare *vt* to launch.

variabile *adj* changeable, variable.

variante *f* variant.

variare *vt*, *vi* to vary, to range.

variazione *f* variation.

varicella *f* chickenpox.

varietà *f inv* variety.

vario *adj* varied, various, miscellaneous.

variopinto *adj* mottled, motley.

varo *m* launch, launching.

vasaio *m* potter.

vasca *f* basin; **~ da bagno** bathtub.

vascello *m* vessel.

vaschetta *f* tub.

vasectomia *f* vasectomy.

vaselina *f* vaseline.

vasellame *m* crockery.

vasetto *m* pot.

vasino *m* potty.

vaso *m* vase; **~ sanguino** blood vessel; **~ del gabinetto** *m* toilet bowl; **(conservato) in ~** *adj* potted; **~ da fiori** *m* flowerpot.

vassoio *m* tray, salver.

vastità *f* magnitude.

vasto *adj* vast.

vecchiaia *f* old age.

vecchio *adj* old.

veci *f* duties; **fa le ~ del direttore** he is the acting manager.

vedere *vi*, *vt* to see, to view; **non ~ l'ora di fare qc** to look forward to doing something; * *vr* **~rsi** to show.

vedova *f* widow.

vedovo *m* widower.

veduta *f* outlook, view.

veemente *adj* vehement.

veemenza *f* vehemence.

vegetare *vi* to vegetate.

vegetariano *adj*, *m* vegetarian.

vegetazione *f* vegetation; **~ densa** *f* overgrowth.

veggente *m/f* seer.

veglia *f* wake, vigil.

veicolo *m* vehicle.

vela *f* sail, sailing; **andare a gonfie vele** *vi* to be successful.

velare *vt* to veil.

veleno *m* poison, venom.

velenoso *adj* poisonous, venomous.

velina *f* tissue; **carta ~** *f* tissue paper.

velismo *m* yachting.

vello *m* fleece.

vellutato *adj* silky.

velluto *m* velvet; **~ a coste** *m* corduroy.

velo *m* veil, ply.

veloce *adj* quick, fast, speedy.

velocemente *adv* fast.

velocità *f* speed, velocity; **eccesso di ~** *m* speeding; **andare a ~ eccessiva** *vi* to speed.

vena *f* vein, seam, streak; **~ nascosta** *f* undercurrent; **~ varicosa** *f* varicose vein.

venale *adj* venal.

vendere *vt* to sell; **~ per strada** *vt* to hawk.

vendetta *f* vendetta, revenge, vengeance.

vendibile *adj* saleable, marketable.

vendicare *vt* to avenge; * *vr* **~rsi** to retaliate.

vendicativo *adj* revengeful, vindictive.

vendita *f* sale; **punto ~** *m* outlet.

venditore *m* seller, vendor.

venerabile *adj* venerable.

venerare *vt* to venerate, to revere.

venerazione *f* veneration, reverence.

venerdì *m* Friday ; **V~ Santo** *m* Good Friday.

venereo *adj* venereal; **malattia venerea** *f* venereal disease.

venial *adj* veniale.

venire *vi* to come; **~ incontro a** *vt* to accommodate.

ventaglio *m* fan.

ventesimo *adj*, *m* twentieth.

venti *adj*, *m* twenty.

venticello *m* breeze.

ventilare *vt* to ventilate.

ventilato *adj* ventilated; **mal ~** *adj* stuffy.

ventilatore *m* fan, ventilator.

ventilazione *f* ventilation.

vento *m* wind; **~ in coda** *m* tailwind; **far ~** *vt* to fan.

ventosa *f* sucker.

ventoso *adj* windy, breezy, blustery, gusty.

ventre *m* stomach.

ventriglio *m* gizzard.

ventriloquo *m* ventriloquist.

ventuno *m* blackjack, pontoon.

veramente *adv* truly, really, actually.

veranda *f* veranda(h), porch.

verbale *m* minutes; *adj* verbal.

verbo *m* verb.

verboso *adj* wordy, verbose.

verdastro *adj* greenish.

verde *adj*, *m* green; **essere al ~** *vi* to be hard-up.

verdetto *m* verdict.

verdura *f* greens; **verdure** *fp* vegetables.

vergine *adj*, *f* virgin.

Vergine *f* Virgo.

verginità *f* virginity.

vergogna *f* shame, disgrace; **pieno di ~** *adj* ashamed.

vergognare *vt* to shame.

vergognoso *adj* shameful, shame-faced, disgraceful, damnable.

verifica *f* verification.

verificare *vt* to verify, to try, t check.

verita *f inv* truth; **per la ~** as matter of fact.

veritiero *adj* truthful.

verme *m* worm.

vermut *m inv* vermouth.

vernice *f* paint, paintwork;

trasparente *f* varnish.
verniciare *vt* to paint.
vero *adj* true, real, veritable.
versante *m* slope.
versare *vt* to spill, to shed, to pour.
versatile *adj* versatile, adaptable, all-round.
versato *adj* conversant.
versione *f* version.
verso *prep* toward(s); * *m* verse.
vertebra *f* vertebra.
vertebrato *adj*, *m* vertebrate.
verticale *adj*, *f* vertical.
vertice *m* apex, vertex, summit.
vertigine *f* dizziness, giddiness, vertigo.
vertiginoso *adj* giddy, dizzy.
verve *f* verve.
vescica *f* blister, bladder.
vescovo *m* bishop.
vespa *f* wasp.
vespasiano *m* urinal.
vestaglia *f* dressing gown.
vestiario *m* apparel.
vestigio *m* vestige.
vestire *m* dressing; * *vt* to clothe, to dress.
vestito *m* dress, frock; **vestiti** *mpl* clothes; * *adj* clad .
veterano *m* veteran.
veterinario *adj* veterinary; * *m* vet, veterinary surgeon.
veto *m* veto; **porre il ~ a** *vt* to veto.
vetraio *m* glazier.
vetrina *f* showcase, window.
vetro *m* glass, windowpane; **~ smerigliato** *m* frosted glass; **~ piano** *m* plate glass.
vetta *f* summit.
via *f* road; **~ a mezzaluna** *f* crescent.
via *prep* via, by.
viadotto *m* viaduct.
viaggiare *vi* to travel.
viaggiatore *m* traveller.
viaggio *m* journey, trip, **viaggi**

mpl travel; **~ per mare** *m* voyage; **in ~** *adv* en route; **di/da ~** *adj* travelling.
viale *m* avenue, mall, drive.
vibrante *adj* vibrant.
vibrare *vi* to vibrate, to shudder.
vibrazione *f* vibration, shudder.
vicepresidente *m* vice-chairman.
viceversa *adv* vice versa.
vicinanza *f* proximity, closeness, **vicinanze** *fpl* vicinity, neighbourhood; **nelle vicinanze** *adj* locally.
vicinato *m* neighbourhood.
vicino *m* neighbour; **da buon ~** *adj* neighbourly;* *adj*, *adv* close, near, nearby; * *prep* near.
vicolo *m* alley; **~ cieco** *m* cul-de-sac.
video *m inv* video.
videotape *m inv* videotape.
vietare *vt* to prohibit.
vigilanza *f* vigilance.
vigile *adj* vigilant, alert.
vigilia *f* eve ; **la ~ di Natale** *f* Christmas Eve.
vigliaccheria *f* cowardice.
vigliacco *m*, *adj* coward.
vigna *f* vineyard.
vigneto *m* vineyard.
vignetta *f* cartoon.
vignettista *m/f* cartoonist.
vigore *m* vigour.
vigoroso *adj* vigorous, pithy, lusty.
vile *adj* base.
villa *f* villa, hall, country house.
villano *adj* rude.
villeggiante *m* holiday-maker.
villeggiatura *f* holiday; **località di ~** *f* holiday resort.
viltà *f* baseness.
vimine *m* wicker; **di vimini** *adj* wicker.

vincere *vt*, *vi* to win.
vincitore *m* winner, victor.
vinile *m* vinyl.
vino *m* wine; ~ bianco/rosso white/red wine; ~ ordinario *m* plonk.
viola *m*, *adj* purple; * *f* viola, violet.
violaciocca *f* wallflower.
violare *vt* to violate.
violazione *f* breach, infringement, violation.
violentare *vt* to rape.
violentatore *m* rapist.
violentemente *adv* wildly.
violento *adj* violent.
violenza *f* violence.
violetto *adj*, *m* violet.
violinista *m/f* violinist, fiddler.
violino *m* violin, fiddle.
violoncello *m* violoncello, cello.
vipera *f* viper, adder.
virare *vi* to turn, to veer.
virgola *f* comma, point.
virgoletta *f* inverted comma; virgolette *fpl* quotation marks.
virile *adj* manly, virile.
virilità *f* virility, manliness, manhood.
virtù *f inv* virtue.
virtuoso *adj* virtuous, righteous.
virulento *adj* virulent.
virus *m inv* virus.
vischio *m* mistletoe.
viscido *adj* slimy; un tipo ~ *m* creep.
viscoso *adj* viscous.
visibile *adj* visible.
visibilità *f* visibility.
visiera *f* visor.
visione *f* vision.
visita *f* visit, examination, tour; ~ medica *f* medical; orario delle visite *m* visiting hours.
visitare *vt* to visit, to examine.

visitatore *m* visitor, caller.
visivo *adj* visual; sussidi visivi *mpl* visual aids.
viso *m* face.
visone *m* mink.
vispo *adj* frisky, bright.
vista *f* sight, vista, vision, view, eyesight; punto di ~ *m* view.
visto *adj* seen; ~ che *conj* seeing that, considering; * *m* visa.
vistoso *adj* showy, flashy, gaudy.
vita *f* life, lieftime, living; waist, waistline; ~ dell'al di là *f* afterlife; privo di ~ *adj* lifeless; ~ sentimentale *f* love life; la durata della ~ *f* lifespan.
vitale *adj* vital.
vitalità *f* vitality.
vitamina *f* vitamin.
vite *f* vine, grapevine; screw.
vitello *m* calf, veal.
vitreo *adj* glassy.
vittima *f* victim, fatality, casualty.
vitto *m* board; ~ e alloggio *n* keep.
vittoria *f* victory, win; una ~ a pari merito *f* a dead heat; ~ facile *f* walkover.
vittorioso *adj* victorious.
vivace *adj* sprightly, lively, skittish, vivacious.
vivacità *f* liveliness.
vivaio *m* nursery.
vivente *adj* living.
vivere *vi* to live, to subsist; ~ di to live on.
vivido *adj* vivid.
vivisezione *f* vivisection.
vivo *m* quick; * *adj* alive, live.
viziare *vt* to indulge, to pamper.
viziato *adj* spoilt.
vizio *m* vice; che induce al ~ *adj* addictive.
vocabolario *m* vocabulary, dictionary.

vocale *f* vowel; * *adj* vocal.
vocativo *adj* vocative.
vocazione *f* vocation, calling.
voce *f* voice, rumour, entry, item; **ad alta ~** *adv* aloud.
vodka *f inv* vodka.
voglia *f* fancy, inclination, craving, birthmark.
voi *pers pron* you.
volano *m* shuttlecock.
volante *adj* flying; * *m* steering wheel.
volantino *m* leaflet.
volare *m* flying; * *vi* to fly.
volatile *adj* volatile.
volente *adv* wanting; **~ o nolente** *adv* willy-nilly.
volenteroso *adj* willing.
volere *vt* to want, to wish; * *m* will, wish(es); **senza ~** *adv* accidentally.
volgare *adj* coarse, vulgar.
volgarità *f* vulgarity, crudity.
volizione *f* volition.
volo *m* flight; **~ charter** *m* charter flight; **in ~** *adj* airborne; **~ di linea** *m* scheduled flight.
volontà *f* will; **spontanea ~** *f* free will; **buona ~** *f* goodwill.
volontario *m* volunteer; * *adj* voluntary.
volpe *f* fox.
volt *m inv* volt.
volta *f* time; vault; **passaggio a ~** *m* archway; **un' altra ~** *adv* again, once more; **qualche ~** *adv* sometimes; **mille**

volte *adv* over and over; **più volte** *adv* many a time; **una ~** *adv* once; **ancora una ~** *adv* once more.
voltagabbana *m/f inv* turncoat.
voltaggio *m* voltage.
voltare *vt* to turn, to turn over.
volteggiare *vi* to whirl, to twirl.
volto *m* countenance.
volume *m* volume, sound, bulk.
voluminoso *adj* bulky.
voluttuoso *adj* sensuous, voluptuous.
vomitare *vi* to vomit, to be sick, *(fam)* to puke, *(fam)* to throw up.
vomito *m* vomit.
vongola *f* clam.
vorace *adj* voracious.
vortice *m* whirl, whirlpool, vortex.
vostro *poss adj*, *pron* your(s).
votare *vt*, *vi* to vote.
votazione *f* poll, vote, voting, ballot; **consultare tramite ~** *vt* to ballot.
voto *m* mark, grade, vow, vote; **~ decisivo** *m* casting vote; **concedere il diritto di ~ a** *vt* to enfranchise;
vulcanico *adj* volcanic.
vulcano *m* volcano.
vulnerabile *adj* vulnerable.
vuotare *vt* to empty, to bale out.
vuoto *m* vacuum, vacancy, void, emptiness, gap, blank; * *adj* unoccupied, empty.

W

wagon-lit *m inv* sleeping car.
walzer *m inv* waltz.
WC *m inv* WC, toilet.

weekend *m inv* weekend.
western *m inv* western (film).
würstel *m inv* frankfurter.

XYZ

xilofono *m* xylophone.
yacht *m inv* yacht.
yankee *m/f inv* yankee.
yard *f inv* yard.
yearling *m inv* yearling.
yen *m inv* yen.
yoga *m* yoga.
yogurt *m inv* yoghurt.
yuppy *m/f* yuppie.
zaffata *f* whiff.
zafferano *m* saffron.
zaffiro *m* sapphire.
zaino *m* rucksack, haversack, knapsack, backpack.
zampa *f* paw; ~ **anteriore** *f* foreleg.
zampata *f* kick; **dare una** ~ *vt* to paw.
zampogna *f* bagpipes.
zangola *f* churn.
zanna *f* fang, tusk.
zanzara *f* mosquito, gnat.
zanzarone *m* daddy-long-legs.
zappa *f* hoe.
zappare *vt* to hoe.
zar *m inv* czar, tsar.
zarina *f* czarina.
zattera *f* raft.
zavorra *f* ballast.
zebra *f* zebra.
zecca *f* mint; tick, louse; **nuovo di** ~ *adj* brand-new.
zelante *adj* zealous.
zelo *m* zeal.
zenit *m inv* zenith.
zenzero *m* ginger.
zeppa *f* wedge; **pieno** ~ *adj* chock-full.
zerbino *m* doormat.
zero *m* nought, zero, nil.
zia *f* aunt.
zibellino *m* sable.
zigomo *m* cheekbone.
zigzag *m inv* zigzag.
zimbello *m* laughing stock.

zinco *m* zinc.
zingaro *m* gypsy.
zio *m* uncle.
zip *m inv* zip.
zitella *f* spinster.
zoccolo *m* hoof, clog.
zodiaco *m* zodiac.
zolfo *m* sulphur.
zolla *f* clod, sod; ~ **erbosa** *f* turf.
zolletta *f* lump; ~ **di zucchero** *f* sugar lump.
zona *f* zone; ~ **di competenza** *f* catchment area (school); ~ **verde** *f* green belt.
zonzo *m*: **andare a** ~ *vi* to saunter.
zoo *m inv* zoo.
zoologico *adj* zoological.
zoologo *m* zoologist.
zoologia *f* zoology.
zoom *m inv* zoom.
zoppicamento *m* limp.
zoppicare *vi* to hobble, to limp.
zoppo *m* cripple; * *adj* lame.
zoster *m*: **herpes zoster** *m* (*med*) shingles.
zotico *m* lout.
zoticone *m* oaf, boor.
zucca *f* pumpkin, marrow, gourd.
zuccherare *vt* to sugar, to sweeten.
zuccherato *adj* sugary.
zucchero *m* sugar; ~ **semolato** *m* caster sugar; ~ **filato** *m* candyfloss; ~ **greggio** *m* brown sugar.
zucchetto *m* skullcap.
zucchina *f* courgette.
zuccone *m* blockhead.
zuffa *f* fray, dust-up, set-to, rough and tumble.
zumare *vi* to zoom.
zuppa *f* soup; ~ **inglese** *f* (*culin*) trifle.
zuppiera *f* tureen.

English-Italian
Dictionary

A

a *art* un, uno, una, un'; * *prep* a, per.

aback *adv* **to be taken ~** sconcertato; essere colto (preso) alla sprovvista.

abandon *vt* abbandonare; * *n* disinvoltura *f*; brio *m*.

abandonment *n* abbandono *m*.

abase *vt* umiliare, mortificare; * *vi* umiliarsi, abbassarsi.

abash *vt* sconcertare, imbarazzare.

abashed *adj* sconcertato, imbarazzato.

abate *vi* placarsi, calmarsi, abbassarsi.

abbess *n* badessa *f*.

abbey *n* badia *f*.

abbot *n* abate *m*.

abbreviate *vt* abbreviare.

abbreviation *n* abbreviazione *f*.

abdicate *vt* abdicare a, rinunciare a.

abdication *n* abdicazione *f*.

abdomen *n* addome *m*.

abdominal *adj* addominale.

abduct *vt* rapire.

abduction *n* rapimento *m*; sequestro *m* di persona.

abductor *n* rapitore *m*.

aberration *n* aberrazione *f*.

abet *vt* **to aid and ~** essere complice di.

abeyance, to be in *vi* essere in disuso; essere in sospeso.

abhor *vt* aborrire, provare orrore per, detestare.

abhorrence *n* orrore *m*.

abhorrent *adj* ripugnante, aborrevole.

abide, by *vi* attenersi a, rispettare, tener fede a.

ability *n* capacità *f*, abilità *f*;

abilities *npl* doti *fpl*.

abject *adj* abietto; umiliante.

ablaze *adj* in fiamme.

able *adj* capace, abile, intelligente; **to be ~ to do** poter fare.

able-bodied *adj* robusto, valido.

abnormal *adj* anormale.

abnormality *n* anormalità *f*, anomalia *f*.

aboard *adv* a bordo, in vettura.

abode *n* domicilio *m*, dimora *f*.

abolish *vt* abolire.

abolition *n* abolizione *f*.

abominable *adj* abominevole; pessimo, orrendo, orribile.

abomination *n* avversione *f*, disgusto *m*; cosa orrenda *f*.

aboriginal *adj* aborigeno.

abort *vi* abortire, fallire; *vt* interrompere.

abortion *n* aborto *m*.

abortive *adj* fallito, mancato.

abound *vi* abbondare.

about *prep* intorno a; **somewhere ~ here** qui intorno da qualche parte; a proposito di; **we talked ~ it** ne abbiamo parlato; * *adv* in giro, qua e là; **to look ~** guardarsi intorno; circa; **~ 20 cars** una ventina di macchine; **to be ~ to** stare per.

above *prep* sopra; * *adv* al di sopra; **~ all** soprattutto; **~mentioned** sopra menzionato.

abrasion *n* abrasione *f*.

abrasive *adj* abrasivo.

abreast *adv* di fianco.

abridge *vt* accorciare, abbreviare, riassumere, compendiare.

abridged *adj* ridotto; ~ **edition** edizione ridotta.

abroad *adv* all'estero; **to go ~** andare all'estero.

abrogate *vt* abrogare, annullare.

abrupt *adj* brusco.

abscess *n* ascesso *m*.

abscond *vi* evadere, scappare, fuggire.

absence *n* assenza *f*, mancanza *f*.

absent *adj* assente; ~ **minded** distratto; mancante.

absentee *n* assente *m/f*.

absenteeism *n* assenteismo *m*.

absolute *adj* assoluto; totale; categorico. ~ **ly** *adv* assolutamente, completamente.

absolution *n* assoluzione *f*.

absolve *vt* scogliere da, assolvere da.

absorb *vt* assorbire, ammortizzare, assimilare.

absorbent *adj* assorbente;.

absorbing *adj* avvincente, molto interessante.

absorption *n* assorbimento *m*.

abstain *vi* astenersi.

abstemious *adj* moderato, frugale; astemio.

abstention *n* astensione *f*.

abstinence *n* astinenza *f*.

abstract *adj* astratto; * *n* riassunto *m*; **in the ~** in teoria, in estratto; sommario *m*; * *vt* estrarre, riassumere.

abstraction *n* astrazione *f*, distrazione *f*.

abstruse *adj* astruso, recondito, oscuro.

absurd *adj* assurdo, ridicolo.

absurdity *n* assurdità *f*, assurdo *m*.

abundance *n* abbondanza *f*, gran quantità *f*.

abundant *adj* abbondante; ~ **in** ricco di.

abuse *vt* insultare; abusare di;

* *n* insulti *mpl*, ingiurie *fpl*, improperi *mpl*; abuso *m*.

abusive *adj* offensivo, ingiurioso.

abysmal *adj* abissale, spaventoso.

abyss *n* abisso *m*, baratro *m*.

acacia *n* acacia *f*.

academic *adj* accademico, universitario, intellettuale; * *n* accademico *m*.

academician *n* accademico *m*.

academy *n* accademia *f*.

accede *vi* acconsentire a; salire a; aderire a.

accelerate *vt, vi* accelerare.

acceleration *n* accelerazione *f*.

accelerator *n* acceleratore *m*.

accent *n* accento *m*.

accentuate *vt* accentuare; mettere in risalto.

accept *vt* accettare, ammettere.

acceptable *adj* accettabile; gradito.

acceptance *n* accettazione *f*; accoglienza *f*.

access *vt* accedere a * *n* accesso *m*.

accessible *adj* accessibile; facilmente reperibile.

accession *n* aggiunta *f*; accessione *f*; ~ **to throne** salita *f*.

accessory *n* accessorio *m*; (*law*) complice *m/f*.

accident *n* incidente *m*, disgrazia *f*; caso *m*.

accidental *adj* fortuito; involontario; ~ **ly** *adv* per caso; senza volere.

acclaim *vt* acclamare * *n* acclamazioni *fpl*; applauso *m*.

acclimatize *vt* acclimatare; * *vi* acclimatarsi, adattarsi.

accommodate *vt* ospitare, alloggiare; venire in contro a; (*differences*) conciliare.

accomodating *adj* conciliante; premuroso.

accommodation n sistemazione f, alloggio m.

accompaniment n accompagnamento m.

accompanist n (mus) accompagnatore m, accompagnatrice f.

accompany vt accompagnare.

accomplice n complice m/f.

accomplish vt compiere, portare a termine, realizzare.

accomplished adj esperto.

accomplishment n completamento m, realizzazione f; talento m, dote f.

accord n accordo m; **with one ~** all'unanimità; **of one's own ~** spontaneamente.

accordance: n **in ~ with** secondo m, in conformità di/a.

according to prep secondo, stando a; conforme a; **~ ly** adv di conseguenza.

accordion n (mus) fisarmonica.

accost vt abbordare.

account n conto m; relazione f, resoconto m; considerazione f; **on no ~** per nessun motivo; in nessun caso; **on ~** in acconto; **on ~ of** a causa di; * vt **to ~ for** rendere conto di; spiegare.

accountancy n ragioneria f, contabilità f.

accountant n ragioniere m, ragioneria f, contabile m/f.

account book n libro m di conti.

account number n numero m di conto.

accrue vi aumentare; maturare.

accumulate vt accumulare; vi accumularsi.

accumulation n accumulo m, mucchio m.

accuracy n esattezza f; accuratezza f; precisione f; fedeltà f.

accurate adj accurato, esatto, preciso; corretto; fedele.

accursed adj maledetto.

accusation n accusa f.

accusative n (gram) accusativo m.

accuse vt accusare.

accused n accusato m, imputato m.

accuser n accusatore m, accusatrice f.

accustom vt abituare.

accustomed adj abituato; solito.

ace n asso m **to have an ~ up one's sleave** avere un asso nella manica.

acerbic adj aspro.

acetate n (chem) acetato m.

ache n dolore m; * vi far male.

achieve vt raggiungere; realizzare.

achievement n realizzazione f; raggiungimento m.

acid adj acido, caustico; * n acido m.

acidity n acidità f.

acknowledge vt riconoscere, ammettere; ricambiare.

acknowledgement n riconoscimento m, ammissione f; (of letter, etc) riscontro m.

acme n culmine m.

acne n acne f.

acorn n ghianda f.

acoustics n acustica f.

acquaint vt informare; **to be ~ed with** conoscere.

acquaintance n conoscenza f; conoscente m/f.

acquiesce vi acconsentire a.

acquiescence n acquiescenza f, consenso m.

acquiescent adj acquiescente, remissivo, condiscendente.

acquire vt acquisire; prendere; **to ~ a taste for** prendere gusto a.

acquisition *n* acquisto *m*.

acquit *vt* assolvere.

acquittal *n* assoluzione *f*.

acre *n* acro *m*.

acrid *adj* acre, pungente.

acrimonious *adj* aspro, astioso, malevolo.

acrimony *n* acrimonia *f*, asprezza *f*.

across *adv* dall'altra parte; * *prep* attraverso.

act *vt* interpretare **to ~ the fool** fare lo stupido; * *vi* recitare; agire; *vr* comportarsi * *n* (*deed*) atto *m*; (*law*) legge *f*; (*theatre*) atto *m*.

acting *adj* **he is the ~ manager** fa le veci del direttore.

action *n* azione *f*.

activate *vt* attivare.

activity *n* attività *f*.

actor *n* attore *m*.

actress *n* attrice *f*.

actual *adj* reale, effettivo; **~ ly** *adv* veramente, addirittura.

acumen *n* perspicacia *f* **business ~** fiuto negli affari.

acute *adj* acuto; fine; intenso; grave; perspicace.

adamant *adj* inflessibile.

adapt *vt* modificare; trasformare; adattare.

adaptable *adj* versatile.

adaptation *n* adattamento *m*.

adaptor *n* presa multipla *f*, riduttore *m*.

add *vt* aggiungere, sommare, addizionare.

adder *n* vipera *f*.

addict *n* tossicomane *m/f*, drogato *m*.

addiction *n* assuefazione *f*, tossicodipendenza *f*.

addictive *adj* che induce al vizio.

addition *n* aggiunta *f*, addizione *f*, **there has been an ~ to the family** la famiglia si è accre-

sciuta.

additional *adj* supplementare.

additive *n* additivo *m*.

address *vt* indirizzare; rivolgere * *n* indirizzo *m*, recapito *m*; discorso *m*.

adenoids *n* adenoidi *fpl*.

adept *adj* abile; * *n* esperto *m*.

adequate *adj* sufficiente; adeguato.

adhere *vi* aderire.

adherent *n* aderente *m/f*.

adhesion *n* adesione *f*.

adhesive *n* adesivo *m*.

adhesive tape *n* nastro adesivo *m*.

adipose *adj* adiposo.

adjacent *adj* adiacente.

adjective *n* aggettivo *m*.

adjoin *vt* essere attiguo/contiguo a.

adjoining *adj* attiguo, contiguo.

adjourn *vt* rinviare; sospendere.

adjournment *n* rinvio *m*; sospensione *f*.

adjudicate *vt* giudicare; decidere su.

adjunct *n* aggiunta *f*, appendice *f*.

adjust *vt* regolare; modificare; aggiustare.

adjustable *adj* regolabile.

adjustment *n* regolazione *f*, modifica *f*, adattamento *m*.

ad-lib *vt* improvvisare; * *adj* improvvisato.

administer *vt* dirigere, gestire, amministrare; somministrare.

administration *n* direzione *f*, gestione *f*, amministrazione *f*; somministrazione *f*; governo *m*.

administrative *adj* amministrativo.

administrator *n* amministratore *m*, amministratrice *f*.

admirable *adj* ammirevole.
admiral *n* ammiraglio *m*.
admiralty *m* ammiragliato *m*, (GB) ministero *m* della marina.
admiration *n* ammirazione *f*.
admire *vt* ammirare.
admirer *n* ammiratore *m*, ammiratrice *f*.
admissible *adj* ammissibile.
admission *adj* ammissione, ingresso.
admit *vt* lasciar entrare; ammettere.
admittance *n* ingresso *m*.
admittedly *adj* bisogna ammettere che; va detto che.
admonish *vt* ammonire.
ad nauseam *adv* fino alla nausea.
adolescence *n* adolescenza *f*.
adolescent *n* adolescente *m/f*.
adopt *vt* adottare.
adopted *adj* adottato.
adoption *n* adozione *f*.
adorable *adj* adorabile.
adoration *n* adorazione *f*.
adore *vt* adorare.
adorn *vt* abbellire, ornare.
adrift *adv* alla deriva.
adroit *adj* abile.
adulation *n* adulazione *f*.
adult *adj* adulto; * *n* adulto *m*, adulta *f*.
adulterate *vt* adulterare.
adulterer *n* adultero *m*.
adulteress *n* adultera *f*.
adulterous *adj* adultero.
adultery *n* adulterio *m*.
advance *vt* anticipare; favorire; *vi* avanzare; progredire; * *n* progresso *m*; in anticipo *m*; dare un anticipo *m*.
advanced *adj* avanzato, superiore.
advantage *n* vantaggio *m*; **to take ~ of** approfittare di.
advantageous *adj* vantaggioso.

advent *n* avvento *m*.
adventure *n* avventura *f*.
adventurous *adj* avventuroso.
adverb *n* avverbio *m*.
adversary *n* avversario *m*.
adverse *adj* sfavorevole.
adversity *n* sfortuna *f*.
advertise *vt* fare pubblicità, reclamizzare.
advertisement *n* pubblicità *f*, inserzione *f*, annuncio *m*.
advertising *n* pubblicità *f*.
advice *n* consiglio *m*; avviso *m*.
advisable *adj* consigliabile; raccomandabile.
advise *vt* consigliare; avvisare.
adviser *n* consigliere *m*, consulente *m/f*.
advisory *adj* consultivo.
advocate *n* avvocato *m*; sostenitore *m* * *vt* sostenere la validità di.
aerial *n* antenna *f*; * *adj* aereo.
aerobics *npl* aerobica *f*.
aerosol *n* aerosol *m*.
aesthetic *adj* estetico.
afar *adv* lontano; **from ~** da lontano.
affable *adj* affabile.
affair *n* faccenda *f*, affare *m*; relazione *f*, avventura *f*.
affect *vt* influire su, incidere su.
affectation *n* ostentazione *f*, pretese *fpl*.
affected *adj* affettato; commosso.
affection *n* affetto *m*.
affectionate *adj* affezionato.
affidavit *n* affidavit *m invar*.
affiliate *vt* affiliare, aggregare.
affiliation *n* affiliazione *f*.
affinity *n* affinità *f*.
affirm *vt* affermare, asserire.
affirmation *n* affermazione *f*.
affirmative *adj* affermativo.
affix *vt* apporre, attaccare.
afflict *vt* affliggere.

affliction *n* sofferenza *f*, infermità *f*.

affluence *n* ricchezza *f*, abbondanza *f*.

affluent *adj* ricco.

afford *vt* permettersi.

affray *n* rissa *f*.

affront *n* affronto *m*, offesa *f*.

aflame *adv* in fiamme *adj* ardente.

afloat *adv* a galla.

aforementioned *adj* suddetto.

afraid *adj* aver paura; temere.

afresh *adv* da capo, di nuovo.

aft *adv* a poppa.

after *prep* dopo * *adv* ~ **all** dopotutto; malgrado tutto.

afterbirth *n* placenta *f*.

aftercare *n* assistenza *f* postoperatoria.

after-effects *npl* ripercussione *f*, conseguenza *f*; reazione *f*.

afterlife *n* vita *f* dell'aldilà.

aftermath *n* conseguenze *fpl*.

afternoon *n* pomeriggio *m*.

after-sales service *n* servizio *m* assistenza *f* cliente.

aftershave *n* dopobarba *m*.

aftertaste *n* sapore *m* che rimane in bocca.

afterwards *adv* dopo, più tardi, in seguito.

again *adv* ancora, di nuovo, un'altra volta; ~ **and** ~ ripetutamente; **then** ~ d'altra parte.

against *prep* contro.

age *n* età *f*, epoca *f*, era *f*; * *adj* **under** ~ minorenne; * *vi* invecchiare.

aged *adj* anziano.

agency *n* agenzia *f*.

agenda *n* ordine del giorno *m*.

agent *n* agente *m/f*.

agglomeration *n* agglomerazione *f*.

aggravate *vt* aggravare; irritare.

aggravation *n* aggravamento *m*.

aggravating *adj* esasperante, irritante.

aggregate *n* insieme *m*; * *adj* complessivo.

aggression *n* aggressione *f*.

aggressive *adj* aggressivo.

aggressor *n* aggressore *m*.

aggreived *adj* offeso.

aghast *adj* spigottito, inorridito.

agile *adj* agile, svelto.

agility *n* agilità *f*.

agitate *vt* turbare, agitare.

agitation *n* agitazione *f*.

agitator *n* agitatore/trice *m/f*.

ago *adv* fa; **how long** ~? quanto tempo fa?

agog *adj* impaziente; ~ **with excitement** emozionato.

agonize over *vi* angosciarsi.

agony *n* dolore *m* atroce.

agree *vt* essere d'accordo con; (*gram*) concordare.

agreeable *adj* piacevole.

agreed *adj* convenuto.

agreement *n* accordo *m*, consenso *m*.

agricultural *adj* agricolo.

agriculture *n* agricoltura *f*.

aground *adv* (*mar*) in secca * *vi* **to run** ~ arenarsi.

ahead *adv* avanti; davanti; in anticipo.

aid *vt* aiuto *m*; assistenza *f*.

aide-de-camp *n* aiutante *m* di campo.

AIDS *n* AIDS *m*.

ailing *adj* sofferente.

ailment *n* indisposizione *f*.

aim *vt* puntare, mirare; * mira *f*; scopo *m*.

aimless *adj* senza scopo.

air *n* aria *f*; * *vt* arieggiare, esprimere.

airborne *adj* decollato, in volo.

air-conditioned *adj* ad/con aria condizionata, climatizzato.

air-conditioning n aria f condizionata.

aircraft n aeromobile m.

air force n aeronautica f militare.

air freshener n deodorante m per l'ambiente.

air gun n fucile m ad aria compressa.

airless adj senz'aria.

airlift n ponte m aereo.

airline n linea f aerea.

airmail n posta f aerea.

airport n aeroporto m.

airstrip n pista f di atterraggio.

air terminal n terminal m.

airtight adj ermetico.

airy adj arieggiato.

aisle n navata f.

ajar adj socchiuso.

alabaster n alabastro m.

alacrity n prontezza f.

alarm n allarme m, sveglia f; * vt allarmare.

alarmist n allarmista m/f.

alas adv ahimè.

albatross n albatro m.

album n album m.

alchemist n alchimista m.

alchemy n alchimia f.

alcohol n alcool m.

alcoholic adj alcolico; * n alcolizzato m.

alcoholism n alcolismo m.

alcove n alcova f.

alder n (bot) ontano m.

ale n birra f.

alert adj sveglio; vigile; * n allarme m; * vt avvertire.

algae npl alghe fpl.

algebra n algebra f.

alias n pseudonimo m; * adv alias, altrimenti detto.

alibi n alibi m.

alien adj estraneo, straniero; * n straniero, extraterrestre.

alienate vt alienare.

alienation n alienazione f.

alight adj essere in fiamme; * vi scendere.

align vt allineare.

alike adj simile.

alimony n alimenti mpl.

alive adj vivo.

alkali n alcali m.

alkaline adj alcalino.

all adj tutto; * adv ~ **at once** tutto d'un tratto; ~ **the same** tuttavia; **not at** ~! prego! * pron **we** ~ **sat down** ci sedemmo tutti quanti.

allay vt dissipare.

allegation n accusa f.

allege vt asserire.

allegiance n lealtà f.

allegorical adj allegorico.

allegory n allegoria f.

allergy n allergia f.

alleviate vt alleviare.

alley n vicolo m.

alliance n alleanza f.

allied adj alleato.

alligator n alligatore m.

alliteration n allitterazione f.

all-night adj aperto/che dura tutta la notte.

allocate vt assegnare.

allocation n stanziamento m.

allot vt assegnare.

allow vt permettere; concedere.

allowable adj ammissibile.

allowance n indennità f.

alloy n lega f.

all-right adv bene.

all-round adj versatile.

allspice n pepe m della Giamaica.

all-time adj senza precedente.

allude vt alludere a.

allure vt allettare * n fascino m.

alluring adj allettante.

allusion n accenno m; allusione f.

alluvial adj alluvionale.

ally n alleato m; * vt allearsi.

almanac n almanacco m.

almighty *adj* onnipotente *m*.

almond *n* mandorla *f*.

almond tree *n* mandorlo *m*.

almost *adv* quasi.

alms *n* elemosina *f*.

aloft *prep* in alto.

alone *adj* solo; * *adv* da solo; **to leave ~** lasciare in pace.

along *prep* lungo; * *adv* **take it ~** prendilo con te; **I knew all ~** sapevo fin dall'inizio.

aloof *adj* distaccato; * *adv* a distanza.

aloud *adj* a voce alta.

alphabet *n* alfabeto *m*.

alphabetical *adj* alfabetico; **~ly** *adv* in ordine alfabetico.

alpine *n* alpino *m*.

already *adv* già.

also *adv* anche, pure.

altar *n* altare *m*.

alter *vt* modificare.

alteration *n* modifica *f*.

altercation *n* lite *f*.

alternate *adj* alternato; * *vt* alternare.

alternating *adj* alternante.

alternative *n* alternativa *f*; * *adj* alternativo; **~ly** *adv* come alternativa.

alternator *n* alternatore *m*.

although *conj* benché.

altitude *n* altitudine *f*.

altogether *adv* tutto sommato.

aluminium *n* alluminio *m*.

always *adv* sempre.

a.m. *adv* del mattino.

amalgamate *vt* amalgamare.

amaryllis *n* (*bot*) amarillide *f*.

amass *vt* accumulare.

amateur *n* dilettante *m/f*.

amaze *vt* stupire.

amazement *n* stupore *m*.

amazing *adj* sorprendente; **~ly** *adv* incredibilmente.

ambassador *n* ambasciatore *m*.

ambassadress *n* ambasciatrice *f*.

amber *n* ambra *f*; * *adj* ambra.

ambidextrous *adj* ambidestro.

ambiguity *n* ambiguità *f*.

ambiguous *adj* ambiguo.

ambition *n* ambizione *f*.

ambitious *adj* ambizioso.

amble *vi* camminare senza fretta.

ambulance *n* ambulanza *f*.

ambush *n* imboscata *f*; **to lie in ~** stare in agguato * *vt* fare un'imboscata a.

amenable *adj* conciliante.

amend *vt* (*law*) emendare.

amendment *n* emendamento *m*.

amends *npl* risarcimento *m*.

amenities *npl* attrezzatura *f*.

America *n* America *f*.

American *adj* americano.

amethyst *n* ametista *f*.

ambiable *adj* affabile.

amicable *adj* amichevole.

amid(st) *prep* in mezzo a, tra.

amiss *adv* male; **don't take it ~** non ti offendere.

ammonia *n* (*chem*) ammoniaca *f*.

ammunition *n* munizioni *fpl*.

amnesia *n* amnesia *f*.

amnesty *n* amnistia *f*.

among(st) *prep* tra, in mezzo a.

amoral *adv* amorale.

amorous *adj* amoroso.

amorphous *adj* amorfo.

amount *n* somma *f*, importo *m*; * *vi* ammontare a.

amp(ere) *n* ampere *m*.

amphibian *n* anfibio *m*;.

amphibious *adj* anfibio.

amphitheatre *n* anfiteatro *f*.

ample *adj* ampio.

amplification *n* amplificazione *f*.

amplifier *n* amplificatore *m*.

amplify *vt* (*sound*) amplificare (*statement*) ampliare.

amply *adv* ampiamente.

amputate *vt* amputare.
amputation *n* amputazione *f*.
amulet *n* amuleto *m*.
amuse *vt* divertire.
amusement *n* divertimento *m*.
amusing *adj* divertente.
an *art* un, uno, una.
anachronism *n* anacronismo *m*.
anaemia *n* anemia *f*.
anaemic *adj* anemico.
anaesthetic *n* anestetico *m*.
anaesthetist *n* anestetista *m/f*.
anagram *n* anagramma *m*.
analogue *adj* analogico.
analogous *adj* analogo.
analogy *n* analogia *f*.
analysis *n* analisi *f*.
analyst *n* analista *m/f*.
analytical *adj* analitico.
analyze *vt* analizzare.
anarchic *adj* anarchico.
anarchist *n* anarchico *m*.
anarchy *n* anarchia *n*.
anathema *n* anatema *m*.
anatomical *adj* anatomico.
anatomy *n* anatomia *f*.
ancestor *n* antenato *m*, avo *m*.
ancestral *adj* ancestrale, atavico.
ancestry *n* stirpe *f*.
anchor *n* ancora *f*.
anchorage *n* ancoraggio *m*.
anchovy *n* acciuga *f*.
ancient *adj* antico.
ancillary *adj* ausiliario.
and *conj* e; **faster ~ faster** sempre più veloce.
anecdote *n* aneddoto *m*.
anemone *n* (*bot*) anemone *m*; (*zool*) **sea ~** attinia *f*.
anew *adv* di nuovo.
angel *n* angelo *m*.
angelic *adj* angelico.
anger *n* rabbia *f*; * *vt* far arrabbiare.
angle *n* angolo *m*; * *vt* pescare con la lenza.
angler *n* pescatore *m*.

anglicism *n* anglicismo *m*.
anglicize *vt* anglicizzare.
angling *n* pesca *f* con la lenza.
angrily *adv* con rabbia.
angry *adj* arrabbiato.
anguish *n* angoscia *f*.
angular *adj* spigoloso.
animal *adj*, *n* animale *m*;.
animate *vt* animare; * *adj* animato.
animated *adj* animato.
animation *n* animazione *f*.
animosity *n* animosità *f*.
aniseed *n* anice *m*.
ankle *n* caviglia *f*; **~ socks** calzini *mpl*.
annals *n* annali *mpl*.
annex *vt* annettere.
annexe *n* annesso *m*.
annihilate *vt* annientare.
annihilation *n* annientamento *m*.
anniversary *n* anniversario *m*.
annotate *vt* annotare.
annotation *n* annotazione *f*.
announce *vt* annunciare.
announcement *n* annuncio *m*.
announcer *n* presentatore *m*.
annoy *vt* infastidire.
annoyance *n* fastidio *m*.
annoying *adj* irritante.
annual *adj* annuo.
annuity *n* annualità *f*.
annul *vt* annullare.
annulment *n* annullamento *m*.
anodyne *adj*, *n* sedativo *m*.
anoint *vt* ungere.
anomalous *adj* anomalo.
anomaly *n* anomalia *f*.
anonymity *n* anonimato *m*.
anonymous *adj* anonimo.
anorak *n* giacca *f* a vento.
anorexia *n* anoressia *f*.
another *adj* un altro, ancora; **one ~** l'un l'altro.
answer *vt* rispondere; **to ~ for** rispondere di; **to ~ to** rispondere a; * *n* risposta *f*.

answerable *adj* responsabile; dover rendere conto di.

answering machine *n* segreteria *f* telefonica.

ant *n* formica *f*.

antagonism *n* antagonismo *m*.

antagonist *n* antagonista *m/f*.

antagonize *vt* inimicarsi.

antarctic *adj* antartico.

anteater *n* formichiere *m*.

antecedent *n* antecedente *m*.

antechamber *n* anticamera *f*.

antedate *vt* precedere; retrodatare.

antelope *n* antilope *f*.

antenatal *adj* prenatale.

antenna *n* antenna *f*.

anterior *adj* anteriore.

anthem *n* inno *m*.

ant-hill *n* formicaio *m*.

anthology *n* antologia *f*.

anthracite *n* antracite *f*.

anthropology *n* antropologia *f*.

anti-aircraft *adj* antiaereo.

antibiotic *n* antibiotico *m*.

antibody *n* anticorpo *m*.

anticipate *vt* prevedere.

anticipation *n* attesa *f*.

anticlockwise *adj* antiorario; * *adv* in senso antiorario.

antics *n* buffoneria *f*.

anticyclone *n* anticiclone *m*.

antidote *n* antidoto *m*.

antifreeze *n* antigelo *m*.

antihistamene *n* antistaminico *m*.

antipathy *n* antipatia *f*.

antipodes *n* antipodi *mpl*.

antiquarian *n* antiquario *m*.

antiquated *adj* antiquato.

antique *adj* antico * *n* pezzo *m* di antiquariato.

antiquity *n* antichità *f*.

antisemitic *adj* antisemitico.

antiseptic *adj*, *n* antisettico *m*.

antisocial *adj* antisociale.

antithesis *n* antitesi *f*.

antler *n* (*zool*) palco *m*.

anvil *n* incudine *m*.

anxiety *n* ansia *f*.

anxious *adj* preoccupato.

any *adj* del, dello, della, dei, degli, delle, qualche, un po', ogni, qualsiasi, qualunque, tutto; * *pron* qualcuno, nessuno, chiunque; ~**thing** qualcosa; niente; * *adv* ~**how** comunque, in ogni modo.

aorta *n* aorta *f*.

apace *adv* velocemente.

apart *adv* a distanza; separatamente; a pezzi; a parte.

apartheid *n* apartheid *f*.

apartment *n* appartamento *m*.

apathetic *adj* apatico.

apathy *n* apatia *f*.

ape *n* scimmia *f*.

aperitif *n* aperitivo *m*.

aperture *n* apertura *f*.

apex *n* vertice *m*.

aphorism *n* aforisma *m*.

aphrodisiac *adj* afrodisiaco.

apiary *n* apiario *m*.

apiece *adv* ciascuno.

aplomb *n* disinvoltura *m*.

Apocalypse *n* apocalisse *f*.

apocryphal *adj* apocrifo.

apolitical *adj* apolitico.

apologetic *adj* (pieno) di scuse.

apologize *vt* scusarsi.

apology *n* scuse *fpl*.

apoplectic *adj* apoplettico.

apoplexy *n* apoplessia *f*.

apostle *n* apostolo *m*.

apostolic *adj* apostolico.

apostrophe *n* apostrofo *m*.

apotheosis *n* apoteosi *f*.

appal *vt* atterrire.

appalling *adj* terribile.

apparatus *n* attrezzatura *f*.

apparel *n* vestiario *m*.

apparent *adj* evidente; * ~**ly** *adv* a quanto pare.

apparition *n* fantasma *m*.

appeal *vi* supplicare; (*law*) appellarsi; * *n* (*law*) appello *m*.

appealing adj attraente; commovente.

appear vi apparire; comparire; sembrare; esibirsi.

appearance n aspetto m; comparsa f.

appease vt placare.

appellant n (law) appellante m/f.

append vt apporre; allegare.

appendage n appendice f.

appendix n appendice f.

appertain vi spettare.

appetite n appetito m.

appetizing adj appetitoso.

applaud vi applaudire.

applause n applauso m.

apple n mela f; **to upset the ~ cart** mandare tutto all'aria.

apple tree n melo m.

appliance n apparecchio m.

applicable adj applicabile.

applicant n candidato m.

application n applicazione f; domanda f.

applied adj applicato.

apply vt applicare; applicarsi; rivolgersi.

appoint vt nominare.

appointment n appuntamento m; nomina f.

apportion vt attribuire.

apposite adj apposito.

apposition n apposizione f.

appraisal n valutazione f.

appraise vt valutare.

appreciable adj notevole.

appreciate vt apprezzare; * vi aumentare di valore.

appreciation n apprezzamento m; comprensione f; aumento m di valore.

appreciative adj grato; caloroso.

apprehend vt arrestare.

apprehension n apprensione f.

apprehensive adj apprensivo, timoroso.

apprentice n apprendista m/f.

apprenticeship n apprendistato m.

apprise vt informare.

approach vt, vi avvicinar(si) a; * n approccio m.

approachable adj avvicinabile.

approbation n approvazione f.

appropriate vt appropriarsi di; * adj adatto.

approval n approvazione f.

approve (of) vt approvare.

approximate adj approssimativo.

approximation n approssimazione f.

apricot n albicocca f; ~ **tree** albicocco m.

April n aprile m.

apron n grembiule m.

apse n abside f.

apt adj appropriato; **~ly** adv appropriatamente.

aptitude n abilità f.

aqualung n autorespiratore m.

aquarium n acquario m.

Aquarius n Acquario m.

aquatic adj acquatico.

aqueduct n acquedotto m.

aquiline adj aquilino.

Arab n, adj arabo m.

arabesque n arabesco m.

arable adj arabile.

arbitrary adj arbitrario.

arbitrate vt fare da arbitro.

arbitration n arbitrato m.

arbitrator n arbitro m.

arcade n arcata f; galleria f.

arch n arco m; * adj principale; malizioso.

archaeological adj archeologico.

archaeologist n archeologo m.

archaeology n archeologia m.

archaic adj arcaico.

archangel n arcangelo m.

archbishop n arcivescovo m.

archbishopric n arcivescovado m.

arched adj ad arco.

archer n arciere m.

archery n tiro m con l'arco.

architect n architetto m.

architectural adj architettonico.

architecture n architettura f.

archives npl archivio m.

archway n passaggio m a volta.

artic adj artico.

ardent adj ardente.

ardour n ardore m.

arduous adj arduo.

area n area f.

arena n arena f.

arguable adj discutibile.

argue vi litigare.

argument n discussione f.

argumentative adj polemico.

aria n (mus) aria f.

arid adj arido.

Aries n Ariete m.

arise vi presentarsi; derivare da.

aristocracy n aristocrazia f.

aristocrat n, adj aristocratico m.

arithmetic n aritmetica f.

arithmetical adj aritmetico.

ark n arca f.

arm n braccio m; * vt armare.

armament n armamenti mpl.

armchair n poltrona f.

armed adj armato.

armful n bracciata f.

armhole n giro m della manica.

armistice n armistizio m.

armour n armatura f.

armoured car n autoblinda f.

armoury n armeria f.

armpit n ascella f.

armrest n bracciolo m.

army n esercito m.

aroma n aroma m.

aromatico adj aromatico m.

around prep intorno; * adv circa.

arouse vt svegliare; stimolare.

arrange vt sistemare; organizzare.

arrangement n sistemazione f; disposizione f.

array n schieramento m, schiera f.

arrears npl arretrati mpl.

arrest n arresto m; * vt arrestare.

arrival n arrivo m.

arrive vt arrivare.

arrogance n arroganza f.

arrogant adj arrogante.

arrow n freccia f.

arse n culo m.

arsenal n arsenale m.

arsenic n arsenico m.

arson n incendio m doloso.

art n arte f; ~s npl lettere fpl, studi mpl umanistici.

artefact n manufatto m.

arterial adj (anat) arterioso; di grande comunicazione.

artery n arteria f.

artful adj furbo; abile.

art gallery n galleria n d'arte.

arthritis n artrite f.

artichoke n carciofo m.

article n articolo m.

articulate vt articolare; * adj chiaro.

articulated lorry n autoarticolato m.

articulation n articolazione f.

artificial adj artificiale.

artillery n artiglieria f.

artisan n artigiano m.

artist m artista m/f.

artistic adj artistico.

artistry n abilità f artistica.

artless adj ingenuo.

art school n scuola f d'arte.

as conj mentre; come; ~ to, ~ fo quanto a.

asbestos n amianto m.

ascend *vt* salire.

ascendancy *n* ascendente *m*.

ascension *n* ascensione *f*.

ascent *n* ascensione *f*.

ascertain *vt* accertare.

ascetic *adj* ascetico.

ascribe *vt* attribuire.

ash *n* (*bot*) frassino *m*; cenere *f*.

ashamed *adj* pieno di vergogna.

ashore *adv* a terra; **to go ~** scendere a terra.

ashtray *n* portacenere *m*.

Ash Wednesday *n* mercoledì *m* delle cenere.

aside *adv* da parte; **~ from** oltre a.

ask *vt* chiedere; **to ~ after** chiedere notizie; **to ~ a question** fare una domanda; **to ~ out** invitare.

askance *adv* **to look ~** guardare qualcuno storto.

askew *adv* di traverso.

asleep *adj* addormentato.

asparagus *n* asparago *m*.

aspect *n* aspetto *m*.

aspersion *n* calunnia *f*.

asphalt *n* asfalto *m*.

asphyxia *n* asfissia *f*.

asphyxiate *vt* asfissiare.

asphyxiation *n* soffocamento *m*.

aspirate *vt* aspirare.

aspiration *n* aspirazione *f*.

aspire *vt* aspirare.

aspirin *n* aspirina *f*.

ass *n* asino *m*.

assail *vt* assalire.

assailant *n* assalitore *m*.

assassin *n* assassino *m*.

assassinate *vt* assassinare.

assassination *n* assassinio *m*.

assault *n* assalto *m*; * *vt* assaltare.

assemble *vt* radunare; montare.

assembly *n* assemblea *f*; montaggio *m*.

assembly line *n* catena *f* di montaggio.

assent *n* benestare *m*; * *vi* approvare.

assert *vt* affermare.

assertion *n* affermazione *f*.

assertive *adj* che sa imporsi.

assess *vt* valutare.

assessment *n* valutazione *f*.

assessor *n* funzionario *m* del fisco.

assets *npl* beni *mpl*.

assiduous *adj* assiduo.

assign *vt* assegnare.

assignation *n* convegno *m* gallante.

assignemnt *n* incarico *m*.

assimilate *vt* assimilare.

assimilation *n* assimilazione *f*.

assist *vt* aiutare.

assistance *n* aiuto *m*.

assistant *n* aiutante *m/f*.

associate *vt* associare; * *adj* consociato; * *n* collega *m/f*.

association *n* associazione *f*.

assorted *adj* assortito.

assortment *n* assortimento.

assuage *vt* attenuare.

assume *vt* supporre.

assumption *n* supposizione *f*.

assurance *n* assicurazione *f*.

assure *vt* assicurare.

asterisk *n* asterisco *m*.

astern *adv* (*mar*) a poppa.

asthma *n* asma *f*.

asthmatic *adj* asmatico.

astonish *vt* stupire.

astonishing *adj* sorprendente.

astonishment *n* stupore *m*.

astound *vt* sbalordire.

astray *adv* **to go ~** perdersi; **to lead ~** portare qualcuno su una brutta strada.

astride *adj* a cavalcioni.

astringent *n*, *adj* astringente *m*.

astrologer *n* astrologo *m*.

astrology *n* astrologia *f*.

astronaut *n* astronauta *m/f*.

astronomer *n* astronomo *m*.

astronomical *adj* astronomico.

astronomy *n* astronomia *f.*
astute *adj* accorto.
asylum *n* asilo *m*; manicomio *m.*
at *prep* a; **~ once** subito; **~ all** affatto; **~ first** dapprima; **~ last** finalmente.
atheism *n* ateismo *m.*
atheist *n* ateo *m.*
athlete *n* atleta *m/f.*
athletic *adj* atletico.
atlas *n* atlante *m.*
atmosphere *n* atmosfera *f.*
atmospheric *adj* atmosferico.
atom *n* atomo *m.*
atomic *adj* atomico.
atone *vi* espiare.
atonement *n* espiazione *f.*
atrocious *adv* atroce.
atrocity *n* atrocità *f.*
atrophy *n* atrofia *f.*
attach *vt* attaccare.
attaché *n* addetto *m.*
attachment *n* accessorio *m*; attaccamento *m.*
attack *vt* attaccare; * *n* attacco *m.*
attacker *n* aggressore *m.*
attain *vt* raggiungere.
attainable *adj* raggiungibile.
attempt *vt* tentare; * *n* tentativo *m.*
attend *vt* frequentare; **to ~ to** occuparsi di.
attendance *n* frequenza *f.*
attendant *n* custode *m/f.*
attention *n* attenzione *f.*
attentive *adj* premuroso.
attenuate *vt* attenuare.
attest *vt* attestare.
attic *n* soffitta *f*, mansarda *f.*
attire *n* tenuta *f.*
attitude *n* atteggiamento *m.*
attorney *n* avvocato *m*, procuratore *m.*
attract *vt* attirare.
attraction *n* attrazione *f*; attrattiva *f.*
attractive *adj* attraente.

attribute *vt* attribuire; * *n* attributo *m.*
attrition *n* usura *f* (per attrito).
aubergine *n* melanzana *f.*
auburn *adj* ramato.
auction *n* asta *f.*
auctioneer *n* banditore *m.*
audacious *adj* audace.
audacity *n* audacia *f.*
audible *adj* udibile.
audience *n* pubblico *m*; udienza *f.*
audit *n* revisione *f* dei conti; * *vt* fare una revisione di.
audition *n* provino *m.*
auditor *n* revisore *m* dei conti.
auditorium *n* auditorio *m.*
augment *vt* aumentare.
August *n* agosto *m.*
august *adj* augusto.
aunt *n* zia *f.*
au pair *n* ragazza *f* alla pari.
aura *n* aura *f.*
auspices *npl* auspici *mpl.*
auspicious *adj* favorevole.
austere *adj* austero.
austerity *n* austerità *f.*
authentic *adj* autentico.
authenticate *vt* convalidare.
authenticity *n* autenticità *f.*
author *n* autore *m.*
authoress *n* autrice *f.*
authoritarian *adj* autoritario.
authoritative *adj* autorevole.
authority *n* autorità *f.*
authorization *n* autorizzazione *f.*
authorize *vt* autorizzare.
autobiography *n* autobiografia *f.*
autocrat *n* autocrata *m.*
autocratic *adj* autocratico.
autograph *n* autografo; * *vt* firmare.
automatic *adj* automatico.
automation *n* automazione *f.*
autonomy *n* autonomia *f.*
autopsy *n* autopsia *f.*

autumn n autunno m.

autumnal adj autunnale.

auxiliary adj ausiliario; (gram) ausiliare; * n assistente.

avail vt to ~ oneself of avvalersi di; * n to no ~ in vano.

available adj disponibile.

avalanche n valanga f.

avant-garde n avanguardia f; * adj d'avanguardia.

avarice n avarizia f.

avaricious adj avaro.

avenge vt vendicare.

avenue n viale m.

average n media f; * adj medio.

aversion n avversione f.

avert vt distogliere da.

aviary n uccelliera f.

aviation n aviazione f.

avid adj insaziabile.

avocado n avocado m.

avoid vt evitare.

avoidable adj evitabile.

await vt aspettare.

awake vt svegliare; * adj sveglio.

awakening n risveglio m.

award vt assegnare; * n premio m.

aware adj consapevole.

awareness n consapevolezza f.

away adv lontano; **far and ~** di gran lunga.

away game n partita f in trasferta.

awe n timore m riverenziale.

awe-inspiring adj imponente.

awful adj terribile.

awkward adj imbarazzante; goffo.

awl n punteruolo m.

awning n tendone m.

awry adv storto.

axe n ascia; * vt ridurre drasticamente.

axiom n assioma m.

axiomatic adj assiomatico.

axis n asse m.

axle n semiasse m.

azalea n azalea f.

azure n azzurro.

B

baa vi belare.

babble vi parlare a vanvera.

babbling n mormorio m.

baboon n babbuino m.

baby n bambino m, bimbo m, neonato m.

babyhood n prima f infanzia.

babyish adj infantile.

baby-minder n bambinaia f.

baby-sit vi guardare i bambini.

baby-sitter n baby sitter m/f.

bachelor n scapolo m; (univ) dottore m, dottoressa f.

back n schiena f; dietro m; retro m; * adj posteriore; arre-trato; * adv indietro; **I'll be ~ soon** sarò di ritorno fra poco; * vt appoggiare; puntare su; * vi fare marcia indietro.

backbencher n (GB) parlamentare m/f di secondo piano.

backbite vt sparlare.

backbone n spina f dorsale.

backchat n impertinenza f.

backcloth n fondale m.

backcomb vt cotonare.

backdate vt retrodatare.

backdoor n porta f posteriore.

backer n sostenitore m.

backfire *vi* fallire. .

backgammon *n* backgammon *m*.

background *n* sfondo *m*; formazione *f*.

backhand *n* rovescio *m*.

backhander *n* bustarella *f*.

backing *n* appoggio *m*.

backlash *n* reazione *f* violenta.

backlog *n* cumulo *m* di lavoro arretrato.

backnumber *n* numero *m* arretrato.

backpack *n* zaino *m*.

backside *n* sedere *m*.

back stage *n* nel retroscena *f*.

back stroke *n* dorso *m*.

backup *adj* supplementare.

backward *adj* all'indietro; lento; arretrato.

backwards *adv* indietro.

backwater *n* angolo *m* sperduto.

backyard *n* cortile *m*.

bacon *n* pancetta *f*.

bacteria *n* batteri *mpl*.

bad *adj* cattivo; brutto; ~ **language** parolacce.

badge *n* distintivo *m*.

badger *n* tasso *m*; * *vt* **to** ~ tormentare.

bad-mannered *adj* maleducato, sgarbato.

badminton *n* badminton *m*.

bad tempered *adj* irascibile.

baffle *vt* confondere.

bag *n* borsa *f*, sacchetto *m*.

baggage *n* bagaglio *m*.

baggy *adj* sformato.

bagpipes *n* cornamusa *f*, zampogna *f*.

bag-snatcher *n* scippatore *m*.

bail *n* cauzione *f*.

bailiff *n* ufficiale *m/f* giudiziario; fattore *m*.

bait *vt* stuzzicare; * *n* esca *f*.

baize *n* panno *m*.

bake *vt* cuocere (al forno).

baker *n* fornaio *m*.

bakery *n* panificio *m*.

baking *n* cottura *f*.

baking powder *n* lievito *m* in polvere.

balaclava *n* passamontagna *m*.

balance *n* equilibrio *m*; bilancio *m*; saldo *m*; * *vt* tenere in equilibrio/in bilico.

balance sheet *n* bilancio *m* di esercizio.

balcony *n* balcone *m*.

bald *adj* calvo.

baldness *n* calvizie *f*.

bale *n* balla *f*; * *vi* vuotare.

baleful *adj* maligno.

balk *vi* recalcitrare.

ball *n* palla *f*; ballo *m*.

ballad *n* ballata *f*.

ballast *n* zavorra *f*.

ballcock *n* galleggiante *m*.

ballerina *n* ballerina *f*.

ballet *n* danza *f* classica.

ballistic *adj* balistico.

balloon *n* palloncino *m*; **hot air** ~ mongolfiera *f*.

ballot *n* votazione *f*; * *vt* consultare tramite votazione.

ballpoint (pen) *n* penna *f* a sfera.

ballroom *n* sala *f* da ballo.

balm *n* balsamo *m*.

balmy *adj* balsamico.

balustrade *n* balaustrata *f*.

bamboo *n* bambù *m*.

bamboozle *vt* raggirare.

ban *n* divieto *m*; * *vt* proibire.

banal *adj* banale.

banana *n* banana *f*; ~ **tree** banano *m*.

band *n* banda *f*; striscia *f*.

bandage *n* fascia *f*.

bandanna *n* fazzolettone *m*.

bandit *n* bandito *m*.

bandstand *n* palco *m* dell'orchestra.

bandy-legged *adj* con le gambe storte.

bang n colpo m * vt, vi sbattere.

banger n salsiccia f; petardo m.

bangle n braccialetto m.

banish vt bandire.

banisters npl ringhiera f.

banjo n banjo m.

bank n riva f; banca f; * vi to ~ servirsi di una banca.

bank account n conto m in banca.

banker n banchiere m.

banking n attività f bancaria.

banknote n banconota f.

bankrupt adj fallito; * n fallito m.

bankruptcy n bancarotta f.

bank statement n estratto m conto.

banner n stendardo m; striscione m.

bans npl pubblicazioni fpl matrimoniali.

banquet n banchetto m.

baptism n battesimo m.

baptistery n battistero m.

baptize vt battezzare.

bar n bar m; sbarra f; * vt sbarrare; * prep tranne.

barb n punta f.

barbarian n barbaro m.

barbaric adj barbaro.

barbecue n barbecue m.

barbed wire n filo m spinato.

barber n barbiere m.

bar code n codice m a barre.

barbiturate n barbiturico m.

bard n bardo m.

bare adj nudo; spoglio; semplice.

bareback adj senza sella.

barefaced adj sfacciato.

barefoot(ed) adj scalzo.

bareheaded adj a capo scoperto.

barely adv appena.

bargain n affare m; * vi contrattare.

barge n chiatta f.

baritone n baritono m.

bark n corteccia f; abbaiare m; * vi abbaiare.

barley n orzo m.

barmaid n barista f.

barman n barista m.

barmy adj suonato.

barn n stalla f.

barnacle n cirripedi m.

barometer n barometro m.

baron n barone m.

baroness n baronessa f.

baroque adj barocco.

barracks n caserma f.

barrage n sbarramento m; a ~ of questions una raffica di domande.

barrel n barile m; canna f.

barrel organ n organetto m.

barren adj infruttuoso; sterile.

barricade n barricata; * vt barricare.

barrier n barriera f.

barrister n avvocato m.

barrow n carriola f.

bartender n barista m.

barter vi, vt barattare.

base n base f; * vt basare * adj ignobile, vile.

baseball n baseball m.

baseless adj infondato.

basement n seminterrato m.

baseness n viltà f.

bash n botta; * vt picchiare.

bashful adj timido.

basic adj fondamentale.

basil n basilico m.

basilisk n basilisco m.

basin n lavandino m.

basis n base f.

bask vt crogiolarsi.

basket n cestino m.

basketball n pallacanestro f.

bass adj basso.

bassoon n fagotto m.

bastard adj bastardo.

bastardy n bastardaggine f.

baste vt (culin) ungere; (sewing) imbastire.

bat n (*zool*) pipistrello m; (*sport*) mazza f.

batch n gruppo m.

bath n bagno m; * vt fare il bagno.

bathe vt lavare; * vi fare il bagno.

bather n bagnante m/f.

bathing cap n cuffia f.

bathing costume n costume m.

bath mat n tappetino m da bagno.

bathos n sentimento m falso.

bathrobe n accappatoio m.

bathroom n (stanza da) bagno m.

baths npl piscina f.

bathtub n vasca f da bagno.

baton n bacchetta f.

battalion n battaglione m.

batter vt colpire violentemente; * n pastella f.

battering ram n ariete m.

battery n pila f, batteria f.

battle n battaglia f, lotta f; * vi lottare, combattere.

battlefield n campo m di battaglia.

battlements npl bastioni mpl.

battleship n nave f da guerra.

bauble n ninnolo m.

bauxite n bauxite f.

bawdy adj spinto.

bawl vi strillare.

bay n baia f; alloro m; * vt latrare.

bayonet n baionetta f.

bay window n bovindo m.

bazaar n bazar m.

be vi essere.

beach n spiaggia f.

beacon n faro m.

bead n perlina f.

beak n becco m.

beaker n (*chem*) bicchiere m, becher m.

beam n trave f; raggio m; * vi sorridere radiosamente.

bean n fagiolo m; chicco m.

beansprouts npl germogli mpl di soia.

bear[1] vt portare; sopportare; partorire; * vi **to ~ right** andare a destra.

bear[2] n orso m.

bearable adj sopportabile.

beard n barba f.

bearded adj barbuto.

bearer n portatore m; titolare m/f.

bearing n portamento m.

beast n bestia f; **~ of burden** bestia da soma.

beastly adj insopportabile.

beat vt battere; * vi palpitare * n battito m; ritmo m.

beatify vt beatificare.

beating n botte fpl; sconfitta f.

beatitude n beatitudine f.

beautiful adj bello; splendido.

beautify vt abbellire.

beauty n bellezza f; **~ spot** neo m.

beaver n castoro m.

because conj perché.

beckon vi chiamare con un cenno.

become vi diventare; divenire.

becoming adj adatto.

bed n letto m.

bedclothes npl coperte fpl.

bedlam n baraonda f.

bedpan n padella f.

bedraggled adj sbrindellato.

bedridden adj costretto a letto.

bedroom n camera f da letto.

bedspread n copriletto m.

bee n ape f.

beech n faggio m.

beef n manzo m.

beefsteak n bistecca (di manzo) f.

beehive n alveare m.

beer n birra f.

beeswax n cera f d'api.

beet(root) n barbabietola f.

beetle n scarabeo m.
befall vt, vi accadere.
befit vt adirsi.
before adv prima di.
beforehand adv prima.
befriend vt prendersi a cuore.
befuddled adj confuso.
beg vt mendicare; supplicare.
beggar n mendicante m/f.
begin vt, vi cominciare, incominciare, iniziare.
beginner n principiante m/f.
beginning n inizio m, principio m.
begonia n begonia f.
begrudge vt invidiare.
behalf n per conto di.
behave vi comportarsi.
behaviour n comportamento m.
behead vt decapitare.
behind prep dietro.
beige adj beige.
being n essere m, esistenza f.
belated adj in ritardo.
belch vi ruttare; * n rutto m.
belfry n campanile m.
belie vt smentire.
belief n fede f; convinzione f; opinione f.
believable adj credibile.
believe vt, vi credere a.
believer n credente m/f.
belittle vt sminuire.
bell n campanello m.
bellicose adj bellicoso.
belligerent adj belligerante.
bellow vi muggire; * n muggito m; urlo m.
bellows n mantice m, soffietto m.
belly n pancia f.
bellyache vi mugugnare.
bellyful n: to have a ~ of avere abbastanza di.
belong vi appartenere.
belongings npl effetti mpl personali.
beloved adj adorato.

below prep, adv sotto.
belt n cintura f; * vi filare.
bemoan vt lamentare.
bemused adj perplesso.
bench n panchina f.
bend vt piegare; * vi piegarsi; * n curva f.
bends n embolia f.
beneath adv, prep sotto.
benediction n benedizione f.
benefactor n benefattore m.
beneficent adj caritatevole.
beneficial adj benefico.
beneficiary n beneficiario m.
benefit n vantaggio m; * vt giovare; * vi trarre vantaggio.
benvolence n benevolenza f.
benevolent adj benevolo.
benign adj benevolo; benigno.
bent n inclinazione f.
bequeath vt lasciare in eredità.
bequest n lascito m.
berrate vt rimproverare.
bereaved adj in lutto.
bereavement n lutto m.
beret n berretto m.
berry n bacca f.
berserk adj forsennato.
berth n cuccetta f; ormeggio m; * vi ormeggiare.
beseech vt implorare.
beset vt assillare.
beside prep a canto a.
besides prep oltre a; * adv inoltre.
besiege vt assediare.
best adj migliore; * adv meglio; * n il migliore.
bestial adj bestiale.
bestow vt conferire.
bestseller n bestseller m.
bet vt, vi scommettere * n scommessa f.
betray vt tradire.
betrayal n tradimento m.
betroth vt fidanzare.
bethrothal n fidanzamento m.
better adj migliore; **so much**

the ~ meglio così; * *adv* meglio; * *vt* migliorare.

between *prep* tra, fra.

bevel *n* smussatura *f*; *vt* smussare.

beverage *n* bevanda *f*.

bevy *n* banda *f*.

bewale *vt* lamentare.

beware *vi* stare attento.

bewilder *vt* disorientare.

bewilderment *n* perplessità *f*.

bewitch *vt* stregare.

beyond *prep* oltre; al di là.

bias *n* tendenza *f*.

bib *n* bavaglino *m*.

Bible *n* bibbia *f*.

biblical *adj* biblico.

bibliography *n* bibliografia *f*.

bicarbonate of soda *n* bicarbonato *m* di sodio.

biceps *n* bicipite *m*.

bicker *vi* bisticciare.

bicycle *n* bicicletta *f*.

bid *vt* offrire; * *vi* dichiarare; * *n* offerto *m*; tentativo *m*.

bidding *n* offerte *fpl*.

bidet *n* bidè *m*.

biennial *adj* biennale.

bifocals *npl* occhiali *mpl* bifocali.

bifurcation *n* biforcazione *f*.

big *adj* grande; grosso; **my ~ sister** mia sorella maggiore.

bigamist *n* bigamo *m*.

bigamy *n* bigamia *f*.

big dipper *n* montagne *fpl* russe.

big-headed *adj* montato.

bigot *n* fanatico *m*.

bigoted *adj* fanatico.

bigwig *n* pezzo *m* grosso.

bike *n* bici *f*.

bikini *n* bikini *m*.

bilateral *adj* bilaterale.

bilberry *n* mirtillo *m*.

bile *n* bile *f*.

bilingual *adj* bilingue.

bilious *adj* biliare.

bill *n* becco *m*; fattura *f*; conto *m*.

billboard *n* tabellone *m*.

billet *n* acquartieramento *m*.

billiards *npl* biliardo *m*.

billion *n* bilione *m*.

billow *vi* gonfiarsi.

billy *n* caprone *m*.

bin *n* bidone *m*.

bind *vt* legare; rilegare.

binder *n* classificatore *m*.

binding *n* rilegatura *f*.

bingo *n* tombola *f*.

binoculars *n* binocolo *m*.

biochemistry *n* biochimica *f*.

biographer *n* biografo *m*.

biographical *adj* biografico.

biography *n* biografia *f*.

biological *adj* biologico.

biology *n* biologia *f*.

biped *n* bipede *m*.

birch *n* betulla *f*.

bird *n* uccello *m*.

bird watcher *n* ornitologo *m*.

birth *n* nascita *f*; parto *m*.

birth certificate *n* certificato *m* di nascita.

birth control *n* controllo *m* delle nascite, contraccezione *f*.

birthday *n* compleanno *m*.

birthmark *n* voglia *f*.

birthplace *n* luogo *m* di nascita.

birthright *n* diritto *m* di nascita.

biscuit *n* biscotto *m*.

bisect *vt* bisecare.

bishop *n* vescovo *m*; (*chess*) alfiere *m*.

bison *n* bisonte *m*.

bit *n* punta *f*; pezzo *m*; morso *m*.

bitch *n* cagna *f*; (*fam*) stronza *f*.

bite *vt* mordere; pungere; **~ the dust** lasciarci la pelle; * *n* morso *m*; puntura *f*.

bitter *adj* amaro; aspro.

bitterness *n* amarezza *f*.

bitumen *n* bitume *m*.

bivouac *n* bivacco *m*.

bizarre *adj* bizzarro.
blab *vt* spifferare.
black *adj* nero; * *n* nero; * *vt* boicottare.
blackberry *n* mora *f*.
blackbird *n* merlo *m*.
blackboard *n* lavagna *f*.
blacken *vi* annerirsi; * *vt* annerire.
blackhead *n* punto *m* nero.
black ice *n* ghiaccio *m* invisibile.
backjack *n* ventuno *m*.
blackleg *n* crumiro *m*.
blacklist *n* lista *f* nera.
blackmail *n* ricatto *m*; * *vt* ricattare.
black market *n* mercato *m* nero.
blackness *n* oscurità *f*.
black pudding *n* sanguinaccio *m*.
black sheep *n* pecora *f* nera.
blacksmith *n* fabbro *m*.
blackthorn *n* prugnolo *m*.
bladder *n* vescica *f*.
blade *n* lama *f*.
blame *vt* incolpare; rimproverare; * *n* colpa *f*.
blameless *adj* irreprensibile.
blanch *vt* (*culin*) scottare; * *vi* sbiancare.
bland *adj* blando.
blank *adj* bianco; vacuo; * *n* vuoto *m*.
blank cheque *n* assegno *m* in bianco.
blanket *n* coperta *f*; * *adj* globale.
blare *vi* strombettare.
blasé *adj* blasé.
blaspheme *vi* bestemmiare.
blasphemer *n* bestemmiatore *m*.
blasphemous *adj* blasfemo.
blasphemy *n* bestemmia *f*.
blast *n* esplosione *f*; raffica *f*; * *vt* far saltare; * *excl* ~! mannaggia!
blast-off *n* lancio *m*.
blatant *adj* sfacciato.

blaze *n* incendio *m*; * *vi* ardere; divampare.
blazer *n* blazer *m*.
bleach *vt* candeggiare; * *n* candeggina *f*.
bleak *adj* tetro; desolato.
bleary(-eyed) *adj* dagli occhi cisposi.
bleat *n* belato *m*; * *vt* belare.
bleed *vi* sanguinare; * *vt* spurgare.
bleeding *n* emorragia *f*; * *adj* sanguinante.
bleep *n* segnale *m* acustico.
bleeper *n* cicalino *m*.
blemish *vt* deturpare; * *n* imperfezione *f*.
blend *vt* mischiare; * *vi* fondersi; * *n* miscela *f*.
blender *n* frullatore *m*.
bless *vt* benedire.
blessed *adj* benedetto.
blessing *n* benedizione *f*.
blight *n* piaga *f*.
blind *adj*, *n* cieco *m*; ~ **alley** vicolo *m* cieco; * *vt* accecare; **Venetian** ~ tenda *f* avvolgibile.
blindfold *vt* bendare; * *n* benda *m*; * *adj* bendato.
blindly *adv* ciecamente.
blindness *n* cecità *f*.
blind spot *n* punto *m* cieco; punto *m* debole.
blink *vt* sbattere le palpebre; * *n* battito *m* di ciglia.
blinkers *npl* paraocchi *mpl*.
bliss *n* felicità *f*.
blissful *adj* stupendo.
blister *n* vescica *f*.
blitz *n* attacco *m* improvviso.
blizzard *n* bufera *f* di neve.
bloated *adj* gonfio.
bloc *n* blocco *m*; * *vt* bloccare.
block *n* blocco *m*.
blockade *n* blocco *m*.
blockage *n* ingorgo *m*.
blockbuster *n* cosa *f* sensazionale.

blockhead *n* zuccone *m*.

bloke *n* tizio *m*.

blonde *adj, n* biondo *m*.

blood *n* sangue *m*.

bloodcurdling *adj* raccapricciante.

blood donor *n* donatore *m* di sangue.

blood group *n* gruppo *m* sanguino.

bloodhound *n* segugio *m*.

bloodless *adj* esangue.

blood poisoning *n* avvelenamento *m* del sangue.

blood pressure *n* pressione *f* del sangue.

bloodshed *n* spargimento *m* di sangue.

bloodshot *adj* iniettato di sangue.

bloodstream *n* circolazione *f* del sangue.

bloodsucker *n* sanguisuga *f*.

blood test *n* analisi *f* del sangue.

bloodthirsty *adj* sanguinario.

blood transfusion *n* trasfusione *f* di sangue.

blood vessel *n* vaso *m* sanguino.

bloody *adj* sanguinante; maledetto; ~ **minded** scontroso.

bloom *n* fiore *m*; * *vi* sfiorire.

blossom *n* fiori *mpl*.

blot *vt* macchiare; asciugare; * *n* macchia *f*.

blotch *n* chiazza *f*.

blotting paper *n* carta *f* assorbente.

blouse *n* camicetta *f*.

blow *vi* soffiare; * *vt* suonare; esplodere; * *n* colpo *m*.

blow-dry *vt* asciugare con il fohn.

blowlamp *n* lampada *f* a benzina per saldare.

blow out *vt* spegnere.

blowout *n* scoppio *m*.

blowpipe *n* cerbottana *f*.

blubber *n* grasso *m* di balena; * *vi* frignare.

bludgeon *n* randello *m*.

blue *adj* azzurro, celeste.

bluebell *n* giacinto *m* dei boschi.

bluebottle *n* moscone *m*.

blue-collar *adj* operaio.

blueprint *n* cianografia *f*.

bluff *adj* brusco; a picco; * *vi* bluffare.

blunder *n* gaffe *f*; * *vi* ~ **into** andare a sbattere contro.

blunt *adj* non tagliente; brusco.

bluntly *adv* senza mezzi termini.

bluntness *n* brutale franchezza *f*.

blur *n* massa *f* indistinta; * *vt* offuscare.

blurt out *vt* lasciarsi scappare.

blush *n* rossore *m*; * *vi* arrossire.

bluster *n* fanfaronata *f*.

blustery *adj* ventoso.

B.O. *n* odore *m* sgradevole.

boa *n* boa *m*.

boar *n* cinghiale *m*.

board *n* asse *f*; (*chess*) scacchiera *f*; vitto *m*; commissione *f*; * *vt* imbarcarsi su; salire su; * *vi* essere a pensione da.

boarder *n* pensionante *m/f*; collegiale *m/f*.

boarding card *n* carta *f* d'imbarco.

boarding house *n* pensione *f*.

boarding school *n* collegio *m*.

boast *vt* vantare; * *n* vanteria *f*.

boastful *adj* si vanta sempre.

boat *n* barca *f*; nave *f*.

boater *n* paglietta *f*.

boatswain *n* nostromo *m*.

bobby *n* poliziotto *m*.

bobsleigh *n* bob *m*.

bode *vt* presagire.

bodice n corpino m.

bodily adj materiale; * adv fisicamente.

body n corpo m; cadavere m; massa f; * pron any~ qualcuno.

bodyguard n guardia f del corpo.

bodywork n carrozzeria f.

bog n palude f; cesso m.

bogey man n orco m, babau m.

bogus adj fasullo.

boil vi bollire; * vt (far) lessare; * n foruncolo m.

boiled egg n uovo m sodo.

boiled potatoes npl patate fpl lesse.

boiler n caldaia f.

boiling point n punto m di ebollizione.

boisterous adj animato.

bold adj audace; ~ type grassetto.

boldness n audacia f.

bollard n colonnina f.

bolster n capezzale m; * vt sostenere.

bolt n chiavistello m; bullone m; fulmine m; * vi svignarsela; * vt ingollare.

bomb n bomba f; vt bombardare.

bombardment n bombardamento m.

bombastic adj magniloquente.

bomber n dinamitardo m.

bombshell n bomba f.

bond n impegno m; legame m; titolo m.

bonded warehouse n magazzino m doganale.

bone n osso m; (fish) lisca f.

bone-dry adj asciuttissimo.

bonfire n falò m.

bonnet n cuffia f; cofano m.

bonny adj carino.

bonus n gratifica f; premio m.

bony adj osseo.

boo vt fischiare.

boob n gaffe f; tetta f.

booby prize n premio per il peggior contendente.

booby trap n trabocchetto m.

book n libro m; quaderno m; * vt prenotare, riservare.

bookbinder n rilegatore m.

bookcase n libreria f.

bookkeeper n contabile m/f.

bookkeeping n contabilità f.

booklet n opuscolo m.

bookmaker n allibratore m/f.

bookmark n segnalibro m.

bookseller n libraio m.

bookshop n libreria f.

bookstall n bancarella f.

bookworm n topo m di biblioteca.

boom n boma f; rombo m; forte incremento m; * vi andare a gonfie vele.

boomerang n boomerang m.

boon n salvezza f.

boor n zoticone m.

boorish adj rozzo.

boost n spinta f; sprone m; * vt rinforzare.

booster n (med) richiamo m; amplificatore di segnale m.

boot n stivale m; **to** ~ dare un calcio.

bootee n scarpetta f.

booth n cabina f.

bootleg adj di contrabbando.

boot polish n lucido m da scarpe.

booty n bottino m.

booze vi alzare il gomito; * n alcol m.

boozer n osteria f.

border n confine m; margine m; aiuola f; * vt fiancheggiare.

borderline n linea f di demarcazione.

bore vt trivellare; annoiare; * n foro m; calibro m; noia f; noioso m.

boredom n noia f.

boring *adj* noioso.
born *adj* nato.
borough *n* comune *m*.
borrow *vt* prendere in prestito.
borstal *n* riformatorio *m*.
bosom *n* petto *m*, seno *m*.
bosom friend amico/ca *m/f* del cuore.
boss *n* capo *m*, padrone *m*.
bossy *adj* autoritario.
botanic(al) *adj* botanico.
botanist *n* botanico *m*.
botany *n* botanica *f*.
botch *vt* fare un pasticcio; * *n* pasticcio *m*.
both *adj* entrambi; ambedue; tutti e due.
bother *vt* infastidire; **a ~** una seccatura.
bottle *n* bottiglia *f*; * *vt* imbottigliare.
bottleneck *n* ingorgo *m*.
bottle-opener *n* apribottiglie *m*.
bottom *n* fondo *m*; sedere *m*.
bottomless *adj* senza fondo.
bough *n* ramo *m*.
boulder *n* macigno *m*.
bounce *vi* rimbalzare * *n* rimbalzo *m*.
bouncer *n* buttafuori *m*.
bound(s) *n* limiti *mpl*; balzo *m*; * *vi* balzare; * *adj* legato; rilegato; **~ for** diretto a; **it was ~ to happen** era da prevedersi.
boundary *n* confine *m*.
boundless *adj* illimitato.
bountiful *adj* abbondante; munifico.
bouquet *n* bouquet *m*.
bourgeois *adj* borghese.
bourgeoisie *n* borghesia *f*.
bout *n* attacco *m*; incontro *m*.
boutique *n* boutique *f*.
bovine *adj* bovino.
bow *vt* chinare; * *vi* inchinarsi; * *n* inchino *m*; prua *f*.

bow *n* arco *m*.
bowdlerize *vt* espurgare.
bowels *npl* intestino *m*.
bowl *n* scodella *f*; * *vt* lanciare.
bowling *n* bocce *fpl*; bowling *m*.
bowling alley *n* bowling *m*.
bowling green *n* campo *m* da bocce.
bow tie *n* farfalla *f*.
box *n* scatola *f*; palco *m*; * *vi* fare il pugile.
boxing *n* pugilato *m*.
boxer *n* pugile *m*.
boxing gloves *npl* guantoni *mpl*.
boxing ring *n* ring *m*.
box office *n* botteghino *m*.
boxroom *n* ripostiglio *m*.
boy *n* ragazzo *m*; fanciullo *m*.
boycott *vt* boicottare; * *n* boicottaggio *m*.
boyfriend *n* ragazzo *m*; fidanzato *m*.
boyish *adj* fanciullesco.
bra *n* reggiseno *m*.
brace *n* apparecchio *m* ortodontico; rinforzo *m*; * *vt* rinforzare.
bracelet *n* braccialetto *m*.
bracing *adj* tonificante.
bracken *n* felce *f*.
bracket *n* mensola *f*; parentesi *f*.
brag *vt*, *vi* vantarsi.
braggart *n* spaccone *m*.
braid *n* treccia *f*; * *vt* intrecciare
brain *n* cervello *m*.
brainchild *n* creazione *f*.
brainless *adj* deficiente.
brainwash *vt* fare il lavaggio del cervello.
brainwave *n* idea *f* brillante.
brainy *adj* geniale.
brake *n* freno *vi* frenare.
brake light *n* fanalino *m* dello stop.
bramble *n* mora *f*.
bramble bush *n* rovo *m*.

bran n crusca f.

branch n ramo m; * vi diramar-si.

branch line n linea f seconda-ria.

brand n marca f; * vt marchiare.

brandish vt brandire.

brand-new adj nuovo di zecca.

brandy n brandy m.

brash adj sfrontato.

brass n ottone m.

brassiere n reggiseno m.

brat n moccioso m.

bravado n spavalderia f.

brave adj coraggioso; * vt sfi-dare; * n giovane guerriero m pellerossa.

bravery n coraggio m.

brawl n rissa f; * vi azzuffarsi.

brawn n muscoli mpl.

bray vi ragliare; * n raglio m.

brazen adj sfacciato.

brazier n bracciere m.

breach n violazione f; breccia f.

bread n pane m.

breadbin n cassetta f porta-pane.

breadboard n tagliere m.

breadcrumb n briciola f.

breadcrumbs n pangrattato m.

breadth n larghezza f.

breadwinner n chi mantiene la famiglia.

break vt rompere; * vi romper-si; **to ~ into** forzare; **to ~ out** scoppiare; evadere; **to ~ up** andare in vacanza; * n rottu-ra f; intervallo m; **a lucky ~** un colpo di fortuna.

breakable adj fragile.

breakage n danni mpl.

breakaway adj scissionista.

breakdown n guasto m; esau-rimento m nervoso.

breaker n frangente m.

breakfast n prima colazione f.

breakthrough n scoperta f de-cisiva.

breakwater n frangiflutti m.

breast n petto m; seno m; mam-mella f.

breastbone n sterno m.

breast-feed vt allattare (al seno).

breaststroke n nuoto m a rana.

breath n fiato n; alito m.

breathe vt respirare.

breathing n respiro m, respi-razione f.

breathalyzer n palloncino m.

breathing space n attimo m di respiro.

breathless adj senza fiato.

breathtaking adj mozzafiato.

breed n razza f; * vt allevare; * vi riprodursi. .

breeder n allevatore m; reat-tore m autofertilizzante.

breeding n allevamento m; buona educazione f.

breeze n brezza f, venticello m.

breezy adj ventoso; brioso.

brevity n brevità f.

brew vt mettere a fermentare; fare un infuso di; * n fermen-tazione f; infuso m.

brewer n fabbricante m di bir-ra.

brewery n fabbrica f di birra.

briar n pipa f di radica.

bribe n bustarella f; * vt cor-rompere.

bribery n corruzione f.

bric-à-brac n bric-à-brac m.

brick n mattone m.

bricklayer n muratore m.

bridal adj nuziale.

bride n sposa f.

bridegroom n sposo m.

bridesmaid n damigella f d'onere.

bridge n ponte m; bridge m.

bridle n briglia f.

brief adj breve; * n dossier; * vt dare istruzioni a.

briefcase n cartella f.

briefs *n* slip; mutandine *fpl*.
brier *n* rosa *f* selvatica.
brigade *n* brigata *f*.
brigadier *n* generale *m* di brigata.
bright *adj* luminoso; vispo.
brighten *vt* ravvivare; * *vi* schiarirsi; rallegrarsi.
brightness *n* luminosità *f*.
brilliance *n* intensità *f*; intelligenza *f* scintillante.
brilliant *adj* brillante.
brim *n* orlo *m*; * *vi* traboccare di.
bring *vt* portare; **to ~ about** causare, provocare; **to ~ up** allevare; sollevare.
brink *n* orlo *m*.
brisk *adj* sbrigativo; attivo.
bristle *n* setola *f*; pelo *m*; * *vi* rizzarsi.
bristly *adj* setoloso.
brittle *adj* fragile.
broach *vt* affrontare.
broad *adj* largo.
broadbean *n* fava *f*.
broadcast *n* trasmissione *f*; * *vt* trasmettere.
broaden *vt* allargare.
broadly *adv* grosso modo.
broad-minded *adj* aperto.
broadside *n* attacco *m* massiccio.
broadways *adv* nel senso della larghezza.
brocade *n* braccato *m*.
broccoli *n* broccoli *mpl*.
brochure *n* depliant *m*; brochure *f*.
brogue *n* scarpone *m*; accento *m* irlandese.
broken *adj* rotto, spezzato; **~ English** parlare un inglese stentato.
broker *n* mediatore *m*, agente *m* di cambio.
brokerage *n* mediazione *f*.
brolly *n* ombrello *m*.

bronchial *adj* bronchiale.
bronchitis *n* bronchite *f*.
bronze *n* bronzo *m*.
brooch *n* spilla *f*.
brood *vi* covare, rimuginare; * *n* covata *f*; prole *f*.
broody hen *n* chioccia *f*.
brook *n* ruscello *m*; * *vt* ammettere.
broom *n* scopa *f*; (*bot*) ginestra *f*.
broth *n* brodo *m*.
brothel *n* bordello *m*.
brother *n* fratello *m*.
brotherhood *n* fraternità *f*.
brother-in-law *n* cognato *m*.
brotherly *adj* fraterno.
brow *n* fronte *f*; **eye~** sopracciglio *m*.
browbeat *vt* intimidire.
brown *adj* marrone; **~ sugar** zucchero greggio; **~bread** pane integrale; * *vt* (*culin*) rosolare.
browse *vi* curiosare.
bruise *vt* farsi un livido a; * *n* livido *m*.
brunette *n* bruna *f*.
brunt *n*: **to bear the ~ of** sostenere il peso di.
brush *n* spazzola *f*; * *vt* spazzolare; scopare; sfiorare.
brusque *adj* brusco.
Brussels sprout *n* cavolino *m* di Bruxelles.
brutal *adj* brutale.
brutality *n* brutalità *f*.
brute *n* bruto *m*; *adj* bruto.
bubble *n* bolla *f*.
bubblegum *n* bubblegum *m*.
buck *n* (*zool*) maschio *m*.
bucket *n* secchio *m*.
buckle *n* fibbia *f*; * *vt* allacciare; * *vi* allacciarsi.
bucolic *adj* bucolico.
bud *n* bocciolo *m*.
Buddhism *m* buddismo *m*.
budding *adj* in erba.

budge *vt* spostare.
budgerigar *n* pappagallino *m*.
budget *n* bilancio *m*.
buff *n* fanatico *m*; * *adj* color paglierino; * *vt* lucidare.
buffalo *n* bufalo *m*.
buffer *n* respingente *m*.
buffet *n* schiaffo; buffet *m*; * *vt* sballottare.
buffoon *m* buffone *m*.
bug *n* insetto *m*.
bugbear *n* spauracchio *m*.
bugle *n* tromba *f*.
build *n* corporatura *f*; * *vt* costruire.
builder *n* costruttore *m*; muratore *m*.
building *n* costruzione *f*; edificio *m*.
bulb *n* bulbo *m*; lampadina *f*.
bulbous *adj* a forma di bulbo.
bulge *vi* essere gonfio; * *n* rigonfiamento *m*.
bulk *n* volume *m*; massa *f*; **in ~** comprare in grandi quantità.
bulky *adj* voluminoso.
bull *n* toro *m*.
bulldog *n* bulldog *m*.
bulldozer *n* bulldozer *m*.
bullet *n* proiettile *m*.
bulletin *n* bollettino *m*.
bulletproof *adj* a prova di proiettile.
bullfight *n* corrida *f*.
bullfighter *n* torero *m*.
bullion *n* oro *m* in lingotti.
bullock *n* torello *m*.
bullring *n* arena *f*.
bull's-eye *n* centro *m* (del bersaglio).
bully *n* bullo *m*; * *vt* fare il prepotente.
bullwark *n* baluardo *m*.
bum *n* culo *m*; fannullone *m*; * *adj* scadente.
bumblebee *n* bombo *m*.
bumpf *n* scartoffie *fpl*.

bump *n* botta *f*; bernoccolo *m*; * *vt* sbattere.
bumper *n* paraurti *mpl*; * *adj* eccezionale.
bumpkin *n* rusticone *m*.
bumpy *adj* accidentato.
bun *n* panino *m* dolce; chignon *m*.
bunch *n* mazzo *m*; grappolo *m*.
bundle *n* fagotto *m*; * *vt* fare un fagotto.
bung *n* tappo *m*; * *vt* tappare.
bungalow *n* bungalow *m*.
bungle *vt* fare un pasticcio; * *vi* fare pasticci.
bunion *n* (*med*) cipolla *f*.
bunk *n* cuccetta *f*.
bunker *n* bunker *m*.
buoy *n* (*mar*) boa *f*.
buoyant *adj* galleggiante.
burden *n* carico *m*; onere *m*; * *vt* opprimere; oberare.
bureau *n* ufficio *m*; secrétaire *m*.
bureaucracy *n* burocrazia *f*.
bureaucrat *n* burocrate *m/f*.
burglar *n* ladro *m*.
burglar alarm *n* antifurto *m*.
burglary *n* furto *m*.
burgle *vt* svaligiare.
burial *n* sepoltura *f*.
burlesque *n* parodia *f*.
burly *adj* ben piantato.
burn *vt* bruciare; * *n* bruciatura *f*, ustione *f*.
burner *n* bruciatore *m*.
burning *n* bruciato *m*; * *adj* in fiamme.
burp *n* rutto *m*; * *vi* ruttare.
burrow *n* tana *f*; * *vt* scavare.
bursar *n* economo *m*.
bursary *n* borsa *f* di studio.
burst *vi* scoppiare; **to ~ into tears** scoppiare a piangere; * *vt* fare scoppiare.
bury *vt* seppellire.
bus *n* autobus *m*.
bush *n* cespuglio *m*.
bushy *adj* folto.

busily *adv* alacremente.
business *n* affari *mpl*; attività *f*.
businesslike *adj* efficiente.
businessman *n* uomo *m* d'affari.
businesswoman *n* donna *f* d'affari.
bus-stop *n* fermata *f* d'autobus.
bust *n* busto *m*; petto *m*.
bustle *vi* affaccendarsi; * *n* trambusto *m*.
busy *adj* occupato.
busybody *n* ficcanaso *m/f*.
but *conj* ma; * *adv* solo; * *prep* tranne.
butcher *n* macellaio *m*; * *vt* macellare.
butcher's shop *n* macelleria *f*.
butler *n* maggiordomo *m*.
butt *n* botte *f*; mozzicone *m*; * *vt* dare una testata; * *vi* **to ~ in** interrompere.
butter *n* burro *m*.
buttercup *n* (*bot*) ranuncolo *m*.
butterfly *n* farfalla *f*.

buttock *n* natica *f*.
button *n* bottone *m*.
buttonhole *n* asola *f*, occhiello *m*.
buttress *n* contrafforte *m*.
buxom *adj* ben in carne.
buy *vt* comprare.
buyer *n* compratore *m*.
buzz *n* ronzio; * *vi* ronzare.
buzzard *n* poiana *f*.
buzzer *n* cicalino *m*.
by *adv* vicino; * *prep* vicino; via; davanti; **~ and large** nel complesso.
bye-election *n* elezioni *fpl* suppletive.
bygone *adj* passato; **let ~s be ~s** mettiamoci una pietra sopra.
by-law *n* norma *f* di regolamento comunale.
bypass *n* circonvallazione *f*.
by-product *n* sottoprodotto *m*.
bystander *n* astante *m/f*.
byte *n* (*comput*) byte *m*.
byway *n* strada *f* secondaria.
byword *n* sinonimo *m*.

C

cab *n* taxi *m*; cabina *f*.
cabbage *n* cavolo *m*.
cabin *n* capanna *f*; cabina *f*.
cabinet *n* armadietto *m*; Consiglio *m* dei Ministri.
cabinet-maker *n* ebanista *m/f*.
cable *n* cavo *m*.
cable car *n* funivia *f*.
cable television *n* televisione *f* via cavo.
cache *n* deposito *m* segreto.
cackle *vi* fare coccodè; ridacchiare; * *n* coccodè; risolino *m* stridulo;.
cactus *n* cactus *m*.
cadaver *n* cadavere *m*.

cadaverous *adj* cadaverico.
caddy *n* (*tea*) barattolo *m* del tè.
cadence *n* cadenza *f*.
cadet *n* cadetto *m*.
cadge *vt* scroccare.
cadger *n* scroccone *m*.
Caesarean *n* cesareo *m*.
café *n* caffè *m*; bar *m*.
caffeine *n* caffeina *f*.
cage *n* gabbia *f*; * *vt* mettere in gabbia.
cagey *adj* riservato.
cajole *vt* convincere con le buone.
cake *n* torta *f*; pasticcino *m*; * *v* incrostare; * *vi* aggrumarsi.

cake shop n pasticceria f.
calamitous adj calamitoso.
calamity n calamità f.
calcify vt calcificare.
calceum n calcio m.
calculable adj calcolabile.
calculate vt calcolare.
calculation n calcolo m.
calculator n calcolatore m.
calculus n analisi f infinitesi-male.
calendar n calendario m.
calf n vitello m.
calibrate vt calibrare.
calibration n calibratura f.
caliber n calibro m.
calico n tela f grezza.
call vt chiamare; telefonare a; indire; * vi **this ~s for a drink** qui ci vuole un brindisi; **I now ~ on Mr Smith to speak** invito Mr Smith a parlare; * n richiamo m; telefonata f; chia-mata f.
call box n cabina f telefonica.
caller n visitatore m.
calligraphy n calligrafia f.
calling n vocazione f.
callous adj insensibile.
callow adj immaturo.
call-up n chiamata f alle armi.
calm n calma f; pace f; * adj cal-mo m; sereno m; * vt calmare.
calorie n caloria f.
calumny n calunnia f.
Calvary n Calvario m.
calve vi figliare.
Calvinist n calvinista m/f.
camber n curvatura f.
camel n camello m.
camellia n camelia f.
cameo n cammeo m.
camera n macchina f fotografi-ca.
cameraman n cameraman m.
camomile n camomilla f.
camouflage n mimetizzazione f.

camp n accampamento m; * vi campeggiare.
campaign n campagna f; * vi fare una campagna.
campaigner n fautore m, sos-tenitore m.
camper n campeggiatore m.
camping n campeggio m.
camphor n canfora f.
campsite n campeggio m.
campus n campus m.
camshaft n albero m a camme.
can vi potere; **I ~'t swim** non so nuotare; * n latta f; lattina f.
canal n canale m.
canary n canarino m.
cancel vt cancellare.
cancellation n cancellazione f.
cancer n cancro m.
Cancer n Cancro m.
cancerous adj canceroso.
candelabra n candelabro m.
candid adj franco.
candidacy n candidatura f.
candidate n candidato m.
candied adj candito.
candle n candela f.
candlelight n lume m di can-dela.
candlestick n candeliere m.
candor n candore m.
candy n caramella f.
candyfloss n zucchero m fila-to.
cane n canna f; bastone m.
canine adj canino.
canister n barattolo m.
cannabis n canapa f indiana.
cannibal n cannibale m/f.
cannibalism n cannibalismo m.
canny adj cauto.
cannon n cannone m.
cannonball n palla f di canone.
canoe n canoa f.
canon n canone m.
cononize vt canonizzare.

canopy *n* baldacchino *m*.
cant *n* discorsi *mpl* ipocriti.
cantankerous *adj* irascibile.
canteen *n* mensa *f*.
canter *n* piccolo galoppo *m*.
cantilever *n* mensola *f*.
canton *n* cantone *m*.
canvas *n* tela *f*.
canvass *vt* fare un giro elettorale.
canvasser *n* propagandista *m/f*.
canyon *n* canyon *m*.
cap *n* berretto *m*; * *vt* tappare; superare.
capability *n* capacità *f*.
capable *adj* capace.
capacity *n* capacità *f*.
cape *n* capo *m*; cappa *f*; mantello *m*.
caper *n* cappero *m*; scherzetto *m*; * *vt* saltellare.
capillary *adj* capillare.
capital *n* lettera maiuscola; capitale *f*; capitale *m*.
capitalism *n* capitalismo *m*.
capitalist *n* capitalista *m/f*.
capitalize *vt* capitalizzare; * *vi* **to ~ on** trarre vantaggio da.
capital punishment *n* pena *f* capitale.
capitulate *vi* capitolare.
caprice *n* capriccio *m*.
capricious *adj* capriccioso.
Capricorn *n* Capricorno.
capsize *vt* ribaltare; * *vi* ribaltarsi.
capsule *n* capsula *f*.
captain *n* capitano *m*.
caption *n* sottotitolo *m*.
captivate *vt* affascinare.
captive *adj*, *n* prigioniero *m*.
captivity *n* prigionia *f*; cattività *f*.
captor *n* rapitore *m*.
capture *n* cattura *f*.
car *n* macchina *f*, automobile *f*.
carafe *n* caraffa *f*.
caramel *n* caramello *m*.

carat *n* carato *m*.
caravan *n* roulotte *f*.
caraway *n* (*bot*) cumino *m*.
carbohydrate *n* carboidrato *m*.
carbolic acid *n* acido *m* fenico.
carbon *n* carbonio *m*.
carbonated *adj* gassato.
carbonize *vt* carbonizzare.
carbon paper *n* carta *f* carbone.
carbuncle *n* foruncolo *m*.
carburettor *n* carburatore *m*.
carcass *n* carcassa *f*.
carcinogenic *adj* cancerogeno.
card *n* biglietto *m*; tessera *f*; carta *f*.
cardboard *n* cartone *m*.
card game *n* gioco *m* di carte.
cardiac *adj* cardiaco.
cardinal *adj* cardinale; * *n* cardinale *m*.
card table *n* tavolo *m* da carte.
care *n* preoccupazione *f*; attenzione *f*; * *vi* interessarsi; **I don't ~** non mi importa.
career *n* carriera *f*.
carefree *n* spensierato *m*.
careful *adj* attento; accurato; prudente.
careless *adj* distratto; negligente.
carelessness *n* disattenzione *f*.
caress *n* carezza *f*; * *vt* carezzare.
caretaker *n* portinaio *m*.
car-ferry *n* nave *f* traghetto.
cargo *n* carico *m*.
carhire *n* autonoleggio *m*.
caricature *n* caricatura *f*; * *vt* fare una caricatura di.
caries *n* carie *f*.
carnage *n* carneficina *f*.
carnal *adj* carnale.
carnation *n* garofano *m*.
carnival *n* carnevale *m*.
carniverous *adj* carnivoro.
carol *n* canto *m* di Natale.
carouse *vi* fare baldoria.

carousel n giostra f.

carp n carpa f.

carpenter n falegname m.

carpentry n falegnameria f.

carpet n tappeto m; moquette f.

carriage n carrozza f; vagone m; portamento m.

carriage-free adj franco di porto.

carriageway n carreggiata f.

carrier n corriere m; (med) portatore; portaerei f; sacchetto m.

carrier pigeon n piccione m viaggiatore.

carrion n carogna f.

carrot n carota f.

carry vt portare; tenere; riportare; approvare; **to ~ on** portare avanti; continuare; * vi trasmettersi.

carrycot n culla f trasportabile.

carry-on n casino m.

carsick n mal m d'auto.

cart n carretto m.

carte blanche n carta f bianca.

cartel n cartello m.

Carthusian n certosino m.

cartilage n cartilagine f.

cartography n cartografia f.

carton n cartone m.

cartoon n vignetta f; cartone m animato.

cartoonist n vignettista m/f.

cartridge n cartuccia f.

carve vt tagliere; incidere; scolpire.

carving n intaglio m.

carving knife n trinciante m.

car wash n lavaggio m auto.

cascade n cascata f.

case n valigia f; custodia f; astuccio m; cassa f; (gram, med) caso m; **in ~** caso mai.

cash n soldi mpl; **in ~** in contanti; * vt incassare.

cash dispenser n sportello m automatico.

cashew n anacardio m.

cashier n cassiere m.

cashmere n cachemire m.

casing n rivestimento m.

casino n casinò m.

cask n barile m.

casket n scrigno m.

casserole n casseruola f.

cassette n cassetta f.

cassette recorder n registratore m a cassette.

cassock n tonaca f.

cast vt gettare; lanciare; affidare; * n gesso m; cast m; stampo m; strabismo m.

castanets n nacchere fpl.

castaway n naufrago m.

caste n casta f.

caster n rotella f.

caster sugar n zucchero m semolato.

castigate vt castigare.

casting vote n voto m decisivo.

cast iron n ghisa f.

castle n castello m.

castor oil n olio m di ricino.

castrate vt castrare.

castration n castrazione f.

casual adj casuale; informale; saltuario; indifferente.

casualty n vittima f.

cat n gatto m.

cataclysm n cataclisma m.

catacombs npl catacombe fpl.

catalogue n catalogo m.

catalyst n catalizzatore m.

catamaran n catamarano m.

catapult n fionda f.

cataract n cataratta f.

catarrh n catarro m.

catastrophe n catastrofe f.

catcall n fischio m.

catch vt afferrare; prendere; sorprendere; sentire; **to ~ cold** prendere freddo; * vi **to ~ fire** prendere fuoco; * n

tranello *m*; gancio *m*; retata *f*.
catching *adj* contagioso.
catch phrase *n* frase *f* di moda.
catchment area *n* (*school*) zona *f* di competenza.
catchword *n* richiamo *m*.
catchy *adj* orecchiabile.
catechism *n* catechismo *m*.
categorical *adj* categorico.
categorize *vt* classificare.
category *n* categoria *f*.
cater *vi* provvedere a.
caterpillar *n* bruco *m*.
catgut *n* corda *f* di minugia.
cathedral *n* cattedrale *f*; duomo *m*.
cathode *adj* catodo; ~ **ray tube** tubo a raggi catodici.
catholic *adj* cattolico; ampio.
Catholicism *n* cattolicesimo *m*.
cat's eye *n* catarifrangente *m*.
cattle *n* bestiame *m*.
caucus *n* comitato *m* elettorale.
cauldron *n* calderone *m*.
cauliflower *n* cavolfiore *m*.
cause *n* causa *f*; motivo *m*; * *vt* causare.
causeway *n* strada *f* rialzata.
caustic *adj* caustico.
cauterize *vt* cauterizzare.
caution *n* attenzione; prudenza *f*; * *vt* ammonire.
cautionary *adj* ammonitorio.
cautious *adj* cauto; prudente.
cavalier *n* cavaliere *m*; * *adj* brusco.
cavalry *n* cavalleria *f*.
cave *n* brocca *f*; caverna *f*.
caveat *n* ammonimento *m*.
cavern *n* caverna *f*.
cavernous *adj* incavato.
caviar *n* caviale *m*.
cavity *n* cavità *f*.
cavort *vt* saltellare.
cease *vt*, *vi* cessare.
ceasefire *n* cessate il fuoco *m*.
ceaseless *adj* incessante.

cedar *n* cedro *m*.
cede *vt* cedere.
cedilla *n* cediglia *f*.
ceiling *n* soffitto *m*.
celebrate *vt* festeggiare.
celebration *n* celebrazione *f*.
celebrity *n* celebrità *f*.
celery *n* sedano *m*.
celestial *adj* celestiale.
celibacy *n* celibato *m*.
celibate *adj* celibe (*man*); nubile (*woman*).
cell *n* cella *f*.
cellar *n* cantina *f*.
cello *n* violoncello *m*.
cellophane *n* cellofan *m*.
cellular *adj* cellulare.
celluloide *n* celluloide *f*.
cellulose *n* cellulosa *f*.
cement *n* cemento *m*; * *vt* cementare.
cemetery *n* cimitero *m*.
cenotaph *n* cenotafio *m*.
censor *n* censore *m*; * *vt* censurare.
censorious *adj* censorio.
censorship *n* censura *f*.
censure *n* censura *f*; * *vt* censurare.
census *n* censimento *m*.
cent *n* centesimo *m*.
centenarian *n* centenario *m*.
centenary *n* centenario *m*.
centennial *adj* centennale.
centigrade *n* centigrado *m*.
centilitre *n* centilitro *m*.
centimetre *n* centimetro *m*.
centipede *n* millepiedi *m*.
central *adj* centrale.
centralize *vt* centralizzare.
centrifugal *adj* centrifugo.
centrifuge *n* centrifuga *f*.
centurian *n* centurione *m*.
century *n* secolo *m*.
ceramic *adj* di ceramica; ~**s** *npl* ceramica *f*.
cereal *n* cereale *m*.
cerebral *adj* cerebrale.

ceremonial *adj* formale; * *n* rito *m*.

ceremonious *adj* formale.

ceremony *n* cerimonia *f*.

certain *adj* certo; sicuro.

certainty *n* certezza *f*.

certificate *n* certificato *m*.

certification *n* attestazione *f*.

certify *vt* certificare; attestare.

cervical *adj* cervicale; * *n* ~ **smear** Pap-test *m*.

cervix *n* collo *m* dell'utero.

cessation *n* cessazione *f*.

cesspit *n* pozzo *m* nero.

chafe *vt* sfregare.

chaff *n* foraggio *m*; pula *f*.

chaffinch *n* fringuello *m*.

chagrin *n* dispiacere *m*.

chain *n* catena *f*; * *vt* incatenare.

chain reaction *n* reazione *f* a catena.

chair *n* sedia *f*, poltrona *f*; * *vt* presiedere.

chairman *n* presidente *m*.

chalice *n* calice *m*.

chalk *n* gesso *m*.

challenge *n* sfida *f*; * *vt* sfidare.

challenger *n* sfidante *m/f*.

challenging *adj* provocatorio; stimolante.

chamber *n* camera *f*.

chambermaid *n* cameriera *f*.

chameleon *n* camaleonte *m*.

chamois leather *n* pelle *f* di camoscio.

champagne *n* champagne *m*.

champion *n* campione *m*; * *vt* difendere.

championship *n* campionato *m*.

chance *n* caso *m*; occasione *f*; probabilità *f*; rischio *m*; * *vt* rischiare.

chancellor *n* cancelliere *m*.

chandelier *n* lampadario *m*.

change *vt* cambiare; trasformare; * *vi* mutare; * *n* cambiamento *m*; resto *m*; spiccioli *mpl*.

changeable *adj* variabile.

changing *adj* mutevole.

channel *n* canale *m*; * *vt* scavare.

chant *n* canto *m*; * *vt* cantare.

chaos *n* caos *m*.

chaotic *adj* caotico.

chap *n* screpolatura *f*; (*fam*) tizio *m*.

chapel *n* cappella *f*.

chaperone *n* accompagnatore *m*.

chaplain *n* cappellano *m*.

chapter *n* capitolo *m*.

char *vt* carbonizzare.

character *n* carattere *m*; personaggio *m*.

characteristic *adj* caratteristico.

characterization *n* caratterizzazione *f*.

characterize *vt* caratterizzare.

charade *n* sciarada *f*.

charcoal *n* carbone *m*, carboncino *m*.

charge *vt* accusare; (*mil*) attaccare; far pagare; * *n* imputazione *f*; (*mil*) carica *f*; tariffa *f*.

chargé d'affaires *n* incaricato *m* d'affari.

charger *n* caricabatteria *m*.

charisma *n* carisma *m*.

charitable *adj* filantropico; caritatevole.

charity *n* carità *f*; beneficenza *f*.

charlatan *n* ciarlatano *m*.

charm *n* fascino *m*; incanto *m*; * *vt* affascinare.

charming *adj* delizioso.

chart *n* tabella *f*; * *vt* tracciare.

charter *n* carta *f*; statuto *m*; noleggio *m*; * *vt* noleggiare.

charter flight *n* volo *m* charter.

chartered accountant *n* commercialista *m/f*.

chase *vt* inseguire; * *n* inseguimento *m*; caccia *f*.

chasm *n* crepaccio *m*.

chassis *n* telaio *m*.

chaste *adj* casto.

chasten *vt* castigare.

chastise *vt* punire.

chastity *n* castità *f*.

chat *vi* chiacchierare; * *n* chiacchierata *f*.

chatter *vi* chiacchierare; * *n*
chiacchiere *fpl*.

chatterbox *n* chiacchierone *m*.

chatty *adj* ciarliero.

chauffeur *n* autista *m*.

chauvinism *n* maschilismo *m*;
sciovinismo *m*.

chauvinist *n* maschilista *m*;
sciovinista *m/f*.

cheap *adj* a buon prezzo.

cheapen *vt* screditarsi.

cheat *vt* imbrogliare; * *n* imbroglione *m*.

check *vt* verificare; controllare;
* *n* limitazione *f*; controllo *m*;
(*chess*) scacco *m*.

checkmate *n* scacco *m* matto.

checkout *n* cassa *f*.

checkpoint *n* posto *m* di blocco.

checkup *n* visita *f* di controllo.

cheek *n* guancia *f*; (*fam*) faccia
f tosta.

cheekbone *n* zigomo *m*.

cheer *n* grido *m* di incoraggiamento.

cheerful *adj* allegro.

cheese *n* formaggio *m*.

cheeseboard *n* piatto *m* per il
formaggio.

cheesecloth *n* tela *f* indiana.

cheetah *n* ghepardo *m*.

chef *n* chef *m*.

chemical *adj* chimico; * *n* prodotto *m* chimico.

chemist *n* chimico *m*; farmacista *m/f*.

chemistry *n* chimica *f*.

cheque *n* assegno *m*.

cheque-book *n* libretto *m* degli
assegni.

chequered *adj* a quadretti; **a
~ career** una carriera movimentata.

cherish *vt* nutrire; avere caro.

cheroot *n* sigaro *m* spuntato.

cherry *n* ciliegia *f*.

cherrytree *n* ciliegio *m*.

cherub *n* cherubino *m*.

chess *n* scacchi *mpl*.

chessboard *n* scacchiera *f*.

chessman *n* pezzo *m* degli scacchi.

chest *n* petto *m*; baule *m*; **~ of
drawers** cassettone *m*.

chestnut *n* castagna *f*; *adj* castano.

chestnut tree *n* castagno *m*.

chew *vt* masticare.

chewing gum *n* chewing-gum
m.

chic *adj* chic.

chick *n* pulcino *m*.

chicken *n* pollo *m*.

chickenpox *n* varicella *f*.

chickpea *n* cece *m*.

chicory *n* cicoria *f*.

chief *adj* principale; * *n* capo *m*.

chiffon *n* chiffon *m*.

chilblain *n* gelone *m*.

child *n* bambino *m*; **~bearing
age** in età feconda.

childhood *n* infanzia *f*.

childish *adj* infantile.

childless *adj* senza figli.

childlike *adj* ingenuo.

children *npl* bambini *mpl*.

chill *adj* freddo; * *n* freddo; * *v*
mettere in fresco.

chilly *adj* fresco.

chime *n* rintocco *m*; * *vi* suonare.

chimney *n* camino *m*.

chimpanzee *n* scimpanzé *m*.

chin *n* mento *m*.

china(ware) n porcellana f.

chink n fessura f; * vt tintinnare.

chip vt scheggiare; * n frammento m; patatina f fritta;
scheggiatura f.

chipboard n agglomerato m.

chiropodist n callista m/f.

chirp vi cinguettare; * n cinguettio m;.

chisel n scalpello m.

chivalrous adj cavalleresco.

chivalry n cavalleria f.

chives npl erba f cipollina.

chlorinate vt clorare.

chlorine n cloro m.

chloroform n cloroformio m.

chlorophyll n clorofilla f.

chock-full adj pieno zeppo.

chocolate n cioccolato m.

choice n scelta f; * adj di prima scelta.

choir n coro m.

choke vt soffocare; * n aria f.

choker n collana f a girocollo.

cholera n colera m.

cholesterol n colesterolo m.

choose vt scegliere.

choosey adj schizzinoso.

chop vt tagliare; spaccare; * n
colpo m secco; costoletta f.

chopper n mannaia f; elicottero m.

chopping board n tagliere m.

chopsticks npl bastoncini
mpl.

choral adj corale.

chord n corda f.

chore n faccenda f.

choreographer n coreografo m.

choreography n coreografia f.

chorister n corista m/f.

chorus n coro m; ritornello m.

Christ n Cristo m.

christen vt battezzare.

christendom n cristianità f.

christening n battesimo m.

christian adj, n cristiano m.

Christianity n cristianesimo
m.

Christmas n Natale m.

Christmas card n biglietto m
di Natale.

Christmas Eve n vigilia f di
Natale.

chromatic adj cromatico.

chrome n metallo m cromato.

chronic adj cronico.

chronicle n cronaca f.

chronological adj cronologico.

chronology n cronologia f.

chronometer n cronometro m.

chubby adj paffuto.

chuck vt gettare.

chuckle vi ridacchiare.

chuffed adj tutto contento.

chug vi sbuffare.

chum n amicone m.

chunk n bel pezzo m.

church n chiesa f.

churchgoer n fedele m/f.

churchyard n cimitero m.

churlish adj sgarbato.

churn n zangola f; * vt agitare.

chute n scivolo m.

chutney n salsa f indiana.

cicada n cicala f.

cider n sidro m.

cigar n sigaro m.

cigarette n sigaretta f.

cigarette case n portasigarette
m.

cigarette end n mozzicone m.

cigarette holder n bocchino m.

cigarette lighter n accendino
m.

cinch n una cosa f sicura.

cinder n tizzone m.

cinecamera n cinepresa f.

cinema n cinema m.

cinnamon n cannella f.

cipher n codice m.

circle n cerchio m; * vt accerchiare.

circuit n giro m; circuito m.

circuitous adj tortuoso.

circular adj circolare; * n circolare f.

circulate vi circolare.

circulation n circolazione f.

circumcise vt circoncidere.

circumcision n circoncisione f.

circumference n circonferenza f.

circumflex n accento m circonflesso.

circumlocution n circonlocuzione f.

circumscribe vt circoscrivere.

circumspect adj circospetto.

circumstance n circostanza f.

circumstantial adj circostanziato.

circumvent vt aggirare.

circus n circo m.

cirrhosis n cirrosi f.

cissy n femminuccia f.

cistern n serbatoio m.

citadel n cittadella f.

cite vt citare.

citizen n cittadino m.

citric adj citrico.

citrus n agrume m.

city n città f.

civic adj civico.

civil adj civile.

civil defence n protezione f civile.

civil engineer n ingegnere m civile.

civilian n (mil) borghese m.

civility n gentilezza f.

civilization n civiltà f.

civilize vt civilizzare.

civil law n diritto m civile.

civil war n guerra f civile.

clad adj vestito.

claim vt rivendicare; pretendere; * n pretesa f; affermazione f.

claimant n (law) citante m/f; pretendente m/f.

clairvoyant n chiaroveggente m/f.

clam n vongola f.

clamber vi arrampicarsi.

clammy adj appiccicoso.

clamour n clamore m; * vi chiedere a gran voce.

clamp n morsetto m; * vt stringere; * vi to ~ down (on) riprimere.

clan n clan m.

clandestine adj clandestino.

clang n rumore m metallico.

clanger n gaffe f.

clap vt applaudire; * n battimano m.

clapping n applauso m.

claptrap n sciocchezze fpl.

claret n chiaretto m.

clarification n chiarificazione f.

clarify vt chiarire.

clarinet n clarinetto m.

clarity n chiarezza f.

clash vi scontrarsi; * n conflitto m; scontro m.

clasp n gancio m; * vt afferrare.

class n tipo m; categoria f; classe f; * vt definire.

class conscious adj classista.

classic(al) adj classico.

classification n classificazione f.

classified adj riservato.

classified advertisements n annunci mpl economici.

classify vt classificare.

classmate n compagno m di classe.

classroom n aula f.

classy adj chic.

clatter vi sferragliare; * n tintinnio m.

clause n proposizione f; clausola f.

claustrophobia n claustrofobia f.

claustrophobic adj claustrofobico.

claw n unghia f; artiglio m; * vt graffiare; to ~ to pieces di laniare.

clay n argilla f.

clean adj pulito; corretto m; * vt pulire.

cleaning n pulizia f.

cleanliness n pulizia f.

cleanness n pulizia f.

cleanse vt pulire.

cleanser n latte m detergente.

clean-shaven adj senza barba.

clear adj chiaro; trasparente; nitido; sgombro; * vt liberare; sgombrare; superare; (law) discolpare; liquidare.

clearance n sdoganamento m; autorizzazione f; sgombro m.

clear-cut adj ben definito.

clearing n radura f.

clearly adv chiaramente.

cleavage n scolatura f.

cleaver n mannaia f.

clef n chiave f.

cleft n crepa f.

clemency n clemenza f.

clement adj clemente.

clench vt stringere.

clergy n clero m.

clergyman n sacerdote m; pastore m; ministro m.

clerical adj (rel) clericale; (com) d'ufficio.

clerk n impiegato m.

clever adj intelligente.

cleverness n intelligenza f.

cliché n frase f fatta.

click vi scattare; * n scatto m.

client n cliente m/f.

clientele n clientela f.

cliff n scogliera f.

climate n clima m.

climatic adj climatico.

climax n culmine m; orgasmo m.

climb vt, vi salire; arrampicarsi; * n salita f; scalata f.

climber n alpinista m/f.

climbing n alpinismo m.

clinch vt concludere.

cling vi aggrapparsi.

clinic n clinica f.

clink vi tintinnare; * n tintinnio m.

clip n (cin) sequenza f; fermaglio m; moletta f; * vt tosare; ritagliare.

clipboard n fermabloc m.

clipper n clipper m.

clippers npl tagliaunghie m; tosasiepi m.

clipping n ritaglio m.

clique n cricca n.

cloak n cappa f; mantella f.

cloakroom n guardaroba m.

clock n orologio m.

clockwise adv in senso orario.

clockwork adj a molla.

clod n zolla f.

clog n zoccolo m; * vt intasare.

cloister n chiostro m.

close vt chiudere; * adv vicino; * adj vicino; intimo; approfondito; fitto; afoso; * n fine f; chiusura f.

closed adj chiuso.

closed-circuit n circuito m chiuso.

close-down n chiusura f; fine f delle trasmissioni.

closely adv strettamente.

closeness n vicinanza f.

close-up n primo m piano.

closing adj conclusivo; finale.

closure n chiusura f.

clot n grumo m; * vi coagularsi.

cloth n tessuto m, stoffa f.

clothe vt vestire.

clothes npl vestiti mpl.

clothes basket n cesto m per il bucato.

clotheshorse n stendibiancheria m.

clothesline n corda f del bucato.

clothes peg n moletta f.

clothing n abbigliamento m.

cloud n nuvola f; nube f; * vt intorbidire.

cloudburst n acquazzone m.

cloud-cuckoo-land *n* mondo *m* dei sogni.

cloudy *adj* nuvoloso; coperto.

clout *n* ceffone *m*; influenza *f*; * *vt* colpire.

clove *n* chiodo *m* di garofano; ~ **of garlic** spicchio *m* d'aglio.

clover *n* trifoglio *m*.

clown *n* pagliaccio *m*.

club *n* randello *m*; mazza *f*; bastone *m*; circolo *m*; club *m*; (*cards*) fiori *mpl*.

clubhouse *n* circolo *m*.

clue *n* indicazione *f*; indizio *m*.

clump *n* ciuffo *m*.

clumsy *adj* goffo.

cluster *n* grappolo *m*; gruppo *m*.

clutch *n* frizione *f*; * *vt* tenere stretto.

clutter *n* disordine *m*; * *vt* ingombrare.

coach *n* corriera *f*; pullman *m*; carrozza *f*; allenatore *m*; * *vt* allenare.

coagulate *vt* coagulare.

coal *n* carbone *m*.

coalesce *vi* unirsi.

coalfield *n* bacino *m* carbonifero.

coalition *n* coalizione *f*.

coalman *n* carbonaio *m*.

coalmine *n* miniera *f* di carbone.

coalminer *n* minatore *m*.

coarse *adj* ruvido; volgare.

coast *n* costa *f*; litorale *m*; * *vt* andare in folle.

coastal *adj* costiero.

coaster *n* sottobicchiere *m*.

coastguard *n* guardacoste *m*.

coastline *n* litorale *m*.

coat *n* capotto *m*; mano *f*; * *vt* ricoprire.

coathanger *n* gruccia *f*.

coax *vt* convincere.

cobalt *n* cobalto *m*.

cobble *n* ciottolo *m*.

cobbler *n* calzolaio *m*.

cobra *n* cobra *m*.

cobweb *n* ragnatela *f*.

cocaine *n* cocaina *f*.

cock *n* gallo *m*; rubinetto *m*.

cock-a-doodle-doo *n* chicchirichì *mpl*.

cock-and-bull story *n* frottola *f*.

cockatoo *n* cacatoa *m*.

cockerel *n* galletto *m*.

cockle *n* cardio *m*.

cockpit *n* cabina *f* di pilotaggio.

cockroach *n* scarafaggio *m*.

cocktail *n* cocktail *m*.

cock-up *n* pasticcio *m*.

cocky *adj* impertinente.

cocoa *n* cacao *m*.

coconut *n* noce *f* di cocco.

cocoon *n* bozzolo *m*.

cod *n* merluzzo *m*.

code *n* codice *m*; * *vt* cifrare.

codeine *n* codeina *f*.

codicil *n* codicillo *m*.

cod-liver oil *n* olio *m* di fegato di merluzzo.

coerce *vt* costringere.

coefficient *n* coefficiente *m*.

coercion *n* forza *f*.

coexist *vi* coesistere.

coexistence *n* coesistenza *f*.

coffee *n* caffè *m*.

coffee break *n* pausa *f* per il caffè.

coffee pot *n* caffettiera *f*.

coffee table *n* tavolino *m*.

coffin *n* barra *f*.

cog *n* dente *m*.

cogent *adj* convincente.

cogitate *vi* meditare.

cognac *n* cognac *m*.

cognate *adj* (*ling*) affine.

cognition *n* cognizione *f*.

cohabit *vi* coabitare.

coherence *n* coerenza *f*.

coherent *adj* coerente.

cohesion *n* coesione *f*.

cohesive *adj* unificante.

coil *n* rotolo *m*; bobina *f*; spiral

f; * *vt* avvolgere; * *vi* attor-cigliarsi.

coin *n* moneta *f*.

coincide *vi* coincidere.

coincidence *n* coincidenza *f*.

coke *n* carbone *m* coke.

colander *n* colapasta *m*.

cold *adj* freddo; indifferente; * *n* freddo *m*; raffreddore *m*;.

cold-blooded *adj* spietato.

cold sore *n* herpes *m*.

coleslaw *n* insalata *f* di cavolo bianco.

colic *n* colica *f*.

collaborate *vt* collaborare.

collaboration *n* collaborazione *f*.

collaborator *n* collaboratore *m*.

collapse *n* crollo *m*; collasso *m*; * *vi* crollare.

collapsible *adj* pieghevole.

collar *n* collo *m*.

collarbone *n* clavicola *f*.

collate *vt* collazionare.

collateral *n* (*fin*) garanzia *f*.

colleague *n* collega *m/f*.

collect *vt* raccogliere; * *vi* radunarsi.

collection *n* raccolta *f*.

collective *adj*, *n* collettivo *m*;.

collector *n* esattore *m*; collezionista *m/f*.

college *n* college *m*; collegio *m*; istituto *m* superiore.

collide *vi* scontrarsi.

collie *n* collie *m*.

colliery *n* miniera *f* di carbone.

collision *n* scontro *m*.

colloquial *adj* familiare.

colloquialism *n* espressione *f* familiare.

collusion *n* collusione *f*.

colon *n* (*med*) colon *m*; (*gram*) due punti *mpl*.

colonel *n* colonnello *m*.

colonial *adj* coloniale.

colonist *n* colonizzatore *m*.

colonize *vt* colonizzare.

colony *n* colonia *f*.

colossal *adj* colossale.

colour *n* colore *m*; **~s** bandiera *f*; * *vt* colorare; tingere.

colour-blind *adj* daltonico.

colourful *adj* dai colori vivaci.

colouring *n* colorazione *f*.

colourless *adj* incolore.

colt *n* puledro *m*.

column *n* colonna *f*.

columnist *n* giornalista *m/f*.

coma *n* coma *m*.

comatose *adj* comatoso.

comb *n* pettine *m*; * *vt* pettinare.

combat *n* lotta *f*; combattimento *m*; * *vt* combattere.

combatant *n* combattente *m/f*.

combination *n* combinazione *f*.

combine *vt* combinare.

combustible *adj* combustibile.

combustion *n* combustione *f*.

come *vi* venire; **to ~ apart** andare in pezzi; **to ~ round** venire; **to ~ in** entrare; **to ~ off** staccarsi.

comedian *n* comico *m*.

comedienne *n* attrice *f* comica.

comedown *n* delusione *f*.

comedy *n* commedia *f*.

comet *n* cometa *f*.

comfort *n* consolazione *f*; conforto *m*; * *vt* confortare.

comfortable *adj* comodo.

comic(al) *adj* comico; buffo.

coming *adj* prossimo; futuro; * *n* avvento *m*.

comma *n* virgola *f*.

command *vt* comandare; disporre di; * *n* ordine *m*; comando *m*.

commandeer *vt* requisire.

commander *n* capo *m*.

commandment *n* comandamento *m*.

commando *n* commando *m*.

commemorate *vt* commemorare.

commemoration n commemorazione f.
commence vt cominciare.
commencement n inizio m.
commend vt lodare.
commendable adj lodevole.
commendation n encomio m.
commensurate adj proporzionato.
comment n commento m; osservazione f.
commentary n commento m;
telecronaca f.
commentate vt commentare.
commentator n telecronista
m/f.
commerce n commercio m.
commercial adj commerciale;
* n pubblicità f.
commiserate vt partecipare al
dolore di.
commiseration n commiserazione f.
commisariat n commissariato
m.
commission n commissione f;
* vt commissionare; incaricare.
commissionaire n portiere m
in livrea.
commissioner n delegato m;
(police) questore m.
commit vt commettere.
commitment n impegno m.
committee n comitato m.
commodity n prodotto m.
common adj comune; * n parco comunale.
commoner n semplice cittadino
m.
common law n diritto m comune.
commonly adv comunemente.
commonplace adj banale.
common sense n buon senso
m.
commotion n trambusto m.
communal adj in comune.

commune vt comunicare.
communicate vt comunicare.
communication n comunicazione f.
communicative adj loquace.
communion n comunione f.
communiqué n bollettino m.
communism n comunismo m.
communist n comunista m/f.
community n comunità f.
community centre n centro m
civico rionale.
commute vt commutare; * vi
fare il pendolare.
compact adj compatto; * n portacipria m.
companion n compagno m.
companionship n cameratismo m.
company n compagnia f; società
f.
comparable adj simile.
comparative adj relativo;
(gram) comparativo.
compare vt paragonare.
comparison n paragone m.
compartment n scompartimento m.
compass n bussola f; compasso
m.
compassion n compassione f.
compassionate adj compassionevole.
compatible adj compatibile.
compatriot n compatriota m.
compel vt costringere.
compelling adj impellente.
compensate vt compensare.
compensation n compenso m;
indennità f.
compére n presentatore m.
compete vt competere.
competence n competenza f.
competent adj competente.
competition n concorrenza;
concorso m; gara f.
competitive adj agonistico;
concorrenziale.

competitor *n* concorrente *m/f*.

compilation *n* compilazione *f*.

compile *vt* compilare.

complacency *n* compiacimento *m*.

complacent *adj* compiaciuto.

complain *vi* lamentarsi.

complaint *n* lamentela *f*.

complement *n* complemento *m*.

complementary *adj* complementare.

complete *adj* completo; * *vt* completare.

completion *n* completamento *m*.

complex *adj* complesso.

complexion *n* carnagione *f*.

complexity *n* complessità *f*.

compliance *n* conformità *f*.

compliant *adj* compiacente.

complicate *vt* complicare.

complication *n* complicazione *f*.

complicity *n* complicità.

compliment *n* complimento *m*; * *vi* complimentarsi.

complimentary *adj* lusinghiero; in omaggio.

comply *vi* attenersi a.

component *adj, n* componente *m*.

compose *vt* comporre.

composed *adj* composto.

composer *n* compositore *m*.

composite *adj* composito.

composition *n* composizione *f*.

compositor *n* compositore *m*.

compost *n* concime *m*.

composure *n* calma *f*.

compound *vt* peggiorare; * *n* composto *m*; (*gram*) parola *f* composta; recinto *m*; * *adj* composto.

comprehend *vt* capire, comprendere.

comprehensible *adj* comprensibile.

comprehension *n* comprensione *f*.

comprehensive *adj* esauriente; globale.

compress *vt* comprimere; * *n* compressa *f*.

comprise *vt* comprendere.

compromise *n* compromesso *m*.

compulsion *n* costrizione *f*; desiderio *m* incontrollabile.

compulsive *adj* incontrollabile.

compulsory *adj* obbligatorio.

compunction *n* scrupolo *m*.

computable *adj* calcolabile.

computation *n* calcolo *m*.

compute *vt* calcolare.

computer *n* elaboratore *m*; computer *m*.

computer programming *n* programmazione *f*.

computer science *n* informatica *f*.

comrade *n* compagno *m*.

con *vt* (*fam*) indurre con raggiri.

concave *adj* concavo.

conceal *vt* nascondere.

concede *vt* ammettere.

conceit *n* vanità *f*.

conceited *adj* vanitoso.

conceivable *adj* concepibile.

conceive *vt* concepire.

concentrate *vt* concentrare.

concentration *n* concentrazione *f*.

concentration camp *n* campo *m* di concentramento.

concentric *adj* concentrico.

concept *n* concetto *m*.

conception *n* concepimento *m*.

concern *vt* riguardare; * *n* preoccupazione *f*; impresa *f*.

concerning *prep* riguardo a.

concert *n* concerto *m*.

concerto *n* concerto *m*.

concession *n* concessione *f*.

conciliate *vt* conciliare.

conciliation *n* conciliazione *f*.

conciliatory *adj* conciliatorio.

concise *adj* conciso.
conclude *vt, vi* concludere.
conclusion *n* conclusione *f*.
conclusive *adj* conclusivo.
concoct *vt* mettere insieme; inventare.
concoction *n* miscuglio *m*.
concomitant *adj* concomitante.
concord *n* armonia *f*; accordo *m*.
concordance *n* concordanza *f*.
concourse *n* atrio *m*.
concrete *n* calcestruzzo *m*; * *adj* concreto; di calcestruzzo *m*; * *vt* rivestire di calcestruzzo.
concubine *n* concubina *f*.
concur *vi* coincidere.
concurrent *adj* simultaneo.
concussion *n* commozione *f* cerebrale.
condemn *vt* condannare.
condemnation *n* condanna *f*.
condensation *n* condensazione *f*.
condense *vt* condensare.
condescend *vi* accondiscendere; degnarsi.
condescending *adj* condiscendente.
condiment *n* condimento *m*.
condition *vt* condizionare; * *n* condizione *f*.
conditional *adj* condizionale.
coditioner *n* balsamo *m*.
condolences *npl* condoglianze *fpl*.
condom *n* preservativo *m*.
condone *vt* perdonare.
conducive *vi* favorire.
conduct *vt* condurre; (*mus*) dirigere; * *n* condotta *f*.
conduction *n* conduzione *f*.
conductivity *n* conduttività *f*.
conductor *n* (*mus*) direttore; (*elect*) conduttore *m*.
conduit *n* conduttura *f*.

cone *n* cono *m*; pigna *f*.
confectioner *n* pasticciere *m*.
confectionery *n* dolciumi *mpl*.
confederacy *n* confederazione *f*.
confederate *adj* confederato; * *vi* confederarsi.
confer *vt* conferire; * *vi* consultarsi.
conference *n* convegno *m*.
confess *vt* confessare.
confession *n* confessione *f*.
confessional *n* confessionale *m*.
confessor *n* confessore *m*.
confetti *n* coriandoli *mpl*.
confidant *n* confidente *m*.
confide *vt* confidare.
confidence *n* fiducia *f*.
confidence trick *n* truffa *f*.
confident *adj* sicuro.
confidential *adj* riservato.
configuration *n* configurazione *f*.
confine *vt* rinchiudere; limitare.
confinement *n* reclusione *f*; parto *m*.
confirm *vt* confermare; (*rel*) cresimare.
confirmation *n* conferma *f*; (*rel*) cresima *f*.
confirmed *adj* inveterato.
confiscate *vt* confiscare.
confiscation *n* confisca *f*.
conflagration *n* conflagrazione *f*.
conflict *n* conflitto *m*.
conflicting *adj* contraddittorio.
confluence *n* confluenza *f*.
conform *vi* conformarsi.
conformity *n* conformità *f*.
confound *vt* sconcertare.
confront *vt* affrontare.
confrontation *n* scontro *m*.
confuse *vt* confondere.
confused *adj* confuso.
confusing *adj* sconcertante.

confusion *n* confusione *f*.
congeal *vi* rapprendersi.
congenial *adj* simpatico.
congenital *adj* congenito.
congested *adj* congestionato.
congestion *n* congestione *f*.
conglomerate *n* conglomerato *m*.
congratulate *vt* congratularsi con.
congratulations *npl* congratulazioni *fpl*.
congregate *vi* radunarsi.
congregation *n* congregazione *f*.
congress *n* congresso *m*.
congruity *n* congruità *f*.
congruous *adj* congruo.
conical *adj* conico.
conifer *n* conifera *f*.
coniferous *adj* (*bot*) conifero.
conjecture *n* congettura *f*; * *vt*, *vi* congetturare.
conjugal *adj* coniugale.
conjugate *vt* coniugare.
conjugation *n* coniugazione *f*.
conjunction *n* congiunzione *f*.
conjuncture *n* congiuntura *f*.
conjure *vi* rievocare; fare giochi di prestigio.
conjurer *n* prestigiatore *m*.
conker *n* castagna *f* d'ippocastano.
con man *n* truffatore *m*.
connect *vt* collegare.
connection *n* collegamento *m*.
connivance *n* connivenza *f*.
connive *vi* essere connivente in.
connoisseur *n* intenditore *m*.
conquer *vt* conquistare.
conqueror *n* conquistatore *m*.
conquest *n* conquista *f*.
conscience *n* coscienza *f*.
conscientious *adj* coscienzioso.
conscious *adj* cosciente.
consciousness *n* conoscenza *f*.

conscript *n* coscritto *m*; * *vt* arruolare.
conscription *n* arruolamento *m*.
consecrate *vt* consacrare.
consecration *n* consacrazione *f*.
consecutive *adj* consecutivo.
consensus *n* consenso *m*.
consent *n* benestare *m*; * *vi* acconsentire a.
consequence *n* conseguenza *f*.
consequent *adj* conseguente; * *adv* ~**ly** di conseguenza; quindi.
conservation *n* conservazione *f*.
conservationist *n* ambientalista *m/f*.
conservative *adj*, *n* conservatore *m*.
conservatory *n* serra *f*; (*mus*) conservatore *m*.
conserve *vt* conservare.
consider *vt* considerare.
considerable *adj* considerevole.
considerate *adj* premuroso.
consideration *n* considerazione *f*.
considering *conj* visto che; * *adv* tutto sommato.
consign *vt* consegnare.
consignment *n* partita *f*.
consist *vi* consistere.
consistency *n* consistenza *f*.
consistent *adj* coerente; * *adv* ~**ly** costantemente.
consolation *n* consolazione *f*.
console *vt* consolare; * *n* quadro *m* di comando.
consolidate *vt* consolidare.
consolidation *n* consolidazione *f*.
consommé *n* brodo *m* ristretto.
consonant *n* (*gram*) consonante *f*.
consort *n* consorte *m/f*; * *vt* frequentare.

consortium n consorzio m.
conspicuous adj cospicuo.
conspiracy n congiura f.
conspirator n cospiratore m.
conspire vi congiurare.
constable n (Brit) agente m/f di polizia.
constabulary n (Brit) corpo m di polizia.
constancy n costanza f.
constant adj continuo; costante.
constellation n costellazione f.
consternation n costernazione f.
constipated adj stitico.
constipation n stitichezza f.
constituency n collegio m elettorale.
const.tuent n componente m; elettore m.
constitute vt costituire.
constitution n costituzione f.
constitutional adj costituzionale.
constrain vt costringere.
constraint n costrizione f.
constrict vt costringere.
constriction n costrizione f.
construct vt costruire.
construction n costruzione f.
construe vt interpretare.
consul n console m.
consular adj consolare.
consulate n consolato m.
consult vt consultare.
consultancy n consulenza f.
consultant n consulente m/f; (med) specialista m/f.
consultation n consultazione f.
consume vt consumare.
consumer n consumatore m.
consumer goods npl beni mpl di consumo.
consumer society n società f consumista.
consummate vt consumare; * adj consumato.

consummation n consumazione f.
consumption n consumo m; (med) consunzione f.
contact n contatto; * vt contattare.
contact lenses npl lenti fpl a contatto.
contagious adj contagioso.
contain vt contenere.
container n contenitore m.
contaminate vt contaminare.
contamination n contaminazione f.
contemplate vt contemplare.
contemplation n contemplazione f.
contemplative adj contemplativo.
contemporaneous adj contemporaneo.
contemporary adj contemporaneo.
contempt n disprezzo m.
contemptible adj spregevole.
contemptuous adj sprezzante.
contend vt sostenere; * vi contendere.
contender n contendente m/f.
content adj contento; * n contentezza; * vt soddisfare.
contents npl contenuto m.
contended adj contento.
contention n tesi f; disputa f; **bone of ~** pomo della discordia.
contentious adj contenzioso.
contentment n contentezza f.
contest vt contestare; * n gara f; concorso m.
contestant n concorrente m/f.
context n contesto m.
contiguous adj contiguo.
continent n continente m.
continental adj continentale.
contingency n contingenza f.
contingent adj, n contingente m; * vi dipendere da.

continual *adj* continuo.

continuance *n* continuazione *f.*

continuation *n* continuazione *f.*

continue *vt, vi* continuare.

continuity *n* continuità *f.*

continuous *adj* continuo.

contort *vt* contorcere.

contortion *n* contorsione *f.*

contour *n* contorno *m.*

contraband *adj, n* contrabbando *m.*

contraception *n* contraccezione *f.*

contraceptive *adj, n* anticoncezionale *f.*

contract *vt* contrarre; * *n* contratto *m.*

contraction *n* contrazione *f.*

contractor *n* appaltatore *m.*

contractual *adj* contrattuale.

contradict *vt* contraddire.

contradiction *n* contraddizione *f.*

contradictory *adj* contraddittorio.

contraption *n* aggeggio *m.*

contrary *adj* contrario; * *n* contrario *m.*

contrast *n* contrasto; * *vi* contrastare.

contrasting *adj* contrastante.

contravene *vt* contravvenire.

contravention *n* contravvenzione *f.*

contretemps *n* contrattempo *m.*

contribute *vt, vi* contribuire.

contribution *n* offerta *f*; contribuzione *f.*

contributor *n* donatore *m*; collaboratore *m.*

contributory *adj* che contribuisce.

contrite *adj* mortificato.

contrition *n* mortificazione *f.*

contrivance *n* congegno *m.*

contrive *vt* escogitare.

control *n* controllo *m*, comando *m*; * *vt* controllare, frenare, dominare.

control room *n* (*TV/radio*) sala *f* di reggia; (*mil*) sala *f* di comando.

control tower *n* torre *f* di controllo.

controversial *adj* controverso.

controversy *n* controversia *f.*

contusion *n* contusione *f.*

conundrum *n* indovinello *m.*

conurbation *n* conurbazione *f.*

convalesce *vi* fare la convalescenza.

convalescence *n* convalescenza *f.*

convalescent *adj, n* convalescente *m/f.*

convection *n* convezione *f.*

convector *n* convettore *m.*

convene *vt* convocare; * *vi* convenire.

convenience *n* comodità *f.*

convenient *adj* comodo.

convent *n* convento *m.*

convention *n* convenzione *f.*

conventional *adj* convenzionale.

converge *vi* convergere.

convergence *n* convergenza *f.*

convergent *adj* convergente.

conversant *adj* versato.

conversation *n* conversazione *f.*

converse *vi* conversare; * *n* inverso *m*; * *adj* apposto.

conversely *adv* al contrario.

conversion *n* (*rel*) conversione *f*; ristrutturazione *f.*

convert *vt* convertire; ristrutturare; * *n* convertito *m.*

converter *n* convertitore *m.*

convertible *adj* convertibile; * *n* auto *f* decappottabile.

convex *adj* convesso.

convey *vt* trasportare; trasmettere.

conveyance *n* trasporto *m*.

conveyancer *n* notaio *m*.

conveyer belt *n* nastro *m* trasportatore.

convict *vt* riconoscere colpevole; * *n* carcerato *m*.

conviction *n* condanna *f*; convinzione *f*.

convince *vt* convincere.

convincing *adj* convincente.

convivial *adj* gioviale.

convoke *vt* convocare.

convoluted *adj* attorcigliato.

convoy *n* convoglio *m*.

convulse *vt* sconvolgere.

convulsion *n* convulsione *f*.

convulsive *adj* convulso.

coo *vi* tubare.

cook *n* cuoco *m*; * *vt* cuocere; (*fam*) falsificare.

cooker *n* cucina *f*.

cookery *n* cucina *f*.

cookerybook *n* ricettario *m*.

cool *adj* fresco; calmo; distaccato; * *n* frescura *f*; calma *f*; * *vt* raffreddare.

coolant *n* refrigerante *m*.

cooler *n* ghiacciaia *f*.

cooling *adj* rinfrescante.

coop *n* stia *f*.

cooperate *vi* cooperare.

cooperation *n* cooperazione *f*.

cooperative *adj* cooperativo; * *n* cooperativa *f*.

coopt *vt* cooptare.

coordinate *vt* coordinare; * *n* coordinata *f*.

coordination *n* coordinazione *f*.

coordinator *n* coordinatore *m*.

cop *n* poliziotto *m*.

cope *vi* cavarsela.

copier *n* copiatrice *f*.

copilot *n* secondo pilota *m*.

copious *adj* abbondante.

copper *n* rame *m*.

coppice *n* boschetto *m*.

copulate *vi* accoppiarsi.

copulation *n* accoppiamento *m*.

copy *n* copia; * *vt* imitare, copiare.

copyright *n* diritti *mpl* d'autore.

coral *n* corallo *m*.

coral reef *n* corallino *m*.

cord *n* corda *f*.

cordial *adj*, *n* cordiale *m*.

corduroy *n* velluto *m* a coste.

core *n* torsolo *m*; nucleo *m*.

co-respondent *n* correo *m*.

coriander *n* coriandolo *m*.

cork *n* sughero *m*; * *vt* tappare.

corkscrew *n* cavatappi *m*.

corn *n* grano *m*; frumento *m*; callo *m*.

corn on the cob *n* pannocchia *f*.

cornea *n* cornea *f*.

corner *n* angolo *m*; * *vt* intrappolare.

cornerstone *n* pietra *f* angolare.

cornet *n* (*mus*) cornetta *f*; cornetto *m*.

cornfield *n* campo *m* di grano.

cornflakes *npl* fiochi *mpl* di granturco.

cornflour *n* farina *f* finissima di granturco.

cornice *n* cornicione *m*.

corny *adj* banale.

corollary *n* corollario *m*.

coronary *adj* coronario; * *n* trombosi *f* coronarica.

coronation *n* incoronazione *f*.

coroner *n* coroner *m*.

coronet *n* coroncina *f*.

corporal *adj* corporale; * *n* caporale *m*.

corporate *adj* collettivo.

corporation *n* società *f*; ente *m*

corporeal *adj* corporale.

corps *n* corpo *m*.

corpse *n* cadavere *m*.

corpulence *n* corpulenza *f*.

corpulent *adj* corpulento.

corpuscle *n* globulo *m*.

correct *vt* correggere; * *adj* corretto.

correction n correzione f.

corrective adj correttivo.

correlate vt correlare.

correlation n correlazione f.

correlative adj correlativo.

correspond vi corrispondere.

correspondence n corrispondenza f.

correspondent n corrispondente m/f.

corridor n corridoio m.

corroborate vt corroborare.

corroboration n corroborazione f.

corrode vt corrodere.

corrosion n corrosione f.

corrosive adj corrosivo.

corrugated adj ondulato; * n ~ **iron** lamiera f ondulata.

corrupt vt corrompere; * adj corrotto.

corruptible adj corruttibile.

corruption n corruzione f.

corset n busto m.

cortège n corteo m.

cortisone n cortisone m.

cosh n manganello m.

cosmetic adj, n cosmetico m.

cosmic adj cosmico.

cosmonaut n cosmonauta m/f.

cosmopolitan adj, n cosmopolita m/f.

cosmos n cosmo m.

cosset vt coccolare.

cost n costo m; * vt costare.

costly adj costoso.

costume n costume m.

cosy adj accogliente.

cot n lettino m.

cottage n cottage m.

cotton n cotone m.

cotton mill n cotonificio m.

cotton wool n cotone m idrofilo.

couch n divano m.

couchette n cuccetta f.

cough n tosse f; * vi tossire.

council n consiglio m.

councillor n consigliere m.

counsel n consiglio; avvocato m.

counsellor n consigliere m.

count vt, vi contare; * n conteggio m; conte m.

countdown n conto m alla rovescia.

countenance n volto m; * vt ammettere.

counter n banco m; * vt rispondere.

counteract vt neutralizzare.

counterbalance vt controbilanciare; * n contrappeso m.

counterfeit vt contraffare; * adj contraffatto.

counterfoil n matrice f.

countermand vt annullare.

counterpane n copriletto m.

counterpart n equivalente m/f.

counterproductive adj controproducente.

countersign vt controfirmare.

countess n contessa f.

countless adj innumerevole.

country n paese m; campagna f.

country house n villa f.

countryman n campagnolo m.

countryside n campagna f.

county n contea f.

coup n colpo m.

coupé n coupé m.

couple n coppia f; * vt associare.

couplet n distico m.

coupon n buono m.

courage n coraggio m.

courageous adj coraggioso.

courgette n zucchino m.

courier n corriere m.

course n corso m; rotta f; portata f; **of** ~ naturalmente; * vi scorrere.

court n corte f; * vt corteggiare.

courteous adj cortese.

courtesy n cortesia f.

courtier n corteggiano m.

court-martial *n* corte *f* marziale.

courtroom *n* sala *f* d'udienza.

courtship *n* corteggiamento *m*.

courtyard *n* cortile *m*.

cousin *n* cugino *m*.

cove *n* baia *f*.

covenant *n* accordo *m*; * *vi* impegnarsi.

cover *n* copertura; coperchio *m*; riparo *m*; * *vt* coprire; nascondere.

coverage *n* (*press, TV, radio*) servizio *m*.

covering *n* copertura *f*.

covering letter *n* lettera *f* di accompagnamento.

covert *adj* nascosto.

cover-up *n* occultamento *m*.

covet *vt* concupire.

covetous *adj* avido.

cow *n* mucca *f*; vacca *f*; * *vt* intimidire.

coward *n* vigliacco *m*.

cowardice *n* vigliaccheria *f*.

cowardly *adj* vigliacco.

cowboy *n* cowboy *m*.

cower *vi* acquattarsi.

cowhide *n* pelle *f* di mucca.

cowl *n* cappuccio *n*.

cowshed *n* stalla *f*.

cowslip *n* primula *f*.

cox *n* timoniere *m*.

coy *adj* civettuolo.

crab *n* granchio *m*.

crab apple *n* mela *f* selvatica.

crack *n* crepa *f*; * *vt* incrinare; *vi* to ~ **down on** porre freno a.

cracker *n* petardo *m*; cracker *m*.

crackle *vi* scoppiettare; * *n* scoppiettio *m*.

crackling *n* cotenna *f* arrostita.

cradle *n* culla *f*.

craft *n* mestiere *m*; arte *f*.

craftiness *n* furberia *f*.

craftsman *n* artigiano *m*.

craftsmanship *n* maestria *f*.

crafty *adj* furbo.

crag *n* rupe *f*.

cram *vt* infilare; stipare; * *vi* affollarsi.

crammed *adj* stipato.

cramp *n* crampo *m*; * *vt* soffocare.

cramped *adj* angusto.

cranberry *n* bacca *f* del muschio.

crane *n* gru *f*.

crank *n* gomito *m*; eccentrico *m*.

crankshaft *n* albero *m* a gomiti.

crash *vt* avere un'incidente con; * *vi* precipitare; scontrarsi; * *n* fracasso *m*; incidente *m*.

crash helmet *n* casco *m*.

crash landing *n* atterraggio *m* forzato.

crass *adj* crasso.

crate *n* cassa *f*.

crater *n* cratere *m*.

cravat *n* foulard *m*.

crave *vt* desiderare disperatamente.

craving *n* voglia *f*.

crawl *vi* andare a gattone; procedere lentamente; adulare; * *n* passo *m* lento; stile *m* libero.

crayfish *n* gambero *m*.

crayon *n* pastello *m*.

craze *n* mania *f*.

crazy *adj* matto; folle.

creak *vi* scricchiolare; * *n* scricchiolio *m*.

cream *n* crema *f*; panna *f*; * *adj* color crema.

creamy *adj* cremoso.

crease *n* piega *f*; * *vt* sgualcire.

crease-resistant *adj* ingualcibile.

create *vt* creare.

creation *n* creazione *f*.

creative *adj* creativo.

creativity *n* creatività *f*.

creator *n* creatore *m*.
creature *n* creatura *f*.
crèche *n* asilo *m* nido.
credence *n* credenza *f*.
credentials *npl* credenziali *fpl*; referenze *fpl*.
credibility *n* credibilità *f*.
credible *adj* credibile.
credit *n* credito *m*; onore *m*; **~s** (*TV, etc*) titoli *mpl* di testa/coda; * *vt* credere; accreditare.
creditable *adj* lodevole.
credit card *n* carta *f* di credito.
creditor *n* creditore *m*.
credulity *n* credulità *f*.
credulous *adj* credulo.
creed *n* credo *m*.
creek *n* insenatura *f*.
creep *vi* strisciare; andare furtivamente; * *n* tipo *m* viscido.
creeper *n* (*bot*) rampicante *f*.
creepy *adj* che fa rabbrividire.
creepy-crawly *n* bestiolina *f*.
cremate *vt* cremare.
cremation *n* cremazione *f*.
crematorium *n* crematorio *m*.
creosote *n* creosoto *m*.
crêpe *n* crespo *m*.
crescent *n* mezzaluna *f*; via *f*.
cress *n* crescione *m*.
crest *n* cresta *f*.
crestfallen *adj* abbattuto.
cretin *n* cretino *m*.
crevasse *n* crepaccio *m*.
crevice *n* fessura *f*.
crew *n* equipaggio *m*.
crib *n* culla *f*; mangiatoia *f*; * *vt* copiare.
crick *n* torcicollo *m*.
cricket *n* grillo *m*; cricket *m*.
crime *n* criminalità *f*; delitto *m*.
criminal *adj*, *n* criminale *m/f*.
crimson *adj* cremisi.
cringe *vi* farsi piccolo dalla paura.
crinkle *vt* spiegazzare.
cripple *n* zoppo *m*; mutilato *m*; * *vt* lasciare mutilato.

crisis *n* crisi *f*.
crisp *adj* croccante; fresco; conciso; * *n* patatina *f*.
criss-cross *adj* intrecciati.
criterion *n* criterio *m*.
critic *n* critico *m*.
critical *adj* critico.
criticism *n* critica *f*.
criticize *vt* criticare.
critique *n* assaggio *m* critico.
croak *vi* gracidare.
crochet *n* uncinetto *m*.
crockery *n* vasellame *m*.
crocodile *n* coccodrillo *m*.
crocus *n* croco *m*.
croft *n* piccola fattoria *f*.
croissant *n* cornetto *m*.
crony *n* amicone *m*.
crook *n* bastone *m*; pastolare *m*; (*fam*) ladro *m*.
crooked *adj* storto; disonesto.
crop *n* coltivazione *f*; raccolto *m*; (*ornith*) gozzo *m*; (*riding*) frustino *m*; * *vt* brucare; rapare.
croquet *n* croquet *m*.
croquette *n* crocchetta *f*.
cross *n* croce *f*; incrocio *m*; * *adj* seccato; * *vt* attraversare; sbarrare; incrociare.
crossbar *n* canna *f*.
crossbreed *n* incrocio *m*.
cross-country *n* campestre *f*.
cross-examine *vt* interrogare.
cross-eyed *adj* strabico.
crossfire *n* fuoco *m* incrociato.
crossing *n* traversata *f*; incrocio *m*; strisce *fpl* pedonali.
cross-purposes *npl* fraintendere.
cross-reference *n* rimando *m*.
crossroad *n* incrocio *m*.
cross-section *n* sezione *f* trasversale.
crossword *n* cruciverba *m*.
crotch *n* forcella *f*; (*anat*) inforcatura *f*; (*garment*) cavallo *m*.
crouch *vi* accovacciarsi.
croup *n* crup *m*.

crow n corvo m; cornacchia f;
canto m; * vi cantare.
crowbar n piede m di porco.
crowd n folla f; * vt affollare.
crown n corona f; cima f; * vt
incoronare.
crown prince n principe m ereditario.
crowning adj supremo.
crucial adj cruciale.
crucible n crogiolo m.
crucifix n crocefisso m.
crucifixion n crocifissione f.
crucify vt crocifiggere.
crude adj grezzo; grossolano.
crudity n volgarità f.
cruel adj crudele.
cruelty n crudeltà f.
cruet n ampolla f.
cruise n crociera f; * vi (taxi) girare in cerca di clienti.
cruiser n incrociatore m.
crumb n briciola f.
crumble vt sbriciolare; * vi sbri-
ciolarsi.
crumple vt accartocciare.
crunch vt sgranocchiare; * vi
scricchiolare; * n scricchiolio
m.
crunchy adj croccante.
crusade n crociata f.
crusader n crociato m.
crush vt schiacciare; frantumare; * n ressa f; cotta f.
crust n crosta f;.
crustacean n crostaceo m.
crutch n stampella f.
crux n nodo m.
cry vi gridare; piangere; * vt gridare; * n grido m; pianto m.
crypt n cripta f.
cryptic adj enigmatico.
crystal n cristallo m.
crystal-clear adj cristallino.
crystallize vt cristallizzare; * vi
cristallizzarsi.
cub n cucciolo m.
cube n cubo m.

cubic adj cubico.
cubicle n cabina f.
cuckoo n cucullo m.
cucumber n cetriolo m.
cud n ruminatura f; **to chew
the ~** ruminare.
cuddle n abbraccio m; * vt coccolare.
cudgel n manganello m.
cue n stecca f.
cuff n schiaffo m; polsino m.
cul-de-sac n vicolo m cieco.
culinary adj culinario.
cull vt scegliere; selezionare e
abbattere.
culminate vi culminare.
culmination n culmine m.
culottes npl gonna f pantalone.
culpability n colpevolezza f.
culpable adj colpevole.
culprit n colpevole m/f.
cult n culto m.
cultivate vt coltivare.
cultivation n coltivazione f.
cultural adj culturale.
culture n cultura f; (agric) coltura f.
cultured adj colto, raffinato.
cumbersome adj ingombrante.
cumin n cumino m.
cumulative adj cumulativo.
cunning adj furbo; * n furbizia
f.
cup n tazza f.
cupboard n armadio m.
curable adj guaribile.
curate n curato m.
curator n conservatore m.
curb n freno m; * vt frenare.
curds npl latte m cagliato.
curdle vt far cagliare.
cure n cura f; guarigione m; * vt
guarire; salare; conciare.
curfew n coprifuoco m.
curio n curiosità f.
curiosity n curiosità f.
curious adj curioso.
curl n ricciolo m; * vt arricciare.

curler n bigodino m.

curlew n chiurlo m.

curly adj riccio.

currant n uva f passa; ribes m.

currency n moneta f; valuta f estera.

current adj attuale; corrente; * n corrente f.

current affairs npl problemi mpl d'attualità.

currently adv attualmente.

curriculum vitae n curriculum vitae m.

curry n curry m.

curse vt maledire; * vi bestemmiare; * n maledizione f; flagello m; bestemmia f.

cursor n cursore m.

cursory adj frettoloso.

curt adj brusco.

curtail vt accorciare.

curtain n tenda f.

curtain rod n bastone m della tenda.

curtsy n inchino; * vi fare un inchino.

curvaceous adj formosa.

curvature n curvatura f.

curve vt curvare; * vi curvarsi; * n curva f.

cushion n cuscino m; * vt attutire.

custard n crema f pasticcera.

custodian n custode m/f.

custody n custodia f; detenzione f.

custom n costume m; consuetudine f; abitudine f; clientela f.

customary adj consueto.

customer n cliente m/f.

customs npl dogana f.

customs duty n tassa f doganale.

customs officer n doganiere m.

cut vt tagliare; ridurre; **to ~ a record** incidere; * vi tagliare; **to ~ teeth** spuntare; * adj reciso; **~ and dried** assodato; * n taglio m; incisione f; riduzione f.

cutback n taglio m; riduzione f.

cute adj carino.

cuticle n pellicina f.

cutlery n posate fpl.

cutlet n cotoletta f.

cut-rate adj a prezzo ridotto.

cut-throat n assassino m; * adj spietato.

cutting n talea f; ritaglio m; scavo m; * adj tagliente; pungente.

cuttlefish n seppia f.

cyanide n cianuro m.

cybernetics n cibernetica.

cyclamen n ciclamino m.

cycle n bicicletta f; ciclo m; * vi andare in bicicletta.

cycling n ciclismo m.

cyclist ciclista m/f.

cyclone n ciclone m.

cygnet n giovane cigno m.

cylinder n cilindro m.

cylindric(al) adj cilindrico.

cymbal n cembalo m.

cynic(al) adj cinico; * n cinico m.

cynicism n cinismo m.

cypress n cipresso m.

cyst n cisti f.

czar n zar m.

czarina n zarina f.

D

dab *n* colpetto *m*; pennellata *f*; * *vt* tamponare.

dabble *vt* sguazzare; * *vi* dilettarsi.

dachshund *n* bassotto *m*.

dad(dy) *n* papà *m*, babbo *m*.

daddy-long-legs *n* zanzarone *m*.

daffodil *n* trombone *m*.

daft *adj* sciocco.

dagger *n* pugnale *m*.

dahlia *n* dalia *f*.

daily *adj* quotidiano; giornaliero; * *n* quotidiano *m*.

dainty *adj* minuto; delicato.

dairy *n* latteria *f*.

dairy farm *n* caseificio *m*.

dairy produce *n* latticini *mpl*.

dais *n* palco *m*.

daisy *n* margherita *f*.

daisy wheel *n* margherita *f*.

dale *n* valle *f*.

dally *vi* dilungarsi.

dam *n* diga *f*; * *vt* arginare.

damage *n* danno *m*.

damaging *adj* nocivo.

damask *n* damasco *m*.

dame *n* (*nob*) gentildonna *f*; (*teat*) vecchia signora *f*.

damn *vt* dannare; maledire; * *interj* accidenti!

damnable *adj* vergognoso.

damnation *n* dannazione *f*.

damning *adj* schiacciante.

damp *adj* umido; * *n* umidità *f*; * *vt* inumidire.

dampen *vt* inumidire.

dampness *n* umidità *f*.

damson *n* susina *f*.

dance *n* ballo *m*; danza *f*; * *vt* ballare; * *vi* danzare.

dance hall *n* sala *f* da ballo.

dancer *n* ballerino *m*.

dandelion *n* dente *m* di leone.

dandruff *n* forfora *f*.

dandy *n* dandy *m*.

danger *n* pericolo *m*.

dangerous *adj* pericoloso.

dangle *vi* dondolare.

dank *adj* freddo e umido.

dapper *adj* azzimato.

dappled *adj* pomellato.

dare *vt* sfidare; osare; * *n* sfida *f*.

daredevil *n* scavezzacollo *m*.

daring *adj* audace; * *n* audacia *f*.

dark *adj* scuro; buio; * *n* buio *m*; oscurità *f*.

darken *vt* oscurare.

dark glasses *npl* occhiali *mpl* da sole.

darkness *n* oscurità *f*.

darkroom *n* camera *f* oscura.

darling *adj* caro; * *n* tesoro *m*.

darn *n* rammendo *m*; * *vt* rammendare.

dart *n* dardo *m*; pince *f*; * *vi* lanciarsi.

dartboard *n* bersaglio *m* per freccette.

dash *n* goccino *m*; trattino *m*; corsa *f*; * *vt* scaraventare; abbattere.

dashboard *n* cruscotto *m*.

dashing *adj* affascinante.

data *npl* dati *mpl*.

database *n* database *m*.

data processing *n* elaborazione *f* dei dati.

date *n* data *f*; appuntamento *m* dattero *m*; * *vt* datare; * *vi* risalire a.

dated *adj* antiquato.

dative *n* dativo *m*.

daub *vt* imbrattare.

daughter *n* figlia *f*.

daughter-in-law *n* nuora *f*.

daunting *adj* scoraggiante.

dawdle *vi* bighellonare.

dawn *n* alba *f*; * *vi* spuntare.

day *n* giorno *m*; giornata *f*; epoca *f*; **by ~** di giorno; **~ by ~** giorno per giorno.

daybreak *n* alba *f*.

daydream *vi* sognare ad occhi aperti.

daylight *n* luce *f* del giorno.

daytime *n* giorno *m*.

daze *vt* stordire; * *n* **in a ~** stordito.

dazed *adj* stordito.

dazzle *vt* abbagliare.

dazzling *adj* abbagliante.

deacon *n* diacono *m*.

dead *adj* morto; intorpidito; scarico; assoluto; **~ tired** stanco morto; **~ loss** caso disperato.

dead drunk *adj* ubriaco fradicio.

deaden *vt* attutire.

dead heat *n* vittoria *f* a pare merito.

deadline *n* scadenza *f*.

deadlock *n* punto *m* morto.

deadly *adj* mortale; micidiale.

deadpan *adj* impassibile.

deaf *adj* sordo.

deaf-and-dumb *adj* sordomuto.

deafen *vt* assordare.

deafening *adj* assordante.

deafness *n* sordità *f*.

deal *n* affare *m*; accordo *m*; legno *m* di abete; **I am a great ~ better** sto molto meglio; * *vi* **to ~ with** occuparsi di; affrontare; sbrigare; * *vt* dare le carte.

dealer *n* commerciante *m/f*.

dealings *npl* rapporti *mpl*.

dean *n* preside *m/f*.

dear *adj* caro; **oh ~!** mamma mia!.

dearth *n* scarsità *f*.

death *n* morte *f*.

deathbed *n* letto *m* di morte.

deathblow *n* colpo *m* di grazia.

death certificate *n* certificato *m* di morte.

deathly *adj* cadaverico.

death penalty *n* pena *f* di morte.

death throes *npl* agonia *f*.

death trap *n* trappola *f* mortale.

death warrant *n* mandato *m* di morte.

debacle *n* fuggi fuggi *m*.

debar *vt* escludere.

debase *vt* svilire.

debatable *adj* discutibile.

debate *n* dibattito *m*; * *vt* dibattere.

debauch *vt* corrompere.

debauched *adj* dissoluto.

debauchery *n* dissolutezza *f*.

debenture *n* obbligazione *f*.

debilitate *vt* debilitare.

debit *n* addebito; * *vt* addebitare.

debonair(e) *adj* gioviale e disinvolto.

debris *n* detriti *mpl*.

debt *n* debito *m*.

debtor *n* debitore *m*.

debunk *vt* demistificare.

debut *n* debutto *m*.

decade *n* decennio *m*.

decadence *n* decadenza *f*.

decadent *adj* decadente.

decaffeinated *adj* decaffeinato.

decant *vt* travasare.

decanter *n* caraffa *f*.

decapitate *vt* decapitare.

decapitation *n* decapitazione *f*.

decay *vi* putrefarsi; deteriorarsi; * *n* decomposizione *f*.

decease *n* decesso *m*.

deceased *adj* deceduto; * *n* defunto *m*.

deceit *n* inganno *m*.

deceitful *adj* falso.

deceive vt ingannare.
decelerate vt decelerare.
December n dicembre m.
decency n decenza f.
decent adj decente.
decentralization n decentramento m.
deception n inganno m.
deceptive adj ingannevole.
decibel n decibel m.
decide vt decidere.
decided adj deciso.
deciduous adj deciduo.
decimal adj, n decimale m.
decimate vt decimare.
decipher vt decifrare.
decision n decisione f.
decisive adj decisivo.
deck n coperta f; * vt decorare.
deckchair n sedia f a sdraio.
declaim vi declamare.
declamation n declamazione f.
declaration n dichiarazione f.
declare vt dichiarare.
declension n declinazione f.
decline vt, vi declinare; * n declino m.
declutch vi premere la frizione.
decode vt decodificare.
decompose vt decomporre.
decomposition n decomposizione f.
decompression n decompressione f.
dicongestant adj decongestionante.
decor n arredamento m.
decorate vt decorare.
decoration n decorazione f.
decorative adj decorativo.
decorator n decoratore m.
decorous adj decoroso.
decorum n decoro m.
decoy n uccello m da richiamo; tranello m.
decrease vt, vi diminuire; * n diminuzione f.

decree n decreto m; * vt decretare.
decrepit adj decrepito.
decry vt condannare.
dedicate vt dedicare.
dedication n dedizione f; dedica f.
deduce vt dedurre.
deduct vt dedurre.
deduction n deduzione f.
deed n azione f.
deem vt giudicare.
deep adj profondo.
deepen vt approfondire.
deep-freeze n congelatore m.
deer n cervo m.
deface vt deturpare.
defamation n diffamazione f.
default n mancanza f; contumacia f; * vi risultare inadempiente.
defaulter n moroso m.
defeat n sconfitta f; * vt sconfiggere.
defecate vi defecare.
defect n difetto m; * vi defezionare.
defection n defezione f.
defective adj difettoso.
defector n rifugiato m politico.
defence n difesa f.
defenceless adj indifeso.
defend vt difendere.
defendant n imputato m.
defensive adj difensivo.
defer vt rimandare.
deference n deferenza f.
deferential adj deferente.
defiance n sfida f.
defiant adj ribelle.
deficiency n mancanza f; insufficienza f.
deficient adj mancante.
deficit n deficit m.
defile vt deturpare; * n passo m stretto.
definable adj definibile.
define vt definire.

definite adj definitivo; **~ly** adv certamente.

definition n definizione f.

definitive adj definitivo.

deflate vt sgonfiare.

deflation n deflazione f.

deflect vt deviare.

deflower vt deflorare.

deform vt deformare.

deformity n deformità f.

defraud vt defraudare.

defray vt coprire.

defrost vt sbrinare.

deft adj abile.

defunct adj scomparso.

defuse vt disinnescare.

defy vt sfidare.

degenerate vi degenerare; * adj, n degenerato m.

degradation n degradazione f.

degrade vt degradare.

degrading adj degradante.

degree n grado m; laurea f.

dehydrate vt disidratare.

dehydrated adj disidratato.

deign vt degnarsi.

deity n divinità f.

dejected adj abbattuto.

dejection n abbattimento m.

delay vt rimandare; * vi ritardare; * n ritardo m.

delectable adj delizioso.

delegate vt delegare; * n delegato m.

delegation n delegazione f.

delete vt cancellare.

deliberate vt considerare; * vi deliberare; * adj premeditato; **~ly** * adv apposta.

deliberation n deliberazione f.

delicacy n delicatezza f; ghiottoneria f.

delicate adj delicato.

delicatessen n salumeria f.

delicious adj delizioso.

delight n delizia f; * vt riempire di gioia.

delighted adj contentissimo.

delightful adj delizioso.

delimit vt delimitare.

delineate vt delineare.

delineation n delineazione f.

delinquency n delinquenza f.

delinquent n delinquente; * adj delinquenziale.

delirious adj delirante.

delirium n delirio m.

deliver vt consegnare.

deliverance n liberazione f.

delivery n consegna f.

delta n delta m.

delude vt illudere.

deluge n diluvio m.

delusion n illusione f.

delve vi frugare.

demagogue n demagogo m.

demand n richiesta f; * vt esigere.

demanding adj esigente.

demarcation n demarcazione f.

demean vt umiliare.

demeanour n contegno m.

demented adj pazzo.

demise n decesso m.

demister n antiappannante m.

democracy n democrazia f.

democrat n democratico m.

democratic adj democratico.

demolish vt demolire.

demolition n demolizione f.

demon n demonio m.

demonstrable adj dimostrabile.

demonstrate vt manifestare; dimostrare.

demonstration n manifestazione f.

demonstrative adj espansivo.

demonstrator n manifestante m/f.

demoralize vt demoralizzare.

demote vt degradare.

demur vi sollevare obiezione.

demure adj contegnoso.

den n tana f, covo m.

denationalize *vt* snazionalizzare.

denial *n* rifiuto *m*; diniego *m*.

denier *n* denaro *m*.

denim *n* tessuto *m* jeans.

denomination *n* confessione *f*.

denominator *n* denominatore *m*.

denote *vt* denotare.

denounce *vt* denunciare.

dense *adj* denso.

density *n* densità *f*.

dent *n* ammaccatura *f*; * *vt* ammaccare.

dental *adj* dentistico.

dentist *n* dentista *m/f*.

dentistry *n* odontoiatria *f*.

dentures *npl* dentiera *f*.

denude *vt* denudare.

denunciation *n* denuncia *f*.

deny *vt* negare; smentire.

deodorant *n* deodorante *m*.

deodorize *vt* deodorare.

depart *vi* partire.

department *n* reparto *m*; sezione *f*.

department store *n* grande magazzino *m*.

departure *n* partenza *f*.

departure lounge *n* sala *f* d'attesa.

depend *vi* dipendere; ~ **on** contare su.

dependable *adj* affidabile.

dependant *n* persona *f* a carico.

dependence *n* dipendenza *f*.

dependent *adj*: **to be ~ on** dipendere da.

depict *vt* rappresentare.

deplete *vt* esaurire.

deplorable *adj* deplorevole.

deplore *vt* deplorare.

deploy *vt* schierare.

depopulate *vt* spopolare.

depopulation *n* spopolamento *m*.

deport *vt* deportare.

deportation *n* deportazione *f*.

deportment *n* portamento *m*.

deposit *vt* depositare; * *n* deposito *m*.

deposition *n* deposizione *f*.

depositor *n* depositante *m/f*.

depot *n* deposito *m*.

deprave *vt* depravare.

depraved *adj* depravato.

depravity *n* depravazione *f*.

deprecate *vt* deprecare.

depreciate *vi* deprezzarsi.

depreciation *n* deprezzamento *m*.

depredation *n* depredazione *f*.

depress *vt* deprimere.

depressed *adj* depresso.

depression *n* depressione *f*.

deprivation *n* privazione *f*.

deprive *vt* privare.

deprived *adj* bisognoso.

depth *n* profondità *f*.

deputation *n* deputazione *f*.

depute *vt* delegare.

deputize *vi* sostituire.

deputy *n* sostituto *m*.

derail *vt* far deragliare.

deranged *adj* sconvolto.

derelict *adj* fatiscente.

deride *vt* deridere.

derision *n* derisione *f*.

derisive *adj* beffardo.

derivation *n* derivazione *f*.

derivative *adj*, *n* derivato *m*.

derive *vt* derivare.

dermatitis *n* dermatite *f*.

dermatology *n* dermatologia *f*

derogatory *adj* spregiativo.

derrick *n* derrick *m*.

descant *n* discanto *m*.

descend *vt* scendere.

descendant *n* discendente *m/f*

descent *n* discesa *f*.

describe *vt* descrivere.

description *n* descrizione *f*.

descriptive *adj* descrittivo.

descry *vt* scorgere.

desecrate *vt* profanare.

desecration n profanazione f.

desert[1] n deserto; * adj desertico.

desert[2] vt abbandonare.

deserter n disertore m.

desertion n diserzione f.

deserve vt meritare.

deservedly adv meritatamente.

deserving adj meritevole.

desiccated adj essiccato.

design vt progettare; * n progetto m; disegno m.

designate vt designare.

designation n titolo m.

designer n disegnatore m.

desirable adj desiderabile.

desire n desiderio m; * vt desiderare.

desirous adj desideroso.

desist vi desistere.

desk n scrivania f.

desolate adj desolato.

desolation n desolazione f.

despair n disperazione f; * vi disperare.

despairing adj disperato.

desperado n disperato m.

desperate adj disperato.

desperation n disperazione f.

despicable adj spregevole.

despise vt disprezzare.

despite prep malgrado.

despoil vt spogliare.

despondency n abbattimento m.

despondent adj abbattuto.

despot n despota m.

despotic adj dispotico.

despotism n dispotismo m.

dessert n dessert m.

destination n destinazione f.

destined adj destinato.

destiny n destino m.

destitute adj indigente.

destitution n indigenza f.

destroy vt distruggere.

destroyer n cacciatorpediniere m.

destruction n distruzione f.

destructive adj distruttivo.

desultory adj sconnesso.

detach vt staccare.

detachable adj staccabile.

detached adj staccato; imparziale.

detachment n distacco m; distaccamento m.

detail n particolare m; dettaglio m; * vt dettagliare.

detain vt trattenere.

detect vt individuare.

detection n scoperta f.

detective n investigatore m.

detector n rivelatore m.

detente n distensione f.

detention n detenzione f.

deter vt dissuadere.

detergent n detersivo m.

deteriorate vi deteriorarsi.

deterioration n deterioramento m.

determination n determinazione f.

determine vt determinare.

determined adj risoluto.

deterrent n deterrente m.

detest vt detestare.

detestable adj detestabile.

detonate vi detonare.

detonation n detonazione f.

detonator n detonatore m.

detour n deviazione f.

detract vi sminuire.

detriment n detrimento m.

detrimental adj dannoso.

deuce n quaranta pari m.

devaluation n svalutazione f.

devastate vt devastare.

devastating adj devastatore.

devastation n devastazione f.

develop vt sviluppare.

development n sviluppo m.

deviate vi deviare.

deviation n deviazione f.

device n congegno m; dispositivo m.

devil n diavolo m.
devilish adj diabolico.
devious adj subdolo.
devise vt escogitare.
devoid adj; ~ **of** privo di.
devolution n decentramento m.
devolve vt devolvere.
devote vt dedicare.
devoted adj devoto.
devotee n appassionato m.
devotion n devozione f.
devour vt divorare.
devout adj devoto.
dew n rugiada f.
dewy-eyed adj con gli occhi languidi.
dexterity n destrezza f.
dexterous adj destro.
diabetes n diabete m.
diabetic adj, n diabetico m.
diabolic adj diabolico.
diadem n diadema m.
diagnose vt diagnosticare.
diagnosis n diagnosi f.
diagnostic adj diagnostico.
diagonal adj diagonale.
diagram n diagramma m.
dial n quadrante m.
dialect n dialetto m.
dialogue n dialogo m.
dialling code n prefisso m.
dialling tone n segnale m di libero.
dialysis n dialisi f.
diameter n diametro m.
diametric(al) adj diametrale.
diamond n diamante m.
diamond-cutter n diamantaio m.
diamonds npl quadri mpl.
diaphragm n diaframma m.
diarrhoea n diarrea f.
diary n diario m; agenda f.
dice npl dado m.
dictate vt, vi dettare.
dictation n dettatura f.
dictator n dittatore m.

dictatorial adj dittatoriale.
dictatorship n dittatura f.
diction n dizione f.
dictionary n vocabolario m.
didactic adj didattico.
die vi morire; **to ~ down** spegnersi; **to ~ out** scomparire.
die n dado m.
diehard n reazionario m.
diesel n gasolio m.
diet n dieta f; alimentazione f; * vi seguire una dieta.
dietary adj dietetico.
differ vi differire; discordare.
difference n differenza f.
different adj diverso.
differential adj, n differenziale m.
differentiate vt distinguere.
difficult adj difficile.
difficulty n difficoltà f.
diffidence n timidezza f.
diffident adj timido.
diffraction n diffrazione f.
diffuse vt diffondere; * adj diffuso.
diffusion n diffusione f.
dig vt vangare; scavare; * n gomitata f; scavo m.
digest vt digerire.
digestible adj digeribile.
digestion n digestione f.
digestive adj digestivo.
digger n scavatore m.
digit n cifra f.
digital adj digitale.
dignified adj dignitoso.
dignitary n dignitario m.
dignity n dignità f.
digress vi divagare.
digression n digressione f.
dilapidated adj scassato.
dilapidation n sfacelo m.
dilate vt dilatare.
dilemma n dilemma m.
diligence n diligenza f.
diligent adj diligente.
dill n aneto m.

dilly-dally vi gingillarsi.
dilute vt diluire.
dim adj fioco; * vt abbassare.
dimension n dimenzione f.
diminish vt diminuire.
diminished adj ridotto.
diminutive adj minuto.
dimly adv vagamente.
dimmer n regolatore m luminoso.
dimple n fossetta f.
din n chiasso m.
dine vi pranzare.
dinghy n gommone m.
dingy adj squallido.
dingo n dingo m.
dinner n cena f.
dinosaur n dinosauro m.
dint n; **by ~ of** a forza di.
diocese n diocesi f.
dioxide n biossido m.
dip vt immergere; * vi essere in pendenza; * n nuotatina f; (culin) salsetta f; cunetta f.
diphtheria n difterite f.
diphthong n dittongo m.
diploma n diploma m.
diplomacy n diplomazia f.
diplomat n diplomatico m.
diplomatic adj diplomatico.
dipsomania n dipsomania f.
dipstick n asta f dell'olio.
dire adj disastroso.
direct adj diretto; * vt dirigere a.
direction n direzione f.
directive n direttiva f.
directly adj direttamente.
director n dirigente m/f.
directory n elenco m.
dirge n canto m funebre.
dirt n sporco m.
dirtiness n sporcizia f.
dirty adj sporco.
disability n menomazione f.
disabled adj invalido.
disabuse vt disingannare.
disadvantage n svantaggio m.

disadvantageous adj svantaggioso.
disaffected adj disamorato.
disagree vi essere in disaccordo.
disagreeable adj spiacevole.
disagreement n discordanza f.
disallow vt respingere.
disappear vi scomparire.
disappearance n scomparsa f.
disappoint vt deludere.
disappointed adj deluso.
disappointing adj deludente.
disappointment n delusione f.
disapproval n disapprovazione f.
disapprove vi disapprovare.
disarm vt disarmare.
disarmament n disarmo m.
disarming adj disarmante.
disarray n disordine m.
disaster n disastro m.
disastrous adj disastroso.
disband vt sciogliere.
disbelief n incredulità f.
disbelieve vt non credere a.
disburse vt sborsare.
disc n disco m.
discard vt scartare.
discern vt discernere.
discernible adj percepibile.
discerning adj perspicace.
discernment n discernimento m.
discharge vt scaricare; licenziare; assolvere; * n scarica f; licenziamento m; secrezione f.
disciple n discepolo m.
disciplinary adj disciplinare.
discipline n disciplina f; * vt castigare; punire.
disclaim vt smentire.
disclaimer n smentita f; disconoscimento m.
disclose vt rivelare.
disclosure n rivelazione f.
disco n discoteca f.
discolour vt scolorire.

discolouration n scolorimento m.

discomfort n disaggio m.

disconcert vt sconcertare.

disconnect vt staccare.

disconsolate adj sconsolato.

discontent n scontentezza f; scontento m.

discontented adj scontento.

discontinue vt interrompere.

discord n disaccordo m.

discordant adj discordante.

discount n sconto; * vt non badare a.

discourage vt scoraggiare.

discouragement n scoraggiamento m.

discouraging adj scoraggiante.

discourse n discorso m.

discourteous adj scortese.

discourtesy n scortesia f.

discover vt scoprire.

discovery n scoperta f.

discredit vt screditare; * n discredito m.

discreditable adj disonorevole.

discreet adj discreto.

discrepancy n discrepanza f.

discrete adj separato.

discretion n discrezione f.

discretionary adj discrezionale.

discriminate vi distinguere; fare discriminazione tra.

discrimination n discriminazione f; discernimento m.

discursive adj discorsivo.

discus n disco m.

discuss vt discutere.

discussion n discussione f.

disdain vt sdegnare; * n disdegno m.

disdainful adj sdegnoso.

disease n malattia f.

diseased adj malato.

disembark vi sbarcare.

disembarkation n sbarco m.

disembodied adj disincarnato.

disenchant vt disincantare.

disenchanted adj disincantato.

disenchantment n disillusione f.

disengage vt disinnestare.

disentangle vt sbrogliare.

disfavour n disapprovazione f.

disfigure vt sfigurare.

disgorge vt riversare.

disgrace n vergogna f; disonore m; * vt disonorare.

disgraceful adj vergognoso.

disgruntled adj contrariato.

disguise vt travestire; mascherare; * n travestimento m.

disgust n disgusto m; * vt disgustare.

disgusting adj disgustoso.

dish n piatto m; pietanza f; * vt servire.

dishcloth n strofinaccio m.

dishearten vt scoraggiare.

dishevelled adj arruffato; tutto in disordine.

dishonest adj disonesto.

dishonesty n disonestà f.

dishonour n disonore m; * vt disonorare.

dishonourable adj disonorevole.

dishwasher n lavastoviglie f.

disillusion vt disingannare; * n disinganno m.

disincentive n: **to act as a ~ to** agire da freno su.

disinclination n riluttanza f.

disinclined adj poco propenso.

disinfect vt disinfettare.

disinfectant n disinfettante m.

disinherit vt diseredare.

disintegrate vi disintegrarsi.

disinterested adj disinteressato.

disjointed adj slegato.

disk n dischetto m.

dislike n antipatia f; * vt non piacere.

dislocate *vt* slogare.

dislocation *n* slogatura *f*.

dislodge *vt* rimuovere.

disloyal *adj* sleale.

disloyalty *n* slealtà *f*.

dismal *adj* tetro.

dismantle *vt* smontare.

dismay *n* sgomento; * *vt* sgomentare.

dismember *vt* smembrare.

dismiss *vt* congedare; licenziare.

dismissal *n* licenziamento *m*; congedo *m*:

dismount *vi* smontare; scendere.

disobedience *n* disubbidienza *f*.

disobedient *adj* disubbidiente.

disobey *vt* disubbidire.

disorder *n* disordine *m*.

disorderly *avv* disordinato.

disorganization *n* disorganizzazione *f*.

disorganized *adj* disorganizzato.

disorientated *adj* disorientato.

disown *vt* rinnegare.

disparage *vt* denigrare.

disparaging *adj* denigratorio.

disparity *n* disparità *f*.

dispassionate *adj* spassionato.

dispatch *vt* spedire; inviare; * *n* invio *m*, spedizione *f*.

dispel *vt* dissipare.

dispensary *n* farmacia *f*; dispensario *m*.

dispensation *n* dispensa *f*.

dispersal *n* dispersione *f*.

dispense *vt* dispensare.

disperse *vt* disperdere.

dispirited *adj* demoralizzato.

displace *vt* spostare.

display *vt* esporre; * *n* mostra *f*; esposizione *f*:

displeased *adj* dispiacere.

displeasure *n* dispiacere *m*.

disposable *adj* disponibile; monouso.

disposal *n* eliminazione *f*.

dispose *vt* disporre.

disposed *adj* disposto.

disposition *n* indole *f*.

dispossess *vt* spossessare.

disproportionate *adj* sproporzionato.

disprove *vt* confutare.

dispute *n* disputa *f*; controversia *f*; * *vt* contestare; disputarsi.

disqualify *vt* squalificare.

disquiet *n* inquietudine *f*.

disquieting *adj* inquietante.

disquisition *n* disquisizione *f*.

disregard *vt* ignorare; trascurare; * *n* indifferenza *f*.

disreputable *adj* poco raccomandabile.

disrespect *n* mancanza di rispetto *m*.

disrespectful *adj* irriverente.

disrobe *vt* svestire.

disrupt *vt* scombussolare.

disruption *n* scombussolamento *m*.

dissatisfaction *n* insoddisfazione *f*.

dissatisfied *adj* insoddisfatto.

dissect *vt* sezionare.

dissection *n* sezionamento *m*.

disseminate *vt* disseminare.

dissension *n* dissenso *m*.

dissent *vi* dissentire; * *n* dissenso *m*.

dissenter *n* dissidente *m/f*.

dissertation *n* dissertazione *f*.

dissident *n* dissidente *m/f*.

dissimilar *adj* dissimile.

dissimilarity *n* dissomiglianza *f*.

dissimulation *n* dissimulazione *f*.

dissipate *vt* dissipare.

dissipation *n* dissipazione *f*.

dissociate *vt* dissociare.

dissolute *adj* dissoluto.

dissolution *n* scioglimento *m*.

dissolve vt sciogliere; dissolvere.
dissonance n dissonanza f.
dissuade vt dissuadere.
distance n distanza f; lontananza f; * vt distanziare.
distant adj lontano; distante.
distaste n ripugnanza f.
distasteful adj sgradevole.
distemper n tempera f; cimurro m.
distend vt gonfiare.
distil vt distillare.
distillation n distillazione f.
distillery n distilleria f.
distinct adj distinto.
distinction n distinzione f.
distinctive adj particolare.
distinguish vt distinguere.
distinguished adj eminente; noto.
distort vt distorcere.
distortion n distorsione f.
distract vt distrarre.
distracted adj distratto.
distraction n distrazione f.
distraught adj stravolto.
distress n angoscia f; pericolo m; * vt addolorare.
distressing adj penoso.
distribute vt distribuire.
distribution n distribuzione f.
distributor n distributore m.
district n distretto m.
distrust n diffidenza f; * vt diffidare.
distrustful adj diffidente.
disturb vt disturbare.
disturbance n disturbo m; disordini mpl.
disturbed adj turbato.
disturbing adj preoccupante.
disuse n disuso m.
disused adj abbandonato.
ditch n fosso m; * vt mollare.
dither vi agitarsi; esitare.
ditto adv idem.
ditty n canzoncina f.
diuretic adj diuretico.

dive vi tuffarsi; lanciarsi; * n tuffo m; bettola f.
diver n tuffatore m.
diverge vi divergere.
divergence n divergenza f.
divergent adj divergente.
diverse adj svariato.
diversify vt diversificare.
diversion n deviazione f.
diversity n diversità f.
divert vt deviare; distrarre.
divest vt spogliare.
divide vt dividere.
divided adj diviso.
dividend n dividendo m.
dividers npl compasso m a punte fisse.
divine adj divino; * vt intuire.
diving n tuffi mpl.
diving board n trampolino m.
divinity n divinità f.
divisible adj divisibile.
division n divisione f.
divisor n divisore m.
divorce n divorzio m; * vi divorziare.
divorced adj divorziato.
divulge vt divulgare.
dizziness n capogiro m; vertigine f.
dizzy adj vertiginoso.
do vt fare; compiere; eseguire.
docile adj docile.
dock n (bot) romice m; bacino m; darsena f; banco degli imputati; * vt mozzare; decurtare; * vi entrare in bacino.
docker n portuale m.
docket n cartellino m.
dockyard n cantiere m navale.
doctor n dottore m; medico m * vt adulterare.
doctrinal adj dottrinale.
doctrine n dottrina f.
document n documento m; * v documentare.
documentary adj, n documentario m.

dodge *vt* schivare; * *n* trucchetto *m*.

doe *n* femmina di daino.

dog *n* cane *m*; * *vt* perseguitare.

dogged *adj* tenace.

dogma *n* dogma *m*.

dogmatic *adj* dogmatico.

dogsbody *n* factotum *m*.

doings *npl* imprese *fpl*.

do-it-yourself *n* bricolage *m*, fai da te *m*.

dole *n* sussidio *m* di disoccupazione.

doleful *adj* afflitto.

doll *n* bambola *f*.

dollar *n* dollaro *m*.

dolphin *n* delfino *m*.

domain *n* dominio *m*.

dome *n* cupola *f*.

domestic *adj* domestico.

domesticate *vt* addomesticare.

domesticity *n* amore *m* per la casa.

domicile *n* domicilio *m*.

dominant *adj* dominante.

dominate *vt, vi* dominare.

domination *n* dominazione *f*.

domineer *vt* spadroneggiare.

domineering *adj* despotico.

dominion *n* dominio *m*.

domino *n* domino *m*.

don *n* docente *m* universitario; * *vi* mettersi.

donate *vt* donare.

donation *n* donazione *f*.

done *adj* fatto; cotto.

donkey *n* asino *m*.

donor *n* donatore *m*.

doodle *vi* scarabocchiare.

doom *n* destino *m*.

door *n* porta *f*.

doorbell *n* campanello *m*.

doorman *n* portiere *m*.

doormat *n* zerbino *m*.

doorstep *n* soglia *f*.

doorway *n* vano *m* della porta.

dope *n* droga *f*.

dopey *adj* inebetito.

dormant *adj* latente.

dormer window *n* abbaino *m*.

dormitory *n* dormitorio *m*.

dormouse *n* ghiro *m*.

dosage *n* posologia *f*.

dose *n* dose *f*; * *vt* somministrare; dosare.

dossier *n* dossier *m*.

dot *n* punto *m*; * *vi* punteggiare.

dote *vi* stravedere.

double *adj* doppio; * *vt* raddoppiare; * *n* sosia *m*.

double bed *n* letto *m* matrimoniale.

double-breasted *adj* a doppio petto.

double chin *n* doppio mento *m*.

double-dealing *n* doppio gioco *m*.

double-edged *adj* a doppio taglio.

double entry *n* (*fin*) partita *f* doppia.

double room *n* camera *f* matrimoniale, camera *f* doppia.

doubly *adj* doppiamente.

doubt *n* dubbio *m*; * *vt* dubitare di.

doubtful *adj* indeciso.

doubtless *adv* indubbiamente.

dough *n* impasto *m*.

doughnut *n* ciambella *f*.

douse *vt* infradiciare.

dove *n* colombo *m*.

dovecot *n* colombaia *f*.

dowdy *adj* scialbo.

down *n* piume *fpl*; * *adv* giù; * *adj* **upside** ~ capovolto.

downcast *adj* avvilito.

downfall *n* rovina *f*.

downhearted *adj* depresso.

downhill *adv* in discesa.

down payment *n* anticipo *m*.

downpour *n* acquazzone *m*.

downright *adj* categorico.

downstairs *adj* al piano inferiore.

down-to-earth *adj* pratico.

downwards *adv* in giù.

dowry *n* dote *f*.

doze *vi* sonnecchiare; * *n* pisolino *m*.

dozen *n* dozzina *f*.

dozy *adj* sonnolento.

drab *adj* grigio; monotono.

draft *n* abbozzo *m*; tratta *f*; * *vt* abbozzare.

drag *n* resistenza *f*; scocciatura *f*; * *vt* trascinare; dragare; * *adj* **in ~** travestito.

dragon *n* drago *m*.

dragonfly *n* libellula *f*.

drain *vt* prosciugare; drenare; svuotare; * *n* scarico *m*; drenaggio *m*.

drainage *n* drenaggio *m*; prosciugamento *m*.

draining board *n* piano *m* del lavello.

drainpipe *n* tubo *m* di scarico.

drake *n* maschio dell'anatra.

dram *n* bicchierino *m*.

drama *n* dramma *m*.

dramatic *adj* drammatico.

dramatist *n* drammaturgo *m*.

dramatize *vt* drammatizzare.

drape *vt* drappeggiare.

draper *n* negoziante *m/f* di stoffe.

drastic *adj* drastico.

draught *n* spiffero *m*; sorsata *f*; * *adj* **on ~** alla spina.

draughtsman *n* disegnatore *m* tecnico.

draw *vt* disegnare; tirare; attirare; pareggiare; estrarre; * *n* sorteggio *m*; lotteria *f*; estrazione *f*; pareggio *m*.

drawback *n* inconveniente *m*.

drawer *n* cassetto *m*.

drawing *n* disegno *m*.

drawing room *n* salotto *m*.

drawl *n* cadenza *f* strascicata; * *vt* strascicare.

dread *n* terrore *m*; * *vt* temere.

dreadful *adj* tremendo.

dream *n* sogno *m*; * *vt, vi* sognare.

dreamer *n* sognatore *m*.

dreamy *adj* di sogno.

dreary *adj* desolato.

dredge *n* draga *f*; * *vt* dragare.

dregs *npl* feccia *f*.

drench *vt* inzuppare.

dress *vt* vestire; condire; * *n* vestito *m*, abito *m*; abbigliamento *m*.

dresser *n* credenza *f*.

dressing *n* vestire *m*; (*med*) fasciatura *f*; (*culin*) condimento *m*.

dressing gown *n* vestaglia *f*.

dressing room *n* camerino *m*.

dressing table *n* toilette *f*.

dressmaker *n* sarto *m*.

dressy *adj* elegante.

dribble *n* bava *f*; (*sport*) dribbling *m*; * *vt* sbrodolare.

dried *adj* secco; essiccato.

drift *n* deriva *f*; tendenza *f*; cumulo *m*; * *vi* andare alla deriva; vagare.

drill *n* trapano *m*; perforatrice *f*; esercitazione *f*; * *vt* trapanare; esercitare.

drink *vt, vi* bere; * *n* bevanda *f*; bibita *f*.

drinkable *adj* potabile.

drinker *n* bevitore *m*.

drinking *n* bere *m*.

drip *vi* sgocciolare; * *n* goccia *f*; (*med*) fleboclisi *f*.

dripping *n* grasso *m* dell'arrosto.

drive *vt* spingere; guidare; azionare; * *n* giro *m* in macchina; viale *m*; grinta *f*; **sales ~** campagna *f* di vendita; trasmissione *f*.

drivel *n* ciance *fpl*.

driver *n* guidatore *m*; autista *m/f*; conducente *m/f*.

driving *n* guida *f*.

driving licence *n* patente *m* di guida.

driving school n scuola f guida.

driving test n esame m per la patente.

drizzle vi piovigginare; * n pioggerella f.

droll adj bizzarro.

drone n fuco m; ronzio m; * vi ronzare.

drool vi sbavare.

droop vi chinarsi; appassire.

drop n goccia f; calo m; * vi lasciar cadere; abbandonare; piantare; calare.

droplet n gocciolina f.

drop-out n emarginato m.

dropper n contagocce m.

droppings npl escrementi mpl.

dross n avanzi mpl.

drought n siccità f.

drove n branco m.

drown vt, vi affogare, annegare.

drowsiness n sonnolenza f.

drowse vi sonnecchiare.

drowsy adj assonnato.

drudgery n sfacchinata f.

drug n medicina f; medicinale f; droga f; stupefacente; * vt drogare.

drug addict n tossicodipendente m/f.

drug pusher n spacciatore m.

drum n tamburo m; ~s batteria f; bidone m; timpano m; * vt, vi tamburellare.

drummer n batterista m/f.

drumstick n bacchetta f; coscia f di pollo.

drunk adj, n ubriaco m.

drunkard n ubriacone m.

drunken adj ubriaco.

drunkenness n ubriachezza f.

dry adj secco; asciutto; * vt seccare; essiccare; asciugare.

dry-clean vt lavare a secco.

dryness n secchezza f; aridità f.

dry rot n fungo m del legno.

dual adj doppio; duplice.

dual-purpose adj a doppio uso.

dub vt doppiare.

dubious adj dubbio; ambiguo.

duchess n duchessa f.

duck n anatra f; * vt immergere; * vi fare una schivata; accucciarsi.

duckling n anatroccolo m.

dud adj inservibile; * n arnese m inservibile.

due adj pagabile; dovuto; atteso; * vi **to fall** ~ scadere; ~ **to** a causa di; * n ~**s** quota f; diritti mpl.

duel n duello m.

duet n duetto m.

duke n duca m.

dull adj ottuso; noioso; spento; * vt ottundere; intorpidire; smussare.

duly adv debitamente.

dumb adj muto.

dumbbell n manubrio m.

dumbfound vt sbigottire.

dumness n mutismo m.

dummy adj finto; * n manichino m.

dump vt scaricare; * n discarica f.

dumping n dumping m.

dumpling n gnocco m di pasta.

dumpy adj tracagnotto.

dunce n somaro m.

dune n duna f.

dung n sterco m.

dungarees npl salopette f.

dungeon n segreta f.

dunk vt inzuppare.

duodenal adj duodenale.

duodenum n duodeno m.

dupe n gonzo m; * vt ingannare.

duplicate n duplicato m; * vt duplicare.

duplicity n duplicità f.

durability n durevolezza f.

durable adj durevole.

duration n durata f.

duress n coercizione f.

during prep durante.

dusk n crepuscolo m.

dust n polvere f; * vt, vi spolverare.

dustbin n bidone m.

dustcart n autocarro m della nettezza urbana.

duster n straccio m.

dustman n netturbino m.

dustpan n pattumiera f.

dust-up n zuffa f.

dusty adj polveroso.

dutch courage n coraggio m dato da alcolici.

dutiful adj deferente; rispettoso.

duty n dovere m; tassa f; dazio m.

duty-free adj esente da dogana.

duvet n piumone m.

dwarf n nano m; * vt eclissare.

dwell vi dimorare.

dwelling n dimora f.

dwindle vi diminuire; affievolirsi.

dye vt tingere; * n colorante m; tintura f.

dyer n tintore m.

dye-works n tintoria f

dying adj morente; * n morte f.

dyke n diga f; (fam) lesbica f.

dynamic adj dinamico.

dynamics n dinamica f.

dynamite n dinamite f.

dynamo n dinamo f.

dynasty n dinastia f.

dysentery n dissenteria f.

dyspepsia n dispepsia f.

dyspeptic adj dispeptico.

E

each adj ogni; ciascuno, * pron ognuno; ciascuno; * adv ciascuno.

eager adj appassionato.

eagerness n passione f.

eagle n aquila f.

eagle-eyed adj dagli occhi di lince.

eaglet n aquilotto m.

ear n orecchio m; **by ~** a orecchio.

earache n mal m d'orecchi.

eardrum n timpano m.

earl n conte m.

early adj primo; precoce; prematuro; * adv presto.

earmark vt destinare.

earn vt guadagnare.

earnest adj serio.

earnings npl guadagni mpl.

earphones npl cuffia f.

earring n orecchino m.

earth n terra f; * vt collegare a terra.

earthen adj di terracotta.

earthenware n terraglie fpl.

earthquake n terremoto m.

earthworm n lombrico m.

earthy adj grossolano.

earwig n forbicina f.

ease n disinvoltura f; tranquillità; **at ~** sentirsi a proprio agio; * vt facilitare; alleviare.

easel n cavalletto m.

easily adv facilmente.

easiness n facilità f.

east n est m; oriente m.

Easter n Pasqua f.

Easter egg n uovo m di Pasqua.

easterly adj orientale.

eastern adj orientale.

eastwards adv verso est.

easy adj facile; **~ going** accomodante.

easy chair n poltrona f.

eat vt mangiare.

eatable adj commestibile.

eau de Cologne n acqua f di Colonia.

eaves npl gronda f.

eavesdrop vi origliare.

ebb n riflusso m; * vi rifluire.

ebony n ebano m.

eccentric adj, n eccentrico m.

eccentricity n eccentricità f.

ecclesiastic adj ecclesiastico.

echo n eco m/f; * vi echeggiare.

éclair n bignè n.

eclectic adj eclettico.

eclipse n ecclissi f; * vt eclissare.

ecology n ecologia f.

economic(al) adj economico.

economics npl economia f.

economist n economista m/f.

economize vi fare economia.

economy n economia f.

ecstasy n estasi f.

ecstatic adj estatico.

eczema n eczema m.

eddy n mulinello m; * vi turbinare.

edge n orlo m; bordo m; * vt bordare; * vi **to ~ forward** avanzare a poco a poco.

edgeways adv di fianco.

edging n bordo m.

edgy adj teso.

edible adj mangiabile; commestibile.

edict n editto m.

edification n cultura f.

edifice n edificio m; costruzione f.

edify vt edificare.

edit vt dirigere; redigere.

edition n edizione f.

editor n direttore m.

editorial adj redazionale; * n editoriale.

educate vt istruire; educare.

educated adj colto.

education n istruzione f; formazione f; pedagogia f.

educational adj didattico.

eel n anguilla f.

eerie adj sinistro.

efface vt cancellare.

effect n effetto m; **~s** effetti mpl; * vt effettuare.

effective adj efficace.

effectiveness n efficacia f.

effectual adj efficace.

effeminacy n effeminatezza f.

effeminate adj effeminato.

effervescent adj effervescente.

effete adj logoro.

efficacy n efficacia f.

efficiency n efficenza f.

efficient adj efficiente.

effigy n effigie f.

effort n sforzo m.

effortless adj facile; disinvolto.

effrontery n sfrontatezza f.

effusive adj espansivo.

egalitarian adj egualitario.

egg n uovo m; * vt **to ~ on** spingere.

eggcup n portauovo m.

eggshell n guscio m d'uovo.

ego n ego m.

egoism n egoismo m.

egoist n egoista m/f.

egotism n egotismo m.

egotist n egotista m/f.

eiderdown n trapunta f di piuma.

eight adj, n otto m.

eighteen adj, n diciotto m.

eighteenth adj, n diciottesimo m.

eighth adj, n ottavo m.

eightieth adj, n ottantesimo m.

eighty adj, n ottanta m.

either pron, adj l'uno o l'altro; * adj entrambi; * conj **~ ... or** o ... o; * adv neanche.

ejaculate vt, vi esclamare; eiaculare.

ejaculation n esclamazione f;

eiaculazione *f*.
eject *vt* espellere.
ejection *n* espulsione *f*.
ejector seat *n* seggiolino *m* eiettabile.
eke *vt* integrare; far bastare.
elaborate *vt* elaborare; * *adj* complicato; ricercato.
elapse *vi* trascorrere.
elastic *adj*, *n* elastico *m*.
elasticity *n* elasticità *f*.
elated *adj* esultante.
elation *n* esultanza *f*.
elbow *n* gomito *m*.
elbow-room *n* spazio *m*.
elder *n* anziano *m*; (*bot*) sambuco *m*; * *adj* maggiore.
elderberry *n* bacca di sambuco.
elderly *adj* anziano.
eldest *adj* maggiore.
elect *vt* eleggere; decidere; * *adj* futuro.
election *n* elezione *f*.
electioneering *n* propaganda *f* elettorale.
electoral *adj* elettorale.
electorate *n* elettorato *m*.
electric(al) *adj* elettrico.
electric blanket *n* coperta *f* termica.
electric fire *n* stufa *f* elettrica.
electrician *n* elettricista *m/f*.
electricity *n* elettricità *f*.
electrify *vt* elettrificare.
electrocute *vt* fulminare.
electrode *n* elettrodo *m*.
electrolysis *n* elettrolisi *f*.
electron *n* elettrone *m*.
electronic *adj* elettronico; ~**s** *npl* elettronica *f*.
elegance *n* eleganza *f*.
elegant *adj* elegante.
elegy *n* elegia *f*.
element *n* elemento *m*.
elementary *adj* elementare.
elephant *n* elefante *m*.
elevate *vt* elevare.

elevation *n* elevazione *f*.
elevator *n* montacarichi *m*.
eleven *adj*, *n* undici *m*.
eleventh *adj*, *n* undicesimo *m*.
elf *n* folletto *m*.
elicit *vt* strappare.
eligibility *n* eleggibilità *f*.
eligible *adj* eleggibile.
eliminate *vt* eliminare.
elimination *n* eliminazione *f*.
élite *n* élite *f*.
elixir *n* elisir *m*.
elk *n* alce *m*.
eliptic(al) *adj* ellittico.
elm *n* olmo *m*.
elocution *n* dizione *f*.
elongate *vt* allungare.
elope *vi* fuggire.
elopement *n* fuga (romantica) *f*.
eloquence *n* eloquenza *f*.
eloquent *adj* eloquente.
else *adv* altro; altrimenti.
elsewhere *adv* altrove.
elucidate *vt* delucidare.
elucidation *n* spiegazione *f*.
elude *vt* eludere.
elusive *adj* inafferrabile.
emaciated *adj* emaciato.
emanate *vi* provenire.
emancipate *vt* emancipare.
emancipation *n* emancipazione *f*.
embalm *vt* imbalsamare.
embankment *n* argine *m*.
embargo *n* embargo *m*.
embark *vt* imbarcare.
embarkation *n* imbarco *m*.
embarrass *vt* mettere in imbarazzo.
embarrassing *adj* imbarazzante.
embarrassment *n* imbarazzo *m*.
embassy *n* ambasciata *f*.
embed *vt* incastrare.
embellish *vt* abbellire.
embers *npl* brace *f*.

embezzle vt appropriarsi indebitamente.

embezzlement n appropriazione f indebita.

embitter vt inasprire.

emblem n emblema m.

emblematic(al) adj emblematico.

embodiment n incarnazione f.

embody vt incarnare.

emboss vt goffrare.

embrace vt abbracciare; * n abbraccio m.

embroider vt ricamare.

embroidery n ricamo m.

embroil vt imbrogliare.

embryo n embrione m.

emend vt correggere.

emendation n correzione f.

emerald n smeraldo m.

emerge vi emergere.

emergency n emergenza f.

emergency exit n uscita f di sicurezza.

emery n smeriglio m

emery board n limetta f di carta.

emetic n emetico m.

emigrant n emigrante m/f.

emigrate vi emigrare.

emigration n emigrazione f.

eminence n eminenza f; reputazione f.

eminent adj eminente.

emirate n emirato m.

emissary n emissario m.

emission n emissione f.

emit vt emettere.

emolument n emolumento m.

emotion n emozione f.

emotional adj emotivo.

emotive adj emotivo; commovente.

emperor n imperatore m.

emphasis n accento m; enfasi f.

emphasize vt sottolineare.

emphatic adj enfatico.

empire n impero m.

empirical adj empirico.

employ vt impiegare; assumere.

employee n dipendente m/f.

employer n datore m di lavoro.

employment n occupazione f.

empress n imperatrice f.

emptiness n vuoto m.

empty adj vuoto; * vt vuotare.

empty-handed adj a mani vuote.

emu n emù m.

emulate vt emulare.

emulsify vt emulsionare.

emulsion n emulsione f.

enable vt permettere.

enact vt rappresentare.

enamel n smalto; * vt smaltare.

enamour vt innamorare.

encamp vi accampare.

encampment n accampamento m.

encase vt racchiudere.

enchant vt incantare.

enchanting adj incantevole.

enchantment n incantesimo m.

encircle vt circondare.

enclose vt allegare; recintare.

enclosure n allegato m; recinto m;

encompass vt comprendere.

encore excl, n bis m.

encounter n incontro m; * vt incontrare.

encourage vt incoraggiare.

encouragement n incoraggiamento m.

encroach vi usurpare; invadere.

encrust vt incrostare.

encumber vt ingombrare.

encumbrance n peso m.

encyclical n enciclica f

encyclopaedia n enciclopedia f.

end n fine f; estremità f; scopo

m; * *vi* finire; terminare; * *vt*
porre fine a.
endanger *vt* mettere in pericolo.
endear *vt* rendere caro.
endearing *adj* tenero.
endearment *n* tenerezza *f*.
endeavour *vt* tentare; * *n* tentativo *m*.
endemic *adj* endemico.
ending *n* fine *f*; (*gram*) desinenza *f*.
endive *n* (*bot*) indivia *f*.
endless *adj* senza fine; interminabile.
endorse *vt* girare; approvare.
endorsement *n* girata *f*; approvazione *f*.
endow *vt* dotare.
endowment *n* fondazione *f*;
donazione *f*.
endurable *adj* sopportabile.
endurance *n* resistenza *f*.
endure *vt* sopportare.
enduring *adj* duraturo.
enemy *n* nemico *m*.
energetic *adj* energico.
energy *n* energia *f*.
enervate *vt* snervare.
enfeeble *vt* indebolire.
enforce *vt* applicare; far rispettare.
enforced *adj* imposto.
enfranchise *vt* concedere il
diritto di voto a.
engage *vt* assumere; innestare;
ingaggiare.
engaged *adj* fidanzato.
engagement *n* fidanzamento
m; impegno *m*.
engagement ring *n* anello *m*
di fidanzamento.
engaging *adj* attraente.
engender *vt* essere causa di.
engine *n* motore *m*; locomotivo
m.
engine driver *n* macchinista
m.

engineer *n* ingegnere *m*, meccanico *m*; * *vt* architettare.
engineering *n* ingegneria *f*.
engrave *vt* incidere.
engraving *n* incisione *f*.
engrossed *adj* immerso.
engulf *vt* inghiottire.
enhance *vt* valorizzare.
enigma *n* enigma *m*.
enigmatic *adj* enigmatico.
enjoy *vt* godere; divertirsi.
enjoyment *m* godimento *m*; divertimento *m*.
enlarge *vt* ingrandire; ampliare.
enlargement *n* ingrandimento
m; ampliamento *m*.
enlighten *vt* fornire chiarimento a.
enlightened *adj* illuminato.
Enlightenment *n* l'Illuminismo *m*.
enlist *vt* arruolare.
enlistment *n* arruolamento *m*.
enliven *vt* ravvivare.
enmity *n* inimicizia *f*.
enormity *n* atrocità *f*.
enormous *adj* enorme.
enough *adj*, sufficiente; *adj*,
* *adv* abbastanza; * *vi* **to be**
~ bastare.
enquire *vt* = inquire.
enrage *vt* fare arrabbiare.
enrapture *vt* estasiare.
enrich *vt* arricchire.
enrichment *n* arricchimento
m.
enrol *vt* iscrivere; immatricolare.
enrolment *n* iscrizione *f*; immatricolazione *f*.
en route *adv* in viaggio.
ensemble *n* complesso *m*.
ensign *n* insegne *f*.
enslave *vt* rendere schiavo.
ensue *vi* seguire; risultare.
ensure *vt* garantire.
entail *vt* comportare.
entangle *vt* impigliare.

entanglement n groviglio m.

enter vt registrare; **to ~ for** iscriversi; * vi entrare; **this does not ~ into it** questo non c'entra.

enteritis n enterite f.

enterprise n impresa f; iniziativa f.

enterprising adj intraprendente.

entertain vt intrattenere.

entertainer n artista m/f.

entertaining adj divertente.

entertainment n trattenimento m; spettacolo m.

enthral vt affascinare.

enthralling adj avvincente.

enthuse vi entusiasmarsi.

enthusiasm n entusiasmo m.

enthusiast n appassionato m.

enthusiastic adj appassionato.

entice vt allettare.

entire adj intero.

entirety n complesso m.

entitle vt intitolare; dare diritto a.

entity n entità f.

entourage n entourage m.

entrails npl interiora fpl.

entrance n entrata f, ingresso m, ammissione f; * vt mandare in estasi.

entrance examination n esame m di ammissione.

entrance fee n quota f di ammissione.

entrant n concorrente m/f; candidato m.

entreat vt implorare.

entreaty n supplica f.

entrenched adj radicato.

entrepreneur n imprenditore m.

entrust vt affidare.

entry n ingresso m, entrata f; accesso m; voce f.

entry phone n citofono m.

entwine vt intrecciare.

enumerate vt enumerare.

enunciate vt enunciare.

enunciation n articolazione f.

envelop vt avvolgere.

envelope n busta f.

enviable adj invidiabile.

envious adj invidioso.

environment n ambiente m.

environmental adj ambientale.

environs npl dintorni mpl.

envisage vt prevedere.

envoy n inviato m.

envy n invidia f.

enzyme n enzima m.

ephemeral adj effimero.

epic adj epico; * n epopea f.

epicure n buongustaio m.

epidemic adj epidemico; * n epidemia f.

epilepsy n epilessia f.

epileptic adj, n epilettico m.

epilogue n epilogo m.

Epiphany n Epifania f.

episcopal adj episcopale.

episcopalian adj, n episcopaliano m.

episode n episodio m.

epistle n epistola f.

epithet n epiteto m.

epitome n personificazione f.

epitomize vt incarnare.

epoch n epoca f.

equable adj costante.

equal adj uguale; * n pari m; * vt uguagliare.

equalize vt livellare; * vi pareggiare.

equalizer n pareggio m.

equality n uguaglianza f.

equally adv ugualmente.

equanimity n serenità f.

equate vt identificare.

equation n equazione f.

equator n equatore m.

equatorial adj equatoriale.

equestrian adj equestre.

equidistant adj equidistante.

equilateral adj equilatero.

equilibrium *n* equilibrio *m*.
equinox *n* equinozio *m*.
equip *vt* attrezzare.
equipment *n* attrezzatura *f*.
equitable *adj* equo.
equity *n* equità *f*.
equivalent *adj* equivalente.
equivocal *adj* equivoco.
equivocate *vi* giocare sull'equivoco.
era *n* era *f*.
eradicate *vt* sradicare.
erase *vt* cancellare.
erect *vt* erigere; * *adj* diritto.
erection *n* erezione *f*.
ermine *n* ermellino *m*.
erode *vt* erodere.
erotic *adj* erotico.
err *vi* sbagliare.
errand *n* commissione *f*.
errand boy *n* fattorino *m*.
erratic *adj* incostante.
erratum *n* errore *m* di stampa.
erroneous *adj* erroneo.
error *n* errore *m*.
erudite *adj* erudito.
erudition *n* erudizione *f*.
erupt *vi* essere in eruzione; erompere.
eruption *n* eruzione *f*.
escalate *vt* intensificare; * *vi* intensificarsi.
escalation *n* intensificazione *f*.
escalator *n* scala *f* mobile.
escapade *n* scappatella *f*.
escape *vt* sfuggire a; scampare; * *vi* scappare; evadere; * *n* fuga *f*; evasione *f*.
escapism *n* evasione *f*.
escarpment *n* scarpata *f*.
eschew *vt* evitare.
escort *n* scorta *f*; * *vt* scortare.
esoteric *adj* esoterico.
especial *adj* particolare.
espionage *n* spionaggio *m*.
esplanade *n* lungomare *m*.
espouse *vt* abbracciare.
essay *n* saggio *m*.

essence *n* essenza *f*.
essential *adj* essenziale.
establish *vt* stabilire; istituire; fondare.
establishment *n* istituzione *f*; azienda *f*.
estate *n* tenuta *f*; patrimonio *m*.
estate agent *n* agente *m/f* immobiliare.
esteem *vt* stimare; * *n* stima *f*.
estimate *vt* valutare; preventivare; * *n* preventivo *m*; valutazione *f*.
estimation *n* giudizio *m*; stima *f*.
estranged *adj* separato.
estrangement *n* allontanamento *m*.
estuary *n* estuario *m*.
etch *vt* incidere all'acquaforte.
etching *n* incisione *f* all'acquaforte.
eternal *adj* eterno.
eternity *n* eternità *f*.
ether *n* etere *m*.
ethical *adj* etico.
ethics *npl* etica *f*.
ethnic *adj* etnico.
ethos *n* norma *f* di vita.
etiquette *n* etichetta *f*.
etymological *adj* etimologico.
etymology *n* etimologia *f*.
eucalyptus *n* eucalipto *m*.
Eucharist *n* eucarestia *f*.
eulogy *n* elogio *m*.
eunuch *n* eunuco *m*.
euphemism *n* eufemismo.
euphoria *n* euforia *f*.
euthanasia *n* eutanasia *f*.
evacuate *vt* evacuare.
evacuation *n* evacuazione *f*.
evade *vt* eludere; evadere.
evaluate *vt* valutare.
evaluation *n* valutazione *f*.
evangelic(al) *adj* evangelico.
evangelist *n* evangelista *m*.
evaporate *vi* evaporare.

evaporated milk n latte m concentrato.

evaporation n evaporazione f.

evasion n evasione f.

evasive adj evasivo.

eve n vigilia f.

even adj liscio; regolare; pari; * adv perfino; addirittura; ancora; * vt appianare.

evening n sera f, serata f.

evening class n corso m serale.

evening dress n abito m da sera.

evenly adv uniformemente.

event n avvenimento m.

eventful adj movimentato.

eventual adj finale; eventuale.

eventuality n eventualità f.

ever adv sempre; mai; **for ~** per sempre.

evergreen n sempreverde m/f.

everlasting adj eterno.

every adj ogni, tutti; * pron **~body** ognuno, tutti; **~thing** tutto; * adv **~where** dappertutto.

evict vt sfrattare.

eviction n sfratto m.

evidence n testimonianza f; prove fpl.

evident adj evidente.

evil adj cattivo; malvagio; * n male m.

evil-minded adj malvagio.

evince vt manifestare.

evocative adj evocativo.

evoke vt evocare.

evolution n evoluzione f.

evolve vt elaborare; * vi evolversi.

ewe n pecora f.

exacerbate vt esacerbare.

exact adj esatto; * vt esigere.

exacting adj esigente.

exactly adj esattamente.

exactness, exactitude n esattezza f.

exaggerate vt esagerare.

exaggeration n esagerazione f.

exalt vt esaltare.

exalted adj esaltato.

examination n esame m; visita f.

examine vt esaminare; visitare.

examiner n esaminatore m.

example n esempio m.

exasperate vt esasperare.

exasperation n esasperazione f.

excavate vt scavare.

excavation n scavo m.

exceed vt eccedere; superare.

exceedingly adv estremamente.

excel vt superare.

excellence n eccellenza f.

Excellency n Eccellenza f.

excellent adj eccellente.

except vt escludere; * prep tranne, eccetto.

exception n eccezione f.

exceptional adj eccezionale.

excerpt n estratto m.

excess n eccesso m.

excessive adj eccessivo.

exchange vt scambiare; * n scambio m.

exchange rate n tasso m di cambio.

exchequer n tesoro m.

excise n imposta f indiretta.

excitable adj eccitabile.

excite vt eccitare.

excited adj emozionato; eccitato.

excitement n eccitazione f.

exciting adj emozionante.

exclaim vt esclamare.

exclamation n esclamazione f.

exclamation mark n punto m esclamativo.

exclude vt escludere.

exclusion n esclusione f.

exclusive adj esclusivo.

excommunicate vt scomunicare.

excommunication n scomunica f.

excrement *n* escrementi *mpl*.
excruciating *adj* atroce.
exculpate *vt* scolpare.
excursion *n* gita *f*, escursione *f*.
excusable *adj* perdonabile.
excuse *vt* scusare; esonerare; * *n* scusa *f*.
execrable *adj* esecrabile.
execute *vt* giustiziare; eseguire.
execution *n* esecuzione *f*.
executioner *n* boia *m*.
executive *adj* esecutivo; * *n* dirigente *m/f*.
executor *n* esecutore *m*.
exemplary *adj* esemplare.
exemplify *vt* esemplificare.
exempt *adj* esente; * *vt* esentare.
exemption *n* esenzione *f*.
exercise *n* esercizio *m*; * *vt* esercitare.
exercise book *m* quaderno *m*.
exert *vt* esercitare; **to ~ oneself** sforzarsi.
exertion *n* sforzo *m*.
exhale *vt, vi* espirare.
exhaust *n* gas *m* di scarico; * *vt* stremare; esaurire.
exhausted *adj* esausto.
exhaustion *n* esaurimento *m*.
exhaustive *adj* esauriente.
exhibit *vt* esporre; * *n* oggetto *m* esposto; reperto *m*.
exhibitor *n* espositore *m*.
exhibition *n* mostra *f*.
exhilarate *vt* rinvigorire.
exhort *vt* esortare.
exhume *vt* esumare.
exile *n* esilio *m*; esule *m/f*; * *vt* esiliare.
exist *vi* esistere.
existence *n* esistenza *f*.
existent *adj* esistente.
existential *adj* esistenziale.
existentialism *n* esistenzialismo *m*.
exit *n* uscita *f*.

exodus *n* esodo *m*.
exonerate *vt* discolpare.
exoneration *n* discolpa *f*.
exhorbitant *adj* esorbitante.
exorcise *vt* esorcizzare.
exorcism *n* esorcismo *m*.
exotic *adj* esotico.
expand *vt* espandere.
expanse *n* distesa *f*.
expansion *n* espansione *f*.
expansive *adj* espansivo.
expatriate *adj, n* espatriato *m*.
expect *vt* aspettare; pensare; pretendere; esigere.
expectancy *n* attesa *f*.
expectant *adj* in attesa.
expectant mother *n* donna *f* incinta.
expectation *n* aspettativa *f*; attesa *f*.
expediency *n* interesse *m*.
expedient *adj* opportuno; * *n* espediente *m*.
expedite *vt* accelerare.
expedition *n* spedizione *f*.
expeditious *adj* sollecito.
expel *vt* espellere.
expend *vt* spendere.
expendable *adj* usabile.
expenditure *n* dispendio *m*.
expense *n* spesa *f*.
expense account *n* conto *m* spese.
expensive *adj* costoso, caro.
experience *n* esperienza *f*; * *vt* sperimentare.
experienced *adj* esperto.
experiment *n* esperimento *m*.
experimental *adj* sperimentale.
expert *adj, n* esperto *m*.
expertise *n* perizia *f*.
expire *vi* scadere; spirare.
expiry *n* scadenza *f*.
explain *vt* spiegare.
explanation *n* spiegazione *f*.
explanatory *adj* esplicativo.
expletive *n* imprecazione *f*.

explicable *adj* spiegabile.
explicit *adj* esplicito.
explode *vi* esplodere.
exploit *vt* sfruttare; * *n* impresa *f*.
exploitation *n* sfruttamento *m*.
exploration *n* esplorazione *f*.
exploratory *adj* preliminare.
explore *vt* esplorare.
explorer *n* esploratore *m*.
explosion *n* esplosione *f*.
explosive *adj*, *n* esplosivo *m*.
exponent *n* esponente *m/f*.
export *vt* esportare; * *n* esportazione *f*.
exporter *n* esportatore *m*.
expose *vt* esporre; smascherare.
exposed *adj* esposto; scoperto.
exposition *n* esposizione *f*.
expostulate *vi* rimostrare.
exposure *n* esposizione *f*.
exposure meter *n* esposimetro *m*.
expound *vt* esporre.
express *vt* esprimere; * *adj* espresso.
expression *n* espressione *f*.
expressionless *adj* inespressivo.
expressive *adj* espressivo.
expropriate *vt* espropriare.
expropriation *n* esproprio *m*.
expulsion *n* espulsione *f*.
expurgate *vt* espurgare.
exquisite *adj* squisito.
extant *adj* esistente.
extempore *adj* improvvisato.
extemporize *vi* improvvisare.
extend *vt* tendere; prolungare.
extension *n* prolunga *f*; (numero) interno.
extensive *adj* esteso.
extent *n* estensione *f*; portata *f*.
extenuate *vt* attenuare.
extenuating *adj* attenuante.
exterior *adj*, *n* esterno *m*.
exterminate *vt* sterminare.

extermination *n* sterminio *m*.
external *adj* esterno.
extinct *adj* estinto.
extinction *n* estinzione *f*.
extinguish *vt* spegnere.
extinguisher *n* estintore *m*.
extirpate *vt* estirpare.
extol *vt* magnificare.
extort *vt* estorcere.
extortion *n* estorsione *f*.
extortionate *adj* esorbitante.
extra *adj* in più; supplementare; maggiore; * *adv* extra; eccezionalmente.
extract *vt* estrarre; * *n* spezzone *m*.
extraction *n* estrazione *f*.
extracurricular *adj* parascolastico.
extradite *vt* estradare.
extradition *n* estradizione *f*.
extramarital *adj* extraconiugale.
extramural *adj* estramurale.
extraneous *adj* estraneo.
extraordinary *adj* straordinario.
extrasensory *adj* extrasensoriale.
extravagance *n* stravaganza *f*.
extravagant *adj* dispendioso; stravagante.
extreme *adj*, *n* estremo *m*.
extremist *n* estremista *m/f*.
extremity *n* estremità *f*.
extricate *vt* districare.
extrinsic(al) *adj* estrinseco.
extrovert *adj*, *n* estroverso *m*.
exuberance *n* esuberanza *f*.
exuberant *adj* esuberante.
exude *vt* emanare.
exult *vi* esultare.
exultation *n* giubilo *m*.
eye *n* occhio *m*; * *vt* scrutare.
eyeball *n* bulbo *m* oculare.
eyebrow *n* sopracciglio *m*.
eyedrops *npl* collirio *m*.
eyelash *n* ciglio *m*.

eyelid n palpebra f.

eyeshadow n ombretto m.

eyesight n vista f.

eyesore n oggetto m sgradevole alla vista.

eyetooth n canino m superiore.

eyewitness n testimone m/f oculare.

eyrie n nido m d'aquila.

F

fable n favola f.

fabric n stoffa f, tessuto m.

fabricate vt fabbricare.

fabrication n fabbricazione f.

fabulous adj favoloso.

facade n facciata f.

face n faccia f, viso m; muso m; quadrante m; * vt affrontare; essere di fronte a; * vi **to ~ up to** fare fronte a.

face cream n crema f per il viso.

face-lift n plastica f facciale.

face powder n cipria f.

facet n sfaccettatura f; aspetto m.

facetious adj faceto.

face value n valore m nominale.

facial adj faciale; * n trattamento m del viso.

facile adj superficiale.

facilitate vt facilitare.

facility n facilità f.

facing n rivestimento m; paramontura f; * adj di fronte

facsimile n facsimile m.

fact n fatto m; **in ~** in realtà.

faction n fazione f.

factor n fattore m.

factory n fabbrica f.

factual adj che riguarda i fatti.

faculty n facoltà f.

fad n pazzia f.

fade vi appassire; sbiadirsi.

faeces feci fpl.

fag n (fam) sigaretta f; (Amer fam) frocio m.

faggot n (culin) involtino m di fegato.

fail vi fallire; mancare; * vt bocciare.

failing n difetto m; * prep in mancanza di.

failure n fallimento m; insuccesso m.

faint vi svenire; * n svenimento; * adj leggero; fievole; vago.

fainthearted adj pusillanime.

fair adj giusto; imparziale; discreto; chiaro; * n fiera f.

fairly adv in modo imparziale; abbastanza.

fairness n imparzialità f; chiarezza f.

fair play n correttezza f.

fairy n fata f.

fairy tale n fiaba f.

faith n fede f.

faithful adj fedele.

faithfulness n fedeltà f.

fake n falso m; imitazione f; * adj fasullo; * vt falsificare; * vi fingere.

falcon n falco m.

falconry n falconiera f.

fall vi cadere; **to ~ asleep** addormentarsi; **to ~ in love** innamorarsi; **to ~ back on** ripiegare su; **to ~ for** cascarci; **to ~ out** litigare; * n caduta f; calo m.

fallacious adj fallace.

fallacy n errore m.

fallibility n fallibilità f.

fallible adj fallibile.

fallout n pioggia f radioattiva.

fallout shelter n rifugio m antiatomico.

fallow adj incolto; ~ **deer** n daino m.

false adj falso.

false alarm n falso allarme m.

falsehood n menzogna f.

falsify vt falsificare.

falsity n falsità f.

falter vi vacillare.

fame n fama f, celebrità f.

famed adj famoso.

familiar adj conosciuto, familiare.

familiarity n familiarità f.

familiarize vt familiarizzarsi.

family n famiglia f.

family doctor n medico m di famiglia.

famine n carestia f.

famished adj affamato.

famous adj famoso.

fan n ventaglio m; ventilatore m; fan m/f, tifoso m; * vt fare vento.

fanatic adj, n fanatico m.

fanaticism n fanatismo m.

fan belt n cinghia f della ventola.

fanciful adj fantasioso.

fancy n voglia f, capriccio m; * adj elaborato.

fancy dress n costume m; ~ **party** festa f in maschera.

fanfare n fanfara f.

fang n zanna f.

fantasize vi fantasticare.

fantastic adj fantastico.

fantasy n fantasia f, sogno m.

far adv lontano; **so** ~ finora; * adj lontano; di gran lunga; estremo.

faraway adj lontano; assente.

farce n farsa f.

farcical adj ridicolo.

fare n tariffa f; cibo m.

farewell excl, n addio m.

farm n fattoria f; * vt coltivare.

farmer n agricoltore m.

farmhand n bracciante m/f.

farmhouse n casa f colonica.

farming n agricoltura f.

farmland n terreno m coltivabile.

farmyard n aia f.

far-reaching adj di vasta portata.

fart n (sl) scoreggia f; * vi scoreggiare.

farther adv più avanti; oltre; * adj ulteriore; * vt favorire.

farthest adv, adj più lontano.

fascinate vt affascinare.

fascinating adj affascinante.

fascination n fascino m.

fascism n fascismo m.

fascist n fascista m/f.

fashion n moda f; modo m; * vt modellare.

fashionable adj alla moda.

fashion show n sfilata f di moda.

fast vi digiunare; * adj veloce, rapido; * adv velocemente; saldamente; * n digiuno m.

fasten vt legare.

fastener, fastening n chiusura f.

fast food n fast food m.

fastidious adj pignolo; difficile.

fat adj, n grasso m.

fatal adj fatale; nefasto.

fatalism n fatalismo m.

fatality n vittima f.

fate n destino m; sorte f.

fateful adj fatidico.

father n padre m.

fatherhood n paternità f.

father-in-law n suocero m.

fatherland n patria f.

fatherly adj paterno.

fathom n braccio m; * vt capire.

fatigue n fatica f, stanchezza f; * vt affaticare.

fatten vt ingrassare.
fatty adj grasso.
fatuous adj fatuo.
fault n difetto m; colpa f; faglia f; * vt criticare.
faultfinder n criticone m/f.
faultless adj impeccabile.
faulty adj difettoso.
fauna n fauna f.
faux pas n gaffe f.
favour n favore m; * vt favorire.
favourable adj favorevole.
favoured adj favorito.
favourite n preferito m.
favouritism n favoritismo m.
fawn n cerbiatto m; * adj, n fulvo m; * vi adulare.
fax n fax m.
fear vi temere, avere paura di; * n paura f.
fearful adj pauroso.
fearless adj intrepido.
feasibility n fattibilità f.
feasible adj realizzabile.
feast n pranzo m; banchetto m; festa f; * vi banchettare.
feat n impresa f; prodezza f.
feather n penna f, piuma f.
feather bed n letto m di piume.
feature n caratteristica f; * vt dare risalto a.
February n febbraio m.
feckless adj irresponsabile.
federal adj federale.
federate vt federare.
federation n federazione f.
fed-up adj stufo.
fee n onorario m.
feeble adj debole.
feebleness n debolezza f.
feed vt nutrire; alimentare; dar da mangiare a; * n pappa f; mangiata f; mangime m; foraggio m.
feedback n feedback m.
feel vt tastare, sentire; credere; provare; * n tatto m; sensazione f.

feeler n antenna f.
feeling n senso m, sensazione f; sentimento m; impressione f.
feign vt simulare, fingere.
feline adj felino.
fell vt abbattere.
fellow n uomo m; tipo m; membro m.
fellow citizen n concittadino m.
fellow countryman n compatriota m/f.
fellow feeling n simpatia f.
fellow men npl simili mpl.
fellowhsip n associazione f; borsa f di studio.
fellow student n compagno m di studi.
fellow traveller n compagno m di viaggio; filocomunista m/f.
felon n criminale m/f.
felony n crimine m.
felt n feltro m.
felt-tip pen n pennarello m.
female adj, n femmina f.
feminine adj femminile.
feminist n femminista m/f.
fen n zona f paludosa.
fence n recinto m; * vt recintare.
fencing n scherma f.
fender n paracenere m.
fennel n (bot) finocchio m.
ferment n fermento; * vi fermentare.
fern n (bot) felce f.
ferocious adj feroce.
ferocity n ferocia f.
ferret n furetto m; * vt **to ~ out** snidare.
ferry n traghetto m.
fertile adj fertile.
fertility n fertilità f.
fertilize vt fecondare; (agric) fertilizzare.
fervent adj fervente.
fervid adj fervente.
fervour n fervore m.

fester *vi* suppurare.
festival *n* festa *f*, festival *m*.
festive *adj* di festa.
festivity *n* festa *f*.
fetch *vt* andare a prendere.
fetching *adj* attraente.
fête *n* festa *f*.
fetid *adj* fetido.
fetish *n* feticcio *f*.
fettishist *n* feticista *m/f*.
fetter *vt* incatenare.
feud *n* faida *f*.
feudal *adj* feudale.
feudalism *n* feudalismo *m*.
fever *n* febbre *f*.
feverish *adj* febbrile.
few *n* poco *m*; * *adj* pochi; ~ **and far between** rari.
fewer *adj* meno.
fewest *adj* il minor numero di.
fiancé *n* fidanzato *m*.
fiancée *n* fidanzata *f*.
fiasco *n* fiasco *m*.
fib *n* frottola *f*.
fibber *n* bugiardo *m*.
fibre *n* fibra *f*.
fibreglass *n* fibra *f* di vetro.
fickle *adj* mutabile.
fiction *n* narrativa *f*; finzione *f*.
fictional *adj* immaginario.
fictitious *adj* fittizio.
fiddle *n* violino *m*; imbroglio *m*; * *vi* giocherellare; * *vt* falsificare.
fiddler *n* violinista *m/f*; imbroglione *m/f*.
fiddling *adj* insignificante.
fidelity *n* fedeltà *f*.
fidget *n* persona *f* irrequieta; * *vi* agitarsi.
fidgety *adj* irrequieto.
field *n* campo *m*.
fieldmouse *n* topo *m* campagnolo.
fieldwork *n* lavoro *m* sul campo.
fiend *n* demonio *m*.
fiendish *adj* diabolico.

fierce *adj* feroce; accanito.
fierceness *n* ferocia *f*
fiery *adj* infocato.
fifteen *adj*, *n* quindici *m*.
fifteenth *adj*, *n* quindicesimo *m*.
fifth *adj*, *n* quinto *m*.
fiftieth *adj*, *n* cinquantesimo *m*.
fifty *adj*, *n* cinquanta *f*.
fig *n* fico *m*.
fight *vt* combattere; lottare; * *n* combattimento *m*; lotta *f*.
fighter *n* combattente *m/f*.
fighting *n* combattimento *m*.
figurative *adj* figurativo.
figure *n* figura *f*; cifra *f*; linea *f*; * *vi* figurare; * *vt* **to ~ out** capire.
figurehead *n* (*naut*) polena *f*; figura *f* rappresentativa.
filament *n* filamento *m*.
filch *vt* rubacchiare.
filcher *n* ladruncolo *m*.
file *n* lima *f*; cartella *f*; archivio *m*; fila *f*; * *vt* limare; archiviare; * *vi* **to ~ past** sfilare davanti.
filial *adj* filiale.
filigree *n* filigrana *f*.
filing cabinet *n* casellario *m*.
fill *vt* riempire; orturare; **to ~ in** completare.
fillet *n* filetto *m*; * *vt* disossare.
filling *n* otturazione *f*; ripieno *m*; * *adj* sostanzioso.
fillip *n* stimolo *m*.
filly *n* puledra *f*.
film *n* film *m*, pellicola *f*; rullino *m*; strato *m* sottile; * *vi* filmare.
film star *n* divo *m* del cinema.
film strip *n* filmina *f*.
filter *n* filtro *m*; * *vt* filtrare.
filter-tipped *adj* con filtro.
filth *n* sudiciume *f*.
filthy *adj* sudicio.
fin *n* pinna *f*.
final *adj* ultimo, finale; * *n* finale *f*.

finale n finale m.
finalist n finalista m/f.
finalize vt definire.
finally n alla fine.
finance n finanza f; * vt finanziare.
financial adj finanziario.
financier n finanziatore m.
finch n fringuello m.
find vt trovare; **to ~ out** scoprire; **to ~ ones feet** ambientarsi; * n scoperta f.
findings npl conclusioni fpl.
fine adj fine, sottile, fino; ottimo; * excl bene; * n multa f; * vt multare.
fine arts npl belle arti fpl.
finely adv finemente.
finery n abiti mpl eleganti.
finesse n finezza f.
finger n dito m; * vt tastare.
fingernail n unghia f.
fingerprint n impronta f digitale.
fingertip n punta f del dito.
finicky adj pignolo.
finish vt, vi finire; * n fine f; traguardo m.
finishing line n traguardo m.
finishing school n scuola f di perfezionamento.
finite adj finito.
fir (tree) n abete m.
fire n fuoco m; incendio m; stufa f; * vt sparare; licenziare.
fire alarm n allarme m antincendio.
firearm n arma f da fuoco.
fire brigade n corpo m dei pompieri.
fire engine n autopompa f antincendio.
fire escape n scala f di sicurezza.
fire extinguisher n estintore m.
firefly n lucciola f.
fireman n pompiere m.
fireplace n caminetto m.

fireproof adj resistente al fuoco.
fireside n angolo m del focolare.
fire station n caserma f dei pompieri.
firewood n legna f da ardere.
fireworks n fuochi d'artificio.
firing n spari mpl.
firing squad n plotone m d'esecuzione.
firm adj saldo; fermo; definitivo; * n ditta f.
firmament n firmamento m.
firmness n fermezza f.
first adj, n primo m; * adv prima; **at ~** sulle prime; **~ly** innanzi tutto.
first aid n pronto soccorso m.
first-class adj prima classe f.
first-hand adj diretto.
first name n nome m.
first rate adj di prim'ordine.
fiscal adj fiscale.
fish n pesce m; * vi pescare.
fishbone n lisca f.
fisherman n pescatore m.
fish farm n allevamento m di pesce.
fishing n pesca f.
fishing line n lenza f.
fishing rod n canna f da pesca.
fishing tackle n attrezzatura f da pesca.
fishmonger n pescivendolo m.
fishy adj sospetto.
fissure n fessura f.
fist n pugno m.
fit n attacco m; accesso m; * adj adatto; in forma; * vt andare bene a; **to ~ out** equipaggiare; * vi **to ~ in** integrarsi.
fitment n accessorio m.
fitness n idoneità f; forma f.
fitted carpet n moquette f.
fitted kitchen n cucina f componibile.
fitter n installatore m.
fitting n prova f; * adj opportu-

no. ~s *npl* accessori *mpl*.

five *adj, n* cinque *m*.

fiver *n (fam)* biglietto *m* da cinque sterline.

fix *vt* fissare; riparare; sistemare; * *n* guaio *m*.

fixation *n* fissazione *f*.

fixative *n* fissativo *m*.

fixed *adj* fisso.

fixtures *npl* impianti *mpl*.

fizz *n* effervescenza *f*; * *vi* frizzare.

fizzy *adj* effervescente.

fjord *n* fiordo *m*.

flabbergasted *adj* sbalordito.

flabby *adj* flaccido.

flaccid *adj* flaccido.

flag *n* bandiera *f*; * *vi* stancarsi.

flagpole *n* pennone *m*.

flagrant *adj* flagrante.

flagship *n* nave *f* ammiraglia.

flail *vt* agitare.

flair *n* disposizione *f* naturale.

flak *n* fuoco *m* contraereo.

flake *n* scaglia *f*; * *vi* scrostarsi.

flaky *adj* scrostato.

flamboyant *adj* stravagante.

flame *n* fiamma *f*; * *vi* divampare

flamingo *n* fenicottero *m*.

flammable *adj* infiammabile.

flank *n* fianco *m*; * *vt* fiancheggiare.

flannel *n* flanella *f*.

flap *n* linguetta *f*; ribalta *f*; panico *m*; * *vt, vi* sbattere.

flare *vi* sfolgorare; * *n* chiarore *m*.

flared *adj* svasato.

flash *n* lampo *m*; flash *m*; * *vi* lampeggiare.

flash cube *n* flash *m*.

flashy *adj* vistoso.

flask *n* fiaschetta *f*; termos *m*.

flat *adj* piatto; sgonfio; stonato; categorico; bemolle; * *n* appartamento *m*; *(auto)* gomma *f* a terra.

flatness *n* monotonia *f*.

flatten *vt* spianare.

flatter *vt* lusingare.

flattering *adj* lusinghiero.

flattery *n* lusinghe *fpl*.

flatulence *n* flatulenza *f*.

flaunt *vt* sfoggiare.

flautist *n* flautista *m/f*.

flavour *n* gusto *m*; sapore *m*.

flavourless *adj* insipido.

flaw *n* difetto *m*.

flawless *adj* perfetto.

flax *n* lino *m*.

flea *n* pulce *f*.

fleck *n* macchiolina *f*.

fledgling *n* uccellino *m*.

flee *vt, vi* fuggire.

fleece *n* vello *m*; * *vt* pelare.

fleet *n* flotta *f*.

fleeting *adj* passeggero.

flesh *n* carne *f*.

flesh wound *n* ferita *f* superficiale.

fleshy *adj* carnoso.

flex *n* filo *m*; * *vt* stirare.

flexibility *n* flessibilità *f*.

flexible *adj* flessibile.

flick *n* colpetto *m*; * *vt* dare un colpetto.

flicker *vi* tremolare; * *n* tremolio *m*.

flier *n* aviatore *m*.

flight *n* volo *m*; rampa *f*; fuga *f*.

flight deck *n* cabina *f* di pilotaggio.

flighty *adj* frivolo.

flimsy *adj* leggero.

flinch *vi* trasalire.

fling *vt* lanciare.

flint *n* silice *f*.

flip *vi*; **to ~ through** sfogliare; * *n* colpetto *m*.

flippant *adj* irriverente.

flipper *n* pinna *f*.

flirt *n* civetta *f*.

flirtation *n* flirt *m*.

flit *vi* svolazzare.

float *vt* galleggiare; * *n* galleggiante *m*.

flock *n* gregge *m*; * *vi* ammassarsi.

flog *vt* frustare.

flogging *n* fustigazione *f*.

flood *n* inondazione *f*; * *vt* inondare; * *vi* straripare.

floodlight *n* riflettore *m*.

floor *n* pavimento *m*; piano *m*; * *vt* pavimentare; sconcertare.

floorboard *n* asse *f* di pavimento.

floor show *n* spettacolo *m*.

flop *n* fiasco *m*.

floppy *adj* floscio.

flora *n* flora *f*.

floral *adj* floreale.

florid *adj* florido.

florist *n* fioraio *m*.

flotilla *n* flottiglia *f*.

flounder *n* passera *f*; * *vi* impappinarsi; dibattersi.

flour *n* farina *f*.

flourish *vt* brandire; * *vi* prosperare; * *n* svolazzo *m*; ostentazione *f*.

flourishing *adj* fiorente.

flout *vt* contravvenire.

flow *vi* fluire; * *n* corrente *f*; flusso *m*.

flow chart *n* organigramma *m*.

flower *n* fiore *m*; * *vi* fiorire.

flowerbed *n* aiuola *f*.

flowerpot *n* vaso *m* da fiori.

flowery *adj* a fiori.

fluctuate *vi* fluttuare.

fluctuation *n* fluttuazione *f*.

flue *n* canna *f* fumaria.

fluency *n* scioltezza *f*.

fluent *adj* scorrevole; corrente.

fluff *n* peluria *f*; * *adj* ~**y** di peluche.

fluid *adj*, *n* fluido *m*.

fluidity *n* fluidità *f*.

fluke *n* colpo *m* di fortuna.

fluorescent *adj* fluorescente.

fluoride *n* fluoruro *m*.

flurry *n* agitazione *f*; raffica *f*.

flush *vi* arrossire; * *vt* tirare l'acqua; * *n* sciacquone *m*; rossore *m*; * *adj* ~ **with** a livello di.

fluster *vt* innervosire; * *n* stato di agitazione *f*.

flustered *adj* agitato.

flute *n* flauto *m*.

flutter *vt* battere; * *vi* svolazzare; * *n* battito *m*.

flux *n* cambiamento *m* continuo.

fly *vi* volare; * *n* mosca *f*.

flying *adj* volante; * *n* volo *m*; aviazione *f*.

flying saucer *n* disco *m* volante.

flypast *n* parata *f* aerea.

flysheet *n* soprattetto *m*.

foal *n* puledro *m*.

foam *n* schiuma *f*; * *vi* schiumeggiare.

foam rubber *n* gommapiuma *f*.

foamy *adj* spumoso.

focal *adj* focale.

focus *n* fuoco *m*.

fodder *n* foraggio *m*.

foe *n* nemico *m*.

foetal *adj* fetale.

feotus *n* feto *m*.

fog *n* nebbia *f*.

foggy *adj* nebbioso.

fog lamp *n* faro *m* antinebbia.

foible *n* debole *m*.

foil *vt* frustrare; * *n* carta *f* stagnola; fioretto *m*.

fold *n* ovile *m*; piega *f*; * *vt* piegare; * *vi* piegarsi.

folder *n* cartella *f*.

folding *adj* pieghevole.

foliage *n* fogliame *m*.

folio *n* foglio *m*.

folk *n* gente *f*.

folklore *n* folklore *m*.

folk song *n* canzone *m* folk.

follow *vt* seguire; **to ~ up** esaminare a fondo.

follower *n* seguace *m/f*.

following *adj* seguente; * *n* seguito *m*.

folly *n* pazzia *f*.

foment *vt* fomentare.

fond *adj* affezionato; grande.

fondent *n* fondente *m*.

fondle *vt* accarezzare.

fondness *n* predilezione *f*; affetto *m*.

font *n* fonte *f* battesimale.

food *n* cibo *m*.

food poisoning *n* intossicazione *f* alimentare.

foodstuffs *npl* generi *mpl* alimentari.

fool *n* sciocco *m*; buffone *m*; * *vt* ingannare.

foolhardy *adj* temerario.

foolish *adj* insensato.

foolproof *adj* infallibile.

foolscap *n* carta *f* protocollo.

foot *n* piede *m*; **to put one's ~ down** imporsi.

footage *n* metraggio *m*.

football *n* calcio *m*.

footballer *n* calciatore *m*.

footbridge *n* passerella *f*.

foothill *n* collina *f*.

foothold *n* punto *m* d'appoggio.

footing *n* punto *m* d'appoggio.

footlights *npl* luci *fpl* della ribalta.

footman *n* lacchè *m*.

footnote *n* postilla *f*.

footpath *n* sentiero *m*.

footprint *n* orma *f*.

footstep *n* passo *m*.

footwear *n* calzatura *f*.

for *prep* per; a favore di; da; **as ~ me** quanto a me; **what for?** perché? * *conj* poiché.

forage *n* foraggio *m*; * *vi* cercare.

foray *n* incursione *f*.

forbearance *n* pazienza *f*.

forbid *vt* proibire.

forbidding *adj* minaccioso.

force *n* forza *f*; **~s** le forze *f* armate; * *vt* forzare.

forced *adj* forzato.

forceful *adj* forte.

forceps *n* forcipe *m*.

forcible *adj* convincente.

ford *n* guado *m*; * *vt* guadare.

fore *n* prua *f*; davanti *m*; * *adj* anteriore.

forearm *n* avambraccio *m*.

foreboding *n* presentimento *m*.

forecast *vt* prevedere; * *n* previsione *f*.

forecourt *n* piazzale *m*.

forefathers *npl* progenitori *mpl*.

forefinger *n* indice *n*.

forefront *n* avanguardia *f*.

foregoing *adj* precedente.

foregone conclusion *n* risultato *m* scontato.

foreground *n* primo *m* piano.

forehead *n* fronte *f*.

foreign *adj* straniero; estero; estraneo.

foreigner *n* straniero *m*.

foreign exchange *n* valuta *f* estera.

foreleg *n* zampa *f* anteriore.

foreman *n* caposquadra *m*, caporeparto *m*.

foremost *adj* più importante.

forename *n* nome *m*.

forenoon *n* mattina *f*.

forensic medicine *n* medicina *f* legale.

forerunner *n* precursore *m*.

foresee *vt* prevedere.

foreseeable *adj* prevedibile.

foreshadow *vt* presagire.

foresight *n* previdenza *f*.

foreskin *n* prepuzio *m*.

forest *n* foresta *f*.

forestall *vt* anticipare.

forester *n* guardia *f* forestale.

forestry *n* silvicultura *f*.

foretaste *n* pregustamento *m*.

foretell *vt* predire.

forethought *n* previdenza *f*.

forever *adv* eternamente, per sempre.

forewarn *vt* preavvertire.

foreword *n* prefazione *f*.

forfeit *n* penitenza *f*; * *vt* perdere.

forge *n* fornace *f*; * *vt* forgiare; contraffare.

forger *n* contraffattore *m*.

forgery *n* contraffazione *f*.

forget *vt* dimenticare.

forgetful *adj* distratto.

forgetfulness *n* smemoratezza *f*.

forget-me-not *n* (*bot*) nontiscordardimé *m*.

forgive *vt* perdonare.

forgiveness *n* perdono *m*.

forgo *vt* rinunciare a.

fork *n* forchetta *f*; biforcazione *f*; * *vi* biforcarsi; * *vt* **to ~ out** sborsare.

forked *adj* biforcuto.

fork-lift truck *n* carello *m* elevatore.

forlorn *adj* sconsolato.

form *n* forma *f*; modulo *m*; banco *m*; classe *f*; * *vt* formare.

formal *adj* formale.

formality *n* formalità *f*.

format *n* formato *m*; * *vt* formattare.

formation *n* formazione *f*.

formative *adj* formativo.

former *adj* precedente; * *pron* **the ~** il primo.

formidable *adj* formidabile.

formula *n* formula *f*.

formulate *vt* formulare.

forsake *vt* abbandonare.

fort *n* forte *m*.

forte *n* forte *m*.

forthcoming *adj* prossimo, imminente.

forthright *adj* schietto.

forthwith *adj* subito.

fortieth *adj*, *n* quarantesimo *m*.

fortification *n* fortificazione *f*.

fortify *vt* fortificare; rafforzare.

fortitude *n* forza *f* d'animo.

fortnight *n* quindici giorni *mpl*.

fortress *n* fortezza *f*.

fortuitous *adj* fortuito.

fortunate *adj* fortunato.

fortune *n* fortuna *f*.

fortune-teller *n* chiromante *m*/*f*.

forty *adj*, *n* quaranta *m*.

forum *n* foro *m*.

forward *adj* in avanti; precoce; **~s** *adv* avanti * *n* attaccante *m*; * *vt* inoltrare.

forwardness *n* sfacciataggine *f*.

fossil *adj n* fossile *m*.

foster *vt* allevare; nutrire.

foster parent *n* genitore *m* affidatario.

foul *adj* disgustoso; * *n* fallo *m*; * *vt* impestare; sporcare.

foul play *n* gioco *m* scorretto; assassinio *m*.

found *vt* fondare.

foundation *n* fondazione *f*.

founder *n* fondatore *m*; * *vi* affondare.

foundling *n* trovatello *m*.

foundry *n* fonderia *f*.

fount *n* sorgente *f*.

fountain *n* fontana *f*.

four *adj*, *n* quattro *m*.

fourfold *adj* quadruplo.

four-letter word *n* parolaccia *f*.

four-poster (bed) letto *m* a baldacchino.

foursome *n* partita *f* a quattro.

fourteen *adj*, *n* quattordici *m*.

fourteenth *adj*, *n* quattordicesimo *m*.

fourth *adj*, *n* quarto *m*.

fowl *n* pollame *m*.

fox *n* volpe *f*; * *vt* lasciare perplesso

foxglove *n* digitale *f*.

foyer *n* foyer *m*.

fracas n rissa f.
fraction n frazione f.
fracture n frattura f.
fragile adj fragile.
fragility n fragilità f.
fragment n frammento m.
fragmentary adj frammentario.
fragrance n fragranza f.
fragrant adj fragrante.
frail adj debole.
frailty n debolezza f.
frame n corporatura f; montatura f; telaio m; cornicia f; * vt incorniciare.
frame of mind n umore m.
framework n struttura f.
franc n franco m.
franchise n concessione f; franchigia f.
frank adj franco; * vt affrancare.
frankness n franchezza f.
frantic adj frenetico.
fraternal adj fraterno.
fraternity n fraternità f.
fraternize vi fraternizzare.
fratricide adj, n fratricida m/f.
fraud n truffa f.
fraudulent adj fraudolento.
fraught adj teso.
fray n zuffa f; * vi consumarsi.
freak n eccentrico m; capriccio m; * adj anormale.
freckle n lentiggine f.
freckled adj lentigginoso.
free adj libero; gratuito; * vt liberare.
freedom n libertà f.
free-for-all n parapiglia f generale.
freehold n proprietà f assoluta.
freelance n collaboratore m esterno.
freely adv liberamente.
freemason n massone m.
freemasonry n massoneria f.
freepost n affrancatura f a ca-

rica del destinatario.
free-range adj ruspante.
fresia n fresia f.
free trade n liberoscambismo m.
freewheel vi andare a ruota libera, andare in folle.
free will n spontanea volontà f.
freeze vt gelare, congelare, surgelare; * vi gelare, congelarsi; * n gelata f.
freeze-dried adj liofilizzato.
freezer n congelatore m.
freezing adj gelido.
freezing point n punto m di congelamento.
freight n nolo m.
freighter n piroscafo m da carico.
French bean n fagiolino m.
French fries npl patatine fpl fritte.
French window n porta f finestra.
frenzied adj forsennato, frenetico.
frenzy n frenesia f.
frequency n frequenza f.
frequent adj frequente; * vt frequentare.
fresco n affresco m.
fresh adj fresco; sfacciato; ~ water acqua dolce; * adv appena.
freshen vt, vi rinfrescare.
fresher n matricola f.
freshly adv appena.
freshness f freschezza f.
fret vi preoccuparsi.
friar n frate m.
friction n frizione f.
Friday n venerdì m; **Good ~** Venerdì m Santo.
fridge n frigo m.
fried adj fritto.
friend n amico m; **Society of ~s** Quaccheri mpl.
friendliness n cordialità f.

friendly *adj* amichevole.
friendship *n* amicizia *f*.
frieze *n* fregio *m*.
frigate *n* (*mar*) fregata *f*.
fright *n* spavento *m*.
frighten *vt* spaventare.
frightened *adj* spaventato, impaurito.
frightening *adj* spaventoso.
frightful *adj* terribile.
frigid *adj* frigido.
fringe *n* frangia *f*.
fringe benefits *npl* vantaggi *mpl*.
frisk *vt* perquisire.
frisky *adj* vispo.
fritter *n* frittella *f*; * *vt* sprecare.
frivolity *n* frivolezza *f*.
frivolous *adj* frivolo.
frizzy *adj* crespo.
fro *adv*: **to go to and ~ between** fare la spola tra.
frock *n* vestito *m*; tonaca *f*.
frog *n* rana *f*.
frolic *vi* sgambettare.
frolicsome *adj* giocoso.
from *prep* da; per.
frond *n* fronda *f*.
front *n* davanti *m*; fronte *m*; lungomare *m*; *adj* davanti.
frontal *adj* frontale.
front door *n* porta *f* d'ingresso.
frontier *n* frontiera *f*, confine *m*.
front page *n* prima pagina *f*.
front-wheel drive *n* trasmissione *f* anteriore.
frost *n* brina *f*, gelo *m*.
frostbite *n* congelamento *m*.
frostbitten *adj* congelato.
frosted glass *n* vetro *m* smerigliato.
frosty *adj* gelido; glaciale.
froth *n* schiuma *f*; * *vi* schiumare.
frothy *adj* schiumoso.
frown *vi* aggrottare le sopracciglia; * *n* cipiglio *m*.

frozen *adj* congelato, surgelato.
frugal *adj* frugale.
fruit *n* frutta *f*; frutto *m*.
fruiterer *n* fruttivendolo *m*.
fruitful *adj* fruttifero; fruttuoso.
fruition *vi*: **to come to ~** realizzarsi.
fruit juice *n* succo *m* di frutta.
fruitless *adj* vano.
fruit salad *n* macedonia *f*.
fruit tree *n* albero *m* da frutto.
frustrate *vt* frustrare.
frustated *adj* frustrato.
frustration *n* frustrazione *f*.
fry *vt* friggere.
frying pan *n* padella *f*.
fuchsia *n* fucsia *f*.
fuck *vt* fottere.
fudge *n* caramella *f* fondente.
fuel *n* combustibile *m*.
fuel tank *n* serbatoio *m* del carburante.
fugitive *adj*, *n* fuggitivo *m*.
fugue *n* (*mus*) fuga *f*.
fulcrum *n* fulcro *m*.
fulfil *vt* compiere.
fulfilment *n* compimento *m*; soddisfazione *f*.
full *adj* pieno.
full-length *adj* lungo; (*film*) a lungometraggio.
full moon *n* luna *f* piena.
fullness *n* abbondanza *f*; ampiezza *f*.
full-scale *adj* su vasta scala.
full-time *adj* tempo pieno.
fully *adv* completamente.
fulsome *adj* insincero.
fumble *vi* brancolare; andare a tentoni.
fume *n* esalazione *f*; * *vi* emettere fumo (o vapore); essere arrabbiatissimo.
fumigate *vt* suffumicare.
fun *n* divertimento *m*.
function *n* funzione *f*.

functional *adj* funzionale.
fund *n* fondo *m*; * *vt* finanziare.
fundamental *adj* fondamentale.
funeral *n* funerale *m*.
funereal *adj* funereo.
fun fair *n* luna park *m*.
fungus *n* muffa *f*.
funnel *n* imbuto *m*.
funny *adj* buffo.
fur *n* pelo *m*.
fur coat *n* pelliccia *f*.
furious *adj* furioso.
furlong *n* 201 metri.
furlough *n* (*mil*) congedo *m*.
furnace *n* fornace *f*.
furnish *vt* arredare; fornire.
furnishings *npl* mobili *mpl*
furniture *n* mobili *mpl*.
furore *n* scalpore *m*.
furrier *n* pellicciaio *m*.
furrow *n* solco *m*; * *vt* solcare.

furry *adj* peloso.
further *adv* più avanti; oltre; ~
to con riferimento a; * *adj* ulteriore; * *vt* favorire.
further education *n* istruzione
f superiore.
furthermore *adv* inoltre.
furthest *adv*, *adj* più lontano.
furtive *adj* furtivo.
fury *n* furia *f*.
fuse *n* fusibile *m*; * *vt* fondere.
fuse box *n* scatola *f* dei fusibili.
fuselage *n* fusoliera *f*.
fusion *n* fusione *f*.
fuss *adj* agitazione *f*; storie *fpl*.
fussy *adj* pignolo; schizzinoso.
futile *adj* futile.
futility *n* futilità *f*.
future *adj*, *n* futuro *m*.
fuzz *n* peluria *f*; (*fam*) polizia *f*.
fuzzy *adj* crespo; sfocato.

G

gab *n*: **to have the gift of the**
~ avere la lingua sciolta.
gabardine *n* gabardine *m*.
gabble *vt* borbottare.
gable *n* frontone *m*.
gadget *n* aggeggio *m*.
gaffe *n* gaffe *f*.
gag *n* bavaglio *m*; gag *f*; * *vt* imbavagliare.
gaggle *n* branco *m*.
gaiety *n* allegria *f*.
gaily *adv* allegramente.
gain *n* aumento *m*; guadagno
m; * *vt* ottenere; guadagnare;
aumentare.
gainful *adj* remunerativo.
gait *n* andatura *f*.
gala *n* festa *f*; gala *m*.
galaxy *n* galassia *f*.

gale *n* bufera *f*.
gall *n* bile *f*.
gallant *adj* gallante.
gall bladder *n* cistifellea *f*.
gallery *n* galleria *f*; tribuna *f*;
museo *m*.
galley *n* galea *f*.
gallon *n* gallone *m*.
gallop *n* galoppo *m*; * *vi* galoppare.
gallows *npl* patibolo *m*.
gallstone *n* calcolo *m* biliare.
galore *adv* a profusione.
galvanize *vt* galvanizzare.
gambit *n* gambetto *m*.
gamble *vt*, *vi* giocare d'azzardo;
* *n* azzardo *m*.
gambler *n* giocatore *m* d'azzardo.

gambling n gioco m d'azzardo.

game n gioco m; partita f; selvaggina f.

gamekeeper n guardacaccia m.

gammon n prosciutto m affumicato.

gamut n (mus) gamma f.

gander n maschio dell'oca.

gang n banda f.

gangrene n cancrena f.

gangster n gangster m.

gangway n passerella f.

gap n spazio m; vuoto m; intervallo m.

gape vi spalancarsi.

gaping adj a bocca aperta; aperto.

garage n autorimessa f, garage m; officina f.

garbled adj ingarbugliato.

garden n giardino m.

gardener n giardiniere m.

gardening n giardinaggio m.

gargle vi fare i gargarismi; * n gargarismo m; collutorio m.

gargoyle n gargolla f.

garish adj sgargiante.

garland n ghirlanda f.

garlic n aglio m.

garment n indumento m.

garnish vt guarnire; * n decorazione f.

garret n soffitta f.

garrison n (mil) guarnigione f.

garrulous adj loquace.

garter n giarrettiera f.

gas n gas m; * vt asfissiare col gas.

gas cylinder n bombola f.

gaseous adj gassoso.

gas fire n stufa f a gas.

gash n squarcio m; * vt squarciare.

gasket n guarnizione f.

gasp vi ansare; * n anelito m.

gas mask n maschera f antigas.

gas meter n contattore m del gas.

gas ring n fornello m a gas.

gassy adj gassoso.

gastric adj gastrico.

gastronomic adj gastronomico.

gasworks n impianto m di produzione del gas.

gate n cancello m.

gateway n porta f.

gate-crasher n intruso m.

gather vt radunare; raccogliere; dedurre.

gathering n raduno m.

gauche adj goffo.

gaudy adj vistoso.

gauge n calibro m; * vt misurare.

gaunt adj emaciato.

gauntlet n guanto m.

gauze n garza f.

gay adj allegro; omosessuale.

gaze vi fissare; * n sguardo m.

gazelle n gazzella f.

gazette n gazzetta f.

gear n cambio m, marcia f; attrezzatura f.

gearbox n scatola f del cambio.

gear lever n leva f del cambio.

gear wheel n ruota f dentata.

gel n gel m.

gelatine n gelatina f.

gelignite n gelatina f esplosiva.

gem n gemma f.

Gemini n Gemelli mpl.

gender n genere m.

gene n gene m.

genealogical adj genealogico.

genealogy n genealogia f.

general adj generale; * adv in ~ generalmente; * n generale m.

general election n elezioni fpl legislative.

generality n generalità f.

generalization n generalizzazione f.

generalize vi generalizzare.

generate vt generare.

generation n produzione f; generazione f.

generator n generatore m.

generic adj generico.

generosity n generosità f.

generous adj generoso.

genetics npl genetica f.

genial adj cordiale.

genitals npl genitali mpl.

genitive n genitivo m.

genius n genio m.

genteel adj snob.

gentile n gentile m.

gentle adj dolce.

gentleman n signore m; gentiluomo m.

gentleness n tenerezza f.

gently adv dolcemente.

gentry n piccola nobiltà f.

gents n toilette per uomini.

genuflect vi genuflettersi.

genuine adj genuino.

genus n genere m.

geographer n geografo m.

geographical adj geografico.

geography n geografia f.

geological adj geologico.

geologist n geologo m.

geology n geologia f.

geometric(al) adj geometrico.

geometry n geometria f.

geranium n (bot) geranio m.

geriatric adj geriatrico.

germ n (med) microbo m.

germinate vi germinare.

gestation n gestazione f.

gesticulate vi gesticolare.

gesture n gesto m.

get vt ottenere; ricevere; prendere; portare; afferrare; * vi arrivare a; diventare; cominciare a; farsi; **to ~ the better of** prevalere su qualcuno.

geyser n (geog) geyser m; scaldabagno m.

ghastly adj orrendo.

gherkin n cetriolino m.

ghost n fantasma m.

giant n gigante m.

gibberish n parole fpl incomprensibili.

gibbon n gibbone m.

gibe vi lanciare frecciate; * n frecciata f.

giblets npl frattaglie fpl.

giddiness n vertigine f.

giddy adj vertiginoso.

gift n dono m; regalo m.

gifted adj dotato.

gift voucher n buono m premio.

gigantic adj gigantesco.

giggle vi ridacchiare; * n risolino m.

gild vt dorare.

gilding, gilt n doratura f.

gill n branchia f; 0,142 litri.

gilt-edged adj di massima sicurezza.

gimmick n trovata f.

gin n gin m.

ginger n zenzero m; rossiccio m.

giraffe n giraffa f.

girder n trave f.

girdle n busto m.

girl n ragazza f.

girlfriend n amica f.

girlish adj di ragazza.

giro n postagiro m.

girth n circonferenza f.

gist n succo m.

give vt dare; regalare; attribuire; dedicare; * vi dare; donare; cedere; **to ~ away** rivelare; **to ~ back** restituire; **to ~ in** cedere; **to ~ off** sprigionare; **to ~ out** distribuire; **to ~ up** rinunciare.

gizzard n ventriglio m.

glacial adj glaciale.

glacier n ghiacciaio m.

glad adj contento; lieto; **I am ~ to see** mi fa molto piacere.

gladden vt rallegrare.

gladiator n gladiatore m.

glamorous adj affascinante; seducente.

glamour n fascino m.

glance n occhiata f; * vi dare un' occhiata a.

glancing adj di striscio.

gland n ghiandola f.

glare n bagliore m; * vi sfolgorare; **to ~ at** fulminare con lo sguardo.

glaring adj accecante; palese.

glass n vetro m; bicchiere m; calice m; **~es** npl occhiali mpl.

glassware n cristalleria f.

glassy adj vitreo.

glaze n smalto m.

glazier n vetraio m.

gleam n lucichio m; * vi luccicare.

gleaming adj lucente.

glean vt racimolare.

glee n gioia f.

glen n vallone m.

glib adj disinvolto.

glide vi planare; * n planata f.

glider n aliante m.

gliding n volo m con l'aliante.

glimmer n barlume m; * vi baluginare.

glimpse n sguardo passeggero; * vt intravedere.

glint vi scintillare; * n scintillio m.

glisten, glitter vi luccicare.

gloat vi gongolare.

global adj globale.

globe n globo m; mappamondo m.

gloom, gloominess n buio m.

gloomy adj cupo; deprimente.

glorification n glorificazione f.

glorify vt glorificare.

glorious adj glorioso.

glory n gloria f.

gloss n glossa f; lucentezza f; * vt chiosare; **to ~ over** mascherare.

glossary n glossario m.

glossy adj lucido.

glove n guanto m.

glove compartment n vano m portaoggetti.

glow vi ardere; rosseggiare; * n incandescenza f.

glower vi guardare con astio.

glucose n glucosio m.

glue n colla f; * vt incollare.

gluey adj colloso.

glum adj cupo.

glut n sovrabbondanza f.

glutinous adj appiccicoso.

glutton n ghiottone m.

gluttony n ghiottoneria f.

glycerine n glicerina f.

gnarled adj nodoso.

gnash vt digrignare.

gnat n zanzara f.

gnaw vt rosicchiare.

gnome n gnomo m.

gnu n gnu m.

go vi andare; andarsene; arrivare; **to ~ ahead** tirare avanti; **to ~ back** ritornare; **to ~ by** passare; **to ~ for** avventarsi; **to ~ in** entrare; **to ~ off** guastarsi; **to ~ on** continuare; **to ~ out** uscire; **to ~ up** salire; * n dinamismo m; tentativo m;

goad vt spronare.

go-ahead adj intraprendente; * n benestare m.

goal n goal m; scopo m.

goalkeeper n portiere m.

goalpost n palo m.

goat n capra f.

goatherd n capraio m.

gobble vt trangugiare.

go-between n intermediario m.

goblet n calice m.

goblin n folletto m.

God n Dio m.

godchild n figlioccio m.

goddaughter n figlioccia f.

goddess n dea f.

godfather n padrino m.

godforsaken adj sperduto.

godhead n divinità f.

godless adj empio.

godlike adj divino.

godliness n santità f.

godly adj pio.

godmother n madrina f.

godsend n dono del cielo; manna f.

godson n figlioccio m.

goggle vi sbarrare gli occhi.

goggles npl occhiali mpl.

going n andatura f; * adj ben avviato; corrente.

gold n oro m.

golden adj d'oro; ~ **rule** n regola f principale.

goldfish n pesce m rosso.

goldsmith n orefice m.

golf n golf m.

golf club n mazza f da golf; circolo m di golf.

golf course n campo m di golf.

golfer n giocatore m di golf.

gondola n gondola f.

gondolier n gondoliere m.

gong n gong m.

gonorrhoea n gonorrea f.

good adj buono; bello; bravo; gentile; * n bene m; ~**s** npl merci fpl.

goodbye! excl arrivederci! * n addio m.

goodies npl chicche fpl.

good-looking adj bello, piacente.

good-natured adj affabile.

goodness n bontà f.

goodwill n buona f volontà; avviamento m.

goose n oca f.

gooseberry n uva f spina.

goosepimples npl pelle f d'oca.

gore n spicchio m; * vt incornare.

gorge n (geog) gola f; * vt rimpinzarsi.

gorgeous adj sontuoso, splendido.

gorilla n gorilla m.

gormless adj tonto.

gorse n ginestra f spinosa.

gory adj sanguinoso.

goshawk n astore m.

gospel n vangelo m.

gossamer n mussolina f.

gossip n pettegolezzi mpl; pettegolo m; * vi chiacchierare.

gothic adj gotico.

gouge vt scavare.

goulash n gulasch m.

gourd n zucca f.

gourmet n buongustaio m.

gout n gotta f.

govern vt governare.

governess n governante f.

government n governo m.

governor n governatore m.

gown n abito m; toga f.

grab vt afferrare.

grace n grazia f; garbo m; proroga f; **to say** ~ dire il benedicite; * vt onorare.

graceful adj aggraziato, garbato.

gracious adj cortese; misericordioso.

gradation n gradazione f.

grade n categoria f; voto m; grado m; * vt classificare; graduare.

gradient n gradiente m.

gradual adj graduale.

graduate vi laurearsi; * n laureato m.

graduation n consegna delle lauree.

graffiti n graffiti mpl.

graft n innesto m; duro lavoro m; * vt innestare.

grain n cereali mpl; granello m; grana f.

gram n grammo m.

grammar n grammatica f.

grammatical adj grammaticale.

gramophone n grammofono m.

granary n granaio m.

grand adj magnifico; alto locato; eccezionale.

grandchild n nipote m/f.

granddad n nonno m.

granddaughter n nipotina f.

grandeur n grandiosità f.

grandfather n nonno m.

grandiose adj grandioso.

grandma n nonna f.

grandmother n nonna f.

grandparents npl nonni mpl.

grand piano n pianoforte m a coda.

grandson n nipotino m.

grandstand n tribuna f coperta.

granite n granito m.

granny n nonna f.

grant vt accordare; ammettere; **to take for ~ed** dare per scontato; * n sovvenzione f; borsa f di studio.

granulate vt granulare.

granule n granello m.

grape n chicco m d'uva; **bunch of ~s** grappolo m d'uva.

grapefruit n pompelmo m.

grapevine n vite f.

graph n grafico m.

graphic(al) adj grafico.

graphics npl grafica f.

grasp vt afferrare; * presa f; padronanza f.

grasping adj avido.

grass n erba f.

grasshopper n cavalletta f.

grassland n prateria f.

grass-roots npl base f.

grass snake n biscia f.

grassy adj erboso.

grate n grata f; * vt grattare; * vi cigolare.

grateful adj grato.

gratefulness n riconoscenza f.

gratification n soddisfazione f.

gratify vt soddisfare.

gratifying adj soddisfacente.

grating n grata f; * adj stridulo.

gratis adv gratis.

gratitude n gratitudine f.

gratuitous adj gratuito.

gratuity n mancia f.

grave n tomba f; * adj grave.

grave digger n becchino m.

gravel n ghiaia f.

gravestone n lapide f.

graveyard n cimitero m.

gravitate vi gravitare.

gravitation n gravitazione f.

gravity n gravità f.

gravy n sugo m dell'arrosto.

graze vi pascolare; * vt scorticare; * n scorticatura f.

grease n grasso m, unto m; * vt ungere, lubrificare.

greaseproof adj: ~ **paper** carta f oleata.

greasy adj untuoso, unto.

great adj grande; meraviglioso; eminente.

greatness n grandezza f.

greed n avidità f.

greedy adj avido; goloso.

Greek n greco m.

green adj, n verde m; ~**s** npl verdura f.

green belt n zona f verde.

greenery n verde m.

greengrocer n fruttivendolo m.

greenhouse n serra f.

greenish adj verdastro.

greet vt salutare.

greeting n saluto m.

greetings card n cartolina d'auguri.

grenade n granata f.

grenadier n granatiere m.

grey adj, n grigio m.

greyhound n levriero m.

grid n grata f; rete f.

gridiron n graticolo m.

grief n dolore m.

grievance n lagnanza f.

grieve vt addolorare.

grievous adj penoso.

griffin n grifone m.

grill n griglia f; * vt cuocere alla griglia.

grille n inferriata f.

grim adj torvo; macabro.

grimace n smorfia f.

grime n sudiciume m.

grimy adj sudicio.

grin n largo sorriso m; * vi fare un largo sorriso.

grind vt macinare; * n trantran m.

grinder n macinino m.

grip n presa f; borsone m; * vt stringere.

gripe n colica f.

gripping adj appassionante.

grisly adj raccapricciante.

gristle n cartilagine f.

gristly adj cartilaginoso.

grit n pietrisco m.

grizzle vi piagnucolare.

groan vi gemere; * n gemito m.

grocer n negoziante m/f di alimentari.

groceries npl spesa f.

grocery n alimentari m.

groggy adj intontito.

groin n inguine m.

groom n palafreniere m; sposo m; * vt governare; aver cura di.

groove n solco m.

grope vi cercare a tastoni.

gross adj obeso; grossolano; lordo; * n grossa f.

grotesque adj grottesco.

grotto n grotta f.

ground n terra f, terreno m; campo m; motivo m; ~s fondi mpl; * vi incagliarsi.

ground floor n pian m terreno.

grounding n fondamento m; basi fpl.

groundless adj infondato.

groundsheet n telone m impermeabile.

groundwork n lavoro m preparatorio.

group n gruppo m; complesso m; * vt raggruppare.

grouse n urogallo m; mugugno m; * vi brontolare.

grove n boschetto m.

grovel vi strisciare.

grow vi crescere; aumentare; diventare; **to ~ up** diventare grande; * vt coltivare; aumentare.

grower n coltivatore m.

growing adj crescente; * n coltura f.

growl vi ringhiare; * n ringhio m.

grown-up n adulto m.

growth n crescita f; tumore m.

grub n larva f; (fam) cibo m.

grubby adj sudicio.

grudge n rancore m; * vt invidiare; dare a malincuore.

grudgingly adv malvolentieri.

gruelling adj estenuante.

gruesome adj agghiacciante.

gruff adj burbero.

grumble vi brontolare; * n brontolio m.

grumpy adj scorbutico.

grunt vi grugnire; * n grugnito m.

G-string n tanga m.

guarantee n garanzia f; * vt garantire.

guard n guardia f; protezione f; * vt fare la guardia a.

guarded adj circospetto.

guardroom n (mil) corpo m di guardia.

guardian n tutore m.

guardianship n tutela f.

guerrilla n guerrigliero m.

guerrilla warfare n guerriglia f.

guess vt, vi indovinare; supporre; * n supposizione f.

guesswork n congettura f.

guest n ospite m/f, invitato m.

guest room n camera f degli ospiti.

guesthouse n pensione f familiare.
guffaw n risata f fragorosa.
guidance n guida f; consigli mpl.
guida vt guidare; * n guida f; manuale m.
guide dog n cane m per ciechi.
guidelines npl direttive fpl.
guidebook n guida f.
guild n corporazione f.
guile n astuzia f.
guillotine n ghigliottina f; * vt ghigliottinare.
guilt n colpa f, colpevolezza f.
guiltless adj senza colpa.
guilty adj colpevole.
guinea pig n porcellino m d'India; cavia f.
guise n sembianza f.
guitar n chitarra f.
guitarist n chitarrista m/f.
gulf n golfo m; abisso m.
gull n gabbiano m.
gullet n gola f.
gullibility n credulità f.
gullible adj credulone.
gully n burrone m.
gulp n boccata f; * vt inghiottire.
gum n gengiva f; colla f; * vt incollare.
gum tree n eucalipto m.
gun n fucile m, pistola f, rivoltella f.

gunboat n cannoniera f.
gun carriage n affusto m.
gunfire n colpi mpl d'arma da fuoco.
gunman n uomo m armato.
gunner n artigliere m.
gunpoint n; **at ~** sotto la minaccia delle armi.
gunpowder n polvere f da sparo.
gunshot n sparo m.
gunsmith n armaiolo m.
gurgle n gorgoglio m; * vt gorgogliare.
guru n guru m.
gush vi sgorgare; * n ondata f.
gushing adj sgorgante; espansivo.
gusset n gherone m.
gust n folata f, raffica f.
gusto n gusto m.
gusty adj ventoso.
gut n intestino m; budello m; **~s** npl budella f; * vt sventrare.
gutter n grondaia f, cunetta f.
guttural adj gutturale.
guy n tizio m; tirante m.
guzzle vt ingozzare.
gym(nasium) n palestra f.
gymnast n ginnasta m/f.
gymnastic adj ginnastico; * n **~s** ginnastica f.
gynaecologist n ginecologo m.
gypsy n zingaro m.
gyrate vi roteare.

H

haberdasher n merciaio f.
haberdashery n merceria f.
habit n abitudine f; tonaca f.
habitable adj abitabile.
habitat n habitat m.
habitation n abitazione f.
habitual adj abituale.

hack n fendente m; scribacchino m; * vt tagliare.
hackneyed adj trito.
hacksaw n seghetto m per metalli.
haddock n eglefino m.
haematology n ematologia f.

haemoglobin n emoglobina f.
haemophilia n emofilia f.
haemorrhage n emorragia f.
haemorrhoids npl emorroidi fpl.
hag n befana f.
haggard adj tirato.
haggle vi contrattare.
hail n grandine f; * vi grandinare; * vt acclamare.
hailstone n chicco m di grandine.
hair n capelli mpl; chioma f; pelo m.
hairbrush n spazzola f per capelli.
haircut n taglio m dei capelli.
hairdo n pettinatura f.
hairdresser n parrucchiere m.
hair-dryer n asciugacapelli m, fon m.
hairless adj senza peli.
hairnet n reticella f.
hairpin n forcina f.
hairpin bend n tornante m.
hair remover n depilatore m.
hairspray n lacca f.
hairstyle n acconciatura f.
hairy adj peloso.
hake n nasello m.
halcyon adj sereno.
half n metà f; * adj metà, mezzo.
half-caste n meticcio m.
half-hearted adj svogliato.
half-hour n mezz'ora f.
half-moon n mezzaluna f.
half-price adj, adv a metà prezzo.
half-time n intervallo m.
halfway adv a metà strada.
half-yearly adj semestrale.
halibut n ippoglosso m.
halitosis n alitosi f.
hall n entrata f; salone m; villa f.
hallmark n marchio m.
hallow vt consacrare.

hallucination n allucinazione f.
halo n aureola f.
halt vt fermare; * vi fermarsi; * n fermata f; sosta f.
halting adj esitante.
halve vt dimezzare.
ham n prosciutto m; radioamatore m.
hamburger n hamburger m.
hamlet n paesino m.
hammer n martello m; * vt martellare.
hammock n amaca f.
hamper n cesto m; * vt ostacolare.
hamster n criceto m.
hamstring n tendine m del ginocchio.
hand n mano f; at ~ a portata di mano; * vt passare; consegnare.
handbag n borsa f.
handbook n manuale m.
handbrake n freno m a mano.
handcuffs npl manette fpl.
handful n manciata f.
handicap n menomazione; handicap m.
handicapped adj andicappato.
handicraft n artigianato m.
handiwork n lavorazione f a mano.
handkerchief n fazzoletto m.
handle n manico m; * vt maneggiare; trattare.
handlebars npl manubrio m.
handrail n corrimano m.
handshake n stretto m di mano.
handsome adj bello; considerevole.
handwriting n scrittura f.
handy adj sottomano; comodo.
handyman n tuttofare m.
hang vt appendere; impiccare; * vi pendere.
hangar n aviorimessa f.
hanger n gruccia f.

hanger-on *n* parassita *m/f*.
hang-gliding *n* deltaplano *m*.
hangman *n* boia *m*.
hangover *n* postumi *mpl* di una sbornia.
hang-up *n* complesso *m*.
hanker *vi* avere molto desiderio di.
haphazard *adj* casuale.
hapless *adj* sfortunato.
happen *vi* succedere; capitare; accadere.
happening *n* avvenimento *m*.
happily *adv* tranquillamente.
happiness *n* felicità *f*.
happy *adj* contento, felice.
happy-go-lucky *adj* spensierato.
harangue *n* aringa *f*; * *vt* aringare.
harass *vt* assillare.
harbinger *n* foriero *m*.
harbour *n* porto *m*; * *vt* covare.
hard *adj* duro; rigido; forte; difficile; ~ **of hearing** duro d'orecchio.
hardboard *n* faesite *f*.
hard-boiled *adj* sodo.
harden *vt* indurire.
hard-headed *adj* pratico.
hard-hearted *adj* duro (di cuore)
hardiness *n* resistenza *f*.
hardly *adv* appena.
hardness *n* durezza *f*.
hardship *n* privazioni *fpl*.
hard-up *adj* al verde.
hardware *n* ferramenta *fpl*.
hardwearing *adj* resistente.
hardy *adj* robusto.
hare *n* lepre *f*.
hare-brained *adj* insensato.
hare-lip *n* labbro *n* leporino.
harem *n* harem *m*.
haricot *n* fagiolo *m* bianco.
harlequin *n* arlecchino *m*.
harm *n* male *m*; danno *m*; * *vt* nuocere a; danneggiare.

harmful *adj* nocivo.
harmless *adj* innocuo.
harmonic *adj* armonico.
harmonica *n* armonica *f*.
harmonious *adj* armonioso.
harmonize *vt*, *vi* armonizzare.
harmony *n* armonia *f*.
harness *n* bardatura *f*; briglie *fpl*; * *vt* bardare.
harp *n* arpa *f*.
harpist *n* arpista *m/f*.
harpoon *n* arpione *m*.
harpsichord *n* clavicembalo *m*.
harrow *n* erpice *m*.
harrowing *adj* straziante.
harry *vt* assillare.
harsh *adj* severo.
harshness *n* severità *f*.
harvest *n* raccolto *m*; * *vt* fare il raccolto di.
harvester *n* (combine) mietitrice *f*.
hash *n* pasticcio *m*.
hashish *n* hascisc *m*.
hassock *n* inginocchiatoio *m*.
haste *n* fretta *f*; **to make ~** affrettarsi.
hasten *vt* accelerare.
hastily *adv* in fretta e furia.
hasty *adj* affrettato.
hat *n* cappello *m*.
hatch *vt* elaborare; * *vi* schiudersi; * *n* boccaporto *m*.
hatchback *n* (*auto*) macchina *f* a tre/cinque porte.
hatchet *n* accetta *f*.
hate *n* odio *m*; * *vt* odiare.
hateful *adj* odioso.
hatred *n* odio *m*.
hatter *n* cappellaio *m*.
hat-trick *n* vincere per tre volte consecutive.
haughty *adj* superbo.
haul *vt* trascinare; * *n* tragitto *m*; retata *f*.
haulage *n* autotrasporto *m*.
haulier *n* autotrasportatore *m*.

haunch n coscia f.

haunt vt frequentare; abitare; * n covo m.

haunted adj abitato dai fantasmi.

have vt avere; possedere; fare; tenere.

haven n rifugio m.

haversack n zaino m.

havoc n danni mpl.

hawk n falco m; * vt vendere per strada.

hawthorn n biancospino m.

hay n fieno m.

hay fever n raffreddore m da fieno.

hayloft n fienile m.

haystack n pagliaio m.

hazard n rischio m; * vt rischiare.

hazardous adj rischioso.

haze n foschia f.

hazel n nocciolo m; * adj nocciola.

hazelnut n nocciola f.

hazy adj sfocato.

he pron egli, lui.

head n testa f; capo m; * vt essere in testa a.

headache n mal f di testa; grattacapo m.

headdress n copricapo m.

headland n capo m.

headlight n fanale m.

headlong adv a capofitto.

headmaster n preside m.

head office n sede f

headphones n cuffia f.

headquarters npl quartier m generale.

headroom n altezza f.

headstrong adj testardo.

headwaiter n capocameriere m.

headway n progresso m; **to make ~** fare progresso.

heady adj inebriante.

heal vt guarire.

health n salute f.

healthy adj sano.

heap n mucchio m; * vt ammucchiare.

hear vt, vi sentire.

hearing n udito m.

hearing aid n apparecchio m acustico.

hearsay n diceria f.

hearse n carro m funebre.

heart n cuore m; **by ~** a memoria.

heart attack n infarto m.

heartbreak n immenso dolore m.

heartburn n bruciore m di stomaco.

heart failure n arresto m cardiaco.

heartfelt adj sincero.

hearth n focolare m.

heartily adv di gusto, di cuore.

heartiness n giovialità f.

heartless adj spietato.

hearty adj gioviale.

heat n calore m; * vt scaldare.

heater n stufa f.

heath n brughiera f.

heathen n pagano m.

heather n erica f.

heating n riscaldamento m.

heat-resistant adj termoresistente.

heatwave n ondata f di caldo.

heave vt strascinare a fatica; * n sforzo m.

heaven n cielo m, paradiso m.

heavenly adj celeste; divino.

heavily adv pesantemente.

heavy adj pesante; intenso; opprimente.

Hebrew adj ebreo, ebraico; * n ebreo m, ebraico m.

heckle vt fare azione di disturbo.

hectic adj movimentato.

hedge n siepe f; * vi premunirsi; tergiversare.

hedgehog n riccio m.

hedonism n edonismo m.

heed vt badare a; * n attenzione f.

heedless adj non curante.

heel n calcagno m; tacco m.

hefty adj pesante.

heifer n giovenca f.

height n altezza f.

heighten vt alzare; aumentare; * vi aumentare.

heinous adj atroce.

heir, heiress n erede m/f.

heirloom n ricordo m di famiglia.

helicopter n elicottero m.

helium n elio m.

hell n inferno m.

hellish adj infernale.

helm n timone m.

helmet n casco m.

help vt aiutare; assistere; soccorrere; * n aiuto m; aiutante m/f; soccorso m; assistenza f.

helper n assistente m/f.

helpful adj utile.

helping n porzione f.

helpless adj incapace.

helter-skelter n scivolo m a spirale.

hem n orlo m.

he-man n fusto m.

hemisphere n emisfero m.

hemlock n cicuta f.

hemp n canapa f indiana.

hen n gallina f.

henceforth adv d'ora innanzi.

henchman n accolito m.

hen-house n pollaio m.

hapatitis n epatite f.

her pron la, lei.

herald n araldo m; * vt preannunciare.

heraldry n araldica f.

herb n erba f aromatica.

herbaceous adj erbaceo.

herbalist n erborista m/f.

herbivorous adj, n erbivoro m.

herd n mandria f; gregge m.

here adv qui, qua.

hereabouts adv da queste parti.

hereafter adv da qui in avanti.

hereby adv con questo.

hereditary adj ereditario.

heredity n eredità f.

heresy n eresia f.

heretic adj, n eretico m.

herewith adv con la presente.

heritage n eredità f; patrimonio m.

hermetic adj ermetico.

hermit n eremita m.

hermitage n eremitaggio m.

hernia n ernia f.

hero n eroe m.

heroic adj eroico.

heroin n eroina f.

heroine n eroina f.

heroism adj eroismo.

heron n airone m.

herring n aringa f.

hers pron suo, di lei.

herself pron se stessa, lei stessa.

hesitant adj esitante.

hesitate vi esitare.

hesitation n esitazione f.

heterogeneous adj eterogeneo.

heterosexual adj, n eterosessuale m/f.

hew vt tagliare.

hexagon n esagono m.

hexagonal adj esagonale.

heyday n tempi mpl d'oro.

hi exclam ciao!

hiatus n lacuna f.

hibernate vi cadere in letargo.

hiccup n singhiozzo m; * vi avere il singhiozzo.

hidden adj nascosto.

hide vt nascondere; * n cuoio m.

hideaway n nascondiglio m.

hideous adj orribile.

hiding n botte fpl.

hierarchy n gerarchia f.

hieroglyphic *adj* geroglifico *m*; ~s *npl* geroglifici *mpl*.

hi-fi *n* stereo *m*; * *adj* hi-fi.

higgledy-piggledy *adj* alla rinfusa.

high *adj* alto.

highchair *n* seggiolone *m*.

high-handed *adj* prepotente.

highlands *npl* zona *f* montuosa.

highlight *n* clou *m*.

highly *adv* estremamente.

highly strung *adj* ipersensibile.

highness *n* altezza *f*.

high tide *n* alta marea *f*.

hijack *n* dirottamento *m*; * *vt* dirottare.

hijacker *n* dirottatore *m*.

hike *n* escursione *f* a piedi.

hilarious *adj* spassosissimo.

hilarity *n* ilarità *f*.

hill *n* collina *f*, colle *m*.

hillock *n* poggio *m*.

hillside *n* pendio *m*.

hilly *adj* collinoso.

hilt *n* impugnatura *f*.

him *pron* lo, lui.

himself *pron* lui stesso.

hind *adj* posteriore; * *n* cerva *f*.

hinder *vt* impedire.

hindrance *n* intralcio *m*.

hindquarters *npl* posteriore *m*.

hindsight *n* giudizio *m* retrospettivo.

hinge *n* cardine *m*, cerniera *f*.

hint *n* allusione *f*; * *vt* alludere.

hip *n* anca *f*.

hippopotamus *n* ippopotamo *m*.

hire *vt* noleggiare; * *n* noleggio *m*.

his *pron* suo, di lui.

hiss *vt* sibilare; * *n* sibilo *m*.

historian *n* storico *m*.

historic(al) *adj* storico.

history *n* storia *f*.

histrionic *adj* istrionico.

hit *vt* colpire; picchiare; sbattere; raggiungere; * *n* colpo *m*; successo *m*.

hitch *vt* to ~ up attaccare; tirare su; * *n* intoppo *m*.

hitch-hike *vi* fare l'autostop.

hitherto *adv* fino a ora.

hive *n* alveare *m*.

hoard *n* gruzzolo *m*; * *vt* accumulare.

hoar-frost *n* brina *f*.

hoarse *adj* rauco.

hoax *n* scherzo *m*; * *vt* ingannare.

hobble *vi* zoppicare.

hobby *n* hobby *m*, passatempo *m*.

hobbyhorse *n* chiodo fisso.

hobnob *vi* mescolarsi.

hockey *n* hockey *m*.

hocus-pocus *n* trucco *m*.

hoe *n* zappa *f*; * *vt* zappare.

hog *n* porco *m*; * *vt* accaparrarsi.

hoipoloi *n* gentaglia *f*.

hoist *vt* issare; * *n* montacarichi *m*.

hold *vt* tenere; mantenere; to ~ up ritardare; (bank) assaltare; * *n* presa *f*; stiva *f*;

hoder *n* possessore *m*; contenitore *m*.

holding *n* podere *m*; ~s azioni *fpl*.

holdup *n* rapina *f*; intoppo *m*.

hole *n* buca *f*, buco *m*, falla *f*; tana *f*; * *vt* bucare.

holiday *n* vacanza *f*.

holidaymaker *n* villeggiante *m*.

holiness *n* santità *f*.

hollow *adj* cavo; falso; * *n* cavità; * *vt* scavare.

holly *n* agrifoglio *m*.

hollyhock *n* malvone *m*.

holocaust *n* olocausto *m*.

holster n fondina f.
holy adj santo, religioso.
Holy Ghost n Spirito m Santo.
homage n omaggio m.
home n casa f; patria f; habitat m; istituto m.
homeland n patria f.
homely adj semplice, familiare.
homeless adj senza tetto.
home-made adj fatto in casa.
homesick n nostalgia f (di casa).
homeward adj verso casa.
homework n compito m.
homicidal adj omicida.
homicide n omicidio m.
homily n omelia f.
homing adj autocercante.
homoeopath adj, n omeopatico m.
homoeopathic adj omeopatico,
homoeopathy n omeopatia f.
homogeneity n omogeneità f.
homogeneous adj omogeneo.
homonym s omonimo m.
homosexual adj, n omosessuale m/f.
honest adj onesto.
honesty n onestà f.
honey n miele m.
honeycomb n nido m d'api.
honeymoon n luna f di miele.
honeysuckle n (bot) caprifoglio m.
honorary adj onorario.
honour n onore m; * vt onorare.
honourable adj onorevole.
hood n cappuccio m.
hoodlum n teppista m/f.
hoodwink vt imbrogliare.
hoof n zoccolo m.
hook n gancio m; **by ~ or by crook** di riffa o di raffa; * vt agganciare.
hooked adj (naso) aquilino; fanatico.
hooligan n teppista m/f.
hoop n cerchio m.

hooter n serena f; clacson m.
hop n saltello m; (bot) luppolo; * vi saltellare; **~ it!** smamma!
hope n speranza f; * vi sperare.
hopeful adj fiducioso.
hopeless adj impossibile; incorreggibile; disperato.
horde n orda f.
horizon n orizzonte m.
horizontal adj orizzontale.
hormone n ormone m.
horn n corno m; clacson m.
hornet n calabrone m.
horny adj incallito.
horoscope n oroscopo m.
horrendous adj orrendo.
horrible adj orribile.
horrid adj odioso.
horrific adj spaventoso.
horrify vt fare inorridire.
horror n orrore m.
horror film n film m dell'orrore.
hors d'oeuvres npl antipasto m.
horse n cavallo m.
horseback adv: **on ~** a cavallo.
horse chestnut n ippocastano m.
horsefly n tafano m.
horseman n cavaliere m.
horsmanship n equitazione f.
horsepower n cavallo m.
horse racing n corse fpl di cavalli.
horseradish n raffano m.
horseshoe n ferro m di cavallo.
horsewoman n ammazzone f.
horticulture n orticoltura f.
horticulturist n orticoltore m
hosepipe n tubo m di gomma.
hosiery n calze fpl.
hospice n ospizio m.
hospitable adj ospitale.
hospital n ospedale m.
hospitality n ospitalità f.
host n ospite m; presentatore m

moltitudine f; (relig) ostia f.

hostage n ostaggio m.

hostel n ostello m.

hostess n hostess f.

hostile adj ostile.

hostility n ostilità f.

hot adj caldo; piccante; focoso.

hotbed n (fig) focolaio m.

hot dog n hot dog m.

hotel n albergo m.

hotelier n albergatore m.

hot-headed adj impetuoso.

hot-house n serra f.

hotline n telefono m rosso.

hotplate n piastra f, scaldavivande m.

hotly adv accanitamente.

hound n segugio m; * vt perseguitare.

hour n ora f.

hour-glass n clessidra f.

hourly adv ogni ora.

house n casa f; (polit) camera f;
* vt sistemare, alloggiare.

houseboat n house boat f.

housebreaker n scassinatore
m.

household n casa f; famiglia f.

householder n capo famiglia
m/f.

housekeeper n governante f.

housekeeping n amministrazione f della casa.

house warming n festa f per
inaugurare la casa.

housewife n casalinga f.

housework n faccende fpl.

housing n alloggiamento m;
incastellatura f.

housing estate n quartiere m
residenziale.

hovel n tugurio m.

hover vi librarsi.

how adv come; ~ do you do!
piacere.

however adv comunque, tuttavia.

howl vi ululare; urlare; pian-

gere; * n ululato m.

hub n mozzo m; (fig) fulcro m.

hubbub n baccano m.

hubcap n coprimozzo m.

hue n tinta f.

huff n: **in a ~** imbronciato.

hug vt abbracciare; * n abbraccio m.

huge adj enorme.

hulk n nave f in disarmo; bestione.

hull n scafo m.

hullo excl ciao!; pronto.

hum vi ronzare; * vt canticchiare * n ronzio m.

human adj umano; * n essere
m umano.

humane adj umanitario.

humanist n umanista m/f.

humanitarian adj umanitario.

humanity n umanità f.

humanly adv umanamente.

humble adj umile; * vt umiliare.

humbly adv umilmente.

humbug n sciocchezze fpl.

humdrum adj monotono.

humid adj umido.

humidity n umidità f.

humiliate vt umiliare.

humiliation n umiliazione f.

humility n umiltà f.

humming-bird n colibrì m.

humorist n umorista m/f.

humorous adj spiritoso.

humour n umorismo m; umore
m; * vt accontentare.

hump n gobba f.

hunch n impressione f; ~**back**
gobbo m; * adj ~**backed** gobbo.

hundred adj, n cento m.

hundredth adj, n centesimo m.

hundredweight n 50,8 kg.

hunger n fame f; * vi **to ~ after** desiderare moltissimo.

hunger strike n sciopero m della fame.

hungrily *adv* avidamente.

hungry *adj* affamato; to be ~ aver fame.

hunt *vi* cacciare; cercare; * *n* caccia *f*; ricerca *f*.

hunter *n* cacciatore *m*.

hunting *n* caccia *f*.

huntsman *n* cacciatore *m*.

hurdle *n* ostacolo *m*.

hurl *vt* scagliare.

hurricane *n* uragano *m*.

hurried *adj* frettoloso.

hurry *vi* affrettarsi, fare in fretta; * *n* fretta *f*.

hurt *vt* ferire; danneggiare; far male; * *n* ferita *f*, lesione *f*.

hurtful *adj* ingiurioso.

husband *n* marito *m*.

hush *n* silenzio *m*; * *vt* quietare.

husk *n* guscio *m*; pula *f*.

husky *adj* rauco; cane *m* eschimese.

hustings *npl* comizi *mpl* elettorali.

hustle *vt* spingere; fare fretta a; * *n* trambusto *m*.

hut *n* baracca *f*.

hutch *n* gabbia *f*.

hyacinth *n* giacinto *m*.

hybrid *adj, n* ibrido *m*.

hydrangea *n* ortensia *f*.

hydrant *n* idrante *m*.

hydraulic *adj* idraulico; ~s *npl* idraulica *f*.

hydroelectric *adj* idroelettrico.

hydrofoil *n* aliscafo *m*.

hydrogen *n* idrogeno *m*.

hydrophobia *n* idrofobia *f*.

hyena *n* iena *f*.

hygiene *n* igiene *f*.

hygienic *adj* igienico.

hymn *n* inno *m*.

hyperbole *n* iperbole *f*.

hypermarket *n* ipermercato *m*.

hypertension *n* ipertensione *f*.

hyphen *n* (*gr*) trattino *m*.

hypnosis *n* ipnosi *f*.

hypnotic *adj* ipnotico.

hypnotism *n* ipnotismo *m*.

hypochondria *n* ipocondria *f*.

hypochondriac *n* ipocondriaco *m*.

hypocrisy *n* ipocrisia *f*.

hypocrite *n* ipocrita *m/f*.

hypocritical *adj* ipocrita.

hypodermic *adj* ipodermico.

hypothesis *n* ipotesi *f*.

hypothetical *adj* ipotetico.

hysterectomy *n* isterectomia *f*.

hysteria *n* isterismo *m*.

hysterical *adj* isterico.

hysterics *npl* crisi *f* isterica.

I

I *pron* io

ice *n* ghiaccio *m*; gelato *m*; * *vt* glassare.

ice-axe *n* piccozza *f*.

iceberg *n* iceberg *m*.

ice-bound *adj* bloccato dal ghiaccio.

ice cream *n* gelato *m*.

ice rink *n* pista *f* di pattinaggio.

ice-skating *n* pattinaggio *m* sul ghiaccio.

icicle *n* ghiacciolo *m*.

icing *n* glassa *f*.

icon *n* icona *f*.

iconoclast *adj, n* iconoclasta *f*

icy *adj* ghiacciato.

idea *n* idea *f*.

ideal *adj, n* ideale *m*.

idealist *n* idealista *m/f*.

identical *adj* identico.

identification *n* identificazione *f*.

identify *vt* identificare.

identity *n* identità *f*.

ideology *n* ideologìa *f*.

idiom *n* frase *f* idiomatica.

idiomatic *adj* idiomatico.

idiosyncrasy *n* peculiarità *f*.

idiot *n* idiota *m/f*.

idiotic *adj* stupido.

idle *adj* pigro; inattivo; infondato.

idleness *n* pigrizia *f*.

idol *n* idolo *m*.

idolatry *n* idolatria *f*.

idolize *vt* idolatrare.

idyll *n* idillio *m*.

idyllic *adj* idillico.

i.e. *adv* cioè

if *conj* se, qualora.

igloo *n* igloo *m*.

ignite *vt* accendere.

ignition *n* iniezione *f*; accensione *f*.

ignition key *n* chiave *f* dell'accensione.

ignoble *adj* ignobile.

ignominious *adj* ignominioso.

ignominy *n* ignominia *f*.

ignoramus *n* ignorante *m/f*.

ignorance *n* ignoranza *f*.

ignorant *adj* ignorante.

ignore *vt* ignorare; fingere di non vedere.

ill *adj* malato; indisposto; cattivo; * **~s** *npl* (*fig*) mali *mpl*.

ill-advised *adj* imprudente.

ill-bred *adj* maleducato.

illegal *adj* illegale.

illegality *n* illegalità *f*.

illegibile *adj* illeggibile.

illegitimacy *n* illegittimità *f*.

illegitimate *adj* illegittimo.

ill-fated *adj* infausto.

ill feeling *n* rancore *m*.

illicit *adj* illecito.

illiterate *adj* n analfabeta *m/f*.

illness *n* malattia *f*.

illogical *adj* illogico.

ill-timed *adj* inopportuno.

ill-treat *vt* maltrattare.

illuminate *vt* illuminare.

illumination *n* illuminazione *f*.

illusion *n* illusione *f*.

illusory *adj* illusorio.

illustrate *vt* illustrare.

illustration *n* illustrazione *f*.

illustrative *adj* illustrativo.

illustrious *adj* illustre.

ill-will *n* malevolenza *f*.

image *n* immagine *f*.

imagery *n* linguaggio *m* figurato.

imaginable *adj* immaginabile.

imaginary *adj* immaginario.

imagination *n* immaginazione *f*.

imaginative *adj* ricco di immaginazione.

imagine *vt* immaginare.

imbalance *n* squilibrio *m*.

imbecile *adj* imbecille.

imbibe *vt* bere.

imbue *vt* imbevere.

imitate *vt* imitare.

imitation *n* imitazione *f*.

imitative *adj* imitativo.

immaculate *adj* impeccabile.

immaterial *adj* irrilevante.

immature *adj* immaturo.

immeasurable *adj* incommensurabile.

immediate *adj* immediato.

immense *adj* immenso.

immensity *n* enormità *f*.

immerse *vt* immergere.

immersion *n* immersione *f*.

immigrant *n* immigrato *m*.

immigration *n* immigrazione *f*.

imminent *adj* imminente.

immobile *adj* immobile.

immobility *n* immobilità *f*.

immoderate *adj* smoderato.

immodest *adj* impudico.

immoral *adj* immorale.

immorality *n* immoralità *f*.

immortal *adj* immortale.

immortality *n* immortalità *f*.

immortalize *vt* immortalare.
immune *adj* immune.
immunity *n* immunità *f*.
immunize *vt* immunizzare.
immutable *adj* immutabile.
imp *n* diavoletto *m*.
impact *n* impatto *m*.
impair *vt* danneggiare.
impale *vt* trafiggere.
impalpable *adj* impalpabile.
impart *vt* comunicare.
impartial *adj* imparziale.
impartiality *n* imparzialità *f*.
impassable *adj* intransitabile.
impasse *n* impasse *f*.
impassive *adj* impassibile.
impatience *n* impazienza *f*.
impatient *adj* impaziente.
impeach *vt* mettere sotto accusa.
impeccable *adj* impeccabile.
impecunious *adj* bisognoso.
impede *vt* ostacolare.
impediment *n* impedimento *m*.
impel *vt* costringere.
impending *adj* incombente.
impenetrable *adj* impenetrabile.
imperative *adj* tassativo; (*gr*) imperativo.
imperceptible *adj* impercettibile.
imperfect *adj* difettoso; imperfetto.
imperfection *n* imperfezione *f*.
imperial *adj* imperiale.
imperialism *n* imperialismo *m*.
imperious *adj* imperioso.
impermeable *adj* impermeabile.
impersonal *adj* impersonale.
impersonate *vt* imitare.
impertinence *n* impertinenza *f*.
impertinent *adj* impertinente.
imperturbable *adj* imperturbabile.
impervious *adj* impervio.

impetuosity *n* impetuosità *f*.
impetuous *adj* impetuoso.
impetus *n* spinta *f*.
impiety *n* empietà *f*.
impinge (on) *vi* urtare; ledere.
impious *adj* empio.
implacable *adj* implacabile.
implant *vt* innestare.
implement *n* utensile *m*; * *vt* attuare.
implicate *vt* implicare.
implication *n* implicazione *f*.
implicit *adj* implicito.
implore *vt* implorare.
imply *vt* implicare.
impolite *adj* scortese.
impoliteness *n* scortesia *f*.
import *vt* importare; * *n* importazione *f*.
importance *n* importanza *f*.
important *adj* importante.
importation *n* importazione *f*.
importer *n* importatore *m*.
importunate *adj* importuno.
importune *vt* importunare.
impose *vt* imporre.
imposing *adj* imponente.
imposition *n* imposizione *f*.
impossibility *n* impossibilità *f*.
impossible *adj* impossibile.
impostor *n* impostore *m*.
impotence *n* impotenza *f*.
impotent *adj* impotente.
impound *vt* sequestrare.
impoverish *vt* impoverire.
impoverished *adj* impoverito.
impracticable *adj* impraticabile.
impractical *adj* privo di senso pratico.
imprecation *n* imprecazione *f*.
imprecise *adj* impreciso.
impregnable *adj* inattaccabile.
impregnate *vt* impregnare.
impregnation *n* impregnazione *f*.
impress *vt* colpire, fare impressione a.

impression n impressione f.

impressionable adj impressionabile.

impressive adj imponente, che colpisce.

imprint n sigla editoriale; * vt imprimere.

imprison vt imprigionare.

imprisonment n reclusione f; **life ~** ergastolo m.

improbability n improbabilità f.

improbable adj improbabile.

impromptu adj improvvisato.

improper adj scorretto.

impropriety n scorrettezza f.

improve vt, vi migliorare.

improvement n miglioramento m.

improvident adj imprevidente.

improvise vt, vi improvvisare.

imprudence n imprudenza f.

imprudent adj imprudente.

impudence n sfrontatezza f.

impudent adj sfrontato.

impugn vt impugnare.

impulse n impulso m.

impulsive adj impulsivo.

impunity n: **with ~** impunemente.

impure adj impuro.

impurity n impurità f.

in prep in; a.

inability n inabilità f.

inaccessible adj inaccessibile.

inaccuracy n inesattezza f.

inaccurate adj inesatto.

inaction n inazione f.

inactive adj inattivo.

inactivity n inattività f.

inadequate adj inadeguato.

inadmissible adj inammissibile.

inadvertent adj involontario.

inadvisable adj sconsigliabile.

inane adj sciocco.

inanimate adj inanimato.

inapplicable adj inapplicabile.

inappropriate adj fuori luogo, inadatto.

inarticulate adj incapace di esprimersi.

inasmuch (as) conj poiché.

inattentive adj disattento.

inaudible adj non udibile.

inaugural adj inaugurale.

inaugurate vt inaugurare.

inauguration n inaugurazione f.

inauspicious adj infausto.

in-between adj intermedio.

inborn, inbred adj innato, congenito.

incalculable adj incalcolabile.

incandescent adj incandescente.

incantation n incantesimo m.

incapable adj incapace.

incapacitate vt rendere incapace.

incapacity n incapacità f.

incarcerate vt imprigionare.

incarnate adj incarnato.

incarnation n incarnazione f.

incautious adj incauto.

incendiary adj incendiario; **~ bomb** bomba f incendiaria.

incense n incenso m; * vt rendere furibondo.

incentive n incentivo m.

inception n principio m.

incessant adj incessante.

incest n incesto m.

incestuous adj incestuoso.

inch n pollice m; **~ by ~** a poco a poco.

incidence n incidenza f.

incident n avvenimento m; episodio m.

incidental adj secondario; fortuito.

incinerator n inceneritore m.

incipient adj incipiente.

incise vt incidere.

incision n incisione f.

incisive adj incisivo.

incisor n incisivo m.

incite *vt* incitare.
inclement *adj* inclemente.
inclination *n* tendenza *f*; inclinazione *f*; voglia *f*.
incline *vi* tendere a; * *n* pendenza *f*.
include *vt* includere.
including *adj* incluso.
inclusion *n* inclusione *f*.
inclusive *adj* incluso.
incognito *adj* in incognito.
incoherence *n* incoerenza *f*.
incoherent *adj* incoerente.
income *n* reddito *m*.
income tax *n* imposta *f* sul reddito.
incoming *adj* subentrante; in arrivo; montante.
incomparable *adj* incomparabile.
incompatibility *n* incompatibilità *f*.
incompatible *adj* incompatibile.
incompetence *n* incompetenza *f*.
incompetente *adj* incompetente.
incomplete *adj* incompleto.
incomprehensible *adj* incomprensibile.
inconceivable *adj* inimmaginabile.
inconclusive *adj* inconcludente.
incongruous *adj* incongruo.
inconsequential *adj* insignificante.
inconsiderate *adj* irriguardoso.
inconsistency *n* incoerenza *f*.
inconsistent *adj* contraddittorio.
inconsolable *adj* inconsolabile.
inconspicuous *adj* poco appariscente.
incontinence *n* incontinenza *f*.
incontinent *adj* incontinente.

incontrovertible *adj* incontrovertibile.
inconvenience *n* scomodità *f*; * *vt* incomodare.
inconvenient *adj* scomodo.
incorporate *vt* incorporare.
incorporation *n* incorporazione *f*.
incorrect *adj* scorretto.
incorrigible *adj* incorreggibile.
incorruptible *adj* incorruttibile.
increase *vt*, *vi* aumentare; * *n* aumento *m*.
increasing *adj* crescente.
incredible *adj* incredibile.
incredulity *n* incredulità *f*.
incredulous *adj* incredulo.
increment *n* incremento *m*.
incriminate *vt* incriminare.
incubate *vt* covare.
incubator *n* incubatrice *f*.
inculcate *vt* inculcare.
incur *vt* contrarre.
incurable *adj* incurabile.
incursion *n* incursione *f*.
indebted *adj* obbligato.
indecency *n* indecenza *f*.
indecent *adj* indecente.
indecision *n* indecisione *f*.
indecisive *adj* indeciso.
indeed *adv* infatti.
indefatigable *adj* infaticabile.
indefinable *adj* indefinibile.
indefinite *adj* indefinito.
indelible *adj* indelebile.
indelicate *adj* indelicato.
indemnify *vt* indennizzare.
indemnity *n* indennizzo *m*.
indent *vt* rientrare dal margine.
independence *n* indipendenza *f*.
independent *adj* indipendente.
indescribable *adj* indescrivibile.
indestructable *adj* indistruttibile.

indeterminate *adj* indeterminato.

index *n* indice *m*.

index card *n* scheda *f*.

index finger *n* indice *m*.

indicate *vt* indicare; * *vi* mettere la freccia.

indication *n* indicazione *f*.

indicative *adj* indicativo.

indicator *n* segno *m*; freccia *f*; rivelatore *m*.

indict *vt* imputare.

indictment *n* imputazione *f*.

indifference *n* indifferenza *f*.

indifferent *adj* indifferente.

indigenous *adj* indigeno.

indigestion *n* indigestione *f*.

indignant *adj* indignato.

indignation *n* indignazione *f*.

indignity *n* umiliazione *f*.

indigo *adj*, *n* indaco *m*.

indirect *adj* indiretto.

indiscreet *adj* indiscreto.

indiscretion *n* indiscrezione *f*.

indiscriminate *adj* indiscriminato.

indispensable *adj* indispensabile.

indisposed *adj* indisposto.

indisposition *n* indisposizione *f*.

indisputable *adj* incontrovertibile.

indistinct *adj* indistinto.

indistinguishable *adj* indistinguibile.

individual *adj* individuale; * *n* individuo *m*.

individuality *n* individualità *f*.

indivisible *adj* indivisibile.

indoctrinate *vt* indottrinare.

indoctrination *n* indottrinamento *m*.

indolence *n* indolenza *f*.

indolent *adj* indolente.

indomitable *adj* indomabile.

indoors *adv* all'interno.

indubitable *adj* indubitabile.

induce *vt* persuadere.

inducement *n* incentivo *m*.

induction *n* induzione *f*.

indulge *vt* accontentare; viziare.

indulgence *n* indulgenza *f*.

indulgent *adj* indulgente.

industrial *adj* industriale.

industrial estate *n* zona *f* industriale.

industrialist *n* industriale *m/f*.

industrialize *vt* industrializzare.

industrious *adj* diligente.

industry *n* industria *f*.

inebriated *adj* ubriaco.

inedible *adj* immangiabile.

ineffable *adj* ineffabile.

ineffective, ineffectual *adj* inefficace.

inefficiency *n* inefficienza *f*.

inefficient *adj* inefficiente.

ineligible *adj* ineligibile.

inept *adj* inetto.

ineptitude *n* inettitudine *f*.

inequality *n* ineguaglianza *f*.

inequitable *adj* iniquo.

inert *adj* inerte.

inertia *n* inerzia *f*.

inescapable *adj* inevitabile.

inestimable *adj* inestimabile.

inevitable *adj* inevitabile.

inexcusable *adj* imperdonabile.

inexhuastible *adj* inesauribile.

inexorable *adj* inesorabile.

inexpensive *adj* economico.

inexperience *n* inesperienza *f*.

inexperienced *adj* inesperto.

inexplicable *adj* inspiegabile.

inexpressible *adj* inesprimibile.

inextricable *adj* inestricabile.

infallibility *n* infallibilità *f*.

infallible *adj* infallibile.

infamous *adj* infame.

infamy *n* infamia *f*.

infancy *n* infanzia *f*.

infant n bambino m.
infanticide n infanticidio m.
infantile adj infantile.
infantry n fanteria f.
infatuated adj infatuato.
infatuation n infatuazione f.
infect vt infettare.
infection n infezione f.
infectious adj infettivo.
infer vt dedurre.
inference n deduzione f.
inferior adj inferiore.
inferiority n inferiorità f.
infernal adj infernale.
inferno n inferno m.
infest vt infestare.
infidel adj, n infedele m.
infidelity n infedeltà f.
infiltrate vi infiltrarsi.
infinite adj infinito.
infinitive n (gr) infinito m; * adj infinitivo.
infinity n infinità f.
infirm adj infermo.
infirmary n infermeria f.
inflame vt infiammare.
inflammation n infiammazione f.
inflammatory adj incendiario.
inflatable adj gonfiabile.
inflate vt gonfiare.
inflation n inflazione f.
inflection n inflessione f.
inflexibility n inflessibilità f.
inflexible adj inflessibile.
inflict vt infliggere.
influence n influenza f; * vt influenzare.
influential adj influente.
influenza n influenza f.
influx n afflusso m.
inform vt informare.
informal adj informale.
informality n mancanza di formalità f.
informant n informatore m.
information n informazioni fpl.

infraction n infrazione f.
infra-red adj infrarosso.
infrastructure n infrastruttura f.
infrequent adj infrequente.
infringe vt infrangere.
infringement n violazione f.
infuriate vt rendere furioso.
infuse vt (fig) infondere; lasciare in infusione.
infusion n infusione f.
ingenious adj ingegnoso.
ingenuity adj ingegnosità f.
ingenuous adj ingenuo.
inglorious adj inglorioso.
ingot n lingotto m.
ingrained adj incancrenito.
ingratiate vi ingraziarsi.
ingratitude n ingratitudine f.
ingredient n ingrediente m.
inhabit vt abitare.
inhabitable adj abitabile.
inhabitant n abitante m/f.
inhale vt inalare.
inherent adj intrinseco.
inherit vt ereditare.
inheritance n eredità f.
inhibit vt inibire.
inhibited adj inibito.
inhibition n inibizione f.
inhospitable adj inospitale.
inhuman adj inumano.
inhumanity n inumanità f.
inimical adj ostile.
inimitable adj inimitabile.
iniquitous adj iniquo.
iniquity n iniquità f.
initial adj, n iniziale f.
initially adv all'inizio.
initiate vt iniziare.
initiation n iniziazione f.
initiative n iniziativa f.
inject vt iniettare.
injection n iniezione f.
injudicious adj imprudente.
injunction n ingiunzione f.
injure vt ferire.
injury n ferita f.

injustice n ingiustizia f.
ink n inchiostro m.
inkling n mezza idea f.
inlaid adj intarsiato.
inland adj interno; * adv nell'entroterra.
in-law n parente m acquisito.
inlay vt intarsiare.
inlet n insenatura f.
inmate n detenuto m.
inmost adj più intimo.
inn n locanda f.
innate adj innato.
inner adj interiore.
innermost adj più intimo.
inner tube n camera f d'aria.
innkeeper n locandiere m.
innocence n innocenza f.
innocent adj innocente.
innocuous adj innocuo.
innovate vi fare innovazioni.
innovation n innovazione f.
innuendo n insinuazione f.
innumerable adj innumerevole.
inoculate vt inoculare.
inoculation n inoculazione f.
inoffensive adj inoffensivo.
inopportune adj inopportuno.
inordinate adj eccessivo.
inorganic adj inorganico.
inpatient n ricoverato m.
input n alimentazione f; input m.
inquest n inchiesta f.
inquire vi indagare; informarsi; **to ~ after** richiedere di.
inquiry n domanda f; inchiesta f.
inquisition n inquisizione f.
inquisitive adj curioso.
inroad n incursione f.
insane adj pazzo, folle.
insanity n follia f; infermità f mentale.
insatiable adj insaziabile.
inscribe vt incidere.
inscription n iscrizione f; dedica f.

inscrutable adj imperscrutabile.
insect n insetto m.
insecticide n insetticida m.
insecure adj malsicuro.
insecurity n insicurezza f.
insemination n inseminazione f.
insensible adj privo di conoscenza.
insensitive adj insensibile.
inseparable adj inseparabile.
insert vt inserire; * n inserto m.
insertion n inserzione f.
inshore adj costiero.
inside n interno m; * adv, prep dentro.
inside out adv alla rovescia.
insidious adj insidioso.
insight n perspicacia f.
insignia n insegne fpl.
insignificant adj insignificante.
insincere adj insincero.
insincerity n insincerità f.
insinuate vt insinuare.
insinuation n insinuazione f.
insipid adj insipido.
insist vt, vi insistere.
insistence n insistenza f.
insistent adj insistente.
insole n soletta f.
insolence n insolenza f.
insolent adj insolente.
insoluble adj insolubile.
insolvency n insolvenza f.
insolvent adj insolvente.
insomnia n insonnia f.
insomuch adv a tal punto che.
inspect vt controllare.
inspection n controllo m; ispezione f.
inspector n ispettore m, controllore m.
inspiration n ispirazione f.
inspire vt ispirare.
instability n instabilità f.
instal vt installare.

installation n installazione f.
instalment n rata f; puntata f.
instance n esempio m.
instant adj immediato; solubile; * n istante m.
instantaneous adj istantaneo.
instead adv invece.
instep n collo m.
instigate vt istigare.
instigation n istigazione f.
instil vt instillare.
instinct n istinto m.
instinctive adj istintivo.
institute vt istituire; * n istituto m.
institution n istituzione f.
instruct vt istruire.
instruction n istruzione f.
instructive adj istruttivo.
instructor n istruttore m.
instrument n strumento m.
instrumental adj strumentale.
insubordinate adj insubordinato.
insubordination n insubordinazione f.
insufferable adj insopportabile.
insufficiency n insufficienza f.
insufficient adj insufficiente.
insular adj insulare.
insulate vt isolare.
insulating tape n nastro m isolante.
insulation n isolamento m.
insulin n insulina f.
insult vt insultare; * n insulto m.
insulting adj insultante.
insuperable adj insuperabile.
insurance n assicurazione f.
insurance policy n polizza f d'assicurazione.
insure vt assicurare.
insurer n assicuratore m.
insurgent adj ribelle; * n insorto m.
insurmountable adj insormontabile.
insurrection n insurrezione f.

intact adj intatto.
intake n immissione f.
integral adj integrante.
integrate vt integrare.
integration n integrazione f.
integrity n integrità f.
intellect n intelletto m.
intellectual adj, n intellettuale m/f.
intelligence n intelligenza f.
intelligent adj intelligente.
intelligentsia n intellighenzia f.
intelligible adj intelligibile.
intemperate adj rigido.
intend vt avere intenzione, intendere; destinare.
intense adj intenso.
intensify vt intensificare.
intensity n intensità f.
intensive adj intensivo.
intensive care unit n centro m di rianimazione.
intent adj assorto, intento; * n intenzione f, intento m.
intention n intenzione f.
intentional adj intenzionale.
inter vt seppellire.
interaction n interazione f.
intercede vi intercedere.
intercept vt intercettare.
intercession n intercessione f.
interchange n scambio m.
intercom n interfono m.
intercourse n rapporti mpl.
interest vt interessare; * n interesse m.
interesting adj interessante.
interest rate n tasso m d'interesse.
interfere vi interferire; intromettersi.
interference n interferenza f intromissione f.
interim adj provvisorio.
interior adj, n interno m.
interior designer n arredatore m.

interjection n (gr) interiezione f.
interlock vi intrecciarsi.
interloper n intruso m.
interlude n intervallo m.
intermediary n intermediario m.
intermediate adj intermedio.
interment n seppellimento m.
interminable adj interminabile.
intermingle vt frammischiare.
intermission n interruzione f.
intermittent adj intermittente.
internal adj interno.
international adj internazionale.
interplay n interazione f.
interpose vt interporre.
interpret vt interpretare.
interpretation n interpretazione f.
interpreter n interprete m/f.
interregnum n interregno m.
interrelated adj correlato.
interrogate vt interrogare.
interrogation n interrogatorio m.
interrogative adj interrogativo.
interrupt vt, vi interrompere.
interruption n interruzione f.
intersect vt intersecare.
intersection n intersezione f.
intersperse vt inframmezzare.
intertwine vt intrecciare.
interval n intervallo m.
intervene vi sopraggiungere; intervenire.
intervention n intervento m.
interview n colloquio m, intervista f.
interviewer n intervistatore m.
intestate adj intestato.
intestinal adj intestinale.
intestine n intestino m.
intimacy n intimità f.

intimate adj intimo; * vt fare capire.
intimidate vt intimidire.
into prep in, dentro.
intolerable adj intollerabile.
intolerance n intolleranza f.
intolerant adj intollerante.
intonation n intonazione f.
intoxicate vt inebriare.
intoxication n ebbrezza f.
intractable adj intrattabile.
intransigence n intransigenza f.
intransitive adj (gr) intransitivo.
intravenous adj endovenoso.
intrepid adj intrepido.
intricacy n complessità f.
intricate adj intricato.
intrigue n intrigo m; tresca f; * vt incuriosire.
intriguing adj affascinante.
intrinsic adj intrinseco.
introduce vt introdurre; presentare.
introduction n introduzione f; presentazione f.
introductory adj introduttivo.
introspection n introspezione f.
introvert n introverso m.
intrude vi intromettersi.
intruder n intruso m.
intrusion n intrusione f.
intuition n intuito m.
intuitive adj intuitivo.
inundate vt inondare.
inundation n inondazione f.
inure vt assuefare.
invade vt invadere.
invader n invasore m.
invalid adj, invalido; nullo; * n invalido m.
invalidate vt annullare.
invaluable adj inestimabile.
invariable adj invariabile.
invasion n invasione f.
invective n invettiva f.

inveigle vt persuadere (con lusinghe).

invent vt inventare.

invention n invenzione f.

inventive adj inventivo.

inventor n inventore m.

inventory n inventario m.

inverse adj inverso.

inversion n inversione f.

invert vt capovolgere.

invertebrate adj invertebrato.

invest vt investire.

investigate vt indagare.

investigation n indagine f.

investigator n investigatore m.

investment n investimento m.

inveterate adj inveterato.

invidious adj ingiurioso.

invigilate vt sorvegliare.

invigorating adj tonificante.

invincible adj invincibile.

inviolable adj inviolabile.

invisible adj invisibile.

invitation n invito m.

invite vt invitare; sollecitare.

inviting adj invitante.

invoice n fattura f; * vt fatturare.

invoke vt invocare.

involuntary adj involontario.

involve vt coinvolgere.

involved adj complicato.

involvement n partecipazione f; complessità f.

invulnerable adj invulnerabile.

inward adj interiore.

iodine n iodio m.

I.O.U. (I owe you) n pagherò m.

irascible adj irascibile.

irate adj irato.

iris n iride f; (bot) iris f.

irksome adj seccante.

iron n ferro m; * vt, vi stirare.

ironic adj ironico.

ironing n roba f da stirare.

ironing board n asse f da stiro.

iron ore n minerale m di ferro.

ironworks n ferriera f.

irony n ironia f.

irradiate vt irradiare.

irrational adj irragionevole.

irreconcilable adj irreconciliabile.

irregular adj irregolare.

irregularity n irregolarità f.

irrelevant adj non pertinente.

irreligious adj irreligioso.

irreparable adj irreparabile.

irreplaceable adj insostituibile.

irrepressible adj irrefrenabile.

irreproachable adj irreprensibile.

irresistible adj irresistibile.

irresolute adj irresoluto.

irresponsible adj irresponsabile.

irretrievable adj irrecuperabile.

irreverence n irriverenza f.

irreverent adj irriverente.

irrigate vt irrigare.

irrigation n irrigazione f.

irritable adj irritabile.

irritant n sostanza f irritante.

irritate vt irritare.

irritating adj irritante.

irritation n irritazione f.

Islam n Islam m.

island n isola f.

islander n isolano m.

isle n isola f.

isolate vt isolare.

isolation n isolamento m.

issue n questione f; emissione f; rilascio m; numero m; prole f; * vt rilasciare; pubblicare; emettere.

isthmus n istmo m.

it pron esso.

italic n corsivo m.

itch n prurito m; * vi prudere.

item n voce f, articolo m.

itemize vt specificare uno per

uno.
itinerant *adj* ambulante.
itinerary *n* itinerario *m*.
its *pron* suo.

itself *pron* si, se stesso.
ivory *adj*, *n* avorio *m*.
ivy *n* edera *f*.

J

jab *n* colpo *m* di punta; * *vt* conficcare.
jabber *n* chiacchierio *m*; * *vi* chiacchierare.
jack *n* cric *m*; fante *m*.
jackal *n* sciacallo *m*.
jackdaw *n* taccola *f*.
jacket *n* giacca *f*.
jack-knife *n* coltello *m* a serramanico.
jackpot *n* il primo premio *m*.
jade *n* giada *f*.
jaded *adj* sfibrato.
jagged *adj* seghettato.
jaguar *n* giaguaro *m*.
jail *n* carcere *m*, prigione *f*.
jailbird *n* carcerato *m*.
jailer *n* carceriere *m*.
jam *n* marmellata *f*; ingorgo *m*; pasticcio *m*; * *vt* bloccare; ficcare; * *vi* incepparsi.
jangle *vi* produrre un rumore metallico.
janitor *n* portinaio *m*; bidello *m*.
January *n* gennaio *m*.
jar *vi* urtare; stonare; * *n* barattolo *m*.
jargon *n* gergo *m*.
jasmine *n* gelsomino *m*.
jaundice *n* itterizia *f*.
jaunt *n* gita *f*.
jaunty *adj* spigliato.
javelin *n* giavellotto *m*.
jaw *n* mascella *f*.
jay *n* ghiandaia *f*.
jazz *n* jazz *m*
jealous *adj* geloso.
jealousy *n* gelosia *f*.
jeans *npl* jeans *mpl*

jeep *n* jeep *f*.
jeer *vi* fischiare; * *n* fischi *mpl*.
jelly *n* gelatina *f*.
jelly-fish *n* medusa *f*.
jeopardize *vt* mettere in pericolo.
jerk *n* sobbalzo *m*; tonto *m*; * *vi* muoversi a scatti.
jerky *adj* a scatti.
jersey *n* maglia *f*.
jest *n* scherzo *m*; * *vt* scherzare.
jester *n* buffone *m*.
Jesuit *n* gesuita *f*.
Jesus *n* Gesù *m*.
jet *n* (*min*) giaietto *m*; getto *m*; jet *m*.
jet engine *n* motore *m* a reazione.
jettison *vt* alleggerirsi di.
jetty *n* molo *m*.
Jew *n* ebreo *m*.
jewel *n* gioiello *m*.
jeweller *n* gioielliere *m*.
jewellery *n* gioielli *mpl*.
Jewess *n* ebrea *f*.
jewish *adj* ebreo.
jib *n* (*mar*) braccio *m*.
jig *n* giga *f*.
jigsaw *n* puzzle *m*.
jilt *vt* piantare.
jinx *n* iettatore *m*.
job *n* lavoro *m*; compito *m*; impiego *m*.
jobless *adj* disoccupato.
jockey *n* fantino *m*.
jocular *adj* gioviale.
jog *vi* fare footing.
jogging *n* footing *m*.

join *vt* unire, collegare; * *vi* unirsi a; confluire; * *n* giuntura *f*.

joiner *n* falegname *m*.

joinery *n* falegnameria *f*.

joint *n* articolazione *f*; pezzo *m* di carne; spinello *m*; * *adj* comune.

jointly *adv* in comune.

joint-stock company *n* società *f* per azioni.

joke *n* battuta *f*; scherzo *m*; * *vi* scherzare.

joker *n* burlone *m*; (cards) jolly *m*.

jolly *adj* allegro.

jolt *vt* sobbalzare; * *n* scossa *f*.

jostle *vt* sballottare.

journal *n* periodico *m*.

journalism *n* giornalismo *m*.

journalist *n* giornalista *m*/*f*.

journey *n* viaggio *m*.

jovial *adj* gioviale.

joy *n* gioia *f*.

joyful, joyous *adj* lieto.

joystick *n* barra *f* di comando.

jubilant *adj* esultante.

jubilation *n* esultanza *f*.

jubilee *n* giubileo *m*.

judge *n* giudice *m*; * *vt* giudicare.

judgement *n* giudizio *m*.

judicial *adj* giudiziario.

judiciary *n* magistratura *f*.

judicious *adj* giudizioso.

judo *n* judo *m*.

jug *n* brocca *f*.

juggle *vi* fare giochi di destrezza.

juggler *n* giocoliere *m*.

juice *n* succo *m*.

juicy *adj* succoso.

juke-box *n* juke-box *m*.

July *n* luglio *m*.

jumble *vt* mescolare; * *n* accozzaglia *f*.

jump *vt, vi* saltare; * *n* salto *m*.

jumper *n* saltatore *m*; maglione *m*.

jumpy *adj* nervoso.

junction *n* incrocio *m*.

juncture *n* congiuntura *f*.

June *n* giugno *m*.

jungle *n* giungla *f*.

junior *adj* più giovane.

juniper *n* (bot) ginepro *m*.

junk *n* giunca *f*; cianfrusaglie *fpl*.

junky *n* drogato *m*.

junta *n* giunta *f*.

jurisdiction *n* giurisdizione *f*.

jurisprudence *n* giurisprudenza *f*.

juror *n* giurato *m*.

jury *n* giuria *f*.

just *adj* giusto; * *adv* proprio; appena; soltanto; ~ **as** altrettanto; ~ **now** attualmente.

justice *n* giustizia *f*.

justifiable *adj* giustificabile.

justification *n* giustificazione *f*.

justify *vt* giustificare.

jut *vi*; **to ~ out** sporgere.

jute *n* iuta *f*.

juvenile *adj* giovanile; minorile; * *n* minorenne *m*/*f*.

juxtaposition *n* giustapposizione *f*.

K

kaleidoscope *n* caleidoscopio *m*.

kangaroo *n* canguro *m*.

karate *n* karatè *m*.

kebab *n* spiedino *m*.

keel *n* (mar) chiglia *f*; * *vi* crollare.

keen *adj* entusiasta; tagliente; acuto.

keenness n entusiasmo m
keep vt tenere; mantenere; trattenere; osservare; * n vito e alloggio; torrione m.
keeper n guardiano m.
keepsake n ricordo m.
keg n barile m.
kennel n canile m.
kernel n gheriglio m.
kerosene n cherosene m.
ketchup n ketchup m.
kettle n bollitore m.
key n chiave f; (mus) tasto m.
keyboard n tastiera f.
keyhole n buco m della serratura.
keynote n nota f di chiave.
key-ring n portachiavi m.
keystone n chiave f di volta.
khaki n cachi m.
kick vt dare un calcio; * n calcio m.
kid n capretto m; ragazzino m; * vt scherzare.
kidnap vt rapire.
kidnapper n rapitore m.
kidnapping n sequestro m di persona.
kidney n rene m; (cul) rognone m.
kill vt uccidere, ammazzare.
killer n assassino m.
killing adj mortale; * n uccisione; * vi fare un bel colpo.
kill-joy n guastafeste m/f.
kiln n fornace f.
kilo n chilo m.
kilogramme n chilogrammo m.
kilometre n chilometro m.
kilt n kilt m.
kin n parenti mpl; **next of ~** parente più stretto.
kind adj gentile; * n genere m.
kindergarten n asilo m.
kind-hearted adj buono.
kindle vt, vi accendere.
kindness n gentilezza f.
kindred adj imparentato.
kinetic adj cinetico.

king n re m.
kingdom n regno m.
kingfisher n martin pescatore m.
kinky adj bizzarro.
kiosk n chiosco m.
kiss n bacio m; * vt baciare.
kit n equipaggiamento m.
kitchen n cucina f.
kitchen garden n orto m.
kite n aquilone m.
kitten n gattino m.
kleptomania n cleptomania f.
knack n abilità f.
knapsack n zaino m.
knave n furfante m; fante m.
knead vt impastare.
knee n ginocchio m.
knee-cap n rotula f.
kneel vi inginocchiarsi.
knell n rintocco m funebre.
knickers npl mutande fpl.
knife n coltello m.
knight n cavaliere m; (chess) cavallo m.
knit vt lavorare a maglia; aggrottare; **to ~ one's brow** aggrottare le sopracciglia.
knitting needle n ferro m da calza.
knitwear n maglieria f.
knob n pomo m; manopola f.
knock vt, vi bussare; colpire; **to ~ down** demolire; * n colpo m.
knocker n battente m.
knock-out n K.O. m.
knoll n monticello m.
knot n nodo m; * vt annodare.
knotty adj nodoso.
know vt, vi sapere; conoscere; riconoscere.
know-all n sapientone m.
knowing adj scaltro; * adv **~ly** consciamente.
knowledge n conoscenza f; sapere m.
knowledgeable adj informato.
knuckle n nocca f.
kudos n gloria f.

L

label *n* etichetta *f*.
laboratory *n* laboratorio *m*.
laborious *adj* faticoso.
labour *n* lavoro *m*; mano d'opera *f*; * *adj* (*pol*) laburista; **to be in** ~ avere le doglie; * *vt* faticare.
labourer *n* manovale *m*.
labyrinth *n* labirinto *m*.
lace *n* pizzo *m*; laccio *m*; * *vt* allacciare.
lacerate *vt* lacerare.
lack *vt, vi* mancare; * *n* mancanza *f*.
lackadaisical *adj* languido.
lackey *n* lacchè *m*.
laconic *adj* laconico.
lacquer *n* lacca *f*.
lad *n* ragazzo *m*.
ladder *n* scala *f*; * *vt* smagliare.
ladle *n* mestolo *m*.
lady *n* signora *f*.
ladybird *n* coccinella *f*.
ladykiller *n* dongiovanni *m*.
ladylike *adj* da signora.
lag *vi* restare indietro; * *vt* rivestire (con materiale isolante); * *n* **time** ~ lasso di tempo *m*.
lager *n* birra *f* bionda.
lagoon *n* laguna *f*.
laid-back *adj* rilassato.
lair *n* tana *f*.
laity *n* laici *mpl*.
lake *n* lago *m*.
lamb *n* agnello *m*.
lambswool *n* lamb's wool *m*.
lame *adj* zoppo.
lamé *n* lamé *m*.
lament *vt* lamentare; * *n* lamento *m*.
lamentable *adj* penoso.
laminated *adj* laminato.
lamp *n* lampada *f*.

lampoon *n* satira *f*.
lampshade *n* paralume *m*.
lance *n* lancia *f*; * *vt* incidere.
lancet *n* bisturi *m*.
land *n* terra *f*, terreno *m*; paese *m*; * *vt* atterrare; sbarcare.
land forces *n* forze *fpl* terrestri.
landing *n* pianerottolo *m*; atterraggio *m*; sbarco *m*.
landing strip *n* pista *f* d'atterraggio.
landlady *n* proprietaria *f*.
landlord *n* proprietario *m*.
landlubber *n* terraiolo *m*.
landmark *n* punto *m* di riferimento.
landowner *n* proprietario *m* terriero.
landscape *n* paesaggio *m*.
landslide *n* frana *f*.
lane *n* stradina *f*.
language *n* linguaggio *m*, lingua *f*.
languid *adj* languido.
languish *vi* languire.
lanky *adj* spilungone.
lantern *n* lanterna *f*.
lap *n* grembo *m*; giro *m*; * *vt* lambire; * *vi* lappare.
lapdog *n* cagnolino *m* di lusso.
lapel *n* risvolto *m*.
lapse *n* svista *f*; intervallo *m*; * *vi* scadere; sgarrare.
larceny *n* furto *m*.
larch *n* larice *m*.
lard *n* lardo *m*.
larder *n* dispensa *f*.
large *adj* grande; **at** ~ in libertà; * *adv* ~**ly** in gran parte.
large-scale *adj* in grande scala.
largesse *n* liberalità *f*.
lark *n* allodola *f*; scherzo *m*.
larva *n* larva *f*.

laryngitis n laringite f.

larynx n laringe f.

lascivious adj lascivo.

laser n laser m.

lash n ciglio m; frustata f; * vt frustare; legare.

lasso n lasso m.

last adj ultimo; scorso; * adv at ~ finalmente; ~ly in fine; * vi durare.

last-ditch adj ultimo.

lasting adj duraturo.

last minute adj dell'ultimo momento.

latch n chiavistello m.

late adj in ritardo, tardi; defunto; * adv ~ly ultimamente.

latecomer n ritardatario n

latent adj latente.

lateral adj laterale.

lathe n tornio m.

lather n schiuma f.

latitude n latitudine f.

latter adj ultimo; ~ly negli ultimi tempi.

lattice n reticolato m.

laudable adj lodevole.

laugh vi ridere; * vt to ~ at ridere di; * n risata f.

laughable adj ridicolo.

laughing stock n zimbello m.

laughter n risata f.

launch vt varare; * n varo; motolancia f.

launching n varo m.

launching pad n rampa f di lancio.

launder vt lavare.

laundrette n lavanderia f (automatica).

laundry n lavanderia f; biancheria f.

laurel n alloro m.

lava n lava f.

lavatory n gabinetto m.

lavender n (bot) lavanda f.

lavish adj sontuoso; * vt colmare di.

law n legge f.

law-abiding adj rispettoso delle leggi.

law and order n ordine m pubblico.

law court n tribunale m.

lawful adj legale.

lawless adj senza legge.

lawn n prato m.

lawnmower n tagliaerba m.

law suit n causa f.

lawyer n avvocato m.

lax adj permissivo.

laxative n lassativo m.

laxity n permissività f.

lay vt porre; posare; stendere; apparecchiare; * adj laico.

layabout n fannullone m.

layer n strato m.

layette n corredino m.

layman n laico m.

layout n disposizione f; impostazione f.

laze vi oziare.

laziness n pigrizia f.

lazy adj pigro.

lead n piombo m; indizio m; ruolo principale; guinzaglio m; filo m; * vt condurre, guidare; **to be in the** ~ essere in testa; * vi andare avanti.

leader n capo m; leader m; guida f.

leadership n direzione f.

leading adj in testa; preminente; ~ **question** n domanda f tendenziosa.

leaf n (bot) foglia f; foglio m.

leaflet n volantino m.

leafy adj frondoso.

league n lega f; campionato m.

leak n perdita f; * vt perdere; divulgare; * vi perdere. **lean** vi pendere; appoggiarsi; * vt appoggiare; * adj magro.

leap vi saltare; balzare; * n salto m; balzare.

leapfrog n cavallina f.

leap year n anno m bisestile.
learn vt imparare.
learned adj colto.
learner n principiante m/f.
learning n cultura f.
lease n contratto m di affitto;
* vt affittare.
leasehold n proprietà f in affitto.
leash n guinzaglio m.
least adj, n minimo m; * adv
meno; **at ~** almeno; **not in the
~** niente affatto.
leather n pelle f, cuoio m.
leave n autorizzazione f, permesso m; licenza f; * vt lasciare; restare; * vi partire.
leaven vt far lievitare.
leavings npl avanzi mpl.
lecherous adj lascivo.
lecture n conferenza f; * vi tenere una conferenza.
lecturer n docente m universitario.
ledge n sporgenza f; cengia f.
ledger n libro m mastro.
lee adj (mar) sottovento.
leech n sanguisuga f.
leek n (bot) porro m.
leer vt guardare con occhi vogliosi; * n espressione f libidinosa.
lees npl sedimento m.
leeward adj sottovento.
leeway n deriva f.
left adj sinistro; **on the ~** a sinistra.
left-handed adj mancino.
leftovers npl avanzi mpl.
leg n gamba f; coscia f; tappa f.
legacy n eredità f.
legal adj legale; * adv **~ly** legalmente.
legality n legalità f.
legalize vt legalizzare.
legal tender n moneta f a corso legale.
legate n nunzio m apostolico.

legation n legazione f.
legend n leggenda f.
legendary adj leggendario.
legible adj leggibile.
legion n legione f.
legislate vt legiferare.
legislation n legislazione f.
legislative adj legislativo.
legislator n legislatore m.
legislature n corpo m legislativo.
legitimacy n legittimità f.
legitimate adj legittimo; * vt
legittimare.
leisure n svago m, tempo m
libero; **~ly** adj tranquillo.
lemon n limone m.
lemonade n limonata f.
lemon tea n te m al limone.
lemon tree n albero m di
limone.
lend vt prestare.
length n lunghezza f; durata; **at
~** esaurientemente.
lengthen vt allungare.
lengthways adv per la lunghezza.
lengthy adj lungo.
lenient adj indulgente.
lens n lente f, obiettivo m.
Lent n quaresima f.
lentil n lenticchia f.
leopard n leopardo m.
leotard n body m.
leper n lebbroso m.
leprosy n lebbra f.
lesbian adj lesbico; * n lesbica
f.
less adj, pron meno; * adv
meno; * prep meno.
lessen vt, vi diminuire.
lesser adj minore.
lesson n lezione f.
lest conj nel timore che.
let vt lasciare; affittare.
lethal adj letale.
lethargic adj letargico.
lethargy n indolenza f.

letter n lettera f.

lettering n iscrizione f.

letter of credit n lettera f di credito.

lettuce n lattuga f.

leukaemia n leucemia f.

level adj piano, piatto, alla pari; * n livello m; * vt livellare, spianare.

level-headed adj equilibrato.

lever n leva f.

leverage n forza f.

levity n frivolezza f.

levy n imposta f; * vt imporre.

lewd adj osceno.

lexicon n lessico m.

liability n responsabilità f.

liable adj responsabile; sogget-to; * adv probabile.

liaise vi mantenere i contatti con.

liaison n coordinamento m.

liar n bugiardo m.

libel n diffamazione f; * vt dif-famare.

libellous adj diffamatorio.

liberal adj liberale.

liberality n liberalità f.

liberate vt liberare.

liberation n liberazione f.

libertine n libertino m.

liberty n libertà f.

libido n libido f.

Libra n Bilancia f.

librarian n bibliotecario m.

library n biblioteca f.

libretto n libretto m.

licence n autorizzazione f; can-none m; patente f.

licentious adj licenzioso.

lichen n (bot) lichene m.

lick vt leccare; * n leccata f.

lid n coperchio m.

lie n menzogna f; * vi mentire; sdraiarsi.

lieu n: **in ~ of** invece di.

lieutenant n tenente m.

life n vita f.

lifeboat n lancia f di salvatag-gio.

life-guard n bagnino m.

life jacket n giubbotto m di sal-vataggio.

lifeless adj privo di vita.

lifelike adj realistico.

lifeline n sagola f di salvatag-gio.

life sentence n ergastolo m.

life-sized adj in grandezza nat-urale.

lifespan n durata f della vita.

lift vt sollevare; revocare; * n ascensore m; montacarichi mpl; passaggio m.

ligament n legamento m.

light n luce f; * adj chiaro; leg-gero; * vt accendere; illumin-are.

light bulb n lampadina f.

lighten vi alleggerire.

lighter n accendino m.

light-headed adj stordito.

lighthearted adj spensierato.

lighthouse n faro m.

lighting n illuminazione f.

lightly adv leggermente.

lightning n fulmine m.

lightning conductor n para-fulmine m.

lightweight adj leggero; * n peso n leggero.

light year n anno m luce.

ligneous adj ligneo.

like adj simile; * prep come; * vt piacere; **I ~ coffee** il caffè mi piace; **he ~s chocolates** gli piacciono i cioccolatini; **which do you ~ best?** quale prefer-isci?

likeable adj simpatico.

likelihood n probabilità f.

likely adj probabile.

liken vt paragonare.

likeness n somiglianza f.

likewise adv altrettanto.

liking n simpatia f.

lilac *n* lilla *m*.

lily *n* giglio *m*; ~ **of the valley** *n* mughetto *m*.

limb *n* arto *m*.

limber *adj* flessibile.

lime *n* calce *f*; tiglio *m*; laim *f*, limetta *f*.

limestone *n* calcare *m*.

limit *n* limite *m*; * *vt* limitare.

limitation *n* limitazione *f*.

limitless *adj* illimitato.

limousine *n* limousine *f*.

limp *vi* zoppicare; * *n* zoppicamento *m*; * *adj* floscio, molle.

limpet *n* patella *f*.

limpid *adj* limpido.

line *n* linea *f*; tratto *m*; ruga *f*; lenza *f*; fila *f*; riga *f*; * *vt* foderare.

lineage *n* stirpe *f*.

linear *adj* lineare.

lined *adj* rigato; foderato.

linen *n* lino *m*.

liner *n* transatlantico *m*.

linesman *n* guardalinee *m*.

linger *vi* indugiare.

lingerie *n* biancheria *f* intima.

lingering *adj* persistente.

linguist *n* linguista *m/f*.

linguistic *adj* linguistico.

linguistics *n* linguistica *f*.

liniment *n* linimento *m*.

lining *n* fodera *f*.

link *n* legame *m*; anello *m*; * *vt* collegare.

linnet *n* fanello *m*.

linoleum *n* linoleum *m*.

linseed *n*: ~ **oil** semi di lino.

lint *n* garza *f*.

lintel *n* architrave *f*.

lion *n* leone *m*.

lioness *n* leonessa *f*.

lip *n* labbro *m*.

lip read *vt*, *vi* capire dal movimento delle labbra.

lip salve *n* burro *m* di cacao.

lipstick *n* rossetto *m*.

liqueur *n* liquore *m*.

liquid *adj*, *n* liquido *m*.

liquidate *vt* liquidare.

liquidation *n* liquidazione *f*.

liquidize *vt* passare al frullatore.

liquidizer *n* frullatore *m*.

liquor *n* bevande *fpl* alcoliche.

liquorice *n* liquirizia *f*.

lisp *vi* essere bleso; * *n* pronuncia *f* blesa.

list *n* lista *f*, elenco *m*; * *vt* elencare.

listen *vi* ascoltare.

listless *adj* apatico.

litany *n* litania *f*.

literal *adj* letterale.

literary *adj* letterario.

literate *adj* che sa leggere e scrivere.

literature *n* letteratura *f*.

lithe *adj* agile.

lithograph, lithography *n* litografia *f*.

litigation *n* causa *f* (giudiziaria).

litigious *adj* litigioso.

litre *n* litro *m*.

litter *n* rifiuti *mpl*; (*zool*) cucciolata *f*.

little *adj* piccolo; * *pron* poco * *adv* ~ **by** ~ gradualmente * *n* poco *m*.

liturgy *n* liturgia *f*.

live *vi* vivere, abitare; **to** ~ **or** vivere di; **to** ~ **up to** essere all'altezza di; * *adj* vivo; inesploso.

livelihood *n* sostentamento *m*

liveliness *n* vivacità *f*.

lively *adj* vivace.

liven up *vt* ravvivare.

liver *n* fegato *m*.

livery *n* livrea *f*.

livestock *n* bestiame *m*.

livid *adj* furibondo; livido.

living *adj* vivente, vita.

living room *n* soggiorno *m*.

lizard *n* lucertola *f*.

load vt caricare; * n carico m.
loaded adj carico.
loaf n pane m; **meat ~** polpettone m.
loafer n bighellone m.
loam n terriccio m.
loan n prestito m; * vt prestare.
loathe vt detestare.
loathing n ribrezzo m.
loathsome adj ripugnante.
lobby n atrio m; gruppo m di pressione.
lobe n lobo m.
lobster n aragosta f.
local adj locale.
local anaesthetic n anestesia f locale.
local government n amministrazione f locale.
locality n località f.
localize vt localizzare.
locally adv nelle vicinanze.
locate vt collocare.
location n posizione f.
loch n (Scot) lago m.
lock n serratura f; chiusa f; sterzo m; (hair) ciocca f; * vt chiudere a chiave.
locker n armadietto m.
locket n medaglione m.
lockout n serrata f.
locksmith n fabbro m.
lock-up n prigione f.
locomotive n locomotiva f.
locust n locusta f.
lodge n portineria f; loggia f; * vi alloggiare.
lodger n pensionante m/f.
loft n soffitta f.
lofty adj altezzoso.
log n tronco m.
logbook n (mar) giornale m di bordo; libretto m di circolazione.
logic n logica f.
logical adj logico.
logo n logo m.

loin n fianchi mpl; (cul) lombata f.
loiter vi bighellonare.
loll vi ciondolare.
lollipop n lecca lecca m.
loneliness n solitudine f.
lonely adj solitario.
long adj lungo; * vi desiderare.
long-distance n: **~ call** interurbano m.
longevity n longevità f.
longing n desiderio m.
longitude n longitudine f.
long-range adj a lungo raggio.
long-term adj a lungo termine.
long wave adj a onda f lunga.
long-winded adj prolisso.
look vt guardare; * vi guardare; sembrare; assomigliare; **to ~ after** occuparsi di; **to ~ for** cercare; **to ~ forward to** non vedere l'ora di fare qc; * n occhiata f; aria f; aspetto m.
looking glass n specchio m.
look-out n (mil) sentinella f.
loom n telaio m; * vi apparire indistintamente.
loop n cappio m.
loophole n scappatoia f.
loose adj allentato; sciolto; staccato; dissoluto.
loosen vt allentare.
loot vt saccheggiare; * n bottino m.
lop vt tagliare.
lop-sided adj sbilenco.
loquacious adj loquace.
loquacity n loquacità f.
lord n signore m.
lore n tradizioni fpl.
lorry n camion m.
lose vt, vi perdere.
loser n perdente m.
loss n perdita f; **to be at a ~** non saper come fare.
lost property office n ufficio m oggetti smarriti.
lot n destino m, sorte f; partita

f; lotto *m*; molto *m*.

lotion *n* lozione *f*.

lottery *n* lotteria *f*.

loud *adj* forte.

loudspeaker *n* altoparlante *m*.

lounge *n* salone *m*, sala *f* d'attesa.

louse *n* pidocchio *m*.

lousy *adj* schifoso; pessimo.

lout *n* zotico *m*.

lovable *adj* adorabile.

love *n* amore *m*; **to fall in ~** innamorarsi; * *vt* amare, voler bene a.

love letter *n* lettera *f* d'amore.

love life *n* vita *f* sentimentale.

lovely *adj* bello.

lover *n* amante *m/f*.

love-sick *adj* malato d'amore.

loving *adj* affettuoso.

low *adj* basso; scadente; malfamato; * *n* depressione *f*; * *vi* muggire.

low-cut *adj* scolato.

lower *adj* inferiore; * *vt* calare; ridurre.

lowland *n* bassopiano *m*.

lowly *adj* umile.

loyal *adj* leale.

loyalty *n* lealtà *f*.

lozenge *n* pastiglia *f*; (*geom*) losanga *f*.

lubricant *n* lubrificante *m*.

lubricate *vt* lubrificare.

lucid *adj* lucido.

luck *n* fortuna *f*.

luckily *adv* fortunatamente.

luckless *adj* sventurato.

lucky *adj* fortunato.

lucrative *adj* lucrativo.

ludicrous *adj* ridicolo.

lug *vt* trascinare.

luggage *n* bagagli *mpl*.

lugubrious *adj* lugubre.

lukewarm *adj* tiepido.

lull *vt* calmare; * *n* tregua *f*.

lullaby *n* ninnananna *f*.

lumbago *n* lombaggine *f*.

lumberjack *n* taglialegna *m*.

luminous *adj* luminoso.

lump *n* zolletta *f*; grumo *m*; nodulo *m*; * *vi* **to ~ together** mettere insieme.

lump sum *n* pagamento *m* unico.

lunacy *n* pazzia *f*.

lunar *adj* lunare.

lunatic *adj*, *n* matto *m*, pazzo *m*.

lunch, luncheon *n* pranzo *m*, (seconda) colazione *f*.

lung *n* polmone *m*.

lurch *n* sobbalzo *m*; * *vt* sobbalzare.

lure *n* richiamo; * *vt* attirare (con l'inganno).

lurid *adj* orrendo; fiammeggiante.

lurk *vi* girare furtivamente.

luscious *adj* appetitoso.

lush *adj* lussureggiante.

lust *n* libidine *f*; * *vi* desiderare.

lustre *n* lustro *m*.

lustful *adj* libidinoso.

lusty *adj* vigoroso.

lute *n* liuto *m*.

luxuriant *adj* lussureggiante.

luxurious *adj* lussuoso.

luxury *n* lusso *m*.

lying *adj* bugiardo.

lymph *n* linfa *f*.

lynch *vt* linciare.

lynx *n* lince *f*.

lyrical *adj* lirico.

lyrics *npl* parole *fpl*.

M

macaroni n maccheroni mpl.

macaroon n amaretto m.

mace n mazza f; macis m/f.

macerate vt macerare.

machination n macchinazione f.

machine n macchina f.

machine gun n mitragliatrice f.

machinery n macchinari mpl.

mackerel n sgombro m.

mackintosh n impermeabile m.

mad adj pazzo.

madam n signora f.

madden vt far impazzire.

madder n (bot) robbia f.

madhouse n manicomio m.

madly adv follemente.

madman n folle m.

madness n follia f.

maestro n maestro m.

magazine n rivista f; caricatore m.

maggot n baco m.

magic n magia f; * adj magico.

magician n mago m.

magistrate n magistrato m.

magnanimity n magnanimità f.

magnanimous adj magnanimo.

magnate n magnate m.

magnesia n magnesia f.

magnesium n magnesio m.

magnet n calamita f.

magnetic adj magnetico.

magnetism n magnetismo.

magnificence n magnificenza f.

magnificent adj magnifico.

magnify vt ingrandire.

magnifying glass n lente f d'ingrandimento.

magnitude n vastità f.

magpie n gazza f.

mahogany n mogano m.

maid n cameriera f.

maiden n fanciulla f; * adj inaugurale.

maiden name n nome m da ragazza.

mail n posta f; * vt spedire (per posta).

mailing list n indirizzario m.

mail-order n vendita f per corrispondenza.

mail train treno m postale.

maim vt storpiare.

main adj principale; * n conduttura f principale.

mainland n continente m.

main-line n (rail) linea f principale.

mainly adv principalmente.

main road n strada f principale.

mainstay n sostegno m.

maintain vt mantenere.

maintenance n mantenimento m; manutenzione f.

maize n granturco m.

majestic adj maestoso.

majesty n maestà f.

major adj maggiore; * n (mil) maggiore m.

majority n maggioranza f.

make vt fare; fabbricare; to ~ for essere diretto a; to ~ up inventare; to ~ up for rimediare; * n marca f.

make-believe n finzione f.

makeshift adj improvvisato.

make-up n trucco m; composizione f.

maladjusted adj disadattato.

malady n malattia f.

malaise n malessere m.

325

malaria n malaria f.

malcontent adj, n malcontento m.

male adj maschile; * n maschio m.

malevolent adj malevolo.

malfunction n cattivo funzionamento m.

malice n malizia f.

malicious adj cattivo.

malign adj malefico; * vt calunniare.

malignant adj maligno.

mall n viale m.

malleable adj malleabile.

mallet n mazzuolo m.

mallow n (bot) malva f.

malnutrition n denutrizione f.

malpractice n negligenza f.

malt n malto m.

maltreat vt maltrattare.

mammal n mammifero m.

mammoth n mammut m; * adj colossale.

man n uomo m; * vt (mil) fornire di uomini.

manacle n manetta f.

manage vt gestire

manageable adj maneggevole.

management n gestione f.

manager n gestore m, manager m.

manageress n direttrice f.

managerial adj dirigente.

managing director n amministratore m delegato.

mandarin n mandarino m.

mandate n mandato m.

mandatory adj obbligatorio.

mandolin n mandolino m.

mane n criniera f.

manful adj valoroso.

manganese n manganese m.

manger n mangiatoia f.

mangle n strizzatoio m; * vt stritolare.

mango n mango m.

mangy adj rognoso.

manhandle vt malmenare.

manhood n virilità f.

man-hour n ora f di lavoro.

mania n mania f.

maniac n maniaco m.

manic adj maniaco.

manicure n manicure f.

manifest adj palese; * vt manifestare.

manifestation n manifestazione f.

manifesto n manifesto m.

manipulate vt manipolare.

manipulation n manipolazione f.

mankind n umanità f.

manliness n virilità f.

manly adj virile.

man-made adj artificiale.

manner n maniera f; ~s educazione f.

manoeuvrable adj maneggevole.

manoeuvre n manovra f; * vt, vi manovrare.

manor n maniero m.

manpower n manodopera f.

mansion n palazzo m.

manslaughter n omicidio m colposo.

mantelpiece n mensola f del caminetto.

manual adj, n manuale m.

manufacture n fabbricazione f; * vt fabbricare.

manufacturer n fabbricante m.

manure n concime m; * vt concimare.

manuscript n manoscritto m.

many adj molti, tanti; ~ a time più volte; how ~? quanti?; as ~ as tanti quanti.

map n carta f, pianta f; * vt tracciare una mappa.

maple n acero m.

mar vt sciupare.

marathon n maratona f.

marauder *n* saccheggiatore *m*.

marble *n* marmo *m*; bilia *f*; * *adj* di marmo.

March *n* marzo *m*.

march *n* marcia *f*; * *vi* marciare.

marchpast *n* sfilata *f*.

mare *n* giumenta *f*.

margarine *n* margarina *f*.

margin *n* margine *m*.

marginal *adj* marginale.

marigold *n* calendola *f*.

marijuana *n* marijuana *f*.

marina *n* marina *f*.

marinade *n* marinata *f*.

marinate *vt* marinare.

marine *adj* marino; * *n* marina *f*.

mariner *n* marinaio *m*.

marital *adj* coniugale.

maritime *adj* marittimo.

marjoram *n* maggiorana *f*.

mark *n* segno *m*; voto *m*; marco *m*; * *vt* macchiare; segnare; correggere.

marker *n* marcatore *m*.

market *n* mercato *m*.

marketable *adj* vendibile.

marketing *n* marketing *m*.

marketplace *n* mercato *m*.

market research *n* ricerca *f* di mercato.

marksman *n* tiratore *m* scelto.

marmalade *n* marmellata *f* d'arance.

maroon *adj* bordeaux; ~ed abbandonato, isolato.

marquee *n* grande tenda *f*.

marriage *n* matrimonio *m*.

marriage certificate *n* certificato *m* di matrimonio.

married *adj* sposato, coniugato.

marrow *n* midollo *m*; (*bot*) zucca *f*.

marry *vt* sposare; * *vi* sposarsi.

marsh *n* palude *f*.

marshal *n* maresciallo *m*; * *vt* schierare.

marshy *adj* paludoso.

marsupial *adj, n* marsupiale *m*.

marten *n* martora *f*.

martial *adj* marziale; ~ **law** stato d'assedio.

martin *n* balestruccio *m*.

martyr *n* martire *m*.

martyrdom *n* martirio *m*.

marvel *n* meraviglia *f*; * *vi* stupirsi.

marvellous *adj* meraviglioso.

marzipan *n* marzapane *m*.

mascara *n* mascara *m*.

mascot *n* portafortuna *m*.

masculine *adj, n* maschile *m*.

mash *n* pastone *m*; purè *m*; * *vt* schiacciare.

mask *n* maschera *f*; * *vt* mascherare.

masochist *n* masochista *m/f*.

mason *n* muratore *m*; massone *m*.

masonry *n* muratura *f*; massoneria *f*.

masquerade *n* mascherata *f*.

mass *n* messa *f*; massa *f*; * *vt* adunare; * *vi* adunarsi.

massacre *n* massacro *m*; * *vt* massacrare.

message *n* massaggio *m*; * *vt* massaggiare.

masseur *n* massaggiatore *m*.

masseuse *n* massaggiatrice *f*.

massive *adj* massiccio.

mass media *n* mass media *mpl*.

mast *n* albero *m*.

master *n* padrone *m*; insegnante *m*; * *vt* dominare; (*fig*) impadronirsi.

masterly *adj* magistrale.

mastermind *n* cervello *m*.

masterpiece *n* capolavoro *m*.

mastery *n* padronanza *f*.

masticate *vt* masticare.

mastiff *n* mastino *m* (inglese).

masturbate *vi* masturbarsi.

masturbation *n* masturbazione *f*.

mat n tappetino m, zerbino m.

match n fiammifero m; partita f, incontro m; pari m/f, uguale m/f; * vt uguagliare; * vi intonarsi; corrispondere.

matchbox n scatola f per fiammiferi..

matchless adj impareggiabile.

matchmaker n sensale m/f di matrimoni.

mate n compagno m; * vt accoppiare; * vi accoppiarsi.

material adj materiale; * n stoffa f, tessuto m; materiale m.

materialism n materialismo m.

maternal adj materno.

maternity n maternità f.

mathematical adj matematico.

mathematician n matematico m.

mathematics npl matematica f.

maths npl matematica f.

matinée n matinée f.

mating n accoppiamento m.

matins npl mattutino m.

matriculate vi immatricolarsi.

matriculation n immatricolazione f.

matrimonial adj coniugale.

matt adj opaco.

matted adj infeltrito.

matter n materia f; faccenda f; **what is the ~?** cosa c'è?; **a ~ of fact** per la verità; * vi importare.

mattress n materasso m.

mature adj maturo; * vi maturarsi.

maturity n maturità f.

maul vt sbranare.

mausoleum n mausoleo m.

mauve adj malva.

maxim n massima f.

maximize vt massimizzare.

maximum adj, n massimo m.

May n maggio m; **~ Day** il primo maggio m; **mayday** S.O.S. m.

maybe adv forse, può darsi.

mayonnaise n maionese f.

mayor n sindaco m.

mayoress n sindaca f.

maze n laberinto m.

me pron mi, me.

meadow n prato m.

meagre adj magro.

meal n farina f; pasto m.

mean adj avaro; meschino; medio; * n mezzo m; **~s** mezzi mpl; **in the ~time, meanwhile** nel frattempo; * vt significare; intendere.

meander vi serpeggiare.

meaning n significato m.

meaningful adj significativo.

meaningless adj senza senso.

meanness n avarizia f.

measles n morbillo m.

measure n misura f; provvedimento m; * vt misurare.

measurement n misurazione f, misura f.

meat n carne f.

meatball n polpetta f di carne.

meaty adj di carne.

mechanic n meccanico m.

mechanical adj meccanico.

mechanics npl meccanica f.

mechanism n meccanismo m.

mechanize vt meccanizzare.

medal n medaglia f.

medallion n medaglione m.

meddle vi immischiarsi.

meddler n impiccione m.

media npl media mpl.

mediate vi mediare.

mediation n mediazione f.

mediator n mediatore m.

medical adj medico; * n visita f medica.

medicate vt medicare.

medicated adj medicato.

medicinal adj medicinale.

medicine n medicina f.

medieval adj medievale.

mediocre adj mediocre.

mediocrity n mediocrità f.

meditate vi meditare.

meditation n meditazione f.

meditative adj meditativo.

Mediterranean adj mediterraneo; * n Mediterraneo m.

medium n mezzo; * adj medio.

medium wave n onde fpl medie.

medley n pot-pourri m.

meek adj mite.

meet vt incontrare; soddisfare; **they met with an accident** hanno avuto un incidente.

meeting n incontro m; riunione f; raduno m.

megalomaniac n megalomane m/f.

megaphone n megafono m.

melancholy n malinconia f; * adj malinconico.

mellow adj maturo; addolcito; * vt maturare; * vi addolcirsi.

melodious adj melodioso.

melodrama n melodramma f.

melody n melodia f.

melon n melone m.

melt vt fondere, sciogliere.

melting point n punto m di fusione.

member n membro m; socio m.

membership n iscrizione f.

membrane n membrana f.

memento n ricordo m.

memo n promemoria m.

memoir n saggio m monografico.

memorable adj memorabile.

memorandum n memorandum m.

memorial n monumento m; * adj commemorativo.

memorize vt imparare a memoria.

memory n memoria f; ricordo m.

menace n minaccia f; * vt minacciare.

menacing adj minaccioso.

menagerie n serraglio m.

mend vt aggiustare, accomodare.

mending n rammendo m.

menial adj servile.

meningitis n meningite f.

menopause n menopausa f.

menstruation n mestruazione f.

mental adj mentale.

mentality n mentalità f.

mentally adv mentalmente.

mention n menzione f; * vt accennare a.

mentor n mentore m.

menu n menu m.

mercantile adj mercantile.

mercenary adj, n mercenario m.

merchandise n merce f.

merchant n commerciante m/f.

merchant navy n marina f mercantile.

merciful adj misericordioso.

merciless adj spietato.

mercury n mercurio m.

mercy n misericordia f.

mere adj puro; **~ly** semplicemente.

merge vi fondersi, confluire.

merger n fusione f.

meridian adj, n meridiano m.

meringue n meringa f.

merit n merito m; * vt meritare.

meritocracy n meritocrazia f.

meritorious adj meritorio.

mermaid n sirena f.

merrily adv gaiamente.

merriment n allegria f.

merry adj allegro; brillo.

merry-go-round n giostra f.

mesh n maglia f.

mesmerize vt ipnotizzare.

mess n disordine m; pasticcio m; * vt **to ~ up** scompigliare.

message n messaggio m.

messenger *n* messaggero *m*.
metabolism *n* metabolismo *m*.
metal *n* metallo *m*.
metallic *adj* metallico.
metallurgy *n* metallurgia *f*.
metamorphosis *n* metamorfosi *f*.
metaphor *n* metafora *f*.
metaphoric(al) *adj* metaforico.
metaphysical *adj* metafisico.
metaphysics *n* metafisica *f*.
mete (out) *vi* ripartire.
meteor *n* meteora *f*.
meteorite *n* meteorite *m*.
meteorological *adj* meteorologico.
meteorology *n* meteorologia *f*.
meter *n* contattore *m*.
methane *n* metano *m*.
method *n* metodo *m*.
methodical *adj* metodico.
methylated spirits *npl* alcol *m*
denaturato.
metric *adj* metrico.
metropolis *n* metropoli *f*.
metropolitan *adj* metropolitano.
mettle *n* fegato *m*.
mew *n* miagolio *m*; * *vi*
miagolare.
mezzanine *n* mezzanino *m*.
microbe *n* microbo *m*.
microchip *n* chip *m*.
microphone *n* microfono *m*.
microscope *n* microscopio *m*.
microscopic *adj* microscopico.
microwave *n* microonda *f*.
mid *adj* metà.
mid-day *n* mezzogiorno *m*.
middle *adj* centrale; * *n* mezzo
m, centro *m*.
middle name *n* secondo nome
m.
middleweight *n* peso *m* medio.
middling *adj* medio; mediocre.
midge *n* moscerino *m*.
midget *n* nano *m*.
midnight *n* mezzanotte *m*.

midriff *n* diaframma *m*.
midst *prep* in mezzo a.
midsummer *n* piena estate *f*.
midway *adv* a metà strada.
midwife *n* ostetrica *f*.
midwifery *n* ostetricia *f*.
midwinter *n* pieno inverno *m*.
might *n* forza *f*.
mighty *adj* possente.
migraine *n* emicrania *f*.
migrate *vi* migrare.
migration *n* migrazione *f*.
migratory *adj* migratore.
mild *adj* mite.
mildew *n* muffa *f*.
mile *n* miglio *m*.
mileage *n* chilometraggio *m*.
milometer *n* contachilometri
m.
milestone *n* pietra *f* miliare.
milieu *n* ambiente *m* sociale.
militant *adj* militante *m/f*.
military *adj* militare; * *n* esercito *m*.
militate *vi* militare.
militia *n* milizia *f*.
milk *n* latte *m*.
milkshake *n* frappé *m*.
milky *adj* latteo; **M~ Way** *n* Via
Lattea *f*.
mill *n* mulino *m*; fabbrica *f*; * *vt*
macinare.
millennium *n* millennio *m*.
miller *n* mugnaio *m*.
millet *n* (*bot*) miglio *m*.
milligramme *n* milligrammo
m.
millilitre *n* millilitro *m*.
millimetre *n* millimetro *m*.
milliner *n* modista *f*.
million *n* milione *m*.
millionaire *n* milionario *m*.
millionth *adj*, *n* milionesimo *m*.
millipede *n* millepiedi *m*.
millstone *n* macina *f*.
mime *n* mimmo *m*; * *vt*, *vi* mimare.
mimic *n* imitatore; * *vt* imitare.

mimicry n imitazione f.

mince vt tritare; * n carne f macinata.

mincer n tritacarne m.

mind n mente f; * vt badare a; * vi preoccuparsi.

minded adj: **open ~** di mente aperta.

mindful adj consapevole.

mindless adj insensato.

mine pron mio; * n miniera f; mina f; * vt estrarre, minare.

minefield n campo m minato.

miner n minatore m.

mineral adj, n minerale m.

mineralogy n mineralogia f.

mineral water n acqua f minerale.

minesweeper n dragamine m.

mingle vt mescolare.

miniature n miniatura f.

minimal adj minimo.

minimize vt minimizzare.

minimum n minima f.

mining n estrazione f mineraria.

minion n servo m favorito.

minister n ministro m; * vi assistere.

ministerial adj ministeriale.

ministry n ministero m.

mink n visone m.

minnow n pesciolino m d'acqua dolce.

minor adj minore; * n minorenne m/f.

minority n minoranza f.

minstrel n menestrello m.

mint n (bot) menta; zecca f; * vt coniare.

minuet n minuetto m.

minus adv meno.

minute n minuto m; **~s** verbale.

minute adj minuscolo.

miracle n miracolo m.

miraculous adj miracoloso.

mirage n miraggio m.

mire n melma f.

mirror n specchio m; * vt riflettere.

mirth n ilarità f.

misadventure n disavventura f.

misanthropist n misantropo m.

misapprehension n equivoco m.

misbehave vi comportarsi male.

misbehaviour n cattiva condotta f.

miscalculate vt calcolare male.

miscarriage n aborto m spontaneo; **~ of justice** errore giudiziario.

miscarry vi abortire.

miscellaneous adj vario.

miscellany n miscellanea f.

mischief n birichinata f; cattiveria f.

mischievous adj birichino; malizioso.

misconception n idea f sbagliata.

misconduct n cattiva condotta f.

misconstrue vt fraintendere.

miscreant adj scellerato.

misdeed n misfatto m.

misdemeanour n trasgressione f.

misdirect vt indirizzare male.

miser n avaro m.

miserable adj infelice.

miserly adj taccagno.

misery n tristezza f, miseria f.

misfit n disadattato m.

misfortune n disgrazia f.

misgiving n apprensione f.

misguided adj malaccorto.

mishandle vt bistrattare.

mishap n incidente m.

misinform vt informare male.

misinterpret vt interpretare male.

misjudge vt calcolare male.

mislay vt smarrire.

mislead vt trarre in inganno.

mismanage vt amministrare male.

mismanagement n cattiva amministrazione f.

misnomer n termine m improprio.

misogynist n misogino m.

misplace vt smarrire.

misprint n errore m di stampa.

misrepresent vt travisare.

Miss n signorina f.

miss vt perdere; mancare; evitare; * n colpo m mancato.

missal n messale m.

misshapen adj deforme.

missile n missile m.

missing adj mancante.

mission n missione f.

missionary n missionario m.

misspent adj sprecato.

mist n foschia f; * vi **to ~ up** appannarsi.

mistake vt sbagliare; * vi sbagliarsi; * n errore m, sbaglio m.

Mister n signore m.

mistletoe n vischio m.

mistreat vt maltrattare.

mistress n amante f; padrona f.

mistrust vt diffidare di; * n diffidenza f.

mistrustful adj diffidente.

misty adj brumoso.

misunderstand vt fraintendere.

misunderstanding n malinteso m.

misuse vt abusare di; * n abuso m.

mite n acaro m.

mitigate vt mitigare.

mitigation n mitigazione f.

mitre n mitra f.

mitten n muffola f.

mix vt mescolare; * n mescolanza f.

mixed adj assortito; misto.

mixed-up adj confuso.

mixer n frullatore m; betoniera f.

mixture n mistura f; miscela f.

mix-up n malinteso m.

moan n gemito m; * vi gemere.

moat n fossato m.

mob n folla f.

mobile adj mobile.

mobile home n casa f viaggiante.

mobility n mobilità f.

mobilize vt (mil) mobilitare.

moccasin n mocassino m.

mock vi beffarsi; * n finto m.

mockery n scherno m.

mocking n beffardo m.

mock-up n modello m.

mode n modo m.

model n modello m; indossatore m; * vt modellare; indossare; * vi posare.

moderate adj, n moderato m; * vi attenuarsi.

moderation n moderazione f.

modern adj moderno.

modernization n modernizzazione f.

modernize vt modernizzare.

modest adj modesto.

modesty n modestia f.

modicum n piccola quantità f.

modification n modifica f.

modify vt modificare.

modulate vt modulare.

modulation n (mus) modulazione f.

module n modulo m.

mohair n mohair m.

moist adj umido.

moisten vt inumidire.

moisture n umidità f.

molar n molare m.

molasses npl melassa f.

mole n neo m; talpa f.

molecule n molecola f.
molest vt molestare.
mollify vt pacificare.
mollusc n mollusco m.
mollycoddle vt coccolare.
molten adj fuso.
moment n momento m.
momentary adj momentaneo.
momentous adj importante.
momentum n momento m.
monarch n monarca m.
monarchy n monarchia f.
monastery n monastero m.
monastic adj monastico.
Monday n lunedì m.
monetary adj monetario.
money n denaro m, soldi mpl.
money order n vaglia m postale.
mongol n mongoloide m/f.
mongrel n bastardo m.
monitor n monitor m.
monk n monaco m.
monkey n scimmia f.
monochrome adj monocromatico.
monocle n monocolo m.
monologue n monologo m.
monopolize vt monopolizzare.
monopoly n monopolio m.
monosyllable n monosillabo m.
monotonous adj monotono.
monotony n monotonia f.
monoxide n monossido m.
monsoon n monsone m.
monster n mostro m; * adj gigantesco.
monstrosity n mostruosità f.
monstrous adj colossale; mostruoso.
montage n fotomontaggio m.
month n mese m.
monthly adj mensile.
monument n monumento m.
monumental adj monumentale.
moo vi muggire; * n muggito m.
mood n (gr) modo m; umore m.

moody adj lunatico.
moon n luna f.
moonbeam n raggio m di luna.
moonlight n chiaro m di luna.
moor n brughiera f; * vt ormeggiare.
moorland n brughiera f.
moose n alce m.
mop n scopa f di filacce; * vt passare lo straccio.
mope vi essere avvilito.
moped n ciclomotore m.
moral adj morale; * npl ~s principi morali.
morale n morale m.
moralist n moralista m/f.
morality n moralità f.
moralize vi moraleggiare.
morass n pantano m.
morbid adj morboso.
more adj più, ancora, altro; **once ~** un'altra volta; * adv **and ~** sempre di più.
moreover adv inoltre.
morgue n orbitorio m.
morning n mattina f; **good ~** buon giorno.
moron n idiota m/f.
morose adj imbronciato.
morphine n morfina f.
Morse Code n alfabeto m Morse.
morsel n boccone m.
mortal adj, n mortale m.
mortality n mortalità f.
mortar n mortaio m.
mortgage n ipoteca f; * vt ipotecare.
mortification n mortificazione f.
mortify vt mortificare.
mortuary n orbitorio m.
mosaic n mosaico m.
mosque n moschea f.
mosquito n zanzara f.
moss n muschio m.
mossy adj muscoso.
most adj più; * pron quasi tutto.

motel n motel m.

moth n tarma f.

mothball n pallina f di naftalina.

mother n madre f.

motherhood n maternità f.

mother-in-law n suocera f.

motherly adj materno.

mother-of-pearl n madreperla f.

mother-to-be n futuro mamma f.

mother tongue n lingua f madre.

motif n motivo m.

motion n moto m, movimento m; cenno m.

motionless adj immobile.

motion picture n film m.

motivate vt motivare.

motivation n motivazione f.

motive n motivo m.

motley adj variopinto.

motor n motore m.

motorbike n moto f.

motorboat n motoscafo f.

motorcycle n motocicletta f.

motorist n automobilista m/f.

motorway n autostrada f.

mottled adj variopinto.

motto n motto m.

mould n muffa f; stampo m; * vt plasmare.

moulding n modanatura f.

mouldy adj ammuffito.

moult vt fare la muta.

mound n mucchio m.

mount n monte m; piedistallo m; * vt montare a; salire.

mountain n montagna f.

mountaineer n alpinista m/f.

mountaineering n alpinismo m.

mountainous adj montagnoso.

mourn vt, vi piangere.

mourner n chi piange la morte di qualcuno.

mournful adj lugubre.

mourning n lutto m.

mouse n topo m.

mousse n mousse f.

moustache n baffi mpl.

mouth n bocca f.

mouthful n boccone m.

mouth organ n armonica f.

mouthpiece n bocchino m; portavoce m/f.

mouthwash n colluttorio m.

mouthwatering adj che fa venire l'acquolina in bocca.

moveable adj movibile.

move * vt spostare, muovere; commuovere; * vi traslocare; * n mossa f, movimento m, trasloco m.

movement n movimento m.

movie n film m.

movie camera n cinepresa f.

moving adj mobile; commovente.

mow vt falciare.

mower n falciatrice f.

Mrs n signora f.

much adj, pron, adv molto.

muck n letame m.

mucous adj mucoso.

mucus n muco m.

mud n fango m.

muddle n confusione f.

muddy adj fangoso.

mudguard n parafango m.

muff n manicotto m.

muffle vt imbacuccare.

mug n tazzone m; boccale m; * vt aggredire.

mugger n rapinatore m.

muggy adj afoso.

mulberry n mora di gelso; ~ **tree** gelso m.

mule n mulo m.

mull vt scaldare con aromi; rimuginare.

multifarious adj svariato.

multiple adj, n multiplo m.

multiplication n moltiplicazione f; ~ **table** tavola pitagorica.

multiply *vt* moltiplicare.
multitude *n* moltitudine *f*.
mumble *vt, vi* borbottare.
mummy *n* mummia *f*; mamma *f*.
mumps *npl* orecchioni *mpl*.
munch *vt* sgranocchiare.
mundane *adj* banale.
municipal *adj* municipale.
municipality *n* comune *m*.
munificence *n* munificenza *f*.
munitions *npl* munizioni *fpl*.
mural *n* pittura *f* murale; * *adj* murale.
murder *n* omicidio *m*, assassinio *m*; * *vt* assassinare.
murderer *n* assassino *m*.
murderess *n* assassina *f*.
murderous *adj* micidiale.
murky *adj* torbido.
murmur *n* mormorio *m*; * *vt, vi* mormorare.
muscle *n* muscolo *m*.
muscular *adj* muscolare.
muse *vt* sognare; * *n* musa *f*.
museum *n* museo *m*.
mush *n* pappa *f*.
mushroom *n* fungo *m*; * *vi* svilupparsi rapidamente.
music *n* musica *f*.
musical *adj* musicale.
musician *n* musicista *m/f*.
musk *n* muschio *m*.
muslin *n* mussola *f*.
mussel *n* cozza *f*.

must *mod aux vb* dovere; * *n* necessità *f*.
mustard *n* senape *f*.
muster *vt* radunare; * *n* appello *m*.
musty *adj* stantio.
mutant *adj, n* mutante *m*.
mutate *vt, vi* cambiare, mutare.
mute *adj* muto.
muted *adj* attutito.
mutilate *vt* mutilare.
mutilation *n* mutilazione *f*.
mutiny *n* ammutinamento *m*; * *vi* ammutinarsi.
mutter *vt, vi* borbottare; * *n* borbottio *m*.
mutton *n* montone *m*.
mutual *adj* reciproco.
muzzle *n* muso *m*; museruola *f*.
my *pron* mio.
myopic *adj* miope.
myriad *n* miriade *f*.
myrrh *n* mirra *f*.
myrtle *n* mirto *m*.
myself *pron* io stesso, me stesso.
mysterious *adj* misterioso.
mystery *n* mistero *m*.
mystic *n* mistico *m*.
mystical *adj* mistico.
mystify *vt* lasciare perplesso.
mystique *n* fascino *m*.
myth *n* mito *m*.
mythology *n* mitologia *f*.

N

nab *vt* acciuffare.
nag *n* ronzino *m*; brontolone *m*; * *vt* assillare.
nagging *adj* brontolone; insistente; * *n* brontolii *mpl*.
nail *n* unghia *f*; chiodo *m*; * *vt* inchiodare.
nailbrush *n* spazzolino *m* da unghie.
nailfile *n* limetta *f*.
nail varnish *n* smalto per unghie.
naïve *adj* ingenuo.
naked *adj* nudo.
name *n* nome *m*; * *vt* chiamare; nominare; stabilire.

nameless adj ignoto.

namely adv cioè.

namesake n omonimo m.

nanny n bambinaia f.

nap n pisolino m; pelo m; * vi schiacciare un pisolino.

napalm n napalm m.

nape n nuca f.

napkin n tovagliolo m.

narcissus n (bot) narciso m.

narcotic adj, n narcotico m.

narked adj scocciato.

narrate vt narrare.

narration n narrazione f.

narrative adj narrativo; * n narrazione f.

narrow adj stretto; * vt restringere; * vi stringersi.

narrow-minded adj meschino; ~**ness** meschinità f.

nasal adj nasale.

nasturtium n nasturzio m.

nasty adj cattivo, sgradevole, maligno.

nation n nazione f.

national adj nazionale; * n cittadino m.

nationalism n nazionalismo m.

nationalist adj, n nazionalista m/f.

nationality n nazionalità f.

nationalize vt nazionalizzare.

nationwide adj a livello nazionale.

native adj natale; indigeno * n nativo m; indigeno m.

native language n madre lingua f.

Nativity n Natività f.

natural adj naturale.

naturalist n naturalista m/f.

naturalize vt naturalizzare.

nature n natura f.

naught n (poet) nulla m.

naughty adj disubbidiente; spinto.

nausea n nausea f.

nauseate vt nauseare.

nauseous adj nauseabondo.

nautical adj nautico.

naval adj navale.

nave n navata f.

navel n ombelico m.

navigate vt, vi navigare.

navigation n navigazione f.

navy n marina f.

Nazi adj, n nazista m/f.

near prep, adj, adv vicino; * vi avvicinarsi a.

nearby adj, adv vicino.

nearly adv quasi.

near-sighted adj miope.

neat adj ordinato.

nebulous adj nebuloso.

necessarily adv necessariamente.

necessary adj necessario.

necessitate vt rendere necessario.

necessity n necessità f.

neck n collo m.

necklace n collana f.

nectar n nettare m.

née adj nata; ~ **Brown** nata Brown.

need n bisogno m; * vt aver bisogno di.

needle n ago m; * vt punzecchiare.

needless adj inutile.

needlework n cucito m.

needy adj bisognoso.

negation n negazione f.

negative adj negativo; * n (gr) negazione f; (phot) negativa f.

neglect vt trascurare.

negligee n négligé m.

negligence n negligenza f.

negligent adj negligente.

negligibile adj trascurabile.

negotiate vt trattare; superare.

negotiation n trattativa f.

Negress n negra f.

Negro adj, n negro m.

neigh vi nitrire; * n nitrito m.

neighbour n vicino m.

neighbourhood *n* vicinato *m*.

neighbouring *adj* confinante.

neighbourly *adv* da buon vicino.

neither *adv, pron, adj* né; * *conj* nemmeno, neanche, neppure.

neon *n* neon *m*.

neon sign *n* insegna *f* al neon.

nephew *n* nipote *m*.

nepotism *n* nepotismo *m*.

nerve *n* nervo *m*.

nerve-racking *adj* snervante.

nervous *adj* nervoso, ansioso.

nervous breakdown *n* esaurimento *m* nervoso.

nest *n* nido *m*; * *vi* nidificare.

nest egg *n* (*fig*) gruzzolo *m*.

nestle *vi* accoccolarsi.

net *n* rete *f*; * *adj* netto.

netball *n* specie di pallacanestro.

netting *n* rete *f* metallica.

nettle *n* ortica *f*.

network *n* rete *f*.

neurosis *n* nevrosi *f*.

neurotic *adj, n* nevrotico *m*.

neuter *adj* (*gr*) neutro; * *vt* castrare.

neutral *adj* neutrale; neutro; * *n* folle *f*.

neutrality *n* neutralità *f*.

neutralize *vt* neutralizzare.

neutron *n* neutrone *m*.

neutron bomb bomba *f* al neutrone.

never *adv* mai; ~ **mind** non fa niente.

never-ending *adj* interminabile.

nevertheless *adv* ciò nonostante.

new *adj* nuovo.

newborn *adj* neonato.

newcomer *n* nuovo arrivato *m*.

new-fangled *adj* stramoderno.

news *npl* notizie *fpl*; notiziario *m*, telegiornale *m*; giornale radio *m*.

news agency *n* agenzia *f* stampa.

newsagent *n* giornalaio *m*.

newscaster *n* annunciatore *m*.

news flash *n* flash *m*.

newsletter *n* bollettino *m*.

newsreel *n* cinegiornale *m*.

New Year *n* Anno *m* Nuovo; ~'s **Day** capodanno; ~'s **Eve** la notte di San Silvestro.

newt *n* tritone *m*.

next *adj* prossimo, successivo; * *adv* dopo; * *n* prossimo *m*; * *prep* accanto a.

nib *n* pennino *m*.

nibble *vt* rosicchiare.

nice *adj* simpatico, piacevole, gentile, bello.

nice-looking *adj* bello.

niche *n* nicchia *f*.

nick *n* taglietto *m*; * *vt* (*sl*) fregare; **in the** ~ **of time** appena in tempo.

nickel *n* nichel *m*.

nickname *n* soprannome *m*; * *vt* soprannominare.

nicotine *n* nicotina *f*.

niece *n* nipote *f*.

niggling *adj* persistente; pignolo; insignificante.

night *n* notte *f*; **by** ~ di notte; **good** ~ buona notte.

nightclub *n* night *m*.

nightfall *n* crepuscolo *m*.

nightingale *n* usignolo *m*.

nightly *adv* ogni notte; * *adj* di ogni notte.

nightmare *n* incubo *m*.

night school *n* scuola *f* serale.

nightshade *n*: **deadly** ~ belladonna *f*.

night shift *n* turno *m* di notte.

night-time *n* notte *f*.

nihilist *n* nichilista *m/f*.

nil *n* nulla *m*, zero *m*.

nimble *adj* agile.

nine *adj, n* nove *m*.

nineteen *adj, n* diciannove.

nineteenth *adj, n* diciannovesimo *m*.

ninetieth *adj, n* novantesimo *m*.

ninth *adj, n* nono *m*.

nip *vt* pizzicare; * *n* pizzico *m*; bicchierino *m*.

nipple *n* capezzolo *m*.

nippy *adj* pungente.

nit *n* lendine *m*; scemo *m*.

nitrogen *n* azoto *m*.

no *adv* no; * *adj* nessuno.

nobility *n* nobiltà *f*.

noble *adj, n* nobile *m*.

nobleman *n* nobiluomo *m*.

nobody *n* nullità *f*; * *pron* nessuno.

nocturnal *adj* notturno.

nod *n* cenno *m* del capo; * *vi* fare un cenno col capo.

noise *n* rumore *m*; fracasso *m*.

noisily *adv* rumorosamente.

noisy *adj* rumoroso.

nomad *n* nomade *m/f*.

nom de plume *n* pseudonimo *m*.

nominal *adj* nominale.

nominate *vt* nominare.

nomination *n* nomina *f*.

nominative (*gr*) *adj, n* nominativo *m*.

nominee *n* candidato *m*.

non-alcoholic *adj* analcolico.

non-aligned *adj* non allineato.

nonchalant *adj* disinvolto.

non-committal *adj* evasivo.

nonconformist *adj, n* anticonformista *m/f*.

nondescript *adj* indefinito.

none *pron* nessuno, niente.

nonentity *n* nullità *f*.

nontheless *adv* nondimeno.

non-existent *adj* inesistente.

non-plus *vt* sconcertare.

nonsense *n* sciocchezze *fpl*.

nonsensical *adj* sciocco.

non-stick *adj* antiaderente.

non-stop *adj* diretto; continuo.

noodles *npl* tagliatelle *fpl*.

nook *n* angolino *m*.

noon *n* mezzogiorno *m*.

noose *n* cappio *m*.

nor *conj* né.

norm *n* norma *f*.

normal *adj* normale.

north *n* nord *m*, settentrione *m*; * *adj* nord.

North America *n* America *f* del nord.

north-east *n* nordest *m*.

northerly *adj* del nord; verso nord.

northern *adj* settentrionale, del nord.

north pole *n* polo *m* nord.

northwards *adv* verso nord.

north-west *n* nordovest *m*.

nose *n* naso *m*.

nosebleed *n* emorragia *f* nasale.

nosedive *n* picchiata *f*.

nos(e)y *adj* curioso.

nostalgia *n* nostalgia *f*.

nostril *n* narice *f*.

not *adv* non.

notable *adj* notevole.

notably *adv* notevolmente.

notary *n* notaio *m*.

notation *n* notazione *f*.

notch *n* tacca *f*; * *vt* intaccare.

note *n* nota *f*; biglietto *m*; * *vt* notare.

notebook *n* taccuino *m*.

noted *adj* famoso.

notepad *n* bloc-notes *m*.

notepaper *n* carta *f* da lettere.

nothing *n* niente; * *adv* per niente; **think ~ of it!** s'immagini!

notice *n* avviso *m*; preavviso *m*; recensione *f*; * *vt* accorgersi di.

noticeable *adj* percettibile.

notification *n* notifica *f*.

notify *vt* notificare.

notion *n* idea *f*; nozione *f*.

notoriety *n* notorietà *f*.

notorious *adj* famigerato.

notwithstanding *conj* benché;
* *adv* cionondistante; * *prep*
nonostante.

nougat *n* torrone *m*.

nought *n* zero *m*.

noun *n* (*gr*) sostantivo *m*.

nourish *vt* nutrire.

nourishing *adj* nutriente.

nourishment *n* nutrimento *m*.

novel *n* romanzo; * *adj* originale.

novelist *n* romanziere *m*.

novelty *n* novità *f*.

November *n* novembre *m*.

novice *n* novizio *m*.

now *adv* adesso, ora; * *conj*
adesso che, ora che; ~ and
then ogni tanto.

nowadays *adv* oggigiorno.

nowhere *adv* in nessun posto.

noxious *adj* nocivo.

nozzle *n* bocchetta *f*.

nuance *n* sfumatura *f*.

nuclear *adj* nucleare.

nucleus *adj* nucleo.

nude *adj*, *n* nudo *m*.

nudge *n* gomitata *f*.

nudist *adj*, *n* nudista *m/f*.

nudity *n* nudità *f*.

nuisance *n* seccatura *f*.

null *adj* nullo.

nullify *vt* annullare.

numb *adj* intorpidito; * *vt* intorpidire.

number *n* numero *m*; * *vt* numerare; contare.

numbness *n* intorpidimento *m*.

numeral *n* numerale *m*.

numerical *adj* numerico.

numerous *adj* numeroso.

nun *n* suora *f*.

nuptual *adj* nuziale.

nurse *n* infermiere *m*.

nursery *n* camera *f* dei bambini; vivaio *m*.

nursery rhyme *n* filastrocca *f*.

nursery school *n* asilo *m* infantile.

nursing home *n* clinica *f*.

nurture *vt* nutrire.

nut *n* noce (walnut), mandorla
(almond), nocciola (hazelnut);
(*mech*) dado; (*sl*) matto *m*;
* *adj* (*sl*) svitato.

nutcrackers *npl* schiaccianoci
m.

nutmeg *n* noce *f* moscata.

nutritious *adj* nutriente.

nut shell *n* guscio *m* di noce.

nylon *n* nailon *m*.

nymphomaniac *n* ninfomane *f*.

O

oaf *n* zoticone *m*

oak *n* quercia *f*.

oar *n* remo *m*.

oasis *n* oasi *f*.

oat *n* avena *f*.

oath *n* giuramento *m*.

oatmeal *n* farina *f* d'avena.

oats *npl* avena *f*.

obedience *n* ubbidienza *f*.

obedient *adj* ubbidiente.

obese *adj* obeso.

obesity *n* obesità *f*.

obey *vt* ubbidire.

obituary *n* necrologio *m*.

object *n* oggetto *m*; * *vt* obbiet-
tare.

objection *n* obbiezione *f*.

objectionable *adj* antipatico.

objective *n* obiettivo *m*.

obligation *n* obbligo *m*.

obligatory *adj* obbligatorio.

oblige *vt* obbligare.

obliging *adj* gentile.

oblique *adj* obliquo.

obliterate *vt* cancellare.

oblivion *n* oblio *m*.

oblivious *adj* ignaro.

oblong *adj* oblungo; * *n* rettangolo *m*.

obnoxious *adj* detestabile.

oboe *n* oboe *m*.

obscene *adj* osceno.

obscenity *n* oscenità *f*.

obscure *adj* oscuro; * *vt* oscurare.

obscurity *n* anonimato *m*.

observance *n* osservanza *f*.

observant *adj* attento.

observation *n* osservazione *f*.

observatory *n* osservatorio *m*.

observe *vt* osservare.

observer *n* osservatore *m*.

obsess *vt* ossessionare.

obsessive *adj* ossessivo.

obsolete *adj* obsoleto.

obstacle *n* ostacolo *m*.

obstinate *adj* ostinato.

obstreperous *adj* turbulento.

obstruct *vt* ostruire.

obstruction *n* ostruzione *f*.

obtain *vt* ottenere.

obtainable *adj* ottenibile.

obtrusive *adj* invadente.

obtuse *adj* ottuso.

obvious *adj* ovvio.

occasion *n* occasione *f*; * *vt* causare.

occasional *adj* occasionale.

occupant, occupier *n* inquilino *m*, titolare *m*.

occupation *n* mestiere *m*; occupazione *f*.

occupy *vt* occupare.

occur *vi* accadere.

occurrence *n* evento *m*.

ocean *n* oceano *m*.

ocean-going *adj* d'alto mare.

oceanic *adj* oceanico.

ochre *n* ocra *f*.

octagon *n* ottagono *m*.

octane *n* ottano *m*.

octave *n* ottava *f*.

October *n* ottobre *m*.

octupus *n* piovra *f*.

oculist *n* oculista *m/f*.

odd *adj* strano; dispari; scompagnato.

oddity *n* bizzarria *f*.

odd jobs *npl* lavoretti *mpl*.

odds *npl* probabilità *f*.

ode *n* ode *f*.

odious *adj* odioso.

odour *n* odore *m*.

odourless *adj* inodore.

odyssey *n* odissea *f*.

oesophagus *n* esofago *m*.

oestrogen *n* estrogeno *m*.

of *prep* di.

off *adv* distante; * *adj* spento; andato a male; * *prep* da.

offal *n* frataglie *fpl*.

offence *n* infrazione *f*; offesa *f*

offend *vt* offendere.

offender *n* trasgressore *m*.

offensive *adj* offensivo.

offer *n* offerta *f*; * *vt* offrire.

offering *n* offerta *f*.

offhand *adj* brusco.

office *n* ufficio *m*.

office block *n* palazzo *m* pe uffici.

office hours *npl* orario *n* d'ufficio.

officer *n* ufficiale *m*.

office worker *n* impiegato *m*

official *adj* ufficiale; * *n* fur zionario *m*.

officiate *vi* ufficiare.

officious *adj* invadente.

off-key *adj* stonato.

off-peak *adj* tariffa ridotta.

off-season *adj* bassa stagione

offset *n* offset *m*; * *vt* bilar ciare.

offshoot *n* germoglio *m*.

offshore *adj* al largo.

offside *adj* in fuorigioco.

offspring *n* prole *f*.

offstage *adj* dietro le quinte.

often *adv* spesso, di frequent

ogle *vt* occhieggiare.

ogre *n* orco *m*.

oil *n* olio *m*; petrolio *m*; * *vt* oleare.

oilcan *n* oleatore *m*.

oilfield *n* giacimento *m* petrolifero.

oil painting *n* quadro *m* a olio.

oil rig *n* impianto *m* di trivellazione per pozzi petroliferi.

oil tanker *n* petroliera *f*.

oil well *n* pozzo *m* petrolifero.

oily *adj* oleoso.

ointment *n* unguento *m*.

O.K., okay *excl* O.K., va bene; * *vt* approvare.

old *adj* vecchio, anziano; precedente.

old age *n* vecchiaia *f*.

old-fashioned *adj* antiquato.

oleander *n* oleandro *m*.

olive *n* oliva *f*; ~ **tree** *n* ulivo *m*.

olive oil *n* olio *m* d'oliva.

omelet(te) *n* frittata *f*.

omen *n* auspicio *m*.

ominous *adj* infausto.

omission *n* omissione *f*.

omit *vt* omettere.

omnipotent *adj* onnipotente.

omnivorous *adj* onnivoro.

on *prep* su, a, sopra; * *adj* acceso.

once *adv* una volta; **at** ~ subito; **all at** ~ improvisamente; ~ **more** ancora una volta.

oncoming *adj* che si avvicina in senso contrario.

one *adj* uno, unico, stesso; * *n* uno *m*.

one-man *adj* individuale.

onerous *adj* gravoso.

oneself *pron* se stesso.

one-sided *adj* unilaterale.

one-to-one *adj* univoco.

one way *adj* a senso unico.

ongoing *adj* in corso.

onion *n* cipolla *f*.

onlooker *n* spettatore *m*.

only *adj* solo; * *adv* solo, solamen-te.

onrush *adj* afflusso.

onset *n* inizio *m*.

onslaught *n* attacco *m*.

onus *n* gravame *m*.

onwards *adj* in avanti.

ooze *vi* trasudare; * *n* melma *f*.

opal *n* opale *m/f*

opaque *adj* opaco.

open *adj* aperto; * *vt* aprire; **to be** ~ **with sb** essere franco.

opening *n* apertura *f*; inaugurazione *f*; breccia *f*.

open-minded *adj* aperto.

openness *n* franchezza *f*.

opera *n* opera *f*.

opera house *n* teatro *m* lirico.

operate *vt* azionare; * *vi* funzionare; operare.

operatic *adj* lirico.

operation *n* operazione *f*; intervento *m*.

operational *adj* operativo.

operative *adj* operante.

operator *n* centralinista *m/f*.

ophthalmic *adj* oftalmico.

opine *vt* ritenere.

opinion *n* opinione *f*, parere *m*.

opinionated *adj* dogmatico.

opinion poll *n* sondaggio *m* di opinione.

opium *n* oppio *m*.

opponent *n* avversario *m*.

opportune *adj* opportuno.

opportunist *n* opportunista *m/f*.

opportunity *n* occasione *f*.

oppose *vt* opporsi a.

opposing *adj* avversario.

opposite *adv* di fronte; * *n* contrario *m*.

opposition *n* opposizione *f*.

oppress *vt* opprimere.

oppression *n* oppressione *f*.

oppressive *adj* oppressivo.

oppressor n oppressore m.
opt vi optare.
optic(al) adj ottico; * npl ~s ottica f.
optician n ottico m.
optimist n ottimista m/f.
optimistic adj ottimistico.
optimum adj ottimale.
option n scelta f, opzione f.
optional adj facoltativo.
opulent adj opulento.
or conj o.
oracle n oracolo m.
oral adj, n orale m; ~ly adv oralmente.
orange n arancia f; ~ tree n arancio m; (colour) arancio m.
orangeade n aranciata f.
oration n orazione f.
orator n oratore m.
orbit n orbita f; * vt orbitare.
orchard n frutteto m.
orchestra n orchestra f.
orchestral adj orchestrale.
orchid n orchidea f.
ordain vt ordinare.
ordeal n prova f ardua.
order n ordine m, comando m, ordinazione f; * vt, vi ordinare.
order form n ordine m.
orderly adj ordinato; * n inserviente m.
ordinance n ordinanza f.
ordinarily adv normalmente.
ordinary adj abituale, comune; ordinario.
ordination n ordinazione f.
ordnance n artiglieria f.
ore n minerale m grezzo.
oregano n origano m.
organ n organo m.
organic(al) adj organico.
organism n organismo m.
organist n organista m/f.
organization n organizzazione f.
organize vt organizzare.
orgasm n orgasmo m.

orgy n orgia f.
oriental adj orientale.
orientate vt orientare.
orifice n orifizio m.
origin n origine f.
original adj, n originale m.
originality n originalità f.
originate vi avere origine.
ornament n ornamento m; * vt ornare.
ornamental adj ornamentale.
ornate adj ornato.
orphan adj, n orfano m.
orphanage n orfanotrofio m.
orthodox adj ortodosso.
orthodoxy n ortodossia f.
orthography n ortografia f.
orthopaedic adj ortopedico; * n ~s ortopedia f.
oscillate vi oscillare.
osprey n falco m pescatore.
ossify vi ossificarsi.
ostensibly adv apparentemente.
ostentatious adj pretenzioso.
osteopathy n osteopatia f.
ostracize vt ostracizzare.
ostrich n struzzo m.
other adj, pron altro; * adv ~ than diversamente.
otherwise adv diversamente altrimenti.
otter n lontra f.
ouch! excl ahi!
ought vb aux dovere.
ounce n oncia f.
our adj nostro.
ourselves pron noi stessi.
oust vt scacciare.
out adv fuori; * prep fuori, per da, senza.
outback n entroterra m.
outboard n fuoribordo m.
outbreak n scoppio m.
outburst n scoppio m.
outcast n emarginato m.
outcome n esito m.
outcry n protesta f.

outdated *adj* sorpassato.

outdo *vt* superare.

outdoor *adj* all'aperto; **~s** *adv* all'aperto.

outer *adj* esterno.

outer space *n* spazio *m* cosmico.

outfit *n* costume *m*; organizzazione *f*.

outgoing *adj* uscente.

outgrow *vt* diventare troppo grande per.

outhouse *n* costruzione *f* annessa.

outing *n* escursione *f*.

outlandish *n* stravagante.

outlaw *n* fuorilegge *m*; * *vt* bandire.

outlay *n* spesa *f*.

outlet *n* scarico *m*; punto *m* vendita.

outline *n* contorno *m*; * *vt* riassumere.

outlive *vt* sopravvivere a.

outlook *n* veduta *f*.

outlying *adj* periferico.

outmoded *adj* sorpassato.

outnumber *vt* superare numericamente.

out-of-date *adj* scaduto; fuori moda.

outpatient *n* paziente *m* esterno.

outpost *n* avamposto *m*.

output *n* produzione *f*; rendimento *m*.

outrage *n* atrocità *f*; sdegno *m*; * *vt* oltraggiare.

outrageous *adj* scandaloso.

outright *adv* nettamente; * *adj* netto; schietto.

outrun *vt* superare.

outset *n* inizio *m*.

outshine *vt* eclissare.

outside *n* esterno *m*; * *adj* esterno; * *adv* fuori, * *prep* fuori di.

outsider *n* estraneo *m*.

outsize *n* taglia forte.

outskirts *npl* periferia *f*.

outspoken *adj* franco.

outstanding *adj* eccezionale; insoluto.

outstretched *adj* disteso.

outstrip *vt* sorpassare.

outward *adj* esterno; apparente.

outweigh *vt* avere più importanza di.

outwit *vt* essere più furbo di.

oval *adj*, *n* ovale *m*.

ovary *n* ovaia *f*.

oven *n* forno *m*.

ovenproof *adj* pirofilo.

over *prep* su, sopra; * *adj* finito; **~ again** da capo; **~ and ~** mille volte.

overall *adj* generale; **~s** *npl* tuta *f*.

overawe *vt* intimidire.

overbalance *vt* sbilanciarsi.

overbearing *adj* prepotente.

overboard *adv* fuori bordo.

overcast *adj* coperto.

overcharge *vt* far pagare troppo.

overcoat *n* soprabito *m*.

overcome *vt* sopraffare.

overconfident *adj* presuntuoso.

overcrowded *adj* sovraffollato.

overdo *vt* esagerare.

overdose *n* overdose *f*.

overdraft *n* conto *m* scoperto.

overdue *adj* scaduto.

overestimate *vt* sopravvalutare.

overflow *vt*, *vi* traboccare; * *n* troppopieno *m*.

overgrown *adj* coperto di vegetazione.

overgrowth *n* vegetazione *f* densa.

overhang *vi* sporgere.

overhanging *adj* sporgente.

overhaul *vt* revisionare; * *n* revisione *f*.

overhead *adv* in alto; * *adj* sopraelevato.

overhear *vt* sentire per caso.

overjoyed *adj* felicissimo.

overkill *n* strafare *m*.

overland *adj, adv* per (via) di terra.

overlap *n* sovrapposizione *f*; * *vi* sovrapporsi.

overleaf *adv* a tergo.

overload *vt* sovraccaricare.

overlook *vt* dare su; chiudere un occhio su; trascurare.

overnight *adv* di notte.

overpass *n* cavalcavia *m*.

overpower *vt* sopraffare.

overpowering *adj* soffocante.

overrate *vt* sopravvalutare.

override *vt* non tenere conto di.

overriding *adj* preponderante.

overrule *vt* prevalere su.

overrun *vt* invadere; * *vi* protrarsi.

overseas *adv* all'estero; * *adj* estero.

oversee *vt* sorvegliare.

overseer *n* sorvegliante *m*.

overshadow *vt* eclissare.

overshoot *vt* andare oltre.

oversight *n* svista *f*.

oversleep *vi* svegliarsi troppo tardi.

overspill *n* eccedenza *f* di popolazione.

overstate *vt* esagerare.

overstep *vt* oltrepassare.

overt *adj* evidente.

overtake *vt* superare.

overthrow *vt* rovesciare; * *n* rovesciamento *m*.

overtime *n* straordinario *m*.

overtone *n* sfumatura *f*.

overture *n* (*mus*) ouverture *f*.

overturn *vt* capovolgere.

overweight *n* eccedenza *f* di peso.

overwhelm *vt* sopraffare, sommergere.

overwhelming *adj* schiacciante.

overwork *vi* lavorare troppo; * *n* lavoro *m* eccessivo.

owe *vt* dovere.

owing *adj* da pagare; * *prep* ~ to a causa di.

owl *n* civetta *f*, gufo *m*.

own *adj* proprio; * *vt* possedere; * *vi* **to ~ up** ammettere.

owner *n* proprietario *m*.

ownership *n* proprietà *f*.

ox *n* bue *m*; ~**en** *npl* buoi *mpl*.

oxidize *vt* ossidare.

oxygen *n* ossigeno *m*.

oyster *n* ostrica *f*.

ozone *n* ozono *m*.

P

pa *n* (*fam*) babbo *m*.

pace *n* passo *m*; * *vi* camminare su e giù.

pacemaker *n* pace-maker *m*.

pacific *adj* pacifico; * *n* pacifico *m*.

pacification *n* pacificazione *f*.

pacifism *n* pacifismo *m*.

pacifist *n* pacifista *m/f*.

pacify *vt* calmare, placare.

pack *n* pacco *m*; branco *m*; * *vt* imballare; stipare di; * *vi* fare le valigie.

package *n* pacchetto *m*; * *vt* confezionare.

package holiday *n* vacanza *f* organizzata.

packet *n* pacchetto *m*.

packing *n* imballaggio *m*.

pact *n* patto *m*.

pad *n* cuscinetto *m*; blocchetto *m*; rampa *f* di lancio; (*sl*) casa *f*; * *vt* imbottire.

padding *n* imbottitura *f*.

paddle *vi* sguazzare; * *n* pala *f*.

paddle steamer *n* battello *m* a ruote.

paddock *n* recinto *m*.

paddy risaia *f*.

padlock *n* lucchetto *m*.

pagan *adj*, *n* pagano *m*.

page *n* paggio *m*; pagina *f*.

pageant *n* corteo *m* in maschera.

pageantry *n* sfarzo *m*.

pail *n* secchio *m*.

pain *n* dolore *m*; * *vt* addolorare.

pained *adj* addolorato.

painful *adj* doloroso.

painkiller *n* antidolorifico *m*.

painless *adj* indolore.

painstaking *adj* coscienzioso.

paint *n* tinta *f*; vernice; * *vt* dipingere; verniciare.

paintbrush *n* pennello *m*.

painter *n* pittore *m*; imbianchino *m*.

painting *n* quadro *m*; pittura *f*.

paintwork *n* vernice *f*.

pair *n* paio *m*, copia *f*.

pal *n* (*fam*) amico *m*.

palatable *adj* gradevole al palato.

palate *n* palato *m*.

palatial *adj* sontuoso.

palaver *n* trambusto *m*.

pale *adj* pallido.

palette *n* tavolozza *f*.

pall *n* drappo *m* funebre; * *vi* diventare noioso.

pallet *n* paletta *f*.

palliative *adj*, *n* palliativo *m*.

pallid *adj* pallido.

pallor *n* pallore *m*.

palm *n* palma *f*.

palmist *n* chiromante *m/f*.

Palm Sunday *n* domenica delle Palme.

palpable *adj* palpabile.

palpitation *n* palpitazione *f*.

paltry *adj* irrisorio.

pamper *vt* viziare.

pamphlet *n* opuscolo *m*.

pan *n* pentola *f*.

panacea *n* panacea *f*.

panache *n* stile *m*.

pancake *n* frittella *f*.

pancreas *n* pancreas *m*.

panda *n* panda *m*.

pandemonium *n* pandemonio *m*.

pane *n* vetro *m*.

panel *n* pannello *m*; giuria *f*.

panelling *n* rivestimento *m* di pannelli.

pang *n* dolore *m* acuto.

panic *adj*, *n* panico *m*.

panicky *adj* allarmista.

panic-stricken *adj* in preda al panico.

panorama *n* panorama *m*.

pansy *n* (*bot*) pensée *f*.

pant *vi* ansimare.

panther *n* pantera *f*.

panties *npl* mutandine *fpl*.

pantihose *n* collant *m*.

pantry *n* dispensa *f*.

pants *npl* mutande *fpl*, slip *m*.

papacy *n* papato *m*.

papal *adj* papale.

paper *n* carta *f*; relazione *f*; giornale *m*; ~s *pl* documenti *mpl*; * *vt* tappezzare.

paperback *n* tascabile *m*.

paper clip *n* fermaglio *m*.

paperweight *n* fermacarte *m*.

paperwork *n* lavoro *m* d'ufficio.

paprika *n* paprica *f*.

par *n* parità *f*; **above ~** sopra la media.

parable *n* parabola *f*.

parachute *n* paracaduta *m*.

parade *n* sfilata *f*, parata *f*.

paradise *n* paradiso *m*.

paradox *n* paradosso *m*.

paradoxical *adj* paradossale.

parafin n kerosene m.

paragon n modello m perfetto.

paragraph n paragrafo m.

parallel adj parallelo; * n parallela f.

paralysis n paralisi f.

paralytic(al) adj paralitico.

paralyze vt paralizzare.

paramount adj sommo.

paranoid adj paranoico.

parapet n parapetto m.

paraphernalia n armamentario m.

parasite n parassita m.

parasol n parasole m.

paratrooper n paracadutista m.

parcel n pacco m; * vt impacchettare.

parch vt inaridire.

parched adj riarso.

parchment n pergamena f.

pardon n perdone m; * vt perdonare.

parent n genitore m/f.

perentage n natali mpl.

parental adj dei genitori.

parenthesis n parentesi fpl.

parish n parrocchia f.

parishioner n parrocchiano m.

parity n parità f.

park n parco m; * vt, vi parcheggiare.

parking n parcheggiare m.

parking meter n parchimetro m.

parking ticket n multa f per sosta vietata.

parlance n gergo m.

parliament n parlamento m.

parliamentary adj parlamentare.

parlour n salotto m.

Parmesan n parmigiano m.

parody n parodia f; * vt parodiare.

parole n libertà f provvisoria.

parricide n parricida m/f; parricidio m.

parrot n pappagallo m.

parsley n prezzemolo m.

parsnip n pastinaca f.

parson n pastore m.

part n parte f; * vt separare; * vi lasciarsi; **to ~ with** disfarsi di.

partial adj parziale.

participant n partecipante m/f.

participate vi partecipare.

participation n partecipazione f.

participle n (gr) participio m.

particle n particella f.

particular adj particolare; pignolo; * n particolare m.

parting n separazione f; riga f; * adj d'addio.

partisan adj, n partigiano m.

partition n parete f divisoria.

partner n partner m/f, socio m.

partnership n associazione f.

partridge n pernice f.

party n partito m; festa f.

pass vt passare; sorpassare; superare; approvare; * vi passare; accadere; **to ~ away** mancare; * n passo m; lasciapassare m; sufficienza f; **to make a ~ at** fare delle avances a.

passable adj passabile.

passage n passaggio m.

passbook n libretto m di risparmio.

passenger n passeggero m.

passer-by n passante m.

passing adj passeggero.

passion n passione f.

passionate adj appassionato.

passion flower n passiflora f.

passive adj, n passivo m.

passkey n passe-partout m.

Passover n Pasqua f ebraica.

passport n passaporto m.

password n parola f d'ordine.

past adj passato; * n passato m * prep davanti; oltre; passato

pasta n pasta f.

paste n pasta f, impasto m; * vt appiccicare.

pastel adj, n pastello m.

parteurized adj pastorizzato.

pastime n passatempo m.

pastor n pastore m.

pastoral adj pastorale.

pastry n pasta f.

pasture n pascolo m.

pasty adj smorto.

pat vi dare dei colpetti leggeri; * n colpetto m.

patch n toppa f; * vt rattoppare; **to ~ up** appianare.

patchwork n patchwork m.

pâté n pâté m.

patent adj palese; brevettato; * n brevetto m; * vt brevettare.

patent leather n pelle f lucida.

paternal adj paterno.

paternity n paternità f.

path n sentiero m.

pathetic adj patetico.

pathological adj patologico.

pathology n patologia f.

pathos n pathos m.

pathway n sentiero m.

patience n pazienza f.

patient adj, n paziente m.

patio n terrazza f.

patriarch adj patriarca.

patrio n patriota m/f.

patriotic adj patriottico.

patriotism n patriottismo m.

patrol n pattuglia f; * vt perlustrare.

patrol car n auto f della polizia.

patron n mecenate m/f; patrono m.

patronage n patrocinio m.

patronize vt trattare con condiscendenza; frequentare.

patter n parlantina f; * vi picchiettare.

pattern n disegno m, modello m.

paunch n pancia f.

pauper n indigente m/f.

pause n pausa f; * vi fare una pausa.

pave vt lastricare.

pavement n marciapiede m.

pavilion n padiglione m.

paving stone n lastra f di pavimentazione f.

paw n zampa f; * vt scalpitare, dare una zampata.

pawn n pedone m; (fig) pedina f; * vt impegnare.

pawn broker n prestatore m su pegno.

pawnshop n monte m di pietà.

pay vt, vi pagare; **to ~ back** rimborsare; **to ~ off** saldare; * n paga f.

payable adj pagabile.

pay day n giorno m di paga.

payee n beneficiario m.

payment n pagamento m.

pay-phone n telefono m pubblico.

payroll n lista f del personale.

pea n pisello m.

peace n pace f.

peaceful adj pacifico.

peach n pesca f; **~ tree** pesco m.

peacock n pavone m.

peak n cima f.

peak hours npl ore; fpl di punta.

peal n scampanio m.

peanut n arachide f.

pear n pera f; **~ tree** n pero m.

pearl n perla f.

peasant n contadino m.

peat n torba f.

pebble n ciottolo m.

peck n beccata f; bacetto m; * vt beccare.

pecking order n ordine m gerarchico.

peculiar adj strano.

peculiarity n peculiarità f.

pedagogic(al) *adj* pedagogico.
pedal *n* pedale *m*; * *vi* pedalare.
pedant *n* pedante *m/f*.
pedantic *adj* pedante.
peddle *vt* spacciare.
pederast *n* pederasta *m*.
pedestal *n* piedistallo *m*.
pedestrian *n* pedone *m*; * *adj* mediocre.
pediatrician *n* pediatra *m/f*.
pediatrics *n* pediatria *f*.
pedicure *n* pedicure *f*.
pedigree *n* pedigree *m*.
pedlar *n* spacciatore *m*.
pee *vi* (fam) pisciare.
peek *vi* sbirciare.
peel *vt* sbucciare; * *vi* spellarsi; * *n* buccia *f*.
peeler *n* sbucciapatate *m*.
peep *vi* squittire; spiare.
peephole *n* spioncino *m*.
peer *n* pari *m/f*; * *vi* scrutare.
peerless *adj* impareggiabile.
peeved *adj* stizzito.
peevish *adj* stizzoso.
peg *n* molletta *f*; picchetto *m*; * *vt* fissare.
pejorative *adj* peggiorativo.
pelican *n* pellicano *m*.
pellet *n* pallottola *f*.
pelt *vt* tempestare; lapidare; * *vi* (fam) **it was ~ing with rain** pioveva a dirotto; * *n* pelle *f* greggia.
pelvis *n* bacino *m*.
pen *n* penna *f*; recinto *m*; * *vt* scrivere; rinchiudere.
penal *adj* penale.
penalty *n* pena *f*.
penance *n* penitenza *f*.
penchant *n* debole *m*.
pencil *n* matita *f*, lapis *m*.
pencil case *n* astuccio *m* per matite.
pendant *n* pendaglio *m*.
pending *adj* in sospeso.
pendulum *n* pendolo *m*.
penetrate *vt*, *vi* penetrare.

pen friend *n* corrispondente *m/f*.
penguin *n* pinguino *m*.
penicillin *n* penicillina *f*.
peninsula *n* penisola *f*.
penis *n* pene *m*.
penitence *n* penitenza *f*.
penitent *adj*, *n* pentito *m*.
penitentiary *n* penitenziario *m*.
penknife *n* temperino *m*.
pennant *n* fiamma *f*.
penniless *adj* senza un soldo.
penny *n* penny *m*.
pension *n* pensione *f*.
pensive *adj* pensoso.
pentagon *n* pentagono *m*.
Pentecost *n* Pentecoste *f*.
penthouse *n* attico *m*.
pent-up *adj* represso.
penultimate *adj* penultimo.
penury *n* indigenza *f*.
peony *n* peonea *f*.
people *n* gente *f*, popolo *m*, persone *fpl*; * *vt* popolare.
pep *n* dinamismo *m*; * *vt* **to ~ up** animare.
pepper pepe *m* peperone *m*; * *vt* pepare.
peppermint *n* menta *f* peperita.
per *prep* per.
per annum *adv* all'anno.
per capita *adj*, *adv* pro capite.
perceive *vt* percepire.
percentage *n* percentuale *f*.
perception *n* percezione *f*.
perch *n* pesce *m* persico; posatoio *m*; * *vi* appollaiarsi.
percolate *vt*, *vi* filtrare.
percolator *n* caffettiera *f* a filtro.
percussion *n* percussione *f*.
peremptory *adj* perentorio.
perennial *adj* perenne.
perfect *adj* perfetto; * *vt* perfezionare.
perfection *n* perfezione *f*.
perfidious *adj* perfido.

perforate *vt* perforare.

perforation *n* perforazione *f*.

perform *vt* svolgere; rappresentare; eseguire; * *vi* esibirsi.

performance *n* rappresentazione *f*; interpretazione *f*; rendimento *m*.

performer *n* artista *m/f*.

perfume *n* profumo *m*; * *vt* profumare.

perfunctory *adj* superficiale.

perhaps *adv* forse.

peril *n* pericolo *m*.

perilous *adj* pericoloso.

perimeter *n* perimetro *m*.

period *n* periodo *m*; ora *f*; punto *m*; mestruazioni fpl.

periodic(al) *adj* periodico.

periodical *n* periodico *m*.

peripheral *adj* periferico.

periphery *n* periferia *f*.

periscope *n* periscopio *m*.

perish *vi* perire.

perishable *adj* deperibile.

peritonitis *n* peritonite *f*.

perjure *vt* spergiurare.

perjury *n* spergiuro *m*.

perk *n* vantaggio *m*.

perky *adj* allegro.

perm *n* permanente *f*.

permanent *adj* permanente.

permeate *vt* permeare; * *vi* filtrare, pervadere.

permissible *adj* ammissibile.

permission *n* permesso *m*.

permissive *adj* permissivo.

permit *vt*, *vi* permettere; * *n* autorizzazione *f*.

permutation *n* permutazione *f*.

perpendicular *adj*, *n* perpendicolare *f*.

perpetrate *vt* perpetrare.

perpetual *adj* perpetuo.

perpetuate *vt* perpetuare.

perplex *vt* lasciare perplesso.

persecute *vt* perseguitare.

persecution *n* persecuzione *f*.

perseverance *n* perseveranza *f*.

persevere *vi* perseverare.

persimmon *n* cachi *m*.

persist *vi* persistere.

persistence *n* perseveranza *f*.

persistent *adj* persistente.

person *n* persona *f*.

personable *adj* prestante.

personage *n* personaggio *m*.

personal *adj* personale.

personal assistant *n* segretaria *f* personale.

personal column *n* annunci mpl personali.

personal computer *n* personal computer *m*.

personality *n* personalità *f*.

personification *n* personificazione *f*.

personify *vt* personificare.

personnel *n* personale *m*.

perspective *n* prospettiva *f*.

perspiration *n* traspirazione *f*.

perspire *vi* traspirare.

persuade *vt* persuadere.

persuasion *n* persuasione *f*.

persuasive *adj* persuasivo.

pert *adj* impertinente.

pertain *vi* **to ~ to** riferirsi a; **~ing to** relativo a.

pertinent *adj* pertinente.

perturb *vt* turbare.

perusal *n* lettura *f*.

peruse *vt* leggere.

pervade *vt* pervadere.

perverse *adj* perverso.

pervert *n* pervertito *m*; * *vt* pervertire.

pessimist *n* pessimista *m/f*.

pest *n* insetto *m* nocivo; peste *f*.

pester *vt* tormentare.

pet *n* animale *m* domestico; beniamino *m*; * *vt* accarezzare.

petal *n* petalo *m*.

petite *adj* minuta.

petition *n* petizione *f*; * *vt* presentare una petizione a.

petrified *adj* impietrito.

petrol *n* benzina *f*.

petroleum *n* petrolio *m*.

petticoat *n* sottoveste *f*.

pettiness *n* meschinità *f*.

petty *adj* insignificante.

petty cash *n* fondo *m* per piccole spese.

petty officer *n* sottufficiale *m* di marina.

petulant *adj* irritabile.

pew *n* banco *m*.

pewter *n* peltro *m*.

phalic *adj* fallico.

phantom *adj, n* fantasma *m*.

Pharaoh *n* faraone *m*.

pharmaceutic(al) *adj* farmaceutico.

pharmacist *n* farmacista *m/f*.

pharmacy *n* farmacia *f*.

phase *n* fase *f*.

pheasant *n* fagiano *m*.

phonomenal *adj* fenomenale.

phenomenon *n* fenomeno *m*.

phial *n* fiala *f*.

philanderer *n* donnaiolo *m*.

philanthropic *adj* filantropico.

philanthropist *n* filantropo *m*.

philanthropy *n* filantropia *f*.

philately *n* filatelia *f*.

philharmonic *adj* filarmonico.

philologist *n* filologo *m*.

philology *n* filologia *f*.

philosopher *n* filosofo *m*.

philosophic(al) *adj* filosofico.

philosophize *vi* filosofare.

philosophy *n* filosofia *f*.

phlegm *n* flemma *f*.

phlegmatic(al) *adj* flemmatico.

phobia *n* fobia *f*.

phoenix *n* fenice *f*.

phone *n* telefono *m*; * *vt* telefonare; * *vt* **to ~ back** richiamare.

phone book *n* elenco *m* telefonico.

phone box, phone booth *n* cabina *f* telefonica.

phone call *n* telefonata *f*.

phoneme (*ling*) *n* fonema *m*.

phonetic *adj* fonetico; **~s** *n* fonetica *f*.

phoney *adj* falso.

phosphate *n* fosfato *m*.

phosphorescent *adj* fosforescente.

phosphorus *n* fosforo *m*.

photocopier *n* fotocopiatrice *f*.

photocopy *n* fotocopia *f*; * *vt* fotocopiare.

photogenic *adj* fotogenico.

photograph *n* fotografia *f*; * *vt* fotografare.

photographer *n* fotografo *m*.

photographic *adj* fotografico.

photography *n* fotografia *f*.

photosynthesis *n* fotosintesi *f*.

phrase *n* frase *f*; * *vt* esprimere.

phrase book *n* frasario *m*.

physical *adj* fisico.

physical education *n* educazione *f* fisica.

physician *n* medico *m*.

physicist *n* fisico *m*.

physics *n* fisica *f*.

physiological *adj* fisiologico.

physiologist *n* fisiologo *m*.

physiology *n* fisiologia *f*.

physiotherapy *n* fisioterapia *f*.

physique *n* fisico *m*.

pianist *n* pianista *m/f*.

piano *n* pianoforte *m*.

piccolo *n* ottavino *m*.

pick *n* piccone *m*; scelta *f*; * *vt* scegliere; cogliere; **to ~ on** prendersela con; **to ~ out** individuare; **to ~ up** raccogliere; rimorchiare; passare a prendere.

pickaxe *n* piccone *m*.

picket *n* picchetto *m*; * *vt, vi* picchettare.

pickle *n* pasticcio *m*; **~s** sottaceti *mpl*; * *vt* mettere sottaceto.

pickpocket *n* borsaiolo *m*.

pickup n pickup m; (auto) camioncino m.

picnic n picnic m.

pictorial adj illustrato.

picture n quadro m; fotografia f; disegno m; * vt immaginare.

picture book n libro m illustrato.

picturesque adj pittoresco.

pie n torta f; pasticcio m.

piece n pezzo m.

piecemeal adv poco alla volta; * adj frammentario.

piecework n lavoro m a cottimo.

pier n pontile m.

pierce vt forare.

piercing adj lacerante.

piety n pietà f.

pig n maiale m, porco m; (fam) stronzo m.

pigeon n piccione m.

pigeonhole n casella f.

piggy bank n salvadanaio m.

pig-headed adj cocciuto.

pigsty n porcile m.

pigtail n treccina f.

pike n lucio m.

pilchard n sardina f.

pile n mucchio m; pila f; ~s emorroidi fpl. * vt impilare; ammucchiare.

pile-up n tamponamento m a catena.

pilfer vt rubacchiare.

pilgrim n pellegrino m.

pilgrimage n pellegrinaggio m.

pill n pillola f.

pillage vt saccheggiare.

pillar n pilastro m, colonna f.

pillion n sellino m posteriore.

pillow n guanciale m.

pillow case n federa f.

pilot n pilota m/f; * vt pilotare.

pilot light n fiammella f di sicurezza.

pimento n pepe m garofanato.

pimp n magnaccia m.

pimple n foruncolo m.

pin n spillo m; ~s and needles n formicolio m; * vt attaccare con uno spillo.

pinafore n grembiule m.

pinball n flipper m.

pincers n pinze fpl.

pinch vt pizzicare; fregare; * n pizzicotto m; pizzico m.

pincushion n puntaspilli m.

pine (bot) n pino m; * vi languire.

pineapple n ananas m.

ping n tintinnio m.

ping-pong n ping-pong m.

pinion n pignone m.

pink n rosa m.

pinnacle n pinnacolo m.

pinpoint vt localizzare con esattezza.

pinstripe n gessato m.

pint n pinta f.

pioneer n pioniere m.

pious adj pio.

pip n seme m.

pipe n tubo m; pipa f; ~s cornamusa m.

pipe cleaner n scovolino m.

pipe dream n sogno m impossibile.

pipeline n conduttura f.

piper n suonatore m di cornamusa.

piping n tubature fpl.

piquant adj piccante; stimolante.

pique n ripicca f.

piracy n pirateria f.

pirate n pirata m.

pirouette n piroetta f.

Pisces n Pesci mpl.

piss vi (fam) pisciare.

pissed adj ubriaco.

pistachio n pistacchio m.

pistol n pistola f.

piston n stantuffo m.

pit n buca f; cava f.

pitch n pece f; campo m; into-

nazione *f*; * *vt* lanciare;
piantare.
pitchblack *adj* buio pesto.
pitcher *n* brocca *f*.
pitchfork *n* forcone *m*.
pitfall *n* tranello *m*.
pithy *adj* arguto; vigoroso.
pitiable *adj* pietoso.
pitiful *adj* pietoso.
pitiless *adj* spietato.
pittance *n* miseria *f*.
pity *n* compassione *f*; peccato *m*;
* *vt* compatire.
pivot *n* perno *m*.
pixie *n* folletto *m*.
pizza *n* pizza *f*.
placard *n* cartello *m*.
placate *vt* placare.
place *n* luogo *m*, posto *m*; * *vt*
posare, mettere; situare; piazzare.
placebo *n* placebo *m*.
placenta *n* placenta *f*.
placid *adj* placido.
plagiarism *n* plagio *m*.
plague *n* peste *f*; * *vt* tormentare.
plaice *n* passera *f* di mare.
plaid *n* tessuto *m* scozzese.
plain *adj* evidente; semplice; in
tinta unita; * *n* pianura *f*.
plain clothes *adj* in borghese.
plaintiff *n* attore *m*.
plait *n* treccia *f*; * *vt* intrecciare.
plan *n* piano *m*; * *vt* pianificare;
organizzare.
plane *n* (*bot*) platano *m*; pialla
f; * *adj* piano; * *vt* piallare; * *vi*
planare.
planet *n* pianeta *m*.
planetarium *n* planetario *m*.
plank *n* tavola *f*.
plankton *n* plancton *m*.
planner *n* pianificatore *m*.
planning *n* pianificazione *f*.
plant *n* pianta *f*; impianto *m*;
stabilimento *m*; * *vt* piantare.

plantation *n* piantagione *f*.
plaque *n* placca *f*.
plasma *n* plasma *m*.
plaster *n* intonaco *m*; gesso *m*;
cerotto *m*; * *vt* intonacare.
plastered *adj* (fam) ubriaco.
plasterer *n* intonacatore *m*.
plastic *adj* plastico; * *n* plastica.
plastic surgery *n* chirurgia *f*
plastica.
plate *n* piatto *m*; targa *f*; piastra *f*; * *vt* placcare.
plateau *n* altopiano *m*.
plate glass *n* vetro *m* piano.
platform *n* piattaforma *f*; binario *m*.
platinum *n* platino *m*.
platitude *n* banalità *f*.
platonic *adj* platonico.
platoon *n* plotone *m*.
platter *n* piatto *m* da portata.
plausible *adj* plausibile.
play *n* gioco *m*; commedia *f*; * *vt*
giocare; suonare; inter-
pretare; * *vi* giocare; suonare;
to ~ down minimizzare.
playboy *n* playboy *m*.
player *n* giocatore *m*; suonatore
m.
playful *adj* giocherellone.
playground *n* cortile *m* per la
ricreazione.
play group *n* asilo *m* infantile.
play-off *n* partita *f* di spareggio.
playpen *n* box *m*.
playwright *n* drammaturgo *m*.
plea *n* supplica *f*.
plead *vt* difendere; * *vi* implorare.
pleasant *adj* piacevole.
please *vi* piacere; * *vt* accontentare; * *excl* per piacere.
pleased *adj* contento, lieto.
pleasing *adj* piacevole.
pleasure *n* piacere *m*.
pleat *n* piega; * *vt* pieghettare

plebeian *adj, n* plebeo *m*.

pledge *n* pegno *m*; * *vt* impegnare.

plenary *adj* plenario *m*.

plentiful *adj* abbondante.

plenty *n* abbondanza *f*.

plethora *n* pletora *f*.

pleurisy *n* pleurite *f*.

pliable, pliant *adj* malleabile.

pliers *npl* pinze *fpl*.

plight *n* situazione *f* (critica).

plinth *n* plinto *m*.

plod *vi* sgobbare; arrancare.

plonk *n* vino *m* ordinario.

plot *n* appezzamento *m*; complotto *m*; trama *f*; * *vt* tracciare; * *vi* complottare.

plough *n* aratro *m*; * *vt* arare; **to ~ back** reinvestire; * *vi* arare.

ploy *n* stratagemma *m*.

pluck *vt* cogliere; pizzicare; spennare; * *n* coraggio *m*.

plucky *adj* coraggioso.

plug *n* tappo *m*; spina *f*; * *vt* tappare.

plughole *n* scarico *m*.

plum *n* prugna *f* (tree) prugno *m*, susina *f* (tree) susino *m*.

plumage *n* piumaggio *m*.

plumb *n* piombo *m*; * *vt* scandagliare.

plumber *n* idraulico *m*.

plume *n* piuma *f*.

plump *adj* paffuto.

plunder *n* saccheggio *m*; bottino *m*; * *vt* saccheggiare.

plunge *vt* immergere; conficcare; * *vi* tuffarsi; precipitare; * *n* tuffo *m*.

plunger *n* sturalavandini *m*.

pluperfect *n* (*gr*) piuccheperfetto *m*.

plural *adj, n* plurale *m*.

plurality *n* pluralità *f*.

plus *n* vantaggio *m*; più *m*; * *prep* più; * *adj* positivo.

plush *n* felpa *f*; * *adj* sontuoso.

plutonium *n* plutonio *m*.

ply *vt* maneggiare; esercitare; incalzare; * *vi* fare la spola tra; * *n* strato *m*; velo *m*.

plywood *n* compensato *m*.

pneumatic *adj* pneumatico.

pneumatic drill *n* martello pneumatico.

pneumonia *n* polmonite *f*.

poach *vi* cacciare di frodo; * *vt* cuocere in bianco.

poached egg *n* uovo *m* in camicia.

poacher *n* bracconiere *m*.

poaching *n* bracconaggio *m*.

pocket *n* tasca *f*; * *vt* intascare.

pocket money *n* paga *f* settimanale.

pod *n* baccello *m*.

podgy *adj* grassottello.

podium *n* podio *m*.

poem *n* poesia *f*.

poet *n* poeta *m*.

poetess *n* poetessa *f*.

poetic *adj* poetico.

poetry *n* poesia *f*.

poignant *adj* struggente.

point *n* punto *m*; virgola *f*; punta *f*; scopo *m*; **~ of view** punto *m* di vista; * *vt* puntare; indicare.

point-blank *adv* a bruciapelo.

pointed *adj* appuntito.

pointer *n* lancetta *f*; pointer *m*; indizio *m*.

pointless *adj* inutile.

poise *n* portamento *m*.

poison *n* veleno *m*; * *vt* avvelenare.

poisoning *n* avvelenamento *m*.

poisonous *adj* velenoso.

poke *vt* dare un colpetto a; * *n* colpetto *m*.

poker *n* attizzatoio *m*; poker *m*.

poker-faced *adj* dalla faccia impassibile.

poky *adj* angusto.

polar *adj* polare.

polarity n polarità f.

polarize vt polarizzare.

pole n palo m; asta f; polo m.

pole vault n salto con l'asta.

polemic n polemica f.

police n polizia f; * vt presidiare.

policeman n poliziotto m.

police station n posto m di polizia.

policewoman n donna f poliziotto.

policy n politica f; polizza f.

polio n polio f.

polish vt lucidare; lustrare; **to ~ off** sbrigare; * n lucido m, cera f; lucidata f; raffinatezza f.

polished adj lucidato; raffinato.

polite adj educato.

politeness n educazione f.

politic adj accorto.

political adj politico.

politician n politico m.

politics npl politica f.

polka n polca f; **~ dot** n pois m.

poll n votazione f; sondaggio m.

pollen n polline m.

pollute vt inquinare.

pollution n inquinamento m.

polo n polo m.

polyandry n poliandria f.

polyester n poliestere m.

polyethylene n polietilene m.

polygamy n poligamia f.

polyglot n poliglotta m/f.

polygon n poligono m.

polyp n polipo m.

polystyrene n polistirolo m.

polytechnic adj, n politecnico m.

polythene n politene m.

pomegranate n melagrana f.

pomp n fasto m.

pompom n pompon m.

pompous adj pomposo.

pond n laghetto m.

ponder vt ponderare.

ponderous adj pesante.

pontiff n pontefice m.

pontoon n pontone m; ventuno m.

pony n pony m.

ponytail n coda f di cavallo.

poodle n barboncino m.

poof n (fam) finocchio m.

pool n pozza f; piscina f; cassa f comune; riserva f; biliardo m; * vt mettere insieme.

poor adj povero; misero; **the ~** i poveri mpl.

poorly adj indisposto.

pop n schiocco m; bevanda f gassata; * adj pop; * vt fare scoppiare; **to ~ in** fare un salto.

pop music n musica f pop.

popcorn n pop-corn m.

Pope n papa m.

poplar n pioppo m.

popper n bottone m automatico.

poppet n tesoro m.

poppy n papavero m.

populace n popolo m.

popular adj popolare; benvoluto.

popularity n popolarità f.

popularize vt rendere popolare, diffondere.

populate vt popolare.

population n popolazione f.

populous adj popoloso.

porcelain n porcellana f.

porch n veranda f.

porcupine n porcospino m.

pore n poro m.

pork n maiale m.

pornography n pornografia f.

porous adj poroso.

porpoise n focena f.

porridge n porridge m.

port n porto m; (mar) babordo m.

portable adj portatile.

portal n portale m.

porter n portinaio m; facchino m.

portfolio n portafoglio m; cartella f.

porthole n oblò m.

portico n portico m.

portion n porzione f.

portly adj corpulento.

portrait n ritratto m.

portray vt ritrarre.

pose n posa f; * vi posare; * vt porre.

posh adj elegante, sontuoso.

position n posizione f; impiego m; * vt sistemare.

positive adj positivo.

posse n squadra f d'armati.

possess vt possedere.

possession n possesso m.

possessive adj possessivo.

possibility n possibilità f.

possibile adj possibile.

post n palo m; posta f; posto m; * vt spedire per posta; affiggere.

postage n affrancatura f.

postage stamp n francobollo m.

postal adj postale.

post box n cassetta f delle lettere.

postcard n cartolina f.

postcode n codice m di avviamento postale.

postdate vt postdatare.

poster n manifesto m, poster m.

posterior n deretano m, posteriore m.

posterity n posterità f.

postgraduate adj di specializzazione (dopo la laurea).

posthumous adj postumo.

postman n postino m.

postmark n timbro m postale.

post-mortem n autopsia f.

post office n ufficio m postale.

postpone vt rimandare.

postscript n poscritto m.

postulate vt postulare.

posture n portamento m.

posy n mazzolino m.

pot n pentola f; vasetto m; erba f; * vt invasare.

potasium n potassio m.

potato n patata f.

potbellied adj panciuto.

potent adj potente.

potential adj, n potenziale m.

pothole n cavità f; buca f.

potion n pozione f.

potted adj conservato (in vaso); condensato.

potter n vasaio m.

pottery n ceramica f.

potty adj (fam) vasino.

pouch n borsa f marsupio.

poultice n impiastro m.

poultry n pollame m.

pounce n balzo m; * vt balzare.

pound n libra f; (lira) sterlina; canile municipale; deposito auto; * vt picchiare, pestare.

pour vt versare; * vi **to ~ with rain** piovere a dirotto.

pout vi fare il broncio; * n broncio m.

poverty n miseria f; povertà f.

powder n polvere f; * vt ridurre in polvere; * vi incipriarsi.

powder compact n portacipria m.

powdered milk n latte m in polvere.

powder puff n piumino m della cipria.

powdery adj farinoso.

power n forza f, potenza f; capacità f; potere m; * vt azionare.

powerful adj potente; possente.

powerless adj impotente.

power station n centrale f elettrica.

practicable adj praticabile.

practical adj pratico.

practicality n senso m pratico.

practical joke n beffa f.

practice n abitudine f; esercizio m; pratica f; **doctor's ~** studio.

practise vi esercitarsi a; praticare.

practitioner n professionista m/f.

pragmatic adj pragmatico.

prairie n prateria f.

praise n elogio m; * vt lodare.

praiseworthy adj lodevole.

prance vi caracollare; pavoneggiarsi.

prank n burla f.

prattle vt blaterare.

prawn n gambero m.

pray vi pregare.

prayer n preghiera f.

preach vt, vi predicare.

preacher n predicatore m.

preamble n preambolo m.

precarious adj precario.

precaution n precauzione f.

precautionary n precauzionale.

precede vt precedere.

precedence n precedenza f.

precedent n precedente m.

preceding adj precedente.

precinct n circoscrizione f.

precious adj prezioso.

precipice n precipizio m.

precipitate vt accelerare; * adj precipitoso.

precise adj preciso.

precision n precisione f.

preclude vt precludere.

precocious adj precoce.

preconceived adj preconcetto.

preconception n preconcetto m.

precondition n condizione f indispensabile.

precursor n precursore m.

predator n predatore m.

predecessor n predecessore m.

predestination n predestinazione f.

predict vt predire.

predictable adj prevedibile.

prediction n predizione f.

predilection n predilezione f.

predominance n predominanza f.

predominant adj predominanza.

predominate vt predominare.

preeminant adj eccezionale.

preen vt agghindarsi.

prefab n casetta f prefabbricata.

preface n prefazione f.

prefer vt preferire.

preferable adj preferibile.

preferably adv di preferenza.

preference n preferenza f.

preferential adj preferenziale.

prefix n prefisso m.

pregnancy n gravidanza f.

pregnant adj in cinta, gravida f.

prehistoric adj preistorico.

prejudice n pregiudizio m; * vt pregiudicare.

prejudiced adj essere prevenuto.

prejudicial adj pregiudizievole.

preliminary adj preliminare.

prelude n preludio m.

premarital adj prematrimoniale.

premature adj prematuro.

premeditate vt premeditare.

premeditate n premeditazione f.

premier n premier m.

premiere n prima f.

premise n premessa f.

premises npl locali mpl.

premium n premio m.

premonition n presentimento m.

preoccupy vt preoccupare.
prepaid adj pagato in anticipo; affrancato.
preparation n preparazione f.
preparatory adj preparatorio.
prepare vt preparare.
preponderance n preponderanza f.
preposition n preposizione f.
preposterous adj assurdo.
prerequisite n presupposto m necessario.
prerogative n prerogativa f.
prescribe vi prescrivere.
prescription n ricetta f.
presence n presenza f.
present n presente m; * adj presente; attuale; * vt presentare.
presentable adj presentabile.
presentation n presentazione f.
presenter n presentatore m.
presentiment n presentimento m.
preservation n conservazione f.
preservative n conservante m.
preserve vt conservare; * n conserva f.
preside vi presiedere.
presidency n presidenza f.
president n presidente m.
presidential adj presidenziale.
press vt, vi premere; stirare; * n pressa f; torchio m; stampa f.
press agent n agente m pubblicitario.
press conference n conferenza f stampa.
pressing adj pressante.
pressure n pressione f.
pressure cooker n pentola f a pressione.
pressure group n gruppo m di pressione.
pressurize vt pressurizzare.
prestige n prestigio m.

presumable adj probabile.
presume vt supporre.
presumption n presunzione f.
presumptuous adj presuntuoso.
presuppose vt presupporre.
pretence n pretesa f.
pretend vi fingere.
pretender n pretendente m/f.
pretentious adj pretenzioso.
preterite n passato m.
pretext n pretesto m.
pretty adj grazioso; * adv piuttosto.
prevail vi prevalere.
prevailing adj attuale.
prevalent adj diffuso.
prevaricate vt tergiversare.
prevent vt prevenire.
prevention n prevenzione f.
preventive adj preventivo.
preview n anteprima f.
previous adj precedente.
pre-war adj dell'anteguerra.
prey n preda f.
price n prezzo m.
priceless adj di valore inestimabile.
price list n listino m prezzi.
prick vt bucare; pungere; * n puntura f; (fam) cazzo m.
prickle n spina f.
prickly adj spinoso.
pride n orgoglio m; branco m.
priest n prete m.
priestess n sacerdotessa f.
priesthood n sacerdozio m.
priestly adj sacerdotale.
prig n borioso m.
prim adj per benino.
primacy n (relig) primazia f.
primarily adj essenzialmente.
primary adj principale.
primate n primate m.
prime n apice m; * adj principale; * vt preparare.
Prime Minister n Primo Ministro m.

primeval *adj* primordiale.
primitive *adj* primitivo.
primrose *n* (*bot*) primula *f*.
prince *n* principe *m*.
princess *n* principessa *f*.
principal *adj* principale; * *n* preside *m*.
principality *n* principato *m*.
principle *n* principio *m*.
print *vt* stampare; * *n* impronta *f*; stampato *m*; stampa *f*; out of ~ esaurito.
printed matter *n* stampe fpl.
printer *n* tipografo *m*; stampante *f*.
printing *n* stampa *f*; stampatello *m*.
prior *adj* precedente; * *n* priore *m*.
priority *n* priorità *f*.
priory *n* prioria *f*.
prise *vt* aprire facendo leva.
prism *n* prisma *m*.
prison *n* prigione *f*.
prisoner *n* prigioniero *m*.
pristine *adj* immacolato.
privacy *n* privacy *f*.
private *adj* privato; confidenziale; * *n* soldato *m* semplice.
private detective *n* detective *m* privato.
privet *n* ligustro *m*.
privilege *n* privilegio *m*.
prize *n* premio *m*; * *vt* valutare.
prize-giving *n* premiazione *f*.
prizewinner *n* premiato *m*.
pro *adj* professionista
probability *n* probabilità *f*.
probable *adj* probabile.
probation *n* periodo *m* di prova; libertà *f* condizionale.
probe *n* sonda *f*; * *vt* sondare.
problem *n* problema *m*.
problematical *adj* problematico.
procedure *n* procedura *f*.
proceed *vi* procedere; ~s *npl* ricavato *m*.

proceedings *n* provvedimenti *mpl*.
process *n* processo *m*, procedimento *m*; *vt* trattare.
procession *n* processione *f*.
proclaim *vt* proclamare.
proclamation *n* proclama *m*.
procrastinate *vt* procrastinare.
procreation *n* procreazione *f*.
procure *vt* procurare.
procurement *n* approvvigionamento *m*.
prod *vi* essere di stimolo a; * *n* colpetto *m*.
prodigal *adj* prodigo.
prodigious *adj* prodigioso.
prodigy *n* prodigio *m*.
produce *vt* produrre; * *n* prodotto *m*.
producer *n* produttore *m*; regista *m/f*.
product *n* prodotto *m*.
production *n* produzione *f*.
production line *n* catena *f* di montaggio.
productive *adj* produttivo.
productivity *n* produttività *f*.
profane *adj* profano.
profess *vt* professare.
profession *n* professione *f*.
professional *adj* professionale; * *n* professionista *m/f*.
professor *n* professore *m*.
proffer *vt* profferire.
proficiency *n* competenza *f*.
proficient *adj* competente.
profile *n* profilo *m*.
profit *n* profitto *m*; * *vi* approfittare.
profitability *n* redditività *f*.
profitable *adj* redditizio.
profiteer *vt* specolare; * *n* speculatore *m*.
profound *adj* profondo.
profuse *adj* copioso.
profusion *n* profusione *f*.
prognosis *n* prognosi *f*.

programme n programma m.

programmer n programmatore m.

programming n programmazione f.

progress n progresso m; * vi procedere.

progression n progressione f.

progressive adj progressivo.

prohibit vt proibire; vietare.

prohibition n proibizione f.

project vt proiettare; * n progetto m.

projectile n proiettile m.

projection n proiezione f.

projector n proiettore m.

prolapse n prolasso m.

proletarian adj, n proletario m.

proletariat n proletariato m.

prolific adj prolifico.

prologue n prologo m.

prolix adj prolisso.

prolong vt prolungare.

prom n (fam) lungomare m;

promenade n passeggiata f.

prominence n prominenza f.

prominent adj prominente.

promiscuous adj promiscuo.

promise n promessa f; * vt promettere.

promising adj promettente.

promontory n promontorio m.

promote vt promuovere.

promoter n promotore m.

promotion n promozione f.

prompt adj tempestivo; * vt suggerire.

prompter n suggeritore m.

prone adj a faccia in giù; soggetto a.

prong n rebbio m.

pronoun n pronome m.

pronounce vt pronunciare.

pronounced adj netto.

pronouncement n dichiarazione f.

pronunciation n pronuncia f.

proof n prova f; bozza f.

prop vt appoggiare; * n sostegno m.

propaganda n propaganda f.

propel vt spingere.

propeller n elica f.

propensity n propensione f.

proper adj appropriato; giusto; decente.

property n proprietà f.

prophecy n profezia f.

prophesy vt profetizzare.

prophet n profeta m.

prophetic adj profetico.

proportion n proporzione f.

proportional adj proporzionale.

proportionate adj proporzionato.

proposal n proposta f.

propose vt proporre.

proposition n proposizione f.

proprietor n proprietario m.

propriety n decoro m.

propulsion n propulsione f.

prosaic adj prosaico.

prose n prosa f.

prosecute vt proseguire; * vi ricorrere in giudizio.

prosecution n azione f giudiziaria.

prosecutor n procuratore m.

prospect n prospettiva f; * vt esplorare.

prospective adj futuro.

prospector n prospettore m.

prospectus n prospetto m.

prosper vi prosperare.

prosperity n prosperità f.

prosperous adj prospero.

prostitute n prostituta f.

prostitution n prostituzione f.

prostrate adj prostrato.

protagonist n protagonista m/f.

protect vt proteggere.

protection n protezione f.

protective adj protettivo.

protector n protettore m.
protégé n protetto m.
protein n proteina f.
protest vt, vi protestare; * n protesta f.
Protestant n protestante m.
protester n contestatore m.
protocol n protocollo m.
prototype n prototipo m.
protracted adj protratto.
protrude vi sporgere.
proud adj orgoglioso.
prove vt dimostrare, provare; vi rivelarsi.
proverb n proverbio m.
proverbial adj proverbiale.
provide vt fornire; **to ~ for** provvedere a.
provided conj:~ **that** a patto che.
providence n provvidenza f.
province n provincia f.
provincial adj provinciale.
provision n fornitura f.
provisional adj provvisorio.
proviso n clausola f.
provocation n provocazione f.
provocative adj provocatorio.
provoke vi provocare.
prow n (mar) prua f.
prowess n prodezza f.
prowl vi aggirarsi.
prowler n chi si aggira furtivamente.
proximity n vicinanza f.
proxy n procura f.
prudence n prudenza f.
prudent adj prudente.
prudish adj puritano.
prune vt potare; * prugna.
prurient adj libidinoso.
prussic acid n acido m prussico.
pry vi curiosare; * vt sollevare con una leva.
psalm n salmo m.
pseudonym n pseudonimo m.
psyche n psiche f.

psychiatric adj psichiatrico.
psychiatrist n psichiatra m/f.
psychiatry n psichiatria f.
psychic adj psichico.
psychoanalysis n psicanalisi f.
psychoanalyst n psicanalista m/f.
psychological adj psicologico.
psychologist n psicologo m.
psychology n psicologia f.
psychopath n psicopatico m.
pshychosomatic adj psicosomatico.
pub n pub m.
puberty n pubertà f.
pubic adj pubico.
public adj, n pubblico m.
public address system n impianto di amplificazione m.
publican n gestore di un pub m.
publication n pubblicazione f.
publicity n pubblicità f.
publicize vt reclamizzare.
public school n scuola f superiore privata.
publish vt pubblicare.
publisher n editore m.
publishing n editoria f.
pucker vt increspare.
pudding n dolce m; budino m; dessert m.
puddle n pozzanghera f.
peurile adj puerile.
puff n soffio m; * vi ansimare, soffiare.
puff pastry n pasta f sfoglia.
puffin n pulcinella f di mare.
puffy adj gonfio.
pug n carlino m.
puke vt, vi vomitare.
pull vi tirare; **to ~ down** demolire; **to ~ in/up** fermarsi; **to ~ off** portare a termine; **to ~ through** cavarsela; * tirata f; attrazione f.
pulley n puleggia f.
pullover n pullover m.

pulp n pasta (di legno) f; polpa f.

pulpit n pulpito m.

pulsate vi pulsare.

pulse n polso m.

pulverize vt polverizzare.

puma n puma m.

pumice n pomice f.

pummel vt prendere a pugni.

pump n pompa f; * vt pompare.

pumpkin n zucca f.

pun n gioco m di parole.

punch n pugno m; perforatrice f; punzonatrice f; * vt dare un pugno; forare.

punctual adj puntuale.

punctuate vt punteggiare.

punctuation n punteggiatura f.

pundit n esperto m.

pungent adj pungente.

punish vt punire.

punishment n punizione f.

punk n punk m.

punt n barchino m.

puny adj gracile; striminzito.

pup n cucciolo m.

pupil n allievo m; pupila f.

puppet n burattino m.

puppy n cagnolino m.

purchase vt acquistare; * n acquisto m; presa f.

purchaser n acquirente m/f.

pure adj puro.

purée n purè m.

purge n purga f; * vt purgare.

purification n depurazione f.

purify vt depurare.

purist n purista m/f.

puritan adj, n puritano m.

purity n purezza f.

purl n rovescio m.

purple adj, n viola m.

purport vt voler sembrare; * n significato m.

purpose n scopo m; **on ~** apposta.

purposeful adj risoluto.

purr vi fare le fusa.

purse n borsellino m; portamonete m.

purser n commissario m di bordo.

pursue vt inseguire; proseguire.

pursuit n inseguimento m; attività f.

purveyor n fornitore m.

pus n pus m.

push vt spingere; **to ~ aside** scartare; **to ~ off** smammare; * vi **to ~ on** perseverare; * n spinta f.

pusher n spiacciatore m.

pussy n (fam) micio m.

pussy willow n (bot) salicone m.

put vt mettere, posare; esprimere; **to ~ away** mettere via; **to ~ down** sopprimere; **to ~ forward** proporre; **to ~ off** rimandare; disanimare; schifare; estinguere, spegnere; **to ~ on** affettare; accendere; organizzare; **to ~ out** spegnere; costruire; contrariare; **to ~ up** alzare; ospitare; fornire, provvedere.

putrid adj putrido.

putt n putting m.

putty n stucco m.

puzzle n rompicapo m, rebus m, puzzle m.

puzzling adj sconcertante.

pylon n pilone m.

pyramid n piramide f.

pyromaniac n piromane m/f.

python n pitone m.

Q

quack *vi* fare qua qua; * *n* qua qua *m*; (*fam*) ciarlatano *m*.

quadrangle *n* quadrangolo *m*; cortile *m*.

quadrant *n* quadrante *m*.

quadrilateral *adj* quadrilatero.

quadruped *n* quadrupede *m*.

quadruple *adj* quadruplo.

quadruplet *n* uno di quattro gemelli.

quagmire *n* pantano *m*.

quail *n* quaglia *f*.

quaint *adj* pittoresco; singolare.

quake *vi* tremare.

Quaker *n* quacchero *m*.

qualification *n* qualifica *f*; riserva *f*.

qualified *adj* qualificato; condizionato.

qualify *vt* qualificare.

quality *n* qualità *f*.

qualm *n* scrupolo *m*.

quandary *n* perplessità *f*.

quantitative *adj* quantitativo.

quantity *n* quantità *f*.

quarantine *n* quarantena *f*.

quarrel *n* litigio *m*; * *vi* litigare.

quarrelsome *adj* litigioso.

quarry *n* preda *f*; cava *f*.

quarter *n* quarto *m*; ~ **of an hour** un quarto d'ora; quartiere *m*; * *vt* dividere in quattro.

quarterly *adj* trimestrale.

quartermaster *n* furiere *m*.

quartet *n* (*mus*) quartetto *m*.

quartz *n* (*min*) quarzo *m*.

quash *vt* stroncare; respingere.

quay *n* molo *m*.

queasy *adj* nauseato.

queen *n* regina *f*.

queer *adj* strano; (*fam*) omoses-

suale; * *n* (*fam*) *m* finocchio *m*.

quell *vt* reprimere.

quench *vt* estinguere, appagare.

query *n* domanda *f*; * *vt* contestare.

quest *n* ricerca *f*.

question *n* domanda *f*; questione *f*; * *vt* interrogare.

questionable *adj* discutibile.

questioner *n* interrogante *m/f*.

question mark *n* punto *m* interrogativo.

questionnaire *n* questionario *m*.

queue *n* coda *f*.

quibble *vi* cavillare; * *n* cavillo *m*.

quick *adj* veloce; * *n* vivo *m*.

quicken *vt* affrettare.

quicksand *n* sabbie *fpl* mobili.

quicksilver *n* mercurio *m*.

quick-witted *adj* sveglio.

quid *n* sterlina *f*.

quiet *adj* silenzioso, tranquillo; * *n* silenzio *m*.

quieten *vt* placare.

quill *n* (*ornith*) penna *f*.

quilt *n* trapunta *f*.

quince *n* cotogna *f*; (tree) cotogno *m*.

quinine *n* chinino *m*.

quintet *n* (*mus*) quintetto *m*.

quintuplet *n* uno di cinque gemelli.

quip *n* battuta *f*; * *vi* motteggiare

quirk *n* bizzarria *f*.

quit *vt* lasciare; smettere; * *vi* dimettersi.

quite adv proprio, piuttosto.

quits *adj* pari.

quiver *vi* tremare; * *n* faretra *f*.

quixotic *adj* donchisciottesco.
quiz *n* quiz *m*; * *vt* interrogare.
quizzical *adj* canzonatorio; interrogativo.
quorum *n* quorum *m*.
quota *n* quota *f*.

quotation *n* citazione *f*; preventivo *m*.
quotation marks *npl* virgolette *fpl*.
quote *vt* citare; indicare.
quotient *n* quoziente *m*.

R

rabbi *n* rabbino *m*.
rabbit *n* coniglio *m*.
rabbit hutch *n* conigliera *f*.
rabble *n* canaglia *f*.
rabid *adj* idrofobo.
rabies *n* rabbia *f*.
raccoon *n* procione *m*.
race *n* corsa *f*; razza *f*; * *vt* gareggiare contro; * *vi* correre.
racer *n* corridore *m*.
racial *adj* razziale.
racialist *n* razzista *m/f*.
racing *n* corsa *f*.
racism *n* razzismo *m*.
rack *n* rastrelliera *f*; * *vi* scervellarsi.
racket *n* racchetta *f*; fracasso *m*; racket *m*.
racy *adj* spigliato.
radar *n* radar *m*.
radial *adj* radiale.
radiance *n* splendore *m*.
radiant *adj* radiante.
radiate *vt* irraggiare.
radiation *n* radiazione *f*.
radiator *n* radiatore *m*; termosifone *m*.
radical *adj*, *n* radicale *m*.
radio *n* radio *f*.
radioactive *adj* radioattivo.
radioactivity *n* radioattività *f*.
radiographer *n* radiologo *m*.
radiography *n* radiografia *f*.
radish *n* ravanello *m*.
radium *n* radio *m*.
radius *n* raggio *m*.

raffia *n* rafia *f*.
raffle *n* riffa; * *vt* mettere in palio.
raft *n* zattera *f*.
rafter *n* puntone *m*.
rag *n* straccio *m*, cencio *m*.
rage *n* colera *f*, furia *f*; * *vi* infuriarsi.
ragged *adj* stracciato.
raging *adj* furioso.
raid *n* irruzione *f*; rapina *f*; * *vt* fare irruzione in; saccheggiare.
raider *n* rapinatore *m*.
rail *n* sbarra *f*; corrimano *m*; rotaia *f*; * *vi* **to ~ against** inveire.
railings *npl* cancellata *f*.
railway *n* ferrovia *f*.
railwayman *n* ferroviere *m*.
rain *n* pioggia *f*; * *vi* piovere.
rainbow *n* arcobaleno *m*.
raincoat *n* impermeabile *m*.
rain fall *n* precipitazione *f*.
rain water *n* acqua *f* piovana.
rainy *adj* piovoso.
raise *vt* sollevare; erigere; alzare; * *n* aumento *m*.
raisin *n* uvetta *f*.
rake *n* rastrello *m*; libertino *m*; * *vt* rastrellare.
rakish *adj* dissoluto.
rally *n* raduno *m*; rally *m*; * *vi* radunare; riunire.
ram *n* montone *m*, ariete; * *vt* speronare; ficcare.

ramble n escursione f; * vi fare escursione; divagare.

rambler n escursionista m/f.

ramification n ramificazione f.

ramify vi ramificare.

ramp n rampa f.

rampage vi scatenarsi.

rampant adj rampante.

rampart n bastione m.

ramrod n calcatoio m.

ramshackle adj sgangherato.

ranch n ranch m.

rancid adj rancido.

rancour n rancore m.

random adj a caso.

range n portata f; autonomia f; gamma f; catena f; * vi variare, estendersi.

ranger n; (forest) ~ guardia f forestale.

rank adj puzzolente, rancido; * n grado; posteggio m; * vt ritenere.

rankle vi bruciare.

ransack vt rovistare.

ransom n riscatto m; * vt riscattare.

rant vi tuonare.

rap vt bussare a; * n bussata f.

rapacious adj rapace.

rape n stupro m; * vt violentare, stuprare.

rapid adj rapido; ~s npl rapida f.

rapidity n rapidità f.

rapier n spadino m.

rapist n violentatore m, stupratore m.

rapport n rapporto m.

rapt adj rapito.

rapture n estasi f.

rapturous adj estasiato.

rare adj raro; al sangue.

rarity n rarità f.

rascal n mascalzone m.

rash adj avventato; * n sfogo, orticaria f.

rasher n fettina f (di pancetta).

rasp n raspa f; stridio m; * vt raspare; vi gracchiare.

raspberry n lampone m; ~ bush lampone m.

rat n ratto m.

ratchet n dente m di arresto.

rate n tasso m; tariffa f; * vt valutare.

rather adv piuttosto.

ratification n ratifica f.

ratify vt ratificare.

rating n valutazione f.

ratio n rapporto m.

ration n razione f; * vt razionare.

rational adj ragionevole; razionale.

rationality n razionalità f.

rationalize vt razionalizzare.

rattan n canna f d'India.

rattle vt innervosire; acciottolare; * vi sferragliare; blaterare; * n rumore m secco; acciottolio m; raganella f; rantolo m; sonaglio m.

rattlesnake n crotalo m.

ratty adj incavolato.

raucous adj rauco.

ravage vt devastare; * n devastazione f.

rave vi farneticare.

raven n corvo m.

ravenous adj famelico.

ravine n burrone m.

ravish vt estasiare; violentare.

ravishing adj incantevole.

raw adj crudo, greggio; gelido.

raw deal n bidonata f.

ray n raggio m; razza f.

raze vt ~ **to the ground** radere al suolo.

razor n rasoio m.

re prep (comm) oggetto.

reach vt raggiungere; * vi estendersi; * n portata f; tratto m.

react vi reagire.

reaction n reazione f.

reactionary n reazionario m.

reactor n reattore m.

read vt leggere; * vi studiare.

readable adj leggibile.

reader n lettore m; antologia f.

readily adv prontamente.

readiness n prontezza f,

reading n lettura f.

reading room n sala f di lettura.

readjust vt regolare; * vi riadattarsi.

ready adj pronto.

real adj vero, reale; ~ly adv davvero.

realism n realismo m.

realist n realista m/f.

realistic adj realistico.

reality n realtà f.

realization n realizzazione f.

realize vi rendersi conto di; * vt realizzare.

realm n regno m.

ream n risma f.

reap vt mietere.

reaper n mietitore m.

reappear vi ricomparire.

rear n parte f posteriore; * adj posteriore; * vt allevare; * vi impennarsi.

rearmament n riarmo m.

rear-view mirror n retrovisore m.

reason n ragione f, motivo m; * vi ragionare.

reasonable adj ragionevole.

reasonably adj abbastanza.

reasoning n ragionamento m.

reassure vt rassicurare.

rebate n rimborso m.

rebel adj, n ribelle m/f; * vi ribellarsi.

rebellion n ribellione f.

rebellious adj ribelle.

rebound vi rimbalzare.

rebuff n rifiuto m; * vt rifiutare.

rebuild vt ricostruire.

rebuke vt rimproverare; * n

rimprovero m.

rebut vt confutare.

recalcitrant adj recalcitrante.

recall vt richiamare; ricordare; * n richiamo m.

recant vt abiurare.

recantation n ritrattazione f.

recapitulate vt, vi ricapitolare.

recapture vt riprendere.

recede vi ritrarsi.

receipt n ricevuta f.

receive vt ricevere.

receiver n ricevitore m.

recent adj recente.

receptacle n recipiente m.

reception n ricevimento m; reception f; accettazione f.

recess n rientranza f; intervallo m.

recession n recessione f.

recharge vt ricaricare.

recipe n ricetta f.

recipient n destinatario m.

reciprocal adj reciproco.

reciprocate vt, vi contraccambiare.

recital n concerto m; recita f.

recite vt, vi recitare.

reckless adj spericolato.

reckon vt calcolare; credere.

reckoning n calcoli mpl.

reclaim vt bonificare; ricuperare.

recline vi essere sdraiato.

reclining adj ribaltabile.

recluse n recluso m.

recognition n riconoscimento m.

recognize vt riconoscere.

recoil vi indietreggiare.

recollect vt rammentare.

recollection n ricordo m.

recommend vt raccomandare; consigliare.

recommendation n raccomandazione f.

recompense n ricompensa f; * vt ricompensare.

reconcilable *adj* conciliabile.

reconcile *vt* riconciliare.

reconciliation *n* riconciliazione *f*.

recondite *adj* astruso.

reconnoitre *vt, vi* fare una ricognizione.

reconsider *vt* riconsiderare.

reconstruct *vt* ricostruire.

record *vt* annotare; registrare; * *n* registro *m*; precedenti penali *mpl*; record *m*; disco *m*; ~s annali *mpl*; archivi *mpl*.

recorder *n* registratore *m*; (*mus*) flauto *m*.

recount *vt* raccontare.

recourse *n* ricorso *m*.

recover *vt* ricuperare; ricoprire; * *vi* riprendersi.

recovery *n* ricupero *m*; ripresa *f*.

recreation *n* ricreazione *f*.

recriminate *vi* recriminare.

recrimination *n* recriminazione *f*.

recruit *vt* reclutare; * *n* recluta *f*.

recruitment *n* reclutamento.

rectangle *n* rettangolo *m*.

rectangular *adj* rettangolare.

rectification *n* rettifica *f*.

rectify *vt* rettificare.

rectilinear *adj* rettilineo.

rectitude *n* rettitudine *m*.

rector *n* rettore *m*.

rectum *n* retto *m*.

recumbent *adj* disteso.

recuperate *vi* ristabilirsi.

recuperation *n* convalescenza *f*.

recur *vi* ripetersi.

recurrence *n* ricorrenza *f*.

recurrent *adj* ricorrente.

red *adj, n* rosso *m*.

redden *vt* arrossare; * *vi* arrossire.

reddish *adj* rossiccio.

redeem *vt* redimere.

redeemable *adj* ammortizzabile.

Redeemer *n* Redentore *m*.

redemption *n* redenzione *f*.

redhanded *adj* in flagrante.

redhot *adj* rovente.

red-letter day *n* giorno *m* memorabile.

redness *n* rossore *m*.

redolent *adj* profumato.

redouble *vt* raddoppiare.

redress *vt* riparare; * *n* riparazione *f*.

redskin *n* pellerossa *m/f*.

red tape *n* (*fig*) burocrazia *f*.

reduce *vt* ridurre; * *vi* diminuire.

reduction *n* riduzione *f*.

redundancy *n* ridondanza *f*; licenziamento *m*.

redundant *adj* ridondante; licenziato.

reed *n* canna *f*.

reedy *adj* acuto.

reef *n* scogliera *f*.

reek *n* puzzo *m*; * *vi* puzzare.

reel *n* mulinello *m*; bobina *f*; * *vi* barcollare.

re-election *n* rielezione *f*.

re-entry *n* rientro *m*.

re-establish *vt* ristabilire.

refectory *n* refettorio *m*.

refer *vi* riferirsi a; consultare; * *vt* rimandare.

referee *n* arbitro *m*.

reference *n* riferimento *m*.

referendum *n* referendum *m*.

refill *n* ricambio; * *vt* riempire.

refine *vt* raffinare.

refinement *n* raffinatezza *f*.

refinery *n* raffineria *f*.

refit *vt* raddobbare; * raddobbo *m*.

reflating *vt* rilanciare.

reflect *vt, vi* riflettere; * *vt* rispecchiare

reflection *n* riflessione *f*; riflesso *m*.

reflector *n* catarifrangente *m*.
reflex *adj, n* riflesso *m*.
reflexive *adj* riflessivo.
reform *vt* riformare; * *n* riforma *f*.
Reformation *n* Riforma *f*.
reformer *n* riformatore *m*.
reformist *n* riformista *m/f*.
refract *vt* rifrangere.
refraction *n* rifrazione *f*.
refrain *vi* astenersi; * *n* ritornello *m*;
refresh *vt* rinfrescare.
refreshment *n* ristoro *m*.
refrigerate *vt* refrigerare.
refrigerator *n* frigorifero *m*.
refuel *vi* rifornirsi di carburante.
refuge *n* riparo *m*, rifugio *m*.
refugee *n* profugo *m*.
refund *vt* rimborsare; * *n* rimborso *m*.
refurbish *vt* rinnovare.
refusal *n* rifiuto *m*.
refuse *vt* rifiutare; * *n* rifiuti *mpl*.
refute *vt* confutare.
regain *vt* riguadagnare.
regal *adj* regale.
regale *vt* intrattenere.
regalia *n* insegne *fpl* reali.
regard *vt* considerare; riguardare; * *n* riguardo *m*.
regarding *prep* riguardo a.
regardless *adv* senza riguardo.
regatta *n* regata *f*.
regency *n* reggenza *f*.
regenerate *vt* rigenerare; * *adj* rigenerato.
regeneration *n* rigenerazione *f*.
regent *n* reggente *m/f*.
régime *n* regime *m*.
regiment *n* reggimento *m*.
region *n* regione *f*.
regional *adj* regionale.
register *n* registro *m*; * *vt* registrare; immatricolare; * *vi*

iscriversi; **~ed letter** *n* raccomandata *f*.
registrar *n* ufficiale *m* di stato civile.
registration *n* registrazione *f*.
registry *n*; **~ office** anagrafe *f*.
regress *vi* regredire.
regression *n* regresso *m*.
regressive *adj* regressivo.
regret *n* rimpianto *m*; rammarico *m*; * *vt* rimpiangere; dispiacersi di.
regrettable *adj* deplorevole.
regular *adj* regolare; fedele.
regularity *n* regolarità *f*.
regulate *vt* regolare.
regulation *n* regolamento *m*.
regulator *n* regolatore *m*.
rehabilitate *vt* riabilitare.
rehabilitation *n* riabilitazione *f*.
rehearsal *n* prova *f*.
rehearse *vt* provare.
reign *n* regno *m*; * *vi* regnare.
reimburse *vt* rimborsare.
reimbursement *n* rimborso *m*.
rein *n* redine *f*.
reincarnation *n* reincarnazione *f*.
reindeer *n* renna *f*.
reinforce *vt* rinforzare.
reinstate *vt* reintegrare.
reinsure *vt* riassicurare.
reissue *n* ristampa *f*.
reiterate *vt* reiterare.
reiteration *n* reiterazione *f*.
reject *vt* scartare; * *n* scarto *m*.
rejection *n* rigetto *m*;
rejoice *vi* rallegrarsi.
rejoicings *npl* festeggiamenti *mpl*.
rejuvenate *vt* ringiovanire.
relapse *vi* ricadere; * *n* ricaduta *f*.
relate *vt* collegare; raccontare.
related *adj* affine; imparentato.
relation *n* relazione *f*; rappor-

to *m*; parente *m/f*.

relationship *n* nesso *m*; relazione *f*; legami *mpl* di parentela.

relative *adj* relativo; **~ly** *adv* abbastanza; * *n* parente *m/f*.

relax *vt* rilassare.

relaxation *n* relax *m*.

relay *n* ricambio *m*; relé *m*; * *vt* ritrasmettere; passare.

release *vt* rilasciare; mollare; emettere; * *n* rilascio *m*; emissione *f*; uscita *f*.

relegate *vt* relegare.

relegation *n* relegazione *f*.

relent *vi* cedere.

relentless *adj* implacabile.

relevance *n* pertinenza *f*.

relevant *adj* pertinente.

reliable *adj* affidabile.

reliance *n* dipendenza *f*.

relic *n* reliquia *f*.

relief *n* sollievo *m*; rilievo *m*.

relieve *vt* alleviare.

religion *n* religione *f*.

religious *adj* religioso.

relinquish *vt* rinunciare a.

relish *n* gusto *m*; condimento *m*; * *vt* gustare.

reluctance *n* riluttanza *f*.

reluctant *adj* restio.

rely *vi* contare su.

remain *vi* rimanere.

remainder *n* resto *m*; avanzo *m*.

remains *npl* resti *mpl*; avanzi *mpl*.

remand *vt* rimandare in carcere; * *n* detenzione *f* preventiva.

remark *n* osservazione *f*; * *vt* osservare.

remarkable *adj* notevole.

remarry *vi* risposarsi.

remedial *adj* correttivo.

remedy *n* rimedio *m*; * *vt* rimediare.

remember *vt* ricordare.

remembrance *n* ricordo *m*.

remind *n* ricordare.

reminder *n* sollecito *m*.

reminiscence *n* reminiscenza *f*.

remiss *adj* negligente.

remission *n* remissione *f*.

remit *vt* rimettere.

remittance *n* rimessa *f*.

remnant *n* scampolo *m*; resto *m*.

remodel *vt* rimodellare.

remonstrate *vi* protestare.

remorse *n* rimorso *m*.

remorseless *adj* spietato.

remote *adj* remoto; vago.

remote control *n* telecomando *m*.

removable *adj* asportabile.

removal *n* trasloco *m*; eliminazione *f*; rimozione *f*.

remove *vt* togliere; rimuovere; eliminare; asportare.

remunerate *vt* rimunerare.

remuneration *n* rimunerazione *f*.

Renaissance *n* Rinascimento *m*.

renal *adj* renale.

render *vt* rendere; interpretare.

rendezvous *n* appuntamento *m*; * *vi* ritrovarsi.

renegade *n* rinnegato *m*.

renew *vt* rinnovare.

renewal *n* rinnovo *m*.

rennet *n* caglio *m*.

renounce *vt* rinunciare.

renovate *vt* rinnovare.

renovation *n* restauro *m*.

renown *n* rinomanza *f*.

renowned *adj* rinomato.

rent *n* affitto *m*, pigione *m*; * *vt* affittare.

rental *n* nolo *m*.

renunciation *n* rinuncia *f*.

reopen *vt* riaprire.

reorganization *n* riorganizzazione *f*.

reorganize vt riorganizzare.

repair vt aggiustare, riparare; * n riparazione f.

reparable adj riparabile.

reparation n riparazione f.

repartee n conversazione f brillante.

repatriate vt rimpatriare.

repay vt restituire; ricambiare.

repayment n rimborso m.

repeal vt abrogare; * n abrogazione f.

repeat vt ripetere; * n replica f.

repeatedly adv ripetutamente.

repel vt respingere.

repent vi pentirsi.

repentance n pentimento m.

repentant adj pentito.

repercussions npl ripercussione fpl

repertoire, repertory n repertorio m.

repetition n ripetizione f.

replace vt rimpiazzare; sostituire.

replacement n sostituto m.

replenish vt rifornire.

replete adj sazio.

replica n replica f.

reply n risposta f; * vt, vi rispondere.

report vt riportare; denunciare; * n rapporto m; pagella f; reportage m.

reporter n cronista m/f.

repose vi riposare; * n riposo m.

repository n deposito m.

repossess vt ricuperare.

reprehend vt rimproverare.

reprehensibile adj riprovevole.

represent vt rappresentare.

representation n rappresentazione f.

representative adj rappresentativo; * n rappresentante m.

repress vt reprimere.

repression n repressione f.

repressive adj repressivo.

reprieve vt concedere una proroga; * n proroga f.

reprimand vt rimproverare; * n rimprovero m.

reprint n ristampa f.

reprisals npl rappresaglie fpl.

reproach n rimprovero; * vt rimproverare.

reproachful adj di rimprovero.

reproduce vt riprodurre.

reproduction n riproduzione f.

reptile n rettile m.

republic n repubblica f.

republican n repubblicano m.

repudiate vt ripudiare.

repugnance n ripugnanza f.

repugnant adj ripugnante.

repulse vt respingere.

repulsion n repulsione f.

repulsive adj ripugnante.

reputable adj stimabile; attendibile.

reputation n reputazione f.

repute vt ritenere; * n reputazione f.

request n richiesta f; * vt richiedere.

require vt richiedere.

requirement n esigenza f.

requisite adj, n occorrente m.

requisition n requisizione f; * vt requisire.

requite vt contraccambiare.

rescind vt rescindere.

rescue vt salvare; * n salvataggio m.

research vi fare ricerca; * n ricerca f.

resemblance n somiglianza f.

resemble vt somigliare.

resent vt risentirsi per.

resentful adj pieno di risentimento.

resentment n risentimento m.

reservation n prenotazione f; riserva f.

reserve *vt* prenotare; riservare; * *n* riserva *f*; riservo *m*.
reservoir *n* bacino *m* idrico.
reside *vi* risiedere.
residence *n* residenza *f*.
resident *adj, n* residente *m/f*.
residual *adj* residuo.
residue *n* residuo *m*.
resign *vi* dimettersi.
resignation *n* dimissioni *fpl*.
resigned *adj* rassegnato.
resilient *adj* elastico.
resin *n* resina *f*.
resinous *adj* resinoso.
resist *vt, vi* resistere.
resistance *n* resistenza *f*.
resolute *adj* risoluto.
resolution *n* determinazione *f*; risoluzione *f*; definizione *f*.
resolve *vt* decidere; risolvere; * *n* risolutezza *f*.
resonance *n* risonanza *f*.
resonant *adj* risonante.
resort *vi* fare ricorso a; * *n* ricorso *m*; località *f* di villeggiatura.
resound *vi* risonare.
resounding *adj* clamoroso.
resource *n* risorsa *f*.
respect *n* rispetto *m*; **in some ~s** sotto certi aspetti; * *vt* rispettare.
respectability *n* rispettabilità *f*.
respectable *adj* rispettabile.
respectful *adj* rispettoso.
respecting *prep* riguardante.
respective *adj* rispettivo.
respirator *n* respiratore *m*.
respiration *n* respirazione *f*.
respiratory *adj* respiratorio.
respite *n* tregua *f*; * *vt* dare respiro a.
resplendent *adj* risplendente.
respond *vi* rispondere.
respondent *n* (*law*) convenuto *m*.
response *n* risposta *f*.

responsibility *n* responsabilità *f*.
responsibile *adj* responsabile.
responsive *adj* che reagisce bene.
rest *n* riposo *m*; pausa *f*; appoggio *m*; resto *m*; * *vt* riposare; * *vi* riposarsi; poggiare.
restaurant *n* ristorante *m*.
restful *adj* riposante.
restitution *n* restituzione *f*.
restive *adj* irrequieto.
restless *adj* irrequieto.
restoration *n* restauro *m*; **the R~** la Restaurazione *f*.
restore *vt* restaurare; restituire.
restrain *vt* trattenere.
restraint *n* restrizione *f*.
restrict *vt* limitare.
restriction *n* restrizione *f*.
restrictive *adj* restrittivo.
result *vi* avere come risultato; * *n* risultato *m*.
resume *vt, vi* riprendere.
résumé *n* riassunto *m*.
resumption *n* ripresa *f*.
resurrection *n* risurrezione *f*.
resuscitate *vt* risuscitare.
retail *vt* vendere al dettaglio; * *adj* al dettaglio;
retailer *n* dettagliante *m/f*.
retain *vt* tenere; conservare.
retainer *n* onorario *m*.
retake *vt* riprendere.
retaliate *vi* vendicarsi.
retaliation *n* rappresaglie *fpl*.
retarded *adj* ritardato.
retch *vi* avere conati di vomito.
retention *n* ritenzione *f*.
retentive *adj* ritentivo.
reticence *n* reticenza *f*.
retina *n* retina *f*.
retinue *n* seguito *m*.
retire *vt* mandare in pensione; * *vi* ritirarsi, andare in pensione.
retired *adj* pensionato.

retirement *n* ritiro *m*; l'andare in pensione.

retort *vt* ribattere; * *n* risposta *f*; storta *f*.

retouch *vt* ritoccare.

retrace *vt* ripercorrere.

retract *vt* ritrattare; ritirare.

retrain *vt*, *vi* riqualificare.

retraining *n* riqualificazione *f*.

retreat *n* rifugio *m*; * *vi* ritirarsi.

retribution *n* retribuzione *f*.

retrieval *n* ricupero *m*.

retrieve *vt* ricuperare; (*comp*) richiamare.

retriever *n* cane *m* da riporto.

retrograde *adj* retrogrado.

retrospect; **in ~** ripensandoci.

retrospective *adj* retrospettivo; * *n* retrospettiva *f*.

return *vt* restituire; * *vi* tornare; * *n* ritorno *m*; resa *f*; guadagno *m*; (ticket) andata e ritorno.

reunion *n* riunione *f*.

reunite *vt* riunire; * *vi* riunirsi.

revalue *vt* rivalutare.

revamp *vt* modernizzare.

reveal *vt* rivelare.

revel *vt* far baldoria.

revelation *n* rivelazione *f*.

revelry *n* baldoria *f*.

revenge *vt* vendicare; * *n* vendetta *f*.

revengeful *adj* vendicativo.

revenue *n* reddito *m*.

reverberate *vi* rimbombare.

reverberation *n* rimbombo *m*.

revere *vt* venerare.

reverence *n* venerazione *f*.

Reverend *n* reverendo *m*.

reverent, reverential *adj* reverente.

revery *n* fantasticheria *f*.

reversal *n* inversione *f*.

reverse *vt* invertire; * *vi* fare marcia indietro; * *n* opposto

m; rovescio *m*; retromarcia *f*; * *adj* inverso; marcia indietro.

reversible *adj* double-face.

revert *vi* ritornare.

review *vt* fare una revisione di; recensire; * *n* revisione *f*; rivista *f*.

reviewer *n* recensore *m*.

revile *vt* oltraggiare, insultare.

revise *vt* ripassare; rivedere.

revision *n* ripasso *m*; revisione *f*.

revival *n* risveglio *m*; ripristino *m*.

revive *vt* rianimare.

revoke *vt* abrogare.

revolt *vi* ribellarsi; * *vt* rivoltare; * *n* rivolta *f*.

revolting *adj* rivoltante.

revolution *n* rivoluzione *f*.

revolutionary *adj*, *n* rivoluzionario *m*.

revolve *vt*, *vi* girare.

revolver *n* rivoltella *f*.

revolving *adj* girevole.

revue *n* revista *f*.

revulsion *n* ripugnanza *f*.

reward *vt* premiare; * *n* ricompensa *f*.

rhapsody *n* rapsodia *f*.

rhetoric *n* retorica *f*.

rhetorical *adj* retorico.

rheumatic *adj* reumatico.

rheumatism *n* reumatismo *m*.

rhinoceros *n* rinoceronte *m*.

rhododendron *n* rododendro *m*.

rhombus *n* rombo *m*.

rhubarb *n* rabarbaro *m*.

rhyme *n* rima *f*; * *vi* fare rima con.

rhythm *n* ritmo *m*.

rhythmical *adj* ritmico.

rib *n* costola *f*.

ribald *adj* sguaiato.

ribbon *n* nastro *m*.

rice *n* riso *m*.

rich *adj* ricco.

riches *npl* ricchezze *fpl*.
richness *n* ricchezza *f*.
rickets *n* rachitismo *m*.
rickety *adj* traballante.
rickshaw *n* risciò *m*.
ricochet *vi* rimbalzare.
rid *vt* sbarazzare.
riddance *n* liberazione; * *excl*
good ~! che liberazione!.
riddle *n* indovinello *m*; setaccio
m; * *vt* crivellare.
ride *vi* cavalcare; andare; * *n*
cavalcata *f*; giro *m*.
rider *n* cavallerizzo *m*; clausola *f* addizionale.
ridge *n* cresta *f*; crinale *m*.
ridicule *n* ridicolo *m*; * *vt* mettere in ridicolo.
ridiculous *adj* ridicolo.
riding *n* equitazione *f*.
riding school *n* scuola *f* di equitazione.
rife *adj* diffuso; imperversare.
riffraff *n* gentaglia *f*.
rifle *vt* svaligiare; * *vi* frugare;
* *n* fucile *m*; carabina *f*.
rifleman *n* bersagliere *m*.
rift *n* spaccatura *f*.
rig *vt* truccare; * *n* impianto *m*
di trivellazione.
rigging *n* (*mar*) cordame *m*.
right *adj* giusto, retto; adatto;
destro; diritto; corretto; * *adv*
completamente; bene; giustamente; * *n* diritto *m*; destra *f*;
* *vt* raddrizzare; correggere;
to be ~ avere ragione.
righteous *adj* virtuoso.
righteousness *n* rettitudine *f*.
rightful *adj* legittimo.
rigid *adj* rigido.
rigidity *n* rigidezza *f*.
rigmarole *n* trafila *f*.
rigorous *adj* rigoroso.
rigour *n* rigore *m*.
rim *n* orlo *m*.
rind *n* buccia *f*; cotenna *f*.
ring *n* anello *m*; cerchio *m*; ring

m; squillo *m*; scampanellata;
* *vt* accerchiare; suonare; * *vi*
telefonare; suonare; risuonare.
ringleader *n* capobanda *m*.
ringlet *n* boccolo *m*.
ringworm *n* tricofizia *f*.
rink *n* pista *f* di pattinaggio.
rinse *vt* sciacquare; * *n* sciacquatura *f*.
riot *n* disordini *mpl*; sommossa
f; * *vi* tumultuare.
rioter *n* rivoltoso *m*.
riotous *adj* chiassoso.
rip *vt* strappare; * *n* strappo *m*;
to let ~ scatenarsi.
ripe *adj* maturo, stagionato.
ripen *vt*, *vi* maturare.
rip off *vt* pelare.
ripple *vi* increspare; * *n* increspatura *f*.
rise *vi* alzarsi; sorgere; lievitare; aumentare; * *n* sorgere
m; ascesa *f*; aumento *m*; salita *f*.
rising *n* sommossa *f*; * *adj* crescente; montante.
risk *n* rischio *m*; * *vt* rischiare.
risky *adj* rischioso.
risqué *adj* spinto.
rissole *n* polpetta *f*.
rite *n* rito *m*.
ritual *adj*, *n* rituale *m*.
rival *adj*, *n* rivale *m*; * *vt* rivaleggiare.
rivalry *n* rivalità *f*.
river *n* fiume *m*.
rivet *n* ribattino *m*; * *vt* rivettare.
rivulet *n* ruscelletto *m*.
roach *n* (cock~) blatta *f*; leucisco *m* rosso.
road *n* strada *f*, via *f*.
roadsign *n* cartello *m* stradale.
roadworks *npl* lavori *mpl* stradali.
roam *vi* gironzolare.

roan *n* roano *m*.

roar *vi* ruggire; * *n* ruggito *m*.

roaring *adj* strepitoso.

roast *vt* arrostire; torrefare; * *n* arrosto *m*.

roast beef *n* rosbif *m*.

rob *vt* derubare.

robber *n* rapinatore *m*.

robbery *n* rapina *f*.

robe *n* tunica *f*; accappatoio *m*.

robin pettirosso *m*.

robot *n* robot *m*.

robust *adj* robusto.

rock *n* roccia *f*; (*mus*) rock *m*; * *vt* cullare; * *vi* dondolare; oscillare.

rocket *n* razzo *m*

rocking chair *n* sedia *f* a dondolo.

rock salt *n* salgemma *m*.

rocky *adj* roccioso; vacillante.

rod *n* bacchetta *f*; bastone *m*.

rodent *n* roditore *m*.

roe *n* uova *fpl* di pesce.

roebuck *n* capriolo *m* maschio.

rogue *n* mascalzone *m*.

roguish *adj* malizioso.

role *n* ruolo *m*;

roll *vt*, *vi* rotolare; * *n* rotolo *m*; rullino *m*; panino *m*; lista *f*.

roller *n* rullo *m*; rotella *f*; bigodino *m*.

roller skate *n* patino *m* a rotelle.

rolling pin *n* matterello *m*.

Roman Catholic *adj*, *n* cattolico *m*.

romance *n* storia *f* d'amore.

romantic *adj* romantico.

romp *vi* giocare chiassosamente; * *n* gioco *m* chiassoso.

rompers *npl* tutina *f*.

roof *n* tetto *m*; * *vt* mettere il tetto.

rook *n* corvo *m*; (chess) torre *f*.

room *n* stanza *f*; spazio *m*; posto *m*.

roomy *adj* spazioso.

roost *n* posatoio *m*; * *vi* appollaiarsi.

rooster *n* gallo *m*.

root *n* radice *f*; * *vt* far radicare; * *vi* attecchire; **to ~ out** eradicare.

rooted *adj* inchiodato.

rope *n* fune *f*; corda *f*; * *vt* legare.

ropey *adj* scadente.

rosary *n* rosario *m*.

rose *n* rosa *f*; rosone *m* di stucco; (watering can) cipolla *f*.

rosebed *n* rosaio *m*.

rosebud *n* bocciolo *m* di rosa.

rosemary *n* rosmarino *m*.

rosette *n* coccarda *f*.

rosé wine *n* vino *m* rosato.

rosewood *n* palissandro *m*.

rostrum *n* podio *m*.

rosy *adj* roseo.

rot *vi* marcire; * *n* marciume *m*.

rotate *vi* rotare.

rotation *n* rotazione *f*.

rote *n*; **by ~** a memoria.

rotten *adj* marcio; schifoso.

rotund *adj* grassoccio.

rouble *n* rublo *m*.

rouge *n* belletto *m*.

rough *adj* ruvido, rozzo; rauco; approssimativo; burrascoso.

rough-and-ready *adj* rudimentale.

rough-and-tumble *n* zuffa *f*.

roughen *vt* irruvidire.

roughly *adv* brutalmente; grossolanamente.

roughness *n* ruvidità *f*.

roulette *n* roulette *f*.

round *adj* rotondo; * *n* cerchio *m*; giro *m*; round *m*; * *prep* intorno a; * *vt* arrotondare.

roundabout *adj* indiretto; * *n* giostra *f*; rotatoria *f*.

roundup *n* retata *f*.

rouse *vt* svegliare; scuotere.

rousing *adj* trascinante.

rout *n* disfatta *f*; * *vt* sbaragliare.

route n itinerario m, percorso m; rotta f.

routine n routine f, tran tran m; * adj comune, abituale.

rove vi vagare.

rover n giramondo m/f.

roving adj vagabondo.

row n baccano m; lite f; * vi litigare.

row n fila f; * vt remare.

rowdy adj turbolento.

rower n rematore m.

royal adj reale.

royalist n realista f.

royalty n reali mpl; royalty m.

rub vt strofinare, sfregare; * n strofinamento m.

rubber n gomma f; caucciù m.

rubber-band n elastico m.

rubbish n spazzatura f, immondizie fpl.

rubble n macerie fpl.

rubic n rubrica f.

ruby adj, n rubino m.

rucksack n zaino m.

rudder n timone m.

ruddy adj rubicondo.

rude adj indecente, brusco, villano.

rudeness n maleducazione f.

rudiment n rudimento m.

rue vt pentirsi di; (bot) ruta f.

rueful adj mesto.

ruffian adj manigoldo.

ruffle vt arruffare.

rug n tappeto m; plaid m.

rugby n rugby m.

rugged adj accidentato; frastagliato; marcato.

ruin n rudere m, rovina f; * vt rovinare.

ruinous adj disastroso.

rule n regola f; regolamento m; * vt governare; decretare; rigare; * vi regnare.

ruler n sovrano m; righello m.

rum n rum m; * adj strambo.

rumble vi brontolare; * vt scoprire; * n rombo m.

ruminate vt ruminare.

rummage vt rovistare, frugare.

rumour n voce f.

rump n groppa f.

rumpus n putiferio m.

run vt correre; dirigere; gestire; organizzare; * vi correre; funzionare; scorrere; collare; * n corsa f; giro m; tragitto m; serie f; recinto m; smagliatura f.

runaway adj, n fuggitivo m.

rung n piolo m; traversa f.

runner n corridore m; guida f.

running adj corrente; * n gestione f.

runny adj sciolto.

run-of-the-mill adj banale.

runway n pista f.

rupture n rottura f; * vt rompere.

rural adj rurale.

ruse n astuzia f.

rush n giunco m; ressa f; premura f; fretta f; * vt fare fretta a; * vi precipitarsi.

rusk n fetta f biscottata.

russet adj marrone rossiccio.

rust n ruggine f; * vt, vi arrugginire.

rustic adj rustico; * n contadino m.

rustle vi frusciare; * n fruscio m.

rusty adj rugginoso.

rut n solco m.

ruthless adj spietato.

rye n segale f.

S

Sabbath *n* domenica *f*.
sable *n* zibellino *m*.
sabotage *n* sabotaggio *m*; * *vt* sabotare.
saccharin *n* saccarina *f*.
sachet *n* bustina *f*.
sack *n* sacco *m*; saccheggio *m*; * *vt* licenziare; saccheggiare.
sacrament *n* sacramento *m*.
sacred *adj* sacro.
sacrifice *n* sacrificio *m*; * *vt* sacrificare.
sacrificial *adj* sacrificale.
sacrilege *n* sacrilegio *m*.
sacrilegious *adj* sacrilego.
sacrosanct *adj* sacrosanto.
sad *adj* triste; deplorevole.
sadden *vt* rattristare.
saddle *n* sella *f*; * *vt* sellare.
saddler *n* sellaio *m*.
sadism *n* sadismo *m*.
sadist *n* sadico *m*.
sadistic *adj* sadico.
sadness *n* tristezza *f*.
safari *n* safari *m*.
safe *adj* salvo; sicuro; ~ **and sound** sano e salvo; * *n* cassaforte *f*.
safe-conduct *n* salvacondotto *m*.
safeguard *n* salvaguardia *f*; * *vt* salvaguardare.
safety *n* sicurezza *f*.
safety belt *n* cintura *f* di sicurezza.
safety pin *n* spilla *f* da balia.
saffron *n* zafferano *m*.
sag *vi* incurvarsi.
saga *n* saga *f*.
sage *n* (*bot*) salvia *f*; saggio *m*; ; * *n* saggio *m*.
Sagittarius *n* Sagittario *m*.
sago *n* (*bot*) sagù *m*.
sail *n* vela *f*; pala *f*; * *vt* con-

durre; * *vi* salpare, navigare.
sailing *n* vela *f*.
sailor *n* marinaio *m*.
saint *n* santa *f*.
saintly *adj* santo.
sake *n*: **for God's** ~ per amor di Dio.
salad *n* insalata *f*.
salad bowl *n* insalatiera *f*.
salad dressing *n* condimento *m* per insalata.
salamander *n* salamandra *f*.
salami *n* salame *m*.
salary *n* stipendio *m*.
sale *n* vendita *f*; svendita *f*.
saleable *adj* vendibile.
salesman *n* commesso *m*.
saleswoman *n* commessa *f*.
salient *adj* saliente.
saline *adj* salino.
saliva *n* saliva *f*.
salivate *vi* salivare.
sallow *adj* giallastro.
sally *n* battuta *f*.
salmon *n* salmone *m*.
salmon trout *n* trota *f* salmonata.
salon *n* salone *m*.
saloon *n* salone *m*; saloon *m*.
salt *n* sale *m*; * *vt* salare.
salt cellar *n* saliera *f*.
saltpeter *n* salnitro *m*.
saltworks *npl* salina *f*.
salty *adj* salato.
salubrious *adj* salubre.
salutary *adj* salutare.
salute *vt* salutare; * *n* saluto *m*.
salvage *vt* ricuperare; * *n* salvataggio *m*.
salvation *n* salvezza *f*.
salve *n* unguento *m*; * *vt* placare.
salver *n* vassoio *m*.
salvo *n* salva *f*.

same *adj, pron* stesso.
sameness *n* monotonia *f.*
sample *n* campione *m;* * *vt* assaggiare.
sampler *n* saggio *m* di ricamo.
sanatorium *n* convalescenziario *m.*
sanctify *vt* santificare.
sanctimonious *adj* moraleggiante.
sanction *n* sanzione *f;* * *vt* sancire.
sanctity *n* santità *f.*
sanctuary *n* santuario *m.*
sand *n* sabbia *f;* * *vt* cartavetrare; cospargere di sabbia.
sandal *n* sandalo *m.*
sandbag *n* sacco *m* di sabbia.
sandblast *vt* sabbiare.
sandpaper *n* carta *f* vetrata.
sandpit *n* buca *f* di sabbia.
sandstone *n* arenaria *f.*
sandwich *n* tramezzino *m,* sandwich *m.*
sandy *adj* sabbioso.
sane *adj* sano di mente.
sangfroid *n* sangue *m* freddo.
sanguine *adj* ottimista.
sanitary towel *n* assorbente *m.*
sanity *n* sanità *f* mentale.
sap *n* linfa *f;* * *vt* fiaccare.
sapling *n* alberello *m.*
sapphire *n* zaffiro *m.*
sarcasm *n* sarcasmo *m.*
sarcastic *adj* sarcastico.
sarcophagus *n* sarcofago *m.*
sardine *n* sardina *f.*
sardonic *adj* sardonico.
sash *n* fusciacca *f;* telaio *m;* **~ window** *n* finestra *f* a saliscendi.
Satan *n* Satana *m.*
satanic(al) *adj* satanico.
satchel *n* cartella *f.*
satellite *n* satellite *m.*
satiate *vt* saziare.
satin *n* raso *m.*
satire *n* satira *f.*

satiric(al) *adj* satirico.
satirist *n* scrittore (etc) *m* satirico.
satirize *vt* satireggiare.
satisfaction *n* soddisfazione *f.*
satisfactory *adj* soddisfacente.
satisfy *vt* soddisfare.
saturate *vt* saturare.
Saturday *n* sabato *m.*
satyr *n* satiro *m.*
sauce *n* salsa *f.*
saucepan *n* pentola *f.*
saucer *n* piattino *m.*
saucy *adj* provocante.
saunter *vi* andare a zonzo.
sausage *n* salsiccia *f;* salame *m.*
savage *adj, n* selvaggio *m;* * *vt* sbranare.
savagery *n* ferocia *f.*
savannah *n* savana *f.*
save *vt* salvare; risparmiare; parare; * *n* parata *f;* * *prep* salvo.
saveloy *n* cervellata *f.*
saver *n* risparmiatore *m.*
saving *n* risparmio *m;* **~s** risparmi *mpl.*
savings account *n* libretto *m* di risparmio.
savings bank *n* cassa *f* di risparmio.
Saviour *n* salvatore *n.*
savour *n* sapore *m;* * *vt* assaporare.
savoury *adj* salato; *n* piatto *m* salato.
saw *n* sega *f;* * *vt* segare.
sawdust *n* segatura *f.*
sawmill *n* segheria *f.*
saxophone *n* sassofono *m.*
say *vt, vi* dire; indicare.
saying *n* detto *m.*
scab *n* crosta *f;* crumiro *m.*
scabbard *n* fodero *m.*
scaffold *n* patibolo *m.*
sfaffolding *n* impalcatura *f.*
scald *n* scottatura; * *vt* scottare.

scale n scaglia f; squama f; scala f; * vt squamare; scalare.

scales n bilancia f.

scallop n (zool) pettine m; smerlo m; * vt smerlare.

scalp n cuoio m capelluto; * vt scotennare.

scalpel n bisturi m.

scamp n peste f.

scamper vi sgambettare.

scampi npl gamberoni mpl.

scan vt scrutare, scandagliare; * vi scandire; * n ecografia f.

scandal n scandalo m.

scandalize vt scandagliare.

scandalous adj scandaloso.

scant adj scarso.

scanty adj scarso, succinto.

scapegoat n capro m espiatorio.

scar n cicatrice f; * vt sfregiare; * vi cicatrizzarsi.

scarce adj scarso; ~ly adv appena.

scarcity n scarsità f.

scare vt spaventare; impaurire; * n spavento m.

scarecrow n spaventapasseri m.

scaremonger n allarmista m/f.

scarf n sciarpa f, foulard m.

scarlet adj, n scarlatto m.

scarlet fever n scarlattina f.

scarp n scarpata f.

scathing adj sprezzante.

scatter vt sparpagliare; * vi disperdersi.

scatterbrain n scervellato m.

scavenger n animale m necrofago.

scenario n copione m.

scene n scena f; luogo m.

scenery n paesaggio m.

scenic adj pittoresco.

scent n profumo m; pista f; * vt profumare; fiutare.

scentless adj inodoro.

sceptic n scettico; ~al adj scettico.

scepticism n scetticismo m.

sceptre n scettro m.

schedule n programma m; orario m; tabella f.

scheduled flight n volo m di linea.

schematic adj schematico.

scheme n piano m; * vi tramare.

schemer n intrigante m/f.

scheming adj intrigante.

schism n scisma m.

schizophrenia n schizofrenia f.

scholar n studioso m.

scholarly adj dotto.

scholarship n erudizione f, borsa f di studio.

scholastic adj scolastico.

school n scuola f; facoltà f; banco m; * vt addestrare.

schoolboy n scolaro m.

schoolgirl n scolara f.

schooling n istruzione f.

schoolmaster n maestro m, insegnante m.

schoolmistress n maestra f, insegnante f.

schoolteacher n maestro m, insegnante m/f.

schooner n schooner m.

sciatica n sciatica f.

science n scienza f.

science fiction n fantascienza f.

scientific adj scientifico.

scientist n scienziato m.

scimitar n scimitarra f.

scintillating adj scintillante.

scissors npl forbice fpl.

sclerosis n sclerosi f.

scoff vi ridere; * vt papparsi.

scold vt sgridare.

scoop n paletta f; mestolo m; colpo m giornalistico; * vt accaparrarsi.

scooter n monopattino m; scooter m.

scope n possibilità fpl, ambito m, capacità f.

scorch vt bruciacchiare; * n bruciacchiatura f.

score n punteggio m; motivo m; scalfittura f; (mus) partitura f; * vt segnare; incidere; (mus) orchestrare.

scoreboard n tabellone m.

scorn vt disprezzare; * n disprezzo m.

scornful adj sprezzante.

Scorpio n Scorpione m.

scorpion n scorpione m.

scotch vt stroncare.

scoundrel n farabutto m.

scour vt sfregare; vi setacciare.

scourge n flagello m.

scout n ricognitore m; * vi andare alla ricerca di.

scowl n sguardo torvo; * vi accigliarsi.

scraggy adj scheletrico.

scramble vi inerpicarsi; * vt (culin) strapazzare; ingarbugliare; * n parapiglia f; gara f di motocross.

scrap n pezzetto m; briciolo m; ferraglia f; baruffa f; * vt demolire.

scrape * vt scorticare; raschiare; * vi grattare; * n raschiatura f; guaio m.

scraper n raschietto m.

scratch vt graffiare; grattare; cancellare; * n graffio m.

scrawl vt scribacchiare; * n graffia n illeggibile.

scream vt, vi urlare; * n urlo m, strillo m.

screech vi strillare, stridere; * n strido m.

screen n paravento m; schermo m; * vt nascondere; proiettare; (fig) vagliare.

screenplay n sceneggiatura f.

screw n vite f; elica f; (sl) secondino m * vt avvitare; spiegazzare.

screwdriver n cacciavite m.

scribble vi scarabocchiare; * n scarabocchio m.

scribe n scriba m.

scrimmage n tafferuglio m.

script n copione m, scrittura f.

Scripture n Sacre Scritture fpl.

scroll n rotolo m di pergamena.

scrotum n scroto m.

scrounge vt, vi scroccare.

scrounger n scroccone m/f.

scrub vt strofinare; cancellare; * n boscaglia f; strofinata f.

scruffy adj trasandato.

scrum n (sport) mischia f.

scrumptious adj delizioso.

scruple n scrupolo m.

scrupulous adj scrupoloso.

scrutinize vt scrutare.

scrutiny n scrutinio m.

scuffle n tafferuglio m; * vi azzuffarsi.

scull vt remare.

scullery n retrocucina m.

sculpt vt, vi scolpire.

sculptor n scultore m.

sculpture n scultura f.

scum n (fig) feccia f.

scurrilous adj scurrile.

scurvy n scorbuto m.

scuttle n secchio m; * vt autoaffondare; * vi sgattaiolare via.

scythe n falce f; * vt falciare.

sea n mare m.

sea breeze n brezza f marina.

seafood n frutti mpl di mare.

sea front n lungomare m.

seagull n gabbiano m.

sea horse n cavalluccio m marino.

seal n foca f; sigillo m; * vt sigillare.

sealing wax n ceralacca f.

seam n cucitura f; vena f.

seaman n marinaio m.

seamanship n tecnica f di navigazione.

seamstress n sarta f.

seamy adj malfamato.

sea plane n idrovolante m.

seaport n porto m di mare.

sear vt cauterizzare.

search vt perquisire; perlustrare; * vi cercare; * n ricerca f; perquisizione f.

searchlight n riflettore m.

seashore n riva f del mare.

seasick vt avere il mal di mare.

seasickness n mal di mare.

seaside n spiaggia f.

season n stagione f; * vt stagionare; condire.

seasonable adj di stagione.

seasoning n condimento m.

season ticket n abbonamento m.

seat n sedia f; posto m; sedile m; sellino m; seggio m; sede f; * vt far sedere.

seat belt n cintura f di sicurezza.

seaweed n alghe fpl.

seaworthy adj in condizione di navigare.

secateurs n forbici fpl per potare.

secede vi ritirarsi.

secession n secessione f.

secluded adj appartato.

seclusion n isolamento m.

second adj secondo; * n secondo m; * vt appoggiare; distaccare.

secondary adj secondario.

secondary school n scuola f secondaria.

secondhand adj di seconda mano.

secondment n distaccamento m.

secrecy n segretezza f.

secret adj, n segreto m.

secretariat n segretariato m.

secretary n segretario m.

secrete vt secernere; nascondere.

secretion n secrezione f.

secretive adj riservato.

sect n setta f.

sectarian n settario m.

section n sezione f, tratto m.

sector n settore m.

secular adj laico; secolare.

secure adj sicuro; * vt assicurare; garantire.

security n sicurezza f.

sedate adj pacato.

sedative adj, n calmante m.

sedentary adj sedentario.

sediment n sedimento m, fondo m.

sedition n sedizione f.

seditious adj sedizioso.

seduce vt sedurre.

seducer n seduttore m.

seduction n seduzione f.

seductive adj seducente.

sedulous adj assiduo.

see vt vedere; capire; accompagnare; * n sede f vescovile.

seed n seme m; * vt seminare.

seedling n piantina m.

seedy adj squallido.

seeing conj: ~ **that** visto che.

seek vt cercare.

seem vi sembrare, parere.

seeming n apparente; ~**ly** adj a quanto pare.

seemly adj decoroso.

seep vi filtrare.

seer n veggente m/f.

seesaw n altalena f; * vi oscillare.

seethe vi bollire.

see-through adj trasparente.

segment n segmento m; spicchio m.

segregate vt segregare.

segregation n segregazione f.

seize vt afferrare; cogliere.

seizure n attacco m; confisca f.

seldom *adj* raramente.
select *vt* selezionare, scegliere;
  * *adj* scelto; esclusivo.
selection *n* scelta *f*, selezione *f*.
self *n* io *m*, se *m* stesso.
self-centred *adj* egocentrico.
self-confident *adj* sicuro di sé.
self-conscious *adj* impacciato.
self-contained *adj* indipendente.
self-control *n* autocontrollo *m*.
self-defeating *adj* futile.
self-defence *n* autodifesa *f*.
self-denial *n* astinenza *f*.
self-discipline *n* autodisciplina *f*.
self-employed *adj* che lavoro in
  proprio.
self-esteem *n* amor *m* proprio.
self-evident *adj* lampante.
self-governing *adj* autonomo.
self-interest *n* interesse *m* personale.
selfish *adj* egoista.
selfishness *n* egoismo *m*.
selfless *adj* altruista.
self-pity *n* autocommiserazione
  f.
self-portrait *n* autoritratto *m*.
self-possessed *adj* composto.
self-respect *n* rispetto *m* di sé.
self-righteous *adj* compiaciuto.
self-sacrifice *n* abnegazione *f*.
selfsame *adj* stesso.
self-satisfied *adj* soddisfatto di
  sé.
self-service *adj* self-service.
self-styled *adj* sedicente.
self-sufficient *adj* autosufficiente.
self-taught *adj* autodidatta.
self-willed *adj* ostinato.
sell *vt* vendere.
seller *n* venditore *m*.
sell-off *vt* liquidare.
sellotape *n* scotch *m*.
sell-out *n* capitolazione *f*.

semantics *npl* semantica *f*.
semblance *n* apparenza *f*.
semen *n* sperma *m*.
semicircle *n* semicerchio *m*.
semicircular *adj* semicircolare.
semicolon *n* punto e virgola *m*.
semiconductor *n* semiconduttore *m*.
semifinal *n* semifinale *f*.
seminal *adj* fondamentale.
seminar *n* seminario *m*.
seminary *n* seminario *m*.
semiprecious *adj* semiprezioso.
semolina *n* semolino *m*.
senate *n* senato *m*.
senator *n* senatore *m*.
send *vt* mandare, inviare; spedire.
sender *n* mittente *m/f*.
senile *adj* senile.
senility *n* senilità *f*.
senior *adj* maggiore, superiore.
seniority *n* anzianità *f*.
senna *n* (*bot*) senna *f*.
sensation *n* sensazione *f*, scalpore *m*.
sense *n* senso *m*; ragione *f*; senno *m*; * *vt* intuire, avvertire.
senseless *adj* insensato; privo
  di sensi.
sensibility *n* suscettibilità *f*.
sensible *adj* assennato; pratico.
sensitive *adj* sensibile.
sensitivity *n* sensibilità *f*.
sensual *adj* sensuale.
sensuality *n* sensualità *f*.
sensuous *adj* voluttuoso.
sensuality *n* sensualità *f*.
sentence *n* frase *f*; sentenza *f*;
  * *vt* condannare.
sententious *adj* sentenzioso.
sentiment *n* sentimento *m*.
sentimental *adj* sentimentale.
sentinel, sentry *n* sentinella *f*.
sentry box garitta *f*.

separable *adj* separabile.
separate *vt* separare; * *adj* separato; **~ly** *adv* separatamente.
separation *n* separazione *f*.
September *n* settembre *m*.
septic *adj* settico.
septicaemia *n* setticemia *f*.
supulchre *n* sepolcro *m*.
sequel *n* seguito *m*.
sequence *n* successione *f*, sequenza *f*.
sequin *n* lustrino *m*.
sequester *vt* segregare.
sequestrate *vt* sequestrare.
seraglio *n* serraglio *m*.
serenade *n* serenata *f*; * *vt* fare la serenata a.
serene *adj* sereno.
serenity *n* serenità *f*.
serge *n* serge *f*.
sergeant *n* sergente *m*.
serial *n* opera *f* a puntate.
series *n* serie *f*.
serious *adj* serio; grave.
sermon *n* sermone *m*.
serpent *n* serpente *m*.
serpentine *n* serpentina *f*.
serrated *adj* seghettato.
serum *n* siero *m*.
servant *n* domestico *m*.
serve *vt*, *vi* servire; * *vt* **to ~ a warrant** notificare.
service *n* servizio *m*; funzione *f*; revisione; * *vt* revisionare.
service station *n* stazione *f* di servizio.
serviceable *adj* pratico.
serviette *n* tovagliolo *m*.
servile *adj* servile.
session *n* seduta *f*; anno *m*.
set *vt* porre; regolare; stabilire; assegnare; * *vi* tramontare; saldarsi; indurirsi; * *n* serie *f*, raccolta *f*, batteria *f*; set *m*; apparecchio *m*; * *adj* fisso; obbligatorio; stabilito; deciso.
settee *n* divano *m*.
setter *n* setter *m*.

setting *n* ambiente *m*, posizione *f*.
settle *vt* sistemare; definire; saldare; appianare; colonizzare; * *vi* depositarsi; insediarsi; concordare.
settlement *n* regolamento *m*; accordo *m*; insediamento *m*.
settler *n* colono *m*.
set-to *n* zuffa *f*.
seven *adj*, *n* sette *m*.
seventeen *adj*, *n* diciasette *m*.
seventeenth *adj*, *n* diciassettesimo *m*.
seventh *adj*, *n* settimo *m*.
seventieth *adj*, *n* settantesimo *m*.
seventy *adj*, *n* settanta *m*.
sever *vt* tagliare, troncare.
several *adj* parecchi.
severance *n* rottura *f*.
severe *adj* severo.
severity *n* severità *f*.
sew *vt*, *vi* cucire.
sewage *n* acque *fpl* di fogna.
sewer *n* fogna *f*.
sewing machine *n* macchina *f* da cucire.
sex *n* sesso *m*; rapporti *mpl* sessuali.
sexism *n* sessismo *m*.
sexist *adj* sessista.
sextant *n* sestante *m*.
sextet *n* sestetto *m*.
sexton *n* sagrestano *m*.
sexual *adj* sessuale.
sexuality *n* sessualità *f*.
sexy *adj* sexy.
shabbiness *n* trasandatezza *f*.
shabby *adj* malandato.
shack *n* baracca *f*.
shackle *vt* ammanettare; * *npl* **~s** pastoie *fpl*.
shade *n* ombra *f*; paralume *m*; tonalità *f*; * *vt* riparare.
shadow *n* ombra *f*; * *vt* pedinare.
shadowy *adj* vago.

shady *adj* ombroso.

shaft *n* asta *f*, albero *m*.

shaggy *adj* ispido.

shake *vt* scuotere; * *vi* tremare; **to ~ hands** dare la mano; * *n* scossa *f*.

shaking *n* scrollata *f*.

shaky *adj* traballante, vacillante.

shallot *n* scalogno *m*.

shallow *adj* poco profondo.

sham *vt*, *vi* fingere; * *n* messa in scena; impostore *m*; * *adj* simulato.

shambles *npl* macello *m*.

shame *n* vergogna *f*; peccato *m*; * *vt* disonorare; far vergognare.

shamefaced *adj* vergognoso.

shameful *adj* vergognoso.

shameless *adj* spudorato.

shammy *n* pelle *f* di camoscio.

shampoo *n* shampoo *m*.

shamrock *n* trifoglio *m*.

shank *n* stinco *m*; gambo *m*.

shanty *n* canzone *f* marinaresca; baracca *f*.

shanty town *n* bidonville *f*

shape *vt* formare; * *n* forma *f*.

shapeless *adj* informe.

shapely *adj* ben fatto.

share *n* parte *f*; azione *f*; * *vt* dividere; condividere.

shareholder *n* azionista *m/f*.

share-out *n* spartizione *f*.

shark *n* squalo *m*, pesce *m* cane.

sharp *adj* affilato, aguzzo; brusco; nitido; acuto; in diesis.

sharpen *vt* affilare, temperare.

sharpener *n* temperamatite *m*.

sharply *adv* bruscamente.

sharp-tempered *adj* irascibile.

shatter *vt* frantumare.

shattered *adj* sconvolto; distrutto.

shatter-proof *adj* infrangibile.

shave *vt* radere; * *vi* radersi.

shaver *n* rasoio *m* elettrico.

shaving *n* (wood) truciolo *m*.

shaving brush *n* pennello *m* da barba.

shawl *n* scialle *m*.

she *pron* ella, lei.

sheaf *n* covone *m*; fascio *m*.

shear *vt* tosare; * *npl* ~s cesoie *fpl*.

sheath *n* guaina *f*; preservativo *m*.

shed *vt* perdere; versare; emanare; * *n* capanno *m*.

sheen *n* lucentezza *f*.

sheep *n* pecora *f*.

sheepfold *n* ovile *m*.

sheep dog *n* cane *m* pastore.

sheepish *adj* imbarazzato.

sheepskin *n* pelle *f* di montone, shearling *m*.

sheer *adj* puro, trasparente; a picco.

sheet *n* lenzuolo *m*; foglio *m*.

sheet lightning *n* lampeggio *m* diffuso.

sheik *n* sceicco *m*.

shelf *n* ripiano *m*.

shell *n* conchiglia *f*; guscio *m*; struttura *f*; * *vt* sgranare; bombardare.

shellfish *n* crostaceo *m*.

shelter *n* riparo *m*; rifugio *m*; * *vt* riparare.

shelve *vt* accantonare.

shelving *n* scaffalature *fpl*.

shepherd *n* pastore *m*.

sherbet *n* sorbetto *m*.

sheriff *n* sceriffo *m*.

sherry *n* sherry *m*.

shield *n* scudo *m*; * *vt* proteggere.

shift *vt* spostare; trasferire; * *n* cambiamento *m*; turno *m*:

shifty *adj* losco.

shilling *n* scellino *m*.

shimmer *vi* luccicare.

shin *n* stinco *m*.

shinbone *n* tibia *f*.

shine *vt* lustrare; * *vi* brillare;

* *n* lucentezza *f.*

shingle *n* ciottoli *mpl*; **~s** *npl* herpes zoster *m.*

shining *adj* lucente.

shiny *adj* lucido.

ship *n* nave *f*; * *vt* imbarcare; spedire.

shipment *n* carico *m.*

shipowner *n* armatore *m.*

shipper *n* spedizioniere *m.*

shipping *n* navigazione *f.*

shipwreck *n* naufragio *m.*

shipyard *n* cantiere *m* navale.

shire *n* contea *f.*

shirk *vt* scansare.

shirker *n* scansafatiche *m/f.*

shirt *n* camicia *f.*

shit *n* (*vulg*) merda *f.*

shiver *n* brivido *m*; * *vi* rabbrividire.

shoal *n* banco *m.*

shock *n* scossa *f*; shock; * *vt* scioccare; * *vi* scandalizzare.

shock absorber *n* ammortizzatore *m.*

shocking *adj* scandaloso.

shoddy *adj* scadente.

shoe *n* scarpa *f*; **horse ~** ferro di cavallo; * *vt* ferrare.

shoehorn *n* calzante *m.*

shoelace *n* laccio *m*, stringa *f.*

shoemaker *n* calzolaio *m.*

shoeshop *n* calzoleria *f.*

shoestring *n* (*fam*) quattro soldi *m.*

shoot *vt* sparare; fucilare; lanciare; (film) girare; * *vi* sparare; * *n* germoglio *m*; partita *f* di caccia.

shooting *n* sparatoria *f*; fucilazione *f*; * *adj* lancinante.

shop *n* negozio *m*; officina *f*; * *vi* fare la spesa; * *vt* tradire.

shoplift *vi* taccheggiare.

shoplifter *n* taccheggiatore *m.*

shopping *n* spesa *f.*

shopping centre *n* centro *m* commerciale.

shore *n* sponda *f.*

short *adj* basso; corto; breve; **~ly** *adv* tra poco.

shortage *n* carenza *f.*

short-circuit *n* corto circuito *m.*

shortcoming *n* difetto *m.*

shorten *vt* accorciare.

shorthand *n* stenografia *f.*

shorts *npl* calzoncini *mpl.*

short-sighted *adj* miope.

short-sightedness *n* miopia *f.*

shortwave *adj* a onde corte.

shot *n* sparo *m*; tiratore *m*; iniezione *f*; foto *f.*

shotgun *n* fucile *f* da caccia.

shoulder *n* spalla *f*; * *vt* accollarsi.

shout *vt*, *vi* gridare; * *n* grido *m.*

shouting *n* grida *fpl.*

shove *vt*, *vi* spingere; * *n* spintone *m.*

shovel *n* pala *f*; * *vt* spalare.

show * *vt* mostrare; esporre; presentare; segnare; * *vt* vedersi; * *n* manifestazione *f*, esposizione *f*; spettacolo *m*; fiera *f*; figura *f*:

show business *n* mondo *m* dello spettacolo.

showcase *n* vetrina *f.*

shower *n* acquazzone *m*; doccia *f*; * *vt* coprire; * *vi* fare la doccia.

show-off *n* esibizionista *m/f.*

showroom *n* show-room *m.*

showy *adj* vistoso.

shred *n* brandello *m*; briciolo *m*; * *vt* stracciare; trinciare.

shrew *n* toporagno *m*; bisbetica *f.*

shrewd *adj* accorto.

shrewdness *n* accortezza *f.*

shriek * *vi* strillare; * *n* strillo *m.*

shrill *adj.* stridulo.

shrimp *n* gamberetto *m.*

shrine n santuario m.

shrink vi restringersi.

shrivel vi rinsecchirsi.

shroud n sudario m; * vt avvolgere.

Shrove Tuesday n martedì m grasso.

shrub n cespuglio m.

shrug n alzata f di spalle.

shudder vi rabbrividire; vibrare; * n brivido m; vibrazione f.

shuffle vt strascicare; mescolare; * n passo m strascicato; mescolata f.

shun vt evitare.

shunt vt (rail) smistare.

shut vt chiudere; * vi chiudersi.

shutter n persiana f; saracinesca f; otturatore m.

shuttle n spola f; navetta f; * vi fare la spola.

shuttlecock n volano m.

shy adj timido.

shyness n timidezza f.

sibling n fratello m, sorella f.

sick adj malato; macabro; * vi vomitare.

sick bay n infermeria f.

sicken vt nauseare; * vi ammalarsi.

sickle n falce f.

sickly adj malaticcio; stucchevole.

sickness n malattia f.

side n fianco m, lato m; faccia f; ciglio m; parte f; squadra f; * adj laterale; * vi parteggiare per.

sideboard n credenza f.

sidelight n luce f di posizione.

sidelong adj di traverso.

side-step vt illudere.

side-track vt sviare.

sideways adj laterale.

siding n (rail) binario m di raccordo.

sidle vi procedere furtivamente.

siege n assedio m.

sieve n setaccio m; * vt setacciare.

sift vt setacciare.

sigh vi sospirare; * n sospiro m.

sight n vista f; spettacolo m; mirino m; ~s attrazioni fpl turistiche.

sightseeing n turismo m.

sign n segno m; gesto m; indizio m; segnale m; * vt, vi firmare.

signal n segnale m; * vt, vi segnalare.

signalman n deviatore m.

signatory n firmatario m.

signature n firma f; (mus) segnatura f.

significance n significato m.

significant adj significativo.

signify vt significare.

signpost n indicazione f stradale.

silence n silenzio m; * vt fare tacere.

silencer n silenziatore m.

silent adj silenzioso.

silhouette n sagoma f.

silicon chip n chip m.

silk n seta f.

silkscreen printing n serigrafia f.

silkworm n bacco m da seta.

silky adj vellutato.

sill n davanzale m.

silly adj sciocco.

silo n silo m.

silt n limo m.

silver n argento m; argenteria f.

silversmith n argentiere m.

silvery adj argentato.

similar adj simile.

similarity n somiglianza f.

simile n similitudine f.

simmer vi sobbollire; **to ~ down** calmarsi.

simper vi sorridere in modo sciocco; * n sorrisetto m sciocco.

simple *adj* semplice; ingenuo.
simpleton *n* sempliciotto *m*.
simplicity *n* semplicità *f*.
simplification *n* semplificazione *f*.
simplify *vt* semplificare.
simply *adv* semplicemente.
simulate *vt* simulare.
simulation *n* simulazione *f*.
simultaneous *adj* simultaneo.
sin *n* peccato *m*; * *vi* peccare.
since *adv* da allora; * *prep* da; * *conj* siccome.
sincere *adj* sincero; **yours ~ly** *adv* distinti saluti.
sincerity *n* sincerità *f*.
sinecure *n* sinecura *f*.
sinew *n* tendine *m*.
sinewy *adj* muscoloso.
sinful *adj* peccaminoso.
sing *vt*, *vi* cantare.
singe *vt* bruciacchiare.
singer *n* cantante *m/f*.
singing *n* canto *m*.
single *adj* solo, unico, celibe, nubile; * *n* singolo *m*; di andata; * *vt* **to ~ out** scegliere.
singly *adv* a uno a uno.
singular *adj* singolare; strano.
singularity *n* singolarità *f*.
sinister *adj* sinistro.
sink *vi* affondare; cedere; abbassarsi; sommergersi; * *vt* scavare; * *n* lavello *m*, acquaio *m*.
sinking *n* naufragio *m*.
sinner *n* peccatore *m*.
sinuous *adj* sinuoso.
sinus *n* seno *m*.
sip *vt* sorseggiare; * *n* sorso *m*.
siphon *n* sifone *m*; * *vt* travasare.
sir *n* signore *m*.
sire *vt* generare.
siren *n* sirena *f*
sirloin *n* controfiletto *m*.
sister *n* sorella *f*; suora *f*.
sister-in-law *n* cognata *f*.

sisterly *adj* da sorella.
sit *vi* sedersi; riunirsi.
site *n* ubicazione *f*; * *vt* collocare.
sit-in *n* sit-in *m*.
sitting *n* seduta *f*.
sitting room *n* salotto *m*.
situated *adj* situato.
situation *n* posizione *f*, situazione *f*.
six *adj*, *n* sei *m*.
sixteen *adj*, *n* sedici *m*.
sixteenth *adj*, *n* sedicesimo *m*.
sixth *adj*, *n* sesto *m*.
sixtieth *adj*, *n* sessantesimo *m*.
sixty *adj*, *n* sessanta *m*.
size *n* dimensioni *fpl*; taglia *f*; misura *f*; numero *m*.
sizeable *adj* considerevole.
sizzle *vi* sfrigolare.
skate *n* razza *f*; patino *m*; * *vi* patinare.
skateboard *n* skateboard *m*.
skating *n* pattinaggio *m*.
skating rink *n* pista *f* di pattinaggio.
skein *n* matassa *f*.
skeleton *n* scheletro *m*.
skeleton key *n* passe-partout *m*.
sketch *n* schizzo *m*; abbozzo *m*; sketch *m*; * *vt* schizzare.
skewer *n* spiedo *m*.
ski *n* sci *m*; * *vi* sciare.
ski boot *n* scarpone *m* da sci.
skid *n* slittamento *m*; * *vi* slittare.
skier *n* sciatore *m*.
skiing *n* sci *m*.
skill *n* capacità *f*, abilità *f*, tecnica *f*.
skilled *adj* abile, specializzato.
skilful *adj* abile.
skim *vt* schiumare; scremare.
skimmed milk *n* latte *m* scremato.
skin *n* pelle *f*; buccia *f*; pellicola *f*; * *vt* spellare; sbucciare.

skin diving n immersione con autorespiratore.
skinned adj scoiato.
skinny adj mingherlino.
skip vi saltellare; * vt saltare; * n saltello m.
skipper n capitano m.
skirmish n scaramuccia f.
skirt n gonna f; * vt aggirare.
skirting board n battiscopa m.
skit n sketch m satirico.
skittish adj ombroso; vivace.
skittle n birillo m.
skive vi svignarsela.
skulk vi aggirarsi furtivamente.
skull n cranio m; teschio m.
skullcap n zucchetto m; papalina f.
skunk n moffetta f.
sky n cielo m.
sky blue n celeste m
sky lark n allodola f.
slylight n lucernario m.
skyscraper n grattacielo m.
slab n lastra f.
slack adj lento; negligente; stagnante.
slacken vt allentare; * vi allentarsi.
slacker n lavativo m.
slackness n negligenza f; mancanza f di tensione.
slag n scorie fpl.
slam vt, vi sbattere; * n colpo m; (cards) slam m.
slander vt calunniare; * n calunnia f.
slanderous adj calunnioso.
slang n slang m, gergo m.
slant vt inclinare; * vi pendere; * n pendenza f.
slanting adj inclinato.
slap n schiaffo m, ceffone m; * adv in pieno; * vt dare uno schiaffo.
slash vt tagliare, sfregiare; * n taglio m.

slat n stecca f.
slate n ardesia f; * vt criticare.
slaughter n macellazione f; massacro m; strage f; * vt macellare; massacrare; trucidare.
slaughterhouse n mattatoio m.
slave n schiavo m; * vi sgobbare.
slave driver n aguzzino m.
slaver vi sbavare.
slavery n schiavitù f.
slavish adj servile.
slay vt uccidere.
sleazy adj squallido.
sled, sledge, sleigh n slitta f.
sledgehammer n martello m da fabbro.
sleek adj lucente, liscio.
sleep vi dormire; * n sonno m.
sleeper n (rail) traversina f; cuccetta f.
sleepily adv con aria assonata.
sleepiness n sonnolenza f.
sleeping adj addormentato.
sleeping bag sacco m a pelo.
sleeping pill n sonnifero m.
sleepless adj insonne.
sleepwalking n sonnambulismo m.
sleep walker n sonnambulo m.
sleepy adj sonnolento, assonnato.
sleet n nevischio m.
sleeve n manica f.
sleight; n ~ of hand destrezza di mano.
slender adj snello; scarso.
slenderness n snellezza f.
sleuth n segugio m.
slice n fetta f; paletta f; * vt affettare.
slicer n affettatrice f.
slick n macchia f d'olio.
slide vi scivolare; * n scivolo m; scivolone m; frana f; diapositiva f.
sliding adj scorrevole.

slight *adj* minuto; * *n* affronto *m*; * *vt* snobbare.

slightly *adv* leggermente.

slim *adj* esile; insufficiente.

slime *n* melma *f*; bava *f*.

slimming *adj* dimagrante.

slimy *adj* viscido, melmoso.

sling *n* fionda *f*; fascia *f*; * *vt* scagliare.

slink *vi* svignarsela.

slip *vi* scivolare; sfuggire; sbagliarsi; * *n* smottamento *m*; scivolata *f*; sbaglio *m*; sottoveste *f*; federa *f*; foglietto *m*.

slipper *n* pantofola *f*.

slippery *adj* scivoloso, sdrucciolevole.

slipshod *adj* sciatto.

slipway *n* scalo *m*.

slit *vt* tagliare; * *n* fessura *f*, spacco *m*.

sliver *n* scheggia *f*.

slob *n* sciattone *m*.

slobber *vi* sbavare.

sloe *n* (*bot*) prugnola *f*.

slog *n* faticata *f*; * *vi* faticare.

slogan *n* slogan *m*.

slogger *n* sgobbone *m*.

sloop *n* scialuppa *f*.

slop *vt* traboccare.

slope *n* versante *m*, pendio *m*; * *vi* essere inclinato.

sloping *adj* inclinato.

sloppy *adj* trasandato; sdolcinato; brodoso.

slot *n* fessura *f*, scanalatura *f*.

sloth *n* accidia *f*.

slothful *adj* accidioso.

slouch *vi* camminare dinoccolato.

slovenly *adj* sciatto.

slow *adj* lento; **~ly** *adv* piano; * *vt*, *vi* rallentare.

slowness *n* lentezza *f*.

slow-worm *n* orbettino *m*.

slug *n* lumaca *f*.

sluggish *adj* fiacco; lento.

sluice *n* chiusa *f*; * *vt* lavare.

slum *n* bassofondi *mpl*; catapecchia *f*.

slumber *vi* dormire; * *n* sonno *m*.

slump *n* crollo *m*, caduta *f*; * *vi* cadere, crollare.

slur *vt* articolare male; * *n* macchia *f*; affronto *m*; (*mus*) legatura *f*.

slush *n* poltiglia *f*.

slut *n* sgualdrina *f*.

sly *adj* astuto; scaltro.

slyness *n* astuzia *f*.

smack *n* schiaffo *m*; schiocco *m*; * *vt* sculacciare, schiaffeggiare.

small *adj* piccolo.

smallish *adj* piccolino.

smallness *n* piccolezza *f*.

smallpox *n* violo *m*.

smalltalk *n* conversazione *f* mondana.

smarmy *adj* (*fam*) untuoso.

smart *adj* elegante, chic; sveglio; svelto; * *vi* bruciare.

smart-aleck *adj* sapientone.

smartly *adv* elegantemente.

smartness *n* eleganza *f*; acutezza *f*.

smash *vt* rompere; frantumare; * *n* fracasso *m*; scontro *m*; successone *m*.

smashing *adj* meraviglioso.

smattering *s* infarinatura *f*.

smear *n* traccia *f*; (*med*) striscio *m*; * *vt* spalmare; sporcare; diffamare.

smell *n* olfatto *m*, fiuto *m*; odore; profumo *m*; puzzo *m*; * *vt* sentire odore di; * *vi* sapere; puzzare.

smelly *adj* puzzolente.

smelt *vt* fondere.

smile *vi* sorridere; * *n* sorriso *m*.

smirk *vi* sorridere compiaciuto; * *n* sorriso *m* compiaciuto.

smite *vt* colpire.

smith n fabbro m.

smithy n fucina f.

smock n blusa f.

smog n smog m.

smoke vt fumare; affumicare; * vi fumare; * n fumo m.

smoked adj affumicato.

smokeless adj senza fumo.

smoker n fumatore m.

smoking adj fumante, fumo; **no ~** vietato fumare.

smoky adj fumoso.

smooch vi sbaciucchiarsi.

smooth adj liscio; omogeneo; * vt lisciare, spianare.

smoothly adv liscio.

smoothness n levigatezza f.

smother vt soffocare.

smoulder vi covare sotto la cenere.

smudge vt imbrattare; * n macchia f.

smug adj compiaciuto.

smuggle vt contrabbandare.

smuggler n contrabbandiere m.

smuggling n contrabbando m.

smut n granellino m di fuliggine; sconcezze fpl.

smutty adj sporco; sconcio.

snack n spuntino m.

snack bar n tavola f calda.

snag n intoppo m.

snail n chiocciola f.

snake n serpente m.

snap vt rompere; schioccare; fotografare; **to ~ sb's head off** rispondere male a qualcuno; * n schiocco ; rubamazzo; * adj improvviso.

snapdragon n (bot) antirrino m.

snappy adj elegante; vivace.

snare n trappola f.

snarl n ringhio m; * vi ringhiare.

snarl-up n intasamento m.

snatch vt strappare; afferrare; cogliere; * n furto m, rapimento m; pezzo m.

sneak; vi fare la spia; **to ~ in** entrare di soppiatto; * n spione m.

sneaking adj segreto.

sneer vi sogghignare; * n sogghigno m.

sneeze vi starnutire; * n starnuto m.

snide adj maligno.

sniff vt annusare; sniffare.

snigger vi ridacchiare; * n risolino m.

snip vt tagliare; * n ritaglio m; affare m.

snipe n beccaccino m.

sniper n franco tiratore m.

snippet n frammento m.

snivel vi piagnucolare.

snivelling adj piagnoloso.

snob n snob m/f.

snobbish adj snob.

snobbery n snobismo m.

snooker n bigliardo m.

snoop vi curiosare.

snooper n ficcanaso m.

snooty adj altezzoso.

snooze n sonnellino m; * vi sonnecchiare.

snore vi russare.

snorkel n respiratore m a tubo.

snort vi sbuffare; * n sbuffata f.

snot n moccio m.

snotty adj moccioso.

snout n muso m.

snow n neve f; * vi nevicare.

snowball n palla f di neve.

snowdrop n (bot) bucaneve m.

snowman n pupazzo m di neve.

snowplow n spazzaneve m.

snowy adj nevoso.

snub vt snobbare; * n affronto m.

snub-nosed adj camuso.

snuff n tabacco m da fiuto.

snuffbox n tabacchiera f.

snug adj accogliente.

so *adv* così, in questo modo; * *conj* affinché.

soak *vt* inzuppare; mettere a mollo.

soap *n* sapone *m*; * *vt* insaponare.

soap box *n* palco *n* improvvisato.

soap opera *n* telenovella *f*.

soap powder *n* detersivo *m*.

soapsuds *npl* saponata *f*.

soapy *adj* insaponato.

soar *vi* librarsi.

sob *vi* singhiozzare; *n* singhiozzo *m*.

sober *adj* sobrio.

sobriety *n* sobrietà *f*.

so-called *adj* cosiddetto.

soccer *n* calcio *m*.

sociable *adj* socievole.

socialism *n* socialismo *m*.

socialist *n* socialista *m/f*.

social work *n* assistenza *f* sociale.

social worker *n* assistente *m/f* sociale.

society *n* società *f*, compagnia *f*.

sociological *adj* sociologico.

sociologist *n* sociologo *m*.

sociology *n* sociologia *f*.

sock *n* calzino *m*, calzettone *m*; pugno *m*; * *vt* picchiare.

socket *n* orbita *f*; presa *f*.

sod *n* zolla *f*; bastardo *m*.

soda *n* soda *f*; selz *m*.

sodden *adj* fradicio.

sodium *n* sodio *m*.

sofa *n* sofà *m*.

soft *adj* morbido, soffice; dolce; indulgente; **~ly** *adv* silenziosamente.

soft drink *n* analcolico *m*.

soften *vt* ammorbidire.

softener *n* ammorbidente *m*.

soft-hearted *adj* dal cuore tenero.

softness *n* morbidezza *f*.

soft-pedal *vt* minimizzare.

soft-spoken *adj* dalla voce dolce.

software *n* software *m*.

soggy *adj* bagnato.

soil *vt* sporcare; infangare; * *n* terreno *m*.

solace *n* consolazione *f*.

solar *adj* solare.

solarium *n* solarium *m*.

solder *vt* saldare; * *n* lega *f* per saldatura.

soldier *n* soldato *m*; **to ~ on** perseverare.

sole *n* pianta *f* del piede; suola *f*; sogliola *f*; * *adj* unico; esclusivo; * *vt* risolare.

solecism *n* (*gr*) solecismo *m*.

solemn *adj* solenne.

solemnity *n* solennità *f*.

solemnize *vt* solennizzare.

solicit *vt* sollecitare.

solicitor *n* avvocato *m*.

solicitous *adj* ansioso.

solicitude *n* sollecitudine *m*.

solid *adj*, *n* solido *m*.

solidarity *n* solidarietà *f*.

solidify *vi* solidificare.

solidity *n* solidità *f*.

soliloquy *n* soliloquio *m*.

solitaire *n* solitario *m*.

solitary *adj* solitario.

solitude *n* solitudine *f*.

solo *n* (*mus*) assolo.

soloist *n* solista *m/f*.

solstice *n* solstizio *m*.

soluble *adj* solubile.

solution *n* soluzione *f*.

solve *vt* risolvere.

solvency *n* solvenza *f*.

solvent *adj*, *n* solvente *m*.

sombre *adj* tetro.

some *adj* di, qualche, alcuno, certo; * *pron* alcuni, certi; * *adv* circa.

somebody *pron* qualcuno.

somehow *adv* in qualche modo.

somersault n capriola f; salto m mortale.

something pron qualcosa.

sometime adv un giorno.

sometimes adv qualche volta.

somewhat adv piuttosto, alquanto.

somewhere adv da qualche parte; circa.

somnambulism n sonnambulismo m.

somnambulist n sonnambulo m.

somnolence n sonnolenza f.

son n figlio m.

sonata n sonata f.

song n (mus) canzone f; canto m.

sonic adj sonico.

son-in-law n genero m.

sonnet n sonetto m.

sonorous adj sonoro.

soon adv presto; **as ~ as possible** appena possibile.

sooner adv prima; piuttosto.

soot n fuliggine f.

soothe vt calmare.

soothing adj calmante; rassicurante.

soothsayer n indovino m.

sop n (fig) concessione f atta a placare.

sophisticated adj sofisticato, raffinato.

sophistication n complessità f.

soporific adj soporifero.

soppy adj sciocco.

soprano n soprano m/f.

sorbet n sorbetto m.

sorcerer n stregone m.

sorceress n maga f.

sorcery n stregoneria f.

sordid adj meschino.

sore n piaga f; * adj indolenzito; doloroso.

sorrel n (bot) acetosa f.

sorrow n dolore m.

sorrowful adj addolorato.

sorry adj dispiacente; pietoso; * vi dispiacersi; * excl scusa, scusi.

sort n genere n, tipo m, specie f; * vt classificare; smistare; risolvere.

so-so adv così così.

soufflé n soufflé m.

sought-after adj richiesto.

soul n anima f.

sound adj sano; valido; profondo; * n suono m, rumore m; volume m; (geog) stretto m; * vt suonare; sondare; * vi suonare.

sound effect n effetto m sonoro.

sounding n scandaglio m.

soundness n sanità f; validità f.

soundproof adj isolato acusticamente.

soundtrack n colonna f sonora.

soup n minestra f, zuppa f.

sour adj acido, acre.

source n sorgente f.

sourness n acidità f.

souse vt mettere in salamoia.

south n sud m, meridione m; * adj sud, meridionale.

southerly, southern adj del sud.

southward(s) adv verso sud.

souvenir n souvenir m, ricordo m.

sovereign adj, n sovrano m.

sovereignty n sovranità f.

sou'wester n capello m incerato.

soviet adj sovietico.

sow n scrofa f.

sow vt seminare.

sowing n semina f.

soya n soia f.

spa n stazione f termale.

space n spazio m; * vt distanziare.

spacecraft n veicolo m spaziale.

spaceman/woman n astronauta m/f, cosmonauta m/f.

spacious adj spazioso.

spade n vanga f, paletta f; ~s picche.

spaghetti n spaghetti mpl.

span n spanna f; * vt attraversare; abbracciare.

spaniel n spaniel m.

spangle n lustrino m.

spank vt sculacciare.

spanner n chiave f fissa.

spar n albero m; * vi bisticciare.

spare vt risparmiare; prestare; * adj di riserva; in più; asciutto; * n pezzo m di ricambio; ~ time tempo libero; ~ wheel ruota di scorta.

sparing adj moderato; ~ly adv frugalmente.

spark n scintilla f; vi provocare

sparkle n scintillio m; vi scintillare

spark(ing) plug n candela f.

sparkling adj frizzante.

sparrow n passero m.

sparrowhawk n sparviero m.

sparse adj rado; scarso.

spartan adj spartano.

spasm n spasmo m.

spasmodic adj spasmodico.

spastic adj, n spastico m.

spate n valanga f.

spatial adj spaziale.

spatter vt schizzare.

spatula n spatola f.

spawn n uova fpl; * vi deporre le uova.

speak vt dire; parlare; vi parlare.

speaker n interlocutore m; oratore m; altoparlante m.

spear n lancia f; * vt trafiggere.

special adj speciale; particolare.

specialist n specialista m/f;

* adj specializzato.

speciality n specialità f.

specialization n specializzazione f.

species n specie f.

specific adj specifico.

specifically adv esplicitamente.

specification n specificazione f.

specify vt specificare.

specimen n campione m.

specious adj specioso.

speck(le) n macchiolina f.

speckled adj screziato.

spectacle n spettacolo m; ~s npl occhiali mpl.

spectacular n colossal m.

spectator n spettatore m.

spectral adj spettrale.

spectre n spettro m.

speculate vi speculare.

speculative adj speculativo.

speech n parola f; parlata f; linguaggio m; discorso m.

speechless adj senza parola.

speed n velocità f, rapidità f; marcia f; * vi procedere velocemente; andare a velocità eccessiva.

speedboat n motoscafo m da corsa.

speeding n eccesso m di velocità f.

speed limit n limite m di velocità.

speedometer n tachimetro m.

speedway n circuito m di gara.

speedy adj veloce, rapido.

spell n incantesimo m; periodo m; * vt dire/scrivere lettera per lettera.

spelling n ortografia f.

spend vt spendere; trascorrere.

spending n spesa f.

spendthrift n spendaccione m.

spent adj usato; esaurito.

sperm n sperma m.

sperm whale n capodoglio m.

spew vt, vi vomitare.

sphere n sfera f.

spherical adj sferico.

sphinx n sfinge f.

spice n droga f; spezie fpl; * vt drogare.

spicy adj piccante.

spider n ragno m.

spider-web n ragnatela f.

spigot n tappo m.

spike n punta f; chiodo m; * vt infilzare; munire di chiodi.

spiky adj spinoso.

spill vt rovesciare, versare.

spin vt filare; prolungare; * vi girare * n giro m; effetto m; giretto m.

spinach n spinaci mpl.

spinal adj spinale.

spindle n fuso m.

sprin-drier n centrifuga f.

spine n spina f dorsale.

spine-chilling adj agghiacciante.

spineless adj smidollato.

spinet n (mus) spinetta f.

spinner n tessitore m.

spinning wheel n filatoio m.

spin-off n prodotto m secondario.

spinster n zitella f.

spiral adj, n spirale f.

spire n guglia f.

spirit n spirito m; coraggio m; ~s liquori mpl.

spirited adj energico, vivace.

spirit lamp n lampada f a spirito.

spiritual adj spirituale.

spiritualist n spiritista m/f.

spirituality n spiritualità f.

spit n spiedo m; sputo m; * vt, vi sputare.

spite n dispetto m; * conj **in ~ of** nonostante, malgrado; * vt fare dispetto a.

spiteful adj dispettoso, maligno.

spittle n sputo m.

splash vt, vi schizzare; * n tonfo m; spruzzo m.

spleen n milza f.

splendid adj splendido.

splendour n splendore m.

splice vt giuntare.

splint n stecca f.

splinter n scheggia f; vi scheggiarsi.

split n fessura f; spacco m; scissione f; * vt spaccare; dividere; * vi spaccarsi.

splutter vi sputacchiare.

spoil vt rovinare; * vi guastarsi; * n bottino m.

spoil sport n guastafeste m/f

spoilt adj viziato.

spoke n raggio m.

spokesman n portavoce m.

spokeswoman n portavoce f.

sponge n spugna f; pan di Spagna; * vt lavare con una spugna; scroccare.

sponger n scroccone m.

spongy adj spugnoso.

sponsor n promotore m; sponsor m/f; * vt promuovere; sponsorizzare.

sponsorship n promozione f, sponsorizzazione f.

spontaneity n spontaneità f.

spontaneous adj spontaneo.

spook n (fam) fantasma m.

spooky adj sinistro.

spool n bobina f.

spoon n cucchiaio m.

spoonful n cucchiaiata f.

sporadic adj sporadico.

sport n sport m; divertimento m; persona f di spirito.

sports car n automobile f sportiva.

sportsman n sportivo m.

sportswear n abbigliamento m sportivo.

sportswoman n sportiva f.

spot n macchia f; puntino m;

pois *m*; foruncolo *m*; posto *m*;
* *vt* macchiare; notare.

spotless *adj* pulitissimo.

spotlight *n* spot *m*, riflettore *m*.

spot-on *adj* esatto.

spotted *adj* a pois; macchiato.

spotty *adj* pieno di foruncoli.

spouse *n* sposo *m*, sposa *f*.

spout *n* becco *m*; * *vi* gettare;
(*fig*) declamare.

sprain *n* slogatura *f*; * *vt* slog-
arsi.

sprat *n* spratto *m*.

sprawl *vi* sdraiarsi/sedersi in
modo scomposto.

spray *n* getto *m*, spruzzo *m*;
spray *m*; mazzolino *m*; * *vt*
spruzzare.

spread *vt* spiegare; spalmare;
cospargere; propagare; * *n*
propagazione *f*; apertura *f*;
banchetto *m*.

spree *n* baldoria *f*.

sprig *n* ramoscello *m*.

sprightly *adj* vivace.

spring *vi* saltare; sorgere; * *n*
sorgente *f*; primavera *f*; salto
m; molla *f*.

springboard *n* trampolino *m*.

springtime *n* primavera *f*.

springy *adj* molleggiato.

sprinkle *vt* cospargere.

sprinkling *n* spruzzatina *f*.

sprint *n* sprint *m*.

sprout *n* germoglio *m*; cavolino
m; * *vi* germogliare.

spruce *n* abete; * *adj* azzimato.

spry *adj* arzillo.

spud *n* (*fam*) patata *f*.

spur *n* sperone *m*, sprone *m*;
* *vt* spronare.

spurious *adj* falso.

spurn *vt* rispingere.

sputter *vi* scoppiettare.

spy *n* spia *f*; * *vt* scorgere; * *vi*
spiare.

spying *n* spionaggio *m*.

squabble *vi* bisticciarsi; * *n*
battibecco *m*.

squad *n* plotone *m*.

squadron *n* squadrone *m*.

squalid *adj* squallido.

squall *n* burrasca *f*; * *vi* strillare.

squalor *n* squallore *m*.

squander *vt* sperperare.

square *adj* quadrato; onesto;
* *n* quadrato *m*; quadro; piazza *f*; (*fam*) matusa *m*; * *vt* squadrare; * *vi* quadrare.

squarely *adv* direttamente.

squash *n* concentrato *m* di
frutta; calca *f*; squash *m*; * *vt*
schiacciare.

squat *vi* acquattarsi; * *adj*
tarchiato.

squatter *n* occupatore *m* abusivo.

squaw *n* squaw *f*.

squeak *vi* cigolare; squittire;
* *n* cigolio *m*, squittio *m*.

squeal *vi* strillare; * *n* strillo *m*.

squeamish *adj* nauseato.

squeeze *vt* premere; strizzare,
spremere; * *n* stretta *f*; strizzata *f*.

squib *n* petardo *m*.

squid *n* calamaro *m*.

squint *vi* essere strabico; * *n*
strabismo *m*.

squirm *vi* contorcersi.

squirrel *n* scoiatolo *m*.

squirt *vi* schizzare; * *vt* spruzzare; * *n* schizzo *m*.

stab *vt* pugnalare; * *n* coltellata *f*; fitta *f*.

stabbing *adj* lancinante.

stability *n* stabilità *f*.

stabilize *vt* stabilizzare.

stable *n* stalla *f*; scuderia *f*; ~s
maneggio *m*; * *adj* stabile.

stack *n* mucchio *m*; comignolo
m; * *vt* accatastare.

staff *n* personale *m*; bastone *m*;
pentagramma *m*.

stag n cervo m.

stage n palco m; stadio m; tappa f.

stagger vi barcollare; * vt sbalordire; scaglionare.

staggering adj sbalorditivo.

stagnant adj stagnante.

stagnate vi stagnare.

stagnation n ristagno m.

staid adj posato.

stain vt macchiare; tingere; * n macchia f; colorante m.

stainless adj inossidabile.

stair n scalino; ~s npl scale fpl.

staircase n scala f.

stake n palo m; puntata f; * vt (fig) rivendicare.

stalactite n stalattite f.

stalagmite n stalagmite f.

stale adj stantio; rafferno.

stalemate n stallo m.

stalk vt inseguire; * n gambo m, torsolo m.

stall n stalla f; bancarella f; stand m; ~s platea f; * vi andare in stallo; bloccarsi.

stallholder n bancarellista m/f.

stallion n stallone m.

stalwart adj prode.

stamen n stame m.

stamina n resistenza f.

stammer vt, vi balbettare; * n balbuzie f.

stamp vt pestare; affrancare; timbrare; * n francobollo m; timbro m.

stampede n fuga f precipitosa.

stance n posizione f.

stand vt mettere; reggere a; sopportare; offrire; * vi stare in piedi; trovarsi; riposare; presentarsi; * n posizione f; stand m; leggio m; **to ~ up** alzarsi.

standard n insegna f; standard m; * adj standard, classico.

stand-in n controfigura f.

standing adj in piedi; permanente; * n rango m.

stand-offish adj freddo.

standstill n punto m morto.

staple n graffetta f; prodotto m principale; * adj base.

stapler n cucitrice f.

star n stella f; asterisco m; divo m.

starboard n tribordo m.

starch n amido m; * vt inamidare.

stardom n celebrità f.

stare vt fissare; * n sguardo m fisso.

starfish n stella f di mare.

stark adj austero.

starling n storno m.

starry adj stellato.

start vt cominciare; iniziare, avviare; * vi cominciare; partire; trasalire; * n sobbalzo m; inizio m; vantaggio m.

starter n starter m, motorino d'avviamento; antipasto m.

startle vt spaventare.

startling adj sorprendente.

starvation n inedia f.

starve vt far morire di fame; * vi morire di fame.

starving adj affamato.

state n stato m; condizione f; agitazione f; * vt affermare; indicare.

stateless adj apolide.

stately adj maestoso.

statement n dichiarazione f; deposizione f; estratto m conto.

statesman n statista m.

statesmanship n abilità f politica.

static adj statico; * n disturbo m.

station n stazione f; * vt stanziare; piazzare.

stationary adj fermo, stazionario.

stationer n cartolaio m.

stationery n cancelleria f.

statistical *adj* statistico.

statistics *npl* statistica *f*.

statuary *adj* statuario.

statue *n* statua *f*.

stature *n* statura *f*; *(fig)* levatura *f*.

status *n* stato *m*, status *m*.

statute *n* statuto *m*.

staunch *adj* convinto.

stave; vi to ~ off allontanare.

stay *n* soggiorno *m*, degenza *f*; sospensione *f* dell'esecuzione; * *vi* rimanere, restare, stare; alloggiare; * *vt* sospendere, fermare.

stead *n*: **to stand in good ~** essere utile a qualcuno.

steadfast *adj* risoluto.

steadily *adv* saldamente.

steady *adj* fermo, saldo; costante; fisso; * *vt* tenere fermo; calmare.

steak *n* bistecca *f*.

steal *vt* rubare.

stealth *n*; **by ~** furtivamente.

stealthy *adj* furtivo.

steam *n* vapore *m*; * *vt* cuocere a vapore; * *vi* fumare.

steamer *n* piroscafo *m*.

steamroller *n* rullo *m* compressore.

steel *n* acciaio *m*.

steelworks *n* acciaieria *f*.

steelyard *n* stadera *f*.

steep *adj* ripido; * *vt* immergere; impregnare.

steeple *n* campanile *m*.

steeplechase *n* steeplechase *m*.

steer *n* manzo *m*; * *vt* guidare; * *vi* sterzare.

steering wheel *n* volante *m*.

stem *n* stelo *m*; * *vt* arrestare.

stench *n* puzzo *m*.

stencil *n* matrice *f*.

stenographer *n* stenografo *m*.

stenography *n* stenografia *f*.

step *n* passo *m*; misura *f*; gradino *m*; * *vi* fare un passo.

stepbrother *n* fratellastro *m*.

stepdaughter *n* figliastra *f*.

stepfather *n* patrigno *m*.

stepmother *n* matrigna *f*.

stepsister *n* sorellastra *f*.

stepson *n* figliastro *m*.

stereo *n* stereo *m*, stereofonia *f*.

stereotype *n* stereotipo *m*.

sterile *adj* sterile.

sterility *n* sterilità *f*.

sterilize *vt* sterilizzare.

sterling *n* sterlina *f*; * *adj* genuino.

stern *adj* severo; * *n* *(mar)* poppa *f*.

sternum *n* sterno *m*.

stethoscope *n* stetoscopio *m*.

stevedore *n* scaricatore *m* di porto.

stew *vt* stufare; * *n* stufato *m*.

steward *n* steward *m*.

stewardess *n* hostess *f*.

stick *n* bastone *m*, bastoncino; asticella *f*; * *vt* incollare; conficcare; * *vi* appiccicarsi; bloccarsi; incepparsi; attenersi a; **to ~ out** sporgere.

sticker *n* adesivo *m*.

sticky *adj* appiccicoso.

stiff *adj* rigido, duro; indolenzito; difficile.

stiffen *vt* irrigidire; * *vi* irrigidirsi.

stiff neck *n* torcicollo *m*.

stiffness *n* rigidità *f*.

stifle *vt*, *vi* soffocare.

stifling *adj* soffocante.

stigma *n* stigma *m*.

stigmatize *vt* stigmatizzare.

stile *n* scaletta *f*.

stiletto *m* stiletto *m*.

still *adj* fermo, immobile; non gassato; * *n* alambicco; **~ life** natura *f* morta; * *adv* ancora;

stillborn *adj* nato morto.

stillness *n* immobilità *f*.

stilt *n* trampolo *m*.

stimulant n stimolante m.
stimulate vt stimolare.
stimulation n stimolazione f.
stimulus n stimolo m.
sting vt pungere; pizzicare; * vi bruciare; * n pungiglione m, puntura f.
stingy adj spilorcio.
stink vi puzzare; * n puzzo m; (sl) putiferio m.
stinker n (sl) fetente m/f.
stint n dovere m.
stipulate vt stabilire.
stipulation n stipulazione f.
stir vt mescolare; agitare; risvegliare; * vi muoversi; * n scalpore m.
stirrup n staffa f.
stitch vt cucire; * n punto m; maglia f; fitta f al fianco.
stoat n ermellino m.
stock n provvista f, stock m; bestiame m; brodo m; stirpe f; ~s npl titoli mpl; * adj solito; * vt tenere; rifornire.
stockade n palizzata f.
stockbroker n agente m/f di cambio.
stock exchange n borsa f valori.
stockholder n azionista m/f.
stocking n calza f.
stockist n fornitore m.
stock market n mercato m azionario.
stock pile n scorta f.
stockroom n magazzino m.
stock taking n inventario m.
stoic n stoico m.
stoical adj stoico.
stoicism n stoicismo m.
stoke vt atticizzare.
stole n stola f.
stolid adj impassibile.
stomach n stomaco m, ventre f; * vt sopportare.
stone n pietra f; * vt lapidare.
stone-deaf adj sordo come una campana.

stony adj sassoso.
stool n sgabello m.
stoop vi chinarsi, abbassarsi.
stop vt arrestare, fermare; impedire; smettere; bloccare; * vi cessare, fermarsi; * n arresto m, pausa f, sosta f; fermata f; punto.
stopover n breve sosta f.
stoppage n sospensione f; trattenuta f; sciopero m.
stopper n tappo m.
stopwatch n cronometro m.
storage n immagazzinamento m.
store n provvista f; deposito m; grande magazzino m; * vt accumulare; immagazzinare.
storekeeper n negoziante m.
storey n piano m.
stork n cicogna f.
storm n tempesta f; temporale m; * vt prendere d'assalto; * vi infuriare.
stormy adj burrascoso.
story n storia f, trama f, racconto m; articolo m.
stout adj robusto.
stoutness n pinguedine f.
stove n stufa f.
stow vt (mar) stivare.
straggle vi estendersi disordinatamente.
straight adj diritto; liscio; onesto; semplice; eterosessuale; * adv diritto; direttamente.
straightaway adv subito.
straighten vt raddrizzare.
straightforward adj franco; chiaro.
strain vt tendere, tirare; slogare; affaticare; passare; * n tensione f; pressione f; sforzo m; (med) strappo m; (biol) razza f.
strainer n passino m.
strait n stretto m.
strait-jacket camicia f di forza.

strand n ciocca f.

strange adj sconosciuto; strano.

stranger n sconosciuto m, forestiero m.

strangle vt strangolare, strozzare.

strangler n strozzatore m.

strangulation n strangolamento m.

strap n cinturino m; spallina f; tracollo m; * vt legare, fasciare.

strapping adj ben piantato.

stratagem n stratagemma m.

strategic adj strategico.

strategy n strategia f.

stratum n strato m.

straw n paglia f; cannuccia f.

strawberry n fragola f.

stray vi smarrirsi; * adj randagio.

streak n striscia f; vena f; * vt striare; rigare.

stream n ruscello m; (fig) fiume; * vt grondare; * vi scorrere.

streamer n stella f filante.

street n strada f.

strength n forza f; resistenza f; gradazione f alcolica.

strengthen vt rinforzare; * vi consolidarsi.

strenuous adj energico; faticoso.

stress n sforzo m, stress m, tensione f; enfasi f; * vt mettere in rilievo.

stressed adj accentato.

stressful adj stressante.

stretch vt tendere, stendere; far bastare; * vi stiracchiarsi; esagerare; * n elasticità f; distesa f; tratto m.

stretcher n barella f.

strew vt spargere.

strict adj severo, rigido; stretto; ~ly speaking a rigor di termini.

strictness n severità f.

stride n passo m; * vt camminare a grandi passi.

strife n conflitto m.

strike vt colpire; sbattere contro; accendere; scoprire; * vi scioperare; rintoccare; * n sciopero m; scoperta f; attacco m.

striker n scioperante m/f.

striking adj che fa colpo.

string n spago m; filo m, corda f; * vt infilare; incordare.

stringent adj rigoroso; stringente.

stringy adj fibroso.

strip vt spogliare; sverniciare; smontare; * vi spogliarsi; * n striscia f; divisa f.

stripe n riga f.

stripper n spogliarellista m/f.

striptease n spogliarello m.

strive vi sforzarsi.

stroke * n colpo m; carezza f; rintocco m; * vt accarezzare.

stroll n passeggiatina f; * vi gironzolare.

strong adj forte; resistente; concentrato.

strongbox n cassaforte f.

stronghold n fortezza f.

strontium n stronzio m.

structure n struttura f; * vt strutture.

struggle vt, vi lottare; * n lotta f.

strum vt (mus) strimpellare.

strychnine n stricnina f.

strut vi pavoneggiarsi; * n supporto m.

stub n mozzicone m; matrice f.

stubble n stoppia f; barba f corta.

stubborn adj cocciuto.

stubbornness n testardaggine f.

stucco n stucco m.

stud n chiodo m; stallone m.

student n studente m.

stud horse n stallone m.

studio n studio m.

studio apartment n appartamento m monolocale.

studious adj studioso.

study n studio m; * vt, vi studiare.

stuff n roba f; * vt riempire; imbottire; farcire.

stuffing n imbottitura f; ripieno m.

stuffy adj mal ventilato m; antiquato.

stumble vi inciampare.

stumbling block n ostacolo m.

stump n troncone m; * vt sconcertare.

stun vt tramortire.

stunning adj splendido.

stunt n acrobazia f; * vt arrestare.

stunted adj striminzito.

stuntman n stunt-man m.

stupefy vt intontire; stupire.

stupendous adj stupendo.

stupid adj stupido.

stupidity n stupidità f.

stupor n intontimento m.

sturdiness n robustezza f.

sturdy adj robusto; solido.

sturgeon n storione m.

stutter n balbuzie fpl; * vt, vi balbettare.

sty n porcile m.

sty(e) n orzaiolo m.

style n stile m; classe f.

stylish adj elegante.

stylus n puntina f.

suave adj garbato.

subconscious adj subcosciente; * n subconscio m.

subcontract vt subappaltare.

subdivide vt suddividere.

subdue vt sottomettere; dominare; * adj ~d pacato, tenue.

subject adj assoggettato; soggetto a; * n suddito m; soggetto m; argomento m; materia f; * vt sottoporre.

subjection n sottomissione f.

subjective adj soggettivo.

subjugate vt soggiogare.

subjunctive adj, n congiuntivo m.

sublet vt, vi subaffittare.

sublimate vt sublimare.

sublime adj sublime.

subliminal adj subliminale.

submachine gun n mitragliatore m.

submarine n sommergibile m.

submerge vt sommergere.

submersion n sommersione f.

submission n sottomissione f.

submissive adj sottomesso.

submit vt presentare; * vi cedere a.

subnormal adj subnormale.

subordinate adj subalterno; (gr) subordinato; * n subalterno m; subordinato m; * vt subordinare.

subordination n subordinazione f.

subpoena n citazione f; * vt citare in giudizio.

subscribe vi abbonarsi; approvare.

subscriber n abbonato m.

subscription n abbonamento m.

subsequent adj successivo.

subservient adj remissivo.

subside vi decrescere; avvallarsi.

subsidence adj avvallamento.

subsidiary n sussidiario m; complimentare.

subsidize vt sovvenzionare.

subsidy n sovvenzione f.

subsist vi vivere di

subsistence n sopravvivenza f.

substance n sostanza f.

substantial adj sostanzioso; sostanziale; notevole.

substantiate vt comprovare.

substantive adj, n sostantivo m.

substitute *vt, vi* sostituire; * *n* sostituto *m*.

substitution *n* sostituzione *f*.

subterfuge *n* sotterfugio *m*.

subterranean *adj* sotterraneo.

subtitle *n* sottotitolo *m*.

subtle *adj* sottile.

subtlety *n* sottigliezza *f*.

subtly *adj* sottilmente.

subtract *vt* sottrarre.

subtraction *n* sottrazione *f*.

suburb *n* sobborgo *m*.

suburban *adj* suburbano.

suburbia *n* periferia *f*.

subversion *n* sovversione *f*.

subversive *adj, n* sovversivo *m*.

subvert *vt* sovvertire.

subway *n* sottopassaggio *m*.

succeed *vi* riuscire; * *vt* succedere.

succeeding *adj* successivo; futuro.

success *n* successo *m*; riuscita *f*.

successful *adj* riuscito; affermato.

succession *n* serie *f*; successione *f*.

successive *adj* consecutivo.

successor *n* successore *m*.

succinct *adj* succinto.

succulent *adj* succulento; * *n* pianta *f* grassa.

succumb *vi* soccombere.

such *adj* tale; ~ **as** come; * *adv* talmente; così.

suck *vt, vi* succhiare.

sucker *n* ventosa *f*; citrullo *m*.

suckle *vt* allattare.

suction *n* aspirazione *f*.

sudden *adj* improvviso.

suds *npl* saponata *f*.

sue *vt* citare; * *vi* intentare causa.

suede *n* pelle *f* scamosciata.

suet *n* grasso *m* di rognone.

suffer *vt* soffrire; tollerare; * *vi* soffrire.

suffering *n* sofferenza *f*.

suffice *vt* bastare.

sufficient *adj* sufficiente.

suffocate *vt, vi* soffocare.

suffocation *n* soffocazione *f*.

suffrage *n* suffragio *m*.

suffragette *n* suffragetta *f*.

suffuse *vi* spandersi su.

sugar *n* zucchero *m*; * *vt* zuccherare.

sugar beet *n* barbabietola *f* da zucchero.

sugar cane *n* canna *f* da zucchero.

sugar lump *n* zolletta *f* di zucchero.

sugary *adj* zuccherato.

suggest *vt* suggerire.

suggestion *n* suggerimento *m*; punta *f*.

suggestive *adj* spinto.

suicidal *adj* suicida.

suicide *n* suicidio *m*; suicida *m/f*.

suit *n* completo *m*; tailleur *m*; causa *f*; colore *m*; * *vt* adattare; andare bene a; contentare.

suitable *adj* adatto, appropriato.

suitably *adv* adeguatamente.

suitcase *n* valigia *f*.

suite *n* suite *f*; appartamento *m*.

suitor *n* corteggiatore *m*.

sulk *vi* tenere il broncio.

sulky *adj* imbronciato.

sullen *adj* scontroso.

sulphate *adj* solfato.

sulphide *n* solfuro *m*.

sulphur *n* zolfo *m*.

sulphuric *adj* solforico.

sultan *n* sultano *m*.

sultana *n* uva *f* sultanina.

sultry *adj* afoso; passionale.

sum *n* somma *f*; **to ~ up** riassumere.

summary *n* riassunto *m*.

summer *n* estate *f*.

summerhouse *n* padiglione *m*.

summit n cima f, vetta f; vertice m.

summon vt convocare.

summons n mandato m di comparizione.

sumptuous adj sontuoso.

sun n sole m.

sunbathe vi prendere il sole.

sunburn n scottatura f.

sunburnt adj scottato.

Sunday n domenica f.

sundial n meridiana f.

sundown n tramonto m.

sundry adj diversi.

sunflower n girasole m.

sunglasses npl occhiali mpl da sole.

sunken adj infossato.

sunless adj senza sole.

sunlight n luce f del sole.

sunny adj assolato, soleggiato; radioso.

sunrise n alba f.

sun roof n tetto m apribile.

sunset n tramonto m.

sunshade n parasole m.

sunshine n luce f del sole.

sunstroke n insolazione f.

suntan n abbronzatura f, tintarella f.

suntan oil n olio m solare.

super adj (fam) fantastico.

superannuation n pensione f.

superb adj superbo.

supercilious adj altezzoso.

superficial adj superficiale.

superfluous adj superfluo.

superhuman adj sovrumano.

superintendent n soprintendente m/f.

superior adj, n superiore m/f.

superiority n superiorità f.

superlative adj, n superlativo m.

superman n superuomo m.

supermarket n supermercato m.

supernatural adj, n sopran-naturale m.

superpower n superpotenza f.

supersede vt soppiantare.

supersonic adj supersonico.

superstition n superstizione f.

superstitious adj superstizioso.

superstructure n sovrastruttura f.

supertanker n superpetroliera f.

supervene vi sopravvenire.

supervise vt sorvegliare.

supervision n sorveglianza f.

supervisor n sorvegliante m/f.

supine adj supino.

supper n cena f.

supplant vt soppiantare.

supple adj flessibile.

supplement n supplemento m; * vt integrare.

supplementary adj supplementare.

supplication n supplica f.

supplier n fornitore m.

supply vt fornire; * n fornitura f.

support vt sostenere; mantenere; appoggiare; * n sostegno m.

supporter n sostenitore m; tifoso m.

suppose vt supporre.

supposed adj presunto.

supposition n supposizione f.

suppository n supposta f.

suppress vt reprimere; sopprimere.

suppression n repressione f.

supremacy n supremazia f.

supreme adj supremo; sommo.

surcharge n sovrapprezzo m.

sure adj sicuro, certo; **be ~ to do something** mi raccomando.

surefire adj infallibile.

sureness n certezza f.

surety n caparra f.

surf n (*mar*) cavalloni *mpl*.
surface n superficie f; * vt asfaltare; * vi risalire in superficie.
surfboard n surf m.
surfeit n sovrabbondanza f.
surge n ondata f; * vi riversarsi.
surgeon n chirurgo m.
surgery n chirurgia f; ambulatorio m.
surgical adj chirurgico.
surly adj burbero.
surmise vt congetturare; * n congettura f.
surmount vt sormontare.
surmountable adj sormontabile.
surname n cognome m.
surpass vt superare.
surplice n cotta f.
surplus n surplus m; * adj di sovrappiù.
surprise vt sorprendere; * n sorpresa f.
surprising adj sorprendente.
surrealism n surrealismo m.
surrealistic adj surreale.
surrender vt rinunciare a; * vi arrendersi; * n resa f.
surreptitious adj furtivo.
surrogate adj, n surrogato m.
surround vt circondare; n borgo m.
survey vt guardare; esaminare; * n indagine f; perizia f; rilevamento m.
survive vt, vi sopravvivere.
survivor n superstite m/f.
susceptibility n suscettibilità f.
susceptible adj predisposto.
suspect vt sospettare; * adj sospetto; * n persona f sospetta.
suspend vt sospendere.
suspense n suspense m; incertezza f.
suspension n sospensione f.

suspension bridge n ponte m sospeso.
suspicion n sospetto m.
suspicious adj sospettoso.
sustain vt sostenere; subire.
sustenance n nutrimento m.
suture n sutura f.
swab n tampone m.
swagger vi pavoneggiarsi.
swallow n deglutizione; rondine f; * vt, vi inghiottire.
swamp n palude f; * vt inondare.
swampy adj paludoso.
swan n cigno m.
swap vt scambiare; * n scambio m.
swarm n sciame m; * vi sciamare.
swarthy adj di colorito scuro.
swastika n svastica f.
swat vt schiacciare.
swathe vt avvolgere.
sway vi ondeggiare; oscillare; * vt influenzare; * n ondeggiamento m; influenza f.
swear vt, vi giurare, vi bestemmiare.
swearword n parolaccia f.
sweat n sudore m; * vt, vi sudare.
sweater n maglione m.
sweatshirt n felpa f.
sweep vt, vi scopare; spazzare; * n scopata f; spazzacamino m; ampio gesto m.
sweeping adj generico, radicale.
sweepstake n lotteria f.
sweet adj dolce, carino; * n caramella f; dolce m.
sweetbreads npl animelle fpl.
sweeten vt zuccherare, addolcire.
sweetener n dolcificante m.
sweetheart n tesoro m.
sweetness n dolcezza f.
swell vi gonfiarsi; * n mare m

lungo; * *adj* eccezionale.

swelling *n* gonfiore *m*.

sweltering soffocante.

swerve *n* sterzata *f*; *vi* sterzare.

swift *adv* rapido; *n* rondone *m*.

swiftness *n* rapidità *f*.

swill *vt* risciacquare; tracannare; * *n* brodaglia *f*.

swim *vt, vi* nuotare; * *n* nuotata *f*.

swimming *n* nuoto *m*.

swimming pool *n* piscina *f*.

swimsuit *n* costume *m* da bagno.

swindle *vt* truffare; * *n* truffa *f*.

swindler *n* imbroglione *m*.

swine *n* suini *mpl*.

swing *vt* dondolare; brandire; influenzare; * *vi* dondolare; penzolare; * *n* oscillazione *f*; altalena *f*; ritmo *m*; swing *m*.

swingeing *adj* drastico.

swinging door *n* porta *f* a vento.

swirl *n* turbinio *m*.

switch *n* interruttore *m*; mutamento *m*; * *vt* cambiare; invertire; **to ~ off** spegnere; **to ~ on** accendere.

switchboard *n* centralino *m*.

swivel *vi* girarsi; * *n* perno *m*.

swoon *vi* svenire; * *n* svenimento *m*.

swoop *vi* scendere in picchiata; fare un incursione; * *n* picchiata *f*; incursione *f*.

sword *n* spada *f*.

swordfish *n* pesce *f* spada.

swordsman *n* spadaccino *m*.

sycamore *n* sicomoro *m*.

sycophant *n* leccapiedi *m/f*.

syllable *n* sillaba *f*.

syllabus *n* programma *m*.

syllogism *n* sillogismo *m*.

sylph *n* silfo *m*.

symbol *n* simbolo *m*.

symbolic *adj* simbolico.

symbolize *vt* simboleggiare.

symmetrical *adj* simmetrico.

symmetry *n* simmetria *f*.

sympathetic *adj* comprensivo.

sympathize *vi* compatire.

sympathy *n* comprensione *f*.

symphony *n* sinfonia *f*.

symposium *n* simposio *m*.

sumptom *n* sintomo *m*.

synagogue *n* sinagoga *f*.

synchronize *vt* sincronizzare.

syndicate *n* sindacato *m*.

syndrome *n* sindrome *f*.

synod *n* sinodo *m*.

synonym *n* sinonimo *m*.

synonymous *adj* sinonimo di.

synopsis *n* sinossi *f*.

syntax *n* sintassi *f*.

sythesis *n* sintesi *f*.

syphilis *n* sifilide *f*.

syringe *n* siringa *f*; * *vt* siringare.

system *n* sistema *m*

systematic *adj* sistematico.

systems analyst *n* analista *m/f* sistemi.

T

tab *n* linguetta *f*; laccetto *m*.

tabby *n* soriano *m*.

tabernacle *n* tabernacolo *m*.

table *n* tavolo *m*; tavola *f*; tabella *f*; **~ d'hôte** pasto a prezzo fisso; * *vt* presentare.

tablecloth *n* tovaglia *f*.

tablespoon *n* cucchiaio *m* da portata.

tablet *n* lapide *f*; compressa *f*;

table tennis *n* ping pong *m*.

taboo *n* tabù *m*.

tabulate *vt* mettere in colonna.

tabulator *n* tabulatore *m*.

tacit *adj* tacito.

taciturn *adj* taciturno.

tack *n* bulletta *f*; (*naut*) bordo *m*; (sewing) punto *m* d'imbastitura; * *vt* fissare con chiodi; imbastire; * *vi* bordeggiare.

tackle *n* paranco *m*; attrezzatura *f*; * *vt* affrontare.

tact *n* tatto *m*.

tactical *adj* tattico.

tactics *npl* tattica *f*.

tactless *adj* indelicato.

tadpole *n* girino *m*.

taffeta *n* taffettà *f*.

tag *n* etichetta *f*.

tail *n* coda *f*; * *vt* pedinare.

tailback *n* coda *f*.

tailgate *n* portellone *m* posteriore.

tailor *n* sarto *m*; * *vt* confezionare.

tailor-made *adj* fatto su misura.

tailwind *n* vento *m* in coda.

taint *vt* infangare; * *n* macchia *f*.

tainted *adj* contaminato.

take *vt* prendere; portare; accettare; contenere; sopportare; * *vi* attecchire; **to ~ after** assomigliare; **to ~ away** togliere; **to ~ back** ritirare; **to ~ down** smontare; demolire; **to ~ in** abbindolare; capire; **to ~ off** decollare; **to ~ on** addossarsi; assumere; **to ~ out** invitare; togliere; **to ~ to** prendere in simpatia; **to ~ up** occupare; cominciare; * *n* ripresa *f*.

takeaway *n* rosticceria *f*.

takeoff *n* decollo *m*; imitazione *f*.

takeover *n* assorbimento *m*.

takings *npl* introiti *mpl*.

talc, talcum powder *n* talco *m*.

talent *n* talento *m*.

talented *adj* di talento.

talisman *n* talismano *m*.

talk *vt, vi* parlare; * *n* conversazione *f*; conferenza *f*.

talkative *adj* loquace.

tall *adj* alto.

tally *vi* corrispondere a.

talon *n* artiglio *m*.

tambourine *n* tamburino *m*.

tame *adj* addomesticato; * *vt* addomesticare; domare.

tamper *vi* manomettere.

tampon *n* tampone *m*.

tan *vi* abbronzarsi; * *n* abbronzatura *f*.

tang *n* sapore *m* o odore *m* forte.

tangent *n* tangente *f*.

tangerine *n* mandarino *m*.

tangible *adj* tangibile.

tangle *vt* aggrovigliare; * *n* groviglio *m*.

tank *n* serbatoio *m*; cisterna *f*; carro armato *m*.

tanker *n* autocisterna *f*; nave *f* cisterna.

tanned *adj* abbronzato.

tantalize *vt* tormentare.

tantalizing *adj* allettante.

tantamount *vi* equivalere a;

tantrum *n* collera *f*.

tap *vt* intercettare; sfruttare; * *vi* bussare; * *n* rubinetto *m*; colpetto *m*.

tape *n* nastro *m*; fettuccia *f*; * *vt* registrare.

tape measure *n* metro *m*, nastro *m*.

taper *n* cerino *m*.

tape recorder *n* registratore *m*.

tapestry *n* arazzo *m*.

tapeworm *n* tenia *f*.

tar *n* catrame *m*.

tarantula *n* tarantola *f*.

target *n* bersaglio *m*; obiettivo *m*.

tariff *n* tariffa *f*.

tarmac n macadam m al catrame.

tarnish vt ossidare.

tarpaulin n telone m incerato.

tarragon n (bot) dragoncello m.

tart adj aspro; * n crostata f; (fam) sgualdrina.

tartan n tartan m.

tartar n tartaro m.

task n compito m.

tassle n tappa f.

taste n gusto m; sapore m; * vt assaggiare; assaporare.

tasteful adj di gusto.

tasteless adj di cattivo gusto; insipido.

tasty adj saporito.

tattoo n tatuaggio m; (mil) parata f militare; * vt tatuare.

tatty adj mal ridotto.

taunt vt prendere in giro; * n presa f in giro.

Taurus n Toro m.

taut adj teso.

tautological adj tautologico.

tautology n tautologia f.

tavern n taverna f.

tawdry adj pacchiano.

tax n tassa f; imposta f; * vt tassare; gravare.

taxable adj imponibile.

taxation n tassazione f.

tax collector n esattore m delle imposte.

tax-free adj esente da imposta.

taxi n taxi m; * vi rullare.

taxi driver n tassista m/f.

taxi rank n posteggio m di taxi.

tax payer n contribuente m/f.

tax relief n agevolazioni fpl fiscali

tax return n dichiarazione f dei redditi.

tea n tè m.

teach vt, vi insegnare.

teacher n insegnante m/f; maestro m; professore m.

teaching n insegnamento m.

teacup n tazza f da tè.

teak n tek m.

team n équipe f, squadra f.

teamwork n lavoro m d'équipe.

teapot n teiera f.

tear vt strappare; * n strappo m.

tear n lacrima f.

tearful adj in lacrime.

tear gas n gas m lacrimogeno.

tease vt stuzzicare; * n burlone m.

tea-service, tea-set n servizio m da tè.

teaspoon n cucchiaino m.

teat n tettarella f.

technical adj tecnico.

technicality n tecnicità f.

technician n tecnico m.

technique n tecnica f.

technological adj tecnologico.

technology n tecnologia f.

teddy (bear) n orsacchiotto m.

tedious adj noioso.

tedium n tedio m.

tee n tee m.

teem vi brulicare.

teenage adj adolescenziale; ~r n adolescente m/f; teenager m/f.

teens npl età fra i 13 ed i 19 anni.

teeth npl denti mpl.

teethe vi mettere i denti.

teetotal adj astemio.

teetotaller n astemia m/f.

telecommunications npl telecomunicazioni fpl.

telegram n telegramma m.

telegraph n telegrafo m.

telegraphic adj telegrafico.

telepathy n telepatia f.

telephone n telefono m.

telephone call n telefonata f.

telephone directory n elenco m telefonico.

telephone number n numero m di telefono.

telephonist *n* telefonista *m/f*.
telescope *n* telescopio *m*.
televise *vt* trasmettere per televisione.
television *n* televisione *f*.
television set *n* televisore *m*.
telex *n* telex *m*.
tell *vt* dire; raccontare; indicare; distinguere; * *vi* parlare; sapere.
teller *n* cassiere *m*.
telling *adj* rivelatore.
telltale *adj* rivelatore; * *n* spione *m*.
temerity *n* audacia *f*.
temper *vt* moderare; * *n* indole *f*; temperamento *m*; collera *f*.
temperament *n* temperamento *m*.
temperamental *adj* capriccioso.
temperance *adj* astinenza dall'alcol.
temperate *adj* temperato.
temperature *n* temperatura *f*.
tempest *n* tempesta *f*.
tempestuous *adj* burrascoso.
template *n* sagoma *f*.
temple *n* tempio *m*; (*anat*) tempia *f*.
temporarily *adv* temporaneamente.
temporary *adj* provvisorio.
tempt *vt* tentare.
temptation *n* tentazione *f*.
tempting *adj* allettante.
ten *adj*, *n* dieci *m*.
tenable *adj* sostenibile.
tenacious *adj* tenace.
tenacity *n* tenacia *f*.
tenancy *n* contratto *m* d'affitto.
tenant *n* inquilino *m*.
tend *vt* tendere; curare.
tendency *n* tendenza *f*.
tender *adj* tenero; sensibile; * *n* tender *m*; offerta *f*; * *vt* presentare; offrire.
tenderness *n* tenerezza *f*.

tendon *n* tendine *m*.
tenement *n* casamento *m*.
tenet *n* principio *m*.
tennis *n* tennis *m*.
tennis court *n* campo *m* da tennis.
tennis player *n* tennista *m/f*.
tennis racket *n* racchetta *f* da tennis.
tenor *n* tenore *m*; * *adj* tenorile.
tense *n* (*gr*) tempo *m*; * *adj* teso; * *vt* tendere.
tension *n* tensione *f*.
tent *n* tenda *f*.
tentacle *n* tentacolo *m*.
tentative *adj* esitante.
tenth *adj*, *n* decimo *m*.
tenuous *adj* tenue.
tenure *n* possesso *m*.
tepid *adj* tiepido.
term *n* termine *m*; trimestre *m*; ~s *npl* condizioni *fpl*: * *vt* chiamare.
terminal *adj* incurabile; * *n* terminale *m*; capolinea *m*.
terminate *vt*, *vi* terminare.
termination *n* recisione *f*.
terminus *n* capolinea *m*.
termite *n* termite *f*.
terrace *n* terrazza *f*.
terrain *n* terreno *m*.
terrestrial *adj* terrestre.
terrible *adj* terribile.
terrier *n* terrier *m*.
terrific *adj* stupendo; enorme.
terrify *vt* terrificare.
territorial *adj* territoriale.
territory *n* territorio *m*.
terror *n* terrore *m*; peste *f*.
terrorism *n* terrorismo *m*.
terrorist *n* terrorista *m/f*.
terrorize *vt* terrorizzare.
terse *adj* conciso.
test *n* prova *f*; collaudo *m*; esame *m*; * *vt* controllare; collaudare; sperimentare.
testament *n* testamento *m*.
testicle *n* testicolo *m*.

testify vi testimoniare.
testimonial n referenze fpl.
testimony n testimonianza f.
test pilot n pilota m collaudatore.
test-tube n provetta f.
testy adj irritabile.
tetanus n tetano m.
tether vt legare; * n laccio m.
text n testo m.
textbook n libro m di testo.
textile adj tessile; ~s npl tessuti mpl.
textual adj testuale.
texture n consistenza f.
than conj che; di;
thank vt ringraziare.
thankful adj grato, riconoscente.
thankfulness n gratitudine f.
thankless adj ingrato.
thanks npl grazie fpl.
thanksgiving n ringraziamento m.
that adj quel; * pron ciò; * dem pron così; * rel pron che; * conj che; **so** ~ affinché.
thatch n copertura f di paglia.
thaw n disgelo m; * vt scongelare.
the def art il.
theatre n teatro m.
theatre-goer n habitué m/f del teatro.
theatrical adj teatrale.
theft n furto m.
their poss adj loro.
them pron gli; loro.
theme n tema m.
themselves pron si; se stessi.
then adv allora; poi; **now and** ~ ogni tanto.
theologic(al) adj teologico.
theologian n teologo m.
theology n teologia f.
theorem n teorema f.
theoretic(al) adj teoretico.
theorist n teorico m.

theorize vt teorizzare.
theory n teoria f.
therapeutic adj terapeutico; ~s npl terapeutica f.
therapist n terapista m/f.
therapy n terapia f.
there adv la, lì.
thereabout(s) adv nei pressi.
thereafter adv in seguito.
thereby adv con ciò.
therefore adv quindi.
thermal adj termale.
thermometer n termometro m.
thermostat n termostato m.
thesaurus n dizionario m dei sinonimi.
these dem adj, dem pron questi.
thesis n tesi f
they pers pron essi
thick adj grosso; spesso; ottuso.
thicken vt ispessire; * vi infittirsi.
thicket n boscaglia f.
thickness n spessore m.
thickset adj tozzo.
thickskinned adj coriaceo.
thief n ladro m.
thigh n coscia f.
thimble n ditale m.
thin adj sottile; magro; * vt diradarsi.
thing n cosa f; ~s npl roba f.
think vi pensare; credere; **to** ~ **over** riflettere su; **to** ~ **up** escogitare.
thinker n pensatore m.
thinking adj ragionevole; * n pensiero m.
third adj, n terzo m.
third-rate adj scadente.
thirst n sete f.
thirsty adj assetato.
thirteen adj, n tredici m.
thirteenth adj, n tredicesimo m.
thirtieth adj, n trentesimo m.

thirty *adj, n* trenta *m*.

this *dem adj, dem pron* questo.

thistle *n* cardo *m*.

thorax *n* torace *m*.

thorn *n* spina *f*.

thorny *adj* spinoso.

thorough *adj* minuzioso; approfondito.

thoroughbred *adj, n* purosangue *m/f*.

thoroughfare *n* strada *f* transitabile.

those *dem adj* quei; * *dem pron* quelli.

though *conj* benché; * *adv* tuttavia.

thought *n* pensiero *m*.

thoughtful *adj* pensieroso; gentile.

thoughtless *adj* sconsiderato.

thousand *adj, m* mille *m*.

thousandth *adj, n* millesimo *m*.

thrash *vt* percuotere.

thread *n* filo *m*; * *vt* infilare.

threadbare *adj* consumato.

threat *n* minaccia *f*.

threaten *vt* minacciare.

three *adj, n* tre *m*.

three-dimensional *adj* tridimensionale.

three-ply *adj* a tre capi.

thresh *vt* trebbiare.

threshold *n* soglia *f*.

thrift *n* parsimonia *f*.

thrifty *adj* parsimonioso.

thrill *vt* entusiasmare; * *vi* fremere; * *n* brivido; fremito *m*.

thriller *n* thriller *m*.

thrive *vi* prosperare.

thriving *adj* fiorente.

throat *n* gola *f*.

throb *vi* palpitare; pulsare; * *n* battito *m*.

thrombosis *n* trombosi *f*.

throne *n* trono *m*.

throng *n* moltitudine *f*; * *vt* affollare.

throttle *n* gas *m*; * *vt* strozzare.

through *prep* attraverso; per; * *adj* finito; di passaggio.

throughout *prep* in tutto; * *adv* dappertutto.

throw *vt* lanciare; gettare; to ~ away butar via; to ~ off sbarazzarsi di; to ~ up vomitare; * *n* lancio *m*.

throwaway *adj* monouso.

thrush *n* tordo *m*; (*med*) candida *f*.

thrust *vt* spingere con forza; * *n* spintone *m*.

thud *n* tonfo *m*.

thug *n* teppista *m/f*.

thumb *n* pollice *m*.

thump *n* colpo *m*; tonfo; * *vt, vi* picchiare.

thunder *n* tuono *m*; * *vi* tonare.

thunderbolt *n* fulmine *m*.

thunderclap *n* rombo *m* di tuono.

thunderstorm *n* temporale *m*.

thundery *adj* da temporale.

Thursday *n* giovedì *m*.

thus *adv* così; perciò.

thwart *vt* ostacolare.

thyme *n* (*bot*) timo *m*.

thyroid *n* tiroide *f*.

tiara *n* diadema *m*.

tic *n* tic *m*.

tick *n* tic tac *m*; segno *m*; zecca *f*; * *vt* spuntare; ticchettare; to ~ over andare al minimo.

ticket *n* biglietto *m*.

ticket collector *n* bigliettaio *m*.

ticket office *n* biglietteria *f*.

tickle *vt* fare il solletico a.

ticklish *adj* che soffre il solletico.

tidal *adj* (*mar*) di marea.

tidal wave *n* onda *f* anomala.

tiddly *adj* brillo.

tide *n* marea *f*; ondata *f*.

tidiness *n* ordine *m*.

tidy *adj* ordinato; * *vt* mettere in ordine.

tie *vt* legare; allacciare; * *vi* pareggiare; **to ~ up** (*mar*) ormeggiare; concludere; * *n* cravatta *f*; pareggio *m*.

tier *n* fila *f*.

tiff *n* battibecco *m*.

tiger *n* tigre *f*.

tight *adj* stretto; sbronzo.

tighten *vt* stringere.

tightfisted *adj* tirchio.

tightrope *n* corda *f* (da acrobata).

tights *n* collant *m*.

tigress *n* tigre femmina.

tile *n* tegola *f*; mattonella *f*; * *vt* piastrellare.

tiled *adj* a piastrelle.

till *vt* coltivare; * *n* cassa *f*.

tiller *n* barra *f*.

tilt *n* pendio *m*; * *vt* inclinare.

timber *n* legname *m*.

time *n* tempo *m*; momento *m*; periodo *m*; ora *f*; era *f*; volta *f*; ~ * *vt* programmare; cronometrare; **to have a good ~** divertirsi.

time bomb *n* bomba *f* a orologeria.

time lag *n* intervallo *m* di tempo.

timeless *adj* eterno.

timely *adj* opportuno.

timer *n* timer *m*.

time scale *n* scala *f* cronologica.

time zone *n* fuso *m* orario.

timetable *n* orario *m*.

timid *adj* timido.

timidity *n* timidezza *f*.

timing *n* tempismo *m*.

tin *n* stagno *m*; scattola *f*; * *vt* inscatolare.

tinfoil *n* carta *f* stagnola.

tinge *n* punta *f*.

tingle *vi* formicolare; * *n* formicolio *m*.

tingling *n* formicolio *m*.

tinker *vi* trastullarsi.

tinkle *vi* tintinnare.

tin opener *n* apriscatole *m*.

tinplate *n* latta *f*.

tinsel *n* fili *mpl* argentati.

tint *n* sfumatura *f*; * *vt* tingere.

tiny *adj* minuscolo.

tip *n* punta *f*; mancia *f*; suggerimento *m*; discarica; * *vt* dare la mancia a; pronosticare; rovesciare; * *vi* rovesciarsi.

tip-off *n* soffiata *f*.

tipsy *adj* brillo.

tiptoe *vi* camminare in punta dei piedi.

tirade *n* tirata *f*.

tire *vt* stancare.

tired *adj* stanco.

tiredness *n* stanchezza *f*.

tireless *adj* instancabile.

tiresome *adj* seccante.

tiring *adj* faticoso.

tissue *n* velina *f*; fazzolettino *m* di carta; (*anat*) tessuto *m*.

tissue paper *n* carta *f* velina.

tit *n* cincia *f*.

titbit *n* leccornia *f*.

titillate *vt* titillare.

title *n* titolo *m*.

title deed *n* atto *m* di proprietà.

title page *n* frontespizio *m*.

titter *vi* ridacchiare; * *n* risatina *f* stupida.

to prep a; secondo; per; da.

toad *n* rospo *m*.

toadstool *n* fungo *m* velenoso.

toast *vt* tostare; brindare; * *n* pane *m* tostato; brindisi *m*.

toaster *n* tostapane *m*.

tobacco *n* tabacco *m*.

tobacconist *n* tabaccaio *m*.

toboggan *n* slittino *m*.

today *adv*, *n* oggi *m*.

toddler *n* bambino *m* che fa i primi passi.

toddy *n* grog *m*, ponce *m*.

toe *n* dito *m* del piede.

toffee *n* caramella *f* mou.

together *adv* insieme.

toil *vi* faticare; * *n* fatica *f*.

toilet *n* gabinetto *m*, toilette *f*.

toilet bag *n* nécessaire *m* da toilette.

toilet bowl *n* vaso *m* del gabinetto.

toilet paper *n* carta *f* igienica.

toiletries *npl* articoli *mpl* da toilette.

token *n* buono *m*; segno *m*; * *adj* simbolico.

tolerable *adj* sopportabile.

tolerance *n* sopportazione *f*; tolleranza *f*.

tolerant *adj* tollerante.

tolerate *vt* tollerare.

toll *n* pedaggio *m*.

tomato *n* pomodoro *m*.

tomb *n* tomba *f*.

tomboy *n* maschiaccio *m*.

tombstone *n* pietra *f* tombale.

tome *n* tomo *m*.

tomcat *n* gatto *m*.

tomorrow *adv*, *n* domani *m*.

ton *n* tonnellata *f*.

tone tono *m*; * *vi* intonarsi; **to ~ down** attenuare.

tone-deaf *adj* che non ha orecchio.

tongs *npl* pinza *f*.

tongue *n* lingua *f*.

tongue-tied *adj* ammutolito.

tongue-twister *n* scioglilingua *m*.

tonic *n* (*med*) ricostituente *m*; acqua *f* tonica.

tonight *adv* stasera.

tonnage *n* tonnellaggio *m*.

tonsil *n* tonsilla *f*.

tonsillitis *n* tonsillite *f*.

tonsure *n* tonsura *f*.

too *adv* troppo, anche.

tool *n* arnese *m*, attrezzo *m*, strumento *m*.

tool box *n* cassetta *f* degli attrezzi.

toot *vi* suonare il clacson.

tooth *n* dente *m*.

toothache *n* mal *m* di denti.

toothbrush *n* spazzolino *m* da denti.

toothless *adj* sdentato.

toothpaste *n* dentifricio *m*.

toothpick *n* stuzzicadenti *m*.

top *n* cima *f*; superficie *f*; tappo *m*; trottola *f*; **big ~** tendone *m*; * *adj* ultimo; migliore; * *vt* sormontare; superare.

topaz *n* topazio *m*.

top hat *n* cilindro *m*.

topic *n* argomento *m*.

topless *adj* a seno scoperto.

top-level *adj* ad alto livello.

topmost *adj* il più alto.

topography *n* topografia *f*.

topple *vi* cadere; * *vt* rovesciare.

top-secret *adj* segretissimo.

topsy-turvy *adv*, *adj* sottosopra.

torch *n* torcia *f*, (*fam*) pila *f*.

torment *vt* tormentare; * *n* tormento *m*.

tornado *n* tornado *m*.

torpedo *n* siluro *m*.

torpid *adj* intorpidito.

torrent *n* torrente *m*.

torrential *adj* torrenziale.

torrid *adj* torrido.

torso *n* torso *m*.

tortoise *n* tartaruga *f*.

tortoiseshell *n* guscio *m* di tartaruga.

tortuous *adj* tortuoso.

torture *n* tortura *f*; * *vt* torturare.

toss *vt* lanciare; sballottare; disarcionare.

total *adj* totale; **~ly** *adv* completamente; * *n* totale *m*; * *vt* ammontare.

totalitarian *adj* totalitario.

totality n totalità f.

totter vi vacillare.

touch vt toccare; commuovere; uguagliare; **to ~ on** sfiorare; **to ~ up** ritoccare; * n tatto m; tocco m; pizzico m; contatto m.

touch-and-go adj incerto.

touchdown n atterraggio m.

touched adj commosso; tocco.

touching adj commovente.

touchy adj permaloso.

tough adj resistente; faticoso.

toughen vt rinforzare.

toupee n parrucchino m.

tour n giro m; tournée f; visita f; * vt fare un giro.

touring n turismo m.

tourism n turismo m.

tourist n turista m/f.

tourist office n ufficio m del turismo.

tournament n torneo m.

tow n rimorchio m; * vt rimorchiare.

toward(s) prep verso.

towel n asciugamano m.

towelling n spugna f.

towel rail n portasciugamano m.

tower n torre f.

towering adj imponente.

town n città f.

town clerk n segretario m comunale.

town hall n municipio m.

towrope n cavo m per rimorchio.

toxic adj tossico.

toxin n tossina f.

toy n giocattolo m; vi **to ~ with** giocherellare.

trace n traccia f; * vt tracciare; rintracciare.

trachea n trachea f.

track n orma f; sentiero m; pista f; binario m; * vt essere sulle tracce di.

tracksuit n tuta f da ginnastica.

tract n distesa f; trattatello m.

traction n trazione f.

tractor n trattore m.

trade n commercio m; industria f; mestiere f; * vt barattare; * vi commerciare.

trade fair n fiera f campionaria.

trademark n marchio m.

trade name n nome m depositato.

trader n commerciante m.

tradesman n fornitore m.

trade union n sindacato m.

trade unionism n sindacalismo m.

trade unionist n sindacalista m/f.

trading n commercio m; * adj commerciale.

tradition n tradizione f.

traditional adj tradizionale.

traffic n traffico m; * vi trafficare.

traffic jam n ingorgo m.

trafficker n trafficante m/f.

traffic lights npl semaforo m.

tragedy n tragedia f.

tragic adj tragico; **~ally** adv tragicamente.

tragicomedy n tragicommedia f.

trail vt trascinare; pedinare; * vi strisciare; * n scia f; orma f; sentiero m.

trailer n rimorchio m; prossimamente m.

train vt addestrare; allenare; * vi fare tirocinio; * n treno m; codazzo m; serie f.

trained adj diplomato; allenato.

trainee n apprendista m/f; tirocinante m/f.

trainer n allenatore m; **~s** npl scarpe fpl da ginnastica.

training n allenamento m; addestramento m.

trait n caratteristica f.

traitor n traditore m.

tram n tram m.

tramp n vagabondo m; * vi camminare pesantemente.

trample vt calpestare.

trance n trance f.

tranquil adj tranquillo.

tranquillizer n tranquillante m.

transact vt trattare.

transaction n operazione f.

transatlantic adj transatlantico.

transcend vt trascendere.

transcription n trascrizione f.

transfer vt trasferire; * n trasferimento m.

transferable adj trasferibile.

transfix vt trafiggere.

transform vt trasformare.

transformation n trasformazione f.

transformer n trasformatore m.

transfusion n trasfusione f.

transgress vi trasgredire.

transient adj transitorio.

transistor n transistor m.

transit n transito m.

transition n transizione f.

transitive adj transitivo.

translate vt, vi tradurre.

translation n traduzione f.

translator n traduttore m.

transmission n trasmissione f.

transmit vt trasmettere.

transmitter n emittente f.

transparency n trasparenza f; diapositiva f.

transparent adj trasparente.

transpire vi traspirare; succedere.

transplant vt trapiantare; * n trapianto m.

transport vt trasportare; * n trasporto m.

transportation n trasporto m.

transvestite n travestito m.

trap n trappola f; (fam) boccaccia f; calesse m; * vt intrappolare.

trap door n botola f.

trapeze n trapezio m.

trappings npl bardatura f.

trash n spazzatura f.

trashy adj di scarto.

trauma n trauma m.

traumatic adj traumatizzante.

travel vi viaggiare; * n viaggi mpl.

travel agency n agenzia f viaggi.

traveller n viaggiatore m.

traveller's cheque n assegno m turistico.

travelling adj intinerante; di viaggio.

travel sickness n mal m di macchina/d'aerea/di mare.

travesty n parodia f.

trawler n peschereccio m.

tray n vassoio m.

treacherous adj sleale.

treachery n slealtà f.

treacle n melassa f.

tread vt calpestare; * vi pestare; * n passo m; battistrada m.

treason n tradimento m.

treasure n tesoro m; vt stimare.

treasurer n tesoriere m.

treat vt trattare; considerare; offrire; curare; * n sorpresina f.

treatise n trattato m.

treatment n trattamento m.

treaty n trattato m.

treble adj triplo; alto; * vt triplicare.

treble clef n chiave f di sol.

tree n albero m.

trek n spedizione f.

trellis n graticcio m.

tremble vi tremare; * n tremito m.

trembling n tremito m.

tremendous adj enorme; tremendo.

tremor n scossa f.

trench n fosso m; trincia f; ~ **coat** n trench m.

trend n andamento m.

trepidation n trepidazione f.

trespass vt transitare abusivamente.

trestle n cavalletto m.

trial n processo m; prova f.

triangle n triangolo m.

triangular adj triangolare.

tribal adj tribale.

tribe n tribù f.

tribulation n tribolazione f.

tribunal n tribunale m.

tributary n affluente m.

tribute n tributo m.

trick n scherzo m; trucco m; inganno m; * vt ingannare.

trickery n astuzia f.

trickle vi gocciolare; * n rivolo m.

tricky adj difficile.

tricycle n triciclo m.

trifle n sciocchezza f; zuppa f inglese; * vi prendere alla leggera.

trifling adj insignificante.

trigger n grilletto m; * vt scatenare.

trigonometry n trigonometria f.

trill n trillo m; * vi trillare.

trilogy n trilogia f.

trim adj snello; * n spuntata f; * vt spuntare.

trimmings npl accessori mpl.

Trinity n Trinità f.

trinket n ninnolo m.

trio n trio m.

trip vi inciampare; * n viaggio m; gita f; trip m.

tripe n trippa f.

triple adj triplo.

triplets npl tre gemelli mpl.

triplicate adj triplice; * n in triplice copia.

tripod n treppiede m.

trite n trito.

triumph n trionfo m.

triumphal adj trionfale.

triumphant adj trionfante.

trivia n banalità fpl.

triviality n frivolezza f.

trolley n carello m.

trombone n trombone m.

troop n squadrone m; ~s npl truppe fpl.

trophy n trofeo m.

tropical adj tropicale.

trot n trotto m; * vi trottare.

trouble vt preoccupare; disturbare; * n problemi mpl; guai mpl.

troubled adj travagliato.

troublemaker n attaccabrighe m/f.

troubleshooter n esperto m.

troublesome adj fastidioso.

trough n mangiatoia f; cavo m.

troupe n troupe f.

trousers npl pantaloni mpl.

trout n trota f.

trowel n cazzuola f.

truant n: to play ~ marinare la scuola.

truce n tregua f.

truck n camion m.

truck driver n camionista m.

truculent adj bellicoso.

trudge vi trascinarsi.

true adj vero; sincero; fedele.

truelove n vero amore m.

truffle n tartufo m.

truly adv veramente.

trump n atout m.

trumpet n tromba f.

truncheon n manganello m.

trunk n tronco m; proboscide f; baule m.

truss n cinto m erniario; * vt legare stretto.

trust n fiducia f; (com) trust m; * vt fidarsi.

trusted *adj* fidato.
trustee *n* amministratore *m*.
trustful *adj* fiducioso.
trustworthy *adj* attendibile.
trusty *adj* fidato.
truth *n* verità *f*.
truthful *adj* veritiero.
try *vt* provare; cercare; verificare; processare; * *vi* provare; * *n* tentativo *m*; meta *f*;
trying *adj* duro.
tsar *n* zar *m*.
T-shirt *n* maglietta *f*.
tub *n* mastello *m*; vaschetta *f*.
tuba *n* tuba *f*.
tube *n* tubo *m*; metrò *m*.
tuberculosis *n* tubercolosi *f*.
tubing *n* tubazione *f*.
tuck *n* pinze *f*; * *vt* infilare.
Tuesday *n* martedì *m*.
tuft *n* ciuffo *m*.
tug *vt* dare uno strattone a; * *n* strattone *m*; rimorchiatore *m*.
tuition *n* lezioni *fpl*.
tulip *n* tulipano *m*.
tumble *vt* ruzzolare; * *n* capitombolo *m*.
tumble-down *adj* cadente.
tumbler *n* bicchiere *m*.
tummy *n* pancia *f*.
tumour *n* tumore *m*.
tumultuous *adj* tumultuoso.
tuna *n* tonno *m*.
tune *n* melodia *f*; * *vt*, *vi* accordare.
tuneful *adj* melodioso.
tuner *n* sintonizzatore *m*; accordatore *m*.
tunic *n* tunica *f*.
tuning fork *n* diapason *m*.
tunnel *n* galleria *f*; tunnel *m*.
turban *n* turbante *m*.
turbine *n* turbina *f*.
turbulence *n* turbolenza *f*.
turbulent *adj* turbolento.
tureen *n* zuppiera *f*.
turf *n* zolla *f* erbosa; to ~ out buttar fuori.

turgid *adj* ampolloso.
turkey *n* tacchino *m*.
turmeric *n* curcuma *f*.
turmoil *n* confusione *f*.
turn *vt* girare; voltare; trasformare; tornire; * *vi* girare; virare; to ~ back tornare in dietro; to ~ down abbassare; rifiutare; to ~ in consegnare; to ~ off spegnere; to ~ on accendere; to ~ out rivelarsi; to ~ over capovolgersi; voltare; to ~ round girarsi; to ~ up arrivare; alzare; * *n* giro *m*; curva *f*; crisi *f*; turno *m*; numero *m*.
turncoat *n* voltagabbana *m/f*.
turning *n* curva *f*.
turnip *n* rapa *f*.
turnover *n* giro *m* d'affari.
turnstile *n* cancelletto *m* girevole.
turntable *n* piatto *m*.
turpentine *n* trementina *f*.
turquoise *adj*, *n* turchese *m*.
turret *n* torretta *f*.
turtle *n* tartaruga *f* acquatica.
turtledove *n* tortora *f*.
tusk *n* zanna *f*.
tussle *n* baruffa *f*.
tutor *n* insegnante *m* privato.
twang *n* suono *m* acuto.
tweezers *npl* pinzette *fpl*.
twelfth *adj*, *n* dodicesimo *m*.
twelve *adj*, *n* dodici *m*.
twentieth *adj*, *n* ventesimo *m*.
twenty *adj*, *n* venti *m*.
twice *adv* due volte.
twig *n* ramoscello *m*.
twilight *n* crepuscolo *m*.
twin *adj*, *n* gemello *m*.
twine *vi* attorcigliarsi; * *n* cordicella *f*.
twinge *n* fitta *f*.
twinkel *vi* scintillare; * *n* scintillio.
twirl *vt* far roteare; * *vi* volteggiare; * *n* piroetta *f*.
twist *vt* attorcigliare; * *vi* slo-

garsi; attorcigliarsi; * n piega f; sviluppo m; twist m.

twitch vi contrarsi; * n tic m.

twitter vi cinguettare; * n cinguettio m.

two adj, n due m.

two-door adj a due porte.

two-faced adj falso.

twofold adj doppio.

two-seater adj biposto.

twosome n coppia f.

tycoon n magnate m.

type n tipo m; carattere m; * vt battere a macchina.

typeface n carattere m tipografico.

typescript n dattiloscritto m.

typewriter n macchina f da scrivere.

typewritten adj dattiloscritto.

typhoid n tifoidea f.

typhoon n tifone m.

typhus n tifo m.

typical adj tipico.

typing n dattilografia f.

typist n dattilografo m.

typographer n tipografo m.

tyrannical adj tirannico.

tyranny n tirannia f.

tyrant n tiranno m.

tyre n gomma f.

U

ubiquitous adj onnipresente.

udder n mammella f.

ugh excl puah!

ugliness n bruttezza f.

ugly adj brutto.

ulcer n ulcera f.

ulterior adj ulteriore.

ultimate adj finale; supremo.

ultimatum n ultimatum m.

ultramarine adj, n oltremarino m.

ultrasound n ecografia f.

umbilical cord n cordone m ombelicale.

umbrella n ombrello m.

umpire n arbitro m.

umpteen adj parecchi.

umpteenth n ennesimo m.

unable adj incapace.

unaccompanied adj non accompagnato.

unaccountable adj inesplicabile.

unaccustomed adj non abituato.

unacknowleged adj senza risposta.

unacquainted adj non al corrente; ignorare.

unadorned adj disadorno.

unadulterated adj puro.

unaffected adj naturale.

unaided adj senza aiuto.

unalterable adj inalterabile.

unaltered adj inalterato.

unambitious adj poco ambizioso.

unanimity n unanimità f.

unanimous adj unanime.

unanswerable adj irrefutabile.

unanswered adj senza risposta.

unapproachable adj inavvicinabile.

unarmed adj disarmato.

unashamed adj sfrontato.

unassuming adj modesto.

unattached adj staccato; libero.

unattainable adj irraggiungibile.

unattended adj incustodito.

unauthorized adj non autorizzato.

unavailable *adj* non disponibile.

unavoidable *adj* inevitabile.

unaware *adj* ignaro.

unawares *adv* alla sprovvista.

unbalanced *adj* squilibrato.

unbearable *adj* insopportabile.

unbecoming *adj* indecoroso, sconveniente.

unbelievable *adj* incredibile.

unbend *vi* distendersi; * *vt* raddrizzare.

unbiased *adj* imparziale.

unblemished *adj* senza macchia.

unblock *vt* sbloccare.

unborn *adj* non ancora nato.

unbounded *adj* sconfinato.

unbreakable *adj* infrangibile.

unbroken *adj* intatto; ininterrotto; insuperato.

unbutton *vt* sbottonare.

uncalled-for *adj* fuori luogo.

uncanny *adj* sconcertante.

unceasing *adj* incessante.

unceremonious *adj* brusco.

uncertain *adj* incerto.

uncertainty *n* incertezza *f*.

unchallenged *adj* incontestato.

unchanged *adj* invariato.

unchanging *adj* immutabile.

uncharitable *adj* severo.

unchecked *adj* incontrollato.

unchristian *adj* poco cristiano.

uncivil *adj* incivile.

uncivilized *adj* selvaggio.

uncle *n* zio *m*.

uncombed *adj* spettinato.

uncomfortable *adj* scomodo.

uncomfortably *adv* in modo disagevole.

uncommon *adj* insolito.

uncompromising *adj* assoluto.

unconcerned *adj* tranquillo.

unconditional *adj* incondizionato.

unconfirmed *adj* non confermato.

unconnected *adj* sconnesso.

unconquerable *adj* invincibile.

unconscious *adj*, privo di sensi; inconscio; * *n* inconscio *m*

unconstrained *adj* disinvolto.

uncontrollable *adj* incontrollabile.

unconventional *adj* non convenzionale.

unconvincing *adj* non convincente.

uncooked *adj* crudo.

uncork *vt* stappare.

uncorrected *adj* non riveduto.

uncouple *vt* sganciare.

uncouth *adj* rozzo.

uncover *vt* scoprire.

unction *n* unzione *f*.

uncultivated *adj* incolto.

uncut *adj* non tagliato.

undamaged *adj* intatto.

undaunted *adj* imperterrito.

undecided *adj* indeciso.

undefeated *adj* imbattuto.

undefined *adj* indefinito.

undeniable *adj* innegabile.

under *prep* sotto; secondo; * *adv* sotto.

under-age *adj* minorenne.

undercarriage *n* carello *m* d'atterraggio.

undercharge *vt* far pagare di meno.

undercoat *n* prima *f* mano.

undercover *adj* clandestino.

undercurrent *n* vena *f* nascosta.

undercut *vt* vendere a minor prezzo di.

underdeveloped *adj* sottosviluppato.

underdog *n* perdente *m*.

underdone *adj* poco cotto.

underestimate *vt* sotto valutare.

underexposed *adj* sottoesposto.

underfed *adj* denutrito.
undergo *vt* subire.
undergraduate *n* studente *m* universitario.
underground *n* (rail) metropolitana *f*; controcultura *f*; * *adj* sotterraneo.
undergrowth *n* sottobosco *m*.
underhand *adj* equivoco.
underlie *vt* essere alla base di.
underline *vt* sottolineare.
undermine *vt* minare.
underneath *prep, adv* sotto.
undernourished *adj* denutrito.
underpaid *adj* mal pagato.
underpants *npl* slip *m*.
underpass *n* sottopassaggio *m*.
underplay *vt* minimizzare.
underprivileged *adj* svantaggiato.
underrate *vt* sottovalutare.
undersecretary *n* sottosegretario *m*.
underside *n* parte *f* di sotto.
undersigned *adj, n* sottoscritto *m*.
understand *vt* capire; credere; * *vi* capire.
understandable *adj* comprensibile.
understanding *n* comprensione *f*; intesa *f*; * *adj* comprensivo.
understate *vt* sminuire.
understatement *n* minimizzare *m*.
understudy *n* doppio *m*.
undertake *vt* assumersi.
undertaker *n* impresario *m* di pompe funebri.
undertaking *n* impresa *f*; assicurazione *f*.
undervalue *vt* sottovalutare.
underwater *adj* subacqueo; sottomarino.
underwear *n* biancheria *f* intima.

underweight *adj* sottopeso.
underworld *n* malavita *f*.
underwrite *vt* sottoscrivere.
underwriter *n* assicuratore *m*.
undeserved *adj* immeritato.
undeserving *adj* indegno.
undesirable *adj* sgradevole.
undetermined *adj* indeterminato.
undigested *adj* non digerito.
undiminished *adj* non diminuito.
undisciplined *adj* indisciplinato.
undisguised *adj* palese.
undismayed *adj* imperterrito.
undisputed *adj* incontrastato.
undisturbed *adj* imperturbato.
undivided *adj* completo.
undo *vt* disfare; slacciare.
undoing *n* rovina *f*.
undoubted *adj* indubbio.
undress *vi* spogliare.
undue *adj* esagerato.
undulating *adj* ondulato.
unduly *adv* eccessivamente.
undying *adj* imperituro.
unearth *vt* dissotterrare.
unearthly *adj* innaturale.
uneasy *adj* inquieto; precario.
uneconomic *adj* antieconomico.
uneducated *adj* incolto.
unemotional *adj* impassibile.
unemployed *adj, n* disoccupato *m*.
unemployment *n* disoccupazione *f*.
unending *adj* interminabile.
unendurable *adj* insopportabile.
unenviable *adj* poco invidiabile.
unequal *adj* disuguale.
unequalled *adj* insuperato.
unequivocal *adj* inequivocabile.
unerring *adj* infallibile.

uneven *adj* ineguale; accidentato.

unexpected *adj* inatteso.

unexplained *adj* inspiegato.

unexplored *adj* inesplorato.

unfailing *adj* immancabile.

unfair *adj* ingiusto.

unfaithful *adj* infedele.

unfaithfulness *n* infedeltà *f*.

unfaltering *adj* risoluto.

unfamiliar *adj* sconosciuto.

unfashionable *adj* fuori moda.

unfasten *vt* slacciare.

unfathomable *adj* insondabile.

unfavourable *adj* sfavorevole.

unfeeling *adj* insensibile.

unfinished *adj* incompiuto.

unfit *adj* inadatto.

unflagging *adj* instancabile.

unfold *vt* spiegare; * *vi* schiudersi.

unforeseeable *adj* imprevedibile.

unforeseen *adj* imprevisto.

unforgettable *adj* indimenticabile.

unforgiveable *adj* imperdonabile.

unfortunate *adj* sfortunato.

unfounded *adj* infondato.

unfriendly *adj* ostile.

unfruitful *adj* infruttuoso.

unfurnished *adj* non ammobiliato.

ungainly *adj* goffo.

ungovernable *adj* ingovernabile.

ungrateful *adj* ingrato.

unhappily *adv* sfortunatamente.

unhappiness *n* infelicità *f*.

unhappy *adj* infelice.

unharmed *adj* illeso.

unhealthy *adj* malsano; malaticcio.

unheard-of *adj* inaudito.

unheeding *adj* disattento.

unhinge *vi* scardinare.

unhook *vt* sganciare.

unhoped-for *adj* insperato.

unhurt *adj* sano e salvo.

unhygienic *adj* insalubre.

unicorn *n* unicorno *m*.

unification *n* unificazione *f*.

uniform *adj* uniforme; * *n* divisa *f*.

uniformity *n* uniformità *f*.

unify *vt* unire; unificare.

unilateral *adj* unilaterale.

unimaginable *adj* inimmaginabile.

unimpaired *adj* intatto.

unpeachable *adj* irreprensibile.

unimportant *adj* trascurabile.

uninformed *adj* non al corrente.

uninhabitable *adj* inabitabile.

uninhabited *adj* disabitato.

uninjured *adj* incolume.

unintelligible *adj* inintelligibile.

unintentional *adj* involontario.

uninterested *adj* indifferente.

uninteresting *adj* privo d'interesse.

uninterrupted *adj* ininterrotto.

uninvited *adj* non invitato.

union *n* unione *f*; sindacato *m*.

unionist *n* sindacalista *m*.

unionize *vt* sindacalizzare.

unique *adj* unico; ~ly *adv* eccezionalmente.

unison *n* unisono *m*.

unit *n* unità *f*; reparto *m*.

unite *vt* unire; unificare.

united *adj* unito.

unity *n* unità *f*; unione *f*.

universal *adj* universale.

universe *n* universo *m*.

university *n* università *f*.

unjust *adj* ingiusto.

unjustified *adj* ingiustificato.

unkempt *adj* scarmigliato.

unkind *adj* scortese; crudele.

unknowingly *adv* inconsapevolmente.

unknown *adj* sconosciuto, ignoto.

unlawful *adj* illecito.

unleash *vt* liberare.

unless *conj* a meno che.

unlicensed *adj* senza licenza.

unlike *adj* dissimile.

unlikely *adj* improbabile; inverosimile.

unlikelihood *n* improbabilità *f*.

unlimited *adj* illimitato.

unlined *adj* sfoderato.

unload *vt, vi* scaricare.

unlock *vt* aprire.

unloveable *adj* antipatico.

unluckily *adv* purtroppo.

unlucky *adj* sfortunato; disgraziato.

unmanageable *adj* intrattabile; poco maneggevole.

unmarried *adj* scapolo (man); nubile (woman).

unmask *vt* smascherare.

unmentionable *adj* innominabile.

unmerciful *adj* spietato.

unmerited *adj* immeritato.

unmindful *adj* dimentico.

unmistakable *adj* inconfondibile.

unmitigated *adj* assoluto.

unmotivated *adj* immotivato.

unmoved *adj* indifferente.

unnamed *adj* anonimo.

unnatural *adj* innaturale.

unnecessary *adj* non necessario.

unneighbourly *adj* non da buon vicino.

unnoticed *adj* inosservato.

unobserved *adj* inosservato.

unobtainable *adj* introvabile.

unobstrusive *adj* discreto.

unoccupied *adj* libero; vuoto.

unoffending *adj* inoffensivo.

unofficial *adj* ufficioso.

unorganized *adj* disorganizzato.

unorthodox *adj* eterodosso.

unpack *vt* disfare.

unpaid *adj* non retribuito.

unpalatable *adj* immangiabile.

unparalleled *adj* senza pari.

unpleasant *adj* spiacevole.

unpleasantness *n* sgradevolezza *f*.

unplug *vt* staccare.

unpolished *adj* non lucidato.

unpopular *adj* impopolare.

unpractised *adj* inesercitato.

unprecedented *adj* senza precedenti.

unpredictable *adj* imprevedibile.

unprejudiced *adj* obiettivo.

unprepared *adj* impreparato.

unproductive *adj* improduttivo.

unprofitable *adj* non redditizio.

unpronounceable *adj* impronunciabile.

unprotected *adj* indifeso.

unpublished *adj* inedito.

unpunished *adj* impunito.

unqualified *adj* non qualificato; incondizionato.

unquestionable *adj* indiscutibile.

unquestioned *adj* indiscusso.

unravel *vt* dipanare.

unreadable *adj* illeggibile.

unreal *adj* irreale.

unrealistic *adj* illusorio.

unreasonable *adj* irrazionale; irragionevole.

unrecognizable *adj* irriconoscibile.

unrefined *adj* greggio.

unrelated *adj* senza nesso; non imparentato.

unrelenting *adj* implacabile.

unreliable *adj* non attendibile.

unremitting adj incessante.
unrepeatable adj irrepetibile.
unrepentant adj impenitente.
unrepresentative adj atipico.
unreserved adj incondizionato.
unrest n agitazione f.
unrestrained adj sfrenato.
unripe adj acerbo.
unrivalled adj senza pari.
unroll vt srotolare.
unruly adj indisciplinato.
unsafe adj pericoloso.
unsaleable adj invendibile.
unsatisfactory adj poco soddisfacente; insufficiente.
unsatisfying adj insoddisfacente.
unsavoury adj poco raccomandabile.
unscathed adj indenne.
unscrew vt svitare.
unscrupulous adj senza scrupoli.
unseemly adj indecoroso.
unseen adj inosservato.
unselfish adj altruista.
unsettle vt scombussolare.
unsettled adj instabile.
unshakable adj irremovibile.
unshaken adj non scosso.
unshrinkable adj irrestringibile.
unsightly adj non bello a vedersi.
unskilful adj inesperto.
unskilled adj non specializzato.
unsociable adj poco socievole.
unsold adj invenduto.
unsound adj cagionevole.
unspeakable adj indicibile.
unstable adj instabile.
unsteady adj vacillante.
unstudied adj spontaneo.
unsuccessful adj non riuscito.
unsuitable adj inadatto; inopportuno.
unsure adj incerto.

unswerving adj ferreo.
unsympathetic adj non comprensivo.
untamed adj indomato.
untangle vt sbrogliare.
untapped adj non sfruttato.
untenable adj insostenibile.
unthinkable adj impensabile.
unthinking adj irriguardoso.
untidiness n disordine m.
untidy adj disordinato.
untie vt sciogliere.
until prep fino a; * conj finché.
untimely adj prematuro.
untiring adj infaticabile.
untold adj mai rivelato.
untouchable n paria m.
untouched adj incolume; non toccato.
untoward adj increscioso.
untranslatable adj intraducibile.
untried adj non messo alla prova.
untroubled adj calmo.
untrue adj falso.
untrustworthy adj indegno di fiducia.
untruth n falsità f.
unused adj inutilizzato.
unusual adj insolito.
unvaried adj monotono.
unveil vt svelare.
unwavering adj incrollabile.
unwelcome adj non gradito.
unwell adj indisposto.
unwieldy adj poco maneggevole.
unwilling adj riluttante; **~ly** adv malvolentieri.
unwind vt srotolare; * vi distendersi.
unwise adj avventato.
unwitting adj involontario.
unworkable adj inattuabile.
unworthy adj indegno.
unwrap vt scartare.
unwritten adj tacito.

up *adv* su.
upbringing *n* educazione *f*.
update *vt* aggiornare.
upheaval *n* sconvolgimento *m*.
uphill *adj* in salita; faticoso.
uphold *vt* sostenere.
upholstery *n* tappezzeria *f*.
upkeep *n* manutenzione *f*.
uplift *vt* sollevare.
upper *adj* superiore; * *n* tomaia *f*.
upper-class *adj* dell'alta borghesia.
upper-hand *n* (*fig*) vantaggio *m*.
uppermost *adj* dominante.
upright *adj* ritto; retto; * *adv* diritto; * *n* montante *m*.
uprising *n* insurrezione *f*.
uproar *n* trambusto *m*.
uproarious *adj* fragoroso.
uproot *vt* sradicare.
upset *vt* rovesciare; turbare; scombussolare; * *n* contrattempo *m*; * *adj* turbato; scombussolato; offeso.
upshot *n* risultato *m*.
upside-down *adv* sottosopra; * *adj* capovolto.
upstairs *adv* di sopra; * *n* piano *m* di sopra.
upstanding *adj* aitante.
upstart *n* parvenu *m*.
uptight *adj* teso.
up-to-date *adj* aggiornato; attuale.
upturn *n* ripresa *f*.
upward *adj* verso l'alto; ~s *adv* verso l'alto; in su.

uranium *n* uranio *m*.
urban *adj* urbano.
urbane *adj* civile.
urchin *n* monello *m*.
urge *vt* insistere; **to ~ on** spronare; * *n* impulso *m*.
urgency *n* urgenza *f*.
urgent *adj* urgente; pressante.
urinal *n* vespasiano *m*.
urinate *vi* orinare.
urine *n* orina *f*.
urn *n* urna *f*.
us *pron* noi; ci.
usable *adj* utilizzabile.
usage *n* usanza *f*; uso *m*.
use *n* uso *m*; impiego *m*; * *vt* usare; adoperare.
used *adj* usato.
useful *adj* utile.
usefulness *n* utilità *f*.
useless *adj* inutile.
uselessness *n* inutilità *f*.
user-friendly *adj* di facile uso.
usher *n* usciere *m*.
usherette *n* maschera *f*.
usual *adj* solito; ~ly *adv* di solito
usurer *n* usuraio *m*.
usurp *vt* usurpare.
usury *n* usura *f*.
utensil *n* utensile *m*.
uterus *n* utero *m*.
utility *n* utilità *f*.
utilize *vt* utilizzare.
utmost *n* massimo *m*; estremo *m*; * *adj* totale.
utter *adj* *vt* pronunciare.
utterly *adv* completamente.

V

vacancy *n* vuoto *m*; stanza *f* libera.
vacant *adj* libero; vacuo.
vacate *vt* lasciare.
vacation *n* vacanza *f*.

vaccinate *vt* vaccinare.
vaccination *n* vaccinazione *f*.
vaccine *n* vaccino *m*.
vacillate *vt* vacillare.
vacuous *adj* vacuo.

vacuum *n* vuoto *m*.

vacuum flask *n* termos *m*.

vagabond *n* vagabondo *m*.

vagina *n* vagina *f*.

vagrant *n* vagabondo *m*.

vague *adj* vago.

vain *adj* vano; vanitoso.

valet *n* cameriere *m* personale.

valiant *adj* coraggioso.

valid *adj* valido.

validate *vt* convalidare.

validity *n* validità *f*.

valley *n* valle *f*.

valour *n* coraggio *m*.

valuable *adj* prezioso; **~s** *npl* preziosi *mpl*.

valuation *n* valutazione *f*; stima *f*.

value *n* valore *m*; * *vt* valutare.

valued *adj* stimato.

valve *n* valvola *f*.

vampire *n* vampiro *m*.

van *n* furgone *m*.

vandal *n* vandalo *m*.

vandalism *n* vandalismo *m*.

vandalize *vt* vandalizzare.

vanguard *n* avanguardia *f*.

vanilla *n* vaniglia *f*.

vanish *vi* svanire.

vanity *n* vanità *f*.

vanquish *vt* sconfiggere.

vantage point *n* punto *m* d'osservazione.

vapid *adj* scipito.

vaporize *vt* vaporizzare.

vapour *n* vapore *m*.

variable *adj* variabile.

variance *n* discordanza *f*.

variant *n* variante *f*.

variation *n* variazione *f*.

varicose vein *n* vena *f* varicosa.

varied *adj* vario.

variety *n* varietà *f*.

various *adj* vario.

varnish *n* vernice *f* trasparente.

vary *vt*, *vi* variare.

vase *n* vaso *m*.

vasectomy *n* vasectomia *f*.

vaseline *n* vaselina *f*.

vast *adj* vasto.

VAT *n* IVA.

vat *n* tino *m*.

vault *n* volta *f*; * *vt* saltare con un balzo.

veal *n* vitello *m*.

veer *vi* virare.

vegetable *n* ortaggio *m*; **~s** *npl* verdure *fpl*.

vegetable garden *n* orto *m*.

vegetarian *adj*, *n* vegetariano *m*.

vegetate *vi* vegetare.

vegetation *n* vegetazione *f*.

vehemence *n* veemenza *f*.

vehement *adj* veemente.

vehicle *n* veicolo *m*.

veil *n* velo *m*; * *vt* velare.

vein *n* vena *f*.

velocity *n* velocità *f*.

velvet *n* velluto *m*.

venal *adj* venale.

vendetta *n* vendetta *f*.

vending machine *n* distributore *m* automatico.

vendor *n* venditore *m*.

veneer *n* impiallacciatura *f*.

venerable *adj* venerabile.

venerate *vt* venerare.

veneration *n* venerazione *f*.

venereal *adj* venereo.

vengeance *n* vendetta *f*.

venial *adj* veniale.

venison *n* carne *f* di cervo.

venom *n* veleno *m*.

venomous *adj* velenoso.

vent *n* presa *f* d'aria; spacco *m*; * *vt* sfogare.

ventilate *vt* ventilare.

ventilation *n* ventilazione *f*.

ventilator *n* ventilatore *m*.

ventriloquist *n* ventriloquo *m*.

venture *n* impresa *f*; *vt* rischiare.

venue *n* luogo *m* d'incontro.

veranda(h) *n* veranda *f*.

verb n verbo m.
verbal adj verbale.
verbatim adj, adv parola per parola.
verbose adj verboso.
verdict n verdetto m.
verge n bordo m; orlo m.
verification n verifica f.
verify vt verificare.
veritable adj vero.
vermin n animali mpl nocivi.
vermouth n vermut m.
versatile adj versatile.
verse n verso m; poesia f.
versed adj pratico.
version n versione f.
versus prep contro.
vertebra n vertebra f.
vertebrate adj, n vertebrato m.
vertex n vertice m.
vertical adj, n verticale f.
vertigo n vertigine f.
verve n verve f.
very adj stesso; solo; * adv molto.
vessel n vascello m; recipiente m.
vest n canottiera f.
vestibule n atrio m.
vestige n vestigio m.
vestment n paramento m.
vestry n sagrestia f.
vet vt esaminare; * n veterinario m.
veteran n veterano m.
veterinary adj veterinario; * n ~ **surgeon** veterinario m.
veto n veto m; * vt porre il veto.
vex vt irritare.
vexed adj irritato.
via prep attraverso; via.
viable adj attuabile.
viaduct n viadotto m.
vial n fiala f.
vibrant adj vibrante.
vibrate vi vibrare.
vibration n vibrazione f.
vicar n pastore m.

vicarage n canonica f.
vicarious adj sofferto al posto di un altro.
vice n vizio m; morsa f.
vice-chairman n vicepresidente m.
vice-chancellor n rettore m.
vice versa adv viceversa.
vicinity n vicinanze fpl.
vicious adj maligno.
victim n vittima f.
victimize vt perseguitare ingiustamente.
victor n vincitore m.
victorious adj vittorioso.
victory n vittoria f.
video n video m.
videotape n videotape m.
vie vi contendersi.
view n vista f; veduta f; punta f di vista; * vt guardare; vedere.
viewer n telespettatore m.
viewfinder n mirino m.
viewpoint n posizione f.
vigil n veglia f.
vigilance n vigilanza f.
vigilant adj vigile.
vigorous adj vigoroso.
vigour n vigore m.
vile adj detestabile.
vilify vt diffamare.
villa n villa f.
village n paese m.
villager n abitante m di paese.
villain n mascalzone m.
vindicate vt scagionare.
vindication n scagionare m.
vindictive adj vendicativo.
vine n vite f.
vinegar n aceto m.
vineyard n vigneto m, vigna f.
vintage adj annata.
vinyl n vinile m.
viola n (mus) viola f.
violate vt violare.
violation n violazione f.
violence n violenza f.
violent adj violento.

violet n (bot) viola f; violetto m.
violin n violino m.
violinist n violinista m/f.
violoncello n violoncello m.
viper n vipera f.
virgin adj, n vergine f.
virginity n verginità f.
Virgo n Vergine f.
virile adj virile.
virility n virilità f.
virtual adj effettivo; **~ly** adv praticamente.
virtue n virtù f.
virtuous adj virtuoso.
virulent adj virulento.
virus n virus m.
visa n visto m.
vis-a-vis prep rispetto a.
viscous adj viscoso.
visibility n visibilità f.
visible adj visibile.
vision n vista f; visione f.
visit vt visitare; * n visita f.
visiting hours npl orario m delle visite.
visitor n ospite m/f; visitatore m.
visor n visiera f.
vista n vista f.
visual adj visivo.
visual aid n sussidi mpl visivi.
visualize vt immaginare.
vital adj vitale; fattale.
vitality n vitalità f.
vitamin n vitamina f.
vitiate vt guastare.
vitriolic adj caustico.
vivacious adj vivace.
vivid adj vivido.
vivisection n vivisezione f.
vocabulary n vocabolario m.
vocal adj vocale.

vocation n vocazione f; **~al** adj professionale.
vocative adj (gr) vocativo.
vociferous adj rumoroso.
vodka n vodka f.
vogue n moda f.
voice n voce f; * vt esprimere.
void adj nullo; * n vuoto m.
volatile adj volatile.
volcanic adj vulcanico.
volcano n vulcano m.
volition n volizione f.
volley n raffica f.
volleyball n pallavolo f.
volt n volt m.
voltage n voltaggio m.
voluble adj loquace.
volume n volume m.
voluntarily adv spontanea-mente.
voluntary adj volontario.
volunteer n volontario m; * vi offrirsi.
voluptuous adj voluttuoso.
vomit vt, vi vomitare; * n vomi-to m.
voracious adj vorace.
vortex n vortice m.
vote n votazione f; voto m; * vt, vi votare.
voter n elettore m.
voting n votazione f.
vouch vi garantire.
voucher n buono m.
vow n voto m; * vi giurare.
vowel n vocale f.
voyage n viaggio m per mare.
vulgar adj volgare.
vulgarity n volgarità f.
vulnerable adj vulnerabile.
vulture n avvoltoio m.

W

wad n batuffolo m; tampone m.
waddle vi camminare come una papera.

wade vi camminare a fatica.
wafer n wafer m; (relig) ostia f.
waffle vi ciarlare; * n cialda f.

waft *vt* portare; * *vi* diffondersi.

wag *vi* scodinzolare; * *vt* dimenare.

wage *vt* intraprendere; ~s stipendio *m*.

wage earner *n* salariato *m*.

wager *n* scommessa *f*; * *vt* scommettere.

waggle *vt* dimenare.

wagon *n* carro *m*; vagone *m*.

wail *n* gemito *m*; urlo *m*; * *vi* gemere.

waist *n* vita *f*.

waistcoat *n* panciotto *m*.

waistline *n* vita *f*.

wait *vt, vi* aspettare; *vi* aspettare; servire; * *n* attesa *f*.

waiter *n* cameriere *m*.

waiting list *n* lista *f* d'attesa.

waiting room *n* sala *f* d'attesa.

waive *vt* rinunciare a.

wake *vi* svegliarsi; * *vt* svegliare; * *n* (*mar*) scia *f*; veglia *f*.

walk *vt* percorrere; * *vi* camminare; passeggiare; * *n* passeggiata *f*; andatura *f*.

walker *n* camminatore *m*.

walkie-talkie *n* walkie-talkie *m*.

walking *n* camminare *m*; * *adj* a piedi.

walking stick *n* bastone *m* da passeggio.

walkout *n* abbandono *m*.

walkover *n* vittoria *f* facile.

walkway *n* passaggio *m* pedonale.

wall *n* muro *m*; parete *f*.

walled *adj* fortificato.

wallet *n* portafoglio *m*.

wallflower *n* (*bot*) violacciocca *f*.

wallow *vi* rotolarsi.

wallpaper *n* carta *f* da pareti.

walnut *n* noce *f*; (tree) noce *m*.

walrus *n* tricheco *m*.

waltz *n* valzer *m*.

wan *adj* pallido.

wand *n* bacchetta *f*.

wander *vi* gironzolare; * *vt* girovagare per.

wane *vi* calare.

wanker *n* uomo *m* insulso; masturbatore *m*.

want *vt* volere; desiderare; * *vi* mancare; * *n* mancanza *f*; miseria *f*; bisogno *m*.

wanting *adj* privo.

wanton *adj* lascivo.

war *n* guerra *f*.

ward *n* corsia *f*.

wardrobe *n* guardaroba *m*.

warehouse *n* deposito *m*.

warfare *n* arte *f* bellica.

warhead *n* testata *f*.

warily *adj* cautamente.

wariness *n* cautela *f*.

warm *adj* caldo; sentito; * *vt* scaldare; * *vi* **to ~ up** scaldarsi.

warm-hearted *adj* affettuoso.

warmth *n* calore *m*.

warn *vt* avvertire.

warning *n* avvertimento *m*.

warning light spia *f* luminosa.

warp *vt* deformare; * *n* curvatura *f*.

warrant *n* mandato *m*; giustificazione *f*.

warranty *n* garanzia *f*.

warren *n* tana *f*.

warrior *n* guerriero *m*.

warship *n* nave *f* da guerra.

wart *n* porro *m*.

wary *adj* diffidente.

wash *vt* lavare; * *vi* lambire; trascinare; lavarsi; * *n* lavata *f*.

washable *adj* lavabile.

washbasin *n* lavabo *m*.

washer *n* rondella *f*.

washing *n* lavaggio *m*; bucato *m*.

washing machine *n* lavatrice *f*.

washing-up *n* lavare i piatti.

wash-out *n* disastro *m*.

washroom *n* gabinetto *m*.

wasp *n* vespa *f*.

wastage *n* spreco *m*.

waste *vt* sprecare; perdere; * *n* spreco *m*; perdita *f*; * *adj* di scarto;

wasteful *adj* sprecone; dispendioso.

waste paper *n* carta *f* straccia.

waste pipe *n* tubazione *f* di scarico.

watch *n* orologio *m*; sorveglianza *f*; guardia *f*; * *vt*, *vi* guardare.

watchdog *n* cane *m* da guardia.

watchful *adj* attento.

watchmaker *n* orologiaio *m*.

watchman *n* guardiano *m*.

watchtower *n* torre *f* di guardia.

watchword *n* parola *f* d'ordine.

water *n* acqua *f*; * *vt* innaffiare.

water closet *n* gabinetto *m*.

watercolour *n* acquerello *m*.

waterfall *n* cascata *f*.

water-heater *n* scaldabagno *m*.

watering-can *n* annaffiatoio *m*.

waterlilly *n* ninfea *f*.

water line *n* linea *f* di galleggiamento.

waterlogged *adj* impregnato d'acqua; inzuppato.

water main *n* conduttura *f* dell'acqua.

watermark *n* filigrana *f*.

watermelon *n* anguria *f*, cocomero *m*.

watershed *n* spartiacque *m*.

watertight *adj* stagno; inattaccabile.

waterworks *npl* impianto *m* idrico.

watery *adj* acquoso.

watt *n* watt *m*.

wave *n* onda *f*, ondata *f*; cenno

m; * *vt* sventolare; salutare con un cenno della mano; * *vi* gesticolare.

wavelength *n* lunghezza *f* d'onda.

waver *vi* oscillare.

wavering *adj* vacillante.

wavy *adj* ondulato.

wax *n* cera *f*; * *vt* dare la cera a.

wax paper *n* carta *f* oleata.

waxwork *n* statua *f* di cera; **~s** *n* museo *m* delle cere.

way *n* strada *f*; direzione *f*; modo *m*; abitudine *f*; * *vt* **to give ~** dare la precedenza.

waylay *vt* fermare.

wayward *adj* ribelle.

we *pron* noi.

weak *adj* debole.

weaken *vt* indebolire; allentare; * *vi* indebolirsi.

weakling *n* mingherlino *m*.

weakness *n* debolezza *f*.

wealth *n* ricchezza *f*.

wealthy *adj* ricco.

wean *vt* svezzare.

weapon *n* arma *f*.

wear *vt* portare; indossare; consumare; **to ~ away** consumarsi; **to ~ down** fiaccare; **to ~ out** logorare; * *vi* durare; **to ~ off** non fare più effetto; * *n* uso *m*; logoramento *m*; usura *f*; abbigliamento *m*.

weariness *n* stanchezza *f*.

wearisome *adj* estenuante.

weary *adj* stanco.

weasel *n* donnola *f*.

weather *n* tempo *m*: * *vt* superare.

weather-beaten *adj* segnato dalle intemperie.

weather forecast *n* previsioni *fpl* del tempo.

weatherman *n* meteorologo *m*.

weathervane *n* segnavento *m*.

weave *vt*, *vi* tessere; intrecciare; * *n* trama *f*.

weaving n tessitura f.

web n tela f; ragnatela f.

wed vt sposare.

wedding n matrimonio m; nozze fpl.

wedding ring n fede f.

wedge n zeppa f; cuneo m.

Wednesday n mercoledì m.

wee adj piccolo.

weed n erbaccia f.

weedkiller n diserbante m.

weedy adj (fam) allampanato.

week n settimana f; **a ~ today** oggi a otto.

weekday n giorno m feriale.

weekend n weekend m; fine settimana m.

weekly adj, n settimanale m.

weep vt, vi piangere.

weeping willow n salice m piangente.

weigh vt, vi pesare.

weight n peso m.

weightlifter n pesista m.

weighty adj importante.

weird adj bizzarro.

welcome adj gradito, benvenuto; * n accoglienza f; benvenuto m; * vt accogliere.

weld vt saldare; * n saldatura f.

welfare n bene m; benessere m.

welfare state n stato m assistenziale.

well n pozzo m; * vi sgorgare; * adj, adv bene; **as ~** anche.

well-behaved adj che si comporta bene.

well-being n benessere m.

well-bred adj beneducato.

well-built adj ben fatto; ben costruito.

well-deserved adj meritato.

well-disposed adj ben disposto.

well-known adj noto.

well-meaning adj ben intenzionato.

well-off adj benestante.

well-to-do adj abbiente.

well-wisher n ammiratore m.

west adj ovest, occidentale; * n ovest m; * adv verso ovest.

westerly adj di ponente.

western adj occidentale; * n (film) western m.

westward n ovest.

wet adj bagnato; umido; piovoso; * n umidità f; * vt bagnare.

wet-nurse n balia f.

whack vt dare una manata a; * n colpo m.

whale n balena f.

wharf n banchina f.

what pron cosa; * adj che, quale.

whatever pron qualsiasi cosa.

wheat n grano m, frumento m.

wheedle vt blandire.

wheel n ruota f; * vi roteare.

wheelbarrow n carriola f.

wheelchair n sedia f a rotelle.

wheeler-dealer n trafficone m.

wheeze vi ansimare.

when adv, conj quando.

whenever adv in qualsiasi momento.

where adv, conj dove.

whereabouts adv dove

whereas conj mentre.

whereby adv per cui.

wherever conj dovunque.

whereupon adv al che.

wherewithal npl mezzi mpl.

whet vt stimolare.

whether conj se.

which adj, pron quale; * rel pron che.

whiff n zaffata f.

while n tempo m; * conj mentre.

whim n capriccio m.

whimper vi piagnucolare; * n piagnucolio m.

whimsical adj fantasioso.

whine vi guaire; * n guaito m.

whinny vi nitrire.

whip n frusta f; * vt frustare.

whipped cream n panna f montata.

whip-round n colletta f.

whirl vi volteggiare; * vortice m.

whirlpool n vortice m.

whirlwind n tromba f d'aria.

whisk n frullino m; * vt frullare.

whiskers npl baffi mpl.

whisky n whisky m.

whisper vt, vi bisbigliare; * n bisbiglio m.

whispering n bisbiglio m.

whistle vi fischiare; * vt fischiettare; * n fischio m.

Whit n Pentecoste f.

white adj, n bianco m.

white elephant n oggetto m costoso ma inutile.

white-hot adj incandescente.

white lie n bugia f pietosa.

whiten vt sbiancare.

whiteness n candore m.

whitewash n bianco m di calce; * vt imbiancare.

whiting n merlango m.

whitish adj biancastro.

whittle away vt ridurre.

who pron chi; * rel pron che.

whoever pron chiunque.

whole adj intero; tutto; completo; * n tutto m.

wholehearted adj incondizionato.

wholemeal adj integrale.

wholesale adj, adv all'ingrosso.

wholesaler n grossista m/f.

wholesome adj salubre.

wholly adv completamente.

whom pron chi; * rel, dir, obj che.

whooping cough n pertosse f.

whore n puttana f.

whose pron di chi; * rel pron il cui.

why adv, conj perché.

wick n stoppino m.

wicked adj cattivo, malvagio, perfido.

wickedness n cattiveria f.

wicker n vimine m; * adj di vimine.

wide adj largo; ~ly adv molto.

wide-angle adj grandangolare.

wide-awake adj completamente sveglio.

widen vt ampliare.

wide-open adj spalancato.

widespread adj diffuso.

widow n vedova f.

widower n vedovo m.

width n larghezza f.

wield vt maneggiare.

wife n moglie f.

wig n parrucca f.

wiggle vt ancheggiare.

wild adj selvatico; selvaggio; furibondo.

wilderness n deserto m; giungla f.

wild life n natura f.

wildly adv violentemente.

wilful adj ostinato.

wilfulness n ostinazione f.

wiliness n scaltrezza f.

will n volontà f; testamento m; * vt volere; pregare; * vi volere.

willing adj volenteroso; disposto.

willingness n disponibilità f.

willow n salice m.

willpower n forza f di volontà.

willy-nilly adv volente o nolente.

wilt vt appassire.

wily adj astuto.

win vt vincere; conquistare; * vi vincere; * n vittoria f.

wince vi rabbrividire.

winch n argano m.

wind n vento m; flatulenza f; fiato m.

wind *vt* avvolgere; caricare.
windbreak *n* frangivento *m*.
windcheater *n* giacca *f* a vento.
windfall *n* bella sorpresa *f*.
winding *adj* serpeggiante.
windmill *n* mulino *m* a vento.
window *n* finestra *f*; vetrina *f*; finestrino *m*.
window box *n* cassetta *f* per i fiori.
window pane *n* vetro *m*.
windowsill *n* davanzale *m*.
windpipe *n* trachea *f*.
windscreen *n* parabrezza *m*.
windscreen washer *n* lavacristallo *m*.
windscreen wiper *n* tergicristallo *m*.
windy *adj* ventoso.
wine *n* vino *m*.
wine cellar *n* cantina *f*.
wine-list *n* lista *f* dei vini.
wine-tasting *n* degustazione *f* dei vini.
wing *n* ala *f*.
winged *adj* alato.
winger *n* ala *f*.
wink *vi* ammiccare; * *n* strizzatina *f*.
winner *n* vincitore *m*.
winning post *n* traguardo *m*.
winter *n* inverno *m*; * *adj* invernale.
winter sports *npl* sport *m* invernali.
wintry *adj* invernale.
wipe *vt* pulire; * *n* passata *f*.
wire *n* filo *m*.
wiring *n* impianto *m* elettrico.
wiry *adj* magro e forte.
wisdom *n* saggezza *f*.
wisdom tooth *n* dente *m* del giudizio.
wise *adj* saggio.
wisecrack *n* spiritosaggine *f*.
wish *vt* volere; desiderare; augurare; * *vi* desiderare; * *n*

desiderio *m*; augurio *m*.
whisbone *n* forcella *f*.
wishful *adj* desideroso.
wisp *n* filo *m*.
wistful *adj* nostalgico.
wit *n* intelligenza *f*; arguzia *f*.
witch *n* strega *f*.
witchcraft *n* stregoneria *f*.
witchhunt *n* caccia *f* alle streghe.
with *prep* con.
withdraw *vt* ritirare.
withdrawal *n* ritiro *m*; prelievo *m*.
withdrawn *adj* distaccato.
wither *vi* appassire.
withering *adj* raggelante.
withhold *vt* trattenere.
within *prep* dentro; * *adv* all'interno.
without *prep* senza.
withstand *vt* resistere.
witless *adj* stupido.
witness *n* testimone *m*; * *vt* autenticare; * *vi* testimoniare.
witness box *n* banco *m* dei testimoni.
witticism *n* arguzia *f*.
wittingly *adv* consapevolmente.
witty *adj* arguto.
wizard *n* mago *m*.
wobble *vi* traballare.
woe *n* dolore *m*.
woeful *adj* triste.
wolf *n* lupo *m*; mandrillo *m*; * *vt* divorare.
woman *n* donna *f*.
womanly *adj* femminile.
womb *n* utero *m*; grembo *m*.
women's lib *n* movimento *m* femminista.
wonder *n* stupore *m*; miracolo *m*; * *vt* chiedersi; domandarsi; * *vi* stupirsi.
wonderful *adj* stupendo.
won't *abbr* di **will not**.
wont *n* costume *m*.
woo *vt* corteggiare.

wood *n* legno *m*; bosco *m*.

wood alcohol *n* metanolo *m*.

wood carving *n* scultura *f* in legno.

woodcut *n* incisione *f* su legno.

woodcutter *n* tagliaboschi *m*.

wooded *adj* boscoso.

wooden *adj* di legno; impacciato.

woodland *n* zona *f* boscosa.

woodlouse *n* onisco *m*.

woodsman *n* tagliaboschi *m*.

woodpecker *n* picchio *m*.

woodwind *n* legni *mpl*.

woodwork *n* falegnameria *f*.

woodworm *n* tarlo *m*.

wool *n* lana *f*.

woollen *adj* di lana; ~s *npl* indumenti *mpl* di lana.

woolly *adj* lanoso; vago.

word *n* parola *f*; notizia *f*; * *vt* formulare.

wordblind *adj* dislessico.

wording *n* formulazione *f*.

word processing *n* elaborazione *f* della parola.

word processor *n* word processor *m*.

wordy *adj* verboso.

work *vt* azionare; * *vi* lavorare; funzionare; * *n* lavoro *m*; opera *f*; ~s *npl* meccanismo *m*; fabbrica *f*.

workable *adj* fattibile.

workaholic *n* lavoratore *m* accanito.

worker *n* lavoratore *m*; operaio *m*.

workforce *n* forza *f* lavoro.

working-class *n* classe *f* operaia.

workman *n* operaio *m*.

workmanship *n* fattura *f*.

workshop *n* officina *f*.

work-shy *adj* indolente.

world *n* mondo *m*; * *adj* mondiale.

worldly *adj* mondano.

worldwide *adj* mondiale.

worm *n* verme *m*; * *vt* insinuarsi.

worn-out *adj* consunto

worried *adj* preoccupato.

worry *vt* preoccupare; importunare; * *n* preoccupazione *f*.

worrying *adj* preoccupante.

worse *adj* peggiore; * *adv* peggio; * *n* peggio *m*.

worsen *vt*, *vi* peggiorare.

worship *n* adorazione *f*; **your** ~ Vostro Onore; * *vt* adorare.

worshipper *n* fedele *m/f*.

worst *adj* peggiore; * *adv* peggio; * *n* peggio *m*.

worsted *adj* pettinato.

worth *n* valore *m*.

worthless *adj* inutile.

worthwhile *adj* valido.

worthy *adj* lodevole.

would-be *adj* aspirante.

wound *n* ferita *f*; * *vt* ferire.

wounded *adj* ferito.

wrangle *vi* litigare; * *n* alterco *m*.

wrap *vt* incartare; * *n* scialle *m*.

wrath *n* ira *f*.

wreath *n* ghirlanda *f*.

wreck *n* naufragio *m*; relitto *m*; * *vt* distruggere.

wreckage *n* relitti *mpl*.

wren *n* scricciolo *m*.

wrench *n* strattone *m*; chiave *m*; * *vt* strappare; (*med*) slogare.

wrestle *vi* lottare.

wrestler *n* lottatore *m*.

wrestling *n* lotta *f* libera.

wretch *n* sciagurato *m*.

wretched *adj* disgraziato; pessimo.

wriggle *vt* muovere; * *vi* agitarsi.

wring *vt* strizzare.

wrinkle *n* ruga *f*; * *vt* stropicciare.

wrist *n* polso *m*.

wristband n polsino m.

wristwatch n orologio m da polso.

writ n mandato m.

write vt, vi scrivere; **to ~ down** segnare; **to ~ off** estinguere; **to ~ up** aggiornare.

write-off n perdita f; rottame m.

writer n autore m; scrittore m.

writhe vi contorcersi.

writing n scrivere m; scrittura f.

writing desk n scrivania f.

writing paper n carta f da lettere.

wrong n torto m; male m; * adj sbagliato; ingiusto m; * vt fare torto a.

wrongful adj ingiusto.

wrongly adv erroneamente.

wry adj beffardo.

X

Xmas n Natale m

X-ray n radiografia f.

xylophone n xilofono m

Y

yacht n yacht m.

yachting n velismo m.

Yankee n yankee m.

yard n yard f; cortile m; cantiere m.

yardstick n criterio m.

yarn n filato m; racconto m.

yawn vi sbadigliare; * n sbadiglio m.

yawning n spalancato.

yeah adv sì.

year n anno m; annata f.

yearbook n annuario m.

yearling n yearling m.

yearly adj annuale.

yearn vi bramare.

yearning n desiderio m intenso; * adj bramoso.

yeast n lievito m.

yell vt, vi urlare; * n urlo m.

yellow adj, n giallo m.

yellowish adj giallastro.

yelp vi strillare; * n strillo m.

yen n yen m.

yes adv, n sì m.

yesterday adv ieri.

yet conj ma; tuttavia; * adv già; ancora.

yew n tasso m.

yield vt fruttare; cedere; * vi cedere; * n resa f.

yoga n yoga m.

yoghurt n yogurt m.

yoke n giogo m; sprone m.

yolk n tuorlo m.

yonder adv laggiù.

you pron tu, lei, voi, loro.

young adj giovane; * n prole f; **~er** adj minore.

youngster n giovane m.

your(s) pron tuo, suo, vostro, loro; **~ sincerely** distinti saluti.

yourself pron ti, si, vi, si.

youth n gioventù f; giovane m.

youthful adj giovanile.

youthfulness n giovinezza f.

yuppie n yuppy m/f.

Z

zany *adj* pazzoide.
zeal *n* zelo *m*.
zealous *adj* zelante.
zebra *n* zebra *f*.
zenith *n* zenit *m*.
zero *n* zero *m*.
zest *n* entusiasmo *m*; buccia *f*.
zigzag *n* zigzag *m*.
zinc *n* zinco *m*.
zip *n* cerniera *f*; zip *m*.

zither *n* cetra *f*.
zodiac *n* zodiaco *m*.
zone *n* zona *f*.
zonked *adj* (*fam*) distrutto.
zoo *n* zoo *m*.
zoological *adj* zoologico.
zoologist *n* zoologo *m*.
zoology *n* zoologia *f*.
zoom *vi* zumare; sfrecciare via;
  * *n* zoom *m*.

English and Italian Verbs

Verbi Irregolari en Inglese

	Preterito	Participio passato		Preterito	Participio passato
arise	arose	arisen	do [he/she/it does]		
awake	awoke	awaked,		did	done
		awoken	draw	drew	drawn
be [I am, you/we/they are, he/she/it			dream	dreamed,	dreamed
is, *gerundio* being]				dreamt	dreamt
	was, were	been	drink	drank	drunk
bear	bore	borne	drive	drove	driven
beat	beat	beaten	dwell	dwelt,	dwelt,
become	became	become		dwelled	dwelled
begin	began	begun	eat	ate	eaten
behold	beheld	beheld	fall	fell	fallen
bend	bent	bent	feed	fed	fed
beseech	besought,	besought,	feel	felt	felt
beseeched	beseeched		mistake	mistook	mistaken
beset	beset	beset	fight	fought	fought
bet	bet, betted	bet, betted	find	found	found
bid	bade, bid	bade, bid,	flee	fled	fled
		bidden	fling	flung	flung
bite	bit	bitten	fly [he/she/it flies]		
bleed	bled	bled		flew	flown
bless	blessed	blessed,	forbid	forbade	forbidden
		blest	forecast	forecast	forecast
blow	blew	blown	forget	forgot	forgotten
break	broke	broken	forgive	forgave	forgiven
breed	bred	bred	forsake	forsook	forsaken
bring	brought	brought	forsee	foresaw	foreseen
build	built	built	freeze	froze	frozen
burn	burnt,	burnt,	get	got	got, gotten
	burned	burned	give	gave	given
burst	burst	burst	go [he/she/it goes]		
buy	bought	bought		went	gone
can	could	(been able)	grind	ground	ground
cast	cast	cast	grow	grew	grown
catch	caught	caught	hang	hung,	hung,
choose	chose	chosen		hanged	hanged
cling	cling	clung	have [I/you/we/they have,		
come	came	come	he/she/it has, *gerundio* having]		
cost	cost	cost		had	had
creep	crept	crept	hear	heard	heard
cut	cut	cut	hide	hid	hidden
deal	dealt	dealt	hit	hit	hit
dig	dug	dug	hold	held	held

435

	Preterito	Participio passato		Preterito	Participio passato
hurt	hurt	hurt	shake	shook	shaken
keep	kept	kept	shall	should	-
kneel	knelt, kneeled	knelt, kneeled	shear	sheared	sheared, shorn
know	knew	known	shed	shed	shed
lay	laid	laid	shine	shone	shone
lead	led	led	shoot	shot	shot
lean	leant, leaned	leant, leaned	show	showed	shown, showed
leap	leapt, leaped	leapt, leaped	shrink	shrank	shrunk
learn	learnt, learned	learnt	shut	shut	shut
			sing	sang	sung
leave	left	left	sink	sank	sunk
lend	lent	lent	sit	sat	sat
let	let	let	slay	slew	slain
lie [gerundio lying]	lay	lain	sleep	slept	slept
			slide	slid	slid
			sling	slung	slung
light	lighted, lit	lighted, lit	smell	smelt, smelled	smelt, smelled
lose	lost	lost	sow	sowed	sown, sowed
make	made	made			
may	might		speak	spoke	spoken
mean	meant	meant	speed	sped, speeded	sped, speeded
meet	met	met			
mow	mowed	mowed, mown	spell	spelt, spelled	spelt, spelled
must	(had to)	(had to)	spend	spent	spent
overcome	overcame	overcome	spill	spilt, spilled	spilt
pay	paid	paid	spin	spun	spun
put	put	put	spit	spat	spat
quit	quitted	quitted	split	split	split
read	read	read	spoil	spoilt, spoiled	spoilt, spoiled
rid	rid	rid	spread	spread	spread
ride	rode	ridden	spring	sprang	sprung
ring	rang	rung	stand	stood	stood
rise	rose	risen	steal	stole	stolen
run	ran	run	stick	stuck	stuck
saw	sawed	sawn	sting	stung	stung
say	said	said	stink	stank	stunk
see	saw	seen	stride	strode	stridden
seek	sought	sought	strike	struck	struck
sell	sold	sold	strive	strove	striven
send	sent	sent	swear	swore	sworn
set	set	set	sweep	swept	swept
sew	sewed	sewn			

	Preterito	*Participio passato*		*Preterito*	*Participio passato*
swell	swelled	swelled, swollen	wake	woke	woken
			wear	wore	worn
swim	swam	swum	weave	wove,	wove,
swing	swung	swung		weaved	weaved
take	took	taken	wed	wed,	wed,
teach	taught	taught		wedded	wedded
tear	tore	torn	weep	wept	wept
tell	told	told	win	won	won
think	thought	thought	wind	wound	wound
throw	threw	thrown	withdraw	withdrew	withdrawn
thrust	thrust	thrust	withhold	withheld	withheld
tread	trod	trodden	withstand	withstood	withstood
understand	understood	understood	wring	wrung	wrung
upset	upset	upset	write	wrote	written

Italian Verbs

Regular Verbs

infinitive

amare	**temere**	**partire** (**capire**)
to love	*to fear*	*to depart* (*to understand*) *

gerund

| amando | temendo | partendo |

past participle

| amato | temuto | partito |

present indicative

amo	temo	parto (capisco)
ami	temi	parti (capisci)
ama	teme	parte (capisce)
amiamo	temiamo	partiamo
amate	temete	partite
àmano	témono	pàrtono (capìscono)

imperfect indicative

amavo	temevo	partivo
amavi	temevi	partivi
amava	temeva	partiva
amavamo	temevamo	partivamo
amavate	temevate	partivate
amàvano	temévano	partvano

past absolute (or preterit)

amai	teméi (temètti)	partii
amasti	temesti	partisti
amò	temé (temètte)	part
amammo	tememmo	partimmo
amaste	temeste	partiste
amàrono	temérono (temèttero)	partrono

future

amerò	temerò	partirò
amerai	temerai	partirai
amer	temerà	partirà
ameremo	temeremo	partiremo
amerete	temerete	partirete
ameranno	temeranno	partiranno

conditional

amerèi	temerèi	partirèi
amerésti	temerésti	partirésti
amerèbbe	temerèbbe	partirèbbe
amerémmo	temerémmo	partirémmo
ameréste	temeréste	partiréste
amerèbbero	temerèbbero	partirèbbero

imperative

ama	temi	parti (capisci)
ami	tema	parta (capisca)
amiamo	temiamo	partiamo
amate	temete	partite
àmino	témano	pàrtano (capscano)

present subjunctive

ami	tema	parta (capisca)
ami	tema	parta (capisca)
ami	tema	parta (capisca)
amiamo	temiamo	partiamo
amiate	temiate	partiate
àmino	témano	pàrtano (capscano)

imperfect subjunctive

amassi	temessi	partissi
amassi	temessi	partissi
amasse	temesse	partisse
amàssimo	teméssimo	partssimo
amaste	temeste	partiste
amàssero	teméssero	partssero

* Third conjugation verbs with -*isc*- suffix include: agire, ammonire, capire, finire, obbedire, percepire, scolpire, sparire, unire.

Some third conjugation verbs can take either form, with or without the -*isc*- suffix. These include: applaudire, assorbire, inghiottire, mentire, nutrire, tossire.

Auxiliary verbs

infinitive	**avere**	**essere**		avevamo	eravamo
	to have	*to be*		avevate	eravate
				avévano	èrano
gerund	avendo	essendo	*past absolute (or preterit)*		
past participle				ebbi	fui
	avuto	stato		avésti	fosti
present indicative				èbbe	fu
	ho	sono		avémmo	fummo
	hai	sei		avéste	foste
	ha	è		èbbero	fùrono
	abbiamo	siamo	*future*		
	avete	siete		avrò	sarò
	hanno	sono		avrai	sarai
imperfect indicative				avrà	sarà
	avevo	ero		avremo	saremo
	avevi	eri		avrete	sarete
	aveva	era		avranno	saranno

conditional

		present subjunctive	
avrèi	sarémmo	àbbia	sia
avrésti	saréste	àbbia	sia
avrèbbe	sarèbbero	àbbia	sia
avrémmo	sarèi	abbiamo	siamo
avréste	sarésti	abbiate	siate
avrèbbero	sarèbbesia	àbbiano	sano

imperative

		imperfect subjunctive	
abbi	sii	avessi	fossi
àbbia	sia	avessi	fossi
abbiamo	siamo	avesse	fosse
abbiate	siate	avéssimo	fòssimo
àbbiano	siano	aveste	foste
		avéssero	fòssero

Irregular and semi-irregular verbs

accendere (*to light*) *past participle*: acceso; *preterit*: accési, accendesti, accése, accendemmo, accendeste, accésero.

accòrgersi (*to notice*) *past participle*: accòrtosi; *preterit*: mi accòrsi, ti accorgesti, si accòrse, ci accorgemmo, vi accorgeste, si accòrsero; *auxiliary*: essere.

affliggere (*to afflict*) *past participle*: afflitto; *preterit*: afflissi, affliggesti, afflisse, affliggemmo, affliggeste, afflissero.

andare (*to go*) *present indicative*: vado, vai, va, andiamo, andate, vanno; *future*: andrò; *imperative*: va'(vai), vada, andiamo, andate, vadano; *present subjunctive*: vada, vada, vada, andiamo, andate, vadano; *auxiliary*: essere.

apparire (*to appear*) *past participle*: apparso; *present indicative*: appaio, appari, appare, appariamo, apparite, appàiono; *imperfect indicative*: apparivo; *preterit*: apparvi, apparisti, apparve, apparimmo, appariste, appàrvero; *future*: apparirò; *conditional*: apparirei; *imperative*: appari, appaia, appariamo, apparite, appaiano; *present subjunctive*: appaia, appaia, appaia, appariamo, appariate, appaiano; *imperfect subjunctive*: apparissi; *auxiliary*: essere.

appèndere (*to* **hang up**) *past participle*: appéso; *preterit*: appési, appendesti, appése, appendemmo, appendeste, appésero.

aprire (*to open*) *past participle*: aperto; *preterit*: apersi (aprii), apristi, aperse (apr), aprimmo, apriste, apèrsero (aprirono).

assistere (*to assist; to be present*) see **esistere**.

assùmere (*to assume; to*

440

appoint) *past participle*:
assunto; *preterit*: assunsi,
assumesti, assunse,
assumemmo, assumeste,
assùnsero.

avvòlgere (*to wind, to wrap*)
see **vòlgere**.

benedire (*to bless*) see **dire**.

bére (*to drink*) *gerund*:
bevendo; *past participle*:
bevuto; *present indicative*:
bévo, bévi, béve, beviamo,
bevete, bévono; *imperfect
indicative*: bevevo; *preterit*:
bévvi (bevéi, bevètti), bevesti,
bévve (bevé, bevètte),
bevemmo, beveste, bévvero
(bevérono, bevèttero); *future*:
berrò; *conditional*: berrei;
imperative: bévi, béva,
beviamo, bevete, bévano;
present subjunctive: béva;
imperfect subjunctive:
bevessi.

cadere (*to fall*) *preterit*: caddi,
cadesti, cadde, cademmo,
cadeste, càddero; *future*:
cadrò; *conditional*: cadrei;
auxiliary: essere.

chièdere (*to ask*) *past
participle*: chièsto; *preterit*:
chièsi, chiedesti, chièse,
chiedemmo, chiedeste,
chièsero.

chiùdere (*to close*) *past
participle*: chiuso; *preterit*:
chiusi, chiudesti, chiuse,
chiudemmo, chiudeste,
chiusero.

cògliere (*to pluck; to collect*)
gerund: cogliendo; *past
participle*: còlto; *present
indicative*: còlgo, cògli, còglie,
cogliamo, cogliete, còlgono;
imperfect indicative: coglievo;
preterit: còlsi, cogliesti, còlse,
cogliemmo, coglieste, còlsero;
future: coglierò; *conditional*:

coglierei; *imperative*: cògli,
còlga, cogliamo, cogliete,
còlgano; *present subjunctive*:
còlga, còlga, còlga, cogliamo,
cogliate, còlgano; *imperfect
subjunctive*: cogliessi.

coincdere (*to coincide*) see
decìdere.

concèdere (*to grant; to admit*)
past participle: concèsso;
preterit: concèssi. concedesti,
concèsse, concedemmo,
concedeste, concèssero.

condurre (*to lead*) *gerund*:
conducendo; *past participle*:
condotto; *present indicative*:
conduco, conduci, conduce,
conduciamo, conducete,
condùcono; *imperfect
indicative*: conducevo;
preterit: condussi, conducesti,
condusse, conducemmo,
conduceste, condùssero;
future: condurrò; *conditional*:
condurrei; *imperative*:
conduci, conduca,
conduciamo, conducete,
conducano, *present
subjunctive*: conduca,
conduca, conduca,
conduciamo, conduciate,
condùcano; *imperfect
subjunctive*: conducessi.

conòscere (*to know; to make
acquaintance of*) *past
participle*: conosciuto;
preterit: conobbi, conoscesti,
conobbe, conoscemmo,
conosceste, conòbbero.

contraddire (*to contradict*)
see **dire**.

coprire (*to cover*) see **aprire**.

corrèggere (*to correct*) see
règgere

còrrere (*to run*) *past
participle*: corso; *preterit*:
corsi, corresti, corse,
corremmo, correste, crsero;

auxiliary: avere or essere.

créscere (*to grow*) *past participle*: cresciuto; *preterit*: crébbi, crescesti, crébbe, crescemmo, cresceste, crébbero; *auxiliary*: essere; *when used transitively*: avere.

cuòcere (*to cook*) *gerund*: cocendo; *past participle*: còtto; *present indicative*: cuòcio, cuòci, cuòce, cuociamo, cuocete, cuòciono; *imperfect indicative*: cuocevo; *preterit*: còssi, cuocesti, còsse, cuocemmo, cuoceste, còssero; *future*: cuocerò; *conditional*: cuocerei; *imperative*: cuòci, cuòcia, cuociamo, cuocete, cuòciano; *present subjunctive*: cuòcia; *imperfect subjunctive*: cuocessi.

dare (*to give*) *present indicative*: do, dai, dà,, diamo, date, danno; *preterit*: diedi (detti), desti, diede, demmo, deste, diedero (dettero); *future*: darò; *imperative*: da' (dai), dia, diamo, diate, diano; *present subjunctive*: dia.

decdere (*to decide*) *past participle*: deciso; *preterit*: decisi, decidesti,decise, decidemmo, decideste, decsero.

devòlvere (*to assign*) *past participle*: devoluto

difèndere (*to defend*) *past participle*: difeso; *preterit*: difési, difendesti, difése, difendemmo, difendeste, difésero.

dipingere (*to paint*) *past participle*: dipinto; *preterit*: dipinsi, dipingesti, dipinse, dipingemmo, dipingeste, dipinsero.

dire (*to say*) *gerund*: dicendo; *past participle*: detto; *present indicative*: dico, dici, dice, diciamo, dite, dìcono; *imperfect indicative*: dicevo; *preterit*: dissi, dicesti, disse, dicemmo, diceste, dìssero; *future*: dirò; *conditional*: direi; *imperative*: di', dica, diciamo, dite, dìcano; *present subjunctive*: dica, dica, dica, diciamo, diciate, dìcano; *imperfect subjunctive*: dicessi.

dirigere (*to manage*) *past participle*: dirètto; *preterit*: dirèssi, dirigesti, dirèsse, dirigemmo, dirigeste, dirèssero.

discùtere (*to discuss*) *past participle*: discusso; *preterit*: discussi, discutesti, discusse, discutemmo, discuteste, discussero.

disdire (*to cancel*) see **dire**.

distìnguere (*to distinguish*) *past participle*: distinto; *preterit*: distinsi, distinguesti, distinse, distinguemmo, distingueste, distinsero.

divìdere (*to divide*) *past participle*: diviso; *preterit*: divisi, dividesti,divise, dividemmo, divideste, divisero.

dolére (**dolérsi**) (*to hurt; to grieve*) *present indicative*: mi dòlgo, ti duòli, si duòle, ci doliamo (dogliamo), vi dolete, si dòlgono; *imperfect indicative*: mi dolevo; *preterit*: mi dòlsi, ti dolesti, si dòlse, ci dolemmo, vi doleste, si dòlsero; *future*: mi dorrò; *conditional*: mi dorrei; *imperative*: duòliti, si dòlga, dogliamoci (doliamoci), doletevi, si dòlgano; *present* *subjunctive*: mi dolga, ti dolga, si dolga, ci doliamo (dogliamo), vi dogliate, si dòlgano; *imperfect subjunctive*: mi dolessi; *auxiliary*: essere.

dovére (*to have to*; *to owe*) *present indicative*: dèvo (dèbbo), dèvi, dève, dobbiamo, dovete, dèvono (dèbbono); *imperfect indicative*: dovevo; *preterit*: dovéi (dovètti), dovesti; *future*: dovrò; *conditional*: dovrei; *present subjunctive*: dèva (dèbba), dèva, dèva, dobbiamo, dobbiate, dèvano (dèbbano); *imperfect subjunctive*: dovessi.

emèrgere (*to emerge*) *past participle*: emèrso; emèrsi, emergesti, emèrse, emergemmo, emergeste, emèrsero; *auxiliary*: essere.

esìstere (*to exist*) *past participle*: esistito; *auxiliary*: essere.

estìnguere (*to extinguish*) see **distìnguere**.

evòlvere (*to evolve*) see **devòlvere**.

fare (*to do*; *to make*) *past participle*: fatto; *present indicative*: faccio, fai, fa, facciamo, fate, fanno; *imperfect indicative*: facevo; *preterit*: féci, facesti, féce, facemmo, faceste, fécero; *future*: farò; con. farei; *imperative*: fa' (fai), faccia, facciamo, fate, facciano. *present subjunctive*: faccia, faccia, faccia, facciamo, facciate, fàcciano; *imperfect subjunctive*: facessi.

fìngere (*to pretend*) see **dipingere**.

fòndere (*to melt*; *to merge*)

past participle: fuso; *preterit*: fusi, fondesti, fuse, fondemmo, fondeste, fùsero.

giùngere (*to arrive*; *to join*) *past participle*: giunto; *preterit*: giunsi, giungesti, giunse, giungemmo, giungeste, giunsero.

godere (*to rejoice*; *to enjoy*) *future*: godrò; godrei.

introdurre (*to introduce*) see **condurre**.

invàdere (*to invade*) *past participle*: invaso; *preterit*: invasi, invadesti, invase, invademmo, invadeste, invasero.

lèggere (*to read*) *past participle*: lètto; *preterit*: lèssi, leggesti, lèsse, leggemmo, leggeste, lèssero.

méttere (*to put*) *past participle*: mésso; *preterit*: misi, mettesti, mise, mettemmo, metteste, misero.

mòrdere (*to bite*) *past participle*: mòrso; *preterit*: mòrsi. mordesti, mòrse, mordemmo, mordeste, mòrsero.

morire (*to die*) *past participle*: morto; *present indicative*: muoio, muori, muore, moriamo, morite, muòiono; *imperfect indicative*: morivo; *preterit*: morii; *future*: morrò (morirò), morrai (morirai); *conditional*: morrei (morirei), morresti (moriresti); *imperative*: muori, muoia, moriamo, morite, muiòano; *present subjunctive*: muòia, muòia, muòia, moriamo, moriate, muoiano; *imperfect subjunctive*: morissi.

muòvere (*to move*) *past participle*: mosso; *preterit*: mòssi, movesti, mòsse, movemmo, moveste, mòssero.

nàscere (*to be born*) *past participle*: nato; *preterit*: nacqui, nascesti, nacque, nascemmo, nasceste, nacquero.

nascòndere (*to hide*) *past participle*: nascosto; *preterit*: nascosi, nascondesti, nascose, nascondemmo, nascondeste, nascòsero.

nuòcere (*to harm*) *past participle*: nociuto; *present indicative*: nòccio, nuoci, nuoce, nociamo, nocete, nòcciono; *imperfect indicative*: nocevo; *preterit*: nòcqui, nocesti, nòcque, nocemmo, noceste, nòcquero; *imperative*: nuòci, nòccia, nociamo, nocete, nòcciano; *present subjunctive*: nòccia, nòccia, nòccia, nociamo, nociate, nòcciano; *imperfect subjunctive*: nuocessi.

offèndere (*to offend*) *see* **difèndere**.

offrire (*to offer*) *past participle*: offerto; *preterit*: offersi (offrii), offristi, offerse (offrì), offrimmo, offriste, offèrsero (offrirono).

opporre (*to oppose*) *see* **porre**.

parére (*to appear*) *past participle*: parso; *present indicative*: paio, pari, pare, paiamo, parete, paiono; *imperfect indicative*: parevo; *preterit*: parvi, paresti, parve, paremmo, pareste, pàrvero; *future*: parrò; *conditional*: parrei; *present subjunctive*: paia, paia, paia, paiamo, paiate, paiano; *imperfect subjunctive*: paressi; *auxiliary*: essere.

pèrdere (*to lose*) *past participle*: pèrso (perduto);

preterit: pèrsi, perdesti, pèrse, perdemmo, perdeste, pèrsero.

persuadére (*to persuade*) *past participle*: persuaso; *preterit*: persuasi, persuadesti, persuase, persuademmo, persuadeste, persuàsero

piacére (*to please*) *past participle*: piaciùto; *present indicative*: piaccio, piaci, piace, piacciamo (piaciamo), piacete, piàcciono; *preterit*: piacqui, piacesti, piacque, piacemmo, piaceste, piacquero; *imperative*: piaci, piaccia, piacciamo, piacete, piacciono; *present subjunctive*: piaccia, piaccia, piaccia, piacciamo (piaciamo), piacciate (piaciate), piacciano; *auxiliary*: essere.

piàngere (*to weep*) *past participle*: pianto; *preterit*: piansi, piangesti, pianse, piangemmo, piangeste, piansero.

piòvere (*to rain*) *preterit*: piòvve (*impersonal*); *auxiliary*: essere *or* avere.

pòrgere (*to hold out, to offer*) *past participle*: pòrto; *preterit*: pòrsi, porgesti, pòrse, porgemmo, porgeste, pòrsero.

porre (*to place*) *gerund*: ponendo; *past participle*: posto; *present indicative*: pongo, poni, pone, poniamo, ponete, pòngono; *imperfect indicative*: ponevo; *preterit*: posi, ponesti, pose, ponemmo, poneste, pòsero; *future*: porrò; *conditional*: porrei; *imperative*: poni, ponga, poniamo, ponete, pòngano; *present subjunctive*: ponga,

ponga, ponga, poniamo, poniate, pòngano; *imperfect subjunctive*: ponessi.

potére (*to be able*) *present indicative*: posso, puoi, può, possiamo, potete, possono; *imperfect indicative*: potevo; *preterit*: poti, potesti; *future*: potrò; *conditional*: potrei; *present subjunctive*: possa, possa, possa, possiamo, possiate, pòssano; *imperfect subjunctive*: potessi.

prèndere (*to take*) *past participle*: préso; *preterit*: prési, prendesti, prése, prendemmo, prendeste, présero.

produrre (*to produce*) *see* **condurre**.

protèggere (*to protect*) *past participle*: protètto; *preterit*: protèssi, proteggesti, protèsse, proteggemmo, proteggeste, protèssero.

règgere (*to support, to last*) *past participle*: rètto; *preterit*: rèssi, reggesti, rèsse, reggemmo, reggeste, rèssero.

rèndere (*to give back*) *past participle*: réso; *preterit*: rési, rendesti, rése, rendemmo, rendeste, résero.

resìstere (*to hold out, stand*) *see* **esìstere**.

rìdere (*to laugh*) *past participle*: riso; *preterit*: risi, ridesti, rise, ridemmo, rideste, rìsero.

ridurre (*to reduce*) *see* **condurre**.

rimanére (*to remain*) *past participle*: rimasto; *present indicative*: rimango, rimani, rimane, rimaniamo, rimanete, rimàngono; *imperfect indicative*: rimanevo; *preterit*: rimasi,

rimanesti, rimase, rimanemmo, rimaneste, rimàsero; *future*: rimarrò; *conditional*: rimarrei; *imperative*: rimani, rimanga, rimaniamo, rimanete, rimàngano; *present subjunctive*: rimanga, rimanga, rimanga, rimaniamo, rimaniate, rimàngano; *auxiliary*: essere.

rispòndere (*to answer*) *past participle*: risposto; *preterit*: risposi, rispondesti, rispose, rispondemmo, rispondeste, rispòsero.

riuscire (*to succeed*) *see* uscire.

rivòlgere (*to turn; to address*) *see* **vòlgere**.

ròmpere (*to break*) *past participle*: rotto; *preterit*: ruppi, rompesti, ruppe, rompemmo, rompeste, rùppero.

salire (*to rise; to climb*) *present indicative*: salgo, sali, sale, saliamo, salite, salgono; *imperative*: sali, salga, saliamo, salite, sàlgano; *present subjunctive*: salga, salga, salga, saliamo, saliate, sàlgano; *auxiliary*: essere; when used transitively, avere.

sapére (*to know; to taste of*) *present indicative*: so, sai, sa, sappiamo, sapete, sànno; *imperfect indicative*: sapevo; *preterit*: seppi, sapesti, seppe, sapemmo, sapeste, séppero; *future*: saprò; *conditional*: saprei; *imperative*: sappi, sappia, sappiamo, sappiate, sàppiano; *present subjunctive*: sappia, sappia, sappia, sappiamo, sappiate, sàppiano; *imperfect* *subjunctive*: sapessi.

scégliere (*to choose*) *past participle*: scelto; *present indicative*: scelgo, scegli, sceglie, scegliamo, scegliete, scélgono; *imperfect indicative*: sceglievo; *preterit*: scelsi, scegliesti, scelse, scegliemmo, sceglieste, scélsero; *future*: sceglierò; *conditional*: sceglierei; *imperative*: scegli, scelga, scegliamo, scegliete, scélgano; *present subjunctive*: scelga, scelga, scelga, scegliamo, scegliate, scélgano; *imperfect subjunctive*: scegliessi.

scéndere (*to go or come down; to fall*) *past participle*: sceso; *preterit*: scesi, scendesti, scese, scendemmo, scendeste, scésero; *auxiliary*: essere; when used transitively, avere.

sciògliere (*to loosen; to solve; to melt*) *past participle*: sciòlto; *present indicative*: sciolgo, sciogli, scioglie, sciogliamo, sciogliete, sciòlgono; *imperfect indicative*: scioglievo; *preterit*: sciolsi, sciogliesti, sciolse, sciogliemmo, scioglieste, sciòlsero; *future*: scioglierò; *conditional*: scioglierei; *imperative*: sciogli, sciolga, sciogliamo, sciogliete, sciòlgano; *present subjunctive*: sciolga, sciolga, sciolga, sciogliamo, sciogliate, sciòlgano; *imperfect subjunctive*: sciogliessi.

sconvòlgere (*to upset*) see **vòlgere**

scoprire (*to discover*) see **aprire**.

scrivere (*to write*) *past participle*: scritto; *preterit*: scrissi, scrivesti, scrisse, srivemmo, scriveste, scrìssero.

scuòtere (*to shake*) *past participle*: scosso; *preterit*: scossi, scotesti, scosse, scottemmo, scoteste, scòssero.

sedére (**sedérsi**) (*to sit*) *present indicative*: siedo (seggo), siedi, siede, sediamo, sedete, sièdono (sèggono); *imperative*: siedi, sieda (segga), sediamo, sedete, sièdano (sèggano); *present subjunctive*: sieda (segga), sieda (segga), sieda (segga), sediamo, sediate, sièdano (sèggano); *auxiliary*: essere.

soffrire (*to suffer*) see **offrire**.

sòrgere (*to rise*) *past participle*: sorto; *preterit*: sorsi, sorgesti, sorse, sorgemmo, sorgeste, sòrsero; *auxiliary*: essere.

sorrìdere (*to smile*) see **rìdere**.

spègnere (*to put out; to switch off*) *past participle*: spènto; *present indicative*: spengo, spegni, spegne, spegniamo, spegnete, spengono; *imperfect indicative*: spegnevo; *preterit*: spensi, spegnesti, spense, spegnemmo, spegneste, spènsero; *future*: spegnerò; *conditional*: spegnerei; *imperative*: spegni, spenga, spegniamo, spegnete, spengano; *present subjunctive*: spenga, spenga, spenga, spegniamo, spegniate, spengano; *imperfect subjunctive*: spegnessi.

spìngere (*to push*) *past participle*: spinto; *preterit*:

spinsi, spingesti, spinse,
spingemmo, spingeste,
spinsero.

stare (*to stay; to be situated*)
present indicative: sto, stai,
sta, stiamo, state, stanno;
preterit: stètti, stésti, stètte,
stémmo, stéste, stèttero;
future: starò; *imperative*: sta'
(stai), stia, stiamo, state,
stiano; *present subjunctive*:
stia, stia, stia, stiamo, stiate,
stìano; *imperfect subjunctive*:
stèssi, stéssi, stésse,
stéssimo, stéste, stéssero;
auxiliary: essere.

strìngere (*to squeeze*) *past
participle*: stretto; *preterit*:
strinsi, stringesti, strinse,
stringemmo, stringeste,
strinsero.

supporre (*to suppose*) see
porre.

tacére (*to be silent*) *present
indicative*: taccio, taci, tace,
taciamo, tacete, tàcciono;
preterit: tacqui, tacesti,
tacque, tacemmo, taceste,
tàcquero; *imperative*: taci,
taccia, taciamo, tacete,
tàcciano; *present subjunctive*:
taccia, taccia, taccia,
taciamo, taciate, tàcciano.

tèndere (*to hold out; to tend*)
past participle: teso; *preterit*:
tesi, tendesti, tese,
tendemmo, tendeste, tsero.

tenére (*to hold*) *present
indicative*: tengo, tieni, tiene,
teniamo, tenete, tèngono;
imperfect indicative: tenevo;
preterit: tenni, tenesti, tenne,
tenemmo, teneste, ténnero;
future: terrò; *conditional*:
terrei; *imperative*: tieni,
tenga, teniamo tenete,
tèngano; *present subjunctive*:
tenga, tenga, tenga, teniamo,

teniate, tèngano; *imperfect
subjunctive*: tenessi.

tògliere (*to remove*) see
cògliere.

tradurre (*to translate*) see
condurre.

trarre (*to pull; to attract; to
fling*) *gerund*: traendo; *past
participle*: tratto; *present
indicative*: traggo, trai, trae,
traiamo, traete, tràggono;
imperfect indicative: traevo;
preterit: trassi, traesti,
trasse, traemmo, traeste,
tràssero; *future*: trarrò;
conditional: trarrei;
imperative: trai, tragga,
traiamo, traete, tràggano;
present subjunctive: tragga,
tragga, tragga, traiamo,
traiate, tràggano; *imperfect
subjunctive*: traessi.

travòlgere (*to overwhelm*) see
vòlgere.

uccìdere (*to kill*) see **decìdere**.

udire (*to hear*) *present
indicative*: odo, odi, ode,
udiamo, udite, òdono;
imperfect indicative: udivo;
preterit: udii; *future*: udirò
(udrò); *conditional*: udirei
(udrei); *imperative*: odi, oda,
udiamo, udite, òdano; *present
subjunctive*: oda, oda, oda,
udiamo, udiate, òdano;
imperfect subjunctive: udissi.

uscire (*to go or come out*)
present indicative: esco, esci,
esce, usciamo, uscite, èscono;
imperative: esi, esca,
usciamo, uscite, èscano;
present subjunctive: esca,
esca, esca, usciamo, usciate,
èscano; *auxiliary*: essere.

valere (*to be worth; to be
effective, of use*) *past
participle*: valso; *present
indicative*: valgo, vale, vale,

valiamo, valete, vàlgono;
imperfect indicative: valevo;
preterit: valsi, valesti, valse,
valemmo, valeste, vàlsero;
future: varrò; *conditional*:
varrei; *imperative*: vali,
valga, valiamo, valete,
valgano; *present subjunctive*:
valga, valga, valga, valiamo,
valiate, vàlgano; *imperfect
subjunctive*: valessi;
auxiliary: essere.
vedere (*to see*) *past participle*:
visto (veduto); *present
indicative*: vedo; *imperfect
indicative*: vedevo; *preterit*:
vidi, vedesti, vide, vedemmo,
vedeste, vìdero; *future*: vedrò;
conditional: vedrei;
imperative: vedi, veda,
vediamo, vedete, védano;
present subjunctive: veda,
veda, veda, vediamo, vediate,
védano; *imperfect
subjunctive*: vedessi.
venire (*to come*) *past
participle*: venuto; *present
indicative*: vengo, vieni,
viene, veniamo, venite,
vèngono; *imperfect
indicative*: venivo; *preterit*:
venni, venisti, venne,
venimmo, veniste, vénnero;
future: verrò; *conditional*:
verrei; *imperative*: vieni,

venga, veniamo, venite,
vngano; *present subjunctive*:
venga, venga, venga,
veniamo, veniate, vèngano;
imperfect subjunctive:
venissi; *auxiliary*: essere.
vncere (*to win*) *past
participle*: vinto; *preterit*:
vinsi, vincesti, vinse,
vincemmo, vinceste, vìnsero.
vivere (*to live*) *past participle*:
vissuto; *preterit*: vissi,
vivesti, visse, vivemmo,
viveste, vssero; *future*: vivrò;
conditional: vivrei; *auxiliary*:
essere; *when used
transitively*: avere.
volere (*to wish, to want; to
intend*) *present indicative*:
voglio, vuoi, vuole, vogliamo,
volete, vògliono; *imperfect
indicative*: volevo; *preterit*:
volli, volesti, volle, volemmo,
voleste, vòllero; *future*: vorrò;
conditional: vorrei;
imperative: vogli, voglia,
vogliamo, volete, vògliano;
present subjunctive: voglia,
voglia, voglia, vogliamo,
vogliate, vògliano; *imperfect
subjunctive*: volessi.
vòlgere (*to turn round*) *past
participle*: volto; *preterit*:
volsi, volgesti, volse,
volgemmo, volgeste, vòlsero.